DATE DUE

A Voice That Spoke for Justice

SUNY Series in Modern Jewish History
Paula E. Hyman and Deborah Dash Moore, Editors

A Voice That Spoke for Justice

THE LIFE AND TIMES OF STEPHEN S. WISE

Melvin I. Urofsky

STATE UNIVERSITY OF NEW YORK PRESS

Albany

For my family, with love and appreciation:
Susan, Philip, Robert, and, of course, Cuz

Published by
State University of New York Press, Albany

© 1982 State University of New York

For information, address State University of New York
Press, State University Plaza, Albany, N.Y., 12246

Library of Congress Cataloging in Publication Data

Urofsky, Melvin I.
   A voice that spoke for justice.

   (SUNY series in modern Jewish history)
   Includes index.
   1. Wise, Stephen Samuel, 1874–1949. 2. Rabbis
—United States—Biography. 3. Zionists—United
States—Biography. I. Title. II. Series.
BM755.W53U76   296.8'346'0924   [B]   81-5676
ISBN 0-87395-538-2   AACR2
ISBN 0-87395-539-0 (pbk.)

Contents

Introduction

In the first half of this century, a talented and charismatic leadership restructured the American Jewish community to meet the demands and opportunities of a pluralistic, secular society. To match the dynamics of the nation, men and women like Louis Marshall, Jacob Schiff, Henrietta Szold, and Louis D. Brandeis created new organizations and refashioned others, often in their own image. This generation of titans is now gone, but their work still guides the current modes of American Jewish life. Among them none articulated the belief that the destinies of the Jewish people and of the United States were inextricably interwined as did Stephen Samuel Wise.

A progenitor of American Zionism, creator of the American and World Jewish Congresses, founder of the Jewish Institute of Religion and, above all rabbi of the Free Synagogue, Wise carved a unique niche for himself at the interface of Jewish communal affairs and those of the broader society. His battles for a free pulpit, for a living Judaism responsive to social problems, for the right—indeed, duty—of rabbis to enter the lists of secular reform, set a pattern from which all American rabbis, those of his generation and their successors, have benefited.

Wise's life, however, is more than a chronicle of an ethnic community's adjustment to the host society. He had a singular vision in which the ethical teachings of the ancient Hebrew prophets merged with the Jeffersonian ideals of an egalitarian society. Jewish communal life could prosper in this land only if it adopted democratic practices, while the promise of America demanded that it adhere to the high standards of social justice elaborated so eloquently in Isaiah and Micah. For Wise, therefore, the battles for democracy in Jewish affairs and against antisemitism were part and parcel of his struggles in progressive and liberal reforms. A free pulpit, an enlightened rabbinate, a socially responsive religion went hand in hand with civic reform, wage and hours legislation, and fair treatment of minorities.

To characterize Wise as a reformer, the friend of Wilson and Roosevelt, Smith and LaGuardia, or as a leader of liberal Judaism and Zionism, the colleague of Heller, Hirsch, and Brandeis, is to fail to see the man whole. One can only understand his Americanism through his passionate Judaism, and his Judaism through his fervent Americanism. This wholeness is best exemplified in his fight against fascism, in which he denounced Hitler as a foe of both the Jewish people and of American ideas. It is this Stephen Wise, an American Jew, whom I have tried to portray in the following pages. As with any historical figure, however, some portions of his life proved easier to illuminate than others, and in at least one eara, the evidentiary record is practically nonexistent.

A controversial figure in his lifetime, Wise has remained the victim of rumors for more than three decades after his death. Three accusations in particular, because of their gravity, demand serious attention. First, Wise allegedly took his doctorate at Columbia under fraudulent circumstances, using another man's work as his own. Fortunately, the contents of a recently discovered box of letters between Wise and Richard Gottheil should establish Wise's sole authorship of his thesis.

A second accusation grew out of the friction between established Jewish organizations and the radical Bergson group during the Second World War, and has been amplified by revisionist historians dealing with the American response to the Holocaust. According to this school, American Jewish leaders in general, and Stephen Wise in particular, collaborated with the Roosevelt administration to cover up evidence of Hitler's Final Solution and thus thwart meaningful efforts to save European Jewry. That Wise was guilty of errors of judgment is certain, especially in his trust of Franklin D. Roosevelt, but the political realities of those years foreclosed many of the options which these critics, with the clarity of hindsight, so forcefully and confidently urge. This matter is explored at length in the chapters on fascism and the Holocaust.

The final set of accusations have, despite all efforts to secure conclusive evidence one way or the other, remained unsubstantiated rumors. Several years ago, Helen Berenson detailed in her memoirs sexual liaisons she allegedly had with Stephen Wise. Many of Wise's colleagues confided that they believed her story to be true; one in particular described Wise as "a womanizer—he loved the girlies." But not one of them could say he had knowledge of an affair, either with Berenson or any one else. Carl Voss, whose joint biography of Wise and John Haynes Holmes proved so valuable to my own work, related that he had heard these same rumors, and in attempting to trace them down had run into the same dead end—much smirking, but no proof.

Interestingly enough, every one of these people testified to the deep love Wise had for his wife, Louise. From the day they met, Wise adored her and daily sent her notes, gifts, and flowers, a pattern from which he rarely deviated through nearly fifty years of marriage. Such evidence does not, of course, preclude the possibility that Wise loved his wife yet nonetheless engaged in extramarital relations. If this were true, then Wise would indeed be guilty of hypocrisy, especially in the light of his numerous sermons and articles on the sanctity of marriage.

The historian, to use Arthur M. Schlesinger, Jr.'s phrase, must at times make a "leap of faith." After marshaling all the available data, one must use critical judgment and informed imagination to fill in the voids of one's knowledge. But if the chasm is too great and the evidentiary blocks too small, the "leap of faith" may prove no better than the rumor-mongering one is trying to overcome. In this case, training as well as intuition protests against labeling Wise a philanderer. Without proof, it seems best to ignore snide whisperings, and to tell Wise's story on the basis of more substantial documentation.

That story first attracted me during my research on Louis D. Brandeis and American Zionism. Brandeis, who also combined a devotion for prophetic idealism and Jeffersonian democracy, found his perfect lieutenant for the Zionist and Congress battles in Stephen Wise, and I determined that, at some later date, I would learn more about Wise's life. In 1974 Dr. Emil Lehman of the Herzl Institute invited me to deliver an address on the centennial of Wise's birth. The Hon. Justine Wise Polier and James Waterman Wise later read that paper, and urged me to undertake a full-scale biography of their father. In the years since then, they have been continuously helpful and informative, answering numerous questions, digging up old letters and photographs, and arranging interviews with men and women who had known or worked with Wise. Both read the first draft of the manuscript, and made many helpful suggestions, but they insisted from the start that I alone would have final say over content and interpretation. I will be eternally grateful to them not only for their help, but for their determination that filial piety had no place in a scholarly biography. Judge Polier's late husband, Shad Polier, was also extremely supportive of this undertaking during the last years of his life.

Among those who shared their memories of Stephen Wise, I would like to thank Gertrude Adelstein, Rabbi Morton M. Berman, the Hon. Eliahu Elath, Dr. Nahum Goldmann, Rabbi Israel Goldstein, Dr. Alfred Gottschalk, Professor Milton Handler, Rabbi Edward Klien, the Hon. Moshe Kol, the Hon. Arthur Lourie, Rabbi Meyer Passow, Dr. Gerhardt Reigner, Dr. Arya Tartakower, and Mr. Jacques Torczyner. I was also fortunate to interview before their deaths Mrs. Rose Halprin, Rabbi Edward I. Kiev, the Hon. Louis Levinthal, the Hon. Golda Meir, Dr. Emanuel Neumann, Mr. Ezra Shapiro, and Mr. Meyer Weisgal. A very special thanks is due Dr. Carl Hermann Voss, who not only worked with Wise and was his first biographer, but who generously shared with me much knowledge of the man, and consistently encouraged me in my own work. Jacques Torczyner, head of the Herzl Institute, not only provided me with lively interviews, but arranged for a travel grant from the Institute. Research was also facilitated by a grant-in-aid from the American Council of Learned Societies, and I wish to thank the Council and its directors for their faith in this project. The manuscript was typed with care and tolerance by my secretaries at the History Department of Virginia Commonwealth University, Janie L. Ghee and Wanda P. Clary.

The main body of the Wise Papers is in the Library of the American Jewish Historical Society, and my work there truly became a pleasure thanks to the librarian, Dr. Nathan M. Kaganoff, and his assistants, Nehemiah Ben-Zev and Martha B. Katz-Hyman. I value the Society's director, Bernard Wax, and assistant director, Stanley Remsberg, not only as friends but for the hospitality they inevitably showed in my often frenetic descents upon the premises. A secondary body of Wise materials is in the American Jewish Archives, and Mrs. Fannie Zelcer made my trips there both profitable and enjoyable. Mrs. Sylvia Landress, head of the Zionist Archives and Library, and her assistants, Esther Togman and Rebecca Sherman, have been so helpful to me over the last several years that my debt can never be repaid. My thanks also go to Dr. William Emerson and his staff at the Franklin D. Roosevelt Library, Mrs. Miriam Leikind of the Abba Hillel Silver Archives, and the many people who make the Manuscript Division of the Library of Congress absolutely the finest research library in the world.

In Israel, I had the research assistance of Ms. Rachel Gershuni in Jerusalem, and I also want to thank Dr. Michael Heymann, director of the Central Zionist Archives, Jerusalem, and his colleague, Dr. I. Phillipp, as well as the head of the Weizmann Archives, Mrs. Nehama A. Chalom, and her assistants, Rhonda Epstein and Shoshana Kafri. The late Meyer Weisgal and his wife Shirley opened their home to me, and in between regaling me with Yiddish jokes and stories about Wise, Weisgal permitted me to examine his private papers. Similarly, Dr. Israel Goldstein and Rabbi Morton Berman also allowed me to examine their personal papers relating to Wise. The staff of the Interlibrary Loan Division at VCU once again tolerated incessant demands, and I am grateful to Janet Howell and Eileen Meagher for their help. At the State University of New York Press, Robert Mandel and Nancy Sharlet were most helpful, while Mary Miles did an outstanding job copyediting the manuscript.

It is my good fortune to have friends who are too polite to refuse requests to read my work, such requests usually arriving several weeks after the manuscript. The valuable comments they made justified, at least in my mind, my behavior, and the final product is far better for my having had the benefit of their knowledge. Jerome Eckstein of the State University of New York at Albany, Susan Estabrook Kennedy of Virginia Commonwealth University, David W. Levy of the University of Oklahoma, and Stephen Whitfield of Brandeis University contributed far more than they can ever know to whatever merits this book may have; the flaws are mine alone.

Throughout the years I have worked on this and other studies, my family has been more than a source of inspriration. They have been a constant joy, reminding me by their very presence of what I hold most dear. In love and gratitude this book is dedicated to my wife Susan, my sons Philip and Robert, and, of course, Cuz.

Richmond, Virginia
February 1981

STEPHEN S. WISE

1

Goodly Beginnings

"My grandfather fought with his congregation for forty years," Stephen Wise would gleefully say, content that his own battles with and for the Jewish people maintained a family tradition that had produced seven generations of rabbis. Wise's grandfather, Reb Joseph Hirsch Weisz (1800–1881) had indeed carried on a running feud during the many years he served as chief rabbi of Erlau in Hungary. A tall, handsome man with a beard extending almost to his knees, he could be brutal in his fanatical defense of Orthodox Judaism. When he saw a member of his congregation smoking on the Sabbath, he crossed the street and knocked the man into the gutter, shouting, "How dare you offend the Sabbath?" Reb Joseph's reputation for learning and piety won him the respect of non-Jews as well, and the Catholic primate of Hungary, Archbishop Bertescovitch, was a close personal friend. Ironically, gentile friends came to his rescue when he was in difficulty with the Jewish community of Erlau and again when he faced civil charges of sedition.

Shortly after Weisz's appointment as chief rabbi of Erlau in 1840, currents of change swept through many of the synagogues of Hungary. Inspired by the liberalizing movement in Germany, religious reformers in Hungary wanted to modernize many of the traditional Jewish rituals and do away with ancient laws and customs that they considered archaic and irrelevant. Reb Joseph set himself firmly against any reform; the word of God, as given to Moses and interpreted by the rabbis, could not be altered to suit the convenience of Jews too lazy to obey the law. For a while, the reformers had the upper hand and forced over twenty rabbis, including Reb Joseph, to resign. The deposed rabbis, led by Weisz, took their case to the civil courts, where it dragged on for almost twelve years. To their aid came Reb Joseph's Catholic friends, including several bishops, and even Emperor Franz Joseph expressed his sympathy for them. In the end, the orthodox group won its case, with the courts ordering their congregations to reinstate them

1

and to pay them back salary. Weisz returned in triumph to the Erlau synagogue with a regiment of soldiers escorting him. The Oberkomandier of the district posted a detachment of guards at the door, and warned the rebellious congregation that he would shoot any person who opposed the rabbi. After accepting apologies, Reb Joseph returned the money to the synagogue, a gesture made more in disdain than as a peace offering.

This special treatment for Weisz derived from the fact that during the Revolution of 1848, he had remained loyal to the crown. After the failure of the Revolution, several Jews in Erlau who bitterly opposed Reb Joseph and his ultra-orthodoxy charged that he had aided the liberals, and at the trial, Catholic leaders once again testified to his loyalty to the emperor.

The strife over reform, both political and religious, left Reb Joseph and his congregation permanently at odds. Even though he retained the post of chief rabbi in Erlau until his death, he went to the synagogue only four times a year on the major holidays. Otherwise he studied and prayed with a group of his followers at his home. It was there that he taught his son Aaron.[1]

Born in Erlau on May 2, 1844, Aaron Weisz inherited his father's brilliance and the gentleness of his mother, Rachel Theresa. As a child he studied Hebrew with his father, and then took rabbinical training in Hungary's finest seminaries, receiving his *s'micha* (ordination) in 1867 from Reb Israel Hildesheimer in Eisenstadt. After pursuing secular studies in Berlin and Leipzig, he received a doctorate from the University of Halle for a dissertation on angels and demons in rabbinic literature. While he was at Leipzig word came of the assassination of the American president, Abraham Lincoln. Weisz reportedly turned to his comrades and quietly said: "Some day I am going to live in the land of Lincoln; I want my children to grow up in freedom." Before he could keep that promise, however, he returned to Erlau, where he served for several years as superintendent of schools; he also met and married Sabine de Fischer Farkashazy.

Sabine would have been an extraordinary woman in any era, but she was especially strong-willed for a Jewess in nineteenth-century Hungary. She belonged to the aristocracy, her father having been titled for developing the great Herend porcelain works. Moreover, she happened to be already married and the mother of two children, Ida and Wilma, when she fell in love with the gentle, handsome, but very impecunious Aaron Weisz. She insisted on getting a divorce so she could marry the young rabbi, and her horrified father quickly took her on a grand tour of Europe, hoping to divert her from this nonsense. But Sabine had determined to marry Aaron Weisz, and the baron finally relented, on condition that Aaron leave the rabbinate and enter the porcelain business where at least he could earn enough to support his family properly.

Aaron and Sabine were married in 1870, but the baron's scheme came to naught. Appalled at the horrible working conditions and tyrannical treatment of the factory workers, Weisz helped organize a strike of the workers against his father-in-law which, if it accomplished nothing for the laborers, terminated his short career as a businessman. His family, in the meantime, had grown with the birth of a son, Otto Irving, in 1872, and then of a second son, Stephen Samuel, on March 17, 1874. Despite these obligations, Aaron determined now to keep the promise made nearly a decade earlier; one month after Stephen's birth, Aaron Weisz left for America by himself, traveling as did so many other immigrants in the overcrowded steerage. Once safely landed in New York, he took a job laying bricks on the new Tribune building until he found a synagogue in Brooklyn, Beth Elohim, delighted to have the son of the famous Reb Joseph Weisz as its rabbi. He stayed there several months improving his English, and then accepted a call to become rabbi of Congregation Rodeph Sholom in Manhattan, the post he held until his death in 1896. In August 1875, fifteen months after he had left Erlau, he finally felt able to bring his wife and children to join him in America.[2]

Sabine and Aaron Wise (an immigration inspector had convinced Aaron that in the United States "Weisz," pronounced "vice," was not a proper name for a rabbi) now set out to make a new life for their four children and the two sons and a daughter who would be born to them in America. Although he had been an ally of his father in defending ultra-orthodoxy in Hungary, Wise considered such a stance inappropriate in the New World. Some of the younger members of Rodeph Sholom already showed a decided preference for reforming, but their new rabbi carefully steered them onto a middle track, a course which utlimately would merge into the Conservative movement. He agreed to modernize the liturgy, edited a revised prayerbook, and even accepted changes in some of the minor rituals, but he insisted on a strong Hebrew component in the Temple's religious school and the preservation of the more important customs. In 1886, he and other "moderate" reformers founded the Jewish Theological Seminary in New York, destined to become the cornerstone of Conservative Judaism in the United States.[3]

Where Reb Joseph had been feared by his congregants, Aaron Wise was as equally loved. Within the growing New York Jewish community he was soon known as a scholar as well as a popular and effective speaker, and under him Rodeph Sholom prospered and grew, moving from its original building hear the corner of Clinton and Houston Streets to a larger and more imposing edifice on Lexington Avenue at 63rd Street. The Wises made their home on East 5th Street, and there Sabine ruled as if she were still a member of Hungary's titled nobility. Her husband did not earn a large salary as a rabbi, but she managed their income well; occasionally, if circumstances grew too strained, she would quietly sell a few pieces of the fine porcelain she had brought over with her from Erlau. Years later Stephen Wise wrote of her: "She tempered my Father's idealism with understanding. She was the perfect balance-wheel in the life of the family. She had great strength of character and all of us found inspiration in her. . . . She had to be a little firmer than she would have liked to have been, because my Father was just a little too kind, as ministers are apt to be in their homes. She was a real influence, a great help and a high inspiration all her days."[4]

With his father, Stephen Wise developed a particularly close relationship. His earliest memory was that of Aaron taking him, as a toddler, on a walk to the synagogue: "I remember walking with him and holding his hand as we walked and thinking it was quite the most wonderful thing that ever could be that I could walk and accompany him." He adored his father, and throughout his life frequently talked about him and what he had learned from him. Most important, though, Aaron Wise recognized that his second son was given to much self-doubt and feelings of inadequacy. Although a robust and healthy lad, he had a cast in one eye, leading other children to call him "Cross-Eye Dick." Moreover, while of above-average intelligence, he stood in the intellectual shadow of his older brother Otto. A mature Stephen Wise wrote in 1931:

> Whatever may be held with respect to the validity of the postulates of modern psychology, I know that I was a younger brother, and that to a most gifted and attractive being, who inevitably, though always compassionate, outshone me in every way. At school he was brillant despite his effortlessness, while I plodded on, as best I could, with distinctly mediocre talents withal never-ending effort. He won all hearts, and our Mother, as often happens, diverted to him not a little of the adoration of her Father whom my elder brother was fancied to resemble. A deep and withering sense of inferiority would have overcome me—in truth it came very near to blighting my life—had it not been for my Father's understanding, compassion, and, in the end, love.

Aaron, as Stephen put it, "sensed and pondered over my need of something to help me overcome a feeling of inferiority which, if left unchecked, was bound to have a disabling effect upon my personality."[5] What Aaron provided was trust, companionship, and constant encouragement. "When you feel life is too much for you," he told his son, "remember to say: 'Always do what you are afraid to do.' " This advice, and above all the love that abounded in the large and noisy Wise family, eventually resolved the difficulty. The youth who was so unsure of his worth and ability grew to become a hurricane of energy, his overachievement compensating for the doubts of his early years.

But if the unsure youth gave few hints of future greatness, his childhood does provide signs of lifelong interests. The young Wise already found himself fascinated by two worlds, and he would move and join these two areas throughout his more than fifty-year career. On the one hand, of course, lay Judaism and the Jewish people, the rich heritage he received from his father. Every night over the dinner table Aaron Wise would talk with his family about the glories and sufferings of Jews, of the stories of distress he heard from new immigrants arriving each day. From the age of seven, Stephen Wise claimed, he knew what he wanted to be: a rabbi, the seventh generation in a line stretching back more than two centuries.[6]

But the life of the secular world, especially politices, also fascinated him. In 1880, only six years old, he carried a torch in parades for General Winfield Scott Hancock, and came home crying over Republican James Garfield's victory. Despite the image of cloistered, aenemic *yeshiva* scholars, Wise was a vigorous lad with more than average strength, which he indulged in wrestling, running, and climbing, as well as dodging carriages and delivery wagons on the crowded asphalt streets. He and his friends walked for miles exploring the bustling city, often winding up at one of the many docks on the East River, where they watched in fascination as longshoremen unloaded cargoes from all over the world. He also learned about a less attractive aspect of the city, the corrupt ward politics of Tammany Hall, with its stuffed ballot boxes and purchased votes. All this took place with little effort at concealment in the Eleventh Ward where the Wises lived.[7]

His education also reflected these twin stands of his life. He entered public school at age six, and walked with his brothers and sisters each day the one block from their home on East 5th Street to P.S. 15. There a teacher named Nathanael Beirs often sent him out after class to fetch hot water for his tea; then they would sit and talk. In his will, Beirs left his favorite pupil a portrait of his grandfather, who had been a professor of surgery at King's College.[8]

The New York schools at that time offered a six-year course of study with an additional year of preparation for those students going on to college. A comprehensive program, it covered everything from arithmetic to zoology, with a special emphasis on writing and speaking the English language. This suited young Wise well, for English literature and language were to fascinate him all his life. He had already learned German, which was spoken in the Wise household, and read Lessing, Schiller, and Goethe. In public school he mastered English, and developed an appetite for reading which provided him great enjoyment all his years. He devoured the classics, Shakespeare, Milton and Locke, Arnold and Wordsworth, memorizing long sections of sonnets, plays, and essays; his later writings and speeches reflected this early training. He also cultivated a taste for theater, and skipped school one day to see Edwin Booth play Hamlet, shortly before the great actor's death in 1888.[9]

Soon afterward, Wise published his first article, an essay on Abraham Lincoln, in which he extolled the "Moses of the Negro race" for rising not through genius but through "perseverance, honesty and unflinching patriotism." The piece overflowed with schoolboy enthusiasm and rhetoric, but the editor of the *Literary Review*, Otto Irving Wise, undoubtedly felt that it had some intrinsic merit.[10] Printing as well as writing fascinated Stephen. He regularly delivered articles his father had written to the office of the *American Hebrew*, and there struck up an acquaintance with the foreman of the print shop, a Scotsman named Cameron. At times Wise would accidentally mix up some of the type, and the paper's owner and editor, Philip Cowen, would grab the boy to send him on his way. Cameron often stopped Cowen, saying "Don't punish the lad; he'll be heard from some day."[11]

At age thirteen, Wise entered the City College of New York, where he stayed for four years. He first took a year of sub-freshman preparation, and then the first three years of the regular course of study, with a concentration in Greek and Latin. His earlier lack of confidence evidently gone, he consistently received high ratings in nearly all his work, and in his junior year he earned several medals for superior work in Latin and Greek. At City College he also received his first opportunity to develop speaking skills. Every morning he and his fellow students gathered in the chapel to listen to or participate in the various student declamations and orations. Wise joined the Clinonian, the college literary society which debated similar groups at other schools. Several of his classmates recalled his oratory as excellent, delivered in a booming voice that impressed all who heard him.[12] By now he had developed a rich baritone voice and a speaking style that gave more than a hint of unusual ability. Here again his father's advice proved useful. At first the would-be orator tried to imitate the "Episcopalian sing song" so prevalent among the city's preachers. "*Sprich wie der Schnabel gewachsen ist*," Aaron told him, "Talk the way your beak grows." Although there have been several attempts to analyze Wise's speaking style and explain his oratorical power, in the end this simple rule is the only one he ever followed consistently, and it was enough.[13]

Simultaneously with his secular studies Wise pursued Hebrew and Jewish topics. Even before entering public school he had learned enough Hebrew from his father to participate in Rodeph Sholom's services. As the boy grew older, his father sent him to study with his good friend, Alexander Kohut. Like Aaron Wise, Kohut had been in the midst of the battle between Reform and Orthodoxy; trying to steer a middle course, he had helped found the Jewish Theological Seminary and taught Talmud there. Now he had a private class of three youngsters who would each achieve exceptional fame in their careers: Stephen Wise; Joseph H. Hertz, Biblical scholar and later Chief Rabbi of England; and his own son, George Alexander Kohut, a leader in the field of Jewish education and bibliography.

George Kohut became Stephen Wise's closest friend, and the relationship lasted until Kohut's death in 1933. Rebecca Kohut, George's stepmother, became almost a foster mother to the young Wise, who spent much time in the Kohut household. She described the two, one to be a man of the world and the other a scholar, as perfect complements to each another. George had, she recalled, "a protective, fraternal solicitude" for his friend, and the two thrived on each other, spending long hours talking and making plans for the future.

Wise, Kohut, and Hertz, although not regularly enrolled students, took a number of courses at the Jewish Theological Seminary. They studied Hebrew under H. Pereira Mendes, Bible with Bernard Drachman, and also took courses with other faculty members. But their work with Kohut remained special, involving love as well as learning. Even after Wise returned from studies in Europe and held a pulpit, he and his two friends continued studying Talmud with the elder Kohut. In 1894, as Alexander Kohut lay dying, he insisted that "his boys" should not be deprived of their lessons. His wife later recalled the old teacher in bed, too weak to hold the volume they were studying and the young men taking turns holding the book for him as he gave them their lessons.[14]

To prepare himself more thoroughly for the rabbinate, Wise left City College at the end of his junior year and transferred to Columbia, so that he could study with Richard J. H. Gottheil, the son of another of his father's friends, Gustav Gottheil, rabbi at the prestigious Temple Emanu-El. Richard Gottheil had singlehandedly built up the Semitics Department at Columbia, and taught Hebrew, Arabic, and Syriac. Wise took all of these, and also wrote his senior thesis under Gottheil on "Judaea Capta," the battle of the ancient Hebrews against Rome. During that year at Columbia, Wise continued his extracurricular interest in oratory and debate, and received several invitations to speak at synagogues around the city. Congregation Beth-El in Greenpoint, Brooklyn, sent out a formal notice that "Mr. Stephen S. Wise, the Great Orator of Columbia College and aspirant for the Ministry" would speak at the synagogue on "Why Am I a Jew?"—all of which must have been heady indeed for the seventeen-year-old would-be rabbi.[15]

As he prepared to graduate from Columbia College in the spring of 1892, young Wise had to decide where and how he would complete his rabbinical training. He had already begun to drift toward Reform, or as he preferred to call it, Liberal Judaism. While remaining sympathetic to more traditional customs, he believed that in the West "Jews could not be expected to maintain the practices and the rites which were a natural part of their life when they were shut out of and away from the world.''[16] The logical place for him to study, therefore, would have been the Hebrew Union College in Cincinnati, then as now the citadel of Reform Judaism in America. Wise wrote to the aging founder-president of the college, Isaac Mayer Wise (to whom he was not related), about the possibility of working under the direction of HUC faculty but not in Cincinnati; he wanted to begin a doctorate in Semitics at Columbia with Gottheil. Later in the summer, Issac Wise reluctantly agreed to so register him, but urged that it would be better if he did his doctorate from afar and joined his classmates at the school. "But as your father seems to think otherwise and your taste runs in the same direction, I submit." Following this letter, the faculty at the college began outlining work for Wise to take.[17]

Before starting his studies, however, Wise prepared to accompany his father to Palestine. Reb Joseph had died in 1881, and his widow had declined Aaron's repeated invitations to join him and his family in New York. Instead, she chose to go to the Holy Land, and wrote her son: "I go not to live there but to die there. There I wish to pray; and there to die, to be laid to rest amid the sacred dust of Jerusalem; to be buried on the slope facing the Holy of Holies." She had settled in Jerusalem in 1882, and for a number of years the Wise family received news of her from Simon Judah Stampfer, a *meshullah* (messenger and alms-gatherer) from the Hungarian Jewish community in Palestine. Aaron Wise wanted to visit her, bringing with him the grandson she had not seen since infancy. Stephen secured a commission from the New York *Sun* to write a series of articles on Palestine, plans were made and tickets purchased, when on the eve of departure a telegram arrived bearing the sad news *"Mutter gestorben"*—"Mother dead."[18] The trip to Palestine was canceled; instead Stephen Wise boarded a train for the Adirondacks to take up an invitation to spend the summer with Thomas Davidson at Glenmore.

Thomas Davidson is an unusual figure in American intellectual history, a wandering scholar or "knight-errant," as William James termed him. Disdainful of material possessions or status, he appeared to his friends and disciples as a modern Socrates, devoted to a rigorous search for truth. What distinguished Davidson from other truthseekers is that he insisted on applying knowledge to practical problems; as Morris Raphael Cohen recalled, Davidson taught "that it is only sheer sloth and cowardice that can urge us to declare certain problems insoluble." The search for truth should not be restricted to so-called intellectuals; every person had the right and the obligation to pursue knowledge. At Davidson's instigation, the Education Alliance began the Breadwinners' College, which provided instruction for working people in the evening and featured, besides Davidson, Morris Cohen, Joshua Frank, and David Muzzey.[19]

In 1882 Davidson had purchased a few acres in the Keene Valley in the Adirondacks and there, at the foot of Hurricance Mountain, built Glenmore, a "summer school of the cultural sciences." In his house and the adjoining cottages and farm buildings he provided lectures and discussions from early April until late November, surrounded by friends and young people whom he invited to participate in a mutual search for knowledge. At Glenmore, Davidson's enthusiasm proved contagious, as he led his disciples in long walks over the hills, singing Scottish songs or reciting poetry and talking with them long into the night before the fireplace.[20]

For Stephen Wise, the summer of 1892 was a time he would remember all his life. The philospher's practicality appealed to the recent college graduate, but even more than that, it opened a new world of reason and idealism. While Davidson was not a specifically "Christian" philosopher, much of what he advocated approximated the views then expressed by Walter Rauschenbusch and other leaders of the Social Gospel movement. For them the true church did not reside in a cathedral but in the shops and factories and markets where people lived and labored. In short time Wise would become the leading advocate of a Jewish version of the Social Gospel, and he would later recall how potent an influence Davidson had been in this direction, how he had made "knowledge and wisdom not idols or fetishes to be worshipped, but instruments to be used for the weal of others." It was Davidson who urged Wise to remember that "Judaism like all living things changes as it grows; that while the letter killeth the spirit keepeth alive. You will devise a twentieth century Judaism fitted to meet the needs of the present day."[21]

That summer passed quickly and happily for Wise, and laid the basis for his close relationship with Davidson until the latter's death in 1900. The Adirondack air proved as beneficial for his body as Davidson's lectures had been for his mind, and his family marveled at his vigor and robustness. But now a decision had to be reached as to where he would study, and following his father's counsel, Wise opted for Europe over Cincinnati. In the fall he boarded a steamer for Bremen, and from there took the train to Vienna, where he would begin work under the great Adolf Jellinek.

Jellinek, then at the pinnacle of his fame, was the chief exponent of *Wissenschaft des Judentums*, the scientific study of Judaism. He introduced his new student from America to commentary and exposition, to research of a kind and intensity Wise had never experienced at either City College or Columbia. Beyond that, Jellinek articulated a concept which, while not original with him, now took on new meaning for Wise. The "community of Israel," the ancient Hebrew idea of *klal Yisroel*, bound all Jews everywhere together, made each one responsible for the well-being of the others. Throughout his life, when explaining why he felt he had to create this organization or fight that battle, why he had to defend German Jewry against Hitler or attack the *shtadlanim* (court Jews) of the American Jewish Committee, Wise would answer in terms of responsibility and community, terms Jellinek would easily have recognized.

Jellinek also showed Wise that a rabbi's sermons need not be limited only to Jewish themes. Aaron Wise had spoken on contemporary social and economic problems to his congregation, but Adolf Jellinek possessed a knowledge and sophistication regarding public affairs far beyond that of Stephen's father. Whenever Jellinek announced that he would speak on current issues, the Great Synagogue of Vienna would be packed, with many non-Jews coming to hear his exposition.

The ties between the elderly scholar and his young pupil soon grew close. Jellinek made Wise his private secretary, and every afternoon dictated letters to him. Afterward, teacher and student conversed in German as they walked slowly along Vienna's spacious boulevards. In the sping of 1893, Wise received *s'micha* personally from Jellinek, and prepared to return to the United States. Before he left, his master gave him a message for American Jewry: The preservation of Jews everywhere would depend upon the strength and courage of Jews in the United States; they would have to fight, with the help of God, to save their brethren. What at the time might have seemed melodramatic rhetoric would in later years appear prophetic.[22]

Thanks to his father, Wise returned to America not only with his rabbinic ordination, but with the possibility of a pulpit awaiting him. The large B'nai Jeshurun congregation on Madison Avenue needed an assistant rabbi to help their aging pastor, Henry F. Jacobs. Wise preached a trial sermon at B'nai Jeshurun in March 1893, on Shabbat Hagadol, the sabbath before Passover, the Jewish holiday celebrating freedom and the delivery of the ancient Hebrews from bondage in Egypt. He took as his text Malachi 4: 5–6, and spoke about the divine whispers each person hears amid the silence of Sabbath peace and rest.

Years later Wise delighted in telling the story of the reaction to this trial sermon. It had deeply impressed the congregation, but one of the trustees protested to the president that the talk must have been written by Aaron Wise, since it was so good, and all Wise had done was deliver it. The president replied that if the young rabbi had sense enough to preach one of his father's good sermons instead of one of his own bad ones, this only proved how fit he was for the post. Wise was elected as junior rabbi, and in April 1893 occupied the B'nai Jeshurun pulpit for the first time as one of the congregation's pastors.

Wise found the saintly Jacobs not only a friend, but a mentor and guide to the daily routine of ministering to a large congregation. But barely had Wise begun to settle into that routine when Jacobs died, throwing the burden of numerous congregational duties onto a rather inexperienced nineteen-year-old junior rabbi. Wise now became a candidate for the vacant position of senior rabbi in the Madison Avenue synagogue, and again his sermons won over the congregation and the trustees. Despite some grumblings that he was much too young for so prestigious a post, an overwhelming majority of the congregants elected him to be their rabbi.[23]

Now he had a pulpit and a congregation of his own, and he set out to prove to the doubters, and to himself, that he was fully worthy of the positon. He performed his first wedding, the first of thousands, on September 6, 1893. He helped the women of the congregation organize a Sisterhood, with the task of providing relief for some of the destitute during that harsh depression winter. In order to encourage young adults to participate in synagogue activities, Wise took the lead in founding a "Society for Religious Study" in December 1893, which in the years to follow heard a variety of Jewish scholars and communal leaders talk on topics of interest. His responsibilities included representing B'nai Jeshurun to the community, and this he did with increasing prominence over the years. He took part in a multitude of memorial services, dedications, and annual meetings, and recognition of his abilities came in election to directorships and offices in a number of communal agencies. He was the leading spirit in the organization of the Jewish Religious School Union in 1896 and its first secretary; he served as a director of the Hebrew Free School Association, and for a while belonged to the advisory board of the Jewish Theological Seminary. In 1899 he was elected secretary of the State Conference of Religions, the only Jew on the executive committee.[24]

Some of the patterns that marked Wise's later ministry were already evident at B'nai Jeshurun. In the religious school he brought in speakers from all walks of Jewish life to meet with the students. He himself now spoke widely in the New York area, frequently exchanging pulpits with rabbis of other congregations. While the majority of his sermons dealt with such standard subjects as "The Spirit of Elijah," the example of his father and of Jellinek, as well as his own inclinations, soon brought current affairs to the pulpit of B'nai Jeshurun. A large streetcar strike in Brooklyn in 1894 led to prolonged violence in which several strikers were killed. Wise went out to Brooklyn to speak to the workers and find out their grievances and what they wanted in order to settle the dispute. The following Sabbath, he spoke on "Strikes and Strikers," and condemned the evil of shooting people who sought nothing more than the right to live decently. After the service Wise saw a small group of the congregation's officers in animated discussion. The treasurer of the temple, a member of an important banking and investment firm, approached the young rabbi and demanded, "What do you know about conditions in that strike?"

Wise responded that he had informed himself as well as he could about the facts and about the living conditions of the strikers. "They are grievously overworked and underpaid.'' When the banker mumbled that he wanted religion, not strikes, in the synagogue, Wise immediately declared, "I shall continue to speak for the workers whenever I come to feel that they have a real grievance and a just cause.'' At that moment, and not a decade later, the Free Synagogue was born.[25]

A portrait of Stephen Wise at this time would have shown a young but impressive figure, leading services in a gown, mitred hat, and a High Church turned collar. He was already a master of ritual and form and knew how to use his deep resonant voice to full advantage. His days were busy, beginning with an early walk to his synagogue study at the corner of Madison Avenue and 65th Street, dressed in a Prince Albert coat and stiff shirt. He spent the morning hours planning services, arranging events, preparing schedules and bulletins, seeing visitors, and representing B'nai Jeshurun at a variety of charitable and service meetings. Then, in the afternoon, sometimes skipping lunch, he hurried across town to Columbia University for his graduate courses in Semitics.[26]

During the decade he also labored on a translation of Solomon ibn Gabirol's eleventh-century treatise on ethics, *The Improvement of Moral Qualities*; about this study a controversy has swirled for decades on the question of whether or not Stephen Wise actually did his own work in earning the doctorate which Columbia University awarded him in 1902.

According to the preface Wise wrote, the original idea came from Alexander Kohut, and for a while he utilized a photographic reproduction of the manuscript in the Bodleian Library at Oxford. During the summer of 1895 he journeyed to England and took up residence in Oxford to work with the original Arabic text. In addition, he consulted four Hebrew manuscript versions, one in Paris, two at the Bodleian, and another at Jews' College in London. The dissertation consisted of a twenty-eight page introductory essay, an English translation of seventy-six pages, two brief appendices, and a reproduction of the Arabic text.[27]

There is no doubt that Wise took graduate courses at Columbia, including several in Arabic, or that he spent the summer of 1895 at Oxford. He also was influenced by his father, who hoped that his son would pursue a scholarly career alongside his rabbinic duties. Wise himself often declared that he would like to have devoted himself to a life of scholarship, "but events turned me in other directions."[28] Many of Wise's colleagues and opponents, few of whom bore the heavy burdens he did, were able to produce scholarly works but considered Wise incapable of serious intellectual pursuits.[29] As early as the 1920s rumors were rife that Wise's dissertation had been ghostwritten. New names were put forth from time to time as the "real author" of the translation, but no hard evidence ever confirmed these suspicions.

The most persuasive case for a ghostwriter has been made by the noted Hebraicist, Professor Jacob Kabakoff. In 1966, Kabakoff published a study of Zvi Gershoni (Henry Gersoni), who had been one of Wise's early Hebrew teachers.[30] In the course of his research he found a letter from Gershoni reported that he was finishing a translation of ibn Gabirol from Arabic into Hebrew, and was also writing a lengthy thesis in English on the treatise. "All this I have sold to a pupil of mine who will publish it together with an English translation of the book in his own name and take the Ph.D. for it next month. I believe it will be a good piece of work."[31]

While the Gershoni letter is certainly interesting, it is far from conclusive and definitely not a "smoking pistol." It is dated more than six years before Wise turned in his dissertation to Columbia, and the final product is an English, not Hebrew, translation of the Arabic. Moreover, the introductory essay of twenty-nine pages hardly constitutes the "lengthy thesis" Gershoni claimed to be writing. Far more convincing evidence favoring Wise's own authorship of the thesis is now available in recently discovered letters between Wise and his mentor, Richard Gottheil. These are letters that could only have been written by a student in the throes of hard work, laboring to master an exceedingly difficult subject.

The first letter in this series is dated July 3, 1894, written in New York amidst a sweltering hot spell. "The Hebrew version," Stephen wrote, "is, Steinschneider to the contrary, quite obscure. Difficult as the Arabic version may prove, I fancy that the two texts will elucidate each other. At all events, within a fortnight my translation of the Hebrew, such as it is, will be finished and then the reading of the Arabic will be facilitated. Occasional expressions wholly baffle me." He then went on to enquire how long it would be until the photographic reproduction of the Arabic text in the Bodleian would be available. At the end of the month, Stephen could report that he had completed a tentative translation of the Hebrew texts, and a comparison of the few pages of the Arabic that had arrived made him believe that his work with the Hebrew would expedite the final translation from the Arabic.[32]

The following summer, 1895, Wise spent at Oxford, and in early July he sent Gottheil the first eighteen pages of the English translation, based on his work of the preceding year and his opportunity to examine the Arabic text. He also began the preparation of plates of Arabic to accompany the English translation, and a number of letters report his progress in finding a printer in Leipzig who was able to do the job.[33] At times he almost despaired of his shortcomings. "I am compelled to realize how much beyond my strength this task is. Much of the text is simple but there are *many* obscure passages. . . . Occasionally I have gone to [Professor Adolf] Neubauer for help, but his eye failing renders him almost useless. . . . And so I grind and grind away, patiently endeavoring to cast some light upon passages whose darkness is nothing less than Egyptian.''[34]

Wise's schedule that summer sounds all too familiar to those who have at one time or another taken a doctorate—long hours poring over obscure and at times illegible texts, working until the early hours of the morning or until thrown out of the library so that the staff could go home, trying to master an endless list of books relating either directly or indirectly to the thesis. By the end of August, as he prepared to leave England, he could report that despite all these difficulties, much had been accomplished. ''The translation is finished, subject of course to a revision at your hand. The [Arabic] text is all in type and all the proofs have been revised by me—the first half twice. . . . I have in addition brought my notes into some order. In the essay, introductory to the work, I shall endeavor to give a clear account of the principles of ibn Gabirol's *Ethics* and as far as I can his sources. This latter task will be hard because he had none, i.e. . . . . no one has thus far been able to carry his ethical principles to any definite authority.''[35]

Shortly after the publication of the book in 1902, Ignaz Goldhizer, a noted Orientalist, wrote a scathing criticism in *Hamazkir*, pointing out what he considered to be numerous errors and literary defects. A more recent evaluation by Dr. Noah Braun suggests that many of Wise's errors noted by Goldhizer may have resulted from working off a Hebrew translation, which magnified the original corruptions of the Arabic text.[36] It would appear, then, that Stephen Wise did do the work himself, but first translated the *Ethics* from Hebrew into English. It is possible that he utilized Gershoni's Hebrew translation, believing his former teacher's work to be superior to older Hebrew texts available. He then went to Oxford and laid out the original Arabic text, the Hebrew version (whether Gershoni's or another copy), and his own English rendered from the Hebrew, and proceeded to revise the English following the Arabic which, with its many defects, made the job very difficult. The criticisms of Goldhizer and Braun both indicate that Wise improperly transliterated some Arab words into Hebrew, and thus misread the meaning. A Hebrew text was indeed used, and it resulted in errors; but Gershoni did not write the thesis, Wise did. At worst, he stands guilty of poor scholarship, but not of fraud.

The question of Wise's scholarly ability, however, is even more muddied. About this time he agreed to write articles for the *Jewish Encyclopedia*, which Gottheil edited.[37] But his name also appears as the translator of the Book of Judges in the 1917 Jewish Publication Society edition of the Bible. At the turn of the century the Society decided to publish an entirely new English translation of the Old Testament which would be free of the Christian biases inherent in the King James and other English versions of the Holy Writ. The preface to the work clearly states that Wise was assigned the translation of Judges, and lists those responsible for the other books, including many leading American Jewish scholars, such as David Philipson, Bernard Drachman, and H. Pereira Mendes.[38]

However, it appears that not only did Wise not do the translation of Judges, but none of the other luminaries did their parts either. According to Dr. Solomon Grayzel, the longtime editor of the Society, the entire translation, with the exception of Psalms, was done by Max L. Margolis, then checked and emended by the editorial committee of the Society. Evidently not one of the invited contributors followed through on his commitments, but their names were nevertheless listed, both as a courtesy to them and to avoid embarrassment to the Society, which had widely publicized that fact that so many noted scholars would be participating in this great undertaking.[39]

Whether or not Stephen Wise had the intellectual abilities to do either of these works is a question that will probably never be completely answered. Despite his oft-repeated wish that he would have preferred a scholarly life, everything in his temperament indicates that the arena of activism and not a scholar's study was his true domain. He was not averse to ideas, nor frightened by them; indeed, his wide range of acquaintances and reading indicate a curious mind, a man eager to learn about new areas.

The period of his first ministry at B'nai Jeshurun can thus be seen as a growing period for Stephen Wise, a time in which he sorted out his ideas and dreams while making himself into an effective rabbi and preacher. These were happy and busy years, marred only by his father's death. On March 30, 1896, while officiating at Passover services, Aaron suddenly complained of not feeling well. The officers of the congregation finally persuaded him to go home, but after a short rest, he returned to the synagogue. Once again he became ill and went home, where he collapsed and died before doctors, summoned from the services, could reach him. Nearly all the rabbis in New York and Brooklyn attended his funeral, at which Kaufman Kohler and Gustav Gottheil eulogized a man truly beloved by the community.[40]

It was a crushing blow for Wise, depriving him not only of parental affection but of the guidance upon which he had so heavily relied. Moreover, much of the responsiblity of supporting his mother and younger siblings now fell on his shoulder; his older brother, Otto, now a lawyer in California, contributed to the financial needs, but Stephen had to deal with the daily problems. There was, however, the satisfaction that his father had seen him ordained and established in a pulpit of his own, thus carrying on the family tradition. Stephen had always wanted to emulate his father, and in later years wrote: "I have been moved to feel that my words were little more than the formulation of his thoughts, my acts were in a very real sense the embodiment of his aims, my deeds the fulfillment of his dreams."[41]

Shortly after Aaron Wise's death, a number of congregants from Rodeph

Sholom began attending services at B'nai Jeshurun and intimating that they would like to see the son take his father's place. Then in November, a formal invitation arrived to preach in the Rodeph Sholom pulpit on December 4. Wise knew that if he wanted it, the position could be his, and he was sorely tempted. As he wrote to Benjamin Blumenthal, the president of Rodeph Sholom, many ties would always bind him to the congregation: "My earliest religious instruction I gained while a pupil in your school; it was within the walls of your majestic synagogue-edifice that I was first privileged to give utterance to my hopes and plans while yet a mere aspirant for the ministry; and above all Rodeph Sholom has been my dearly beloved father's home for throughout the larger part of my life." But he would not deliver the sermon lest "it might appear to some that I was a candidate for the vacant position and for such a suspicion I must refrain from affording the slightest basis."[42]

Wise recognized that while there might be a short-term satisfaction in succeeding to his father's place, in the long run the disadvantages would outweigh the benefits. He would be seen as "Aaron's boy" for years to come, his every word and action compared to what his father might have said or done. At B'nai Jeshurun, or wherever else he might go, he would be the rabbi; at Rodeph Sholom the shadow of his father would always be there behind him.

His father's death proved, in many ways, a cleavage in Stephen Wise's life. Behind him now lay his youth, his doubts about his own abilities, his entrance into the world of Jewish affairs. In the years immediately following Aaron's death, Wise entered a new phase of his career, and took several steps that profoundly altered his life.

2

The Cause and the Lady

A tale is told that a few days before the first Zionist Congress met in Basle in 1897, Professor Joseph Klausner met an American rabbi and asked him if there were any Zionists in the United States. "Yes," came the answer, "there are two. A mad man named Stephen Wise and a mad woman, Henrietta Szold."[1] While the story may be apocryphal, it succinctly captures the status of Zionism in the United States at the end of the nineteenth century.

The movement to recreate a Jewish homeland had at its roots the deep religious yearning for redemption that had been part of Jewish life for nearly two milennia, mixed with the political nationalism that had swept across Europe in the nineteenth century. Both strands had come together in the rather fantastic figure of Theodor Herzl. An assimilated Austrian Jew, Herzl had had little to do with organized Jewish life until as a reporter he witnessed the degradation of Captain Alfred Dreyfuss in 1895. As the army drummed Dreyfuss out of its ranks, the howling mob screamed "A bas les Juifs!" Shortly afterward, Herzl published *Der Judenstaat* (The Jewish State), which called for the establishment of a Jewish homeland to solve the problem of antisemitism. Within a few months, Herzl's vision had captured the imagination of European Jews, especially those of Russia and Poland, where a proto-Zionist movement, Ohave Zion, had already begun.

Herzl's strategy called for the securing of an international charter to help Jews build their new home, but *Der Judenstaat* was vague concerning where this new Jewish state would be. As Herzl learned more about the Jews of eastern Europe, he quickly realized that only Palestine held the emotional and religious ties that could sustain the dream of return. The first Zionist Congress, therefore, adopted the Basle Programme, which would provide the rationale of the movement of the next fifty years: "Zionism strives to create for the Jewish People a home in Palestine secured by public law." To

17

this end the movement would assist settlement by Jews in Palestine, the development of local agencies to support the Zionist work, and the raising of a national consciousness among Jews everywhere. At the end of the Congress, Herzl confided to his diary: "At Basle I founded the Jewish state. If I said this out loudly today I would be greeted by universal laughter. In five years, perhaps, and certainly in fifty years, everyone will perceive it."[2]

Not all Jews welcomed Herzl and his Zionism. Those in western Europe had been emancipated from their ghettos and relieved of restrictive laws by Napoleon almost a century earlier. They had worked hard to secure a place in the secular society, to safeguard their right to be seen as German or French or English rather than as Jewish. This newly resurgent Jewish nationalism scared them, and they feared that they would be branded as aliens, as traitors who had turned against their host countries. After all, how could they be loyal to France or England if they worked to create a Jewish state in Palestine? "Whoever disputes my claim to the German fatherland," wrote Gabriel Riesser, "disputes my right to my thoughts and feelings, to the language I speak, the air I breathe." Orthodox Jews condemned Herzl for violating God's will because only the messiah would be able to redeem the Jewish people; Reform Jews denounced the attempted revival of an anachronistic nationalism. Hermann Adler, the chief rabbi of Engand, called Zionism an "egregious blunder," while the chief rabbi of Vienna, Moritz Gudemann, railed against the "Kuckucksei of Jewish nationalism."[3]

In the United States the general reaction to Zionism was even more hostile than in Europe. To many American Jews, this country was in fact a new Zion, one which lacked repressive laws against Jews and which had never had any institutionalized antisemitism. In migrating here from Europe, Jews had chosen the United States over Palestine as the land of their hopes and dreams. While life for the new immigrants had been hard, the opportunities for success existed, and within one generation Jews had begun to climb out of tenements and sweatshops into the middle and upper classes. The age-old dream of redemption in Palestine was relegated to a messianic vision, a ritual chant of "Next year in Jerusalem" dutifully recited each year at the Passover *seder*.

For no group was this more true than for Reform Jews. The modernizing movement, begun in Germany in the 1830s and 1840s, reached its peak in the United States in the 1880s. For Reform Judaism, the departure of Jews from Palestine had not been an exile, but a dispersion in order to carry the ethical message of God throughout the world. The mission of Judaism was universal, and should not be shackled by attempts to restore an ancient state, an atavism which had outlived its usefulness in God's grand scheme of history. The United States, a land of freedom, provided the perfect soil upon which a liberal, universal, and modern Judaism could grow. Rabbi

Emil Hirsch, on the 250th anniversary of the arrival of Jews in America, declared: "Our Reform Judaism has come to understand in fullest measure this concordance of its own genius with that of the institutions and goals of America. We feel that if anywhere on God's footstool our messianic vision will be made real, it is in this land where a new humanity seems destined to rise."[4] This anti-Zionism in the Reform movement would last until the eve of World War Two. Thelogical arguments were buttressed by the fears of prominent Reform laymen that Zionism would create a dual loyalty among American Jews, and would thus undermine their freedom and security. Zionism, according to Jacob Schiff, "places a lien upon citizenship" and would create "a separateness which is fatal." Publisher Adolph Ochs constantly disparaged Zionism and ordered that the movement should receive little space and no support in the pages of the *New York Times*.[5]

There were, however, a few Reform rabbis who supported Zionism. Bernhard Felsenthal argued that Jews could not be a light to the nation unless there was a united Jewish nation in a country of their own. Caspar Levias and Max Schloessinger urged their colleagues to recognize that Zionism had strong spiritual as well as secular features. "Reform Judaism will be Zionistic," prophesied Schloessinger, "or it will *not be at all!*" Gotthard Deutsch attacked as Philistine the contention that Jerusalem had no meaning for modern Jewry, while Maximillian Heller of New Orleans strongly supported the cause. In June 1900, Gustav Gottheil, who had emigrated from Germany three decades earlier, declared: "There is no such thing as an anti-Zionist. A man need not be a supporter of our ethics, but how can anyone in whose veins flows Jewish blood oppose the movement? Every true Jewish heart is naturally Zionistic."[6] But Reform Jews who were Zionists were a tiny minority in the late 1890s, exceptions in a movement that would remain hostile to the cause of Jewish nationhood for decades to come. It was this battle that would occupy much of Stephen Wise's energy and time.

What exactly turned Stephen Wise into a Zionist is difficult to say. As a child, he heard a great deal about Palestine, since his grandmother had gone to live in Jerusalem after Reb Joseph's death. Messengers collecting alms for the Holy Land were frequent in Aaron Wise's house, but the settlers they spoke about were poor, pious Jews who studied Torah in Palestine while living on *chalukah* (charity) gathered in the Diaspora, not the young pioneers who went out to settle the land.

Nor was Wise influenced by the large proto-Zionist Ohavei-Zion groups on the lower East Side. Although he grew up on East 5th Street, the east side of the Russian and Polish immigrants lay further to the south, and by his own admission, Wise knew little of them. Socially his family moved more in the uptown circle of German-speaking Jews, in which the Gottheils were prominent. The elder Gottheil, a close friend of Aaron, had been one of

Stephen's teachers when the youth attended after-school religious classes at Emanu-El. Gustav's son Richard was Wise's teacher at Columbia and supervisor of his thesis; only twleve years older than Wise, Richard Gottheil would become a close friend of his student as well as a colleague in the Zionist movement. In fact in 1897, Richard Gottheil was the leading Zionist in the United States, and Stephen Wise his energetic assistant.

The value of the Gottheils and Wise to the movement was quickly recognized by the eastern European Jewish immigrants who comprised the bulk of the membership in local Zionist clubs. The elder Gottheil was rabbi of prestigious Temple Emanu-El, his son a professor at a leading American university, while Wise ministered to B'nai Jeshurun, another important "uptown" synagogue. These connections to the more Americanized groups within the Jewish community held out hope that the movement could attract other Jews besides the Yiddish-speaking "downtowners." But at the same time Wise and Gottheil differed in an important way from their followers.

The Yiddish-speaking intellectuals who supported Zionism considered political Zionism, the need for establishing a Jewish homeland to provide refuge from persecution, as only one part, and perhaps the least important part, of the cause. If they were socialists, they dreamed of creating a new Jewish society based not so much on religion as on social justice and economic egalitarianism. Even while a state was little more than the utopian wish of the Basle Program, they argued heatedly over its economic organization, over how land would be distributed, about a classless society in which all people—men and women—would be equal. Other Zionists followed the teachings of Asher Ginsberg, who under the pen name of Achad Ha'am saw a home in Palestine as the catalyst in a cultural rebirth of the Jewish people.

The more Americanized Zionists—and they were very few at this time—followed the political philosophy of Theodor Herzl and Max Nordau. Wise's first known Zionist statement, made shortly after the initial Zionist Congress in the summer of 1897, shows how little he either knew about or understood these other elements of Zionism, which in the end would be at least as important as the political component:[7]

> Zionism looms large on the horizon of the Jewish outlook. No better testimony can be borne to the just and equitable protection which is accorded to every dweller in our free land regardless of race or religion, than our very inability to understand the necessity for founding a little Jewish principality within the confines of Palestine. The American Jew longs for no Palestine. He gives his individual allegiance to this land which alone can satisfy his very passion for liberty in conviction and freedom of soul.

Why then shall Zion be rebuilt? And, rebuilt it must be, unless the United States raises its voice in the councils of nations so that the Jew may everywhere be permitted to live and labor in safety and peace.

Surely the American heart will sympathize with the unhappy plight of the millions of Jews in Russia, Roumania, Bulgaria—omitting the mention of sundry lands—self-styled *Kulturvolke* who are not permitted to till the soil, lest they eke out a substance and being driven to resort to small barter and traffic by inhuman laws, are reproached because they have the hardihood to gain success.

Wise seemingly believed that it might not be necessary to rebuild Zion if only the nations of the world would allow Jews everywhere "to live and labor in safety and peace." According to Louis Lipsky, who would be associated with Wise in both the Zionist movement and the American Jewish Congress for the next fifty years, Wise "was never able to rid himself of the overwhelming influence of Theodor Herzl and the prejudices of that early period." It blinded him to the spiritual and cultural interest of the immigrant masses, but it also provided him with strength, and "gave what he said when he spoke on Jewish subjects a tone and dignity and purpose it could have acquired from no other source."[8]

Throughout his life Wise rarely engaged in the intricate ideological debates which the East Side Zionists so loved. Like so many American progressives, discussion of means without regard to ends bored him; he wanted to know the problem, how it should be solved, and which methods could best implement the solution. Thus, when Louis Brandeis rose to the leadership of the American Zionists in August 1914, he found Wise a willing lieutenant totally in sympathy with his hard-headed, pragmatic approach. In the 1890's, however, Wise tackled the problem of organization, a morass that plagued American Zionism for years to come.

Gottheil and Wise, following the Herzlian directive at the First Zionist Congress, took the lead in attempting to merge the numerous small Zionist societies into some cohesive and effective pattern. While nearly all the Zionist clubs recognized the need for organization and cooperation, each group—the Uptown East Side Zion Society, the Patriots of Palestine, or the Daughters of Zion—insisted on retaining near-total freedom of action. The first step involved bringing together the several Zionist societies in the New York area. On December 15, 1897, they formed the Federation of Zionist Societies of Greater New York and Vicinity with Richard Gottheil as president, Herman Rosenthal and Joseph T. Bluestone as vice-presidents, and Stephen Wise as secretary. Before they could take the next step, however, the New York federation practically fell apart over a jurisdictional dispute.

Rabbi Bluestone believed a Zionist faternal order would attract members, since many Jews seemed interested in joining fraternal societies at the time. He therefore proceeded to organize the Free Sons of Zion. Gottheil and Wise called in Bluestone and tried to point out to him that a new group, outside the framework of the New York Federation, could only undermine their efforts to impost unity and cohesiveness on American Zionism. Bluestone refused to listen, withdrew from the Federation, and set up a rival group, the United Zionists, which, after a short and not very succcessful existence, died a natural death. While it functioned, however, it hampered the work and prestige of the Federation.[9]

Gottheil and Wise pressed on, however, trying to spread the Zionist idea, extending the movement's activities and organization. They called a conference of Jewish merchants to inform them of the increasing wine production in Palestine at the vineyards supported by Baron de Rothschild near Rishon l'Tzion. More important, they finally managed to convene a conference of American Zionist groups in New York on July 4 and 5, 1898, at the B'nai Zion Club on Henry Street. One hundred delegates attended, twenty from outside New York representing thirteen cities. After much debate, they drew up a constitution for a Federation of American Zionists which endorsed the Basle Programme and submitted to the jurisdiction of the World Zionist Organization, which then had its headquarters in Vienna. The convention chose Richard Gottheil as the president of the FAZ and Wise as "honorary secretary," a term he later jocularly interpreted as meaning "unpaid."[10]

The Federation did provide American Zionism with a central organization, or to be more precise, an address, for it had the same structural defects as its New York predecessor. The FAZ had its basic unit of membership the local society, not the individual Zionist. The primary loyalty of each member, therefore, lay not with the national organization but with his or her club. Many of these groups were short-lived, and they were unable to contribute either money or reliability to the Federation, which remained weak and ineffectual.

These weaknesses, however, were not apparent in the glow of comradeship and accomplishment that suffused the convention. Despite the opposition of the Americanized German Jewish elite, despite the indifference of the majority of the Jewish community, despite the factionalism and petty jealousies among the local clubs, a national organization had been forged and three fully accredited delegates, each of course paying his own way, boarded a steamer to journey to the Second Zionist Congress, which met in Basle at the end of August 1898.

The Second Congress proved the most productive of the early Zionist gatherings. On the recommendation of the Executive, the Congress voted to establish the Jewish Colonial Trust, which for the next fifty years would act as the movement's bank, transferring funds, arranging for payment of land puchase, and in general aiding the development of *yishuv*, the Jewish settlement in Palestine. The Congress also created the General Hebrew Language Society to foster the study and growth of Hebrew as a modern language. Despite opposition to Jewish nationalism especially among the more assimilated communities, the number of recognized Zionist groups had increased in one year from 117 to 913. The 349 delegates cheered wildly when Herzl declared that the movement must "capture the Jewish communities."

Few cheered louder than the young American delegation, particularly Stephen Wise, for whom the Congress and especially Theodor Herzl were a revelation. "For the first time in my youthful life I got a glimpse of world Jewry. There I sought and met for the first time with great men who were great Jews, with great Jews who were great men. . . . Suddenly as if by magic I came upon a company of Jews who were not victims or refugees or beggars, but proud and educated men, dreaming, planning, toiling for their people. Veritably I suffered a rebirth, for I came to know my people at their best. Thrilled and gratified, I caught a glimpse of the power and the pride and the nobleness of the Jewish people, which my American upbringing and even service to New York Jewry had not in any degree given me. I was a Jew by faith up to the day of the Congress in Basle and little more. At Basle I became a Jew in every sense of that term. Judaism ceased to be a type of religious worship. The Jewish people became my own."[11]

Wise was particularly enthralled by Herzl, to whom he had written earlier in the year about the lack of support for Zionism among American rabbis. He now met Herzl, and would evermore be his disciple. The Zionist founder, wrote Wise, reminded him of an ancient prophet, a Hebrew king. He wrote of Herzl in glowing terms for the New York *Journal*, for which he had agreed to report the Congress. Enthusiastically, he described the final session at 5:00 in the morning; as Herzl finished the closing speech, the day dawned and Herzl shone in the brilliance of the rising sun.[12]

A jubilant Wise returned from the Congress eager to carry out Herzl's command to "capture the communities." In the next two years he spoke frequently at Zionist meetings, writing articles for the *American Hebrew* in the United States and contributing occasional pieces to the *Jewish World* of London and the Viennese *Die Welt*, the official organ of the World Zionist Organization. Herzl urged him to work even more strenuously, for if the large American Jewish community could be won over to Zionism, it would immeasurably strengthen the movement. But as Wise perceived and tried to explain to the European leaders, "the well to do, the rich, the Americanized, more or less educated and cultured [Jews] cannot be won over or stormed at in public meetings"[13] Only a slow educational process could reach them; how slow that would be even Wise could not imagine.

Given the fact that he ministered to a relatively large congregation, participated in a number of New York Jewish activities, and worked on his doctorate, Wise still expended immense energy on Zionism during this period. He traveled through much of New England and the Atlantic coastal states selling shares in the Jewish Colonial trust, trying to win new members to the movement, and becoming the most effective Zionist orator in the country.[14] In Boston, an overflow crowd packed the Balwin Place synagogue, and according to one news reporter present, "the large audience was held spellbound by a tall and stately young man with arresting classic countenance, piercing eyes, and a voice that reverberated throughout the auditorium and stirred the emotions of every person present." At another meeting, even the anti-Zionist reporter conceded that Wise's "fine eloquence and manifest great Jewish heart gained for him a place in the affections of his hearers which nothing can efface." Although he was only twenty-five years old, Wise was cited by Herzl himself as the foremost Zionist speaker in America.[15]

At least some of this effort bore fruit. At the second conference of the FAZ in June 1899, Wise could report to the one hundred delegates that 125 societies had now affiliated, 100 more than the year before, and that 10,000 men and women had paid the *shekel*, the dues payment. But balancing these gains was the poor financial condition of the Federation, which barely had enough money to pay its bills, and the continued organizational weakness that precluded effective national action.[16]

This weakness soon affected relations between the Federation and the World Zionist Organization. The parent body, starved for funds, believed that despite the exertions of Wise and Gottheil, more could be done. Over Gottheil's protest, Herzl sent two of his lieutenants to the United States to spread Zionist propoganda. Both Michael Singer and Joseph Zeff proved singularly inept, insisting on using the rhetoric of a Europe racked by antisemitism in a nation relatively free of that curse. Moreover, the WZO Executive had no hesitation in dealing with strong local societies, bypassing the Federation and further undermining its position.

While Wise maintained good personal relations with Herzl, the deteriorating position of the FAZ constantly frustrated him. Finally, in November 1899, he resigned as honorary secretary of the Federation, but as he quickly explained to Herzl, the release from "that onerous work" would allow him to be of more service to the cause. The fact of the matter, however, was that his enthusiasm had been dampened by the continuous infighting among the Zionist groups. "I am getting pretty tired," he confided to Isidore Morrison, his successor as honorary secretary of the FAZ. "There is so much bickering and dissatisfaction and fault-finding that the best of good nature is put to a severe test. As you know I have sacrificed a great deal in behalf of the cause. I have frequently neglected my personal business, have made a number of enemies, and have otherwise gone to greater lengths than a great many would have done in order to upbuild a respectable Zionist organization in this country. And now to see that all these efforts and sacrifices are not only not appreciated but even sneered at and my motives questioned is enough to disgust anybody."[17]

Here it is possible to see one of Stephen Wise's less admirable traits, the tendency to personalize every battle, every difference of opinon. Perhaps part of his greatness stemmed from his throwing his entire being, body and soul, into every cause he championed; no one could ever doubt his sincerity, his belief, his commitment whenever he took up the fight for Zionism or child labor reform or good government. But he had difficulty understanding why others could not see the light so clearly as he did, and he frequently construed their criticisms of his positions as personal attacks on him.

At the turn of the century there was great opposition to Zionism among many American Jews, and Wise came in for his share of criticism from those who differed with him about the merits of Jewish nationalism. Even within his own congregation few members accepted their rabbi's Zionism. Jewish nationalism as it was being expounded by its European ideologues and American interpreters such as Gottheil and Wise, had little appeal to those trying to make a new life in America, one free from the prejudices and persecutions of Europe.

Wise, Gottheil and others sought to define Zionism not only in terms of a refuge from tyranny, but as an affirmation of New World idealism. In a speech to a large Zionist rally at Cooper Union in June 1900, Wise exhorted the crowd to be good Zionists and good Americans at the same time. "Say that you are an American Jew," he declared, "and strive for the best principles of the race, and you will be respected and the Zionist name honored." He himself swore that there would be no one in this country who would "strive more for the glorious ideals of Zionism."[18]

This would be his last major Zionist speech in New York of several years, because his energies and attention turned to other interests. On a speaking tour of the West Coast for the Federation, he had glimpsed a new and intriguing part of America, one not only geographically but culturally removed from the New York he knew—and loved—so well. A chance now came to learn more about this semi-frontier country, but an even more important change in his life had already begun—the result, fittingly enough, of one of his responsibilities as a rabbi.

In January 1899, a member of B'nai Jeshurun died and the bereaved family asked a cousin to inform the rabbi so that funeral arrangements could be made. Since there was no telephone, the young woman walked from her home on 68th Street to the address she had been given. After being announced, she waited a few moments in the parlor until the young rabbi came downstairs to join her. As Stephen Wise later recalled, the minute he set eyes on Louise Waterman he fell in love with her; it took the lady a little while longer to make up her mind. To his friends and family as well as to hers, it seemed a most improbable match, yet their love flourished on a commonality of interests and a passion for justice and decency. Their romance continued throughout the nearly five decades of their marriage.

The Waterman family had begun to emigrate from Bruck, near Erlanger in Bavaria, to the New World in the 1840's. Sigmund Wasserman (as they then spelled the name), a talented poet arrived first and became one of the first instructors of German language and literature at Yale College. During the four years he taught there he also studied medicine; he received his medical degree in 1848, the first Jew ever to graduate from Yale. He then moved to New York where he established his practice, served as police surgeon for thirty years, and also taught at a medical school.[19]

Sigmund's two brothers, Leopold and Julius, soon followed him to New Haven. Writing home, Leopold described the terrible conditions on board the frigate *Everhard*, but, he added, "no matter what my lot may be, I shall never regret having sought a new home, where only one comes to the recognition of true human dignity, and in free employment of one's own strength can become the master of one's own fortune".[20] Within ten years Leopold established a prosperous business, held extensive property, and engaged in a large trans-Atlantic commerce. A business trip to Europe in the summer of 1854 ended in his tragic death, as the steamship *Artic*, on which he was a passenger, sank off Newfoundland after colliding with another vessel.

Leopold's business partner had been his brother Julius, who, as soon as he had been able to earn proper living, had sent for his fiancée, Justine Meyer, brought her to New Haven, and there married her. A craftsman by training, Julius joined Leopold in establishing a highly successful hoop-skirt factory. When his business interest expanded, Julius decided to move to New York, just before the birth of his third child, Louise. There his son and two daughters were raised in comfortable surroundings. Julius enjoyed good music and liked to read; he brought *Don Quixote* and Byron's poems with him from Germany, and the markings in the books show that he had used them to help him learn English. Justine Waterman seems to have been the chief influence in her daughter's youth. At a time when few women were educated beyond the simple necessities of polite society, she knew three languages (which she taught to Louise), and read widely and avidly, another trait she passed on to her children. Most important, Louise admired her mother's passion for truth, her disgust with fraud or deceit.[21]

As a result, Louise Waterman set extremely high standards for herself. Nicknamed "Quicksilver" because of her gay spirits, by her late teens she had matured into a serious, intelligent, and quite beautiful young woman. She was educated at Comstock, one of New York's better finishing schools where she mastered French and German and received some training in music and art. In later years she would put this education to good use, translating the works of Edmond Fleg and Aimé Pallière into English; she also developed into a fair artist, one praised by critics and whose works would be exhibited in galleries and museums. But there was always that serious streak, those Alpine standards. Her schoolmates married one by one, but Louise waited, spurning beaus who did not measure up to her ideals, declaring it would be better not to marry than to accept someone she could not respect and admire.

As far as religion went, it did not go far at all. Julius was devoutly agnostic, and took out a membership in Temple Emanu-El only for burial privileges. The family rarely attended services, nor did the parents ever force their children to do so. For a time, Louise could be found on Sunday mornings at an Episcopal Sunday School accompanying her best friend. Judaism evidently offered her little, nor did she seek or find solace in it after her mother's death in 1890. Instead, she retreated into her books and art until she met Felix Adler, the founder of the Ethical Culture Movement.[22]

A rabbi and the son of a famous rabbi, Adler had come to eschew both formal theology and ritual. He left the rabbinate to seek a Universal Truth based on the insights of man rather than on divine commandments. His moral passion, which derived in large part from Judaism's prophetic teachings, appealed to Louis Waterman's own idealism. Adler induced her, much to her family's chagrin, to give art courses in ghetto settlement houses, to do what she could to help the people living in tenement slums. He not only taught her, but became a friend; years later, when their paths had diverged, she would still write him occasional notes, affirming that he always would hold a special place in her life.[23]

But now, suddenly, this woman with impossible standards, with practically no identification or even sympathy with Judaism, found herself attracted to Stephen Wise. They both read and appreciated the Stoics and admired Emerson and Thoreau. Her work at the University Settlement House carried out the precept of the social gospel he preached. Throughout the spring of 1899 Wise wooed her, lending her books, going for walks, contriving to stop in and see her at odd moments.

Louise and Stephen grew ever more oblivious of anything and anybody but each other, and her family, at first annoyed, soon became concerned and then frantic. She came from good Bavarian stock, he from Hungary; she enjoyed all the advantages of wealth, while he was a poor rabbi—not even a banker or lawyer or businessman. Worst of all, he belonged, in fact was a leader, of that crazy Zionist movement. Even Louise and Stephen recognized with some bemusement the ludicruous improbability of their romance; her relatives were not at all amused. With the death of her father, her elder brother and sister, Leo and Jennie, now headed the family, and they told her in all seriousness that she owed it to the Waterman name to avoid such a misalliance. When such reasoning failed, the family resorted to an old but tested remedy. With almost unseemly haste, she was packed off to spend the summer in Europe with relatives, in the hope that time and distance would put an end to this infatuation.[24]

The remedy failed. In her trunks Louise carried not only books Wise had given her to read, but a small gold medallion in the form of a six-pointed star, with the Hebrew letters for "Zion" within its border. It was the emblem of the Zionist movement, a token to remind her not only of him but in what he believed. She wore his gift that summer, much to the dismay of her relatives, who could not understand how a girl of otherwise fine sensibilities had chosen a man so far beneath her station, and a demented Zionist at that. One evening an uncle came to take her to the opera, and he beamed with avuncular pride as the lovely young woman came down the stairs to join him. The he spied the medallion, and asked her what it was. Louise explained that it was a gift, and stood for Zionism. He told her to take if off, for he would not be seen in public, and certainly not at the opera, in the company of one flaunting a flag, as it were, of that wretched Jewish nationalism. "I certainly would not want to embarrass you, uncle," Louise said, "but I will not take it off. I do hope you enjoy the opera." And she turned on her heel and went back upstairs.[25]

With her return from Europe that fall, Wise renewed his courtship, now certain that she loved him in return. But he also had news for her, and how she responded was suddenly terribly important to him.

While Louise had been in Europe, Wise had decided to go west to California. His older brother Otto had established a successful law practice in San Francisco, and had written to the family in glowing terms about life and opportunity on the Pacific Coast. In addition, nascent Zionist groups had been pressing the Federation to send them some speakers, in order to bolster their own programs and attract new members. Rather than suffer through a long hot New York summer pining for his love, Wise boarded a train, intent on discovering a new part of America, spreading the Zionist message, and spending time with his brother.

The trip turned out to be more successful and enjoyable than anticipated. The spectacular scenery of the Rocky Mountains and coast states enthralled him, the audiences at his Zionist meetings responded enthusiastically, and the reunion with Otto proved joyous indeed. And in the crowds of a Zionist meeting in Portland, Oregon were members of Congregation Beth Israel, who determined to secure this dynamic young preacher for their pulpit.

Much to their surprise, Rabbi Wise responded positively to their overtures. His request for a salary of $5,000 a year did not seem exorbitant, nor did his stipulation that he be free to pursue Jewish and non-Jewish interests provided they did not interfere with his responsibilities to the congregation. By July 22 a guarantee fund to cover the salary had reached $3,000; a week later the full amount had been subscribed. The officers of Beth Israel wrote to inform him that at a special meeting of the Congregation on July 30, the members had unanimously voted to offer him a five-year contract as "Rabbi, reader and teacher," commencing in August 1900. "We have known of you for some years as a gentleman of highest standing in the community in which you have so successfully labored, as well also as a man of well-known piety, of learning and of eloquence. . . . With God's blessing, we feel sure, that during the five years of your ministrations among us, [the Congregation] will make such advances as will easily make it the leading congregation on this western coast." They also added their hope that Wise would be able to visit Portland again before going back to New York, both to see the city and explore in person its possibilities, and so that other members of Beth Israel could meet the man they hoped would be their new rabbi.[26]

Upon receipt of this letter in San Francisco, Wise immediately wrote two responses. The first was highly formal, notifying the officers that he would give "searching and prayerful deliberation" to their offer, and that upon his return to New York, he would consult with the leaders of his present congregation, B'nai Jesherun, with members of his family and with friends. He regretted that he would not be able to visit Portland *en route* to New York, pleading that his mother, who had come with him to visit Otto, did not feel well enough for the additional journey. All of this was, of course, quite proper, but on that same day he wrote privately and confidentially to Solomon Hirsch, Beth Israel's president, that "if God spares me I am fully and finally resolved to make my future home in Portland. I have considered the matter in its every bearing and now the feeling is become mine that in undertaking to labor among the Jewish residents of Portland, I shall be doing that to which the hand of God points as my nearest and holiest duty." He assured Hirsch that his mother's health was really not up to the journey, but aside from that consideration, "I should hardly deem it wise to come to your City at this time, seeing that in this event I should be obliged to signify publicly my acceptance of the charge, and this step I feel I owe it to my Congregation to defer until after I return."[27]

Why Wise decided, seemingly so precipitately, to move across the continent, away from the large concentration of Jews in New York where he had already developed a growing reputation, is difficult to determine. He himself referred to the matter only once, nearly a half century later, when he claimed that his "conservative congregation [had failed] to support its youthful, pioneering Zionist rabbi."[28] The facts, however, do not give any evidence that B'nai Jeshurun offered the slightest obstacle to his Zionist work, or stopped him from holding Zionist meetings in the building, even if individual members did not rush to pay the shekel. Some people believed he left so that the prestigious cathedral temple of Reform Judaism, Emanu-El, would be able to call him to its pulpit, something that would be more difficult if he remained rabbi of a neighboring Conservative congregation. To Louise he wrote, while in San Francisco, of the great opportunity that existed in Oregon: "A number of cities within 500 miles of Portland have their Jewish communities but no minister and nothing of religious teaching and striving. These I shall try to build up. It will be hard work, but I welcome it." Again, on his return to New York, he declared: "I wish to begin work all over again, in a new (religiously) untilled and explored land, and I am persuaded that with God's help and blessing, I shall be able to further the cause of Israel and spread the gospel of Zion.[29]

When his Zionist colleague as well as academic sponsor Richard Gottheil expressed fears that Stephen would waste his life in Oregon, Wise responded that "if I do good hard concientious work in Oregon, I shall not be wholly forgotten by the people who have come to know me during the past six years. As you know, Professor, there are many reasons why I shall seek another field of work. Portland may not be the *ideal* for me, insofar as it may seem too small and too far removed, but it is a good place and certainly more extensive and promising than the limited sphere in which I am now permitted to work. The people . . . will not be adverse to my lending my services in Oregon and surrounding states in the matter of building up and strengthening the half-organized and disorganized smaller Jewish communities, which are to be found in a radius of 500 to 1000 miles of Portland. With all the work which is in store for me in the Northwest, I yet think I shall have abundant time for study, and I mean to study, because even though I cannot be a scholar, I wish to indulge my scholarly taste and read widely and deeply in Jewish and kindred lore. . . . The truth is I am absolutely resolved to leave New York and go to Portland."[30]

Here one can see the restless ambition and energy that dominated Wise's entire life. Success of a kind had perhaps come too easily in New York, thanks in part to his family connections as well as his native talent. He had helped found the Zionist movement in America, held national office at age twenty-three and had been elected to the Zionist Executive a year later. Had he chosen to stay in New York, to "play it safe," there were few professional rewards that could not have been his for the asking. But Stephen Wise could never rest content with a level of success that would have satisfied others; he constantly needed new challenges, new opportunities that would not only test him to his limits, but that would bring recognition of the heights he had scaled. The frontier, the Jewish frontier in America, seemed to lie in the West.

Word of the Portland offer leaked out even before he returned to New York. The Portland *Hebrew Standard* referred to him in very complimentary terms as the "bishop of Oregon," a term Wise found enjoyable, if not quite appropriate. In September he discussed the matter at great length with the trustees of B'nai Jeshurun and with Louise. Despite the New York congregation's entreaties that he stay, Wise appeared determined to accept the Portland offer, provided Louise would come with him.[31]

Much to his relief and joy, the thought of moving across continent, of giving up family and friends and status, did not faze Louise at all. After all, Wise now had, as he put it, "splendid opportunities for pioneer work," and wasn't this what she has always sought—a man larger than life, a champion willing to face the unknown for just causes? In turn, as Thomas Davidson told him, he had found his Beatrice, one who would be there encouraging him in his tilts at prejudice and injustice, deflating him if his ego got out of hand, bristling at the barbs of his detractors, providing a calm home, a shelter from the storms he created.

If Louise had been won over, Jennie and Leo remained to be convinced. In January of 1900, they began to face the inevitable. After a lengthy meeting in which Wise described his "prospects" as well as his great love for their sister, they still held back on an engagement, but tacitly assented to his courtship.[32] In the meantime, they asked Felix Adler to find out what he could about this tall, courteous, and extremely persistent young man. Adler knew that Wise, like himself, had spent a summer at Glenmore with Thomas Davidson, and so contacted their mutual teacher and friend for his appraisal of Louise's suitor. Adler passed Davidson's glowing report on to the Watermans:[33]

> The fact is, I am so fond of Stephen Wise personally, that I cannot, perhaps, be trusted to judge him impartially. I have known him for the past six or seven years, and my respect and affection for him have grown all that time. He is loyal in his personal relations, and socially attractive. I cannot think of him as doing a mean thing. When roused, he is an eloquent and powerful speaker, with a delightful sense of humor.

> He is still young—only twenty-seven, I think—and may have some of the faults of the young and inexperienced, delight in sense of power and perhaps desire for popularity, though the last is not especially prominent.

> He is distinctly a stirring man, original and forcible, with great schemes in his mind. I always leave him with the sense that I have been facing a brisk, bracing wind.

At the beginning of July 1900, Louise Waterman and Stephen Wise announced their engagement, and the couple began coping with the innumerable details that precede a wedding. Together they went to the graves of her parents and his father, symbolically beseeching their blessing. Wise would have preferred marriage before leaving for Oregon, but Louise convinced him that in the first few months of his new pastorate, he should be able to give all his time and energy to the demands of the congregation.

While not wishing to be separated from his fiancée, he had to agree that her suggestion made good sense. A lovelorn Wise bade her goodbye, and left by train for Portland at the end of the month.

Wise's West Coast ministry almost ended before it began. His melancholia suddenly gave way to severe physical distress when he was seized by an attack of appendicitis in Duluth. He insisted upon continuing the journey, with the conductor and his fellow passengers tending and comforting him. Finally, the pain almost unendurable, he agreed to enter a hospital in Helena, Montana, where the doctors feared they might have to operate on a patient so ennervated by the trip as to make the procedure dangerous. Rest and medication, however, soon reduced the inflammation, and Wise resumed his journey westward. On the train he wrote, only half-jokingly, that he doubted he could wait until November, when their wedding was scheduled. "I really think we will have the arrangements changed," he suggested, "and you, love, come out to me in Portland to be married. In fact I have been seriously thinking to be sick, sending for you as a nurse, and then keeping you with me."[34]

Upon his arrival, the entire Jewish community went out of its way to welcome the new rabbi. They filled his hotel room with dozens of roses and other flowers, and vied to entertain him in their homes. He wrote to Louise about his reception, and his trip to the temple:[35]

> Last night, I took dinner at the beautiful home of the Hirsch's. After dinner we drove in a blinding rain to the Temple. Dr. Bloch read the Service—I taking no part, because not yet installed, although I was very eager to praise God for his countless loving kindnesses—and I do from out of the silent depths of my heart. The Synagogue interior, which I had forgotten, was a revelation and delight to me—simple and beautiful and commodious. The organ was well-played and the choir expectionally good. Despite the rain a goodly attendance was present. The Services are very different from those of the Madison Avenue Synagogue, mainly in English, but the English is mouthed and badly pronounced. I shall introduce the Union Prayer Book. It is quite certain that after a time it will be possible for me to induce the congregation to engage Dr. Bloch as my reader and assistant. For the holidays in the absence of Dr. Bloch from Portland, I am to have the assistance of a Jewish lawyer who will read the prayers.

> One thing impressed me last night, as I looked at the men and women before me: We feel, and justifiably, that this is an age of materialism. Still there is hope! Does not the gathering of people in large numbers for worship, for worship of *something*, show that these people, though they understand it not, are not satisfied with their gold and houses. They yearn for something—their spirits are in quest of something. We must give it—God and righteousness—a God of righteousness. If we fail now, God pity us. I tremble when I think of

the awfulness of the responsibility—we can and ought to do so much—we are doing so little.

He also assured her that he was taking care of himself. "I am really in good health and absolutely rested. I am very careful about my diet. The doctor, who has gotten to be very chummy, allows me to have fish and fowl but I shall stick to the old regimen eating nothing but bouillon, hominy, rice, chocolate, cocoa, toast or oysters and eggs. I eat nothing else, no meats, vegetable, fruits, fish, etc. I want to finish my work nicely and get back to you, my angel, strong and well enough to begin my task as dictator and Imperator in Rex."[36]

After being installed and officiating at the High Holy Day services, Wise hastened eastward at the beginning of November. On the ninth, he went to Tiffany's to purchase "two plain rings," one of which he inscribed "30:12," referring to their favorite verse in Psalm 30: "Thou didst turn for me my mourning into dancing. Thou didst loose my sackcloth and gird me with gladness." Stephen Wise married Louise Waterman on November 14, 1900 in her family's home. Two rabbis officiated—Gustav Gottheil, his father's old colleague and Wise's teacher, and Kaufman Kohler, a leader of the Reform movement and a longtime friend of the Waterman family. At the reception afterward, Kohler took the bride aside and told her: "My dear, you have married a promising young man who will, I am sure, go far. But he will accomplish much more if you can cure him of his *meshugass*, this lunacy of Zionism. To rid him of that will be the greatest service you can do him—and yourself."[37] Louise smiled sweetly, but said nothing. Soon afterward, Rabbi and Mrs. Stephen S. Wise boarded a train for their new home and new life together in Portland.

3

Bishop of Oregon

It is doubtful whether Solomon Hirsch, Ben Selling, or any of the other enthusiasts who had secured Stephen Wise's consent to become rabbi of Beth Israel had any idea of the impact he would have on that congregation. They knew, of course, of his speaking abilities, that he was finishing a doctorate at Columbia, and that his congregation in New York thought so highly of him that some members tried, despite his protests, to have the Portland group release him from his contract.[1] Moreover, one could hardly be in Wise's presence for more than a few moments without recognizing the enormous nervous energy which he could barely contain. Even so, Wise's accomplishments in Portland far exceeded the fondest hopes of his sponsors.

The Jewish presence on the West Coast dated back to the early exploration and survey expeditions. With the gold rush of the 1850s and the completion of the transcontinental railroad lines, Jewish communities had sprung up in nearly all of the larger cities and towns, while relatively isolated families or groups of families could be found in smaller settlements. Portland's Jewish population in 1900 did not exceed 1,500 or 2,000 people; Beth Israel, founded in 1858 and the largest congregation, had between eighty and ninety families. In addition to the Reform Beth Israel, two smaller Orthodox synagogues served the community, but probably half the Jewish population did not formally affiliate with any congregation. The growth of Beth Israel had been due in large measure to the dedicated work of a handful of men, notably Solomon Hirsch, a businessman who had also become a power in state politics and served for three years as U. S. Minister to Turkey. As president of the congregation, Hirsch had been the moving force in bringing Wise to Portland, and until his death in the fall of 1902, provided the young rabbi with sound advice about the congregants, access to influential people in the wider community, and above all, generous support for the innovations Wise introduced. But even he had not anticipated the ideas of independence and action that the new minister brought with him.

A hint might have been found in Wise's reluctance to sign a contract with Beth Israel. Shortly after wiring his acceptance of the call, he wrote Hirsch and suggested foregoing a formal contract: "I, for my part, feel assured that you will never ask anything which is not just and reasonable, nor will I ever insist upon anything which you cannot cheerfully concede to me. Our mutual relations are to be of too high and holy a nature to be brought within the stipulations of a contract. Unless we can work together in a spirit of mutual confidence and helpfulness, it will be impossible for us to promote the spiritual interests of the Congregation."[2] While Hirsch sympathized with this desire to base relations solely on trust rather than rely on a legal document, he gently explained that the subscribers to the guarantee fund for the rabbi's salary had themselves signed a pledge which included a clause calling for a contract within six months of acceptance of the offer.

Moreover, the trustees were not acting in self-interest but in order to create the best possible atmosphere in which rabbi and congregation could function harmoniously. They had agreed at their last meeting to grant Wise two months of summer vacation, and to have him participate in all board meetings relating to religious or educational matters. They did not want to keep his predecessor on even as an assistant, since Jacob Bloch was "somewhat contentious." Wise thus had little choice but to accede. All he requested was that the contract be kept as short and simple as possible, and on December 22, 1899, he signed a one-page agreement and mailed it off to Hirsch.[3]

The historian of Beth Israel, Julius Nodel, believes that the trustees wanted a formal contract because they feared Wise would change his mind, that the blandishments of his New York congregation, family ties, and the wealth and opportunities of New York's large Jewish population would lead him to renege on his acceptance and stay in the East. Wise's constant assurances to Hirsch, however, as well as his private letters to Louise and Richard Gottheil, indicate just the opposite—that he meant exactly what he told Hirsch, that he wanted to have a ministry in Oregon different from the usual rabbi–congregation formalities.

At his installation as rabbi of Beth Israel on September 7, 1900, however, Wise quite clearly indicated that he wanted a level of independence far beyond that normally exercised by a rabbi. The commodious sanctuary was jammed that evening, despite inclement weather, both by members and nonmembers of the congregation as well as by a large sprinkling of non-Jews. After greetings from Hirsch and the charge by Rabbi Jacob Voorsanger of San Francisco, the new rabbi strode up to the pulpit, an unruly lock of hair hanging over his forehead, struck the lectern with a clenched fist, and in a booming voice declared: "I name but one condition. I ask it as my right. You will and must allow it. You would not respect me if I should waive it for a single hour. This pulpit must be free! *This pulpit must be free!"*

This manifesto must be seen in the context of prevailing pulpit restrictions at the turn of the century. Wise himself had felt few constraints while at B'nai Jeshurun, nor had his father been silenced at Rodeph Sholom. At other Jewish and non-Jewish congregations, however, many ministers were compelled either formally or informally to clear their sermon topics with the boards of trustees. The rabbi or pastor may have been allowed a free hand in all matters of ritual or religious interpretation, but especially in those churches or synagogues with a large wealthy clientele, comments on social issues were neither encouraged nor welcome, save if the speaker endorsed the prevailing conservative ethos. While it would be difficult to determine the actual number of congregations in which this type of censorship prevailed, there are sufficient examples of its existence to describe it as more than an isolated phenomenon.

In his installation sermon, Wise consciously and emphatically allied himself with the Social Gospel movement, and indicated that at Beth Israel, more than had been the case in New York, he would be speaking out on current social topics, that he would be trying to make his congregation aware of how the ethical teachings of Judaism related to the economic problems of everyday life. Portland still had about it much of the lawless character of a frontier town, and Wise warned his congregation that he intended to address such issues, whether they be discomfited or not. But he also invited them to join him in this crusade. "Be my good angels," he implored, "and help me bear my burden. Our acts, our angels are—I ask your lives, your works, your conduct, your character."[4]

The response to the installation services and to his speech more than pleased him. To Louise he wired: "Deeply impressive installation. Enthusiastically welcomed. Never felt beter. Love." A number of Christian clergy made it a point to pay special visits to the new rabbi and praise his comments. The trustees of Beth Israel could hardly believe it when in the next several weeks before the High Holy Days of Rosh Hashanah and Yom Kippur, weeks usually "slow" in terms of attendance, crowds filled the synagogue for each service.[5] After returning from New York with his bride, Wise launched into his pastoral work, with impressive results.

First he set out to meet his congregation, and did a great amount of pastoral calling, more so than he had done at B'nai Jeshurun or would do during the Free Synagogue years. In part this resulted from the small-town nature of Portland, a community which expected to call upon its ministers and to have them return such calls. He worked diligently with the various service organizations of the congregation, including the Ladies Sewing

Society and the Altar Guild, and affiliated groups such as the Council of Jewish Women. He completely revamped the religious school curriculum and insisted upon hiring only competent teachers; volunteers would be welcome, provided they knew the material and could teach. Within a year, attendance at the temple school increased sixty percent.

Attendance at services also showed a healthy growth. Some of those at the Friday evening services came initially out of curiosity, to hear this new wonder about whom everyone spoke. Rarely were their expectations disappointed. Wise began an ongoing sermon series entitled "Present-Day Problems in Ancient Settings," in which he tied current social and economic issues to biblical events and teachings. Topics that had never been discussed at Beth Israel, such as Zionism, woman suffrage, and child labor, now became familiar issues in Wise's sermons, and with gratifying results for the congregation. Within three years, membership nearly tripled to more than 200 families. Wise also suggested a new catagory of associate membership for unmarried men, and within a year had signed up over forty members. The indebtedness of the congregation, which had amounted to more than $30,000 at the beginning of 1901, was totally erased in two years. The operating budget of Beth Israel climbed to $33,000 for 1903, but the temple's income easily exceeded that figure and the trustees delightedly announced a surplus of more than $4,000.[6]

This revitalization of Beth Israel also derived in part from Wise's definite shift toward the Reform, or as he preferred to call it, the Liberal wing of Judaism. At B'nai Jeshurun, an essentially Orthodox congregation had modified its ritual to the point of a right-wing Conservatism, but never went further than that. At Beth Israel, Wise found a congregation willing to embrace Reform completely. He introduced the Union Prayer Book, the official liturgy issued by the Union of American Hebrew Congregations, and trained a cantor to provide the appropriate music for a Reform service. He downplayed ritual,and instead emphasized the commitment of Liberal Judaism to social justice, the importance of ethics over theology.

Such precepts, moreover, should be applied not only in the secular world, but within the congregation. It had been the practice at Beth Israel, and at many other temples, to sell seats within the sanctuary, with the better pews—those closer to the Ark of the Law—commanding a premium over those at the side or in the back. As a result, a class division existed during services, with the well-to-do easily indentified by their location in the synagogue. Wise preached that a Jew's place in a House of God should not depend in any way on his wealth; let each man voluntarily pay what he could afford, and sit equally in the eyes of the Lord. The trustees, with a great deal of hesitancy, finally agreed to try this plan for the High Holy Days in 1905. Much to their surprise, voluntary contributions provided a thousand dollars more than the sale of seats had yielded a year earlier.[7] Here again, one of the major ideas of the Free Synagogue, the equal seating of all congregants, first worked successfully in Oregon. All those accomplishments won much notice for Beth Israel and its rabbi. Jacob Voorsanger, who toured the West Coast on behalf on the Reform movement, termed Beth Israel "the banner congregation. . . . All honor to Dr. Stephen Wise, whose unflagging enthusiasm leads his congregation from height to height." Even across the continent, the work in Portland received notice. Richard Gottheil wrote of all the "good reports" he heard of Wise's activities, and only hoped "that your contentment equals that of the people whose spiritual welfare is in your keeping."[8]

Gottheil also prodded his student to finish his degree, a task that had received little priority in the last few years at B'nai Jeshurun, especially after Theodor Herzl and Louise Waterman had entered the scene. Just before leaving for Portland, however, Wise had gotten the manuscript of ibn Gabirol's *Ethics* into shape for his defense, and had passed the committee examination on July 19, 1900. In those days a thesis had to be published, and for most candidates this meant subsidizing the printer. Even though Gottheil arranged for *Ethics* to be published by Columbia University Press as part of its Oriental Studies Series, endless details had to be arranged, including an extremely careful final proofing of the Arabic plates. Gottheil proved indispensable as well as persistent, taking on much of the work with the printers in order to hasten the task.[9] In May 1902, the book appeared. Gottheil deposited it in the university library, thus fulfilling the last of the degree requirements, and Columbia awarded Stephen Wise his doctorate. Although he dedicated the work as a whole to the memory of his father, the first copy he inscribed to Louise, "my wife, my love, my sweetheart, my precious angel," and in the lower right-hand corner of the flyleaf, he jotted the numbers he had had engraved on her wedding band.[10]

It is fortunate that Wise finished the dissertation when he did, for even with his phenomenal energy, he would have been hard pressed to handle scholarly tasks in addition to his other enterprises. He not only ministered to his congregation in Portland, but as he had promised, traveled widely in the Northwest, even up to Alaska, speaking to and assisting small and isolated Jewish communities. Zionism usually crept into his talks one way or another. In February 1901, for example, he spoke to the Council of Jewish Women and within a week had garnered a hundred new members; through his efforts, the Orthodox Ohavei Shalom congregation resolved to join *en masse*. But his move to the West Coast perforce made it impossible for him to be as active in national Zionist affairs as when he had lived in New York, and some of his former associates chastised him for his supposed abandonment of duty. "I share the anger of many of your friends at your having become so completely lost," wrote Isidore Morison. "You could have no idea how much we have missed you here. We had so much work for you, work which no one else could do as well as you." The fact that Wise recruited new members, that he spread the idea of Jewish nationalism on the West Coast, did not seem important to provincial New Yorkers.[11]

Wise had good cause to absent himself from the daily business of the Federation of American Zionists. During his years in Portland the organizational difficulties of the FAZ went from bad to worse, and relations between the American body and the World Zionist Organization deteriorated further. By early 1904, Gottheil was futilely demanding that the world leaders make up their minds: either the FAZ would be the representative of organized Zionism in the United States or it would not, and the WZO should designate another group. When Wise traveled to Europe in the spring of 1904, he rediscovered at first hand how little the European Zionists thought of their American colleagues. The English government had offered to provide land in East Africa for Jewish settlement, the first recognition Zionism had ever received from a major power, but the proposal split the organization and nearly destroyed the movement. Wise admitted his own ambivalence on the matter: much as he understood the historic attachment to Palestine, East Africa would at least provide an immediate refuge for persecuted Jews in Russia and eastern Europe.[12] Whatever his views, however, they mattered little to the Europeans on the Greater Actions Committee, who did not even bother to ask him what Americans thought about the proposal. Wise wrote an angry letter to Gottheil, informing him that he too would resign from the GAC. "I cannot and will not work with men who refuse to place in me their fullest confidence. That Herzl and his colleagues fail to take counsel with the only American member of the Greater Actions Committee then present in Vienna, touching the state of affairs in America, constitutes an indignity to which no gentleman can submit with honor. . . . I am as much a member of the Greater Actions Committee as Herzl or any man. It was and is his duty to deal with me, with us, frankly and honestly—I am not a Russian underling nor yet a Turkish landowner who must be kept in the dark as to the real purpose of things."[13]

Herzl tried to calm the irate young American, assuring him that it had never been his intention or that of any member of the GAC to exclude Wise from discussions of affairs in the United States. But, he added, one had to admit that bookkeeping in the Federation had been sloppy, and the bad relations between WZO and FAZ was not all one-sided. Wise reluctantly absolved Herzl from personal blame, but refused to budge on his accusations that the Europeans saw American Zionists as distinctly second-class citizens in the movement. As for the efficiency of the Federation, he declared he could not be held responsible for the condition of the organization, "seeing that my residence in Oregon 3000 miles from New York precludes the possibility of any real participation in the [FAZ] management. I have made that mistake long enough. I shall not make it all over again."[14]

Shortly before Wise left Vienna, he and Herzl went for a leisurely walk, the city parks beautiful in the mild spring weather. "Veiss, how old are you?" Herzl asked.

"I am just thirty years," came the reply.

Placing his arm around the younger man's shoulders, Herzl declared, "Veiss, you are a young man; I am an old man [Herzl was 44]. I shall not live to see the Jewish State, but you, Veiss, are a young man. You will live to see the Jewish State."[15]

A few weeks later came word of Herzl's death, his heart worn out by the endless toil and constant infighting he had had to endure in the cause of the Jewish people. For Wise, Herzl's death marked the end of an era. The Viennese Jew, with his dream of Jewish restoration and of Jewish pride, had caught the young American's imagination and loyalty; none of Herzl's lieutenants had his stature or his charisma, they inspired no loyalty. "My heart is sore and bitter," Wise wrote Gottheil upon learning of Herzl's death, and he repeated his intention to resign office in the movement. "I want to work for the cause as I did from '97 to 1900, and I will, but when I do, it must be by the side of men," not the puny leaders who now wanted to fill Herzl's place.[16] Herzl had been a father figure for Wise, coming along shortly after Aaron had died; it would take another authority figure with a commanding personality to rouse him from his Zionist doldrums, but the advent of Louis Brandeis onto the American Zionist scene was still nearly a decade in the future.

In the meantime, Wise discovered that a rabbi need not limit his activities to the synagogue nor even to Jewish affairs. If nothing else, Stephen Wise believed thoroughly and passionately in the commitment of Liberal Judaism to social betterment; first through Beth Israel and then in overtly secular activities, he made it plain to one and all that he intended to practice what he preached. His preachings, as Carl Voss has noted, derived in large part from the works of Social Gospel leaders such as Josiah Strong, Washington Gladden, Lyman Abbott, and Walter Rauschenbusch. Within a few months of his arrival in Portland, Wise reported to Richard Gottheil that "I took an active part of the battle, not yet over, with the vicious elements of the town, much to the displeasure of some of the congregation."

The battle involved efforts by some of the gambling interests to have Portland declared an "open town," one with licensed brothels and gaming halls. Beth Israel's rabbi joined with a number of other clergymen and citizens to oppose the enabling resolution, and the turnout of ministers proved sufficient to dampen the ardor of city councilmen for the motion. "I must have my farewell shot at those who are weeping and wailing," he wrote, "because we Puritans dare to restrict (not abolish) the evils of gambling and prostitution. I mean to present the moral aspects of the whole problem—that's what I'm here for. . . . I feel the call to speak. I should despise myself as a coward if I remain silent."[17]

Never one to remain silent when "called to speak," Wise attacked the gambling and liquor interests from the pulpit of Beth Israel and in guest editorials he wrote for the Portland *Journal*. In a sermon before a packed synagogue entitled "Shall the City Be Wide Open?," he lashed out at those who not only profited directly from gambling and vice, but at those who tolerated it as well. "There will always be scarlet women," he declared, "that is just as long as there are scarlet men." People could not look the other way, they had to stand up and say, "This cannot be; this must not be!" Yet privately, as he wrote to Louise, "sometimes I think nothing can avail against the entrenched powers of the world's evil and darkness." At other times, however, he believed "that if enough men spoke out freely and truly, much of the world's evil and wrong would be corrected." In this last sentence, he summed up the progressive philosophy of reform: If only people recognized and understood the problems, their inherently good nature would be moved to remedy the situation.[18]

Whatever his private doubts may have been, his barbs evidently hit close to home. The head of the gambling syndicate in the city approached Solomon Hirsch to complain about Beth Israel's rabbi meddling in political affairs, and asked Hirsch to force Wise to desist from his attacks. Hirsch delcared that not only could he not stop him, he would not even try, but the gentleman was certainly free to discuss the matter with the rabbi himself. The gambler never did, but one day as the Beth Israel rabbi relaxed in a Turkish bath, he heard a voice in the next booth speak rather bitterly about "that Dr. Wise . . . If I ever get near that son of a bitch, I'll shoot holes through him." For once in his life, Stephen Wise had the good sense not to speak; instead he dressed quickly and hastened home, where he congratulated Louise on the fact that no one carried guns in a Turkish bath.[19]

Wise's intervention also prevented the introduction of public hangings. The city's sheriff had proposed charging five dollars for admission to watch a convicted murderer named Belding be hanged, with the proceeds going to the benefit of the criminal's young son. "Did you ever hear of anything more ghastly?" Wise asked. "I shall go to the sheriff tomorrow to say that this must not be. If necessary, I will go to the Courts and to the Governor to prevent it." Sheriff Storey, whom Wise described as "a bulky, uncouth 'statesman,' " quickly backed down, and later announced to the press that a "wise man changes his mind, but a fool never."[20]

In the years he spent in Oregon, Stephen Wise gained a reputation as a clergyman unafraid to speak out on social issues, ranging from woman suffrage to union rights. He became a leading citizen of Portland, consulted by civic leaders, and invited to dine with President Theodore Roosevelt when he came to visit the city. Roosevelt's tour of the Northwest, shortly after the Kishineff pogrom in Russia, led the young rabbi to advise the president to speak out against antisemitism, to set an example of moral outrage by the civilized nations of the world against such massacres.[21]

Perhaps his most notable reform work while he was in Oregon involved child labor, which only then was becoming recognized as an evil. Children had always worked in this country, but a great difference existed between sons and daughters working on their parents' farms and girls and boys sent off at a young age to labor twelve hours a day in factories. Progressive investigators reported horrible stories of children kept awake during the long night in southern mills by having cold water dashed in their faces, of little girls in canning factories "snipping" sixteen hours a day in the never-ending race with tireless machines. Few states had restrictions on child labor before 1898, but in the decade following a coalition of labor unions, women's clubs, the National Consumers League, and other groups pushed through legislation in most states limiting the hours children could work and regulating the conditions of their labor.[22]

Canning constituted a major industry in Oregon, and some of the worst abuses could be found in the fish canneries along the Columbia River. Thomas Eliot, pastor of the Unitarian Church in Portland, invited Wise to join him and others interested in the problem of child labor when they investigated the conditions inside the canneries. What he saw sickened him, and he immediately joined the campaign for a child labor law. But he realized, as some of his colleagues did not, that a radical bill, while morally desireable, might be politically unfeasible. Better to get some restrictive legislation on the books which could then be expanded and strengthened rather than propose an ideal bill, only to see it inevitably defeated. He paid several visits to the executive council of the State Federation of Labor, warning them that an unreasonable bill would not go through the legislature. Recognizing the wisdom of his advice, the labor leaders withdrew their earlier demands and, as Wise had predicted, a moderate measure passed easily. In 1903, Governor George E. Chamberlain named him as a member of the Board of Child Labor Commissioners.[23] In the three years he served on the panel, Wise did much to enforce the law and to secure more stringent measures to limit child labor and its abuses.

His concern for children, which would mark his ministry not only in Portland but later in New York, was not limited only to problems of child labor. Thanks in part to Louise, as well as to his investigations in the fish canneries, Wise realized that neglected children not only suffered great emotional and physical harm, but their continued ill-treatment posed a threat to social stability. He became an outspoken advocate of new concepts in dealing with youthful offenders, promoting such ideas as juvenile courts, parole, and indeterminate sentencing. Here again he widened his circle of acquaintances among reformers, joined with them to create the Oregon Conference of Charities and Corrections, and was elected first vice-president.

His endeavors as a progressive reformer did not endear him to all, of course, and within Beth Israel a certain amount of grumbling could be heard. Some of the members had direct and indirect interests in the canneries, gambling houses, and saloons that Wise attacked. Others felt a rabbi "belongs in the synagogue and not in public meeting halls," that he "should preach on the Torah and the Talmud, not on bawdy houses on the East side or on the poor Chinese in Portland." Some of his critics feared change in general; others worried that a Jew should be in the forefront of reform. As one of his congregants said, "Business is terrible. Why must *you* always be the leader?" Such an attitude frequently caused him private despair, but then he would remember his father's advice—"Always do what you are afraid of doing." As he wrote to Louise, "The harder the post, the higher the duty of sticking to it, of holding out till the grim end." All in all, however, the majority of the congregation and its leaders backed their rabbi, and agreed with him that "in no respect has this pulpit been more loyal to the synagogue nor more obedient to its spirit than in trying to carry out the message of Israel to all men seeking to apply it to the problems and perplexities and crises of our age. . . . In the words of the Hebrew prophets, 'Justice, justice shalt thou pursue.' "[24]

Outside of Beth Israel, other groups warmly welcomed his reform activities. Those Christian ministers committed to the ideas of the Social Gospel, for example, found Wise a helpful ally in their battles, and in addition, a pioneer in interfaith dialogue and understanding. At their invitation, he often occupied church pulpits to explain Judaism to Christian audiences. This he did proudly, not apologetically, and the Reverend Alexander Blackbirn of the First Baptist Church wrote Wise that he respected and admired him for his strong belief in his faith, and his courage in declaring not only what he believed, but what he did not believe.[25]

These efforts to promote interfaith harmony, which included Jewish-Christian "union" services at Thanksgiving, did not mean that Wise had to remain silent when Christian groups offended him or insulted Judaism. When one minister dubbed him "Caiphas," Wise took up the challenge. In an hour-long speech he explained why he rejected the alleged messiahship of Jesus, and then attacked the idolotrous features of orthodox Christianity. He condemned a proposal for a National Church Federation which would have excluded not only Jews but Unitarians and Universalists, the two sects most willing to cooperate with the synagogue. In Portland itself, he noted, "there is no ministerial association which includes all the ministers of religion. There is a ministerial association, or body of men calling themselves by the name, which is made up only of the ministers of the evangelical churches. . . . For my part I have endeavored to bear up under the great denial with becoming fortitude. What I do regret for the sake of the members of the Ministers Association of Portland is that by so narrowing and restricting the terms of admittance into their fellowship, they have for more than a generation shut themselves out from the opportunity for communion" with many of the noble men in the liberal churches. "The churches have got to learn and to teach," he declared, "that religion is an interchangeable term for life; that religion should be coterminous with the area of life; that religion should spell daily conduct; that religion is the moral habit of the soul." Lest anyone miss the Social Gospel message, Wise hammered his point home in a sermon entitled "Is It Possible to Have a Fellowship of Churches?":[26]

> What light and help are the churches giving today in the matter of the solution of the tremendous social and industrial economic problems which engage the thought of men? Tens of thousands of children of eight and ten and twelve years are in the factories and in the mills of the South and North, the East and West. What are the churches doing to free these little white slaves? What are the churches doing to save these little beings damned, it would seem, rather than born into the world? What in the last years have the churches of this city done together in order to suppress the boxes and stalls in the drinking places which are the nurseries of immorality? What will the churches of our city do in the impending civic contest in order that righteousness may be at the helm of our civic affairs? What have the churches in our state been doing to avert the shame and infamy that blotted our escutcheon? What are the churches in the land doing to call a halt to the lowering of the tone of ideals of our nation?

In this, as many of his utterances, he echoed the thoughts if not the actual words of his heroes, Theodore Parker and Henry Ward Beecher.

Wise's ideas and personality attracted another group of non-Jews, the civic reformers of Portland, who recognized in him a potentially attractive political figure. In his sermons to Beth Israel and in speeches to other groups, Wise's approach to the issues of the day appealed strongly to those whom we classify as "progressives," men and women who in one way or another sought to ameliorate the social, political, economic, and moral problems brought about by the rapid industrialization and urbanization of the country. They knew firsthand of his work in child labor and civic improvement, and applauded his opposition to American imperialism in the Philippines. When Wise delivered the Fourth of July oration at the Lewis and Clark Exposition in 1905, he used the occasion to compare, in typically progressive terms, the older values of American society and the dangers of the new colossus. "Ours is become a nation too great to offend the least, too mighty to be unjust to the weakest, too lofty and noble to be ungenerous to the poorest and lowest." He railed against the corruption so prevalent in Amerian politics, and the economic divisions that grew more pronounced each year. "The standards in a democracy," he pleaded, "are to be based not on money but manhood, not dissent but assent, not acquisition but aspiration, not color but character. Caste and Class cannot be suffered to endure in a democracy which must needs fall as these triumph, for by the side of class goes mass, high caste implies low caste, and caste spells outcaste. The American democracy is a democracy of brotherhood and brotherliness."[27]

Although, as he admitted, his reform work could certainly be labeled "political" in its broadest terms, Wise nonetheless resisted repeated requests to run for political office. Mayor Harry Lane offered him a post in the city cabinet, and several of the state's Democratic leaders wanted to put him up as the reform candidate for the United States Senate against the entrenched Republican machine. He did not deny that the offer tempted him, for as he later explained, "To me neither religion nor politics was remote or sequestered from life. Religion is a vision or ideal of life. Politics is a method. To say that the minister should not go into politics is to imply that ideal and reality are twain and alien. Politics is what it is because religion keeps out of it."[28] But despite the appeal, Wise recognized that much of his effectiveness resulted from his independence, his freedom from fealty to a political organization. As a rabbi denouncing corruption from a pulpit, he could be a force for good in city and state; as a candidate, even a sucessful one, he would have obligations and ties to interests, and even his reformist statements would be seen as insincere, phrases mouthed to cultivate public favor.

All this activity in the congregation, completing his doctorate, serving outlying Jewish communities, establishing relations with Christian groups and in progressive reform eventually took their toll. His youth, his enormous energy and robust physical appearance deceived him and led him to believe that he could work sixteen or more hours a day indefinitely. In September 1903 he suffered a physical collapse from which it took him nearly a year to recover. Most of that winter he spent at the Traymore Hotel in Atlantic City, trying to rebuild his strength. Often even a short stroll on the boardwalk overtaxed him, and his main activity for several months consisted of reading, especially in Shakespeare.[29]

Although he made no secret of his physical problems, he seemingly could not convince some wellwishers who saw his absence from Portland as a sign of dissatisfaction with Beth Israel and who wished to lure him to their congregations. To all such suggestions, he affirmed his desire to return to Portland. "My people have been more than kind to me, having lately offered me a considerable increase in the already generous remuneration which they accord me. Instead of accepting that which came as a free-will offering on their part, I have asked that they allow me the service of an assistant minister, and that the congregation is prepared to do. So you will see that I have every reason to go back to Portland and resume my labor there." In the spring, although he had not fully regained his health, his doctors approved a trip to Europe so he could spend come time resting at one of the health spas near Heidelberg. Neither he nor they expected him to get so involved and wrought up by Zionist politics.[30] But undoubtedly the worst part of his illness was the enforced absences he had to endure from his family, for the Portland years were extremely happy ones for him and Louise.

Although Louise had been willing to follow him to the West, she had done so with an outward smile and some inner trepidation. New York, the New York of upper-class German Jewry, represented a cultured, comfortable milieu, one in which she could indulge her intellectual and artistic tastes. Portland lacked many of the social amenities she had always taken for granted, and absolutely nothing in her background had prepared her for the rule of *rebbitzen*, a rabbi's wife. A beautiful, indeed an exquisite woman, her family feared that she would waste away in Oregon.

They need not have worried. There were, of course, some problems adjusting to the social responsibilities of being a rabbi's wife. Once, when her husband invited two very Orthodox rabbis for dinner and suggested that fish be served, she innocently ordered scallops, a non-kosher seafood that would have deeply offended the strictly observant guests. Fortunately, Wise returned in time to learn of this and to change the menu.[31] Her innate charm and graciousness, however, soon won her many friends in the congregation and in the town, dissipating any lingering fears of loneliness.

Above all, the passion of their courtship blossomed into a fuller and deeper understanding and love, and as Wise told her: "All I had ever hoped and dreamed of peace and joy and comradeship that could ever come to any man through marriage has come to me and more. . . . I looked for spiritual companionship, for moral sustainment in you when I asked you to be my wife. This, more than this, I have found. If there has been any change for the better in the character of my work during the past two years, I owe it to you and you alone."[32]

In the very center of the storms raised by Wise's causes, he and Louise created a haven of peace and quiet. After living for a brief time in a hotel suite, they moved into a large but simple house, with a veranda overlooking the lawn and a rose garden. Here he had a study and she set up a studio for her painting. She also made their home a meeting place of teachers, artists, social workers, all of whom helped to provide the intellectual stimulation they both craved. Within a short time, other rooms in the house had to be converted into nurseries. On December 7, 1901, Louise gave birth to their first child, James Waterman, and on April 12, 1903 to their daughter, Justine Louise.

If Stephen had been an adoring suitor and husband, he became a positively impossible father, doting on every real or imagined accomplishment of his offspring. But his love for Louise, and his joy in James and Justine, made his frequent absences from home all the more difficult. His responsiblities as a child labor commissioner and his outreach work with Jewish communities forced him to travel more than he wished, so he resorted to endless notes and letters, sometimes three or four in a day, scribbled to Louise in trains and hotels and stations. "My dearest sweetheart," ran one missive, "here I am in Eugene. Are you pleased, angry or amused at my writing so often—the third time in seven or eight hours? May I not write as often now as I did in the old days, seeing that I am husband as well as lover?" When in turn Louise traveled to New York with James to visit her family, her disconsolate husband wrote one letter after another, telling "how rebellious my heart has been at the thought of you leaving me and taking my boy from me." One compensation for his physical breakdown was that he was able to spend several months of his recuperation in the company of his wife and children.[33]

The births of her two children had one other effect upon Louise; it served to reawaken that moral fervor which Felix Adler had first recognized. Social services were rare in Portland in 1902, and although the Wises easily afforded private medical care for their children, Louise wondered what poor families did when their sons and daughters required attention. She soon discovered that the poor had no access to doctors or nurses other than through a few charity clinics, so she introduced a practice already in effect in New York, that of sending visiting nurses into the slums and tenements to provide pre- and postnatal care, as well as to advise families on necessary health and sanitary measures. Not only did Louise have to raise the funds to support the first nurse, she also had to convince the poor women who had never had any experience with nurses to allow this stranger to examine them and their children. From this beginning grew the Visiting Nurse Association of Portland. In the report Louise wrote of the service after its first year, one can discern a counterpoint to her husband's angry sermons. Where he lashed out at corruption and vice and degradation, she chastised those who failed to respond to the cries of the needy and the suffering. Just as Wise's work at Beth Israel anticipated his ministry at the Free Synagogue, so his wife's ventures in Portland presaged the larger schemes she undertook to relieve distress and suffering, plans gentle and compassionate in their ends, yet carried out efficiently and most effectively.[34]

Stephen and Louise Wise enjoyed their years in Oregon. Friendships made in the congregation and in the city would last throughout their lives. In later years, members of Beth Israel visiting New York frequently dropped in at the Free Synagogue to see their former rabbi, and whenever one of his speaking tours brought him to Portland, large crowds would turn out to welcome him. But by 1905 Wise had in large part "conquered" Portland; he had become, as one wit put it, the "Bishop of Oregon." He needed new challenges, new avenues in which to expend his energies and ambitions. Only New York City, with its two million Jews, could provide the proper setting.

4

Emanu-El

"Have you heard," a gleeful Sol Stroock wrote to Wise, "that a certain set of gentlemen headed by Leonard Lewisohn are strongly advocating that an invitation be sent to a certain rabbi who formerly occupied one of our New York pulpits but who is now in a western city, urging this rabbi to accept a call to Emanu-El?"[1]

For many of Stephen Wise's friends and admirers, it seemed only natural that the most promising young rabbi in America should eventually be called to the pulpit of New York's Emanu-El, the cathedral synagogue of American Reform Judaism. Founded in 1849, Emanu-El counted amoung its members nearly all the leading families of the German-Jewish aristocracy, and the wealth and prestige of its congregants conferred a status and influence upon its rabbi unmatched by the pulpit of any other congregation in the nation. But the conservatism of this elite, its desire to avoid controversy, especially anything that might conceivably reflect adversely on Jews or Judaism, led to a muted, some would say stifling, atmosphere. Emanu-El liked its religion and its rabbi to be inspirational but peaceful, uplifting but noncontroversial. For anyone as committed to a Jewish Social Gospel outlook or to liberal political ideas as Wise, Emanu-El must have seemed the enemy incarnate.

Rumors connecting him and Emanu-El had begun to circulate even before he left New York. Some people believed that he was going to Oregon only to make it easier for Emanu-El to offer him its pulpit. Yet as early as the fall of 1900, a theme developed in Wise's private letters which exploded in 1905—namely, that Temple Emanu-El stood for all he loathed in Reform Judaism, a rich complacency indifferent to the ills of the world, deaf to the ethical commands of the Hebrew prophets. Upon hearing that the president of Emanu-El, James Seligman, had been interested in his inaugural sermons at Beth Israel, Wise wrote to Louise that "Emanu-El will never get a *man* in its pulpit until the snobs forget the millionairedom long enough to acquire

49

some respect for a man who is not rich, but is some other thing. They must learn that a 'call' to Emanu-El is not an 'honor' but a burden and responsibility, and that if 'honor' there be, it belong to the God whom congregation and minister should serve."[2]

The famous battle with Louis Marshall and the trustees of Emanu-El in 1905 did not reflect a momentary aberration or a burst of idealism. Wise knew Emanu-El intimately. As a youth he had studied there with Gustav Gottheil; as rabbi of B'nai Jeshurun he had observed it closely, and had, in fact, preached a guest sermon there in May 1900. Louise, of course, agreed, although Leo and Jennie Waterman found their brother-in-law's attitude puzzling, if not actually a signal of mental disorder akin to Zionism. Yet if Wise had no desire to be "called" to Emanu-El, fate kept putting him and the cathedral synagogue on a collision course. Psychologists might argue that he actually wanted to have the Emanu-El pulpit, but believing that he could not, chose to tackle the trustees head-on; if so, he certainly avoided one opportunity after another in his first two years in Portland.

Emanu-El by then was looking for a rabbi, either to replace Joseph Silverman or to serve as his associate. In order to look over as many men as possible, most of whom yearned for the "call," the trustees invited a number of rabbis to deliver guest sermons when they were in New York, speeches rightly characterized as "trial sermons." Wise also received such an offer, and promptly said no. As he explained, "To preach there under the present circumstances is to offer oneself for the pulput. . . . I would not as much as raise my finger, let alone preach a trial sermon—the very term is an abomination—in order to be elected as minister of Emanu-El. What would a sermon prove as to my fitness to meet such an enormous responsibility? At best I would preach well and please people, damn it—what index would that offer to my real powers and gifts in other directions, if I have any?"

And yet Emanu-El did offer a challenge, "a responsibility appalling in its magnitude." To occupy its pulpit provided that opportunity of "serving and of leading the Jewish community of New York," a task Wise both feared and wanted. He would not "try out" for the position, but as he wrote, "I will never again preach in Temple Emanu-El *save as its minister*."[3]

In 1903, as he recuperated in Atlantic City from his breakdown, Emanu-El once again approached him. James Seligman wrote that the trustees had decided to offer a course of twelve or more Sabbath sermons by visiting rabbis. Each of the visiting rabbis would receive $200 plus expenses, and Seligman hoped Wise would accept the invitation. At first, Wise welcomed the letter, for it would provide a break from the monotony of recuperation; one sermon would be easy to prepare and deliver without taxing his limited physical strength. Then, as he wrote Louise, a rereading of the invitation depressed him, and he had decided to decline on grounds of ill health, for it would, "I presume, be considered insolent if I stated my real views." The mention of a specific albeit generous fee "is the Rockefeller-Morgan method of buying up everything in sight including men's scruples." The $200 could be interpreted either as a bribe or as balm to the unsucessful, for he had no doubt that the guest lecture series was but the trial sermon dressed up somewhat. He mused, however, on the idea of accepting the invitation, and then delivering a sermon attacking the trustees for their materialistic and insulting policies.[4]

Nearly fifteen men had participated in this "oratorical contest" when Emanu-El again asked Wise to deliver one or more guest sermons in November 1905; this time he agreed. The reasons for his change of heart are not to be found in his letters, although one can make reasonable guesses about them. He had accomplished what he could in Oregon, and needed the greater stage of New York; the pulpit of Emanu-El would allow him to become, overnight, a leading if not the leading rabbi in New York. There is also little doubt that Wise expected, perhaps even hoped, for a confrontation with the Emanu-El trustees. In any event, by the fall of 1905 he had made up his mind that, as rabbi of Emanu-El or not, he would leave Portland and return to the East. He told Adolphe Wolfe, the president of Beth Israel, that he doubted if Emanu-El would call him, or that he would accept in the unlikely case it did. Instead, he planned "to found a new and free and living Synagogue movement." On the train to New York, he wrote Louise: "No one but you will ever believe that I would not lift a finger to become Rabbi of Emanu-El. I will preach for them. They must do or leave undone the rest."[5]

Wise mounted the pulpit of Emanu-El on Sunday morning, November 26, and spoke on "The New Conscience," an open espousal of the cause of progressive reform, but couched in the language of morality. Depending upon how one wanted to interpret the talk, it was either a call to apply the teachings of Judaism in civic affairs or an evocation of the good that people could do in life if they chose to follow their consciences. That same evening, he lectured to a large crowd at the Cooper Union on William Lloyd Garrison, applauding the great abolitionist's stand for morality despite overwhelming public disapproval. Afterward, Garrison's daughter wrote to him how thrilled she had been by the talk, not thinking it possible for anyone who had not personally known her father to have caught the true heroism of his life.[6]

As far as Emanu-El's trustees were concerned, their search had ended. Stephen Wise represented just the type of rabbi they had been searching for—young, handsome, free from any connection with Hebrew Union College in Cincinnati (the rival center for leadership of American Reform Judaism), well-known in New York Jewish circles, and an outstanding orator. A committee of five men, representing a majority of the trustees, arranged to call on Wise on November 30 at the Waterman house, where he and Louise were staying. James Seligman, president of the congregation, M. H. Moses, chairman of the trustees, Daniel Guggenheim, Isaac Spiegelberg, and Louis Marshall, honorary secretary to the trustees, and in fact the dominant personality in the congregation, wanted to know if Wise would be willing to accept a call to Temple Emanu-El and what conditions, if any, he would demand. Marshall prefaced the discussion with the caveat that any offer the committee made would be subject to congregational approval which, they assured him, would be nominal and confirmatory. The powers of Emanu-El had, so it seemed, reached their decision.[7]

Wise had awaited this moment, with dread or anticipation, for many years. Now he carefully took out two small pieces of paper he had scribbled upon earlier in the day, and slowly began going over what he expected should he accept Emanu-El's call. First, there had to be a unanimous election by the trustees and by the congregation for a term of three to five years; afterward, if he and Emanu-El were happy with one another, he would stay on indefinitely. He intended to participate in the services, not leaving the conduct of the ritual to a reader; he would preach three times a month, with his messages aimed not only at Jews but at non-Jews as well; he would require a secretary, as he had at Beth Israel. He would, with the concurrence of the trustees, invite guest preachers to occupy the Emanu-El pulpit, and these would include not only other rabbis, but men prominent in public affairs, arts, and letters, as well as religion. He wanted Emanu-El's members to be exposed to as many viewpoints as possible. He also indicated that at some point in the future, he hoped to establish a downtown division to minister to the needs of the immigrant Jewish masses. To all these requests, the trustees, although raising some eyebrows, agreed; after all, they wanted a dynamic rabbi, and while some of his ideas were new (at least to Emanu-El), none could really be considered dangerous or heretical. Now came the crucial issue.

"If I go to Emanu-El, the pulpit must be free while I preach therein."

Immediately Louis Marshall objected. "Dr. Wise, I must say to you at once that such a condition cannot be complied with; the pulpit of Emanu-El has always been and is subject to and under the control of the board of trustees."

"If that be true, gentlemen," Wise shot back, "there is nothing more to say."

A great deal, however, remained to be said. The trustees pressed him to explain just what he meant by a "free pulpit." Emanu-El, Marshall explained, was part of the conservative, or as it is now called, "classical" wing of Reform movement. It would be a source of serious controversy if its rabbi should preach orthodoxy or radical reform, Ethical Culture or Zionism, or should indulge in sensational preaching on political or economic subjects, thus "converting the pulpit into a forum of character entirely foreign to the purpose for which the congregation was organized."

All this, of course, was like waving a red flag before Wise's eyes, and he decided to lay out what he wanted to do as clearly and as explicitly as possible; here was his opportunity, longed for even while denied, to confront the complacency and irrelevance of Emanu-El with his own fiery brand of Liberal Judaism. "I have in Oregon," he declared, "been among the leaders of a civic reform movement in my community. Mr. Moses, if it be true, as I have heard it rumored, that your nephew, Mr. Herman, is to be a Tammany Hall candidate for a Supreme Court judgeship, I would, if I were Emanu-El's rabbi, oppose his candidacy in and out of my pulpit. Mr. Guggenheim, as a member of the Child Labor Commission of the State of Oregon, I must say to you that if it ever came to be known that children were being employed in your mines, I would cry our against such wrong. Mr. Marshall, the press stated that you and your firm are to be counsel for Mr. Hyde of the Equitable Life Assurance Society. That may or may not be true, but knowing that Charles Evans Hughes's investigation of insurance companies in New York has been a very great service, I would in and out of my pulpit speak in condemnation of the crimes committed by the insurance thieves."

"But," stammered one trustee, "politics is *never* discussed in the pulpit of Temple Emanu-El."

At this Wise practically exploded. "The election of Mr. Jerome [the crusading district attorney of New York] was not a matter of politics but of morals. He was not only a candidate for political position, but the inspiring and fearless leader of a revolt against the tyranny of bosses and grafters, a revolt looking to the restoration to the people of the civic rights and liberties plundered by the political gangs. Jerome is not a politician but a civic prophet. The Hebrew prophets were politicians in the sense in which Mr. Jerome is, furtherers of civic and national righteousness. As a Jewish minister I claim the right to follow the example of the Hebrew prophets and stand and battle in New York as I have stood and battled in Portland for civic righteousness."[8]

At Wise's request, Marshall the next day sent him a formal statement of the trustees' position, "that the pulpit should always be subject to and under the control of the board of trustees," warning that this was "not a mere figure of speech, or any empty formula." Marshall probably knew that several of the trustees chafed under his control ("Emanu-El," as one person noted, "lives under Marshall Law") and were urging Wise to ignore the seemingly inflexible postion put forth by Marshall. Jacob Schiff called at the Waterman residence, and asked Wise to accompany him on a walk up Fifth Avenue. The short, bearded, impeccably dressed Schif, with his German accent, urged the younger man to take the post, "Of course they want to restrict your sermons, but you take it anyhow. After you're elected, tell them to go to hell—and I'll back you up." That evening, James Seligman and Daniel Guggenheim called to ask Wise to reconsider. Just because Marshall said there was control, they argued, did not make it so. In the more than half-century of Emanu-El's history, not one rabbi had ever complained of being muzzled. "You know and respect Dr. Gottheil," they noted. "Do you think he would have remained at Emanu-El for so many years if we had told him what he could or could not say?" Had Wise entertained even the slightest temptation at this point, it was immediately dispelled when he looked up to see Louise standing just outside the parlor door, shaking her head in scornful disdain.[9]

Shorty after his vistors left, Wise sat down and wrote out his answer to Louis Marshall:[10]

Dear Sir: If your letter of December first be expressive of the thought of the trustees of Temple Emanu-El, I beg to say that no self-respecting minister of religion, in my opinion, could consider a call to a pulpit which, in the language of your communication, shall always be subject to, and under the control of, the board of trustees. I am, Yours very truly,

Stephen S. Wise

At this point, the entire episode could have been drawn to a close. Congregations, including Emanu-El, had had offers to prospective rabbis turned down in the past, because they could not or would not meet certain demands. Wise now knew he could have been Emanu-El's rabbi, and his confrontation with the trustees had vindicated his own and Louise's belief in his honor and integrity. He had a congregation in Portland, but he had already indicated that irrespective of the Emanu-El decision, he would leave Oregon within a year and return to New York. What happened next can be seen as showing both Wise's best and worst sides. His friends hailed him for having the courage of his principles; his detractors labeled him a publicity seeker. Both groups looked at the same events for their interpretations, and both were right. Throughout his career Wise not only wanted to do the brave and right and good thing, as he so often did, but he wanted it to be known, to be flung in the teeth of the complacent and aloof.

Soon after his return to Portland, Wise composed a lengthy "open letter" to the members of the Temple Emanu-El "on the question of freedom of the Jewish pulpit," which he proceeded to read aloud on Friday evening, January 5, 1906, to Beth Israel. Reviewing the chain of events of the preceding November and December, he condemned the entire idea of controlled pulpit as offensive not only to the rabbi but to the congregation as well. Why employ a man whose qualifications supposedly included a lengthy study of religion and ethics, and then tell him that he can only preach those ethical and religious ideas which do not affront the members of the congregation? In a debate over ethics, it became inevitable that the rabbi, be he right or wrong, must always yield. He then set forth in ringing words the duties of a rabbi:

> The chief office of the minister, I take it, is not to represent the views of the congregation, but to proclaim the truth as he sees it. How can he serve a congregation as a teacher save as he quickens the minds of his hearers by the vitality and independence of his utterances? But how can a man be vital and independent and helpful, if he be tethered and muzzled? A free pulpit, worthily filled, must command respect and influence; a pulpit that is not free, howsoever filled, is sure to be without potency and honor. A free pulpit will sometimes stumble into error; a pulpit that is not free can never powerfully plead for truth and righteousness. In the pursuit of the duties of his office, the minister may from time to time be under the necessity of giving expression to views at variance with the view of some, or even many, members of the congregation. Far from such differences proving the pulpit to be in the wrong, it may be, and oftimes is, found to signify that the pulpit has done its duty in calling evil evil and good good, in abhorring the moral wrong of putting light for darkness and darkness for light, and in scorning to limit itself to the utterance of what the prophet has styled "smooth things," lest variance of views arise. Too great a dread there may be of secession on the part of some members of a congregation, for after all, differences and disquiet, even schism at the worst, are not so much to be feared as that attitude of the pulpit which never provokes dissent because it is cautious rather than courageous, peace-loving rather than prophetic, time-serving rather than right-serving. The minister is not to be the spokesman of the congregation, not the message-bearer of the congregation, but the bearer of a message to the congregation.

He then published his letter, together with Marshall's December 1 message stating the trustees' attitude, and distributed this pamphlet across the country under the title of *An Open Letter . . . on The Freedom of the Jewish Pulpit.* The first copy of the pamphlet, as with his dissertation, he gave to Louise, "without whose inspiration and steadying strength this could not have been written. With Dodi's* love, January 17, 1906."

Wise's sense of timing provided legitimate ammunition to those charging him with seeking publicity. He read the open letter to Beth Israel and arranged for its publication before it had even reached Emanu-El, where the trustees responded almost apopletically. Rabbi Joseph Silverman, M. H. Moses, and Louis Marshall all condemned him, and pointed out that no call had ever been extended to Dr. Wise. "The open letter came to us an un-

---

*"Dodi" was Louise's pet name for Stephen, one later used by their children as well; it is derived from the Hebrew for "my beloved."

mitigated surprise,'' Marshall told a reporter, ''especially that the reverend gentleman should have seen fit to have read an open letter which is magnified in its surprising nature . . . since there had emanated nothing from us which called for any response or comment.'' Marshall pointed out that at no time in the discussions had the trustees ever asked the rabbi to compromise his principles. They had affirmed that in the event of irreconcilable views between rabbi and congregation, one or the other would have to give way, and it could not be the congregation. The entire policy of the board was to prevent such a confrontation, thus protecting both rabbi and congregation.[11]

The sophistry of the Emanu-El spokesmen in declaring that no offer had been made fooled no one. It had been an open secret that the ''oratorical contest'' had been designed to find an associate for Rabbi Silverman, and much of New York Jewry knew that the trustees had approached Stephen Wise in order to tender him the pulpit. In his response to reporters' queries, Wise noted that he never claimed to have received a call from Emanu-El; rather, he recited again the gist of the November 30 meeting, noting that he had made it impossible for the trustees to extend a call by insisting upon a free pulpit.[12] He did not volunteer any reason, however, why he felt it necessary to rush his open letter into such a wide circulation, why he had to publicize his disagreement with Emanu-El.

While a desire for publicity, probably to pave the way for his next step, undoubtedly played some role in the decision, it should not be assumed that he tilted at imaginary windmills. Schiff's and Seligman's comments notwithstanding, Louis Marshall had meant exactly what he had said regarding control of the pulpit; for him the wishes and needs of the congregation always took precedence over rabbinical inclinations. Where Wise saw the rabbi as exhorting the congregation, urging it to action, making it uncomfortable with a less than perfect *status quo*, Marshall viewed the rabbinical task as one of ministering, of comforting, of bringing solace. Obviously, both functions could be performed; the question was one of priories and interpretations.

Few rabbis were willing to challenge the Emanu-El attitude, nor did many laymen understand the real issues involved. Less than a half-dozen fellow rabbis wrote to Wise. ''Think of the pity and the shame of it,'' he told Max Raisin, ''not a single rabbi in New York has spoken a word. The complacency with which the men who occupy the pulpits of the larger congregations wear their muzzles is to me unspeakably sad.'' More typical was the attitude of Richard Gottheil, who believed it had been ''injudicious and inadvisable'' to raise the issue of the free pulpit. As Wise wrote to one well-wisher, ''the battle for freedom in the Jewish church is only begun.''[13] He had determined to found a new synagogue, a free synagogue, one that embodied all the hopes and ideals of social responsiblity he had developed in his years in Oregon, but that would now minister to the large Jewish population of New York.

It is possible that because of the large, and largely unorganized, nature of New York's Jewish community, Wise deliberately generated so much publicity about his tilt with Emanu-El. Despite his seven years at B'nai Jeshurun, Wise had not developed the type of reputation that would now enable him to found his own synagogue. He was known as a good preacher, a compassionate pastor, and a hard worker, but he did not have that charismatic aura which would bring people flocking to his banner. In one swoop, he now assumed the mantle of a leader, a man with cause. Louis Marshall unwittingly provided the one thing Wise had lacked to begin his new enterprise—an enemy, a counterpoint, a foil to his ideals. So long as Emanu-El ignored social concerns, sold its pews to the highest bidders, and nominally controlled the pulpit, Wise's gospel made sense. One could hardly call for a free pulpit unless muzzled ones existed; one could not advocate a pewless synagogue unless one could point to temples where a a man's wealth bought him a coveted place in God's house. Years later, when the two men had to some extent patched over their differences, Marshall accepted an invitation to speak at the Free Synagogue. In introducing him, Wise humorously but not inaccurately described Marshall as "the author and founder of the Free Synagogue."*

Before the Wises could leave for New York, they had to bid a painful farewell to Portland, and Beth Israel was loath to lose its rabbi. A number of congregants actively and passionately sought to dissuade Wise from his planned course of action. David Solis Cohen, a Portland attorney, summed up much of the argument when he pleaded that Oregon needed him far more than New York did. "Nowhere can you do so much good for the principles you have at heart. . . . I put my plea on the broad basis of your opportunity for your peple, not only of the west but of the entire country, by making the Beth Israel pulpit reverse the ancient condition, and become the 'source of light.' "[14]

But Wise would not be deterred. He resigned from the board of child

---

*Wise loved to add a postscript to this story. In the mid-twenties, the Walden School occupied a house adjacent to the Free Synagogue, and the children often played on the second-story roof, near Stephen's study. One day they were particularly boisterous, and he called out the window: "Children, would you try to be just a little less noisy? I have a meeting in my study." The noise subsided somewhat, but then eventually grew in volume. Again Stephen went to the window and called, "Boys and girls, I beg you to be a little more quiet at play." Suddenly a little girl called back: "My grandfather could not muzzle you, and you are not going to muzzle us!" Shortly afterward, Stephen found out that the little girl was the daughter of James Marshall. As he wryly noted, "Thus again out of the mouths of babes and sucklings."

labor commissioners, and prepared to endure a series of farewell dinners, including one on October 10 attended by the governor, both United States senators, and the mayor of Portland, replete with background music by the Webber String Orchestra. Only one sour note marred his departure, and it indicates how much of his ministry was shaped by the force of his own personality. As an inducement to bring Wise to Portland, Beth Israel's trustees had voted to have him participate in board meetings. Now, as he prepared to leave, the trustees decided that in the future the rabbis should not be members of the board. Despite Wise's strong protest—"Gentlemen, I see I have *wasted* six years in Portland"—the trustees adopted the measure. Their argument, that no one could ever measure up to his stature, only made him despair of how congregations tended to view their rabbis as hired men.[15]

Despite this, a real affection existed between Stephen Wise and his congregants at Beth Israel, and this affection, as well as sadness, was clearly revealed in his farewell sermon. "It is hard to give up a ministry among you, for I am only a man, and I love Beth Israel and Portland and Oregon." He proudly reviewed what he and they had accomplished in six years, from creating a free pulpit to involving themselves in the struggle for social betterment. In a cadence reminiscent of the ancient Hebrew prophets, Wise gave his valedictory at Beth Israel, enjoining his followers to remember the Biblical command "to love truth and peace, truth before and better than peace, truth even at the cost of peace." As he finished, he blessed them, and his words of farewell were those with which Samuel parted from his people—"only fear the Lord and serve Him in truth with all your hearts."[16]

The years of training and preparation were now over. If one believes that people are destined to fulfill certain roles, to achieve—or at least attempt—great things, then Stephen Wise had spent his first thirty-two years preparing for this moment when he would undertake to breathe a new spirit and meaning into Jewish life in America.

5

The Free Synagogue

The New York Stephen and Louise returned to in October 1906 had changed considerably from the city they had left six years earlier, although in many details, both good and bad, it had remained the same. Hundreds of thousands of immigrants, especially Jews from eastern Europe, had poured into New York at the height of the new wave of immigration, fleeing from hunger and persecution, searching for freedom and opportunity in the *goldenah medina* of America. Here they found that freedom and opportunity, but at a great cost. Packed into overcrowded and unsanitary tenements, working in unheated and unventilated sweatshops twelve or more hours a day, they slowly crept up the social and economic ladder. In the meantime, they created a vibrant Yiddish-speaking culture, with theaters, newspapers, and literary journals; the intellectual level of conversation in the coffeshops of Houston Street matched that found in many Park Avenue salons, and certainly exceeded it in exuberance.

New York's Jewish community at this time consisted on the one hand of this large mass of immigrant Jews from eastern Europe—Yiddish-speaking, politically socialist-oriented, Orthodox if religious, working-class, and numbering about two million. The other large bloc of New York Jews lived uptown; these were the Germans who had immigrated between 1840 and 1880, and who had found a niche in American society. Acculturated, English- and German-speaking, upper-class, conservative and Reform, they and the downtowners played out a curiously ambivalent relationship. To the Germans, the eastern European newcomers represented all that they had tried to leave behind—archaic religious customs, a barbarous language, a miserable existence. They feared that the crudity and the size of this new immigration would undermine their own hard-earned status and created antisemitism in a country that had been relatively free from that old curse. For the residents of Clinton and Orchard Streets, the uptown aristocracy—the *yahudim*—were hardly Jews, but near-apostates, their Reform temples (especially Emanu-El) barely distinguishable from churches, their business success making them part of the oppressing capitalist class. Yet at the same time, each saw themselves in the other. The Germans had been immigrants only a generation earlier; they had worked hard and succeeded; they had grasped at America's freedom and opportunity, just as the Jews from Russia and Poland now hoped to do. Even while they castigated the uptowners, the downtowners wanted to emulate them, to succeed as they had.

And "our crowd" could not, and would not, forget its origins, its Jewishness. The Schiffs and Lewisohns and Seligmans never abandoned their faith; whatever the customs they may have ignored, they kept the commandments regarding charity, the obligation of one Jew for another. They used their wealth openly and generously to establish hospitals, clinics, relief societies, and family services for the benefit of their coreligionists, and in 1906 founded the American Jewish Committee to work both at home and overseas in the defense of the Jewish people. Yet even here, the ambivalence could be seen. The downtowners need the help, they recognized the Jewishness of their benefactors, and yet like all recipients of charity, resented the donors; the *yahudim* worked very hard and gave large sums of money; they did more than just a minimal amount, yet they looked down on those whom they helped. The Germans had been here long enough to establish themselves and the Eastern Europeans had just arrived, so no middle existed, no group that might have served as a buffer and a bridge between these two blocs.[1]

Stephen Wise hoped he could minister to both groups, that he might serve as a conduit, although he never nursed the delusion that he or any other person could overcome the enormous gap between *yahudim* and *yiddin*. Rather, as a rabbi he believed that he had to speak to all Jews, rich and poor, newcomer and established, German and Russian, downtowner and uptowner. There are few indications that Wise ever paid much attention to speculative theological questions, but if one wanted to identify a lodestar in his religous thought, it would have to be the unity of the Jewish people. In all the battles he fought, no matter how he castigated his opponents or denounced them as misguided, they remained Jews, and he always recognized them as such. To found a new synagogue that catered only to one faction of New York Jewry would violate a cardinal tenet of his faith; the Free Synagogue not only had to be free and open, it had to reach out to the community. There was work to be done for the immigrants, but as Richard Gottheil reminded him, "Uptown needs whatever influence you can bring to bear more than downtown does."[2] And it would be primarily uptown where Wise could find the financial backing to begin his work.

At the end of December 1906, Wise announced that he would give a series of public lectures in which he would explain his plans and his beliefs. The new synagogue, he told a reporter, would be liberal in its creed, welcoming Jews and non-Jews to services; there would be no distinction in memberships based upon wealth; the congregation would be expected to support a program of social welfare activites in the larger community; and the pulpit, which would be free, would be used to speak out against the evils of time. "Nathan the Prophet," he declared, "did not preach in carefully veiled and dexterously unoffending phrases about the crime of Cain nor make a polite and cryptic reference to ancient violators of the sixth commandment. Instead of that, stern as conscience, brave as manhood, terrible as justice, inexorable as truth, he thundered into the ear of the king: 'Thou has killed Uriah the Hittite!' " Wise would employ no "dexterously unoffending phrases." for he wanted the Free Synagogue to be a living house of God. "Without liberty of truth-seeking the Church becomes a cemetery, with no Ezekial to resurrect these dead bones of life. Without pulpit liberty the Church degenerates into a mortuary chapel and the preacher is degraded into a pensioner and parasite of certain classes."³ There is little doubt what Wise had in mind; he often referred to Emanu-El as "an urban gateway to a suburban cemetery."

The series of six addresses began on Sunday morning, January 27, 1907, in the Hudson Theater, which its owner, Henry B. Harris, made available to Wise at no charge. The Times Square entertainment palace bore little resemblance to a house of worship, and the audience that day did not conform to any known congregational models. Orthodox, Conservative, and Reform Jews mingled with atheists and free thinkers, socialists and agnostics. Some were wealthy, more were poor, and all were curious about what this firebrand from the West had to say. For his first talk, Wise asked, "What is a Free Synagogue?" and he made it clear that while all men and women, Jew and non-Jew alike, would be welcome, the Free Synagogue, unlike Ethical Culture (with which some people mistakenly confused Wise's ideas) would be

a Jewish society, for I am a Jew, a Jewish teacher. The Free Synagogue is not be an indirect or circuitous avenue of approach to Unitarianism; it is not to be a society for the gradual conversion of Jewish men or women to any form of Christianity. We mean to be vitally, intensely, unequivocally Jewish. Jews who would not be Jews will find no place in the Free Synagogue, for we its founders wish to be not less Jewish but more Jewish in the highest and noblest sense of the term

But this Jewishness was to be expressed democratically, not dogmatically. There would be no pew or dues system wherein wealth determined place, but an equality of men and women in a house of God. What they learned there, moreover, would not be confined, but expanded and built upon through social service. "I could not abide the reproach," Wise later wrote, "that in most synagogues social service is left to the sisterhoods." The Free Synagogue would, therefore, be Jewish, democratic, socially conscious, and active, as well as free.[4]

He continued this lecture/service series into early March, speaking on a variety of issues. The sixth and last talk, "Is the Bible in Danger?," was one of the few times in his career when he addressed himself to a specifically theological /scholarly problem, the question of scientific and textual criticism of the Holy Scriptures. Wise bluntly declared that the Bible was indeed in danger, but not from the so-called "higher criticism" as much as from its friends. The frenetic defense of divine authorship diverted attention from the real importance of the Bible, its content and message. "The Bible of the twentieth of Exodus or the nineteenth of Leviticus," he said, "or the sixth of Micah or the fifth of Amos or the twenty-third and fifty-first Psalms can never be lost nor endangered."[5]

Throughout February and March, he spent much of his time in private meetings with well-to-do Jews, seeking their financial support for the Free Synagogue, and proved his effectiveness as a fund-raiser. Among the original subscribers to the Free Synagogue, Jacob Schiff, Adolf Lewisohn, and James Speyer (all members of Emanu-El) contributed $10,000 a piece; Henry Morgenthau gave $5,000; and several other men, including Wise's boyhood friend Sol Stroock, pledged $1,000. On April 15, the congregation formally organized at a meeting in the Hotel Savoy. Henry Morgenthau as acting chairman and publisher Charles Bloch as acting secretary announced a signed membership list of 192 families and individuals, with pledges toward the first year's budget already in hand of more than $9,000. The gathering unanimously elected Stephen Wise as rabbi, but only after he insisted that he receive no salary during the first year. The constitution and by-laws summed up the tenets of Wise's faith:[6]

Desirous of vitalizing and reasserting a fundamental ideal of Israel, the founders of the Free Synagogue resolve that it shall not at any time for any reason impose any fixed pecuniary dues, tax or assessment upon its members, nor shall pews or sittings be owned by members; but it shall be supported fully by voluntary contributions.

Believing that Judaism is a religion of perpetual growth and development, we hold that, while loyal to the fundamental teachings thereof, we are and by virtue of the genius of Israel ought to be free to interpret and restate the teachings of Israel of the past in the light of the present, and that each such succeeding generation in Israel is free to reformulate the truth, first trusting in the providence of the God of our fathers.

Believing that the power of the synagogue for goods depends, in part, upon the inherent right of the pulpit to freedom of thought and speech, the founders of the Free Synagogue resolve that its pulpit shall be free to preach on behalf of truth and righteousness in the spirit and after the pattern of the prophets of Israel.

Part of Stephen Wise's genius was his ability not only to dream great visions, but to develop the practical details for turning ideals into realities. That night he outlined the specific tasks confronting the more than one hundred men and women gathered at the Savoy. They would need a meeting place more suitable for religious worship than the Hudson Theater, room for the office staff, a lending library, and a religious school. That same evening, the members resolved to establish both uptown and downtown branches, thus enabling Wise to minister, as he had hoped, to both *yahudim* and *yidden*. Rabbi Emil Hirsch of Chicago's Sinai Temple and one of the leading Liberal rabbis in the country had been visiting in New York, and at Wise's invitation attended the meeting. Carried away by enthusiasm, he asked "for the privilege of being regarded by all of you as a non-resident assistant rabbi of the Free Synagogue." No free pulpit then existed in New York, Hirsch declared, and the city's Jewish community therefore had all the more need for the "uncompromising free Judaism" which he expected would develop under Stephen Wise's "magnificent leadership."[7]

The Free Synagogue proved successful far more quickly than anyone had expected. By the end of the year, all New York Jewry seemed to be talking about the new venture and the brillant sermons of its rabbi. Charles Bloch judged Wise's first High Holy Day sermons, "The Call to Higher Life," the best he had ever heard, a sentiment echoed by many others.[8] At the beginning of 1908 the executive committee made arrangements to move services out of the Hudson Theater and into the Universalist Church of Our Father on West 81st Street. Wise began the practice of inviting guests to occupy the Free Synagogue pulpit or in exchanging sermons so that his people would have the opportunity to hear a diverse range of opinions.[9] And within five weeks of the first service in the Hudson Theater, a downtown branch of the Free Synagogue opened on the lower East Side, renting the main auditorium of Clinton Hall for meetings on Friday and Sunday evenings.

While the uptowners looked more to Wise's oratory and his interpretation of political and secular events, the residents of the ghetto wanted to see how Jewish he was. Jacob Minkin noted that Wise fortunately chose not to make his East Side debut at the famous Educational Alliance, which the radicals and would-be radicals considered a bastion of reaction. Nevertheless, these so-called revolutionaries nearly rioted when Wise brought along a hand-organ—*a hand organ* —and on Friday night, into the heartland of Orthodoxy! Still, even though suspicious, they stayed. Wise rose and read a few verses in Hebrew, his voice deep and resonant, the Hebrew carrying a warmth and intensity suited to its prophetic message. He began his sermon, and for all the great Yiddish orators on the East Side, no one had ever heard such a torrent of eloquence in English before. He said little new or startling to people who read their Bible and Talmud, their Yiddish papers and journals, and modern writers like Perez Smolenskin and Ahad Ha'am. But how he said it, his sincerity, his passion for justice, won many of them over, and they came back again and again to the the

Friday evening services and the Sunday night forum on social problems. In the ten years that the downtown branch existed, attendance climbed from 250 a night to betwen 500 and 600. Wise's success alarmed many of the Orthodox, who saw his Reform services as alien to Judaism. The older generation, confirmed in its traditionalism, ignored him; but their sons feared his invasion, perhaps as Irving Howe suggests, because they were more than a trifle drawn to his eloquence and sophistication. To counter the modernism Wise symbolized, they formed Young Israel, an activist association dedicated to making Orthodox Judaism meaningful in modern-day terms.[10]

The Orthodox were not the only ones upset by Wise's success. Samuel Schulman, the rabbi of Temple Beth-El and an inveterate foe of Wise, caustically commented that "the way to start a Free Synagogue is to cultivate a voice, place a pitcher of ice water on a stand, and marry an heiress." It was a mark of Wise's self-confidence and the obvious success of the Free Synagogue that news of Schulman's sarcastic remark only made him smile; Louise, on the other hand, could never forgive anyone for attacking her husband. About a week later, as the Wises walked on Fifth Avenue, they met Schulman. Louise said not a word as the two men chatted for several minutes, and then Wise (who did not smoke) pulled a cigar out of his pocket and give it to Schulman. As soon as they were around the corner, Louise exclaimed: "How could you do that, Stephen, after the way he spoke about us last week?" "Well, you see, my dear," came the cheerful reply, "that was last week."[11]

Here one can see another and very important aspect of Wise's character. His was not a temperament "slow to anger"; rather, he could and did explode, often with slight provocation. But he calmed down, and forgave or apologized, with equal speed. His friends and opponents recognized this mercurial nature and discounted his outbursts. He had many opponents during his life, but very few enemies. Through all the years he and Louis Marshall fought over Emanu-El and the American Jewish Congress and the Jewish Agency, for example, they remained on cordial personal terms. Part of Wise's attractiveness—and effectiveness—over the years may have derived from this emotional openness, this refusal to bottle up grievances; he was open and honest in his fights, and expected the same from those opposing him.

At the Free Synagogue Wise developed a congregational policy unique in its time, one that became the ideal if not the reality for American synagogues in the decades to come. He somehow managed to create a workable equilibrium between two potentially conflicting goals. On the one hand, the rabbi would be a leader, a speaker of truth to the congregants' conciences, and Wise often championed causes which many of the members opposed. On the other, the rabbi would be a supporter of democracy and equality. Like most men who possess large egos, Wise had more than a trace of the autocrat. Yet at the same time he truly believed in democracy and equality in Jewish life, and challenged the prevailing dominance of the wealthy elite in congregational life. There is no evidence that he ever recognized the inherent friction in these goals, and his oratorial prowess and personal popularity made it unnecessary for him or the Free Synagogue to face what other strong-willed rabbis sometimed did, the clash of their views with that of a democratically organized congregation of equals. In his forty-two-year tenure as rabbi of the Free Synagogue, Wise and his congregants rarely fought, not because they always agreed, but because each had too much respect and affection for the other to let minor disagreements mushroom into major quarrels.

Despite the resentment of Samuel Schulman and others, the Free Synagogue flourished, outgrowing the facilities available at the Universalist Church. In 1910, while Wise was in England, Felix Adler's Ethical Culture Society completed a building of its own and give up its lease of Carnegie Hall on Sunday mornings. The executive committee immediately voted to move services to that auditorium, and on Rosh Hashonah Eve of 1910, October 3, the Free Synagogue began what eventually became a thirty-year residency. Carnegie Hall provided a dignified setting; it could hold well over 3,000 people, and here Wise's voice could play over its full range. Now every Sunday morning between 1,600 and 2,000 people would participate in the services, the number always including guests, non-members, and visitors from out of town who came out of curiosity. For special events and guest speakers, the hall would be filled, with the overflow shifted into a basement auditorium where they listened to services piped in through a loudspeaker. No seats were ever reserved, and even the most prosperous and prominent members soon learned that unless they came early, they could wind up in the back, or in the galleries, or even in the basement.

From the beginning, the work of the Free Synagogue divided into three major areas—religious, educational, and social services. Wise, of course, had ultimate responsiblity for everything, but proved singularly adept at delegating authority to capable men and women. He kept almost complete control of the religious activities of the synagogue until the 1930's, when he began devoting most of his time to the fight against fascism. Arrangements for guest speakers, services, and ritual remained his special domain, one in which he paid great attention to detail and from which he derived an equally great pleasure. Although not known for having an impressive singing voice, he had a good ear, and when the choir performed horrendously one Friday evening at Clinton Hall, he immediately demanded improvement from its director.[12] The guest speakers who occupied the Free Synagogue pulpit over forty years came from all walks of life—business, the professions, politics, reform—and presented a wide spectrum of opinion. Every one came at Wise's personal invitation; to each of them he promised and provided a free pulpit, whether he agreed with their opinions or not.

One of his most successful and innovative, as well as controversial, ventures proved to be the union service. In the fall of 1910 Wise joined with John Haynes Holmes of the Church of the Messiah and Frank Oliver Hall of the Church of the Divine Paternity to sponsor non-sectarian union services each Sunday evening on "Religion and the Social Problem." Hundreds of people had to be turned away from the first meeting, where Judge Ben Lindsey of the Juvenile Court of Denver spoke on "The Battle with the Beast." In subsequent series on "The Application of Religious Principles to the Social Life" and "Social Justice," the audiences heard from John Mitchell of the United Mine Workers, Social Gospel advocate Washington Gladden, Dean George W. Kirchwey of Columbia Law School, conservationalist Gifford Pinchot, Paul Underwood Kellogg of *Survey*, Bishop Charles D. Williams of Detroit, and many others.

The success of the union services, in fact their very existence horrified many Jews. Samuel Schulman, ever eager to find fault with Wise, pontificated that "if Jews can meet in common worship with the Christians one night in the week, why not every night? If one service can be shared with the Christians, why not all? And then what becomes of historic Judaism?" The *Maccabaean*, the official organ of American Zionism, carried a vicious attack accusing Wise of ignoring centuries of Jewish tradition as well as the thousands of martyrs to the faith, all for the glory of "coquetting with some Christians and to show them that we are not different from them—not even in religion." Jacob Schiff, whose generosity had helped get the Free Synagogue underway, denounced the interfaith gatherings. "Christians are still persecuting Jews with atrocious cruelty in Russia," he declared. "Why then is it seemly for Jews to meet with Christians in common worship in New York? First the atrocities must cease!"

Wise, Holmes, and Hall tried to reason with Schiff; the Christians of New York were not persecuting the Jews in Russia, and the two Christian denominations involved, Unitarian and Universalist, fostered religious liberty and opposed intolerance. In a lengthy letter to Schiff, Wise attempted to explain that the common worship played a secondary role to the main purpose of showing "that the synagogue and church can stand together . . . to bring the light of religion to bear upon the tasks and problems of our age." While Schiff had a right to object to the services, Wise asked him to think about how his comments might be interpreted, "to bear in mind what great damage may be done to the highest interests of American Israel if it should go out . . . that you, as a leader of the Jewish people in America, have taken a position which meant that you look with disfavor upon the union of Jews and Christians for the furtherance of aims common to the church and synagogue." Schiff could not be presuaded, and withdrew his support from the Free Synagogue, reserving his contributions only for social services.[13]

Not all of Wise's experiments proved successful, at least not in the long run. In the fall of 1907 he abandoned the traditional Saturday morning rituals because of the poor attendance, and substituted instead a Sunday morning service. A number of Reform congregations had chosen Sunday services in the latter part of the nineteenth century, some in an open effort to make the entire religious program as Christian as possible, others because many Jews now had to work on Saturday, and would be more likely to attend services on Sunday. In the move to Sunday, Wise downplayed the reading of the Torah, the five books of Moses, in favor of selections from the prophetic writings, which buttressed his desire to make Liberal Judaism more responsive to ethical and social considerations. "Herein we erred," he later wrote, "for, as I have long seen, even the form of the Torah, the Scroll of the Law, had become too precious to the tradition of the synagogue to be lightly, indeed on any account, abolished."[14]

Another failing in the Free Synagogue services resulted directly from the very cause of its success, the brilliant preaching of its rabbi. Services at the Free Synagogue, according to some members, could be deadly dull except for the sermon. The Union Prayer Book then in use was a product of the classical period of American Reform; it tried to be decorous and succeeded primarily in being boring, the heavy-handed English translations of the traditional Hebrew liturgies catching little of the poetry and exaltation of the originals. While the musical accompaniment to the services eventually improved when Abraham Binder took over the choir and organ, it nonetheless remained a minor feature. The Free Synagogue service revolved around the sermon, and as a result, led to a dichotomy between the religious and the secular, a division totally alien to traditional Judaism, which saw the divine as an integral part of the daily. Wise preached that religion must address itself to contemporary moral problems, and there is no doubt that he, more than any other rabbi of his time, brought contemporary issues to the attention of his congregation. They heard about the prophets, about the moral injunctions of Judaism, but in a manner and setting that rarely gave them a feel for the religion, for the "Jewishness" which Wise mistakenly assumed was there.[15] Eventually he recognized this, and in later years sought to provide a more religious component in the work of the Free Synagogue. By then, his congregation and many others were moving in directions few observers of Liberal Judaism had anticipated at the turn of the century.

Perhaps the most unique contribution of the Free Synagogue can be found in its true commitment to social service, a concept nearly ignored by most congregations in 1907 and still honored more in the abstract than in practice. The eighth point of the 1885 Pittsburgh Platform, the original credo of American Reform Judaism, resolved: "We deem it our duty to participate in the great task of modern times, to solve on the basis of justice and righteousness, the problems presented by the contrasts and evils of the present organization of society." For all that he was at odds with many of his Reform colleagues, Wise took this precept to heart. Some of his ideas worked, others did not; some of the ventures inaugurated by him and his colleagues broke new ground, others proved of only temporary value. But in every instance, even if mistakes were made, they could answer detractors with "We at least are trying. What are you doing?"

It is impossible to talk of the Free Synagogue's social service work without reference to Sidney Goldstein, who throughout Wise's ministry in New York served as his director of the Social Service Division. Goldstein's dedication and effectiveness made Wise's dream into a successfuly reality.[16]

Sidney Emanuel Goldstein entered Hebrew Union College in 1897, and went through the entire eight-year preparatory and rabbinic program, receiving his ordination in 1905. At the College, he "found little if any understanding or appreciation of social conditions and programs and the movements for social justice." Impelled by a fierce need to help people, he began to do extracurricular volunteer work with Boris Bogen, then director of Cincinnati's Federation of Philanthropies. Bogen taught Goldstein about the various needs of and services available to the the city's poor Jews, and through people he met at the agencies, kept abreast of the latest thought and developments in the field of social work. Just before his graduation, Goldstein had to deliver a sermon at one of the nearby Reform temples, and since it was the Passover season, he took as his text "Let My people go in order that they may serve Me." He pleaded for the emancipation of the millions of poor working people who suffered want and injustice at the hands of the country's large corporations. No sooner had he said "Amen" than Kaufman Kohler, who had recently become president of the College, rushed to the pulpit and began to pray, earnestly beseeching the Lord to save the congregation from the heresies they had just heard.

The incident confirmed Goldstein in his decision to enter the field of social work rather than become a practicing rabbi. After graduation he moved to New York and became assistant superintendent of Mount Sinai Hospital under Dr. Sigmund S. Goldsmith, an extremely able man with wide social interests. Goldstein's duties included meeting patients upon admission, visiting them in the wards, and seeing them again at discharge. He soon learned that although Mount Sinai provided superior medical and nursing services, the staff had little awareness of the social problems of the men, women, and children they treated as patients. To point out that hospitals had to take these factors into consideration, Goldstein wrote a pioneering article entitled "The Social Function of the Hospital" in 1906.[17] Doctors, nurses, and administrators, he urged, should remember that patients were not isolated units, mere medical cases, but members of families, with social and economic problems that greatly affected their overall mental and physical well-being.

Wise, still in Oregon, read the piece and wrote to Goldstein saying that he wanted to meet him on his next trip to New York. When Wise arrived in the city late in the year, he told Goldstein of his plans for a new synagogue, one that not only preached and taught, but also practiced what it preached. He invited Goldstein to join him and be responsible for the Social Service Division. At first, the Free Synagogue could only afford Goldstein on a part-time basis at $1,200 a year, and to earn a living he took on another job, as rabbi of a small congregation in Bensonhurst, Brooklyn. Not until 1912 would the Free Synagogue be able to secure enough funds to bring Goldstein in on a full-time basis. Thus began an association which lasted throughout Wise's life; even after Wise's death Goldstein stayed on at the Free Synagogue, directing the program he had done so much to shape. He once asked Wise to account for their long and harmonious partnership. Wise replied: "In two ways: first, my own inexhaustible patience of spirit; and second your own incredible power of endurance."[18]

In his memoirs Goldstein described the aims of the Social Service Division as threefold; namely, to socialize the membership, making it aware of and involved in the problems of the larger community; to relate the synagogue as a whole to community needs, programs, and agencies; and to further social movements and advance social causes. To accomplish these tasks, Goldstein and Wise devised a number of projects to involve the congregation. Philanthropy by itself satisfied neither of the rabbis; the congregants had to involve themselves personally in the work, so they could see, face to face, how the other half lived. Many of the programs, such as a survey of homes of the children attending religious school at the downtown branch, relied entirely on volunteers. Members of the synagogue, from both branches, visited the homes of 150 children to see what, if any, improvements could be made and/or what practical help could be given. In some instances, immediate financial aid was provided; in others, the immigrant parents had to be taught how to do certain tasks, or informed of services available to them at little or no charge.[19]

Because Goldstein had pointed out the need for social awareness in hospitals, the providing of social care to the Jewish sick became one of the first projects of the Division. Although the directors of Mount Sinai were more than willing to cooperate, Goldstein and Wise decided that a more needy group, and one that would offer the Free Synagogue greater opportunites for service, could be found in Bellevue Hospital. To Bellevue came the cases that could not be treated at other hospitals and people who, for one reason or another, could not be admitted elsewhere. A city institution, Bellevue handled about 6,000 Jewish patients each year, and its overworked Department of Social services welcomed the offer of outside assistance. A plan evolved so that within twenty-four hours of admission, every Jewish patient would be visited by either a trained medical–social worker or a volunteer and interviewed regarding nonmedical problems and the conditions at home. Where feasible, plans were then made for help both during the hospital stay and after discharge.

Over the years, Goldstein expanded his program. He lectured frequently to the congregation on social service work and on specific needs. He ran a training course for the volunteers, gathered gifts of clothing and established cooperative relations with courts and prisons. Although some of the older charitable agencies initially looked askance at the Free Synagogue "do-gooders," Goldstein's professionalism and the obvious effectiveness of his efforts soon won acceptance for the Division. When the New York Federation of Jewish Philanthropies organized in 1917 as an umbrella agency for fund-raising and charitable work, the Free Synagogue joined as a constituent agency, the only synagogue in New York able to do so. Goldstein's preparatory work in establishing a volunteer program with professional standards now proved its worth. The Division of Social Service henceforth received an annual allotment from the Federation which allowed it to expand its work.

Funds for the program came from a variety of sources. At every service, whether in Carnagie Hall, Clinton Hall, or the Bronx branch, one of the rabbis or a congregant would talk about some aspect of the program and then pass a basket for donations. Part of the general budget of the Free Synagogue was earmarked for the Division, and outside funds came in from the Federation and from some municipal agencies, such as the Youth Board, which underwrote specific programs. Moreover, Wise urged his congregants to make specials gifts to the Divison in honor of happy events, such as birthdays and weddings, and to provide for the program in their wills. Many nonmembers also made contributions to the work; even after Jacob Schiff withdrew his support from the synagogue over the question of union services, he still made donations to the Division. The Free Synagogue underwrote all the administrative costs; every penny that came in as a donation or allocation went to aid the needy. By 1909, Goldstein operated on a budget of $10,000; three years later the Division expended $15,000, and found new opportunities for service everywhere it looked.[20]

Problems existed, of course, not the least of which involved the large number of Jewish poor needing help. Goldstein, as a professional, knew that if his division tried to help everybody, it would soon lose all effectiveness; he wisely decided to build up each project before embarking upon another, otherwise he would be spreading his limited resources much too thinly to be of any use. Wise, on the other hand, found the problem overwhelming. He wanted to help everyone, and his papers bulge with hundreds of letters he wrote to Goldstein, Morris Waldman (director of the United Jewish Charities), and other social workers on specific cases. "I made an appeal yesterday to enable us to purchase a wooden leg for Samuel Rosenberg," he wrote to Waldman; when one woman lamented that her only son had been posted to the Phillipines, Wise had no hesitation in asking the Secretary of War to transfer the boy.[21] He dug often and deeply into his own pocket, and over the years he paid out tens of thousands of dollars. While the rich *yahudim* gave more in total dollars, Wise gave more in proportion to his income than did many of the great philanthropists. His goodheartedness, however, often got in the way of the professionals, especially when someone they had turned down with just cause would hie over to Wise's study and pour out a tale of woe, knowing the rabbi would be a soft touch. "For you to pay Mrs. Stern's rent," his friend Morris Waldman lectured him in exasperation, "would be encouraging pauperism. You are paying the penalty of all well-known philanthropists. The knowledge of your goodness of heart among the poor is common property. May I suggest that you leave responsiblity with us?"[22]

Stephen was not the only Wise involved in social work. Just as Louise had labored alongside him in Portland, now she created a part of the Free Synagogue which would be uniquely hers. In 1916, Louise met a Jewish couple at a dinner party who lamented that their home had not been blessed with children. "Why not adopt a child?" she asked, only to be dumbfounded by their answer: No agency existed for this purpose; orphaned Jewish children were placed in asylums, with no means of uniting them with would-be adoptive parents. Soon afterward she confirmed what the couple had told her, that there were thousands of Jewish boys and girls in institutions, and there no means of placing them in homes where their lives and those of their parents could be immeasurably enriched. Louise set out to remedy the situation, and together with other women established the Child Adoption Committee of the Free Synagogue, the first agency of its kind to handle adoption for Jewish orphans. Two entries from her diary, one in 1917 and the second in 1920, provide an idea of Louise's dedication to her project, how much she, like her husband, believed that true religion ultimately meant "doing justly and loving mercy":[23]

> A red-letter day! Adolph Lewisohn gave me one thousand dollars to begin my baby-caring work. I can keep twenty babies out of the asylums for a year on that and soon we shall get more and make a big work of it. How I hate those awful asylums where so many poor helpless babies die who might live and ought have the chance such as my babies did.

> Baby adoption work grows almost too big for my strength—yet what joy it was to see one of our babies going away today with a lovely mother looking as rosy and round as an apple. The joy compensates for the sacrifices of time and strength.

In the first quarter-century of work, the Free Synagogue's Child Adoption Committee placed nearly 2,000 children and processed more than 10,000 applications from would-be parents. More important than the statistics is the fact that the Committee set a pattern other Jewish agencies soon followed. Within her lifetime, Louise Wise saw Jewish orphan asylums practically disappear as adoption took the place of institutionalization. "Child adoption," Wise wrote proudly of his wife's work, "should be magnified as one of the outstanding phases in the solution in the problem of the homeless child."[24]

The work of the Free Synagogue, its branches, and its social service programs, occupied much of Wise's time, and no matter how involved he became in other activities, the Free Synagogue remained the center of his life, his forum for more than four decades. He worried about its finances, attendance, and program as a parent would about a child's major and minor illnesses or cuts or bruises. During the Depression, for example, Wise reacted typically; he insisted on a reduction in his own salary. When things went well, he rejoiced greatly, for few men have the pleasure of seeing their dreams brought to fruition.[25] Of all the organizations he founded, none personified what he believed in or stood for as did the Free Synagogue, and when asked to identify himself, he always declared: "I am the rabbi of the Free Synagogue."

6

Rabbi of the
Free Synagogue

The years in which Stephen Wise founded and built the Free Synagogue were happy ones for him. The success of his enterprise propelled him to the forefront of the American rabbinate, and made him a model from which many younger rabbis drew inspiration. Israel Goldstein recalled that when he entered the profession, Wise and Emil G. Hirsch were the great figures, two rebels who blazed a trail of freedom within the Jewish pulpit.[1] In this period, the decade between the founding of the Free Synagogue and American entry into the First World War, Wise entered his maturity, successful as a rabbi, involved in Jewish and secular affairs with at least three or four battles going on at all times—the minimum needed to keep him happy—and a home life where love and enthusiasm abounded.

A reporter has given a colorful portrait of Wise during these years:[2]

Imagine a tall, spare, active, swarthy athlete of early middle age, his frame well covered with muscle of the long sinuous springy sort, the whole surmounted by a massive head, framed in a leonine mass of wavy, blue-black hair. The dark eyes are keen and piercing, yet alight with sympathy and kindliness. The big, full forehead, the big aquiline nose, the big outjutting chin, the big, steely jaws, give altogether a picture of enormous driving power, of indomitable will. At first glance, the young man seems a typical football-player, the sort you would pass the ball to as a forlorn hope for a line plunge when the powerful enemy have you down, six to nothing. His step is light, his movements quick and resilient. But there is more in him than that. The kindling eye, the broad mobile mouth bespeak the orator. The smile that illuminates the eyes and ripples away from the twin rows of large even white teeth evidence the hopeful, cheery, buoyant youth.

When this "cheery, buoyant youth" and Louise first returned to New York in late 1906, they moved in with Leo and Jennie in the spacious brownstone at 46 East 68th Street; this was the house which Julius Waterman had left jointly to his three children. Leo and Jennie, now reconciled to the marriage, were delighted to have Louise and her family "back home," and they gave over much of the house to the Wises—living quarters on the second floor, a nursery on the third, and a study for Stephen on the fourth. They lived this way for two years, Stephen and Louise reluctant to buy a place of their own as long as he drew no salary and the fate of the Free Synagogue remained in doubt. While Jennie and Leo did all they could to make everyone feel comfortable, they found their own orderly and peaceful lives totally disrupted. Dozens of callers came to see the rabbi during the week, the telephone rang perpetually, and two very boisterous children constantly escaped their nurse to burst in on committee meetings or even an occasional wedding ceremony. John Haynes Holmes recalled that in the fall of 1907 he went to pay a courtesy call on Wise at the Waterman home. He no sooner range the bell than he heard the commotion of children running madcap down the hall. They threw open the door even as their nurse tried vainly to restrain them.

"Who are you?" demanded six-year-old Jimmie. "And what do you want? Did you come to see my Daddy or my Mummy?"

"Daddy, you silly," exclaimed his four-year-old sister Justine. "He's the only one around here who's important."[3]

The longer they stayed, the more Stephen and Louise felt they were intruding on Leo and Jennie's life, and at the same time, were themselves constrained and unable to live as freely and informally as they desired. Finally they found a roomy, comfortable house at 23 West 90th Street; Louise used part of her inheritance to purchase it and here the Wises made their home for the next three decades. In addition, in 1908 they bought a few acres on Buck Island at Lake Placid, in the scenic Adirondack Mountains of upstate New York, and named it Camp Willamette after the Oregon river they had so loved. In the next few years they build a small home there, to which they went every summer and as often other times as they could, for its delightful quiet repaired body and nerves worn down by strife. They deliberately kept the furnishings simple and the room limited, not wanting it to be too accessible lest their rest be interrupted.

If Louise's upbringing had been in the restrained decorous fashion of the German–Jewish aristocracy and Stephen's had been only a little less formal, they raised their own children in an atmosphere which, to some observers, must have appeared perilously close to chaotic. Neither Justine nor James remember any restraints on them other than mild indications that certain activities had not pleased their parents. Stephen and Louise flooded their children with affection and support, and then let them grow up as they wanted to, free to make their own decisions and mistakes, knowing their parents were there for support and guidance whenever they might be needed. Both children adored their father and resented any intrusion on that part of his time which they saw as belonging to them.[4]

That time came early in the morning, when he would wake the children for their baths. If they got up quickly, he would sit with them for a few minutes and talk; if they were drowzy, they would find him gone, waiting for them at the breakfast table. There would be more conversation while they ate, and then Wise walked the two children, both with their collies in tow to school so they could have more time together. During the trek he explained what he was doing and answered the children's questions about his work, about things in general, or about any problems they might be having. At first they walked from the house on 90th Street down to the Ethical Culture School on West 64th, near Central Park, but that route ended when Jimmie and a close friend proved too much for the teachers to handle. The principal called in the parents of both boys to explain the situation, and said that one of the youths would have to leave. Louise indignantly stood up, outraged that her first-born should not be considered well-behaved, and declared "I won't even let my son stay in this school!"

So now instead of walking south, the entourage—Stephen, James, Justine, and two dogs—walked north the mile and a half to the Horace Mann School, then located at 120th Street and Broadway. Occasionally they would meet a member of the congregation who would stop Wise to talk for a few minutes, unaware of two small children looking daggers at him. Particularly vexing was Meyer Weisgal, then a young man of 18 or 19, who ran a newspaper stand near Columbia University in the mornings and worked at the Zionist offices in the afternoons. Jim and Justine did not mind if their father, who took possession of both dogs at the schoolhouse door, *shmoozed* (chatted) with Weisgal on his way home, but they deeply resented any and all intrusions on their time with him.[5]

As Jim and Justine grew up, they exhibited all the characteristics their parents prized—a fierce independence of spirit, an inquisitive nature, a deep caring for other people, and a commitment to social justice. They could also be hellions. Both attended a variety of schools changing from one to another both voluntarily and involuntarily; Jim especially, despite his innate intelligence, found it difficult to settle down to studies. Wise at all times felt confident, however, that as the headmaster of the Loomis School said, Jim had "good stuff in him" and would "come out alright someday."[6] Justine, who Jim recalls as "a perfect angel," reacted both with fists and outrage if anyone attacked or even insulted her brother or parents. If Stephen and Louise needed any evidence of how strong-willed their daughter could be, they found it in 1913.

That year the Wises planned to go first to Europe and then on to Palestine, but because of a cholera scare in the Middles East, they decided to leave the children in Germany. They signed Jim into a boarding school. One would have thought that Justine, the "perfect angel," would have accepted this arrangement while Jim, the rebellious one, would have balked.

As it turned out, Jim became great friends with an English boy at the school, had plenty of time to read, memorized lengthy sections of Shakespeare, and all in all had a thoroughly enjoyable time. Ten-year-old Justine, on the other hand, hated it. She had a strict governess who made her practice the piano for hours, and she resented the comments of her Waterman relatives, who still believed that cousin Louise had married beneath her. So the little "angel" saved up her money and sent a cable to her parents in Palestine that she was going to run away forever unless they came for her. Fortunately, Stephen and Louise were about to return to Europe, so they wired instructions for the governess to bring Justine to meet them in Rome.[7]

In addition to wife and children, Wise had other family responsibilities which he took seriously. His aging mother now moved around, visiting with one or the other of her children, but preferring Wise's home. There she would often stay as long as six months at a time, reigning like a queen, speaking only in German. Her grandchildren remember her as strong–willed but neither nasty nor interfering, absolutely doting on her son who, more than any of her children, assumed responsibility for her in her old age. He kept in touch with brothers and sisters, and especially his younger brother Joe, whom he helped through the trauma of a marital breakup and subsequent divorce. Nor did he ignore his wife's side of the family. When Louise's close friend and cousin Jo and her husband, Carl Grossman, were in financial straits, Wise did all he could, albeit in vain, to prevent the bank from foreclosing on their loan. This pattern of assuming responsibility, whether for his family or his people characterized Wise's entire life.[8]

The maintenance of the 90th Street house with its cook, maid, and governess, the tuition in private schools for the children, the summer place in the Adirondacks and trips to Europe in 1910 and 1913 took far more money than the modest salary Wise drew from the Free Synagogue. From the time he returned to New York until the eve of World War Two, he supplemented his and Louise's income by going on the lecture circuit. Lectures then constituted a form of entertainment as well as an educational function, and Wise proved a popular speaker, invited back year after year to such series as the prestigious Ford Hall Forum in Boston. A fellow speaker on the lecture circuit, William McAndrew, wrote him that "I found your footprints at Manchester, New Hampshire. I was on the program for Saturday morning. One enthusiastic man from upstate said to me, 'I would have not waited this morning but for the reason the New York speaker we had yesterday filled me with the desire to hear more people from the same place.' I packed him off at the earliest train so as not to destroy the inspired memory he had at the time." By 1911 Wise found himself so deluged with invitations that he turned the management of his speaking engagements over to the

William Feakins Agency, and told Feakins that for 1912 he wanted to cut back his schedule to no more than forty speeches.[9]

Inevitably one must come to Wise's oratorical ability, a talent that impressed itself on all who heard him. Free Synagogue congregants and his Zionist colleagues often declared that he was the greatest speaker of his time. In an age that valued oratory, Wise ranked with the best. Efforts to explain, to analyze, his speaking ultimately fail, just as explanations for the greatness of a Beethoven or a Rembrandt fail; one must hear or see, one must personally experience an art to enjoy and appreciate it. Perhaps the best description of his speaking, one that points out not only its strengths but also shows why it is impossible to analyze, came from his son, who in 1928 under the pen name of "Analyticus" wrote *Jews Are Like That!*, which includes a chapter on Stephen Wise:[10]

> It is this dramatic intensity of conviction which, rather than any studied or conscious method of oratory, makes him supremely effective as a speaker. Indeed, his prepared and published addresses are with few exceptions singularly unmoving. His written oratorical style is as bad as the best of George William Curtis. He has an almost pathological addiction to antitheses, a delight in epigrams which borders on the abnormal, and when conscious of himself and of his flawless oratorical manner he is at his worst.

> It is only when, forgetting the polished phrases and the impressive periods which he had designed, he suddenly loses himself in the deep fervor of his belief, in the white heat of his emotion, that his eloquence rises to really lofty heights. Then alone, when he throws aside prepared notes and pours the torrent of his passionate conviction into truths which he hardly seems to utter but which rather utter themselves through him, does he speak in the grand manner. At such moments one may say of him that despite, rather than because of, his oratorical gifts, he is a great speaker.

Wise himself, while well aware of his talents, loved to tell stories deprecating his oratorical skills. He once met Mark Twain, who was walking down Fifth Avenue with William Dean Howells. Wise raised his hat in greeting and Howells stopped, asking if he would like to meet the great writer. When Wise said, "Of course I would," Howells turned to Twain and presented him: "This is Rabbi Wise, whom we heard speak the other night for suffrage at the Carnegie Hall meeting." Twain's reply was half grunt, half groan: "Yes, I remember. I heard him speak for equal suffrage, and I am still for it!" One evening at a party, Simeon Strunsky offered everybody wine. Wise declined, saying, "I never drink wine; it interferes with my speaking." Rollo Ogden at once brought a glass to him, exclaiming: "Here, Dr. Wise, drink this glass of wine at once!" Wise led the guests in the ensuing laughter. When he heard legitimate criticism of his speaking, however, such as that he spoke too slowly and used overlong sentences, he welcomed the comments, always willing to correct defects.[11]

But if one cannot, through analysis, re-create an art, surely it is helpful in knowing the man to see how he worked, how he put his speeches together, what he thought of his accomplishments. Wise's mind may have lacked the rigor and discipline of a true scholar, but it had an amazing spongelike quality. He wanted to know about everything, and kept clipping files on a large variety of subjects he spotted in newspapers and magazines. When he heard of something he wanted to know more about, he would write to get further information or a more precise quotation. Whenever he met people, new acquaintances or old friends, he would pump them for the latest news on subjects with which they were familiar. Bernard G. Richards, who worked closely with him for fifteen years in the American Jewish Congress, recalled that whenever he met with him Wise would demand: "What do you think of this? What do you know about that?" No time in his crowded schedule would be wasted; even trips in taxicabs would be converted into briefings. If there should be some free time, he would leave his office and walk across the street into Central Park. There he would jot down ideas as they came to him on slips of paper; when he returned to his office he would dictate memoranda from these slips, and then throw them into a drawer or folder for future use. He once explained his method of preparation:[12]

I have twenty to thirty, and perhaps even more, envelopes on my desk containing material on things about which some day I am going to preach. As I read and think, I make memoranda and put the items into the different envelopes. A great deal of this material I shall never use, but again it is a case of a sermon ripening rather than of being delivered and prepared *ad hoc* or delivered impromptu, except for a few days' preparation. I ought to add that while I read and read. . . I depend more or less upon myself. I use quotations less, not because I have come to think less of those whom I read, but because the only way I can help people is by uttering the things that are in and that grow out of my own soul.

The final preparation of my sermon runs like this: By Wednesday or Thursday preceding the Sunday morning of my sermon. . . I work at my material and then try, though I do not always succeed, to dictate an abstract of the address by Thursday or Friday. If I cannot do that, I try to stay in my study all of Saturday, usually until late in the night, leaving it for early Sunday morning to map out a 500 to 1000 word summary of what I am going to say. I rarely, if ever, read a sermon in its entirety, though upon a few great occasions I have done that. The difficulty about reading, for me, is that the members of my family tell me that I am a wretched reader, excepting of the Bible, and that when I read I might just as well be reading another man's output as my own. It does not seem, they claim, a part of me. It is not I. . .

I have found, upon the few occasions when an address or sermon was finished days or weeks before delivery, that my mind ceased to occupy itself with the problem or the sermon once the thing was written out. There is, for me, a finality in the typewritten form of a sermon which somehow seems to call a halt to the creative power of one's spirit.

In fact, however, the speech, any speech, was never really finished in his mind. He opened a talk one evening by telling his audience:[13]

When I make a speech, I actually make three speeches. The first is the one I prepare before I see my audience, and let me tell you, it's an excellent speech. Then I face the audience, and I somehow feel that this is not the right speech for this audience. So I tear up my first speech and deliver an impromptu one. There again it's a wonderful speech. Then comes the time for me to go home and think of what I should have said. That is the best speech of all. So, if you want to hear a good speech, walk home with me tonight.

How effective was he? Such distinguished contemporaries as Norman Thomas and Ralph Sockman called him a great orator and "the outstanding speaker in the Jewish pulpit." Ben Lindsey termed him "the greatest pulpit original we have," while Harold Truslow Ross named him as one of the six twentieth-century preachers "who have earned places in world oratory." His close friend and colleague, John Haynes Holmes, ranked him with Robert Ingersoll and Williams Jennings Bryan, and noted that Wise's inspiration rose to match his audience:[14]

Thus, in addressing a small group of fifty or a hundred people, he was seldom at ease. He had a keen sense of humor, a contagious gaiety of spirit, great charm of personality, but a certain unfitness in a room many sizes too small for him. But let the gathering leap to a thousand people, and the speaker catches fire. Five thousand people, and the element in question is suddenly consumed in the mounting flame of eloquence. Twenty thousand, and the speaker has found himself. He moves now with ease, and immeasurable passion. He soars into the vast empyrean, on the beating wings of the spirit. The larger the audience, the more wonderful the range and effectiveness of the speaker's utterance. This was Wise's unique distinction. I know of no other orator who ever met this test, and with such notes of triumph.

That Wise enjoyed his speaking is beyond doubt. He once said, "Nothing would give me greater pleasure than to die while preaching a sermon. But preferably at the end."[15]

Yet one must be careful to distinguish between form and substance. Some of Wise's critics maintained that he never really said anything, but did so in a beautiful manner. Comparisons to another great Jewish preacher, Abba Hillel Silver (who would later be his bitter foe), inevitably led to comments that Wise had the better voice, but Silver had the better mind. Wise himself never claimed anything more for his oratory than that it was an instrument, at times an extremely powerful and effective one, to be used in the battles against vice and corruption and prejudice.[16] If he rarely ventured into the realm of abstract philosophical argument, he had a firm grasp of the problems of everyday life, and could portray these in such a manner as to move his audience to action.

A rabbi, even one accustomed to speaking in great causes or before large meetings, must also perform pastoral work. There are times when he must be not the great orator but the wise counselor, the consoling minister, the joyful friend. For all his work in secular reform, in the American and World Jewish Congresses, in founding the Jewish Institute of Religion, in lecturing and writing and being a public personality for more than four decades, Wise saw himself first and always as *rabbi* of the Free Synagogue. He took his responsibilities to his congregants seriously and performed his duties well. One can say that a doctor is brilliant because of the number of lives he saves, or that a lawyer is successful because he wins so many cases. To evaluate a rabbi one must resort to testimony, to glimpses of him at work as seen through the eyes of others, to the judgments of those to whom he has ministered.

Take, for example, the evidence of a colleague, who recalled that despite all the magnificent orations that he heard Wise deliver at great meetings,[17]

I value as the most beautiful diadem a funeral message he delivered one day after the death of a mother in childbirth. Now the thundering voice was tender and gentle. Now the crusader for righteousness had become a loving friend and the messenger of compassion. I still see him turning to the grief-stricken husband saying, "Do you think that you are alone in your grief? Do you believe that your sorrow is only your burden? Oh, my dear young friend, all of us are smitten, all of us weep with you, all of us share in your enormous grief." Suddenly the mourning husband and family discovered the kinship of sorrow, the community of suffering. They were no longer isolated in a dark world of death, rather they were brothers and sisters in a family of sympathy and devotion, in a world shining with the light of loving-kindness and everlasting life.

Henry Bloch wrote to Wise after his wife's funeral: "With my heart overflowing with sorrow, yet I was so comforted in the thought that you, who knew so well that lovely, beautiful, gladsome girl—my precious pollyanna—should say the last farewell. I know that your heart dictated what you said, for you spoke with such a depth of feeling, with so much sincerity and fervor, and in such intimate affection for the one I so dearly loved. I shall always cherish tenderly and reverently the memory of your touching words." Wise knew also that one of the most difficult things surrounding death is bringing the living back to a normal routine of life. "It really is not honoring to the dead," he wrote to one widow, "to be unable to survive them. One must go on because of it, and you know best that

Sidney would not have wished you to fail to go on with renewed courage and purpose." No matter how busy, he always found the time for that little touch, that special note, which brought some measure of consolation to the bereaved.[18]

Nor were his notes restricted to times of sorrow. Whenever congregants or friends had children, he wrote, usually in his large sprawling longhand and in green ink, not to the parents but to the newborn. Typical is one letter sent to Edward Lubbin:[19]

Dear Little Edward: I am delighted to hear from you and to learn that you were born on St. Patrick's Day. That happens to be my birthday as well as St. Patrick's, and now there are three saints who celebrated the 17th of March —you and Patrick and I.

I hope you are going to have a happy beautiful life that will bring joy and blessing to yourself and to your parents. Please give your mother and father my affectionate congratulations, and hoping sometimes when you come to town I may see you.

Although fees from officiating at weddings, funerals, and other ceremonies can often constitute a substantial portion of a minister's income, from the beginning Wise refused to accept personal payment for these functions. Instead, he took whatever amount might be offered (there were no set fees) and put it into a special fund which he administered for charitable purposes.[20] In cases where close or longtime friends were involved, he absolutely refused to take any money, even for his fund, and indignantly sent back the check with a note indicating how insulted he felt. He and Louise did, at times, suggest that a *simcha* (a happy event, such as a birth, Bar Mitzvah, or wedding) could be appropriately celebrated by sharing some of the joy through giving to a charity, but no evidence at all exists that Wise ever deviated from his habit of refusing to keep fees.

This pastoral work illustrates how caring a person Stephen Wise was. In the hundreds of letters he answered relating to human problems, he invariably tried to steer a course that would hurt the least number of people and that might turn a potentially sorrowful situation into one for good. How, wrote one man, should he and his wife deal with fact that they had an adopted daughter? Should they lie to the child, and risk her discovering the truth later on, or should they be honest, and thus hurt the girl? For Wise, this dichotomy made no sense. Tell the child, he urged, at as young an age as possible, thus minimizing the shock; at the same time, affirm that adoption brings with it a special gift of love. He suggested that the couple follow the advice of the Child Adoption Committee, that when telling their daughter, they could say: "Parents must take any child born to them; but you were chosen by us, and we wanted just you, whom we now have." For parents troubled by their children marrying out of the faith, he counseled love and understanding; rejection would only drive the couple further away, while compassion might bring both the Jewish and non-Jewish partner back to family and into the Jewish people. Children had to have the right to choose, to make mistakes; the greatest gift a parent could give to a child was to provide freedom. "What greater wrong," he asked,[21]

> can I do my child than to withhold from him the freedom of choice, than so to keep in and confine his spirit but he needs beat his wings in vain without knowing the atmosphere that magnifies his freedom and liberates the soul? Guide if you will the light of youth, but beware of the danger of maiming and crippling life through so definitely and completely mapping it out as to deny the soul of youth the peril of adventure, the joy of combat, the glory of hopeless daring.

Numerous recollections again attest to this trait. Israel Goldstein noted: "You couldn't help loving him for the lovableness of his own nature. He could take a little child around and spend a considerable amount of time just with a little child. He had a tremendous gift for human understanding and human sympathy. He was really, by God's gift, a pastor."[22] When Reinhold Niebuhr reviewed *Challenging Years*, he wrote: "Only one aspect in Wise's life is not mirrored in these pages—his capacity for sympathy in every case of individual need which came to his attention. . . .This busy man could take infinite pains to alleviate the distress of any unfortunate who sought his aid. This touch of the lamb in the lion should have appeared somewhere in the records to make it complete." Even in small things he sought not to hurt. One of his students recalled Wise standing over a red-faced, yowling infant and saying to the adoring parents, "*That* is a baby!"[23] Perhaps his longtime friend and disciple Nahum Goldmann summed it up best:[24]

> Political leaders are motivated by many things, some by will for power, others by a wish to utilize their talents, others by vanity and the desire for fame. Stephen Wise was motivated essentially by his human goodness. Not only did he love the Jewish People; he loved every individual Jew. He would turn his hand to finding help for a poor refugee, arranging for the adoption of an orphan, or providing for a destitute widow as willingly as to solving a great social problem. . . . Other Jewish leaders may have been more revered, feared, or admired than he, but none was so beloved.

Finally, in looking at Stephen Wise as rabbi, there is the rabbinic function of interpreting Judaism. Traditionally, this involved the application of *halachah*, the laws of the Torah as interpreted by the sages, to particular situations, and Judaism is rich in *responsa*, the commentaries of rabbis over the centuries on how specific laws should be interpreted. Since Liberal Judaism emphasizes the prophetic teachings over ritual requirements, there are far fewer *responsa* in its literature, and Wise did not involve himself in *halachic* debates. Unlike the Orthodox, he did not claim a finality for

Jewish teaching; rather Judaism, to be alive, had to change and grow to meet new conditions.[25]

Perhaps this lack of certainty regarding ultimate truths denies one the inner spiritual peace, the assurances about God, claimed by those who have no doubts. Abraham Cronbach relates an incident he observed while serving as assistant rabbi for the Downtown branch during these years. The confirmation class had requested a special consecration hour, in which boys and girls spoke openly and simply about their beliefs. During the discussion, Wise entered the room unseen, sat down in the rear, and signaled Cronbach to continue. For a long while he sat and listened to the children, and then joined with them. He told them that in his crowded life, he often found it difficult to experience God's presence. Between God and him, he said, there was "a barrier, a thick wall which he was unable to penetrate." Much as he desired it, the experience was not his. Cronbach interpreted this to mean that "God is near the hearts of the lowly, but to be lowly is for some of us impossible. Some of us have duties by which lowliness is precluded. The boon of humility was not consonant with Stephen Wise's gigantic work. His mission in life did not permit him to experience the divine." One might equally argue, as Carl Voss has done, that the remark,made in deep humilty, may well have reflected a unique awareness of God and closeness to Him, that between man and God there must always be a barrier.[26] Certainly an undated "Prayer" in Wise's papers would indicate that while he may not have been "lowly," he did possess a humble yet exalted understanding of the interaction of God and man:

> Who will presume to speak of futility in the role of spirit, who will say that aspiration is unavailing because it seems to be what the world calls futile? How can prayer be futile, for through prayer one reaches out—as is possible in no other way—into the life of another, one reaches out into the life of all. Prayer might almost be defined as the mingling of the stream of life of the individual with the seas of infinite life; the steam of the soul is not lost or spent, but regained and enriched through commingling with the tides of life, infinite and eternal . . . .
>
> I pray not that I may have, but that I may be. I pray not that God may give me, but that I may give myself to God. Nor shall I cease to pray when God withholds from me, for from men God may not withhold the infinite and eternal of themselves. Prayer is the joy, high and unutterable, of the soul's outreaching to Him who is the Soul of Souls.

For Wise, God was at the center of Judaism, but Judaism was not an inward-looking but an outward-reaching religion, one that dominated and affected all of his life and activities. Perhaps his clearest statement on this came in an article he wrote during the twenties for *Christian Century*:[27]

I have found life worth living, for I am a Jew. No Heinesque notion that Judaism is a misfortune ever found lodgment in my being. For my Jewishness, never forgetting disabilities and discriminations and limitations, has been the supremely enriching joy of my days. The story is told of a Jew who, being asked to write on elephants, prepared a voluminous treatise of "Elephants and the Jewish Problem." I am like that Jew, for I cannot write on the things that have led me to find life worth living without "draggin in" the Jewish question. For Jewishness has colored my life, has been more than color, for it has been of the very substance and texture of my being.

Not that being a Jew is happiness unmixed. For priceless though *gaudium certaminus* [the glory of the contest] be, it is hard to find oneself in battle array all one's days, either in defense against an attacking world or waging war against such as are the enemies within their own people. The burden of striving with the foes of Israel must need rest heavily upon those who like myself view their freedom as opportunity and challenge to do battle for them that are in bondage as most Jews in one sense or another still are.

He once commented that the world's greatest sin was indifference, and of that sin he could not be accused. Judaism, especially the teachings of the prophets, would not allow him to stand by passively as long as injustice and bigotry oppressed people, and here he found the link to American ideals, the connection that not only justified but mandated his involvement in secular reforms. "I have tried," he stated, "and will try while I live to bring the best of American life into the the life of my people in this land, and in turn to move my people to give of their highest and finest to the life of this new world."[28] A complete concord existed between American ideals and Jewish ethics, and the American Jew would find no tension in fulfilling his obligations both as an American and as a Jew. The idea of harmony between Americanism and Judaism was, of course, a standard tenet of Reform Judaism in this country, but no other rabbi of his time practiced this belief with as much fervor as did Wise. In the years following the founding of the Free Synagogue, its rabbi threw himself energetically into Jewish affairs and into the world of progressive reform as well.

Wise's involvment in Jewish matters might well be compared to a great love affair, in which one can find traces of jealousy, rancor, and discord as well as deep devotion and sacrifice. Of his devotion and sacrifice, the record is clear; the jealousy and discord need to be discussed, for they too are found in his long career as a Jewish leader. Some people have suggested that unless Wise could be the unquestioned leader, he sought out the opposition, starting a new synagogue or seminary or organization that would be his. Certainly Wise found it more to his liking to be a leader rather than a follower, yet when he perceived greatness in others, such as Louis Brandeis, he proved a reliable and trustworthy lieutenant. Perhaps the problem might better be viewed in terms of a jealous lover, convinced of the rightness of his own beliefs and expecting his beloved to live up to great standards. There is no doubt that he loved the Jewish people and guarded their welfare to the utmost limits of his abilities and energies for more than fifty years, that he preached a doctrine of high ethical behavior derived from the prophetic tradition, and that he expected his people to live up to the standards of their glorious past. When, in his eyes, they did not, he fought with them as a lover would, less in anger than in sorrow.

What gave him the right, then and even more so later in his life, to assume this responsibility, to lecture his brethren on what they should and should not do? Had his fellow Jews elected him as their spokesman? Were there no others as well or better qualified to speak in behalf of American Jewry? In part, Stephen Wise assumed his authority from the Bible, from the example of the Hebrew prophets. He never claimed that God had spoken to him, commanding him to speak harsh truths; rather, God had commanded the Jewish people to live righteously, and *kol Yisrael arevim zeh lazeh*—all Jews are responsible one for the other. He as a Jew, and especially as a rabbi and teacher, and a special obligation to remind his people of the ethical covenant they had entered. At times his interpretation of the role struck some people as *chutzpah* (nerve) or even arrogance.

One example of this special role can be found in an incident when the American Standard Bible Committee invited Dr. Harry Orlinsky to participate in the translation of the Old Testament; Orlinsky was the first Jew ever to be asked to work on this Christian project. At first he refused, reluctant to get involved in disputations with Protestant collegues over potentially Christological passages. When a second invitation came, Orlinsky, then a faculty member at the Jewish Institute of Religion, went to ask Stephen Wise what he thought. As Orlinsky, perhaps the leading Biblical scholar of his generation, recalled:[29]

> Dr. Wise rose from his high-back chair, a sort of throne, and standing over me at his full height, like a lion over his prey (when in action he always looked taller than he really was), he explained to me, in the manner of an urgently exhorting Jeremiah, that it was not I as an individual the International Council of Relígous Education (an arm of the National Council of Churches of Christ) had invited to help make the new official translation of the Hebrew Bible for the Protestant community of the United States and the world over, but I as a representative of the Jewish people. For how could a translation of the Hebrew Bible be attempted seriously—he asked me rhetorically—without the direct participation and assistance of a descendant of those who wrote the original in the first place? Who was I—he continued—to say "No" to this historic invitation? Only the Jewish people had the authority to decide in the matter, and—he assured me—the Jewish people say "Yes!".
>
> Not only that. Dr. Wise made it very clear that as a representative of the Jewish people—he, who was not known for his observance of sundry rules and regulations pertaining to traditional Judaism, was telling this to me!—that as the representative of the Jewish people I was not to work with the Committee

on the Sabbath, and that I was not to partake of unkosher food (*trefah* is the term he used) in the company of my Christian collegues. I was to consider myself not an individual Jewish scholar but a scholar spokesman for the Jewish people.

Interestingly, Orlinsky also consulted Rabbi Mordechai Kirshbloom, a leading Orthodox figure, who seconded Wise's advice.

Why did this assumption that he—Stephen Wise—could speak for Jewish people seem so natural? Why didn't Orlinsky or Rabbi Kirshbloom resent Wise's attitude of authority? By the 1940s, of course, Wise's sacrifice and labors in defense of Jewry had legitimized his claims to speak for his brethren. Yet within a few years after the founding of the Free Synagogue, this trait had already become apparent.

Wise may have castigated his fellow Jews for their deficiencies, but he also, and with great vigor, rushed to defend them from attack. When a series of magazine articles appeared criticizing Jews (including one entitled "The Jew As An Enemy of Peace"), Wise declared in a sermon: "It is our duty to meet every attack on honor, righteousness and justice, to make ourselves kings among men, and knightly administrators of justice to humanity at large. This is the correct Jewish spirit. Let no Jew be afraid of his religion, but respect himself as a Jew and by his conduct entitle himself to the respect of other races."[30]

Here, as in other areas, he did his best to practice what he preached. When some fellow Jews showed alarm at a proposal to create a Jewish university club in New York, lest it be considered a token of Jewish clannishness, the rabbi of the Free Synagogue asked whether it might better be viewed as a protest over the exclusion of Jews from some of the upper-caste Fifth Avenue clubs. Jews should not see this snobbishness as their dishonor, but rather as the shame of those who practiced it. Jews, especially those who on occasion were invited in to these gentile sanctuaries, should proudly refuse to enter. He himself had recently been invited to the famed Lake Mohonk Peace Conference as a guest and speaker, but when he learned that the host resort normally denied accomodations to Jews, he refused to attend. The real tragedy, he said, lay with those Jews who would not stand up for their rights, but instead made lame excuses for the discriminatory policy of the hotel.[31]

Jews had to be ever vigilant in their own defense, and they had the right, indeed the obligation, as Americans as well as Jews to demand publicly what legally and morally belonged to them. While Louis Marshall, Jacob Schiff, and the American Jewish Committee did their work quietly, Wise believed in open confrontation. Thus the Committee lobbied successfully behind the scenes to have Congress rescind the Russo-American Trade Treaty in protest against antisemitic restrictions placed by the Russian government on American Jewish citizens traveling in Russia. Wise visited the White House to urge President William Howard Taft to insist that Russia treat all American citizens equally or forego the commercial advantages of doing business with the United States. He then told reporters the gist of his conversation with the president, noting that "the Jew would rightly forfeit the respect of the American people if he uncomplainingly endured a grave violation of his rights as an American citizen by a nominally friendly power."[32] Both the Committee and Wise agreed on ends but not means, and this difference would erupt again in the battles over the American Jewish Congress during the First World War and the American Jewish Conference of World War Two.

As the years wore on, Wise became more and more identified as a vocal defender of Jewish rights, whether protesting exclusionary social customs or trying to save the life of Leo Frank, who ultimately was lynched by a southern mob.[33] He never asked that Jews be treated with special consideration, and condemned attempts by Jews or non-Jews to appeal to a so-called "Jewish vote." By the time he emerged as the leading Jewish figure in America to oppose Hitler and fascism in the 1930s, he had already set this pattern, which in large measure justified his claims to speak for his people.

A rabbi speaks not only *for* but above all *to* his people, and Wise condemned intolerance and ethical blindness among Jews as well as gentiles. He attacked the American Jewish Committee because of its undemocratic nature, and opposed the original charter of the New York Kehillah because he considered it unrepresentative of the city's Jewish population. During these years, he also waged battle against what he considered the illiberal attitudes and policies of the established organs of American Reform Judaism.

Wise attended his first meeting of the Central Conference of American Rabbis in Philadelphia in July 1901, while he was rabbi of Portland's Beth Israel. Evidently leaders of the Conference welcomed this promising young man, elected him to the executive committee (a position he would not hold again until 1932), and named him to the important committees on nominations and the president's message. A proposal that the CCAR cooperate with the Zionist movement caused much discussion, and Wise, considering his Zionist activities, took a rather mild position. Perhaps he realized that a strong pro-Zionist stand would find few adherents and would only alienate potential allies, or perhaps he believed that slow education would, in the end, win over the body. In any event, he peacefully suggested "that a thoughtful study of Zionism should be made by the Conference and that it ought not to be hastily or contemptuously dismissed." The resulting compromise called for a paper to be presented at the following year's meeting on the subject of Jewish colonization.[34]

Not until 1909 would Wise again play a prominent role in Conference affairs, having attended meetings irregularly and when there not participating in discussions. This time, however, a longwinded paper on "The Working

Man in the Synagogue" by Rabbi Soloman Foster of Newark, New Jersey roused his ire. Foster had gone on interminably quoting one passage after another from rabbinic literature on the dignity of labor, and endorsing one sage's comment that the synagogue should not take sides in labor disputes. The synagogue, Foster grandly declared, should be an agency to propagandize working-class people in order to bring them closer to religion. The entire speech all too accurately reflected the abstract attitude of many Reform rabbis toward social problems; Foster did not advocate a single specific proposal for dealing with labor or its problems.[35]

Wise immediately claimed the floor, and made no effort to be conciliatory:[36]

> You ask me, "What have you done about the synagogue and the working man?" I will tell you what I did. I was asked last summer to have a part in the baker's strike in New York. I investigated it. I did not talk about general principles. I went down and found Jewish bakers treated almost like slaves. I told their Jewish masters that it was an outrage. And that strike was settled by the strikers gaining, as they ought to have gained, every single point they contended. They did not ask enough. They did not ask even human conditions. They asked for the minimum. And it was given to me to present their claims to their employers.
>
> We must be true to Judaism. The synagogue deals with this world. Its characteristics have been called the thought and spirit of this-worldliness. . . . A year ago it was said in one of the Jewish seminaries, "It is alright to speak about great moral principles but you must not apply them." That is a new idea to me. We are told the rabbi may deal with these things, but not as a representative of the synagogue. Why not? If the synagogue has laid down these principles, why should we not speak out frankly and fairly as men?

In the ensuing questions, he vigorously attacked the failure of Reform congregations to live up the social justice tenets of Judaism, and pointed to the Free Synagogue's Social Service Division as a model.

Wise's activities in the CCAR were sporadic over the next few years. He evidently resigned after the battle at the 1909 convention, only to rejoin in 1911 at the personal invitation of the new president, his longtime critic, Samuel Schulman. In the meantime, he continued to propagandize for social service, both in a series of lectures to the Jewish Religious Union in London in 1910 and before the Eastern Council of Reform Rabbis. As Sidney Goldstein noted, "It is certainly time that some of our Jewish ministers strive to do what all the Christian ministerial organizations have done."[37]

He resumed attendance at the CCAR in 1914, and found the trip to Detroit well worth his effort. While the older members continued to pose or ignore his views, many of the younger rabbis wanted to know more about the work of the Free Synagogue and its Social Service Division. Recent graduates of the Hebrew Union College invited him to be their guest of honor at a luncheon, and as he told Louise, were "extraordinarily friendly to me, far more than I had dreamed." Their response even led him to believe that if he wanted to devote his time to working with younger rabbis, the Conference could ultimately come under his control. Sidney Goldstein, who also attended the meeting, had a more realistic attitude, and urged Wise not to pin his hopes on the College. Rather, and here we find the first evidence of how early he had thought of founding a new seminary, Goldstein reminded Wise of his idea of a school attached to the Free Synagogue. He even proposed bringing over the great English scholar, Israel Abrahams, which in fact is just what Wise did when he opened the Jewish Institute of Religion nearly a decade later. But Wise, at least for a short while, would try to work within the CCAR and with the College. In asking for support from Martin Meyer, a West Coast rabbi whom Wise greatly liked and admired, he wrote: "We can succeed in smashing the old ring and making the Conference count in American Israel in a way which it has never before counted. The younger men are with me; they know that I am not an office seeker and I am not hunting for honors in the Conference. I am merely trying as you would to make it serviceable and the younger men stood with me splendidly. . . . The future lies with a few of us like you, [J. Leonard] Levy and myself."[38]

Wise learned soon enough that the old order was not yet ready to die. At the Detroit meeting he had proposed that the Conference sponsor an annual lectureship at the Hebrew Union College. By this device he hoped to introduce new ideas and bypass the control of David Philipson and Kaufman Kohler. The CCAR's executive committee agreed to establish the lectureship, but then conceded that the choice of lecturer and subject would be left entirely to the discretion of the college faculty and administration, which meant in effect that President Kohler could choose whom he liked. The CCAR committee, to which Wise had been named, would be responsible only for raising funds. Wise exploded, declaring that he would not serve either as chairman or member on such a hamstrung committee, and that the executive committee had no right to so distort the intention of the original proposal.[39]

A few days later came word that Professor Horace Meyer Kallen of the University of Wisconsin, a rising young philosopher, author of the doctrine of cultural pluralism, and a Zionist, had been invited by the College Literary Society to speak on "The Meaning of Heroism," only to have the offer rescinded at the last moment by Kohler. Here was more proof of the perversity of the college and of the reactionaries who controlled American Reform. "Is nothing to be said or done about this?" Wise asked Max Heller. "Are you satisfied with that spirit at the College and are you going to sit silent under it? I ask you not only as a graduate of the College and as my fellow Zionist, but as the father of a College student. Is there nothing to be done to end once and for all that bigoted attitude which stifles every expression of opinion that differs from the gentlemen of the College who are still living in 1840, including Kohler and Philipson?''[40]

At the 1915 biennial meeting of the Union of American Hebrew Congregations (the sponsoring body of the college), the resentment of many people at Kohler's arbitrary rule boiled over, and a special "Executive Conference" met on February 15 to hear the grievances. Wise and Max Heller managed to secure a resolution, later endorsed by the college's board of governors, which stated that while the president would continue to determine who might speak in the chapel he would not object to Zionist addresses delivered elsewhere in the building, nor would he prevent students from delivering sermons on Zionism providing they were religious in tone and content. Within a month, however, Wise received news that a student, who turned out to be James Heller, had not been allowed to deliver a sermon on a Zionist subject. Upon visiting Cincinnati, he discovered that there had been a "misunderstanding" rather than a deliberate muzzling of the talk. But the situation remained hopeless at the college, and he saw little that could be done to improve it.[41]

Nor did things seem much better with the Conference, despite his original optimism. Because Louise was sick, he did not go to the 1915 meeting, but reports of the gathering led him to believe that pettiness and provincialism still ruled. This time he did not resign, although he had few illusions that in time he could bring the Conference around to a more modern view of Judaism and the world; but as he told Heller, he had an obligation to try.[42] Besides, by the fall of 1915 the reactionary attitude of Reform leaders seemed a minor irritation to Wise, whose secular activities had made him a frequent and welcome guest at the White House, and whose Zionist interest had been rekindled by a brilliant new leader.

7

The Rabbi as Progressive

If, as Stephen Wise often declared, the synagogue had to be a part of and not apart from the secular world, then the rabbi of a living and free synagogue had to play an active role not only in the life of the congregation, but in the city and state outside the walls of the temple. In the years following the establishment of the Free Synagogue, he fully lived this creed, engaging in battles for municipal reform, woman suffrage, the rights of labor, racial equality and other causes. More than any other rabbi of that time, Wise was an active and important figure in American progressivism.

From the late 1890s to the armistice ending the First World War, the United States witnessed dozens of efforts to ameliorate the impact of industrialism, urbanization, and modernism. Few countries ever underwent such rapid social and economic change as did the United States in the decades following the Civil War. Railroad mileage shot up from 38,601 miles in 1866 to 193,346 miles in 1900, while the freight carried on these tracks doubled and then doubled again. The gross national product in these years increased twelvefold, with the seemingly overnight creation of new industries in steel, oil, and mineral production. Value of exports from American mills and factories climbed from $434 million in 1866 to $1.5 billion at the turn of the century, while imports doubled. To staff the new mills and factories, millions of immigrants, especially from southern and eastern Europe, came to America, seeking political freedom as well as economic opportunity.[1]

The huge wealth generated by this Industrial Revolution came at a great price in human suffering, with the benefits inequitably distributed. For each new millionaire, thousands of people lived in abject poverty. The industrial might of America rested on the bowed backs of men, women, and children laboring ten, twelve, or even more hours every day in squalid and often dangerous conditions. Around the corners from the great town houses rising on Park and Madison Avenues, stinking slums housed two or three families to a flat, with eight people not infrequently crowded into a single room.[2] Not only did the new industrialism weigh heavily on individual laborers, but the concentration of economic power threatened the democratic system itself. Reformers like Louis D. Brandeis and Herbert Croly warned that liberty could not survive in a society dominated by billion-dollar monopolies in which the individual had no protection from the arbitrary powers of big business or of corrupted legislatures.

Progressivism can best be described, in Samuel Hays's phrase, as the response to industrialism, but it took many different forms. Some reformers concentrated on alleviating the lot of workers, while others engaged in battles for conservation of natural resources or urban planning or woman suffrage or any one of the dozens of causes. Nearly all wanted to adjust the political system, expanding the right to vote, cleaning up corrupt municipal or state governments, and extending democratic procedures. Some wanted to control big business by breaking up monopolies and then regulating a small-unit economy, while others believed that bigness was here to stay and should be controlled by the countervailing power of big government. Although reformers frequently differed on means, they agreed that the traditional values of democracy and individual opportunity stood endangered, and that heroic measures were needed to restore the pristine values cherished by Jefferson and the other founding fathers.

For Wise, progressivism constituted an essential part of his philosophy, a natural complement to the Social Gospel and Liberal Judaism. As an activist he could never be chained to a pulpit, even a free pulpit; advocacy of even the loftiest ideal had no value unless acted upon not only by the congregation but by its rabbi as well. As a citizen concerned with American values, Stephen Wise plunged into reform, and for the rest of his life would divide his time between Jewish and secular activities. And because of his temperament, his tendency to invest reform with a moral mandate, Wise often found himself at the cutting edge, a focus of both reform hope and conservative resentment.

At a time when the rights of labor to organize and to bargain collectively had not won wide recognition, he championed labor unions and frequently took the side of labor in strikes. Often he proved able to intercede in a dispute, and over the years developed into a capable and respected mediator.[3] But he never hid his belief that workers were entitled to fair wages and decent, safe working conditions. If anyone questioned the need for such reforms, the Triangle Fire should have silenced their doubts.

At 4:45 on Saturday afternoon, March 26, 1911, the 600 workers of the Triangle Shirtwaist Factory, which occupied the top three floors of a ten-story building on Washington Place, were preparing to quit work for the week. Ninety-five percent of the employees were young women who labored nine and a half hours a day, six days a week, for an average weekly wage of

$15.40. Because the management suspected pilfering and wanted to keep out union organizers, the heavy iron rear doors had been locked so that all the workers might be searched as they left through the front. On the eighth floor, one of the male laborers lit a cigarette and tossed away the match, which landed on a pile of scraps soaked with cleaning fluid. The scraps burst into flames, and the men tried to stamp out the fire, but it soon spread to stacks of finished cloth. The workmen then raced to the standpipe, only to find the fire hose had rotted away. In desperation they tried to open the standpipe to flood the floor, but the valve had rusted shut and could not be turned. In a few minutes the inferno engulfed all three floors of the sweatshop and the workers panicked. With the fire doors locked, many climbed onto window ledges and either jumped or fell to their deaths; by the time the flames were extinguished, 146 workers, nearly all women, had died, and the East side plunged into mourning.

The day after the fire, Wise spoke at the first of several protest meetings. Nearly two dozen labor and philanthropic groups gathered at the headquarters of the Women's Trade Union League to discuss relief measures for victims and their families. More important, they wanted an investigation into how the tragedy had occurred, and legislation to make sure such a disaster would not happen in the future. Wise warned the gathering not to rely on the city's regular procedures. "We have seen the terrible evidence of what officials can do," he charged, "in avoiding the search for facts. . . . I want the citizens of New York to find out for themselves, though the medium of a committee named at a general mass assembly. If this thing were avoidable, I want to see those responsible punished. If it was due to some corrupt failure to enforce the law, I want to see that determined. And I do not trust public officials to determine it for us; it is our own task to do that for ourselves." That same evening, speaking at the Holy Trinity Church in Brooklyn, he warned that while relief funds should be gathered, much more than charity was needed. "This disaster . . . demands that justice be done to the workers of the nation."

On Sunday, April 2, many New Yorkers gathered to mourn the victims and to see that such needless deaths were prevented in the future. In the forenoon, the cloakmakers assembled in the Grand Central Palace to mark their sorrow and anger. At three that afternoon, the eyes of the city turned toward the Metropolitan Opera House, which Anne Morgan had rented on behalf of the Women's Trade Union League. First the galleries filled, mainly with the East Siders, workingmen and women who daily had to face the same intolerable conditions that had existed in the Triangle factory. Below them in the orchestra came men in high hats and fine suits, their wives wearing furs and feathers. The division at the Opera House could not have been clearer, and several of the scheduled speakers worried whether the social gap could be bridged. The balconies wanted justice and demanded retribution; would the prosperous occupants of the orchestra do any more than provide charity?

Jacob Schiff called the meeting to order, and announced that the relief committee had received a sum he termed "the public's conscience money." Following Schiff came Monsignor White, the Director of Charities of the Roman Catholic Diocese of Brooklyn and Bishop David H. Greer, both of whom declared that the churches had the obligation to support labor unions in their fight for safety and justice. "Hereafter the laws as to fire protection must be enforced," said Greer, "not for a few weeks or a few months but for all time, faithfully, continuously, and effectively. If this is not done the responsibility—the sin—is on the public, on us."

Hearing this ringing declaration, the audience broke into cheers, only to fall silent immediately when Wise suddenly rushed forward on the stage holding up both arms and began shouting: "Not that! Not that! This is not a day for applause but for contriteness and redeeming penitence.

"It is not the action of God but the inaction of man that is responsible. The disaster was not the deed of God but the greed of man. This was not inevitable disaster which could not be foreseen. Some of us foresaw it. We have laws that in a crisis we find are no laws and we have enforcement that when the hour of trial comes we find is no enforcement. Let us lift up the industrial standards until they will bear inspection. And when we go before the legislatures let us not allow them to put us off forever with the old answer, 'We have no money.' If we have no money for the necessary enforcement of the laws which safeguard the lives of workers, it is because so much of our money is wasted and squandered and stolen."

The applause Wise had earlier silenced now roared forth from both galleries and orchestra. When he could be heard again, he reminded the audience that the purpose of the meeting was not charity, but "redress in justice, remedy in prevention." But when the committee presented its resolutions calling for better fire protection and more factory safety inspectors, the galleries began hissing. They had heard too many resolutions that had led nowhere, seen too many nobly phrased proposals end up in legislative wastebaskets. Shouting began and the meeting threatened to break up in disorder when Rose Schneiderman stood up to speak, her voice choking in tears. Only a year earlier, she had led a strike at the Triangle factory, only to see the police beat the picketers and throw them in jail; many were among the women who had burned to death a week before. What Wise had begun, she now finished. She charged that the workers had waited patiently for fair-minded people to come to their aid, but there had been no aid. They had waited for elected officials to provide justice, but there had been no justice. "Public officials have only words of warning for us, warning that we must be intensely orderly and must be intensely peaceable, and they have the workhouse just back of all their warnings. The strong hand of the law beats us back when we rise—back into the conditions that make life unbearable. I can't talk fellowship to you who are gathered here. Too much blood has been spilled. I know from experience it is up to the working people to save themselves. And the only way is through a strong working-class movement." There was not applause as she walked back to her seat, only silence, sorrow, and shame.[4]

Fortunately, the leaders of the rally recognized that not only were strong measures called for, but a wide range of support would be there to back their efforts, not only in the working classes but among the more genteel elements as well. The Committee on Safety, which included Wise, Anne Morgan, Amos Pinchot, George W. Perkins, Mary Dreier, and others, together with many civic and union groups, kept up a steady pressure on the legislature, which finally, on June 30, 1911, created a special Factory Investigating Commission of nine members. Its chairman and vice-chairman were two young men whose careers would often intersect with Wise's, Robert F. Wagner and Alfred E. Smith. Realizing that the public would not be satisfied with a whitewash of existing conditions, the Commission honestly and energetically carried out its mandate, taking testimony from workers and union organizers, visiting the sweatshops, utilizing as expert consultants men and women who for years had beem vainly trying to warn the public about the unsafe conditions at the Triangle and other factories. Wise kept a close watch on the hearings, occasionally consulting with some of its members, and on one occasion lashing out at the city's Fire Prevention Bureau as "a home for 'out-of-works,' " after the fire commissioner had tried to absolve his agency of any blame in the tragedy. When the Commission turned in its report, the legislature acted promptly, tripling the number of the factory inspectors and doubling the appropriation for the Labor Department; moreover, the state's safety standards for factories were tightened considerably in the hope of avoiding any more Triangle disasters.[5]

Neither Wise nor any of his colleagues on the Committee claimed credit for these modest gains; the deaths of 146 workers had created a climate that demanded, at the very least, safe conditions in factories. But the battle for labor rights, or as progressives preferred to call it, "the fight for industrial democracy," went on. "The church must demand," Wise declared, "that men shall neither be over-employed nor unemployed, that the work of women must not be done under conditions that are physically hurtful and morally menacing, that no man or woman shall cease to compromise with the iniquity of child labor." To his congregation, he put the matter bluntly: "It is the business of the church to link itself with the fortunes of unionized industry."[6] He stood willing to back labor even in circumstances where little or no public sympathy existed. In fact, one of the most trying times for both

Wise and his good friend, John Haynes Holmes, came at the same time the Factory Investigating Commission was exposing the terrible conditions of New York sweatshops.

A year before, on October 1, 1910, a dynamite blast had rocked the *Los Angeles Times* building, and many people blamed the explosion on organized labor because of the anti-union activities of *Times* publisher Harrison Gray Otis. A subsequent investigation led to the arrest of James and Joseph McNamara, brothers who had been extensively involved in union organizing. The two were indicted for the deaths of twenty-one workers who had perished in the blaze caused by the explosion, and AF of L president Samuel Gompers asked Clarence Darrow to defend the men. The State's case was so overwhelming, however, that Darrow, after exhausting negotiations with the prosecution, entered a plea of guilty. This development shocked labor's friends, but most of them took the attitude of Louis Brandeis, that organized labor would have suffered more from a protracted trial ending in a guilty verdict, and that "the public will soon realize the distinction between the law-abiding and the law-breaking unionist, and the great value of unionism to society will be more fully recognized."[7]

In seeking to defend union rights, Wise argued that the denial of justice would inevitably breed more violence. "As long as labor organizations are denied a hearing save just before election seasons; as long as they are treated with scorn and contumely; as long as they are cast out and denied, it is not to be wondered at that the leaders, finding themselves and their organizations outlawed, should in turn be guilty of outlawry; that being cast out, they should resort to the weapon of the outcast; that being denied a hearing after the manner of orderly and reasoning friends, they should make themselves heard after the manner of destructive and unreasoning foes." Holmes went even further, comparing the McNamaras' violence to that of John Brown at Harper's Ferry or the Russian Nihilists in assassinating Alexander II. In fact, he declared, he would rather be in the McNamaras' cell at San Quentin than in the office of the president of the Steel Trust.[8]

The following month, *American Industries*, the organ of the National Association of Manufacturers, editorially attacked both Wise and Holmes as the "the McNamaras of the pulpit," alongside a cartoon depicting them as the Dr. Jeckyl and Mr. Hyde of organized labor. Although the journal quoted both men extensively, it went after Wise in particular. "If the rabbi knew more of the subject," the editors charged, "he would feel as other citizens do, that organized labor is the Big Noise of the country. When labor leaders are not clamoring for more pay and less work, they are clamoring for less work and more pay."[9]

The editorial infuriated Wise, who considered it libelous and immediately wanted to sue. Holmes reluctantly agreed to go along with whatever course of action his friend decided upon, but informed him that he had no money to pay lawyers. Recognizing the burden that a protracted legal battle would entail, Wise called upon a close friend of the family for advice. Benjamin Cardozo, later to win fame on the New York bench and as Oliver Wendell Holmes' successor on the United States Supreme Court, agreed that both the title of the editorial and the statement that Wise and Holmes had condoned violence and assassination constituted a libel. But Cardozo, anticipating the Supreme Court by more than six decades, noted that a civil action would be difficult "where the subject of the libel is criticism of the public utterance of a man occupying a public or quasi-public position." Cardozo suggested that the "cruel and unjust interpretation of the meaning of your words" was so manifest that intelligent people, reading the article through, could easily see how the journal had distorted Wise's views.[10]

It was sound advice; if Wise wished to attack wrongdoers, he would have to be prepared for them to counterattack. Far better to let his words and actions speak for him, leaving the public to judge his true intent. Time and again he would find opponents condemning him for his pro-union activities, interpreting his speeches as incitements to disorder. When he backed transit workers in their demand for more pay, for example, the *New York Times* editorialized that "to stir up trouble where peace prevails, to incite wage earners apparently satisfied with the terms and conditions of their employment to demand higher wages, better conditions, and if these are refused, to go on strike, is to make an ill use of such notable talents as Rabbi Stephen S. Wise possesses. . . . [He] volunteers his counsels of discontent and disturbance."[11]

The McNamara case did have one positive outcome, however. Friends of labor realized that unless industrial labor conditions improved, frustrated workers would be more tempted, perhaps even provoked, into greater violence. Factory and mill conditions had to be explored and publicized, with labor, industry, and the public educated about the unpleasant facts and the necessary remedies. Wise and Holmes, Jane Addams, Lillian Wald, and other reformers met with the editors of *Survey* and drew up a petition to President William Howard Taft. The McNamara case, they argued, had struck "the social conscience of the nation." The signers pointed out that America's industrial growth had outpaced social and legal developments, that an imbalance in the social order had led to "a profound restlessness" among larger groups of workers who believed society denied them any means to pursue their own legitimate interests. "The American people must think these things through. We need more light . . . on that larger lawlessness which is beyond the view of the criminal court." Specifically, the petition asked for the formation of a federal commission on industrial relations with authority to investigate trade unions, industrial associations, federal and state bureaus, and the conditions that led to the prolonged and bloody strikes. In conclusion, it warned that "today as fifty years ago a house divided against itself cannot stand. We have to solve the problems of democracy in its industrial relationships and to solve them along democratic lines.''

On December 29, 1911, a delegation headed by Wise and Jane Addams presented the petition to Taft at the White House. The president greeted them warmly, and hinted that he might incorporate their proposal in his next message to Congress. In fact, Taft was under considerable pressure from many groups to establish an investigative commission, and he saw it as a potential political asset in the forthcoming presidential election. He did propose a Commission on Industrial Relations in his State of the Union Message on February 2, 1912, and the Congress, aware of a public sentiment in favor of the idea, approved the measure in August. Taft's appointees, however, ran aground in the Senate, where progressives charged that he had stacked the commission with pro-business and anti-labor men, and it fell to Woodrow Wilson to designate the members in the spring of 1913.[12]

Wise carried his fight for labor into many a hostile quarter for, after all, there would be little gain in preaching to the converted. Those who through ignorance or greed refused to recognize the justice of labor's demands had to be educated. Thus he stirred up a storm at the 1914 meeting of the Central Conference of American Rabbis when he denounced as ''reactionary'' those rabbis who paid lip service to the ideal of social justice but denied the principles of the minimum wage, industrial insurance, workmen's compensation, old-age pensions and the right to organize. He attacked them for catering ''to the wealthy employers of labor who so largely support the synagogue. You are afraid of what the rich may say if we take a stand for social justice. You quote the Scriptures that 'Justice, justice shalt thou preach,' but you are afraid to practice what you preach.''[13]

The analogy of Nathan confronting the king might well apply to Wise's first—and only—invitation to speak at the annual banquet of the New York Chamber of Commerce in 1911. Here gathered the leaders of American industry men who could, if they wanted to, change the entire path of labor-management relations in the country. And Wise could, if he wanted to, ingratiate himself with them, develop good relations which might, over a period of time, allow him to educate and persuade these captains of industry to follow a more enlightened road. As he pondered his options, J. P. Morgan leaned over and offered the rabbi one of the long expensive Havana cigars, the famous ''Corsairs'' which the banker had specially made for his private stock. Wise casually accepted the cigar and put it in his pocket. Morgan, about to light his own, asked ''Aren't you going to smoke the cigar?''

''I don't smoke,'' Wise replied.

''Then why did you take the cigar?''

"Oh, the janitor at the Free Synagogue smokes, and I am going to give it to him."*

Morgan's irritation soon turned to anger as he listened to Wise castigate the audience for its insensitivity to the problems of those less fortunate than themselves. The biblical command to seek justice fell on captains of industry as much as on clergyman. It was one of his best speeches, although the audience failed to appreciate it, and as much as any talk he ever gave, it summed up his credo as a progressive:[14]

> Not only ought the barter or trade side of the business be completely moralized, but we need to ethicize what might be called the process of creating and production, of distribution and consumption. No business order is just nor can it long endure if it be bound up with the evil of unemployment on the one hand and over-employment on the other, the evil of a man's underwage and a child's toil, and all those social maladjustments incidental to our order which we lump together under the name of proverty. Let us not imagine that we can shift to the shoulders of over-worked charity the burdens that can be born only by the strength of under-worked justice. Yes, the stricken ask not the occasional tonic of charity, but the daily meat and substance of justice. We are never to forget that ours is a democracy, that a democracy, in the words of a high servant of the commonwealth means "the use of all the resources of nature by all the faculties of man for the good of all the people . . . "

> The conscience of the nation is not real unless the nation safeguard the workingmen, safeguard him from the peril of over-work, as well as from the occasional accidents of industry. The conscience of the nation is not vital unless we protect women and children in industry, and protect them with half the thoroughness and generosity with which, for many decades, we have protected infant industries. We have not the right to speak of the importance of conserving the opportunity for initiative on the part of the individual as long as masses of individuals are suffered to perish without the opportunity of real life. The aim of democracy is not to be the production of efficient, machine-like men in industry. The first business of democracy is to be the industry of turning out completely effective, because completely free and self-determining, citizens.

Would it have been better to be more conciliatory, to secure a place within the councils of power, and from there exert whatever influence he could? Did his comments affect any in the audience, or did it just leave them annoyed that some crank radical masquerading as a man of the cloth had disturbed their otherwise peaceful and pleasant surroundings? Considering

---

*It is unlikely that Wise did this to insult Morgan. Throughout his life he would accept cigars when offered to him, and then give them to congregants, friends, or just acquaintances, like the janitor at his synagogue.

that it would take another quarter-century and the power of the national government to win labor its rights in places like U.S. Steel, the chances of Wise or anyone working from within were small. The lash of outrage might or might not advance labor's cause, but at least workers knew that someone had spoken for them, that not all ministers ignored their plight. And, as Wise candidly admitted, he felt better for speaking the truth as he saw it. He had to live by his own lights, and while he enjoyed popularity, he did not fear to offend public opinion.

If labor had few friends in those days, Negroes had even fewer. Southern states, with northern acquiescence, had eliminated nearly all the rights gained by freedmen during the Reconstruction. Jim Crow laws governed public facilities, while grandfather clauses and literacy tests disenfranchised the blacks. The Supreme Court itself gave blessing to the doctrine of "separate but equal," which immediately translated into "segregated and unequal." Race riots swept over the nation; in the summer of 1908 mobs beat and killed Negroes and burned their homes in Springfield, Illinois, within sight of the Lincoln house. Lynchings took place in the South almost casually at the rate of more than two a week during the first decade of the century. On February 12, 1909—the hundredth anniversary of Lincoln's birth—sixty people, including many of the nation's leading progressives, signed a call to action to end this flagrant abuse of human and civil rights. Stephen Wise's name was on the list, as was that of John Haynes Holmes.

According to Mary White Ovington, one of the founders of the National Association for the Advancement of Colored People, few white ministers would even discuss racial questions at the time. Wise and Holmes did agree with the ideal of racial equality, and although Wise never played a prominent role in NAACP affairs, he continued to fight in his own way for its ideals. The Free Synagogue may have been the only congregation in the city to have its rabbi eulogize Booker T. Washington on the black leader's death. When D. W. Griffith produced and released "Birth of a Nation" in 1915, Wise was one of the few whites to protest the distorted and hateful portrait Griffith had drawn of black people. Perhaps Wise saw an analogy between the sufferings of the Jew and the Negro. But he also recognized that in "denying justice to the Negro . . . in the end the white race will suffer most. No race can violate the moral law with impunity; no race can for years and generations pursue courses that are unjust without mutilating its own moral nature and sinking to a lowered level of life."[15] In later years he saw to it that the American Jewish Congress defended not only Jewish rights, but the liberties of all persecuted groups, and that group became the first and most consistent national Jewish organization to ally itself with the cause of civil rights.

Another reform that interested Wise was woman suffrage and the whole question of women's role in society. There is a remarkably modern tone in a sermon Wise delivered nearly seven decades ago:[16]

> The women's movement is not a feminist movement at all but a human movement. If the same measure of unrest obtained among men today we should not speak at all of a great masculine unrest but of a mighty human awakening . . . . The awakening of women is not a national or a sexual movement, but is international and worldwide in scope and as deep as it is wide. . . .

> Any man who declares that because a woman does or does not do a thing she does not interest him implies that woman does not exist for him except as a sex animal. It is significant that the man who holds this conception of a woman's position deplores the passing of the veil and wishes woman screened and immured. But no man should dream of perpetuating this obsolete view of womanhood upon a new civilization which will have none of his profoundly and insulting attitude toward womanhood. To say that woman's greatest charm is her mystery is to deny the right to live frankly, openly, forthrightly. It is to surround the woman with the veil of seclusion and to consign her once more to the twilight out of which she is to emerge at times only to do the pleasure of her lord and master.

Yet there are internal contradictions in Wise's own life and views regarding women which were never resolved in his own mind nor in his public statements, and one must remember that he was, after all, a product of his times and environment. There are statements and actions which strike one immediately as extremely broadminded and liberal, far ahead of his contemporaries, alongside those which appear equally narrow. He called for equality for women, yet declared that women inherently were more moral than men, and therefore had to protect the moral standards of the nation. He was one of the first to speak out for allowing women to enter the rabbinate, yet never did anything to implement this idea. He wanted men to treat their wives as full human beings, and certainly encouraged and sustained Louise in her reform activities; at the same time he retained a very traditional and romantic view of her, and as their son commented, always kept her on a pedestal. He denounced new styles of dancing, especially the tango, as immoral, and condemned women who engaged in such activities. While declaring that no objection should be raised "to frank and serious discussion of sex problems" on the stage, he chastised actors and especially actresses who took parts dealing with sexual matters.[17]

To his credit, Wise recognized that many of the qualities and activities of women which he criticized resulted from societal patterns. In one sermon he asked "Is Woman a Parasite?" and declared that, with the exception of working women, the answer would have to be "yes." But, he went on, "woman is free to do as man pleases, free within the limits of man's pleasures and man's economic determinism."[18] Only when men—and society dominated by men—broke out of this mold could habits be changed. Yet even if he recognized this as the root of the problem, an ambivalence remained, one that would be even more pronounced in the post-suffrage 1920s when the entire nation engaged in a great debate over manners and morals.

Undoubtedly the most daring and dramatic part of Wise's career involved his willingness to participate in the hurly-burly of politics. It was unusual for a rabbi to speak out for labor and blacks and women, to call for social reform, but some people rationalized these idiosyncracies in an impersonal and abstract way. Child labor constituted a social problem, and historically ministers had condemned society's evils; the antislavery movement, for example, had counted numerous ministers in its ranks. Old Testament prophets such as Isaiah had spoken out time and again in opposition to the evil ways of the ancient Israelites. Wise, however, chose to remember the prophet Nathan declaring to the king, "Thou art the man!" When the rabbi of the Free Synagogue began attacking corrupt politicians by name, pious hands were thrown up in horror at the thought of dragging the temple into the political muck.

He was far from the first man of the cloth to enter the political fray; in 1892 the Rev. Charles H. Parkhurst had led the attack against Tammany Hall and its chief sachem, Richard Croker. Ultimately, when Tammany abuses had grown too large even for New Yorkers to swallow, they had elected Seth Low as a reform mayor, and Croker tactfully retired to his estate in Ireland, rich from years of plunder. Low, for all his virtues, had been unable to govern the city, and in 1903 Tammany roared back to power, installing George Brinton McClellan, Jr., as its figurehead mayor. Everyone knew that Charles F. Murphy ruled New York from Tammany headquarters on East 14th Street, or in his private dining room upstairs at Delmonico's, behind the big oak table supported by carved tigers, the symbols of Tammany's power.

Wise well knew about Tammany corruption; he had seen it firsthand as a child. But even he was appalled when Croker decided to return to New York in a bid to regain his seat as chief. The Democrats organized a welcome dinner, and nearly all the city's officeholders, including its judges—most of whom owed their appointments to the machine—purchased seats at the affair. Wise denounced their action "as a sullying of the judicial ermine," and termed the dinner "New York's night of shame." The phrase caught on, and the Democratic chieftains soon realized that the time had not yet come for Croker to be "rehabilitated." Several years later Lewis Nixon, one of the more honest Tammany leaders, told Wise that his attack had scotched plans to reinstate Croker.[19]

McClellan was followed as mayor by Judge William J. Gaynor, who had started out opposing Tammany and ended up accepting the machine's nomination on a fusion line. Although Gaynor won, he found himself faced by a totally uncontrollable Board of Estimate, the real locus of power in the city. In four years he held office, the irascible mayor time and again confronted Wise, Parkhurst, and other clergymen who demanded that he clean up the cesspool of New York's financial affairs and put an end to the corruption in the police department. All too often Gaynor mistook criticism of conditions as a personal attack upon himself, and thus wound up defending the worst aspects of Tammany graft.

Gaynor was, however, a popular figure with the immigrant Jews, and it is doubtful whether Wise or other reform leaders really understood the services political machines provided to the immigrants, although they well reckoned the cost to both the beneficiaries as well as the victims of the system. During his years on the bench, Gaynor had shown sympathy and understanding to the problem of newcomers, and his criticism of Police Commissioner Theodore Bingham, whom many suspected of antisemitism, had led to Bingham's forced retirement. In his 1909 campaign, Gaynor denounced police harassment of pushcart peddlers, and as mayor, curbed policemen in their use of clubs and warned them against arrest for trivial offenses; in his first year in office, the total number of arrests and summonses in the downtown wards dropped 40 percent. Moreover, Gaynor's approach to vice seemed more realistic to the immigrants than the high-toned attacks of Parkhurst and Wise. Thus the mayor found a great deal of support when he attacked Wise, charging "although he is a preacher, he seems to be without charity or truthfulness."[20]

But Wise kept up the pressure, and the truth of his charges about police corruption was vindicated by the events following the murder of gambler Herman Rosenthal on July 16, 1912. Rosenthal had been harassed by police, especially Lieutenant Charles Becker, for not paying enough protection money. At the instigation of Herbert Bayard Swope, then a young reporter with the New York *World*, Rosenthal had dictated a long affidavit exposing the ties between police and the underworld; word of this document had led to his murder as he walked out of a restaurant, with seven policemen standing by as he was gunned down. The next day the *World* published the affidavit which named Becker, the very man Police Commissioner Rhinelander Waldo had put in charge of the investigation. Gaynor stuck by the hapless Waldo, directing him not to suspend or dimiss Becker, but merely transfer him until all the facts could be uncovered. He also declared that policemen should not associate with known criminals, a directive which gave journalists and cartoonists a field day at Gaynor's expense.[21]

Only District Attorney Charles S. Whitman seemed determined to find out the truth, and he discovered that because of a personal feud, the mayor's office would not help him, and in fact threw one obstacle after another in his path. Apprised of the situation, Wise called for the creation of a public commission to assist Whitman. The Citizens Committee which Wise helped to organize provided the public pressure Whitman needed, and in the next two years the district attorney secured a number of indictments and convictions in graft cases connected to the police department. Afterward, Whitman wrote Wise that "I appreciate more than I can tell you your attitude in the matter. The knowledge that men like you have understood and supported me during the most trying experience I have ever known has been of itself a real inspiration."[22]

Wise, however, was not content to expose corruption or denounce the corrupt; civic reform meant not only throwing out the crooks, but securing honest and efficient municipal administration as well. Here he took a step which, over the years, brought down more censure on his head than anything else he did. He decided he would openly support candidates for public office, men whom he believed could provide the enlightened leadership he and other progressives sought. Wise never called upon Jews to vote for a candidate because that candidate was Jewish or because he, a rabbi, had endorsed him. At all times he tried to make clear that he backed a man for public office because of ability and experience. Yet if a rabbi or a priest or a minister, or a black or Czech or Irishman, spoke up for a candidate, most people in the audience inferred that an ethnic seal of approval had been bestowed, that a rabbi in effect had said: "It would be good for the Jews if this man were elected." As one of America's leading rabbis, Wise could not avoid such an implication, and he was neither naive nor stupid enough to believe that it did not exist; he knew his value to candidates derived from his identification and influence within the Jewish community. But his decision to back or oppose men came from his judgment of their suitabilities for the office; no non-Jew was ever denied his endorsement because of religion alone. "The only excuse for a Jewish vote," he once explained, "is to keep bad Jews out of office. We can leave it to the fairness of the American public to elect good Jews."[23]

In 1913 Wise threw himself into the mayoral battle between reformer John Purroy Mitchel and Tammany's Edward E. McCall. In a speech before 2,500 representatives of the Clerical and Lay Conference of New York, he urged other ministers to get more involved in politics, and then scorchingly denounced McCall as the machine's tool. "They say McCall is not purchaseable," he charged. "It reminds me of a story of a certain Massachusetts senator of whom they said: 'He is not for sale. Sam Bowles won't sell him.' The boss of Tammany Hall has nominated McCall because he believes he will be a safe and profitable investment for him. Judge McCall denies that he is Murphy's man. He is right. There is no such thing as

Murphy's man. No man can be a man and Murphy's man at the same time."[24]

With a great deal of satisfaction, he saw Mitchel elected, although the new mayor failed to be the man who could master New York; two more decades of corruption and frustration would be needed before Fiorello H. LaGuardia emerged. Mitchel, in Amos Pinchot's words, held down the mayorality "respectably and creditably," but while not permitting Tammany to extend its power, proved unable to whittle it down either. Yet, as Wise believed, "the personal integrity of Mitchel, the change of atmosphere in city government, and the beginning of the appointment of decent, responsible public servants" did make a difference. Moreover, Wise found himself consulted from time to time on appointments, and occasionally on more pressing if not so weighty matters. One morning, just as he was about to leave home, the phone rang, and Wise heard Mitchel exclaim, "Dr. Wise, this is John Mitchel. Where in hell is Armenia? Some representatives of Armenia are coming to this office in a few minutes and I don't know where Armenia is and what these fellows want." The rabbi calmed the mayor down, and then dictated a short statement of welcome to the delegation, which Mitchel later delivered in his most eloquent fashion.[25]

Since Tammany's influence extended beyond the city's five boroughs, Wise fought the machine on the state level as well. In Oregon his reform work had brought him to the attention of state officials, and the nature of several of his interests in New York necessitated state rather than local action. As early as 1910 he had been appointed to the State Commission on Congestion by Governor Charles Evans Hughes, who also happened to be a neighbor and friend at Lake Placid. The following year he began devoting some of his sermons to attacks on the inaction of Governor John A. Dix and on the Tammany men in the state legislature for bottling up reform measures. In the 1913 election, Wise denounced Tammany's gubernatorial candidate, William Sulzer, with as much gusto as he had used in his pronouncements on McCall. The victor, Martin H. Glynn, turned out to be less of an improvement in the state government than Mitchel was at City Hall. Glynn's clumsy use of patronage and his mania for economizing at the expense of the poor soon earned him the rabbi's contempt. Wise derived much more satisfaction in the administration of the next governor, Charles S. Whitman, his ally from the Becker-Rosenthal days, and prevailed upon Whitman to veto a bill that would have exempted the canning industry from nearly all of the protective labor laws.[26]

What was Wise seeking through all this activity? On one level, he wanted no more and did no more than many of his fellow progressives, people who worked as lawyers or reporters or doctors or city planners instead of as ministers. They wanted to improved the quality of life for the multitudes whose sweat and blood made it possible for the middle and upper classes to enjoy the fruits of the Industrial Revolution. They wanted to restore democracy, to wipe away the corruption generated by new and unscrupulous wealth and to awaken the public from its indifference. The fact that Wise wore, as it were, a rabbinical collar may have confused some people, and upset those who believed that the church should be so wholly separated from the state that political matters ought never to be discussed from the pulpit. But if one sees the close connection of progressive reform and the Social Gospel, it becomes much easier to understand Stephen Wise's willingness to enter the political fray. He once explained his views to Theodore Rousseau, an aide to Mayor Mitchel:[27]

> I have been trying to formulate myself just what it is I have in mind when I say as I do that church and synagogue together want to have a large and impressive part in the shaping of the civic life of a community. I need not say to you that I believe in the wisdom of the wall as between church and state. . .but it is the business of the church and synagogue to have a large part in lifting up the tone of the city's life. The man in the pulpit . . .must speak unafraid in what he believes to be the truth and the right. This may at times involve him in serious disagreement with the officials of the city, for the preacher must dare to speak of wrong when wrong is done by a city's head or heads. It may not be the popular nor the pleasant thing to do, but the man who dares to speak in the name of God must dare to speak nothing less than the truth however much it hurts. . . . I think it also necessary to emphasize that church and synagogue must not limit themselves to fault-finding. While they must dare to speak the truth as regards wrong when wrong is done, they must also and even primarily be generous and appreciative when city officials do their duty finely and faithfully.

Thus politics was but an extension of religion, and if it involved battles, Wise being Wise plunged into the melee. In his whole life he loved nothing better than to battle for the causes he believed in and the people for whom he cared.

8

Wilson and the New Freedom

Many of his critics and not a few of his friends considered Stephen Wise so egocentric a personality that he could never play the role of supporting actor to another star; he had to occupy center stage, as it were, or he would walk out. Thus, his opponents contended, he could not work with Marshall and the Emanu-El board, so he founded the Free Synagogue; he could not cooperate with the American Jewish Committee so he created the American Jewish Congress; he fought with Hebrew Union College and, finding he could not master Kohler and Philipson, he opened the doors of the Jewish Institute of Religion. There is just enough truth in this charge to make it sound plausible; Wise was strong and tended to dominate his surroundings. He believed fiercely in his principles and would not compromise them, especially when opposed by those as strong and as self-assured as he; often, therefore, he found that in order to sustain what he believed in, he had to strike off on his own. But when he found someone strong and charismatic, with dreams to match his own, Wise gladly labored as a lieutenant rather than as commander-in-chief. He had accepted Theodor Herzl's leadership at the turn of the century, and during the progressive era found two more men of vision and daring whom he could follow.

Thomas Woodrow Wilson, more than any president before him, personified the denominational impulse in politics, the tendency to view and act on political matters according to the dictates of his stern Presbyterian upbringing. After a false start in the law, which he had hoped would lead to a political career, Wilson had discovered talents for writing, and his historical studies quickly found a large and receptive popular audience. Friends arranged for him to be brought to Princeton as professor of political economy and jurisprudence, and in 1902 he was elected the first nonministerial president of the university. His bold innovations marked him as one of the nation's outstanding educators, and his fight against the exclusive dining clubs won him renown as a reformer. Within the

Democratic Party he emerged as a spokesman of the conservative wing against Bryanite populism, and his extensive speaking tours gradually brought him to the attention of local party leaders looking for an alternative to the Great Commoner. In 1910 Wilson, who had never given up his dream of politics, agreed to run for governor of New Jersey on the Democratic ticket, the reluctant choice of hard-pressed state party boss Jim Smith. The conservative but pragmatic Wilson soon recognized that with progressivism sweeping the nation, he would have to adopt some of the programs advocated by reformers if he wanted to win. Cutting loose from the machine that had nominated him, Wilson began preaching moral indignation, social uplift, and political reform, which appealed to progressives of both parties. A brilliant campaigner, he captured the governorship with a 50,000-vote majority.[1]

Wise, who had been a nominal Republican since his youth, was one of those progressives attracted to Wilson. On the Sunday before the 1910 election, Wise lectured at the Trenton YMCA and although his subject was not political, he stopped to comment that he expected the Princeton president to be elected governor the following Tuesday. Moreover, he predicted: "He will not complete his term of office as governor. In November 1912 he will be elected President of the United States. In March 1917 he will be inaugurated for the second time as President. He will be one of the great Presidents of American history."[2]

The two men met for the first time on February 10, 1911, when Wise went to hear Wilson speak. "He is clear-minded, thoughtful and incisive," he noted in his diary. "He thinks and knows how to put his thoughts." The next day, Wise and Henry Morgenthau, the Free Synagogue president and one of Wilson's early boosters, spent nearly 45 minutes with Wilson at the latter's hotel, discussing politics and reform. The New Jersey governor also accepted an invitation to speak at the Free Synagogue's annual banquet in late April. As Wise prepared to leave, Mrs. Wilson came over to talk with him for a few minutes. She had read reports of his sermons, and wanted to thank him for the kind things he had been saying about her husband.[3]

Wilson spoke at the dinner on "Politics and Morals," and his sentiments so matched those of Wise that by October the Free Synagogue's rabbi stood ready to leave the Republican Party if Wilson won the 1912 Democratic presidential nomination. Wise's loyalty went over completely to Wilson in December when he brought him to New York to speak before an overflow crowd at Carnegie Hall. Wilson took as his theme "The Rights of the Jews," and in the course of his remarks made a point which Wise maintained throughout his life—"They are not Jews in America; they are American citizens." And as American citizens, they should not be subject to the indignities which the Russian government had inflicted upon American Jews traveling in that country.[4]

The Russian treatment of visiting Jews had been a sore point for several years, and the American Jewish Committee had been leading the campaign to have the old Russo-American Trade Treaty revoked unless the Czar's government changed its policy.[5] Wise and other Jewish spokesmen were also urging Congress and President Taft to take action, not because Jews as such had been insulted, but because American citizens who happened to be Jewish had been the victims of a policy that insulted all Americans. The constant pressure as well as public sentiment proved irresistible, and in late December the American government served notice that it intended to abrogate the treaty. Upon hearing the news, Wise wrote to President Taft "I know that in this matter you have acted as President of the United States and as an American citizen. But in addition to that the people of Israel will for many years bless the day which found the Chief Magistrate of the first nation on earth prepared to insist upon abrogation of a treaty because one group of American citizens, and that group Jewish, was dealt with unjustly."[6]

Despite these laudatory words and his relatively cordial relations with Taft personally, Wise grew increasingly disenchanted with the Grand Old Party. In early 1912, while attacking Tammany in a sermon, he paused to note that "because the Republican Party was once the party of human liberation, men wrongly assume that it always marches under equally high standards."[7] Soon afterward, he traveled to upstate New York to lecture on "Religion and Industrial Justice," and then took a horse-drawn sleigh to the Lake George home of philanthropist George Foster Peabody. Before a roaring fire, the two men talked well past midnight, and then again in the morning when Peabody drove his guest to the train station. Both agreed that Wilson represented the only hope for liberals; should the Democrats refuse to nominate Wilson, progressives might have to unite in a new third party.[8]

By May, Wise openly touted Wilson as the best man for the presidency; he considered Taft much too conservative and Theodore Roosevelt too erratic. When Adolph Ochs, publisher of the *New York Times*, joined Wise, Abram Elkus, and Henry Morgenthau (by now an important financial backer of the Wilson boom) at lunch one day, Wise heatedly criticized the *Times* and other supposedly independent journals, for their failure to give the public a fair picture of the Jersey governor. Whenever Wilson came to New York, Wise went to visit him, and Wilson evidently enjoyed this new friendship and the encouragement that accompanied it.[9]

When the Republican convention met in June in Chicago, delegates feared a prolonged fight between Taft and Roosevelt. Rumors circulated that in order to avoid a crippling struggle, a majority would gladly swing to Charles Evans Hughes, former governor of New York and now an associate justice of the United States Supreme Court. Judge William H. Wadhams journeyed to Hughes' summer camp on Lake Placid to urge him to run, while Frederick C. Tanner waited impatiently in Chicago for permission to place Hughe's name before the delegates. The justice proved reluctant, however, and went over to discuss the matter with Wise, whom he had come to know both as a neighbor and as a reformer. Hughes had prepared a statement explaining why he could not consider the nomination. If men were to step down from the bench to elective office, court decisions might become subject to political considerations, and would certainly seem so in the public eye. When Wise asked Hughes whether an extraordinary crisis might "make it your duty to accept the nomination," Hughes emphatically replied, "No man is as essential to his country's wellbeing as is the unstained integrity of the courts." After writing out his statement, Hughes asked Wise to deliver it to the press, and to explain his feelings in the matter.[10] Without Hughes as an available compromise, the Republicans went about destroying one another. Taft's political henchmen rigged the credentials committee to disqualify Roosevelt backers, and the Rough Rider led his troops out of the party to do battle for the Lord at Armageddon.

The Democrats, tasting their first victory in twenty years, almost tore each other apart, but William Jennings Bryan finally swung his influence behind Wilson, who beat out Missouri's Champ Clark on the 46th ballot.[11] Wise and his family were at Placid when word came by telegram on July 2, and he joyously ran to tell his brother-in-law, Leo Waterman. When little eleven-year-old Jimmy heard, tears trickled down his face. "That settles Roosevelt," he said, "and I prayed for Clark."

"Why did you do that?" his father asked.

"Because you said that if Clark were nominated, Roosevelt would be elected. And you're a turncoat, because you've always been a Republican and now you're going to vote Democratic."

That night, as the children went up to bed, Jim threatened to pray for Roosevelt. "Don't do that, Jim" his father urged. "Instead, do as I will do, pray that God may give us the best man, the man best fitted to lead this great nation to honor."

"That's Teddy all right," Jim shot back as he ran upstairs.[12]

While Wise liked Wilson the man, the Democratic platform on which he was to run seemed far too evasive on key issues, and no real reflection of the progressive fervor he believed Wilson had. He began sounding out some of his reform friends to see whether some sort of supplemental statement might be made, one that did not repudiate the official platform so much as ignore it. Unless Wilson did something to reassure progressives, many of them would be tempted to join Roosevelt's new party, with its ringing moralism and clearcut demands for reform. As Lillian Wald told Wise, Wilson seemed surrounded by too many party hacks and conservative advisors; much as she wanted to believe in Wilson, the candidate had given her very little to go on so far.[13]

Wise nonetheless endorsed Wilson on July 19, terming him the only real progressive in the presidential race. With Wilson, he declared, "The Democratic Party has been reborn [and] is once again to become. . .a party of genuine and substantial progress." When one of Roosevelt's aides questioned Wise, whom he had always believed to be a supporter of the former president, about the statement, the rabbi responded in a lengthy letter that he still admired the Bull Moose candidate. But the Republican Party had become corrupt and machine-controlled, and he did not believe that Roosevelt could function outside the party apparatus. Teddy might be reform-minded, but the Republicans were not; the only real alternative for progressives, therefore, was Wilson.[14]

As the campaign developed Wilson realized that if he were to win, he had to put to rest the doubts among his supporters and the large body of still undecided progressives. Fortunately, a meeting with Louis D. Brandeis and subsequent advice from him gave Wilson's speeches a new edge and clarity that hitherto had been lacking. Before a conference with Brandeis at Sea Girt, Wilson had muttered noble but vague generalities about trusts and the economic system; he disliked monopolies, but did not know what to do about them. Roosevelt, on the other hand, was proposing to recognize the historic and economic inevitability of monopolies, but regulate them through strong governmental control. Brandeis convinced Wilson that monopolies could be broken up, that competition could be restored, and that a small government could then regulate competition in such a way as to prevent the re-emergence of trust. Consulting frequently with Brandeis, Wilson now put steel in his speeches. He called for the rebirth of the older American values instead of materialism; he called for the re-establishment of a country in which the individual, and not the giant corporation, mattered most as against helplessly allowing humanity to be crushed by industrialism.[15]

This was what Wise and other progressives had been waiting to hear. Following one of his increasingly frequent talks with Wilson, a happy Wise reported to George Foster Peabody that he and the candidate stood in total agreement on all the important issues. When the Civic Forum arranged a meeting in Carnegie Hall to allow voters to hear the different party viewpoints, Wise spoke in behalf of the Democrats, a reflection of his close ties to Wilson. He consulted with Brandeis to be sure he understood the concept of regulating competition, and asked if Wilson wanted him to emphasize anything in particular. Evidently Wilson suggested a meeting at the University Club, but Wise, aware of the club's restrictive policy, wrote, "I regret that I am under the necessity of saying that I could not call at the University Club. No self-respecting Jew can cross its threshhold." Wilson, who probably knew little or nothing of the club's procedures, recognized in this note a kindred spirit, and respected Wise all the more for it.[16]

Finally the country voted, and Wilson won a majority of the electoral if not the popular vote. A contented Wise noted in his diary: "I feel good over Wilson's victory. It would be easier now to do what I fear I may have to do before four years are over, namely go over to the Progressive Party. Had Teddy won I never could have done it, because of all things on earth I hate to go on to the winning side. I feel that I may have been a little help to Wilson, in the fight both before and after his nomination. I must write to him that I want nothing of him but that I do want to give him my support throughout his term of office."[17]

Wilson answered that letter with equal warmth, addressing him as "my dear friend," wanting the rabbi to "know how proud I have been to be supported by you." Wise offered his children the letter as a keepsake, and Justine quickly claimed it; Jimmy still smarted from the defeat of his idol. In January came an invitation to have luncheon with the president-elect at Trenton. As they went into the dining room, Wilson courteously gestured for his guest to be seated, but Wise remained standing, declaring "You will have to learn to be seated first at the White House." "Perhaps," came the response, "but won't you let me be a gentleman a little longer?" As they talked during the meal, Wise, aware of the horde of office-seekers beseiging Wilson, told the president-elect that he ought to feel relieved that one man at least had come to see him who did not want an appointment. "Are you sure?" Wilson asked. "Absolutely sure." "Well, Rabbi, let's shake hands again." Years later, Wilson's secretary Joseph P. Tumulty told Wise that on March 4, 1921, as the sick and weary Wilson prepared to leave the White House for the last time, he sat for a few minutes pondering his eight turbulent years. "Some friends, a very few," he mused aloud to Tumulty, "have never asked anything for themselves and given me every service." He named only a handful of people, including Stephen Wise.[18]

While Wise himself did not seek office, and in fact put off all requests that he intercede for various job-seekers, there were some issues he wanted to discuss. Senator William Borah, in consultation with Wise and other progressives, had led the fight in the Senate to bottle up Taft's nominations to the Industrial Commission, so that the new president would be able to name the members. Wise and some of the other signers of the original petition had met in mid-December to formulate their ideas, and they objected to the fact that Taft had included no women in his list, that he had named no political economists, and that the so-called "public" members were in fact business representatives. Taft had not chosen a single one of the petitioners for the commission. Borah also reported that labor spokemen were pressing him for assurances that union representatives would sit on the new group. Wise conveyed these concerns to Wilson at the luncheon, and the president-elect asked him to assure Samuel Gompers of the AF of L that labor would be treated fairly when he sent in a new list for the Industrial Commission.[19]

Wise had two other items on his agenda which he hoped Wilson would consider. He wanted Wilson to call a conference of people familiar with Russian persecution of Jews to aid in formulating the new administration's policy. Wilson reminded Wise of his attitude as expressed in the speech to the Free Synagogue, but said he could do nothing until he had appointed a secretary of state. The two men also discussed having an informal group of men and women involved in social welfare areas provide advice on matters requiring federal action. Wise lamented the fact that Roosevelt's Progressive Party had made so many reform measures into partisan questions, and hoped that the Democrats would not avoid dealing with pressing social problems because of this. Wilson saw no reason why some of the more imperative items of the Progressive Party agenda could not be adopted, provided the party leaders were not involved. All in all, it was a satisfactory conference, and when Wise left the meeting, reporters crowded around him to find out what he had discussed with Wilson. "Oh," he answered smiling, "I came to urge him to accept the election to the presidency."

A few days after Wilson's inauguration, Wise left, with his family, for Europe en route to Palestine. With him he took a personal letter of introduction from the new president, asking that American diplomatic officers extend to Wise any and all courtesies and assistance. While traveling, news of Wilson's activities reached Wise irregularly, but what little he heard troubled him. He could not know that the president was carefully laying the groundwork for the major reform proposals he would submit to Congress in December, but the list of appointments stunned him. "What is the matter? Have you heard anything?" he wrote to Henry Morgenthau. "As far as I have seen, no Jew has been appointed to a single place of importance. It seems almost a deliberate slight. . . . I have been terribly tempted for a week to write to Washington and tell him of my astonishment and pain at his failure, seemingly premeditated, to name some distinguished members of his party to high office, seeing that they were among the first to support him at a time when prospects seemed dubious."[20]

Actually, Wilson had been seeking Jews to appoint, but with little success. Opposition from the financial community as well as from party chieftains forced him to abandon plans to name Brandeis Attorney-General, and Brandeis himself refused the chairmanship of the Industrial Commission. Secretary of State Williams Jennings Bryan met twice with Simon Wolf, who represented several Jewish organizations in Washington, but none of the names they discussed filled the administration's need to establish fruitful contacts with leading Jewish groups. Moreover, Wilson had offered Henry Morgenthau the post of ambassador to Turkey, but Morgenthau, like Wise, had not sought nor wanted any office from the president.[21] Only when Morgenthau came to Europe did Wise learn of the offer, and discovered that Wilson had again sought Morgenthau for the position.

In early August, Morgenthau, resting at Aix-les-Bains, contacted Wise in Paris and asked if he could meet him to discuss the matter. They both journeyed to Dijon, where the rabbi urged his congregant and friend to accept. The Wises had just been in Palestine, and he reminded Morgenthau that as ambassador to Turkey he would be able to help the Jewish community in the Holy Land. Morgenthau said he would be back in the States in September, and if the job were still open, he would then reconsider. Much to Morgenthau's surprise, Wise immediately wired the president that Morgenthau would accept if asked again, and three days later Wilson cabled the invitation.[22] As it turned out, when war broke out a year later, Ambassador Morgenthau did provide crucial assistance to the Jews of Palestine.

Wise neither possessed nor claimed the type of influence with the White House such as Brandeis or Edward M. House exercised, but he had ready access to the president, and from time to time performed services of one kind or another for Wilson. In late November 1913, for example, a newspaper article claimed that the administration had abandoned efforts to negotiate a new commerical treaty with Russia which would preclude religious or racial discrimination against American citizens. Wise went to Washington to see Wilson, and handed the president a copy of the piece. Wilson became furious, and denounced the report as an "absolutely malicious invention." While agreeing that the White House could not be troubled with repudiating every false rumor, Wise urged that Russia should not think for a moment that the administration was not in earnest on this subject. Together president and rabbi drafted a statement which the latter gave out to the press after the conference, reiterating the determination of the American government to secure a proper treaty. At the same meeting, Wilson suggested that Wise meet with Secretary of State Bryan to see if something could be done about Turkish policies restricting Jewish land ownership in Palestine. As Henry Morgenthau wrote him after hearing about the conference: "Is it not great that you can go to Washington and feel at home with all of them?"[23]

Wilson's legislative programs also cheered Wise, as the president eventually moved to implement his campaign promises. He adroitly maneuvered tariff reductions through Congress despite efforts by the powerful protectionist lobby, and then brought together all the wings of the party in support of a complete overhaul of the federal banking system. In early 1914 Wilson presented his long-waited message on business to Congress, and while calling for more potent antitrust legislation, the president also held out the olive branch to corporate leaders, urging them that the war between business and government should come to an end. Upon reading the speech, Wise wrote Wilson praising him for his "unerring analysis of present-day industrial conditions, and if the leaders of industry in the nation do not meet you in the right spirit it will be incredibly short-sighted on their part. Your friends are all happy and proud of this epochal state paper." To Morgenthau he noted that "if the business men of the nation refuse to accept that offer of peace, they deserve a double dose of Roosevelt."[24]

Wise also rejoiced in Wilson's veto of the literacy test in the Smith-Burnett Bill, a measure designed to restrict immigration from southern and eastern Europe, and which would in effect have severely limited the number of Jews from those areas entering America. "To have vetoed the bill was in itself a service," Wise wrote to the president, "but to have done it in such a way as to make it increasingly difficult for the matter ever to be revived is to have rendered a really great service to the nation." Here he totally misread the mood of the country, for the growing nativist sentiment could not be stopped, and Congress passed the bill over Wilson's second veto in 1917.[25]

Wise's friendship with Wilson and his access to the administration were soon to prove of inestimable value, for when war broke out in August 1914, a new leader came to the fore in American Zionism, and Wise reclaimed his own role in the movement.

9

Zionism Redivivus

Although Wise never lost his interest in Zionism, the first few years after his return to New York found him almost totally uninvolved in the movement. Nearly all his energy and time went into either Free Synagogue or secular reforms, for there was little in American Zionism between 1907 and 1913 to attract a man of his vigor. After the death of Herzl the movement languished in Europe and America, with its only sign of life the slow growth of a handful of colonies in Palestine. No charismatic leader inspired the masses, no great event caught their imagination. The Federation of American Zionists stagnated, its leaders constantly ignored by the Europeans, who seemed concerned only about the rather irregular remittances of funds.[1]

Wises's dormant interest in Jewish nationalism awoke during the trip he and Louise took to Palestine in 1913. The heavy-handedness of Turkish rule struck him even before he set foot on land at Jaffa. The Sultan's immigration officers would not allow the couple to debark from their ship until they promised in writing to leave the Holy Land within a matter of weeks. Wise at first refused, and prepared to appeal through the State Department to, as he put, "avert the insult to me as American and Jew," but grudgingly gave in when he learned the appeal would take at least a month to process. He and Louise reached Jerusalem on the eve of Passover, and immediately went to the tomb of his grandmother. Her prayers had been answered and her grave, in a place of honor, faced the Temple Mount. Remembering his father's wishes, Wise arranged for a new tombstone bearing the additional inscription, "the Mother of Aaron Wise."

Stephen and Louise toured Judea, Samaria, and on up to the Galilee, visiting many of the nearly forty settlements established since 1870. This was a totally new experience for Wise, actually seeing the land, the work of reclaiming and rebuilding barren soil, the proud young Jews, men and women who had left Europe to live and labor on the soil of their ancestors.[2] He returned to America determined to work once again, if not in the

Federation, at least for Palestine. The device he chose, an investigatory commission whose report would explain the possibilities of Palestinian development, accurately reflected the progressive impulse—a team of experts, a clearcut statement of problems and solutions, followed by the prescribed actions.

Wise began work on his project soon after his return to the United States, approaching Jacob H. Schiff, Henry Morgenthau, and several other well-to-do Jews to finance "a social survey as it were of Jewish affairs within and without Jerusalem."[3] The first problem occurred after the so-called "language controversy" at the Haifa Technikum. The German directors of the school insisted all technical subjects be taught only in German, leading to a wave of indignation by the Zionist settlers and a strike by the Hebrew Teachers Association. For them, Hebrew constituted part of the Jewish renaissance in Palestine, an integral factor of the nation-building process. In February 1914, in the face of determined resistance by the *yishuv* (the Jewish settlement), the Technikum's board backed down agreeing that all courses at the school would be taught in Hebrew.

The controversy left Jacob Schiff upset and resentful. He had contributed generously to the building of the school by the Hilfsverein der Deutsche Juden, and did not see why the Zionists had to act so unreasonably; a German-sponsored school, he thought, ought to be able to teach in German. He understood neither the importance of Hebrew to the settlers nor the fact that the Technikum was part of the German *Drang nach Osten*, designed to be a showpiece of *Deutsche Kultur* in the Ottoman Empire. He wrote to Wise in late January 1914 that he found the recent events in Palestine so disturbing as to alter his attitude toward the projected survey. The two men met for lunch a few days later, and Wise tried to explain the Zionist's reasons for insisting on Hebrew, but to no avail. Schiff expected his philanthropies to be clear and straightforward, and did not like to see any of his projects embroiled in controversy.[4]

Either Schiff failed to make clear that he intended to withdraw his sponsorship or Wise did not recognize the financier's meaning, for he continued to act as if Schiff's backing for a quarter of the estimated $10,000 survey would still be forthcoming.[5] Wise proceeded to put together a three-man commission consisting of Meyer Bloomfield, a student of industrial organization; Dr. Milton J. Rosenau, who would examine medical and sanitation facilities; and Boris D. Bogen of the United Jewish Charities. Lee K. Frankel, one of the country's oustanding Jewish social workers, had originally agreed to participate, but because of his close ties to Schiff, he withdrew when he realized that Schiff no longer intended to remain a sponsor. The commission planned to sail for Palestine and spend at least a month there in the summer of 1914.

On April 30, Wise met once again with Schiff, and this time the banker made it quite clear that he had no intention of subscribing $2,500, attributing his change of heart to the language controversy. Wise was momentarily stunned by Schiff's decision; not only would the money have to be made up, but he feared that the other backers would follow Schiff's example. He immediately set about securing other supporters, but he also exchanged several bitter letters with Schiff which left the two men permanently alienated from each other.[6]

In the meantime, Louis D. Brandeis agreed to serve as a sponsor, and in mid-June Wise gave out a formal announcement of the commission which, he said, would leave in the near future for Palestine. On June 17 he sent $500 checks to each of the three men as an advance on their expenses.[7] Rosenau sailed for England in July, and planned to spend a few weeks there until joined by the other two; he was in London, and Bloomfield and Bogen about to sail, when war broke out in Europe, aborting the project. At the same time, the war initiated a new and fruitful period in Wise's lifelong commitment to Zionism.

Much has been written about Louis Dembitz Brandeis, his leadership of American Zionism during the war period, and how he transformed the moribund Federation of American Zionists into the politically potent Zionist Organization of America. There has also been much controversy over how and why he became a Zionist.[8] Certainly little in his family background or personal experience suggested any prior commitment either to Judaism or to Jewish Nationalism. Around 1910, when he served as mediator in New York garment strike, he met for the first time large numbers of Jewish immigrants from eastern Europe, and came into contact with the vibrant, dynamic, and democratic culture they had created in this country. Shortly afterward, Jacob deHaas, who had once served as Herzl's English secretary, interested Brandeis in the idea of Zionism, and the Boston attorney began reading extensively in the English and German literature on the subject. By 1913 he had formally joined the Federation and even appeared on a platform with Nahum Sokolow during the latter's tour of America, but he had resisted all overtures to take any sort of leadership role either in Massachusetts or nationally. It had been a coup of sorts for Wise to get Brandeis to become one of the underwriters of his Palestinian survey project, although undoubtedly the format of the survey appealed to the man who stood in the forefront of the efficiency movement.

Brandeis would have a major and enduring influence on Stephen Wise, extending from the revitalization of American Zionism begun in August 1914 until the jurist's death in October 1941. In Brandeis, Wise found a man of intellectual brilliance whose idealism was matched by an ability to implement practical programs. To the traditionalists, Brandeis may not have seemed much of a Jew, but the rabbi of the Free Synagogue saw him as the embodiment of the prophetic virtues, a man who sought justice and loved mercy. Friend and foe recognized the People's Attorney as one of the leading reformers in the nation, respected by both Wilsonian and Rooseveltian progressives. When Brandeis assumed an active role in Zionist affairs, he epitomized Wise's ideal, a man who could at one and the same time be effective as a Jew and as an American, harmonizing the best of both traditions. Brandeis himself declared that his "approach to Zionism was through Americanism. . . . Zionism is essentially a movement of freedom, a movement to give the Jews more freedom, a movement to enable Jews to exercise the rights now exercised by practically every other people in the world."[9]

This movement of freedom, however, had failed to make much impression on American Jews by the summer of 1914. At the annual convention of the Federation of American Zionists in Rochester that June, the secretary reported a membership of little over 12,000, and the proposed budget of $12,150 exceeded anticipated revenues by $2,600. After Richard Gottheil's resignation, no one wanted the onerous job of president, and Harry Freidenwald, a Baltimore ophthalmologist, served as honorary president. Before the convention, Gottheil had written beseechingly to Horace Meyer Kallen on the sad state of Zionist leadership, begging him to use his friendship with Brandeis to bring him into a more Zionist role. Such a step, Gottheil declared, "would be worth more to us than anything else we could do."[10] But Brandeis steadfastly refused such overtures.

When war broke out late that summer, some of the heaviest fighting on the eastern front took place in areas of Jewish population, and American Jews quickly set about raising funds to aid their distressed brethren. But the *yishuv* in Palestine also faced disaster, its fragile economy threatened by the closing of European markets. While the American Jewish Committee called for aid to European Jews, the *yahudim* evidently had little interest in relief for Palestine, and Zionists recognized that if any help were to go to the settlers, it would have to come from them. On August 30, 1914, various Zionist groups assembled in an extraordinary conference at the Hotel Marseilles in New York. At the urging of Jacob deHaas and Horace Kallen, Brandeis had finally agreed to chair the conference, and most of those assembled in the hot, crowded room expected little other than some oratory on the seriousness of the situation and the establishment of an emergency fund. For a while, the scenario went as expected. After explaining the dangers facing Jews in Europe and Palestine, Brandeis announced the creation of the Provisional Executive Committee for General Zionist Affairs to develop a relief program; he contributed $1,000 toward the fund, and then Nathan Straus added another $5,000. Now, according to the script, Brandeis would contact his rich friends for more money while everyone else went home.

Instead, Brandeis, pleading his ignorance of the many organizations represented, asked the assembly to stay on and meet with him that evening and the following day. He needed to know more about them, their leaders, their memberships, their administrative arrangements. For the next day and a half, Brandeis sat patiently in a crowded hotel suite, absorbing fact after fact about Zionism and Jewish life in America, occasionally asking a question or repeating a strange-sounding Hebrew or Yiddish name. When he finally adjourned the meeting late on August 31, his orderly mind might well have been reeling from the realization that nearly all the groups present had poor organization, modest enrollments, miniscule financial resources, and very, very few people to do real work. But the shock to the men and women representing American Zionism was immeasurably greater; rather than a figurehead, the extraordinary conference had brought them a man who had the ability, determination, and reputation to be their leader, and who intended to be just that.[11] The Hotel Marseilles meeting marked a turning point in the fortunes of American Zionism and in the life of Stephen Wise, for from that time on, he would remain a leading figure in the movement, first as Brandeis's lieutenant, then as his successor in the Provisional Committee, ultimately assuming the mantle of full leadership in the dark days of Hitler, British perfidy, and another world war.

Brandeis brought into Zionism a number of people who, like himself had earned reputations as reformers and hitherto rarely participated in Jewish affairs, such as Felix Frankfurter, Julian W. Mack, Eugene Meyer, and Nathan Straus, Jr. But he also recognized the talent of two people who had long despaired over the sad state of Zionist affairs—Henrietta Szold and Stephen Wise. With Wise especially, Brandeis created an instant rapport, for the two men shared many ideas on secular reform and were devoted to Woodrow Wilson. What Wise had lamented in Zionism—the lack of purpose, the poor administration, the failure to develop an effective organization—Brandeis now set about to rectify. In the next year and a half the new leadership worked wonders, trebling and then trebling membership again, raising hundreds of thousands of dollars, and making Zionism a visible and potent force on the American Jewish scene. Brandeis, of course, stood at the focus of this upheaval, galvanizing the movement into action, but much of the credit for the actual implementation of the program must be shared with his two chief lieutenants, Julian Mack and Stephen Wise. They were the ones who oversaw the administrative details, and Wise especially took on the most extensive speaking tours of his life to raise relief money and generate support for Jewish nationalism. All the work proved exhilarating to Wise, following Brandeis from one triumph to another, discovering that the ideals he so cherished might, in the end, prove victorious.

In only one area did Wise prove reluctant to follow his leader—when Brandeis asked him to chair the committee on funds. Wise tried to beg off, but Brandeis insisted that he had only a few good men on whom he could rely, and he needed help. But as funds failed to materialize, Wise attempted to explain why someone else should chair this important committee: "I must make very clear to you that there is no man in New York who would be less likely to succeed in interesting rich New Yorkers in the [Zionist] movement than would I. Access to them is denied me not because of the heterodoxy of my pulpit but because of the social, and economic and ethical economic heterodoxies in my teaching which I am happy, if not proud, to say have made me wholly unacceptable to the rich Jews of New York. They do not support me in any measure."[12]

Brandeis, no stranger to ostracism because of his own reform activities, knew exactly what Wise meant, and within a few weeks would learn more about the power of the German-Jewish elite in communal affairs. In October, Brandeis and Wise attended several meetings with the *yahudim* in an effort to develop a larger base for relief work, and the new Zionist leader had a firsthand lesson in the realities of this strange world.[13] After one particularly exasperating session, Wise wrote to Richard Gottheil that "it seems rather regrettable that [Brandeis] should, so soon after his entrance into Jewish affairs, learn of the meannesses and pettinesses of our so-called leaders. . . . The whole thing is a sorry commentary upon American Jewish affairs and more especially upon American Jewish leadership." It came as no surprise to Wise when, at the insistence of the *yahudim*, his name was deliberately omitted from the membership of the American Jewish Relief Committee, nor that a number of prominent Jews now attacked Brandeis for his Zionist work. "The least we can do," he told Horace Kallen, "is to stand loyally behind him to carry out his far-reaching plans. I was with him for two days, and the one fear that I had—that he might be completely disgusted when he discovered the chaos in which the movement actually is—has been dissipated. He is thoroughly aware of the conditions, and appears to be inexorably intent in remedying them."[14]

Brandeis set about in true progressive fashion to mold American Zionism along the lines already proven successful in reform work. His motto of "Men! Money! Discipline!" aptly summed up his methods. There had to be a large membership in order to carry out the Zionist program and to demonstrate that Zionist goals were supported by many in the Jewish community. This large membership could then raise sufficient money not only for relief work but to support Zionist settlements in Palestine and other projects. Discipline meant the orderly use of people and money to carry out the political program. For those familiar with progressive crusades, the Brandeisian approach appeared familiar; for the masses of old-line Zionists, used to endless and sterile ideological debates, the American emphasis on efficiency and result was astounding and confusing. There could be no better indication of the great gulf between Americanized Jews and their newly arrived brethren from eastern Europe than this dichotomy between theory and practice. The Europeans loved theory, perhaps because they had had so little opportunity for practice; the Americans quickly reached beyond their ideological bases, and then concentrated exclusively on carrying out their program. For Wise especially, the Brandeisian method, its philosophical synthesis of Zionist and American ideals—"To be good Americans we must be good Jews; to be good Jews we must become Zionists!"—its emphasis on practical work and results, all summed up what he had hitherto found lacking in American Zionism.

Wise himself now became a regular visitor to the State Department, verifying reports on the status of Jewish communities in Europe and Palestine, meeting with Secretary Bryan to arrange for shipment of foodstuffs or with Secretary of the Navy Josephus Daniels to secure the use of American destroyers to deliver food, medicine, and money to the *yishuv*. One day as he waited in a Washington anteroom to see an official, he jotted a note to Louise: "It is hard and wearing, but I should feel that I were perfidious as a Jew and disloyal as an American not to have my part."[15]

Alongside Brandeis, Wise saw Zionism achieve a position of influence in American Jewish life far beyond the wildest expectations of the original founders of the FAZ. No better indicator of how far the movement had come in one short year under Brandeis's leadership can be found than in comparing the morbid spirit of the lackluster 1914 convention with the triumphant celebration of the 1915 meetings in Boston. The city fathers prepared a near royal welcome for the delegates. Special floral arrangements, featuring the Star of David, decorated the Public Gardens; local groups, both Jewish and non-Jewish, held numerous receptions for the Zionists; and the Boston newspapers gave extensive coverage to the convention. Ten thousand people filled all the seats and every inch of standing room in Mechanics Hall to hear the main speakers, especially Brandeis and Wise.[16]

Not everyone found the newly potent Zionist movement so appealing. Henry Morgenthau, for example, cautioned Wise that many of the speeches dealing with hopes for Palestine could prove disastrous; as ambassador he had already spent many hours trying to quiet the fears among Turkish officials that the Zionists supported the Allies in order to gain the Holy Land after the war. Jacob Schiff, Louis Marshall, and the leaders of the American Jewish Committee also looked askance at the Provisional Committee,[17] but undoubtedly the greatest concern occurred in the ranks of Reform Judaism, whose anti-Zionist leadership found itself and its principles suddenly on the defensive.

Wise originally wanted to press an all-out attack on the Cincinnati group led by Kaufman Kohler and David Philipson, but Brandeis urged a more cautious policy. Let Zionism catch on, he counseled, and the Cincinnati crowd would eventually be cut off and isolated, thus rendering it harmless. In early March 1915, Wise agreed to cancel a speaking engagement in Cincinnati, seconding Brandeis's idea that "Philipson and men of his stamp must be left severely and contemptuously alone." A month later though, in response to insistent demands that he speak, Wise went to the Queen City and received a warm welcome there. The Jewish press, including some non-Zionist publications, even berated Kohler and Philipson for their lack of courtesy toward Wise, who, for his part, spoke in a calm and friendly manner, stressing the need for unity among American Jews. The Brandeis strategy seemed to be paying off; the outright hostility of Reform leaders compared poorly to the open and conciliatory statements of Wise, Julian Mack, and other Zionists.[18] Slowly, the Cincinnati crowd was isolated, not only from American Jews as a whole, but in the end even within the Reform movement.

Wise, even while acknowledging the efficacy of Brandeis's method, wanted to move things along at a somewhat faster pace. It was less a matter of tactics than of psychology. "One of the most important things we could do in American Israel," he told Horace Kallen, "is to end the delusion under which too many Liberal Jews have been led to rest by the Philipsonians, that a follower of Liberal Judaism cannot be a Zionist." Slowly, in speeches and sermons, Wise began hitting at the claim that Zionists could neither be good Reform Jews nor good Americans. "I know that I can be a loyal American," he told his congregation. "Zionism is not a religion. It is not un-American. But it is touched by the spirit of religion." He reveled when Wilson appointed Brandeis to the Supreme Court, gleefully asking what Philpson, Schulman, and others thought about the president naming a Zionist to the Court, a man they had denounced as un-American.[19] At a meeting of the Eastern Council of Reform Rabbis in mid-1916, Wise urged his colleagues to embrace a program devoted to social action, democracy in American Jewish life, and Zionism. Shortly afterward he delivered his strongest attack in nearly two years. "That Zionism is irreligious," he charged, "it is left in the main for religionless Jews to assert. That Zionism is un-American is an indictment drawn up principally by Americans . . . of doubious if not infirm loyalty." He scathingly denounced both classic Reform and the *yahudim* for their failure to recognize the legitimacy of Jewish nationalism in the contemporary world.[20]

The battle came to a head in 1917, at the annual gathering of the Central Conference of American Rabbis in Buffalo that June. President William Rosenau of Balitmore reiterated the classic Reform position: "We as rabbis who are consecrated to the service of the Lord," he intoned, "have no place in the movement in which Jews stand together on racial or national grounds, and for a political state or even a legally assured home. . . . The time has come for this Conference to publish the statement that it stands for an Israel whose mission is religious, and that in the light of that mission, it looks with disfavor upon any movement the purpose of which is other than religious.'' The Zionists were immediately on their feet shouting their oppositon, and Wise delivered an impassioned and moving appeal to his colleagues:[21]

> In the twenty years history of this Conference there has never been an attempt made to compel anyone to accept Zionism as the lawful and permissible interpretation of Liberal or Reform Judaism. But year after year we have heard Zionism attacked. You are making Reform Judaism proscriptive of us who are Zionists. Perhaps you feel you have the right, perhaps you feel Zionists are a menace to liberalism and Judaism, but I warn you to be mindful of the Conference. If you pass this resolution no matter how you order it or mitigate it, the moment you say that we who are Zionists are anti-religionists, that we are enemies of religious Judaism, that moment we must regretfully and with absolute conviction say, ''We can no longer stay with the Conference.'' I stand here today not as a Zionist, but as a Reform Rabbi. I would not have you say that a Reform teacher or rabbi has forfeited the right to be a teacher of Reform Judaism because he has subscribed to a Zionist platform. I appeal not for Zionism, but for the inclusiveness and comprehensiveness of Liberal Judaism. Will Liberal Judaism after a century of distinguished and outstanding history make the monumental blunder of saying to men who love and serve, ''We bid you go forth''? I ask not for the sake of Zionism, but that the honor, dignity and noble history of Reform Judaism shall not be marred and undone now.

Although the Zionists could not defeat the President's report, they did secure a concession in a substitute resolution that downplayed Rosenau's demand and instead called for Jewish unity.

Following the meeting, Wise admitted that the Zionists had not secured the statement they had sought, but as for the anti–Zionist claim, ''another such victory and they are undone.'' Zionism had not been hurt at Buffalo, he declared, ''but Liberal Judaism, and the hurt was inflicted by those leaders of Jewish Reform to whom Jewish is an adjective rather than substance.''[22] Yet the fact remained that the Zionists had shown themselves far stronger at Buffalo than ever before in CCAR history, and although it would be years until the Zionists ''controlled'' the Conference, the era of anti-Zionist supremacy in the Reform movement had passed.

Closely tied to the Zionist resurgence was the fight to establish an American Jewish Congress. To some extent, it marked the coming to maturity of the eastern European immigrants, and their desire to have a major say in the community, but it also reflected the efforts of the Zionists to become a leading force among American Jews.[23] At the heart of the controversy lay two conflicting philosphies: the aristocratic leadership of an elite, endorsed by the American Jewish Committte, as opposed to the fervent belief in democracy, the right and ability of people to govern themselves. Horace Kallen once described the *yahudim* and their attitudes in these words: "They distrusted the rank and file. They were afraid of the publicity. They were afraid of having their 'Americanism' impugned. . . . The class as a whole showed distrust of democracy, fear of frankness, a consciousness of moral and social security. They insisted that whatever could be done, could be done quietly, by wire pulling, by use of the influence of individuals, by the backstairs methods of the *Sh'tadlan* of the Middle Ages and of the Russian ghetto."[24] For Stephen Wise, Louis Brandeis, and the other leaders of the congress movement, Jewish life in this country would remain cramped and undeveloped until a democratic and representative structure allowed the masses to express their innate creativity and passion for freedom and social justice.

The idea of an organization representative of all American Jews was mentioned in the announcement of the August 1914 Zionist conference. At the Hotel Marseilles meeting, Nachman Syrkin introduced a resolution, backed by many of those present, that the Provisional Committee "take the initiative, within the shortest time possible, to call a convention of Jewish organizations and Jewish committees" for the purpose, among other things, of discussing "the entire Jewish situation in regard to the change of the condition of the world after the war." That same day, Brandeis wrote Louis Marshall informing him of the establishment of the Provisional Committee, and inviting the American Jewish Committee to cooperate in calling a conference representative of the entire community. Marshall, rather annoyed at the presumption of this upstart group, nonetheless replied that he and his colleagues would be willing to meet with Brandeis to discuss the matter.[25]

The American Jewish Committee had always viewed foreign affairs as its special domain, an area of policy that had to be handled with discretion, certainly not something to be debated in an open hall. The AJC had, in fact, already decided to call some sort of conference open to the major Jewish organizations, but one which the *yahudim* could control and which would not be subject to passions inflamed by unstable rabble-rousers. "The problems with which we have to deal," Marshall declared, "are of so delicate a nature that the mob cannot grapple with them." Marshall was also aware of a growing sentiment throughout the community for some sort of umbrella agency. The large faternal organization B'nai B'rith had already called for a national Jewish conference, as had the Labor Zionists. The *Jewish Daily News*, the *Wahrheit*, and the *Jewish Leader* editorially endorsed similar plans, and even within the Committee a few men, notably Judah Magnes and Harry Friedenwald, spoke out in favor of the congress idea.[26] The seemingly instantaneous acceptance of the Provisional Committee's invitation in reality masked a clever ploy to buy time; as long as the AJC seemed willing to cooperate with the Zionists, Brandeis and Wise would be unable to do anything until they had in fact met.

There is not doubt what most of the *yahudim* thought of the entire proposal. "The holding of a Jewish Congress," Jacob Schiff lamented, would
mean "nothing less than a decision . . . that we are Jews first and
Americans second." A conference of "conservative and thoroughly tried
men" would accomplish more than a congress led by Zionist agitators. The
congress movement, Marshall warned, gave "flamboyant orators an opportunity to make themselves conspicuous for a moment irrespective of the permanent injury which they inflict upon Jewry." The very term "congress'
frightened the Committee leaders, implying as it did elections, parties, campaigns, open debates, and worst of all, airing internal Jewish problems
before the world.[27] Because of its elitist attitude, the Committee, whatever
the wisdom of its policy, gave the game away from the start. In the public
mind, the Committee stood for secrecy, exclusion, and autocracy, while
Brandeis and Wise called for a free, democratic and self-governing
deliberative body.

Yet both Brandeis and Wise also had some misgiving, not over principle
but over execution. The administrative work in organizing enrollments,
elections, and thousands of other details necessary to convene an assembly
representative of three million American Jews required manpower and
resources far beyond those available to the Zionists in winter of 1914/1915.
The delaying tactics of the Marshall group also served the needs of the congress proponents, who wanted to build up Zionist ranks before undertaking
additional responsibilities. Brandeis and Wise stood committed to the idea,
yet unable to divert sufficient attention or resources to begin the work. In
discussing the matter with Wise, Horace Kallen accurately noted that while
the Zionists had the proper sentiment and the *yahudim* adequate money,
neither group had the organization necessary to undertake the management
of such a large-scale project. Brandeis pushed Wise to step forward and be
the leader of the congress movement, a step Wise feared might be politically
maladroit. As he told his brother, "I am a clerical . . . I am an ultra-liberal,
and . . . I am a New Yorker." Moreover, he feared his Zionist affiliation
might scare off those opposed to or worried about Jewish nationalism. Yet
the eloquent addresses he made in support of the congress, such as his
response to David Philipson at the 1915 UAHC meeting, constantly propelled
him forward toward this unsought responsibility.[28]

Not all Zionists favored the congress, while others saw it solely in terms of
increasing the prestige and membership of their own organizations. Julian
Mack and Richard Gottheil were initially cool to the idea, while Judah
Magnes, after a futile attempt to reconcile the two groups, angrily resigned
from the Provisional Committee, accusing the Zionists of fomenting disuni-
ty among American Jews. Only Horace Kallen and Felix Frankfurter, of all
the Zionist leaders, worked energetically with Wise and Brandeis to support
the movement, and in so doing formed the nucleus around which the pro-

congress groups could coalesce. According to Bernard Richards, the downtown Jews might never have gone against the power, influence, and wealth of the *yahudim* were it not for the fact that Brandeis and Wise provided a leadership and prestige that, in the eyes of the masses, balanced that of Marshall and Schiff.[29]

The record also indicates that the masses wanted to push ahead far faster than their leaders. Throughout this period, Brandeis and Wise, aware of the administrative and organizational problems, often held back until they were forced to act by their followers. In February and March 1915, for example, pressure mounted in the Yiddis press for the Provisional Committee to call for a congress; finally, Joseph Barondess summoned together a number of officers of organizations whose memberships consisted primarily of eastern Europe immigrants. On March 21, the Jewish Congress Organizing Committee (COC) came into being with Gedalia Bublick, editor of the *Jewish Daily News*, as chairman. Faced with this *fait accompli*, the Provisional Committee officially endorsed the congress movement and joined the COC a few days later.

For both Wise and Brandeis, who had frequently taken positions in advance of popular support, the entire congress episode proved difficult. For the first time in his life, Wise worked closely with a leader he trusted and admired, but found himself having to rein in his instincts. He had wanted to tackle the Reform leaders head-on, but had seen the wisdom of Brandeis's strategy of isolation. Now he ached to confront the *yahudim* over a really important issue, democracy in Jewish life, but recognized that Brandeis's evaluation of the situation made caution, even in the face of pressure from below, the course of greatest wisdom. How uncharacteristic to find him writing that "we must move very carefully, and I shall so advise Brandeis."[30]

In June, on the eve of the great Zionist convention in Boston, the American Jewish Committee announced that in response to popular will, it would convoke a Washington meeting in early November of no more than 150 representatives of Jewish organizations, with a special committee of seven, appointed by the Committee, to select those groups which would officially participate. At the Zionist gatherings, one speaker after another denounced the Committee proposal as autocratic, and the convention adopted a resolution calling for an American Jewish Congress.[31]

With this mandate, the movement for a congress took on a new urgency. A series of meetings between Brandeis and Cyrus Adler indicated that neither side would compromise, and produced nothing more than an exchange of charges between the Zionists and the Committee. Wise did not take part in the direct talks, but consulted with Brandeis frequently, urging him to stand fast for the principles they both held dear. Adler, in his memoirs, claims that the negotiations would have succeeded except for

Wise, whom, he charged "wished all Jewish life in America and the world over to be controlled by Zionists"[32] Adler and his associates failed to understand that the times had changed, that the Jewish community, now composed primarily of recent immigrants from eastern Europe, demanded a new political structure, that the newcomers took the promise of American life seriously in their insistence upon participation and democracy. The leaders of the Committee did not see that they too could have a role in the new structure, that the masses did look up to them, did respect them for their ability and power and the sacrifices they had made to help their people; but they would not accept the continued domination by an autocratic elite. "It is conceivable that my days of usefulness are at an end," Louis Marshall mused, "that my vision is too circumscribed." Marshall, in fact, did learn and grow, but his analysis was all too true for many of the *yahudim* on the Committee.[33]

In fact, the next few months proved a nightmare for the Committee leaders. One after another of the organizations invited to the Washington conference declined to attend, and castigated the Committee for its antidemocratic policy. Now both Brandeis and Wise began to speak out more openly and forcefully, attacking the Committee's proposal of a closed conference and demanding support for the congress. "This congress must be a thoroughly democratic instrument," Brandeis declared, "democratic in its basis, its convening and in the regulations which shall guide its conduct. How else should we be justified in claiming that the voice of this congress is the real expression of the actual majority of the Jews of this country? How else could we expect the effective and enthusiastic cooperation necessary to achieve whatever such a congress might will?"[34]

On October 3, Wise rose in the pulpit of the Free Synagogue to give one of the strongest defenses of the congress idea yet heard. He began on a conciliatory note, conceding the integrity and selflessness of the American Jewish Committee leaders, but then launched into an attack on the philosophy behind their proposal for a conference. No one group could determine ahead of time which bodies should be allowed representation, nor what the agenda should be, nor that it proceed in private. "Privileges must be sought in secret," he charged; "rights may be demanded in the open. We have nothing to conceal either from ourselves or from the peoples of the earth, nor can wise and popular support, which surely is indispensable, be secured for any undertakings on behalf of the people as long as they are made to feel that they are not trusted by their self-appointed elders." He then discussed some of the items which the Committee believed should be kept muted, such as the growing persecution of Jews in Rumania, and the support of Jewish settlement in Palestine. These were surely matters that concerned all Jews, and were not the private domain of either the Committee or the Zionist organization. "It is not a sign of greatness but a token of littleness," he concluded, "it is not a sign of vision but a token of vulgarity to insist upon the superimposition of one's own will upon a whole community. But the arrogance of the few is a little thing by the side of the supineness of the many if the many suffer themselves to lapse into degradation of uncomplaining and unchallenging acquiescence in the will of the few." The congress had not been preordained, he warned, and would not inevitably come about. Those who supported democracy in Jewish life would have to exert themselves to ensure that the ideal became a reality; if they failed to do so, the forces of autocracy would surely win by default.[35]

That same day, leaders of the congress movement, the Committee, and twenty other organizations met under the auspices of B'nai B'rith, whose president, Adolph Kraus, had been trying for months to find a compromise acceptable to all sides. After nine hours of charges and countercharges, the exhausted participants went home convinced that American Jewry would soon be split. In fact, however, public opinion had already swung to the side of the congress proponents. On October 10, the deadline for response to the Committee's invitation, so few organizations had accepted that the Committee had to abandon the Washington conference. Wise was ecstatic over this moral victory, and while the congress group would not push for immediate results, they were "determined that the old bureaucratic and oligarchic management of American Jewish affairs shall cease."[36]

The question of timing had, in fact, become the focal point of a possible compromise. Committee leaders let it be known that they might not object to a congress held *after* the war, a proposal that split many of the congress adherents. Wise, like Brandeis, considered this a minor issue compared to the Committee accepting the principle of a democratically-elected congress. But, as Charles Cowen reminded them, the masses of American Jewry were restless, and might look upon delay as a sellout to the *yahudim*; the only way to meet this difficulty, he suggested, was to call the congress at the earliest possible day. Here again, the pressure of their followers left the congress leaders little room for maneuvering. Brandeis decided to push ahead because, as he explained, "a congress after the termination of hostilities may mean a congress after the time has passed when Jews could accomplish something by participating in a [peace] conference." In fact the leaders had little choice but to move ahead, despite misgivings about inadequate manpower and resources, for the momentum could not be halted.[37] Throughout the winter of 1915/1916, plans were made and implemented to call the first American Jewish Congress. On January 24, 1916, thousands of people jammed Carnegie Hall to indicate their support, and the message to the leaders could not have been clearer: "We want a congress now!" As Horace Kallen commented to Wise, "I feel more and more we cannot back down, and we dare not let go.''[38] Brandeis and Marshall continued to meet privately, with the AJC trying to salvage some of its influence, but the congress movement could not be stopped, and the COC scheduled a preliminary conference in Philadelphia for March 26 and 27, 1916.

The elation Wise and others felt over this move was tempered, however, by President Wilson's nomination of Louis Brandeis to the Supreme Court on January 28, 1916. None doubted that the People's Attorney deserved the honor, but they all feared losing his leadership from Zionist and congress affairs. Because of the bitter feelings generated by the confirmation struggle, Brandeis did withdraw from the spotlight, but he continued to direct the congress movement through the personally trying weeks and then months of Senate hearings. In letters and memoranda to Wise, Lipsky, Richards, and others, he helped mold the pro-congress passion into a workable structure. When Jacob Schiff charged that the congress would inevitably bring political antisemitism in its wake, it was Brandeis who declared that the best answer to Schiff would be "the dignified, solemn, worthy conduct of the conference and of everyone connected with it.''[39] In fact, Brandeis devoted so much time to the congress that Horace Kallen, who had originally worried about the chief withdrawing from Jewish affairs, now reassured Wise that little would change. But Wise would not be calmed. Brandeis, he told Kallen, "took over the leadership of the Jewish people of the world over and that in the moment of greatest need, it may become necessary to give him up . . . . What shall we do without Brandeis? There is no one else in sight big enough and commanding enough to take his place.''[40]

But as Brandeis withdrew from public leadership, Wise moved to the fore as the champion of democracy in Jewish life. His associates wanted him to chair the Philadelphia convention, an idea that horrified his brother Otto. "Please do not preside," Otto begged. "It would be a grave mistake for you to do so. You are a very positive person, and the office of chairman demands a conciliatory temperament.[41] Otto's judgment ultimately came to be shared by others, and much to his relief, Wise found himself on the floor as a delegate, with a major and active role to play when the conference opened on March 26. A total of 367 delegates from 83 cities and 28 states attended, representing more than one million American Jews. After Nathan Straus called the gathering to order, he called on Wise to deliver the keynote address.

In a rousing speech on "American Israel and Democracy," Wise declared that the creation of the congress marked a new day for American Jewry, one which would be characterized by democracy and equality. Criticizing those who would deny to the Jewish community the "substance of democracy," he asserted that the people "are resolved to be free of their masters whether these be malevolent tyrants without, or benevolent despots within. . . . Let it be said that whatever may have been the necessities of the past, the time is come for a leadership by us to be chosen, a leadership that shall democratically and wisely lead rather than autocratically command.'' As he sat down, the delegates roared to their feet, shouting and whistling and clapping, until the chairman finally gavelled them back to order.

During the next two days, Wise rarely left the floor of the conference, constantly talking to the other delegates, soothing ruffled feelings, proposing compromises over minor as well as major issues. When a national executive committee of seventy was chosen, a number of people objected that their town or city had no representative. Wise calmly pointed out that seventy people could not represent all three million American Jews, but it was the best they could do for now. He urged the dissidents to accept the proposals in a spirit of harmony, and the resolution unaminously passed. Many people now wanted him to serve as chairman of the executive committee, a proposal he wasted no time in vetoing both publicly and privately. When it came time for the conference to adjourn, Wise again took the podium to commend the spirit and actions of his colleagues, for their actions had proven American Jewry ready and able to exercise democracy in determining its own future. "We have named our goals," he declared "and now it lies in the hands of God and our own will to reach those goals. May this day mark the dawn of a new era for a greater, nobler, freer Israel.[42]

Congress adherents now redoubled their efforts to bring new organizations into the movement. Wise and his colleagues spoke to B'nai B'rith and other fraternal groups which, one after another, joined the congress bandwagon. The American Jewish Committee found its position undermined every way it turned. The *American Israelite*, which normally endorsed AJC policies, admitted that the congress "is the greatest movement, numerically, that has ever occurred in this country, and perhaps any other. None other has ever received such wide-spread support."[43] In June, three members of the American Jewish Committee, including Harry Friedenwald, one of its founders, resigned in protest against the Committee's antidemocratic stance, especially its opposition to the congress. Groups that had previously affiliated with the Committee broke those ties and then announced their support of the proposed congress.

Within the Committee, Marshall, Schiff, and their colleagues finally recognized that the congress movement could not be stopped, and set about saving what they could of their leadership in the Jewish community. While democratic elections would surely mean they no longer controlled events, even worse was the possibility of their becoming leaders of a minority faction. So they chose a strategy of emphasizing "unity" among American Jews. They recognized, as did Wise and Brandeis, that the American Jewish Committee represented a powerful segment of the community, a segment that could not be ignored by a truly democratic and representative congress. Indeed, throughout the fight no one had ever suggested that the *yahudim* should be excluded from Jewish affairs, but merely that they would have to share power with others. The Committee now decided to go along with the congress, and on June 16, invited congress officials and representatives of other organizations to a meeting one month later at the Hotel Astor in New York to discuss the issue. At the gathering the Committee not only salvaged its defeat, but achieved a certain victory.

Brandeis led the congress delegation to the meeting, and soon realized that a trap had been set. Committee members, with Louis Marshall presiding benignly, attacked the newly confirmed Supreme Court justice for his arbitrary manner in refusing to compromise, and suggested that it was beneath his dignity as a judge, and certainly offensive to the honor of the court, to have him participating in such free-for-alls. The next day the *New York Times* carried a sanctimonious editorial praising Brandeis's integrity but regretting that he had to bear the brunt of the attack directed against his colleagues.[44] What Wise and others had feared most now came to pass. Without consulting any of the Zionist or congress leaders, Brandeis resigned all his offices in the Joint Distribution Committee, the American Jewish Relief Committee, the Provisional Committee, and the Jewish Congress Organizing Committee, of which he was honorary chairman. "There is at least this compensation," he told Hugo Pam. "My enforced withdrawal did not come until after the triumph of the congress movement has been assured, and the desired unity of the Jews of America has been made possible." A horrified Wise telegraphed Brandeis that he was "shocked and pained" and that the resignation "would undo congress victory and assure triumph to the foes of democracy. . . . Your faithful associates," he pleaded, "have right to expect such eventful decision will be held in abeyance until after conference with them." But Brandeis would not be budged, nor would he meet with anyone to discuss the matter.[45]

Moreover, recognizing that continued fighting among Jews could only bring harm, Brandeis resolved to compromise with Marshall. Ironically, the private meetings between these two men did bring the Committee around to accepting the congress, but they occurred in a manner redolent of the secrecy which Brandeis for so long had attacked. Marshall agreed to a congress, but one that would be temporary with a limited program. There would be democratic elections, but to ensure organizational representation, 25 percent of the seats would be reserved for national Jewish bodies. The Committee thus conceded much, but it also won much. By limiting the congress to a temporary body dealing with war-related issues, the Committee might yet emerge after the war with its power intact. Brandeis had great difficulty forcing his followers to accept the agreement. The Yiddish press damned the arrangement, and many of the Zionist leaders lost heart. A discouraged Wise, still angry over Brandeis's abrupt resignation, refused to participate in the negotiations. Wise, Horace Kallen, Bernard Richards, and others lamented to one another the loss of Brandeis's leadership and his seeming abandonment of the principles for which they had fought so long and so hard. "Our people," said Kallen, "have sold our birthright for a mess of pottage."[46]

Yet for all their anger and self-pity, there is little doubt that Brandeis acted correctly, in substance if not in style. Although trapped at the Hotel Astor meeting, his new role of associate justice would have, at some time, required him to give up his extrajudicial activities. It is a measure of his devotion to Zionism and the congress that he retained his posts in Jewish organizations long after he had resigned from secular reform groups. While he might have avoided some bitter feelings had he met with Wise and the others before announcing his decision, in the end he could have decided no other way. Similarly, his agreement with the American Jewish Committee might have conceded less, but not significantly, and he realized that once in the congress the Committee would be bound by its actions, a not unimportant consideration.

Within a few months of this summer tempest, work on the American Jewish Congress was well underway. By December 1916, 140 delegates representing a real cross-section of American Jewry met to work out the administrative and procedural methods for electing a congress the following spring. As Brandeis anticipated, the Zionists easily outvoted the *yahudim*, and elected Nathan Straus over Louis Marshall as permanent chairman. Plans were set for the congress to convene no later than September 1917, and Wise and his colleagues had begun to appreciate the wisdom of Brandeis's action when suddenly, once again, events completely upset everyone's plans. In April 1917 the United States, which had carefully maintained its neutrality for more than two and half years, entered the world war on the side of the Allies.

10

War . . .

The war that erupted in Europe in August 1914 killed not only millions of men, women, and children, but humanity's dream of a world free from the scourge of battle. It had been nearly a hundred years since the Napoleonic wars, a century that, although marked by minor skirmishes from time to time, had seemed to be reaching toward a sense of international community. The dream of progressive reformers included the vision of a world in which disputes between nations would be settled in a civilized manner, by recourse to mediation or binding arbitration. Secretary of State William Jennings Bryan had, in fact, negotiated a number of bilateral arbitration agreements before the assassination of the Austrian archduke ignited the general conflagration.

Wise had been but one of many progressives who believed that war would disappear in the onward march of progress and reason. In 1912 he had opposed universal military education of school-age children, and lauded a proposal for an international congress of all the religious groups to work for peace. He praised the efforts of writer-traveler George Kennan to inform Americans about Asian civilization, so that they would stop thinking of non-white groups as inferior, useful only for colonization and exploitation. Time and again he lectured his congregation on the need of powerful nations to pursue peace. "In the matter of international relations," he declared, "a democracy must lift itself to the level of the highest moral obligation. Whether it be true or not that a King can do no wrong, a democracy will do wrong unless it will do the right."[1] When in the spring of 1914 it appeared as if the United States might go to war with Mexico over that nation's internal affairs, Wise averred that Wilson could easily "lose the support of the thinking men and women of the nation" if war came. After the occupation of Vera Cruz, however, Wilson and Bryan accepted the offer of three Latin American countries to mediate, and the White House sent Wise a message that "there will be no war." He read the note to his congregation, which burst into applause, and he then lauded Wilson as a "noble stateman . . . who will prevent any war." Because of this "promise of peace," Wise exclaimed, "my cup of joy is overflowing."[2]

Only a few months later, the nightmare of war descended over Europe. In neutral America some citizens backed the Allies, others defended Germany, and still another group loathed the conflict and feared possible American involvement. Wise favored the Allies, but feared that militarists in the United States would drag the country into the fray. "We anti-militarists must more than ever have the courage of our convictions," he told George Foster Peabody. "We must not suffer any compromise hereafter. Whether we like it or not we must oppose the big navy policy and it will not be easy to do that." Late in 1914, together with a number of other reformers including John Holmes, Paul Kellogg, Lillian Wald, Florence Kelley, Max Eastman, and Jane Addams, Wise helped found the Anti-Preparedness Committee, which later grew into the American Union against Militarism. The Union represented, according to Miss Wald, "conservative Quakerism, socialism, the church, the press, literature and social work."[3] It included, in fact, nearly every shade of antiwar thought in the country; some of its members would later go to jail rather than support American involvement while others, like Wise, would change their minds after April 1917. But in the intervening years, Wise made many speeches for the Union in opposition to those calling for a larger army or navy.

In late 1914, however, Woodrow Wilson remained firm in his desire to keep the United States out of the conflict. He ignored Theodore Roosevelt, Augustus Gardner, and other early advocates of "preparedness," and in his annual message to Congress reaffirmed the nation's historic position of neutrality vis-à-vis European disputes, "We shall not alter our attitude," he vowed, "because some amongst us are nervous and excited." This was the word pacifists had hoped for, and Wise immediately wrote Wilson praising him for this brave and noble stand. "You have made it not only easier," he said, "but a more joyous task to hold before the minds of the people those ideals which your Administration has done much to vitalize." Wilson, under attack from the preparedness advocates, gratefully acknowledged such support from Wise and other friends.[4]

Throughout 1915, Wise kept up his attacks on those who wanted to push America into combat. Time and again he preached on the urgent need for peace rather than war. "The business of democracy," he declared, "is not to wage war. There is no room in democracy for war and military ideals." Instead of preparing to fight, he urged, let the nation prepare for peace, to shake itself free of the jingoists and the armaments advocates, and back the president in his efforts to bring an end to the slaughter in Europe.[5] Before a large student rally at Columbia University, he urged schools "not to move our youth to share those dreams of military glory which in their results are proving an unutterable curse to European lands," and he rejoiced when Wilson's "Lusitania" notes proved successful in reducing German-American tensions and averting war.[6]

At this time one could not characterize Stephen Wise as an extreme pacifist, as was his close friend Holmes, who utterly rejected the option of war under any circumstance. In 1911, for example, Wise had warned the Free Synagogue that one should not become a "peace at any price" advocate in a sermon, taking as his text "Crying peace when there is no peace." One could not "barter away the immediate jewel of the soul, not so much for peace as for that spurious thing which Milton calls ignoble ease and peaceful sloth. . . . The work of peace is not always righteousness." But if a nation ultimately had to go to war, it nonetheless should resist provocation to do so until only the most compelling reasons remained why young men had to fight and die. In his 1915 Rosh Hashonah sermon, he praised Wilson for recognizing this truth, and despite the personal calumny heaped upon the president by the warmongers and preparedness champions, remaining true to the vision of peace. Wise admitted that German conduct had placed a "severe strain on the patience of a patient people," but urged that America not plunge into a war because of "a people reft for a time of the power of national self-mastery."[7]

This situation, however, deteriorated when Wilson, for security and political reasons, took the first steps toward putting the nation on a more effective defense status. As Congress prepared to convene in December 1915, Wilson made preparedness the chief objective of his legislative program, calling for increases in naval and military appropriations and other measures. The president believed, as did a number of his advisors, that a submarine war with Germany was not only possible but perhaps inevitable. And, as Wise recognized, political considerations, the necessity to undercut Theodore Roosevelt and others critical of the country's alleged military weaknesses, also played a role in Wilson's decision. "I think it must be said," Wise wrote to Henry Morgenthau, "that if Wilson had dared to come out against military preparedness at this time, Roosevelt might have swept the country on a military preparedness platform. But we must pay a terrible price in order to avert the Roosevelt bogie. For the first time I find myself actively unable to agree with and support the President. You may be sure that I may say so and in no uncertain terms."[8]

This he did in an anguished letter to Wilson on November 12:[9]

> From time to time during the last two years it has been my privilege to write to you in order to express my agreement with the things you have said and done. I therefore regard it as my duty to tell you how deeply I deplore the necessity under which you have found yourself of accepting and advocating a preparedness program. Up to the last moment I had hoped that against the preparedness campaign you might throw the weight not only of your great of-

fice but of your equally great hold upon the respect of the whole people. I have felt, as have many others among your friends, that if you had found it possible to stand out the people, having learned to trust your wise and just judgment, would have been ready to follow your leadership as they have done since the beginning of the war. . . .

I should not, my dear Mr. President, have written in this way nor would I burden you with my thoughts and questions if I did not feel in conscience bound to dissent in pulpit and on platform from your position. I regret this not only on personal grounds but because I believe that issues of deepest moment are at stake touching which you will not expect that even the most revering of friends should remain silent.

Wilson's response a few days later indicated that he would not back down, but admitted the distress he felt over having to differ with some of his friends. Despite these differences, however, he hoped that he and Wise could continue to be friends and respect each other's views.[10]

The preparedness idea gained momentum, and Wise found the cause of peace losing ground both in the government and among the public.[11] The president stumped the country in early 1916 in support of his legislative package, and the pacifists found their position eroding. The National Defense Act of 1916 expanded the National Guard, brought it under greater federal control, and also increased the size of the regular army. Congress authorized huge increases in the navy over a three-year period and also created the United States Shipping Board with a $50 million appropriation to build, purchase, or lease merchant ships. "I am discouraged about the whole situation at Washington," Wise lamented. "I think some of us will simply have to face the necessity of taking an utterly uncompromising position. It is the only position we can take and be true to such light as is given." When a huge preparedness parade took place in New York in mid-May, he was one of only two clergyman in the city to condemn it.[12]

But while opposing the president's preparedness program, Wise did not oppose the president, especially Wilson's bid for re-election in 1916. In some ways, this undercut his ability to take "an utterly uncompromising position," for if he supported Wilson generally, his criticism of preparedness would have to be muted. Moreover, since he believed that Wilson was sincerely trying to keep the nation out of war, he could not be too harsh in his judgment of the man. Despite occasional talk of a third-party peace movement by Wise and others, the accomplishments of the administration in terms of reform and commitment to social justice could not be denied. Despite the terrible outlook for Wilson early in the year, Wise felt that by November the American people would recognize the president's great service to the cause of progressivism as well as to peace.[13]

Wise, together with Amos Pinchot, helped organize the Wilson

Volunteers, a group of progressives, many of them former Republicans, who now endorsed the Democratic Wilson over the GOP candidate, Charles Evans Hughes, and then campaigned in the Northeast for Wilson. "I was for Hughes as Governor and I stood by his side," Wise declared, "but it would be a great mistake to elect him President of the United States now. He has revealed an amazing lack of vision regarding the problems and the tasks and difficulties which face us."[14] The Republican Party, Wise charged had become an instrument of privilege, and had thus driven him and other "disgusted Republicans" to support Wilson "because of the enemies he had made . . . and because he had made a good job out of [his term in office]." Shortly after Wilson squeaked out his electoral victory, Wise wrote to a friend: "Heartfelt congratulations of each of us to the other on Wilson's re-election. It means a great deal to us, a great deal to democracy and a tremendous deal with respect to the Jewish interest . . . The way may now prove open in the next four years to still greater distinction of the chief."[15]

In the months following the election both Wise and Wilson, each in his own way, worked desparately to keep the United States out of the war, but it was evident in their words, both public and private, that they saw American involvement as inevitable, a mere question of time. The rabbi's "utterly uncompromising position" slowly gave way to a pragmatic, even fatalistic view of world affairs. In February 1917, as Germany stepped up its U-boat campaign, Wise spoke at Cornell University and at the Free Synagogue about the "necessity of doing battle against the graver of two evils, the lesser being war and the graver Prussianism."[16] He called upon German-Americans to try to influence the Kaiser's government to desist from its war-like acts of provocation, and gradually he moved to the point where the *New York Times* could describe him as "a worker for world peace but not an extreme pacifist." He told a crowd in the latter part of March that "we are on the verge of war. I pray God it may not come, but if it does the blame will not rest upon us, but upon German militarism." Right to the last, he continued to praise Woodrow Wilson for all he had done to avert American involvement in the fray.[17]

But where some of the anti-preparedness advocates slowly tempered their stand because of the changing international scene, others grew more rigid in their total and unremitting opposition to war. At meetings of the American Union against Militarism, former allies and friends began hurling accusations against one another, and in the end Wise felt he had to resign. The climax came when he read portions of a sermon he planned to deliver to explain his change of mind to his congregation, and he asked the Union members what they thought of it. Perspiration ran down his face as Crystal Eastman, Lillian Wald, Amos Pinchot, Norman Thomas, and others flayed what they saw as his abandonment of the true faith. They reminded him that at a large pacifist rally in early 1916, he had told the overflow audience that he had brought his son to hear him say that no matter who else supported the war, he never would. Oswald Garrison Villard declared that Wise had once written the finest tribute to his grandfather, William Lloyd Garrison, that had yet been published, and that Wise had pledged his allegiance to Garrison's nonresistant doctrine. If Wise delivered the sermon, Villard promised, he would never speak to him again.[18]

On Monday, April 2, 1917, Woodrow Wilson walked into the chamber of the House of Representatives to address a specially convened joint session of Congress. Armed neutrality, he declared, was no longer possible, and there was no choice but to recognize the fact that the actions of the Imperial German Government in recent months constituted war against the United States. The American people would now respond, he promised, but it would not fight for profits or territory or conquest, but for the rights of man. "The world must be made safe for democracy. Its peace must be planted upon the tested foundations of political liberty . . . It is a fearful thing to lead this great peaceful people into war, into the most terrible and disastrous of all wars, civilization itself seeming to hang in the balance. But the right is more precious than peace, and we shall fight for the things which we have always carried nearest our hearts—for democracy, for the right of those who submit to authority to have a voice in their own Governments, for the rights of small nations, for a universal dominion of right by such a concert of free peoples as shall bring peace and safety to all nations and make the world itself free at last." It was a magnificent speech, and even Wilson's bitterest foes conceded that he had epitomized all that was fine and noble in the American spirit. As members of Congress cheered, a somber and sad Wilson slowly left the hall.[18]

The following Sunday, April 8, Wise rose in the Free Synagogue pulpit; it was draped in an American flag which, he said, would remain there until "the morning of the dawn of peace for humanity." His words that day reveal the inner turmoil of many pacifists who now felt they had to support not war, but this war, a war to make the world safe for democracy. He reiterated his abhorrence of war, his antipathy toward militarism, and his firm belief that war, no matter how noble its aims, was the most terrible of earth's sorrows. For Wilson he had nothing but praise, terming the president's war message "the world's Magna Carta, spoken for peoples of every race and faith and tongue." He called upon his congregation and the American people to forget past differences and to unite in this great crusade. In the midst of this plea for unity, however, Wise proudly and bravely referred to his friend and fellow founder of American Union against Militarism:[20]

I would refer today to my pride, yea more than pride, in the word and action of a friend, honored and cherished, the minister of the Unitarian Church of the Messiah of this city, one of the bravest and noblest preachers of our time.

We are not of one mind touching this war, though for years we have been antimilitarist fellow-workers. He has taken the perhaps more uncompromising position that war is never justified and that non-resistance must be the rule of life for individuals and nations from which there can be no departure without compromise and without sin. Nothing could be more splendid than his courage, unless it be the fine determination of the people of his church, even though they are not at one with him, not to suffer any denial of his freedom of utterance within their pulpit. Prussianism is become the shame and confusion of the great German people because of its insistence that all men shall think alike and speak alike, because of its insistence upon the regimentation of the intellectual and spiritual life of the people. I thank God for the consequences-scorning nobleness of a minister of religion, ready to lay down his office and to brave the frowns of the world rather than compromise with the truth as God gives it to him to see the truth. But the congregation of the Church of the Messiah matches the nobleness of its leader, for, though it does not stand with him any more than I do in non-resistant neutrality toward this war, it sets a new standard for the liberty of the pulpit to which it is the abiding distinction of John Haynes Holmes to have given a new honor and a new glory.

These words have a special poignancy, for they not only reveal the depth of Wise's friendship, love, and respect for Holmes, but also a wistfulness, possibly a yearning that Holmes could stand so firmly for a principle which he, Wise, had once so strongly espoused. Many of Wise's former colleagues in the peace movement could forgive him for the change of mind, at least at first, because in this sermon and other talks he acknowledged the sincerity and integrity of those still opposed to war. When he resigned from the Union against Militarism, he told Lillian Wald that the union's members must do their work as he felt he must do his, and she responded that "perhaps you will agree with more things that are promoted through the Union than you disagree with. You know that your colleagues will welcome you should you, after further consideration, find this to be true."[21]

But eventually mutual respect gave way to mutual antagonism, as Wise, convinced of the righteousness of the cause, began to attack those still opposing the war. He condemned antiwar senator Robert M. LaFollette as playing into German hands for political reasons, and declared LaFollette "did not know the Prussian mood as I know it through repeated visits to the Old World." A tone of strident denunciation crept into his various talks around the country in which he condemned those who still adhered to pacifism as fools and scoundrels. "They can do little for peace and democracy," he charged, "who speak and act with regard to the war as if two bands of ruffians were causelessly scrimmaging in the streets, as if nothing more were at stake than the outcome of a futile struggle between two equally guilty war groups. They can do little either for peace and democracy who are indifferent to the origin of a war, which is nothing else than a mightily organized assault upon the right of the lesser peoples to choose their own way of life instead of having it made in Germany for them.''[22]

This turnabout was not one of Stephen Wise's finer moments, and it soured relations between him and a number of former friends for years to come. One can, perhaps, explain his behavior—his love of America, his faith and trust in Woodrow Wilson, his opposition to Prussian militarism, and his perpetual tendency to see everything in terms of absolute right and wrong. To explain, however, is not to justify, although his intolerance in this case was matched by those every bit as fanatical in defense of their beliefs as he was of his. But unlike the majority favoring the war, Wise drew a careful distinction between the brutal policies of the German government and the German people. He attacked the "Hun," but did not read the German people out of the human race. He never succumbed to the war-induced hysteria that branded all those somewhat different in their political or economic beliefs as alien or un-American. And Wise also did not abandon the cause of reform after April 1917.

The war, as several scholars have noted, did not end reform but accelerated activity, and in some cases victory, for specific causes. Wise's speeches during 1917 and 1918 certainly reflected this ongoing concern. He urged the administration to establish an insurance program for servicemen, spoke out for woman suffrage and equal rights for Negroes. He also went on extensive speaking tours to rally support for the war effort and took the opportunity to endorse international as well as internal application of progressive reform ideals.[23]

In the midst of his public activity, Wise tried not to neglect his family, although the many demands on his time often kept him away from home. Whenever possible, he took Louise with him, but she had war work to do, together with managing the Child Adoption Service. Jim, caught up by the patriotic fervor, wanted to enlist but was turned away because of his age. A freshman at Princeton and a member of the ROTC there, he pestered his parents continuously for their permission to join the army. Wise wondered whether Jim really wanted to serve or merely wanted to escape the classroom grind. Learning that a shipyard in Connecticut need unskilled laborers, Wise proposed that he and Jim spend their summer vacation working in the yard, and if Jim still wanted to join the army at the end of the summer, he could have his parents' assent.

The Wises took a small cottage in Stanford, and every day Stephen, Jim and some of Jim's friends from college went to work at Shippen Point. The labor was not easy, but Wise welcomed the chance to lose some weight and build up his stamina and muscle tone. All told, they spent six weeks working from 7:00 A.M. to 4:30 P.M. for the daily wage of three dollars. Wise's identity remained unknown to his fellow-workers until a telegram arrived one day asking him to address a meeting in Washington. Newspaper reporters and photographers soon converged on the yard, snapping away and asking his fellow workers about Wise. The men were uniform in their praise, calling Wise a "good scout" and "the youngest old man" they ever saw, one who "doesn't spare himself in the least." "There are no frills to him," said one co-worker, "and he puts on no airs. His son is a good deal like his daddy."

On his last day, the rest of the workers gathered at the gate to bid him farewell, and asked him to give a speech. "Boys," he said, "may I not feel in all the years to come that you will think of me as your friend? We cannot tell what is going to happen to any of us so if ever the occasion should arise and you think you need a friend, won't you come to regard 'No. 186' as your friend?" Interrupted by frequent applause Wise recounted the story of why he had gone to work in the shipyard, and how much he had learned about workingmen and their thoughts. "I have always respected men who work with their hands," he said. "I respect them more than ever today."

After some comments about supporting the president and the war program, he held up his wages for four weeks worth of work, which amounted to $76.13, and asked the men whether he should give it to the Red Cross or to a workshop fund. The laborers unanimously urged him to give it to the Red Cross, so he turned and handed the envelope to Louise to forward to the Red Cross. The next day Jim returned to Princeton, with his parents' permission to enlist in the army in December, when he would turn 17. By then, however, the war had ended.[24]

The war years thus found Wise in a positon of influence both in the Jewish and non-Jewish worlds, and especially in the field of Zionist endeavor, it would be hard to find a time when his labors would again prove so fruitful. For Jewish leaders in general, the war from the start had held out the tantalizing vision of a new order in Europe, one in which the shackles of discrimination and persecution would be struck away. The Zionists however, had little hope at first other than that a neutral America might prevail upon Turkey to allow the Palestinian settlements to receive aid. Because the Sublime Porte was allied with Germany, American Zionists, whatever their sympathies in the war, took great care to emphasize their friendliness toward Turkey and their lack of any designs upon Palestine. Wise asked his friend Ambassador Henry Morgenthau to assure the Turks that the Zionists wished no harm to the Ottoman Empire and desired nothing more than for the settlements to exist peacefully under Turkish rule.[25] The Provisional Committee offficially declared that "Zionism is not a movement to wrest from the Turks the sovereignty of Palestine." As late as February 1917, Wise was still warning his colleagues that Jews in the Holy Land remained hostage to Turkish whims, and that Zionist leaders, even if they denounced Prussian autocracy, had to be careful not to offend the sultan.[26]

Once the United States had entered the conflict, the situation grew even more complex for the Zionists. On the one hand, Congress had declared war against Germany but not against Turkey, and the Wilson administration wanted to preserve neutral relations with the Ottomans. At the same time, no one doubted that the Allies, if victorious, would carve up the Turkish Empire, and Palestine's future would rest in the hands of Britain, France, and possibly the United States. A few days after America entered the war, Wise went to Washington to meet with Colonel Edward M. House, Wilson's confidant and advisor on foreign affairs, in order to explore the administration's views. House proved far more encouraging than Wise had expected, immediately grasping the possibilities of a new order in the Middle East. Perhaps England could trade concessions with France and Russia, House suggested, in order to get control of Palestine. Moreover, he hinted, one should not discount the possibility of an American protectorate over the Holy Land. An excited Wise reported that "things could hardly be better from our point of view," and he optimistically predicted that the British army would in all likelihood soon occupy Palestine.[27] It would be another eight months, however, before General Allenby's troops marched into Jerusalem, eight months of frantic activity by Zionist leaders in which old plans and assumptions would have to be rethought and in some instances radically altered.

The first matter to be dealt with was the American Jewish Congress, which had been scheduled to convene in September 1917. American entry into the war brought renewed protests from the *yahudim* that a Congress meeting during the war would only pose new dangers to Jewish interests. Henry Morgenthau urged Secretary of State Robert Lansing to prevail upon Justice Brandeis to abandon the Congress until peace arrived, while Simon Wolf announced publicly that administration officials had told him that the Congress would be disastrous to American Jewry. On June 29, Wise went to the White House to find out whether the president in fact had any strong views on the Congress issue. Wilson assured Wise that in principle he did not object to the Congress, but that many of his advisors questioned the timing of its meeting. He himself wondered whether it might better serve all their interests if the Congress were not canceled but delayed until the war situation became clearer. Wise had met with Brandeis shortly before, and the two Zionist leaders had anticipated that this might be Wilson's response. They understood that the main problem of the American Jewish Congress would not be a discussion of Jewish rights in Europe, but of the future of Palestine. It would be almost impossible to prevent that subject from coming up at the Congress, and it was understandable why, with the United States neutral *vis-à-vis* Turkey, the State Department feared such a public debate. Wise had written out a statement which he gave to Wilson, and the president, after making a few minor changes, authorized the rabbi to give it out to the press. Upon emerging from the Oval Office, Wise told reporters:[28]

> A contrary impression having gained currency, I am authorized to say that the President has learned with interest of the proposed American Jewish Congress. While it may seem necessary to the gentlemen who have called the Congress to postpone it for some little time from the date fixed—September 2—because of the urgency at this time of public business, the President is persuaded that the American Jewish Congress will wisely and prudently serve Jewish interests, and that its deliberations and policies will be in accord with and helpful to the aims and policies of the American Government.

Jacob Schiff and other opponents of the Congress were delighted, and read into the presidential statement their own hopes that the Congress would never meet.[29] Wise recognized this, and despite Wilson's endorsement of the principle of the Congress, knew that unless some sort of activity could be maintained until the end of the war, the masses would lose heart. He would have preferred to hold the session, but one could not say no to the president. Horace Kallen, like many others, saw the postponement as one more example of Jews failing to stand up for their rights. "The Congress should be held," Kallen declared. "The failure to hold it will mean disaster to us and our shame before the whole of the American people. It will be a breaking of our pledge and . . . . that is the one thing that cannot be done." As Wise reported to Brandeis after a meeting of the large Congress executive, "I am sorry to say that all our Zionists were against us, Lipsky and Rosenblatt making strong speeches against postponement." Ironically, Wise had found himself allied with Louis Marshall arguing for restraint. Although the committee finally voted to delay the Congress, Wise felt little elation. "I have really come to mourn over the necessity," he wrote Kallen, "but we saw no other way out. Now as far as possible we must repair the hurt which we have had to do for our own cause."[30]

For Wise, of course, this meant adding one more item to the roster of subjects he dealt with in his increasingly frequent speeches. In fact, when Brandeis had suggested earlier in the year that Wise devote an entire month strictly to Congress fund-raising, Stephen uncharacteristically retorted that he had no more time for anything, that he was already working full-time and more on each of several tasks.[31] Wise actually tried to reduce this load in the spring, suggesting that Dr. Harry Friedenwald of Baltimore take over the chairmanship of the Provisional Committee. When Brandeis heard of this, he called Wise down to Washington and in his most persuasive and charming manner appealed to him to stay at the head of American Zionism, at least until the proposed reorganization of the movement could be effected. Richard Gottheil and others also pressed Wise to stay on for, besides Brandeis, he alone had the prestige necessary to lead the organization. Wise reluctantly agreed, but insisted that once the reorganization took place, either Judge Julian Mack or Professor Felix Frankfurter would have to take over.[32]

One reason why Rabbi Stephen Wise the public man undoubtedly felt such pressure during these months is that his mother, now eighty-one, had grown increasingly ill, and the responsibility for her care fell entirely on his shoulders. During the summer and fall of 1917, Sabine Wise's condition deteriorated, and her son tried to spend as much time as possible with her until the end came on November 28. Ironically, this personal sorrow had as a counterpoint great joy for both Wise and the Zionist movement.

In 1904 Herzel, in his last meeting with the young Wise, had suggested that "it is from and through England that salvation will come to our people." Now in 1917 Herzl's prophecy appeared to come true, for as British troops moved across the Sinai and up into Palestine, His Majesty's Government put the final touches on a statement about the future of the Holy Land. While a great deal has been written about the Balfour Declaration, the role of American Zionists in its evolution is often overlooked. No one suggests other than that the majority of the credit rightly belongs to Chaim Weizmann and his colleagues in London, but because the British War Cabinet did not want to act without Woodrow Wilson's approval, the final steps could not have been taken without American Zionist intervention.[33]

British motives behind the Balfour Declaration have been the subject of an endless debate, but a few things are clear. First, Great Britain wanted to protect its imperial lifeline to the East, the Suez Canal, by extending its power east of Egypt into Palestine. At the same time, it hoped to check French ambitions of spreading Gallic influence south from Lebanon. A third factor involved the real or imagined influence of Jewish opinion in the United States and elsewhere, which looked askance at the wartime alliance of liberal, democratic England with reactionary, autocratic Russia. By promising Palestine to the Jews after the war, British policymakers believed that Jewish support for the Allies supposedly could be strengthened and a similar plan by the Germans forestalled. Finally, a form of Christian Zionism had existed in Britain among members of the upper class since the 1830s; there was a belief that God had indeed promised the Holy Land to the Jews and that this promise ought to be honored by man.

While Chaim Weizmann lobbied in London, American Zionists with no knowledge of his activities also began discussing the possibility of Britain taking over Palestine and allowing Jews to settle there. At a meeting with Colonel House in late January 1917, even before American entry into the war, Wise presented a memorandum which he, Brandeis, and Felix Frankfurter had prepared, outlining a possible British policy for Palestine. At their conference in April, House proved even more receptive to this idea. By the late spring, Wise and others within the Zionist leadership had learned of Weizmann's activities, and were eagerly discussing the possibility. "The British Government," Wise said, "has always for centuries been most friendly to Jews. I think that the feeling of Jews everywhere, save possibly in the enemy countries, is one of gratitude and affection for Great Britain. I know I have always hoped and prayed that there might come to pass a Jewish commonwealth in Palestine under the British flag." When Wise went to the White House on June 29 to talk to Wilson about the American Jewish Congress, he also broached the subject of a possible British statement. The president reminded Wise that he had always had a "deep interest in Zionism," a fact which the rabbi said greatly assured Zionist leaders. "Whenever the time comes," Wilson said, "and you and Justice Brandeis feel that the time is ripe for me to speak and act, I shall be ready."[34]

That time came in September, and despite Wilson's pledge, his action almost aborted the British plan. A draft of the proposed statement had been forwarded by Whitehall to the American president for his comments, and Wilson, preoccupied by sagging war production, had almost offhandedly said he thought the war situation too unsettled for a strong declaration. Wilson's response threw the British War Cabinet and English Zionists into a dither. Chaim Weizmann fired off cable after cable to Brandeis imploring him to do something, anything, before the Jewish people lost this great opportunity. Brandeis and Wise met with Colonel House to explain the importance of Wilson's approval, which they secured before the end of October. Wise and Jacob deHaas also edited the proposal to read "a national home for the Jewish people" instead of "a national home for Jews," the latter phrase a red flag sure to infuriate non-Zionists. A few days later, November 2, 1917, Arthur James Balfour forwarded a note to James Lord Rothschild, informing him that His Majesty's Government would do all it could to establish a Jewish homeland in Palestine. The charter which Theodor Hertzl had called for twenty years earlier had been secured.[35]

News of the declaration, followed by Allenby's dramatic capture of Jerusalem, stunned most American Jews, who had received few hints in advance. At first no one seemed able to believe it, but as the realization sank in, expressions of joy and approval abounded in the Jewish press: "The daily prayers of Israel for the restoration of Zion have at last been answered." "The greatest occurrence in modern Jewish history." "There is joy this day in Israel. Shout it in the ear of every fellow Jew." Among the Yiddish papers only *Der Morgen-Journal*, reflecting ultra-Orthodox opinion, expressed reservations. *Dos Yiddishe Folk* declared that "for the first time in 2,000 years, we again enter the arena of world history as a nation."[36]

New York Jews celebrated the event with a great parade, with Wise and Nathan Straus marching at the head. That evening thousands crowded into a Carnegie Hall festooned with American, British, and Zionist flags, while several thousand more listened to the speeches and songs on loudspeakers outside the building. Wise reminded them that in 1914 the German chancellor had dismissed the nonaggression treaty on Belgium as "a scrap of paper." Holding a copy of the Balfour Declaration, Wise declared that it too was only a scrap of paper, "but it is written in English. It is signed by the British Government and therefore is sacred and inviolable. . . . It is true to the finest traditions of the British people, and is a symbol of the will of the Allies to right wrongs, however ancient, to undo injustice, however hoary, to supplant the Prussian ideal of rule by might with the changelessly true principle of justice and right. It will always be honored in the observance, not the breach." Writing thirty years later, after Great Britain had reneged on its promises and six million Jews had died, many of them because they could not enter the homeland promised by England, Wise wrote in his memoirs: "I was wrong, and I quote that sentence all the more readily because of the bitter tension today between the British government and the Jewish people. Whatever may happen today, the fact uncancellable remains that it was England which, in the Cromwellian tradition and by the Balfour Declaration, was the first nation after more than eighteen hundred years, since the year 70 A.D., to recognize 'the Jewish people.' "[37]

But while Woodrow Wilson had privately approved the Balfour Declaration, he refrained from a public endorsement at the urging of Secretary of State Robert Lansing. The State Department continuously reminded Wilson that the United States had not declared war against Turkey, and it would be inappropriate to approve the postwar disposition of Ottoman lands. The Secretary, personally opposed to the whole Zionist idea, also pointed out that not all Jews favored restoration, while many "Christian sects and individuals would undoubtedly resent turning the Holy Land over to the absolute control of the race credited with the death of Christ." Moreover, the president in his famous "Fourteen Points" speech in January 1918 had called for no annexation of territory and the principle of self-determination, both of which were violated by the Balfour Declaration.[38]

Brandeis and Wise recognized Wilson's problem, and throughout the spring and summer of 1918 worked to convince him of the political and moral need to indicate his approval. Finally, Wise suggested that Rosh Hashonah, the Jewish New Year, might be an appropriate time for a presidential statement, and Wilson, for reasons still unclear, agreed. On August 31, the president sent a letter to the chairman of the Provisional Committee:[39]

My dear Rabbi Wise:

I have watched with deep and sincere interest the reconstructive work which the Weizmann Commission has done in Palestine at the instance of the British Government, and I welcome the opportunity to express the satisfaction I have felt in the progress of the Zionist movement in the United States and the Allied countries since the declaration of Mr. Balfour on behalf of the British Government, of Great Britain's approval of the establishment in Palestine of a national home for the Jewish people, and his promise that the British Goverment would use its best endeavors to facilitate the achievement of that object, with the understanding that nothing would be done to prejudice the civil and religious rights of non-Jewish people in Palestine or the rights and political status enjoyed by Jews in other countries. I think that all America will be deeply moved by the report that even in this time of stress the Weizmann Commission has been able to lay the foundation of the Hebrew University of Jerusalem with the promise that that bears of spiritual rebirth.

Wise's fellow Zionists were delighted with his having secured the president's statement. "The nations of the world," exalted Felix Frankfurter. "no less than the people of Israel, will arise and call you blessed." Letters from rabbis and laymen poured in on both Wise and Wilson, praising the statement. Some Reform rabbis resented the message and that it had gone to Wise, and he suspected that the American Jewish Committee was less than happy that the president had dealt with the Zionists rather than with it.[40]

The Balfour Declaration and American endorsement of it undoubtedly marked high points of Zionist activity during the war, but they should not obscure the fact that Wise presided over and took an active role in the basic restructuring and reorganization of the Zionist movement in America. Louis Brandeis may have been the "Chief," and responsible for the ideas, but nothing could have been implemented without Wise's phenomenal energy and dedication to the cause. The experience he gained during these years contributed enormously to his growth as a leader. He had always been a dynamic speaker, able to move people by the force and passion of his words and the impetuosity of his actions. Now he had to deal with governments and their leaders, with results that could greatly help or harm the cause of Jewish nationalism. He learned that one had to balance a variety of factors, to weigh options and consequences, that there was a role in Jewish affairs for the man of caution and discretion. While Wise did not change over completely, he did learn, and fortunately he had as his tutor Louis Brandeis, a man with an exquisite sensitivity to nuance and tone.

Shortly after the Balfour Declaration, for example, the British government asked Chaim Weizmann to head an official Zionist Commission to Palestine to survey conditions there; Weizmann immediately cabled Brandeis ask for a strong and influential American delegation. Wise went to Washington to confer with Colonel House to see if there would be any objections to American participation, and the president's advisor emphatically listed all the problems, chief of which was that America was not at war with Turkey. Moreover, administration endorsement of American representation might lead to embarassing complications, including British assumptions that the United States would share responsibility for the future of Palestine. Send money, House advised, but stay off the mission.[41]

American Zionists tried to convey this message to Weizmann, but he continued to importune them for at least a token representative, an observer if nothing more, who could at least share in the responsibility and decision-making not as an official member of the British mission but as a Zionist. The State Department reluctantly agreed that there would be no problem with an observer, and Brandeis urged Wise to go. Communications between the English and American Zionists had been less than satisfactory, and Wise could do important work in cementing better relations as well as in securing firsthand knowledge of the character and ability of Weizmann and his colleagues. Moreover, Wise had the advantage of being one of the few American Zionist leaders who had ever been to Palestine, so his observations there would be of great value.

The offer tempted him enormously, for in early 1918 the Zionists felt that their time had come. In the United States the movement had progressed to become a potent force in Jewish affiars, with 186,000 enrolled members and a leadership with entree to the White House. The Zionist Commission would be taking the first and crucial steps in turning the Balfour Declaration into a reality, and potentially could wield great influence. As head of the Provisional Committee, Wise undoubtedly appeared the most likely person to represent American Zionism in this venture.

But just as Brandeis had refused to leave the bench to go, so Wise also declined. He doubted, as he told Brandeis, whether Weizmann wanted a partner so much as someone who would promise greater American financial support. "Under the circumstances I feel I can render more important service to the cause by remaining at home and continuing to give to the work of the office of the movement a very considerable portion of my time and strength, such as I have devoted for the past few months." If this decision would embarrass Brandeis—that is, not having the Provisional Committee chairman willing to go—then Wise offered to step down from that office. Brandeis immediately wrote back that while he regretted the decision, it would be "hurtful to the cause" for Wise to give up the leadership.[42] In the end, a New York lawyer, Walter Meyer, went along on the Commission without any official status, in the nominal capacity of an assistant to Weizmann.

For the European Zionists, this incident was indicative of what they saw as a lack of real Zionist commitment and passion on the part of American Jews. In crucial moments in the life of the movement, Weizmann and his colleagues dropped all their other obligations to go and do Zionism's work; Brandeis refused to leave the Court and Wise, while willing to give a great deal of his time, had other commitments which he would not surrender. If American Jews were truly devoted to Zion, the Europeans charged, they should have done as Weizmann did.

There is some truth to this argument, but it also reveals the differences between European and American Zionism as well as the ignorance of European Jews about the situation in the United States. For Weizmann, Nahum Sokolow, and the other leaders of the movement in Europe, the only solution to the Jewish problem—to *their* Jewish problem—was restoration in Palestine. They saw themselves as the proto-government of a state-in-the-making, and as citizens of that state, well before 1948 and in fact even prior to 1917. No matter what else they did for vocation or avocation, the needs of Zionism took precedence. For Wise, Zionism was a great cause, the greatest in his life, and one to which he would devote more time and energy in his career than to anything else. But while he too saw Zionism as a solution to the Jewish problem, it was not his Jewish problem. He was a proud American citizen, with no intention of resettling in Palestine. He believed in Zionism because he, as a Jew, had obligations to other Jews, to help those suffering from persecution and misfortune find peace and security. Zionism, however, was more than a rescue operation; it proposed a spiritual as well as cultural and political rebirth of the Jewish people. This was the goal of the Europeans' existence; for the Americans, it was important, but they saw it as only a part of their total lives and commitments.

Moreover, what the Europeans failed to see was that in continuing these other obligations, the Americans developed the influence they could use to further the movement. Had Brandeis stepped down from the Supreme Court, had Wise severed all his non-Zionist ties, they would have been powerless. The masses of recently arrived Jews supported the Brandeis–Wise leadership precisely because they were Americanized, because they had stature in the eyes of the non-Jewish world. When the State Department tried to prevent the Hadassah Medical Unit from going to Palestine in 1918, for example, Wise and Brandeis, because of their personal contacts with Wilson—contacts based on non-Zionist interests—were able to get the president to override Secretary of State Lansing.[43] Had they reduced themselves to one-cause persons, they would not have done this, nor given much other service to Zionism over the years.

While all these activities certainly raised Wise's influence and stature, they also began to take a toll in the spring of 1918. He continued as the active rabbi of the Free Synagogue, a leader in the Jewish Congress movement, and chairman of the Zionist Provisional Committee. In addition, he went on extensive speaking tours for Zionism, for the Congress, for Wilson's re-election, to sell war bonds, and to bolster support for the war program. He had played a central role in negotiating the Balfour Declaration on the American end, and commuted regularly to Washington to confer with Justice Brandeis, President Wilson, and other administration officials.

In early summer some of this pressure was relieved with the election of Julian Mack as president of the newly created Zionist Organization of

America, but the burden of preparing and effecting the reoganization had fallen largely on Wise's shoulders. Many of the old-line Zionists resisted having to cede some of their power and prerogatives to a centralized federation, and Wise, as Brandeis's chief lieutenant as well as chairman of the Provisional Committee, became the target of their resentments. With great happiness he turned over the leadership to Mack, a friend whom he admired and respected.[44] There was no question, of course, but that Wise would still play a major role in American Zionist affairs.

The vacation he took in the summer, working at the Shippen Point Yard, seemed to have had at least a temporary effect in alleviating his tensions, but by fall he was back to the old relentless pace. In late September, some of his Zionist colleagues worriedly reported to Brandeis that Wise had been in "a very nervous and irritable condition for some weeks." Fortunately, the guns of war fell silent at 11:00 A.M. on November 11, 1918, ending four years of wanton killing, maiming, and destruction. If Wise thought, however, that the Armistice would allow him to resume a quieter and more normal life, he soon learned differently. Within a month he would leave for Europe as one of the heads of the American Jewish delegation to the Paris Peace Conference.

11

.... and Peace

The Armistice brought not only the blessing of an end to destruction but also the hope that a new world order based on justice and righteousness might take the place of the older corrupt relationships among nations. For Jews and especially for Zionists peace brought great opportunities to secure legally assured civil and political rights in Europe and to turn the Balfour Declaration from a promise into a reality. American Zionists would play a crucial role in the postwar settlement of the Palestine question, and Stephen Wise, now confirmed in his role as an American Jewish leader, would take his first steps toward becoming a figure of importance for world Jewry.

The future of Palestine dominated Zionist thoughts, and they wondered how much they could demand. Would a minimal program draw greater support and find easier acceptance, or was it worth the risk to gamble for a maximal program, attempting to get all that the Zionists had ever wanted, since such an opportunity might not come again? Horace Kallen believed that in the public mind a presumption existed that "Zion is to be a state. . . . If we destroy it we shall have killed the idea itself and have reduced the settlement in Palestine to a new ghetto which will differ in no way from the old ones. For this reason, honesty and tactics both require us to stand publically by the 'great programs.' "[1]

But to achieve the "great programs," the Zionists would have to present their case before the victorious Allies, and convince them to write into the peace terms the promise made by the British in November 1917. Although Brandeis undoubtedly stood as the pre-eminent and most influential Zionist in the United States, his position on the Supreme Court precluded his taking an active role in Jewish presentations to the peacemakers; instead he relied on his lieutenants to safeguard Zionist interests. Felix Frankfurter worked behind the scenes, utilizing his legal skills to draft and polish Jewish demands, while Julian Mack and Stephen Wise moved among the representatives of the great powers, cajoling, soothing, arguing, persuading. The personal relations Wise had established with President Wilson, Colonel House, and other administration figures stood him in good stead, but he also showed how much and how well he had learned in his association with Brandeis.

The "Chief," in fact, had called Wise in immediately after the Armistice and asked him to go to Europe as head of the Zionist delegation and as his personal representative.[2] This time Wise did not object, for he too recognized that the great decisions would be made in Europe, and that his greatest service to the Zionist cause would be to use his talents and connections at the Peace Conference. Moreover, relations between American and European Zionists had grown rather strained in the preceding months. Weizmann's softness toward Great Britain, a trait that would later cost him the leadership of the Zionist Organization, had already manifested itself in his minimalist approach regarding what the Balfour Declaration meant, and in statements indicating that he would not press England on questions of geographic boundaries or internal administration in Palestine. The man who had so masterfully dealt with great leaders in 1917 now bombarded American Zionists with pleas for help, declaring that nothing could be done without the active assistance and actual physical presence of some American Zionist leaders in England. It is your duty, he wired Brandeis, "to take your share in national responsibility by your presence here."[3] His seeming inability to make decisions upset the American leaders. Wise had to go to Europe, therefore, not only to represent American and Zionist interests at the Peace Conference, but to calm Weizmann, reassure him of American commitments, and at the same time, size up the man firsthand.

Wise hesitated over one matter, however; while appreciating the need to leave for Europe as soon as possible, he wanted to see the long-deferred plans for the American Jewish Congress come to fruition. Congress leaders had reluctantly acceded to Wilson's wartime request for delay, but with the end of hostilities had immediately scheduled the Congress to meet in Philadelphia on December 15. Although he hoped to delay his departure until after mid-December, Wise realized that the Congress would function without him; he was needed in London, and therefore would leave as soon as he could arrange all the necessary details. But a few days before he left Wise, together with Louis Marshall, Julian Mack, and Bernard Richards, went to the White House to confer with President Wilson on the planned program of the Congress, to see whether there might be anything on their agenda that would embarrass the American government, and how, in the president's opinion, they might best advance their program. The four men spent the morning of Sunday, December 6, putting the final touches on a memorandum setting forward proposals for Jewish rights in Europe and

Palestine, and late in the afternoon met with Wilson in the Red Room. The president arranged five chairs in a circle, and then listened attentively to the ideas and dreams of the Jewish leaders.

"Mr. President," they asked, "how can we best advance our case?"

"Gentlemen," he replied, "spread your conversations as widely as possible." As the meeting broke up, Wilson took his old friend aside for a moment, speaking to him in a confident and reassuring manner, and the others heard the president say, "Don't worry, Dr. Wise, Palestine is yours."[4]

The American Jewish Congress, representing some 3.5 million American Jews, convened in Philadelphia on December 15, and it turned out to be all that Wise, Brandeis, and its other advocates had hoped it would be. The *yahudim* now made their peace with fellow-delegates representing the eastern Europe immigrants. "We here in America sympathize with every Jewish aspiration," Louis Marshall told the cheering crowd. "Many of us who in the past have been disconnected with the Zionist organization, have nevertheless felt that it would be a privilege to assist in the rehabilitation of the land of our fathers. . . . There are some of us who have in the past been classified as anti-Zionists—which we never were—who have gladly inaugurated works in the Holy Land for the purpose of developing it agriculturally and educationally." Nor did the masses reject the uptowners. The Congress chose Marshall and Harry Cutler of the American Jewish Committee as vice-presidents and Jacob Schiff as treasurer. For its delegation to the Peace Conference, the Congress named Julian W. Mack, who had been elected chairman of the Congress, Stephen Wise, Louis Marshall, Jacob deHaas, Nachman Syrkin of the Labor Zionists, Joseph Barondess, Morris Winchevsky, Harry Cutler, and Rabbi Bernard Levinthal, together with Bernard G. Richards as secretary. The delegation would present proposals for a Jewish "bill of rights" in Paris and for the implementation of the Balfour promise.[5]

Word of the Congress resolutions reached Wise in London a few days after his arrival, and he discussed them over tea with Arthur Balfour at the Foreign Office. Balfour sounded out Wise on American intentions in the Middle East, and wanted to know which government the Zionists wanted to receive the protectorate over Palestine. Wise reiterated the official position that the Unites States sought no new territories, and he assured Balfour that American Zionists, and he believed the government as well, favored a British administration in the Holy Land.[6] In a letter to his daughter after this meeting, Wise wrote: "You can't imagine how deeply interesting was the conference with Mr. Balfour, sitting before a fine fire at his side discussing great questions. He is so wise, so poised, so learned. He takes a fine position with respect to the Palestine problem. The British Government will take over the trusteeship of Palestine if forced to do so by the pressure of disinterested peoples. Everything depends on the President."[7]

Balfour was not the only "notable" Wise conferred with during his nearly three weeks in London. Louise, who had accompanied him on this trip, wrote home after taking a solitary dinner at a cafeteria on Regent Street that her husband was dining that evening "with princes and lords, who only have male persons at dinner, the princes of Arabia not being civilized as yet." Everywhere he went, and with everyone he met, Wise took the opportunity to discuss Jewish issues which would come before the Peace Conference. "How wonderful it seems," Louise mused, "that one so close to us as Daddy should mean so much in the development of the history of his people."[8]

And everywhere Wise and Louise went, they saw evidence of the suffering caused by four years of war. "I am on the verge," she wrote to Jim, "nay in tears most of the days. Boys like you—tall, strong, dear boys so maimed and crippled for 50 years or more to come. Their mothers, wives, sweethearts lead them about so tenderly and sadly, but the boys smile and smile and seemed determined to carry on without thought of complaint. When I look at them and say to myself, 'Germany, this devil's work is yours!' I find it hard not to hate the whole nation that brought misery on a peaceful world."[9] Wise, also appalled at this suffering, began to reconsider his earlier pacifism, and wondered if he had been right in changing his mind. Over the next few years he would move closer to Holme's position of opposing any and all wars, ultimately declaring that he had made a mistake in 1917.

An even less satisfactory part of his London stay, however, involved his conferences with European Zionist leaders. Unlike Brandeis, Mack, and Frankfurter, he had had some acquaintance with the European movement dating from Herzl's time, and his experience had left him disenchanted with Zionist politics and administration. The intervening years, he discovered, had changed little. Brandeis's fears about Chaim Weizmann seemed to be confirmed. Time and again Weizmann stated that he should not have to bear the responsibility of leadership alone; Brandeis should head the Jewish cause, and the Justice should personally go to the peace tables. Weizmann believed he could be most effective in Palestine; he knew just what to do there, and would gladly take charge. Wise assured him that while the Americans had "a hundred confidences" in him, they were unwilling to give him unlimited powers anywhere.[10]

Wise would later report that a great gulf of misunderstanding separated the two groups. "The Zionist movement in Europe," he declared, "admits that there is a Zionist movement in America, because occasionally, much too occasionally, remittances come to hand, but if those remittances for any reason should cease to float into the coffers of London or Paris, we should speedily be cut off from London or France. Our friends there do not know us, do not believe in us, and do not believe in the reality of our Zionism." Chaim Weizmann stood out among those most guilty of this, and Wise charged that the English chemist, despite his demands for greater American involvement, did not comprehend that America had a serious and important part to play in the future development of the movement, a role other than mere financing of the *yishuv*. The caution that Weizmann displayed toward the British in his demands for Palestine also upset Wise, as well as the fact that the Europeans had not bothered to consult their American colleagues on these matters. Pointing to the future, Wise warned that unless better communication could be established between London and New York, great damage would occur; indeed, only the acts of a benevolent Providence had prevented such damage before. Finally, he cautioned that a relatively minor matter, the postwar reorganization of the Actions Comité, had become fraught with all sorts of dangers reflecting personal rivalries and local jealousies. Wise seem particularly upset by Weizmann's insistence that all powers be lodged in a single executive office. Brandeis and Julian Mack were appalled by this development as well as by Wise's comments on the slipshod administrative arrangements he had seen.[11]

Early in January 1919, the Wises traveled on to Paris, where he received the Legion of Honor from the French government. During their stay in Paris, Wise devoted most of each day to lobbying for the Zionist cause and for Jewish rights in Europe, but continued to be frustrated by the activities of his European colleagues. At Weizmann's request, for example, Wise secured a thirty-minute appointment for the English leader with Colonel House, only to learn that Weizmann had asked several other people if they would gain him access to the president's advisor. As a result an annoyed House, who had agreed to Wise's original request, cut Weizmann's time to a quarter-hour. An angry Wise told Weizmann never to do this again, for it made him and the Zionists look bad. Joseph Cowen, Weizmann's aide, tried to soothe Wise by explaining that it was just "the Zionist way of doing things." Wise and the two Englishmen then argued heatedly over the need for the Zionists to cooperate with each other, and for the London office to stop trying to bypass the American delegation on all matters.[12] Weizmann in the end made some conciliatory gesture, and then pressed Wise to make an appointment for him with Woodrow Wilson, and insisted that he wanted to talk to the president alone.

On January 14 the two men received a call to present themselves at Wilson's hotel suite late in the afternoon. Wise met with his old friend first, and discovered that the president, who had recently dismissed a petition from anti-Zionist American Jews, had begun to worry about the Arab reaction to the Jewish restoration in Palestine. Wise guessed that the Arabists in the State Department had been hard at work, and suggested that Wilson send for T. E. Lawrence, the famed "Lawrence of Arabia," who could attest to the expressions of friendship to Zionism which the Emir Feisal had made. He also reported on the dinner he had attended in London with Feisal and other Arab leaders, and on the memorandum which the prince òf the Hedjaz was preparing for the Zionists. Wise then called in Weizmann, introduced him to Wilson, and went to wait in the anteroom. Weizmann soon discovered that the American president was well-informed on the problems in the Middle East and sympathetic to Zionist aims; Wise and Brandeis had done their work well. Following the meeting, a delighted Weizmann told Wise "Your super *goy* is all right.!"[13]

A few days later, Wise prepared to leave for America, confident that his nearly five weeks in London and Paris had been fruitful for the cause. Both publicly and privately he averred that the political situation, at least regarding Jewish claims at the Peace Conference, looked good. "A Jewish Palestine," he told Max Heller, "is taken for granted by the Allied peoples, just the same way as a renascent Poland or a restored Serbia. That is nothing less than a God-given miracle!" He did, however, urge his fellow Zionists not to magnify this achievement beyond reason. There might be a Jewish Palestine approved in the peace treaty, but not an independent Jewish state. It would be up to the Jews in the *yishuv* and elsewhere to fill in the details of Palestine's future.[14]

After the exhilaration and accomplishments of Europe, he found sorrow and disappointment awaiting him at home. While crossing the Atlantic he learned that his older brother Otto had died, and that the family was delaying the funeral until his arrival. Where he had seen Wilson idolized and cheered in Europe, in America he found partisan critics of the president sniping away at his peace proposals and calling for him to return to America.

When Wilson did return from Europe late in February 1919, the American Jewish Congress asked for an appointment with him to learn the status of its presentations to the Allies. On March 2, Wise, together with Marshall, Mack, and Richards, went to the White House. Wilson had invited Wise to meet with him alone about twenty minutes before the scheduled interview with the Congress delegation, and he assured the New York rabbi that all had gone well for the Zionists. He later authorized the four men to announce his continued personal approval of the Balfour Declaration, and "that the Allied nations, with the fullest concurrence of our own government and people, are agreed that in Palestine should be laid the foundation of a Jewish commonwealth." The statement was all that the Zionists could have hoped for, but as Wise privately noted, "I wish I might be assured that the Jewish people will be equal to the opportunity."[15]

The meeting did, however, have one unfortunate result. In order to accommodate the president's schedule, the Congress delegation had agreed to meet with Wilson on a Sunday morning. Given the short notice he had, Wise asked former ambassador Henry Morgenthau, as president of the Free Synagogue, to occupy the pulpit that day, explaining that he had to go to

Washington. Morgenthau at one point had been friendly to Zionism, and as ambassador to Turkey in the early years of the war had proved of inestimable help in transferring American relief funds to the *yishuv*, but by 1919 he had become staunchly anti-Zionist. When he picked up the newspaper on Monday morning and read that he had substituted for Wise in order for the rabbi to plead the Zionist case with Wilson, he felt wronged and called Wise to tell him that he would resign as president of the congregation. Wise immediately went to Morgenthau's home and tried in vain to dissuade him. As Morgenthau wrote to the executive committee, he did not question either his own or Wise's freedom of thought and expression, and hoped that the "friendly and cordial relations" that had long existed between them would continue, but he had to forego "the happy and inspiring association with Dr. Wise because our views of Zionism . . . are so diverse and apparently irreconcilable." Although there would be many resignations from the Free Synagogue over the years (Wise once quipped that he could measure how effective a sermon had been by the number of withdrawals), few were as generous as Morgenthau in acknowledging the basic premises of the Free Synagogue, that in an independent pulpit the rabbi would have full freedom to express his views, whatever they might be, while the congregants had equal freedom to accept or reject those ideas. Whatever disagreements Stephen Wise might have with Henry Morgenthau over the years on Zionism or other issues, he always admired the integrity of a man who had helped him found the Free Synagogue and who remained faithful to its premises.[16]

There was little time, however, to lose worrying over Morgenthau's resignation, because Wise spent the next several months stumping the country for both Zionism and for Wilson's vision of a new world order. Shortly after his return he had attacked Wilson's critics in a speech before the League for Political Education. "It may not be long," he declared, "before the American people will apply the term 'moral treason' to the aims and acts of that coterie of gentlemen so eager to 'smash Wilson' as to forget that he is still President of the United States, meeting in councils of utmost delicacy and difficulty with representatives of countries other than our own. But one must not forget that there is some satisfaction felt abroad over every American who tries to 'show up the President.' The non-German Prussians of London, Paris and Rome take comfort in the sayings and doings of their fellow Prussians. These Prussians have a common tongue whether their native speech be English, French or Italian. Its accents are always unmistakably Bourbon."[17]

In the spring of 1919 Wise went on an extensive speaking tour of the midwest with former President William Howard Taft, who together with the Rev. A. A. Berle, Sr. and Amos Pinchot, had founded the League to Enforce Peace. In city after city Wise defended Wilson's peace program and called for American support of the League of Nations, although he quickly learned that there was far less unanimity about the League in America than he had seen in Europe. The League, he told his audiences, provided the only sane method of settling international conflicts, the only realistic means to combat the spirit of militarism. War, he declared, could only be countenanced as a last resort to enforce peace if all other methods, including arbitration, failed. And in every town he visited, he spoke to Jewish groups, discussing the relation of the League to Zionism, and the protection it would afford to Jews and other minority groups in Europe.[18]

Jewish affairs, however, which had been marked by a high degree of harmony and unity in 1918 and early 1919, reverted to their normal internecine quarreling. The whole question of the American Jewish Congress, for example, threatened to split the community much as it had in 1915 and 1916. During the peace conferences, the Congress relied on its delegation, especially Louis Marshall and Julian Mack, who returned to Europe for the second session of the Supreme Allied Council. There was, after all, little the Congress could do until it knew how much, if any, of its program had been adopted. But by July 1919 Wise perceived evidence that the *yahudim* already considered the Congress moribund, with the American Jewish Committee waiting in the wings to reclaim its alleged leadership of American Jewry. The Zionists, moreover, who had been so supportive of the Congress before the war now seemed to have their attention diverted to other matters. and the Congress suffered from lack of manpower and money.[19]

When a formal session of the Congress was called for May 1920, both sides braced for a bitter fight. Louis Marshall charged "the Jews, too, seem to have eaten of the insane root . . . An attempt will doubtlessly be made at the coming session of the Congress to convert it into a permanent body to deal with all Jewish matters. Such a resolution would be contrary to the conditions on which the Congress was called." He predicted that although Judge Mack would try to stick to the original agreement, a group of "hotheads" would either try to override him or call a rump session afterward. In either case, Marshall declared, he would sever his relations with the Congress. Jacob Schiff reached a similar conclusion, but was even blunter about the "correct" policy—namely "to strengthen the American Jewish Committee so that it may . . . deal with the various Jewish problems without regard to what others may do or to the misrepresentation and vituperation to which it may be subjected." Both Marshall and Schiff, as well as observers such as Julius Simon, recognized that Stephen Wise belonged in the group planning to turn the Congress into a permanent institution. After all, he had opposed Brandeis's original compromise to limit the Congress to a temporary agency; under no circumstances should the *yahudim* regain their hegemony over American Jewish affairs.[20]

No one, however, expected the brawl which the Congress session turned out to be. It convened in Philadelphia on May 30, 1920, and the tumult started almost immediately when Judge Mack, as chairman, called upon Marshall to read his report on the activities of the delegation to the Peace Conference. Marshall carefully explained how the group had tried to carry out its mandate and how hard its members had worked to protect Jewish rights, an effort in which for the most part they had been successful. As he finished, Benjamin Zuckerman of New York jumped up and in a bitter harangue in Yiddish, charged that the Marshall group had "betrayed the Jewish race and misrepresented the Congress." All efforts by Mack to restore order in the next hour failed as groups of delegates shouted charges and countercharges against one another. That evening the level of tension and noise rose so much that Wise, temporarily in the chair and banging the gavel vigorously, threatened "to adjourn this session and abandon the Congress for all time" unless the audience came to order. Wise finally shouted the meeting back to some semblance of parliamentary order. The original American Jewish Congress then adjourned *sine die*, thus conforming to the original Brandeis-Marshall agreement.[21]

A large number of delegates, including Wise, immediately reconvened in a "conference for the formation of an American Jewish Congress." This time the men and women cheered Wise as he urged that the gains made in bringing democracy to Jewish life should not be lost. American Jewry should not return "to the undemocratic, un-American, un-Jewish method of dictation from above, however well-meaning in intent, however soft-spoken in manner." An executive committee was chosen, charged with preparing plans for an ongoing body. To show they wanted the *yahudim* to participate, they elected Marshall and Schiff to the committee, but the two men, upon learning of this, immediately and emphatically declined.[22] Wise while elated over this move to continue the ideas which the Congress represented, nonetheless recognized that a difficult task confronted the new executive committee. "The [old] Congress is gone," he wrote to Brandeis, "but I am not sure the new one is born. It is hard to say what will come of it. Of course the JDC and the Committee people will not be with us, and I find there is nothing else considerable in Jewish life save for those elements, numerically weak but strong in some respects, and ourselves."[23] Not until 1922, however, would Wise, Louis Lipsky, and their colleagues be able to create this new and enduring American Jewish Congress.

A more perplexing and difficult issue involved the growing strains between American and European Zionists and the tensions among the American groups. Even within the ruling faction, Wise and others had began to grumble in late 1918 about Jacob deHaas's role in controlling access and information to Brandeis. "Frequently one is unable to perform one's best services," Wise told Julian Mack, "because we are a little in the dark and do not quite command the confidence of the Chief." When

Brandeis prepared to visit London, Paris, and Palestine in the summer of 1919, taking along only deHaas as an aide, Wise tried in vain to convince the jurist that he needed a larger entourage, ten or more men who could help him and who would also have independent judgment.[24]

Another sore point involved the efforts of Brandeis and Mack to reach rapprochement with Marshall and Schiff in order to bolster Zionist plans for the rebuilding of Palestine. In September, after Brandeis's return from the Holy Land, he and Marshall, in a continuation of meetings begun in late 1917 after the Balfour Declaration, spent several days analyzing what Brandeis had seen and learned. Of all the *yahudim*, Marshall enjoyed the greatest prestige with Zionist leaders for his open mind and his integrity in carrying out the instructions of the American Jewish Congress as one of its delegates to the Peace Conference. When Wise learned of the extent of these negotiations and the willingness of Brandeis to give Marshall a major role in Palestinian work, he protested stongly. At the ZOA convention in Chicago in September 1919, although he defended the administration's general policies, he privately let it be known that he intended to withdraw as vice-president so as not to hamper Mack and Brandeis in their negotiations with the *yahudim*, a development he feared and mistrusted.[25]

Wise recognized that there would have to be some means of bringing well-to-do Jews into Zionist work, but feared the antidemocratic prejudices of the *yahudim* would undermine the idealism of Zionist endeavors. He had no alternative except to try to raise more money from the less wealthy Jews, a policy he admitted had little chance of success. American Zionists, he complained, had failed to build a necessary financial and institutional base, and the ZOA's Palestine Restoration Fund had taken on the character of a charity drive. Zionism's aims made it imperative, he argued, to keep all aspects, even the raising of money, on a high moral plane. Although the postwar recession reduced Zionist income, Wise still opposed the Mack/Brandeis plans for soliciting money from the wealthy elite.[26]

By the summer of 1920, in fact, Wise found himself more and more frustrated by Zionist politics. Wilson's stroke in October 1919 had cut off access by Wise and now he could no longer handle important matters directly with the president. The resignation of Robert Lansing as Secretary of State reduced at least some of the anti-Zionist animus in Washington, but his successor, Bainbridge Colby, while friendly to the Zionists, had little interest in or familiarity with Middle East policy. Brandeis's opening to the *yahudim* depressed Wise, who nonetheless remained allied with the jurist in emphasizing the need for practical work over ideological squabbling. He also identified strongly with Brandeis's increasing skepticism about the integrity and intentions of Chaim Weizmann and the London Office.[27] But when Brandeis asked Wise to go to England in the late spring, he refused, saying it would be impossible for him to work closely with Weizmann since he distrusted the Englishman. Moreover, he declined to join the American delegation to the Zionist conference in London that summer, and tried to warn Brandeis that Weizmann planned to undermine American influence, reducing the movement in the United States to little more than a collection agency. Wherever Wise looked that summer, he saw the unity and high purpose of the war years fading before the pettiness of old-time Zionist politicking, while the desperate need for funds in Palestine subverted the chance of American Zionism to restructure the community. Before Mack left for the London meeting, Wise indicated that he planned to go on a much-needed vacation to the Pacific Northwest and Alaska, and would step down as vice-president of the ZOA at the next convention.[28]

If despair fathered the idea of resignation, anger brought it to life. In a deliberate slap at Wise, the Weizmann group dropped his name from among the American members of the WZO Greater Actions committee, a group Wise had originally served on under Herzl. He expected this sort of treatment from the Europeans, he told Nathan Straus, but what really hurt was the fact that his American colleagues had not fought for him. The various explanations offered by Louis Lipsky and others as to why they thought they were doing Wise a favor failed to placate him, and on August 11 he sent in his resignation to Julian Mack, refusing to discuss the matter with anyone, including Brandeis. When Mack appealed to him in terms of loyalty to Brandeis, now under attack from the Weizmannites, Wise exploded:[29]

> Do you know of any man who has been more loyal to Justice Brandeis than I have been? My loyalty, I dare affirm, has been the loyalty not so much of a captain to the general of the army battling in a great cause as the loyalty of self-forgetting friendship. I have asked nothing of Justice Brandeis. I have given him much more than he or you know. I have made serious sacrifices at the behest of my devotion to him. I have never alluded to this before. I would not allude to it now, but your appeal to me to be loyal to Justice Brandeis constrains me to cry that loyalty to Justice Brandeis has been one of the mainsprings of my public activity and my private life during the six years we have worked together.

No doubt Wise assumed that his devotion to Brandeis and his service to the Zionist movement deserved better treatment than he had been accorded. Wise believed that the American delegation should have come to his defense when Weizmann dropped his name from the Actions Committee list; by not doing so, they in effect denigrated his service. Few people could give more of themselves than Stephen Wise to a cause, but he needed recognition in turn, both the recognition of mass adulation and the respect of his peers. By failing to defend him in London, they hurt him in the worst possible way.

Mack read Wise's letter of resignation as first vice-president to members of the ZOA executive committee on August 29, 1920. Brandeis immediately claimed the floor, and declared that only a total misunderstanding of circumstances at the London Conference could have led Wise to believe that his friends and associates had deserted him. The executive committee, he said, could not for a moment consider allowing Wise to retire. The committee then unanimously passed a resolution affirming its appreciation of his services and the continued need of them in Zionist work.[30] Brandeis and Mack immediately left to see Wise in person, and convinced him to stay on, for as he well knew, the entire Brandeis program was under strong attack and he, better than anyone, could defend it before other Zionists.

The events leading up to the 1921 Cleveland convention reflected the polarization that still affected American Zionism. In essence, the Brandeis group emphasized efficiency over ideology, accomplishments over politicking; they insisted that funds for Zionist work be administered honestly and effectively in an accountable manner. They were, above all, Americanized Jews devoted to Zion more in the abstract than in personal terms. While they had led the fight for democracy in American Jewish life, they had kept power in the ZOA in the hands of only a few men, all of whom deferred to Brandeis and his ideas. The masses of Jews at first willingly followed the Brandeis–Wise–Mack leadership, since it had revivified American Zionism and then gave the immigrants a voice through the American Jewish Congress. But the newcomers always harbored a suspicion that the Americianized leadership lacked *yiddishkeit*, a true feeling for things Jewish, that they failed to see the great spiritual and emotional aspects of Zionism, and instead reduced the movement for restoration to a passionless abstraction, a charity. The truth is in between, but by 1919 friction had developed to the point where an administration motion presented by Wise had been defeated, and the Brandeis group, for the first time, tried to create better lines of communication with the eastern European immigrants. Yet no one wanted to depose the Brandeis leadership, and as one of the insurgents wrote to Wise: "I want you to know that even in the time when we voted down your motion, personally we admired and loved you as we always have."[31]

At the 1920 London Conference, Brandeis, because of the growing tension between the Weizmann clique and his group, decided that Americans would not participate in the leadership of world Zionist affairs until Weizmann either resigned or overhauled a corrupt and inept administration. This time even some of Brandeis's most ardent supporters felt he had gone too far. The young Abba Hillel Silver did not repudiate the Justice, but complained of Brandeis's failure to consult with the executive committee before deciding on such a radical change in policy. Together with Wise, Silver worked out a proposal calling for greater involvement of the executive with the officers. Although Wise still considered himself part of the Brandeis leadership, he confessed that the situation confused him. "I believe Brandeis is not at fault," he wrote, "and I am not even sure Weizmann is at fault. The [London] conference marked the parting of the ways, the end of the old agitation epoch and the beginning of the new efficiency epoch after thirty years."[32]

But old Zionist politicians die hard, and the Weizmann group had plenty of life left in it. Weizmann accused the Americans of trying to undermine the WZO by refusing to join in the new Keren Hayesod, the Foundation Fund, and he appealed to American Zionists to maintain their loyalty to the world movement, with its true vision of Jewish restoration, rather than to a pale shadow led by assimilationists who knew nothing of the inner Jewish spirit. Although there was much empty rhetoric in this appeal, Weizmann did touch upon enough sore points that the Brandeis administration felt it had to answer the indictment. Brandeis asked Wise personally to defend their policies at the ZOA convention in Buffalo in late November 1920.

In a tense atmosphere, Wise's performance tipped the scales one last time for the adminstration. As he approached the podium on Sunday evening, November 27, the audience rose to give him a tremendous ovation, a token of the delegates' affection and respect and, in some ways, a compensatory gesture for the insult he had felt earlier in the year. According to the *American Hebrew*, throughout the speech one could sense "the wildest excitment and experience of feeling" among the crowd. Wise carefully attempted to rebut Weizmann's charges of separatism:[33]

> There is no such thing as a European Zionist point of view against an American Zionist point of view. The European and the American points of view, as far as they are two, are not to be merged into one point of view. In one word we deny, and we have the right in the light of the past, and the resolve of the future, to say that no Monroe Doctrine or any other doctrine separates us from an insoluble oneness. If there is a difference, and I deny that there is a difference, between some of the European and American Zionists, it lies in this: Some of our brothers, just as well-meaning, just as devoted as we are or fain would be, are for Zionism first and for Zion second. We Americans are for Zion first, and for Zionism second. In other words, not Zion for the sake of Zionism, but Zionism for the sake of Zion.

He reminded his listeners of the tremendous devotion and achievements of the leadership, and then engineered a resolution of thanks and support to Louis Brandeis, a proposal which none of the delegates could oppose. A delighted Brandeis warmly thanked Wise: "You have performed a very big service to the Jewish people. Your address is an educational document of the first order. . . . I hope it will have as wide a circulation abroad as it is sure to have here. Your generous reference to me is just what I should have wished."[34] The convention elected Mack as president, and Wise, who declined to stand for office, as honorary vice-president; it also named him, along with Mack and Harry Friedenwald, to the Greater Actions Committee. But the Buffalo convention was the last triumph of the Brandeis faction for the next ten years.

Despite this "victory," Wise and others saw quite clearly that something had to be done to ameliorate the growing discord between the leadership and the masses. He and Mack began to talk with the so-called "opposition" to discover what real differences were, and what steps might be taken to overcome them. Brandeis, on the other hand, stood immovably on principle, although on one issue—Weizmann's untrustworthiness—he and Wise agreed fully. With the leadership split as to strategy, there was little Wise or anyone else could do to halt the deteriorating situation. On March 29, 1921, ten members of the ZOA executive committee refused to endorse a statement prepared by Julian Mack which defended American policies against Weizmann's charges. The suggestion that a sort of coalition administration be formed only brought a sharp rebuke from Justice Brandeis, who called not for cooperation but expulsion of the dissidents. By the time Weizmann arrived in the United States at the beginning of April, even Wise believed that it would be impossible to compose the differences. Although Weizmann was ostentatiously cordial to Wise, the American rabbi found the Europeans as unwilling to compromise as were Brandeis and his colleagues.[35]

The break came in April 17, when Weizmann unilaterally proclaimed the establishment of the Keren Hayesod in the United States over objections of the ZOA leadership to the fund's failure to separate donation and investment monies so as to ensure responsible fiscal management. Brandeis now came to rally his troops in person. "Our aim is the kingdom of heaven," he thundered, paraphrasing Cromwell, "we take Palestine by the way. But we must take it with clean hands; we must take it in such a way as to ennoble the Jewish people. Otherwise it will not be worth having."[36]

In an effort to split the Americans, Weizmann insisted that Wise join him for lunch, and invited the New York rabbi to head the dissident cause. Wise tried to convince Weizmann that the only reason Zionism had caught on in the United States was because Brandeis had assumed the leadership; that even if Weizmann could force the Brandeis group out, no one else in the country had the status or ability to forge a dynamic Zionist organization. Weizmann contemptuously dismissed the importance of the Brandeis leadership: "The ship that takes me back to Europe will also return to America again. This is not my last trip to America but my first." Wise left the meeting convinced more than ever that the Englishman lacked principle, and wanted either to rule or ruin the Zionist movement.[37]

The end came in June 1921. Judge Mack opened the ZOA convention in Cleveland, and called for the election of officers. Wise rose to second the nomination of Mack as convention chairman, and in the course of his remarks said: "I would like to hear one man in this room arise and say that

Judge Mack is not capable of fairness toward everyone here.'' Immediately a number of people started shouting objections, and Wise, seeing Judge Bernard Rosenblatt in the crowd, declared ''This is not a New York police court!'' only to have Rosenblatt fire back, ''Neither is it the Free Synagogue!'' Although Mack was elected, a little while later the adiminstration lost a vote of confidence over the issue of establishing the Keren Hayesod.[38]

When the uproar died down, Julian Mack reached in his pocket and took out a piece of paper Brandeis had given to him before the convention, to be used in case the vote went against the leadership. It was a letter of resignation. Brandeis would remain a Zionist, a ''humble soldier in the ranks,'' but he could not hold office in an organization that denied basic principles of honesty and justice. Mack then read off, name by name, a list of thirty-seven other members of the executive committee who also submitted their resignations including himself, Mary Fels, Nathan Straus, Abba Hillel Silver, Felix Frankfurter, Horace Kallen, and Stephen Wise. As Mack read the list, silence settled over the astounded audience, the muffled sobbing of some delegates punctuating the tolling of the names. The end of an era had come in American Zionism.[39]

For Wise, the results of Cleveland were hardly surprising, and he analyzed the debacle in a long letter to Mary Fels. He recognized that the administration had made political mistakes, that he had misjudged the grievances of some groups and underestimated the power of Weizmann's appeal, but at least it had tried to act in a decent principled manner. What troubled him most, he said, was not the deceit practiced by Weizmann and his crowd, but the ''moral obtuseness of the delegates, the imperviousness of the majority to the moral considerations we urged.''[40]

In fact, ''moral considerations'' played only a minor role in the Cleveland schism, as Wise came to understand once the passions of the moment subsided. Of all the members of the Brandeis leadership, none was more loyal to ''the Chief'' than Wise, yet he would be the first to make peace with the dissidents in the next few years. He never really trusted Chaim Weizmann, though, and the two men would not settle their differences for another two decades.

The two camps stood so far apart because of differing views over what Zionism meant, what its goal should be, and the role it ought to play in the lives of individual Jews as well as in the corporate life of the Jewish people. Brandeis had revivified Zionism by making the movement in the United States an extension of the ideals and principles he found most valuable in the American tradition. In an era in which reformers strove for efficiency and rationalization in all aspects of society, it is not surprising that he expected Zionism to be logical or for its leaders to employ modern methods.

Perhaps the most significant aspect of Brandeisian Zionism is the single-minded concentration on a practical goal, the development of a Jewish homeland in Palestine; all questions essentially boiled down to whether or not a given action or policy furthered this goal. It was an effective approach, one that appealed to Wise and other Americanized Jews because it provided a concrete sense of accomplishment in their work. Wise epitomized this when he said that the Americans put "Zion before Zionism."

But Zionism also had a meaning related to, yet separate from, Zion. To the Americans, as Weizmann complained, "Zionism is not a movement which gives them a definite viewpoint of the world, which gives them a definite outlook on Jewish life."[41] Zionism constituted a total framework in the Europeans' lives, their dreams, their work, their achievements. Zionism, as opposed to just Zion, could tap a great reservoir of Jewish memory and emotion; the rebuilding of a Jewish homeland in Palestine went far beyond the limits of logic. For Jews, there is a common historical and psychological experience, and Weizmann's messianic outlook, his near-mystical approach to restoration, struck a responsive chord in that totality. There is perhaps no better word to use than *Yiddishkeit*—an all prevading sense of Jewishness—to describe the key to that appeal. Weizmann and Brandeis were both stubborn, proud prima donnas, but in the end Brandeis lacked *Yiddishkeit*, while Weizmann had it. And for the common Jew, that was more important than adherance to sound principles of accounting.

But Stephen Wise, whose ideals as a progressive attracted him to Brandeis, also had *Yiddishkeit*; despite his impassioned speeches in defense of the administration, he understood that the differences between the two groups involved more than bookkeeping. When Weizmann tried to split the Brandeisists, he instinctively went to the one member of the Americanized leadership most able to identify with the common Jew, the one they not only respected but also held in affection. Zionism, as Wise knew, had to be more than the rebuilding of the land; it had to rebuild the Jewish people as well; this was a goal the Europeans instinctively understood. A great gulf did divide Minsk from Washington, although in the end it would be the emotional commitment of the Europeans combined with pragmatic approach of the Americans that made the success of the movement possible.

For all his ongoing devotion to Brandeis, Stephen Wise understood and shared this emotional component of Zionism. In the 1920's, Brandeis continued to condemn the Weizmannites and adamantly refused to engage in the work of the Zionist organization as long as Louis Lipsky "and his ilk" controlled the movement; the principles to which he adhered could not be compromised one iota. It was part of Brandeis's great strength, but it made the emotional, the subjective side, of Zionism a closed book to him. Wise stayed out for a while, but he could not condemn people, even if they were "misguided." Just as he had fought with Louis Marshall and Jacob Schiff, so he would fight with Weizmann and Lipsky, but he knew and openly admitted their great commitment to the welfare of their people.

The years from the Hotel Marseilles conference in August 1914 to the schism at the Cleveland convention in June 1921 are properly called the Brandeis years in American Zionism, but they also marked the Brandeis era in Stephen Wise's life as well. He entered the period as a maverick rabbi, his influence limited primarily to a middle-class stratum of the New York Jewish community; he left it an acknowledged leader of American Jewry and a growing figure in world Jewish affairs. From Brandeis he learned much, especially the need to consider the long-term consequences of his actions. Although he would continue to be accused of rashness and impetuosity, in fact he looked carefully at what he did and said in later years, not out of timidity, but in order to be sure his words and deeds had the greatest impact, that they led to the desired results. The Wise who left the Cleveland convention was a far different person than the one at the Hotel Marseilles; he was a man who had grown enormously in ability and influence. At age 47, he entered the prime of his life, with much great work still to do.

12

"Slightly Dispirited"

Historians have long debated the character of the decade between the end of the Great War and onset of the Great Depression. The Roaring Twenties, the Nervous Decade, and other epigrams have been coined in efforts to capture the mercurial nature of the times. One thread, however, does run through all the various accounts—namely, rapid social, economic, and political change. In these frenzied years, the United States did not "return to normalcy," but plunged forward into a new urbanized, industrialized world, one that at time seemed bereft of any moral values or cultural anchors. For reformers especially, the decade belonged to Philistines and reactionaries, all the hope of the progressive years washed away by war. Wise caught this mood in a letter he wrote in the fall of 1920, about a month before the presidential election:[1]

> Things are rather dull and uninspiring in America just now. Harding is an impossible person, and yet he is inevitable as president. He is a person without even an elementary understanding of the rudiments of English to say nothing of the rudiments of national and international policies. His nomination is the gravest insult ever leveled at the American people, but the people do not understand that they will make him president. . . . The real fight is not against Cox but against Wilson. The country has come around to your state of mind with regard to Wilson, failing to understand that his faults are almost wholly those of manner and that he is distinctly great and will have a very great place in history.

Yet less than two years earlier, Wise had been riding a crest of optimism. He had returned from his postwar trip to Europe aboard the *S. S. Adriatic*, which was also bringing 3,000 American soldiers home. Irene Castle, the famous dancer, organized nightly entertainments for the passengers and troops, but one evening in the midst of the show a bell rang, and the spotlight swung to focus on an improvised rostrum. Wise held up a radiogram he had just received from Wilson at Versailles, reporting that the Allied Supreme Council had just adopted the proposal for a League of Nations. Pandemonium broke loose, as soldiers and civilians cheered and wept. A few months later, when Wilson returned from his second trip to Europe, a jubilant Wise wrote that his heart rejoiced "in the victory of justice which you have won for our country, the *pax Americana* which is to bless the whole world."[2]

Very quickly, though, Wise saw special-interest groups rally to promote their own agendas and the spirit of wartime cooperation give way to reaction and selfishness. In his speaking tour on behalf of the League to Enforce Peace, he discovered that Wilsonian ideals had failed to penetrate the public consciousness. By early 1920, as he ruefully wrote ex-President Taft, things looked "pretty bad" for the peace treaty.[3] By then, however, the extent of the reaction had been borne home to him right in the Free Synagogue, in a ruckus precipitated by one of Wise's longtime causes, the right of labor to organize.

The controversy, symptomatic of the clash between wartime reform and postwar reaction, centered in the steel mills, where union organizers rallied the workers in a fight against low wages, the twelve-hour day, and the seven-day week. During the war, the Wilson administration had encouraged not only the right to unionize, but had also attempted, with limited success, to impose government guidelines regarding hours and wages. Despite the support of the War Labor Policies Board headed by Felix Frankfurter, the American Federation of Labor had been unable to make much headway in the steel mills. The industry, headed by U.S. Steel president Elbert H. Gary, had a long and often violent history of opposing any and all union activities, and Gary stood determined not to give way to what he saw as the forces of Bolshevism. While conceding that hard labor conditions existed in the mills, Gary claimed that economic necessity mandated the traditional twelve-hour shift. Moreover, he said, the working men, left to themselves without the agitation of outsiders, preferred the long hours because of the higher wages they were thus able to earn.[4] By the summer of 1919, a combination of unkept promises by the government and incessant harassment by the operators drove the workers toward a confrontation with Big Steel.

From the start, Wise stood with labor, and he offered his services to AF of L president Samuel Gompers. Not even Wise, however, recognized the extent of anti-union sentiment in the iron and coal fields. When he proposed speaking in Duquesne in behalf of the union in late August, the mayor of that city declared that "Jesus Christ himself could not speak in Duquesne for the American Federation of Labor!"[5] Wise's pro-union activities evoked numerous letters accusing him of fomenting rebellion and anarchy. He responded in a sermon to the Free Synagogue on Sunday, October 5, 1919, on "Bolshevists at Home: Who are They?"

Wise wasted little time in coming to his point: "Garyism is today the most prolific breeder of revolutionary and Bolshevik sentiment in our land." Gary, he declared, was "a perfect representative of the eighteenth and early nineteenth centuries, a very interesting survival, and though Judge Gary may win [the strike], the eighteenth century is going to lose. In ten years or less we shall laugh at the Garys, and the Gary autocracy will be as obsolete as the Hohenzollern autocracy." Wise carefully reviewed the background of the steel strike, which had begun on September 22, the long list of worker grievances, the terrible conditions in the mills, and the refusal of steel magnates to deal equitably with the men. The steel operators had their own organization, and fairness required that the workers be allowed to have their union. The failure to permit unions to function had led to lawlessness and violence, and the blame rested squarely on the companies. Wise plainly declared that he had no sympathies with the economic philosophies of either the radical International Workers of the World in the United States or with the new communist regime in Russia. "I am as unalterably opposed to Bolshevism as I was to Prussianism. To me Lenin and Trotsky are no less odious than Czar or Kaiser. The Lenin-Trotsky regime spells ruthless despotism; therefore to me it is loathesome and intolerable." But labor unions would not bring on a Bolshevik regime in America; if social revolution came, it would be brought by the arrogance of Gary and his like.

It is doubtful whether Wise ever gave an angrier or more impassioned sermon in the Free Synagogue. He declared he would go to Pittsburgh or anywhere to say the same things, and he dared the steel operators to sue him for libel. "If I am libelling them, they have their redress. I am a responsible person, and can be found any day. No man could say to me what I am saying of them and go unchallenged in court." When at one point the audience applauded a reference to alleged serfdom in the mills, Wise scolded them: "Please, never do that again. I am not trying to get your applause; I want you to think."[6]

He had no illusions about the reaction to this talk. When he left his house that morning, he had told his wife, "Today I am going to light a million dollar blaze," anticipating that many of the wealthy and more conservative members of the congregation would repudiate their pledges for a new synagogue structure. He did not have to wait long. The cancellations caused the Free Synagogue to defer building its own home, and several members sent in their resignations. Wise wrote to each one of them asking them to delay any action until the following Sunday, when he would explain his ideas more fully. If, at that time, they felt they should withdraw, he would not try to stop them. "I rather think" he suggested, "that you will feel that my word about Garyism, though it meet not with your approval, could not be as hurtful as to deny to another the right of freedom of speech or pulpit because he happens not to agree with you or others."[7] Most of the letters he received, even if critical, came couched in polite and normally friendly terms, and Wise responded in a similar vein. One criticism that infuriated him, however, was that he had no right to say such things since they would endanger Jews in America.[8] To this charge and others Wise addressed himself on October 12.

Wise took as his title "How Ought the Pulpit to Deal with the Industrial Situation?" and he made no effort to evade any of the criticisms leveled against him in the previous week. He repeated his charge about the Garys of America being the cause of Bolshevism, and pointing his finger at the audience, which included a number of wealthy manufacturers, he asked: "Why are some of you disturbed about an attack on Judge Gary? Why so sensitive in respect to my references to him? I know the reason, perhaps, as well as some of you. Because he is to many of you become a symbol, because he is fighting your battle, the battle which you would fight on the morrow if you dared; because you imagine that if Garyism can win, unionism will be defeated and all workingmen's organizations smothered." As to the charge that had harmed his fellow Jews, he responded: "If I am to be silent on every great moral issue because I am a Jew, if my lips are to be sealed when truth and conscience bid me speak lest I hurt the Jewish name, than I wish to live in some place, small or large, near or far, where a man can live without forefeiting his self-respect."

Were he persuaded that his outspokenness would harm the Jewish people, "I would not be silent, but would instantly take myself out of the Jewish pulpit. I am ready to make the test. I offer my congregation the privilege of passing upon the question whether or not I ought to remain as their leader and continue to be free to speak as I have spoken. I shall not be offended by any action which my people may choose to take. If it seems best in their sight that I withdraw from their ministry, as God is my witness, and as I believe that God will judge between me and them that assail me, I will withdraw with nothing but friendship and goodwill and affection for every member of my congregation, whether I continue to serve it or whether the hour has come for my withdrawal."[9]

It was not a threat to resign, for a resignation had been in the hands of the executive committee since the founding of the Free Synagogue. It is doubtful, in fact, if Wise expected anything other than a vote of confidence from his congregration, for what else had he been teaching and preaching to them for a dozen years but that only in a free pulpit could a minister of the Lord speak truth to power? Despite the dissatisfaction aroused by the Gary speech and the withdrawal of pledges from the building fund, in the end only nine members actually resigned. And while the executive committee, as Wise noted, wished he "were a little more amiable and gentle in manner, somewhat more irenic in speech," they had followed this man, had worked with him to create an exciting institution free from the fetters of wealth, one in which their minds could be challenged and their consciences aroused, even while their spirits were comforted. Some members of the executive committee disagreed with their rabbi's views, but none questioned his right to express them. When the committee met a few days later, it quickly and unanimously rejected any thought of resignation. As for whether the members endorsed Wise's views, they declared that in the Free Synagogue the rabbi spoke *to* the congregation, not *for* it. While congratulations over "victory" came in from many people, including Louis Brandeis and George Foster Peabody, the battle had actually been won much earlier, at some undefined point when Wise's commitment to a free pulpit came to be shared in fact as well as in theory by his followers.[10]

While Wise no doubt took satisfaction from his vote of confidence, there was little else of joy connected with the steel strike. By January 1920 the union movement had practically collapsed, although reverberations would be felt from the uproar for years to come. When invited to speak in Pittsburgh in April for the ZOA, Wise declined on the grounds that his identification with the strikers might hurt the Zionist cause. Later in the year, his lecture bureau scheduled Wise to speak in Pittsburgh to the men's club of Temple Rodef Shalom on "Jewish Problems." When Wise indicated his preference for discussing industrial matters, the engagement was quickly cancelled.[11] America's descent into the so-called "Red Scare" was scarcely its finest hour.

Wise, of course, fought the hysteria in every way he knew, and especially in speeches and sermons. The deportation of aliens appalled him, and he called for increased efforts to teach newcomers American ideals. Reactionary groups such as the Daughters of the American Revolution and the Key Men of America put his name on a list of those "considered so subversive that they were to be banned from speaking." The so-called National Security League declared that Wise "was not a patriot," and the local chapter at the University of Michigan, upon learning that the New York rabbi was to speak on campus, threatened to disrupt the meeting. Economist Isador Lubin met Wise at the train station to alert him to the danger, and asked if he wanted to cancel the program. An indignant Wise drew himself up to his full height and thundered at Lubin, "I will speak! I will not be threatened by the National Security or Securities League!"[12]

Many progressives including Wise feared that the general tide of reaction would not only sweep away earlier reform gains, but would bring conservative forces into power. They watched in despair as an incapacitated Wilson refused to compromise on minor issues and thus sent the entire treaty and the League of Nations down to defeat. A befuddled Democratic Party seemed incapable of deciding who it wanted to run in 1920, or the principles on which it should stand. The ticket of Governor James Cox of Ohio and former assistant Secretary of the Navy Franklin Roosevelt never had a chance, but beleaguered liberals had little choice but to back them as infinitely preferable to the boss-picked Republican slate of Warren Harding and Calvin Coolidge. Wise contributed some time in speaking for a Cox-Roosevelt Independent League, and on the local level worked to elect candidates free from the taint of Tammany.[13]

In the midst of the campaign, however, he learned that the Indiana State Democratic Committee had appealed to the Jewish voters of the state to cast their ballots against Harding because he had opposed Louis D. Brandeis's appointment to the Supreme Court. The thinly disguised message, that Harding was therefore antisemitic, appalled Wise, and he issued a statement condemning the Indiana Committee's actions. In words that would have earned him the approbation of the American Jewish Committee, Wise declared that "there is no Jewish vote and there will not be a Jewish vote. Jews, like members of all other religious and racial groups, vote as Americans." Harding had voted against Brandeis, Wise explained, not because of religion but because "Brandeis had become the greatest leader of sound, constructive liberalism in America. . . . I believe that Senator Harding would have voted against Mr. Brandeis if the latter had been a Protestant, Catholic or unbeliever."[14]

On November 2, Harding and Coolidge inundated the Democratic ticket, 16,152,000 to 9,147,000, with 404 electoral ballots to 127, the most smashingly one-sided victory since the election of 1820. Both houses of Congress went over to Republican control and many local reformers, including Al Smith of New York, were buried in the Republican landslide. "I was not surprised," Wise wrote to his daughter Justine, then a college student at Barnard. "I predicted a five to six hundred thousand majority in the state of New York for Harding, and it is nearly eleven hundred thousand." The only bright spot was the fine showing made by Al Smith, who even though defeated, ran over a million votes ahead of the national ticket. "I have so much to do, dear child, and I am just slightly dispirited."[15]

There was indeed much for Wise to be dispirited about, as America entered the frenzy of Republican prosperity. Not only the political situation dismayed him, the entire moral fabric of the nation seemed to unravel, as the high purpose and idealism of the Wilson administration gave way to crass materialism under Harding and Coolidge. The sanctity of home and marriage appeared threatened by the new status of women, while theater and literature denigrated the old standards of human conduct. Organized religion stood by helplessly, unable to sustain the old morality or provide a meaningful substitute. In a speech at Bryn Mawr College, Wise conceded that modern youth had revolted against organized religion because church and synagogue demanded too little, while the moral codes of Moses and Jesus demanded too much. "Modern youth finds the churches warring against each other instead of banding together for the common purpose of mankind's spiritual life," he said. "They find the church unchallenging, unexacting and undemanding. . . . In one manner or another, the church is silent in the face of the great inequities of our social order. You revolt because the church asks nothing of you." Yet if youth abandoned religion, what would serve as an anchor in their lives? "To be shrineless is to be purposeless," he warned. "There is no easy way through Egypt to Canaan. The mountain of the law must stand between the land of endeavor and the land of accomplishment."[16]

Even more alarming to Wise was the apparent disintegration of family life and personal morality which threatened the foundation of society. While Wise had long called for political and civic equality of women, like many other progressives he continued to expect women to remain the guardians of family purity and the protectors of decency. As women moved out of home and into the business world, many of them demanded greater freedom in terms of lifestyle and personal behavior. The flapper became the epitome of the "new woman," and her behavior appalled Wise, who attacked the whole syndrome in a number of sermons. One in particular, "The Daughters of Nice People," is worth looking at closely, for it summed up his horror at what the "new woman " supposedly meant for society and morality.

"I believe much in the present-day life of women is due to a half-conscious revolt against standards, some women making the terrible blunder not of insisting that men's standards shall be even as their own, but of acquiescing in the lower standards of men. It is as if women were to say: 'You need not be as clean as we have been, but we shall be as unclean as you have been!'"He acknowledged a reaction to the "social hypocrisy of other days with its conspiracies of silence and deceit, of wile and strategem. But the absence of high candor in one generation is no excuse for the next generation lapsing into the so called frankness which is little better than unashamed indecency and bestiality." The excesses of smoking and drinking, "lewd dancing" and "semi-nude dressing," the common use of cosmetics and all-night parties, had reduced the daughters of nice people to a level little better than women of the street. Yet even though he admitted that these excesses constituted a reaction to the hypocrisy of the Victorian era, Wise's own double standard showed plainly in an offhand reference to the sons of nice people who "will hardly be worth saving if the daughters continue to be as they are becoming."[17]

Wise's attitude in the 1920s reflected those of many progressives who had rather naively believed that progress could be achieved with little or no social upheaval, that humankind could travel an eternally upward road without losing that which had been good and noble in the past. They tended to identify that which they valued in middle-class life as the normative good, and were shocked and frightened when their assumptions were rejected by the children of "nice people." They failed to understand that the homebound role of middle-class women in the nineteenth century had reflected particular social and economic needs, that despite the granting of suffrage and the easier material life of women in the twentieth century, they would remain second-class human beings as long as they remained isolated in a rigidly defined role. Then as later, to be separate meant they could not be equal. Wise, like many liberally minded men, wanted to have his cake and eat it also. He endorsed the legal and civil equality of women, yet expected them to remain on a lofty pedestal in social moral matters.

Some progressives did try to come to grips with the full implication of women's equality, recognizing that marriage, for example, as defined in earlier times might have to be recast in form as well as substance, to allow for the growth and freedom of each partner. One such proposal came from Judge Benjamin B. Lindsey of Denver, whose pioneering work in children's court had made him particularly sensitive to the stresses of family life in the new era. In 1927 he and Wainwright Evans published a book entitled *Companionate Marriage* which summed up many ideas on reforming family life. Lindsey and Evans called for liberalization of the divorce laws to permit easier dissolution of unhappy unions, legalized dissemination of birth control information and devices, and a trial marriage in which couples could decide on the depth of their feelings and commitment to each other before opting for children and a permanent arrangement.

The proposal horrified Wise, who attacked it vigorously in speeches, articles, and a series of public debates with Lindsey. Both men agreed on the need for more equitable divorce laws as well as accessible contraception, but Wise saw the companionate arrangement as undermining the essential premise of marriage. In one symposium on Lindsey's proposal, Wise declared that "a marriage without risks or liability will be a better name for companionate marriage. It cannot be marriage as long as its essence is childlessness. Childbirth will then be the awful result of such an arrangement rather than the glorious consummation of marriage. . . . The rule that you must make marriage 'go' is infinitely better than the rule if you cannot make it go, go to Reno. Companionate marriage means exchanging your partner. Marriage means to change yourself." Lindsey proposed, according to Wise, legal sanction for temporary sexual unions, thus eroding the sanctity of family life.[18]

The Lindsey proposal was but one of the numerous assaults on marriage and morality in the 1920s, but it did have the virtue, as Wise freely admitted, of dealing with problems of family life and of individual freedom and responsibilty. It openly confronted the fact that many unions resulted from sexual needs, a base which might not support long–term commitments. But if the sexual component of marriage had been hidden or ignored in the Victorian scheme, novelists and playwrights now rushed to remedy this defect in the hunger for "openness" in the 1920s. For the first time, sexuality openly became a part of the American literary scene, and while artists dealt boldly but creatively with the subject, hacks and businessmen rushed to exploit the new candor.

Wise reacted as did many ministers, strongly condemning what he deemed immorality and filth. An avid threater-goer and reader, he found it personally degrading to have his favorite forms of entertainment corrupted by an undue emphasis on sex. "What are the facts about the theatre of New York today?" he asked the Free Synagogue. While there were some good plays, he conceded, there were also too many sleazy productions such as "The Demi-Virgin," which he termed "theatrical filth, gutter garbage of the foulest ranking kind. As I sat through a performance I thought of the degradation of a great art." The theater, he declared, reflects and at the same time affects life. Certain plays "are not merely salacious. They embody the vulgarity of all that is most vulgar and decadent on Broadway brought into the theatre. Now we are beginning to get a beautifully vicious circle . . . [in] that life is transferred to the theatre, so that they who know and live it may see it over again and find it good. And they who do not know it may be tainted and corrupted."[19]

Nor did modern literature hold much attraction for him, especially the works of novelist John Erskine, whose *Helen of Troy* and *Galahad* he characterized as "the most vicious books" he had read in a generation. They ridiculed tradition, repudiated any and all moral law, and in essence declared "that the quest of the human life is the quest of the evil, the bad, the vicious." In a symposium on literature and psychology in 1925, Wise lamented the failure of modern college students to read those classics which he had enjoyed in his youth, such as Arnold, Emerson, and Thackeray, with their edifying moral messages. He blamed this moral decline on the vogue of Sigmund Freud, which had replaced the earlier Kantian imperative of "Thou must, thou shall, thou canst" with "You may." Freudianism, he charged, "is a digging down into the sewage of our moods and appetites, dreams and passions."[20]

As a rabbi, Wise objected above all to anything that fomented anti-simitism and thus generated a physical danger as well as moral decay. Toward the end of December 1927 he perceived such a threat in Cecil B. DeMille's movie based on the life of Jesus entitled *The King of Kings*, which he termed "the Hollywood Oberammergau" for its vicious and distorted portraits of Jewish figures. For weeks he tried to get the producers, who ironically were Jewish, to alter the most objectionable parts of the film, warning that if it were shown in eastern Europe, it could easily loose a new pogrom. During this struggle, Wise found himself at odds with the B'nai B'rith Anti-Defamation League, which seemed willing to settle for meaningless changes in the dialogue captions. In the end, the film appeared in the United States with minor alterations, but the producers did withdraw it from circulation in eastern Europe.[21]

The real issue centered on how a free society, in an era of so-called openness, could act to prevent liberty from degenerating into license. Time and again Wise declared his opposition to censorship, yet as the moral level of theater and literature apparently declined, he not infrequently came close to supporting some type of censorship. "I would be glad if tomorrow the most strict and rigid censorship were to intervene," he said on one occasion, "not for play producers, but for the garbage distributors flourishing in our theatre today," Wise shared the sentiments of his good friend John Haynes Holmes, who wrote him: "I have never been a champion of censorship, but if something isn't done to stop the flood of filth in our theatres and bookshops, I can almost contemplate with philosophical resignation the closing of all the theatres and publishing houses."[22]

Wise remained acutely aware of the dangers of censorship and how easily one could misinterpret the true motivations of playwright or producer. A case in point is the 1923 play *The God of Vengeance*, which dealt with the life of several characters in a brothel. The production sparked a number of protests and the New York District Attorney's office secured an injunction to close the play on charges of indecency. Wise defended the work on the grounds that its essential message was highly moral. The sordid atmosphere did not exist to titillate the prurient, but to highlight the need for truth and purity. In a sermon, he called for the play to continue. "There are those who will misunderstand it," he admitted. "There are those who will mock and laugh and sneer in places where there is room for only tears and for horror. But I cannot find it in my heart to say other than this: 'The God of Vengeance' is a strong play, dealing with the most unpleasant things and yet dealing with them in such a way as to command the good and only the good." In the end the Court of Appeals dismissed the charges, and allowed the play to reopen with no restrictions.[23]

His fears of censorship also led Wise to oppose the so-called "Clean Books" bill introduced in the New York legislature in 1923. While acknowledging the mass of objectionable material, people had to think of the long-term results of censorship, and in a sermon to the Free Synagogue Wise spelled out what, in the end, can be seen as his controlling view of censorship in a free society:[24]

If we assent to censorship, we will find all of our freedom gone. It is the easiest and cheapest way out of an obligation to ask the State to do everything for us, and censorship is one of the stupid stratagems of democracy to find a way out of responsibility. Censorship is negative action. Negation will not help you to protect your children from the immoral and indecent play and book.

I hate obscene things as much as you do, but I am afraid censorship is not the way to stop them. I am an old-fashioned freedomist. I would infinitely rather have those things than any limitation on the freedom of thinking, writing and publishing. It is the passion of the day to limit freedom.

One can see through all this Wise's real ambivalence, not on the need for a high moral tone but on how to achieve that goal. He and other ministers called constantly for adherence to lofty ideals, a message that had but little impact in the 1920s. Many of the more zealous moralists had no qualms about the civil liberties issues involved, but although Wise was occasionally tempted by censorship, he would not risk freedom for short-term results. Even in the area of antisemitism, he once declared that he would not raise his voice against Henry Ford's *Dearborn Independent*, lest the most precious freedom of speech and press be diminished.[25]

Much of the problem, as Wise saw it, resulted from a lack of moral leadership in the government. How could anyone expect the common citizen to lead an idealistic life when high officials in Washington so blatantly violated the law? "I'm afraid in the present temper of the American people," he wrote, " it is hopeless to expect anything better. It is in truth a sad day in American life." Wise missed the moral tone of the progressive years; unless and until the country had leaders of Wilson's stature and vision, there was little hope of improving the moral climate of the nation. A people could not be expected to be better than its leaders.[26]

Thus, throughout the decade progressives sought political means to renew the reform impulse, but with little success. If it is true that a nation may reach heights of vision and achievement but once in a generation, then the American people had burned itself out in Wilson's great crusade, and now needed a rest from "uplift." To Wise, however, a country, like an individual, could not and should not surrender to material or intellectual or moral sloth. Greatness came only to persons who strove mightily for it, not to those who were content to wallow in luxury while social problems remained, or who wanted to get rich through speculative schemes. It could hardly be expected that a nation preoccupied with the stock market and totally indifferent to government scandals would demand a leadership calling for sacrifice and idealism, and this fact bore down heavily on Wise and other progressives.[27]

Harding's death in the summer of 1923 stunned the nation, and Wise momentarily had hopes that the stern New Englander who now sat in the White House might bring some probity back into government. Within a few months it became clear that Coolidge, even more than Harding, stood prepared to turn the entire country over to the control of the business community, for after all, as the president said, "The business of America is Business." Progressives began looking to the 1924 election in the vain hope that a revivified Wilsonianism could triumph over the worship of Baal.

William Gibbs McAdoo had long wanted to claim Wilson's mantle, but had been unable to act so long as the former president, who was also his father-in-law, still lived. After Wilson's death in 1923, McAdoo began planning for the Democratic convention, and asked Wise for his help, suggesting as well that the rabbi go to the convention either as a delegate or an alternate, with the right to speak from the floor. Although Wise agreed to attend the convention, by June 1924 he had swung his support over to Alfred E. Smith, who had been re-elected governor in 1922 and who had built a fine record of reform achievement in the Empire State. Smith was, Wise believed, the only real liberal among the contenders.[28]

The Democrats met in New York in late June, and the convention soon turned into a nightmare for both the Wilsonians and the party managers. McAdoo and Smith fought to a deadlock, neither one able to gather the necessary two-thirds vote, and finally a weary group of delegates chose Wall Street lawyer John W. Davis on the 103rd ballot. Progressives including Wise fought in vain for a strong platform and for a resolution condemning the Ku Klux Klan; only a few bright spots, such as Newton D. Baker's speech in support of the League of Nations, highlighted an altogether dismal and prolonged affair. While Davis appeared personally honest, he seemed much too conservaive and unimaginative to bear the Wilsonian standard. Given a choice between Coolidge and Davis, a number of progressives deserted both the Democrats and the Republicans to cross over to the LaFollette third-party candidacy. Although Wise personally admired the Wisconsin senator as a fighting liberal, he found the new alliance unappealing, a mottled group of factions more united by what they were against than what they were for.[29]

Wise's own indecision lasted well into the fall. At the end of September he told Holmes that the still awaited "the light which somehow does not seem to come." In the end, Wise reluctantly cast his vote for Davis, but only after he had delivered a stinging attack on the Republican ticket the Sunday before the election in a sermon that saw more than a dozen people walk out of Carnegie Hall in protest. Coolidge swamped Davis, but as Wise told Newton Baker, he felt no sense of personal grief as he had in 1920, when the electorate had turned its back on Woodrow Wilson.[30]

Wise did not, however, desert the Democratic camp. LaFollette's death put an end to the Progressive Party, and no outstanding liberals moved to create a new coalition. Moreover, it soon became clear that Al Smith would capture the 1928 Democratic nomination, and Smith's record in New York had won him the respect of many reformers. Smith, had two marks against him: he was Catholic and he opposed prohibition. Wise favored the ban on liquor and considered Smith's wetness regrettable but not controlling. As for Smith's religion, Wise deemed it not only irrelevant but a non-issue that had no place in the campaign. In March 1928 he told one correspondent that no person should be disqualified for public office because of religious beliefs, and specifically mentioned Smith as a man eminently qualified for the presidency. Wise and many others completely underestimated the depth of anti-Catholic feeling in the country; it was a bias that was carried home to him after a radio speech he gave in October calling for tolerance. In the next few days the rabbi's mail was inundated with letters accusing him and the Catholic Church of all manner of foul deeds and schemes. "I am amazed that a man of your standing and as a Jew," ran one typical message, "should stand before the microphone and praise the religion which is not a religion, but a great money-making scheme on the part of the heads of the Roman Catholic Church. By the way, do you know where all the little Catholic orphans come from?"[31]

In his pre-election sermon, Wise declared that he would vote "as an American for men of all faiths," supporting Smith, a Catholic, for the presidency, Franklin D. Roosevelt, a Protestant, for the governorship, and Herbert H. Lehman, a Jew, for lieutenant-governor. He would vote for Smith not because he was a Catholic or in spite of it. "The choice is really between two conceptions of America," he declared, "the difference between the conception of the present President who has said that the business of America is business and the conception of the next President of the United States, who believes that the business of America is America! The difference is between the conception of the Democratic candidate who believes in the regulation of business by government and the conception of the Republican Party which has led to the control of government by business!"[32]

Republican prosperity and anti-Catholic prejudice gave Hoover, who personally detested such bias, over 21 million popular votes to Smith's 15 million. The religious issue proved so strong that Hoover even broke into the normally solid South, and Smith garnered less than 90 electoral votes. In the days following the election Wise wrote letter after letter to friends bemoaning the sad state of the country and sounding out sentiment for a new party, one that would be dedicated to social and moral ideals. The Democrats had failed to provide leadership, and if liberals ever hoped to gain power, they would have to do so through some new vehicle. But everywhere that Wise turned he found his friends, like him, more than "slightly dispirited."[33]

13

The Jewish Institute
of Religion

The Balfour Declaration, the battle for the Congress, the invigoration of American Zionism, and its ensuing schism all had profound impact upon the Jewish community in the United States; the assumptions and relationships that had governed in the prewar years had been, if not shattered, severely strained. The earlier attitudes of Reform leaders in particular appeared irrelevant to Wise, and he watched anxiously to see how the major organs of the movement would adapt to new realities. As the decade wore on, however, he and other Reform rabbis began to despair over the leadership of Reform Judaism in America. Solomon Goldman of Chicago asked: "With what forward-looking movements is Reform Judaism identified? Where in the United States is the Reform temple regarded as the symbol of the pain and travail that accompany the birth of new ideas?"[1] Although Wise never left the Reform movement, he in effect left it far behind. Not until after World War Two would the organized arms of American Reform finally catch up to the policies he had enunciated years earlier in respect to Zionism, social welfare, and the relation of religion to everyday life.

Wise was meanwhile becoming an institution of his own, a model of forceful speaking and action, a rabbi who tried not only to explain the prophetic teachings but to apply them to modern life and its problems. Nearly every week brought one or more letters from young rabbis seeking his advice on personal or professional matters. These ranged from the question of fees for ministerial services to soothing the ruffled feelings of an assistant rabbi passed over for a senior pulpit to counseling young men about how they could be most effective.[2] Frequently he received letters from young rabbis despairing of accomplishing anything in their congregation, asking Wise if they should move on to try elsewhere. Invariably he responded as he did to Israel Goldstein: "I am persuaded that it is your duty to stay where you are and do your work. . . . I have no doubt there are many and serious difficulties which lie before you. I have no doubt that opportunities not a few are coming and will come to you, the acceptance of any one of which would mean ease, comfort and speedily earned personal distinctions. But if you would have my counsel as a friend and older colleague in the ministry, I would say to you your highest duty lies where you are in the continuance of the work which you are doing."[3]

His obvious influence and standing with many other rabbis, especially the younger men, and his equally obvious failure to move the established agencies of the Reform movement, led Wise to re-examine a long-dormant idea, the founding of a new, liberal and independent seminary. The first reference to this notion is in a letter to his wife in 1909:

> A lovely young boy came to me yesterday from Cincinnati—he is so unhappy at the [Hebrew Union] College. The boy is dejected and almost sullen. Now, Madam, please hold your breath while I tell you something. Why shouldn't I have a school for the training of Jewish ministers?. . .The practical experience, training and discipline they could get under me! I am just aflame with the idea and I will do it, and you'll help me and it will be blessed of God.

A year later he discussed the idea again, this time with Richard Gottheil, pointing out that he hoped for diversity in his school rather than the mental lockstep that prevailed in Cincinnati.[4]

But the burden of the Free Synagogue, secular responsibilities, and then the wartime duties of Zionism led to deferring the seminary plan until 1920. By then Wise's fight with Reform leaders had gone on long enough for him to recognize that he had little chance of capturing the CCAR or Hebrew Union College to his views. In the spring of that year he began discussing the idea with a number of people, including George Kohut and Mordecai Kaplan, and above all with officers and trustees of the Free Synagogue. At a special meeting on November 2, 1920, the board gave its blessing to the plan and appointed a committee to investigate the feasibility of establishing a rabbinical training institute. What is noteworthy about the discussion at this meeeting is the concept of the rabbinate as a profession, akin to medicine and law, and one that requires a broad-based liberal education. At that time, both Hebrew Union and the Jewish Theological Seminary accepted youths as young as twelve or fourteen, who then went through a preparatory department before entering rabbinical studies. Wise believed that no one should begin theological studies until after receiving an adequate college education. The program of the Jewish Institute of Religion (JIR) began and remained a professional, post-baccalaureate course of instruction.[5]

A second distinguishing feature of JIR can be found in Wise's determination that, for students and teachers alike, it be intellectually and spiritually catholic, embracing all shades of Jewish belief and practice. Over the years teachers and students representing Orthodox, Conservative, Reconstructionist, and Reform viewpoints met to discuss their ideas and to learn from one another. Probably no other seminary in the world, of any denomination, welcomed the chance to examine new and different ideas in an atmosphere of complete academic freedom as did JIR. Wise never acted in a doctrinaire fashion, and this liberal spirit infused his school as well. Still another characteristic that set the Institute apart derived from one of the basic premises of the Free Synagogue: that in order to carry out the precepts of prohetic Judaism, one had to participate in the life and problems of the society at large. The Social Service program of the Free Synagogue provided the model for JIR, and Sidney Goldstein played a major role in developing that part of the curriculum dealing with community agencies and societal issues.[6]

In 1921 Wise and the trustees of the Free Synagogue began their work in earnest. Enough funds were secured to tide the Institute over its first two years, thanks to the generosity of Adolph Lewisohn, Abram Elkus, and Bertha Guggenheimer. Because the Free Synagogue House (a building housing administrative, educational, and social service offices but not a sanctuary) was not yet complete, Temple Israel offered the use of its classrooms for the first year. After that, the Institute and the Free Synagogue shared the same quarters for a number of years. Dr. Emil Hirsch of Chicago donated a large number of books, and Wise gave his own library to form the core from which the school's own collection would ultimately grow.[7]

The trustees of the Free Synagogue recognized that in the long run JIR would require greater financial support than they could provide. They delegated Abram Elkus, then president of the synagogue, to meet with the executive board of the Union of American Hebrew Congregations, the parent body of Reform Judaism, in order to seek support akin to that which UAHC provided for Hebrew Union College. The memorandum Elkus presented enumerated the considerations (other than the parochialism of HUC) that had led Wise and the Free Synagogue to propose a new seminary: the size of the Jewish population of New York, the opportunity for "laboratory practice" in this heterogeneous community, the intent to enroll only college graduates, the need for social service training, and the commitment to academic freedom. The Union responded in a cautious but not hostile manner, and appointed a subcommittee to examine the problems of cooperation and support. Three meetings took place, and at the third the Institute backers proposed that the new JIR become an activity of the Union, co-equal with the College, between which there could be exchanges of faculty and students. Wise would place his talents in the service of the Union to raise funds for both schools. The Union would be expected to provide a minimum of $45,000 annually for the first three years, and in return would have one-fifth of the seats on the Institute's board of trustees. It was to be understood by all parties that the Jewish Institute of Religion would at all times retain complete autonomy.[8]

This plan, which seemed rational and fair to Wise and his colleagues, struck the Union's executive committee as patently unreasonble. The committee clearly indicated its belief that Hebrew Union College more than met the needs of American Jewry, whose "best interest. . .will be conserved not by founding a new institution, but by strengthening the present support of the College." The Union also objected to the plan that called for it to provide so much financial assistance without control of the school. This lack of control, of course, was essential in Wise's view, to prevent JIR from becoming an East Coast version of HUC, a school which in his opinion lacked any claim to academic freedom or intellectual vitality. It is likely that Wise, Lee Frankel, Abram Elkus, and the other founders of JIR expected that the Union would not agree to their terms, that the offer had been made primarily to appear willing to cooperate and thus forestall charges of fractionalization. To a friend Wise wrote: "As I expected it has come to pass. The enclosed communication. . .is a notice of war. I have done my best and my conscience is clear. We have now done all that could be done. The truth is perhaps we never should have expected that there would be any attempt on the part of those in authority to foregather with us. . . . But we shall go on. If I live the Institute will be established, its doors to be thrown open on October 4th."[9]

Wise's apprehensions of war unfortunately proved accurate, and relations between the Union and JIR remained soured for years. Charles Shohl, president of the UAHC, sent out a circular letter to the Union's two hundred constituent congregations urging them not to cooperate with Wise in his efforts to launch and support the new seminary. Some rabbis did, in fact, preach sermons attacking Wise and JIR, while others, including Abba Hillel Silver and Max Heller, strongly rebuked Union officials for their shortsightedness.[10] It is unlikely that Shohl's efforts accomplished anything other than confirming Wise's belief in the absolute necessity of a new school free from the narrowmindedness of the Union and its College. He set about diligently securing funds, and in the summer of 1922 sailed for Europe to recruit faculty.

The trip proved particularly invigorating for him. After the year-long hassle with the Union, he was now free to move, to act, and to do so on his own terms. He felt rejuvenated, he wrote Max Heller, away "from the atmosphere of American Jewish pettiness and rabbinical malignities." Notes and memoranda he jotted from time to time caught this feeling of elation and optimism, as he met with Israel Abrahams, Claude Montefiore, Ismar Elbogen, and other scholars.[11]

When Wise returned to New York at the end of August, he found his desk piled with letters of support and a number of applications for admission. He joyously wrote to Martin Meyer: "I spent one of the happiest moments of my life in my study this morning with seven different men, every one of them a joy to meet, and evocative of highest hope. Not one of these boys would have dreamed of going to Cincinnati. One morning has convinced me of the need of the work we ought to do. . . . I almost tremble at the immensity of the task before us."[12]

The task indeed proved immense, and in the twenty-seven years after JIR's founding in 1922, it provided him with some of his greatest burdens as well as some of his happiest moments. As Michael Meyer aptly notes, Stephen Wise was the heart of the Jewish Institute of Religion. He recruited the faculty and the students, taught classes, raised funds, placed graduates, and fought constantly to ensure that JIR and its rabbis received their proper due from the community. He treated each of the students as his own child, and they reciprocated with love and respect. From the beginning, however, he considered himself unworthy of being the president of the Institute. He was no theologian, and despite his work on ibn Gabirol, no scholar either. For all his claims of envying the academic life, Wise was too much the activist ever to be constrained by the patience and contemplation of a scholarly role. Yet unlike some activists, he truly respected scholars, and wanted to find a leading theologian to head JIR. He had, in fact, originally offered the presidency to Emil Hirsch, but Hirsch turned 70 in 1922 and felt physically unequal to the task. The Chicago rabbi did accept the honorary presidency and agreed to be visiting professor of theology, but died in January 1923 before giving a single lecture. Similarly, the eminent English scholar Israel Abrahams also felt too advanced in years to assume the burden, although he came to New York to receive the school's first honorary degree in 1924 and stayed to give a series of lectures.[13]

The man Wise sought most persistently for the presidency was Mordecai Kaplan, perhaps the most original American Jewish philosopher of the twentieth century. Kaplan, then at the Jewish Theological Seminary, had a well-deserved reputation as a thinker, scholar, and teacher, but his iconoclastic theological views set him apart from his colleagues in the Conservative movement. The eclectic JIR appeared an obvious home for Kaplan, and for several years Wise and Kaplan talked and talked, but to no end. Many years later Kaplan admitted that perhaps he should have gone to JIR, but feared that men like Henry Slonimsky and Chaim Tchernowitz were as opposed to his Reconstructionist philosophy as were the faculty of the Jewish Theological Seminary.[14] Finally, in 1927, upon the unanimous demand of the faculty, Wise stopped signing "acting president" after his name and assumed the title along with the the functions of the president, a position he occupied until his death. Throughout all these years Wise tied together the elements that made up the school: board, faculty, and students.

The board of trustees derived primarily from the leadership of the Free Synagogue or from a group of Wise's close friends, and it changed little over the years. Lee K. Frankel, an insurance executive, served as the first chairman until 1927, to be succeeded by U.S. Court of Appeals Judge Julian W. Mack, Wise's colleague and friend from the Zionist years. Mack, a warm and outgoing man, held this office until his death in 1943. Although he and Wise agreed on most issues, Mack tended to emphasize the scholarly nature of a rabbinical seminary, while Wise sought to make it more of a professional school.[15] Following Mack, Judge Joseph W. Levine of the Free Synagogue headed the trustees during Wise's final years. Nearly all the board members were from New York, and they shared one thing in common: respect for and the devotion to Stephen Wise. They had no obligation to raise funds, although most of them contributed generously to the school. There was one scholar on the board, however—Wise's boyhood friend George Kohut. Wise turned to him frequently for advice on matters relating to faculty appointments, new courses, and book purchases.

Wise's relations with the teachers seemed to have been relatively good. They complained to him, as they would have to any president, about low pay and student problems, but they also recognized that Wise played an important role in advancing Jewish learning and in defending Jewish causes. Moreover, one could not deny the high quality of people he brought to the Institute, some on a visiting basis, others for longer periods of service. The list of brilliant people who at one time or another taught at the Jewish Institute of Religion included Harry Wolfson, Salo Baron, Julian Oberman, Ralph Marcus, Shalom Spiegel, Israel Abrahams, David Yellin, Mordecai Kaplan, Ismar Elbogen, and many others. It was a fabulous and opulent intellectual repast, in many cases far too rich for the students. As one of them commented, in Chaim Tchernowitz they had one of the great Talmudic scholars of the world but they could not understand him; "what we needed was *aleph bes!*"[16]

The teacher they had no trouble in understanding was Wise himself, who had a profound effect on the students during their years at the Institute and thereafter. Every Thursday he met with them for the course on "Problems of the Ministry," which the students referred to as "Schmoos Session with the Chief." Here Wise spent some time on the daily practical matters confronting a rabbi, but for the most part he dealt with the broader problems of the Jewish people and especially of Zionism. Over the years, Wise invited hundreds of community, state, national, and world leaders to share their views with his boys. In what other seminary could students meet with labor leaders such as William Green, Sidney Hillman,, or Jacob Potofsky; social workers ranging from Mary Simhkovitch to John Lovejoy Elliot; social reform advocates including Norman Thomas, Morris Hillquit, Rev. Henry A. Atkinson, and Father John A. Ryan; Zionist leaders of the rank of Chaim Weizmann and Vladimir Jabotinsky; as well as political leaders of every party? And at all times Wise himself would tell of his own past and current battles.[17]

On Friday, Wise led the class in "Homiletics," where the greatest preacher of American Judaism gave his students lessons and advice drawn from his own years of experience. He repeated over and over again his father's advice that they should be themselves, and attempted to prevent them from modeling their style after his. "One Stephen Wise is enough!" he declared, yet there is not doubt that, as Carl Voss noted, a whole crop of miniature Stephen Wises soon sprouted in synagogues around the country. One day a student preached on "The Prophetic Tradition of Judaism," and imitated Wise so effectively that the entire class had difficulty restraining their laughter. At the climax of the oration, the would-be rabbi declaimed: "It is our bounden duty to maintain the prophetic tradition in Judaism, that prophetic tradition which began with Isaiah and continues with Stephen Wise." He sat down and awaited Wise's verdict. Shaking his leonine head slowly back and forth, Wise glowered at the student for a few moments and then grinned: "Why drag in Isaiah?"[18]

But despite such moments of flippancy, Wise could be a merciless critic. He would sit there listening, his eyes closed and his head nodding, so that often the students feared he had dropped off to sleep; but the minute the practice sermon ended, he would be on his feet, remembering every detail of content and delivery.[19] Did the student rely too much on *The Nation, The New Republic*, or some other current journal? "When did you last read Maimonides? Or Spinoza or Josephus? They, too, had a word for our age." He urged them to listen to other preachers, including non-Jewish ministers such as S. Parkes Cadman or Harry Emerson Fosdick or even the revivalist "Gypsy" Smith. Above all, they should study "the unmatched prince of the pulpit," his close friend John Haynes Holmes of the Community Church.

The students accepted Wise's suggestions and criticisms no matter how harsh they might be, because they knew that he spoke to them from a loving and caring heart. They were far less tolerant of the biting critiques they received from other faculty. Professor Joel Blau once attacked a practice sermon of Philip Bernstein's, declaring that it sounded like an editorial from *The Nation*; on another occasion in the chapel, he kept making faces and depracatory asides while Bernstein preached on pacifism. Finally the young student could stand it no longer and before the entire sudent body told Blau: "You have no right to criticize me. Your conduct today is unworthy of a rabbi and a teacher. You should be ashamed of yourself." Blau promptly reported the incident to Wise, who called both men in to his study. There he "scolded" Bernstein for his rudeness and told him to "apologize," but the twinkle in his eye did not go unnoticed.[20]

There developed a camaraderie between Wise and the Institute students akin to that of father and sons. Each year on his birthday, Wise took the students to a Hungarian restaurant on the East Side, where Holmes presided as master of cermonies. They came to him with their problems and joys, both academic and personal, and on more than one occasion he lent them money out of his own pocket so they could get married or remain in school. In later years he went out of his way to accept their invitations to preach in their synagogues, or to install them in new pulpits. Some JIR graduates in- · dicated the affection and respect they had for Wise by naming their first sons after him.

There is no doubt that nearly all the students came to the Institute because of Wise. Philip Bernstein, for example, while working as a clothing salesman after school, learned that Julius Morgenstern, head of Hebrew Union College, would be in Rochester for a sermon, and arranged to meet him. Berstein informed the visitor that he was thinking of entering the rabbinate, and wanted to know what qualities were necessary. Morgenstern rather pompously replied: "Saintliness, nobility of character and lofty idealism." The younger man thanked him and to himself said "Bernstein, stay in the pants business."

A month or so later in the spring of 1922, Bernstein learned that Stephen Wise, about to open a new rabbinical seminary, would be speaking in nearby Syracuse. He traveled there to meet him, and after the banquet went to the head table to introduce himself. Gates Thalheimer, the president of the synagogue, cordially offered Bernstein a cigar, but the latter, who did not smoke, declined. Wise, however reached over and grabbed the cigar. "When you are a rabbi, " he said, "always accept cigars offered by the rich members of the congregation and give them to poor members." "That's the kind of ethics I like," Bernstein thought, and decided to enroll in the opening class at JIR.[21]

Another student of an entirely different sort who also came to the Institute because of Wise was Jacob X. Cohen. A well-known sanitary engineer and one of the original members of the Free Synagogue, Cohen had helped found the Bronx branch and then served as its first president. Always interested in urban and social reform, Cohen became more and more involved in Judaism. When Wise opened the Institute, Cohen went to speak to him, and poured out his dream of doing something to help his fellow Jews. Wise summed up the situation in a moment, and told Cohen he must come to JIR and become a rabbi, no matter that he was 35 and had a wife and daughter. Wise arranged for Cohen to serve as executive secretary of the Free Synagogue while he studied next door at the Institute, and after his ordination in 1928, Cohen became associate rabbi and Wise's alterego in several undertakings, including the American Jewish Congress. Bernstein and Cohen were indicative of the wide heterogeneity in the student body, a group as varied as its faculty, and which for a while included Wise's son Jim.[22]

The essential weakness of the JIR was its lack of a strong financial base. It had neither an endowment nor a subsidy from the UAHC, and depended for its yearly operating revenues upon Wise's success in fund-raising; when the Depression hit at the end of the decade, Wise could barely keep the Institute afloat.

He had started out believing, perhaps naively, that he would have no difficulty raising funds. In April 1923 he described the task as "pretty easy," and predicted he "wouldn't have the least difficulty in getting $100,000 a year for the next two or three years." Within ten years, he believed, there would be enough put aside to purchase a building. By that fall he had given up most of his outside lecturing save for JIR-related matters. He often agreed to speak in a community for nothing but travel expenses provided he had the opportunity to meet privately afterward with some of the town's leading Jewish citizens to ask them to support the Institute.[23] Although by May 1924 he had raised approximately $45,000 for the building fund, Wise had discovered that the ongoing task was much harder than he had earlier anticipated. "If the Jews of New York and of the country gave me the support to which I believe I am entitled," he complained, "I would not have to spend my time and strength to go through the country begging for money with which to maintain the work of JIR." He discovered that not all communities wanted to hear about the Institute, and some congregations would not even let him raise the subject. By early 1928, the mood of Wise's letters definitely took on more pessimistic tone. To Morton Berman, one of the JIR's first graduates, Wise wrote:[24]

> I am desperately worried about the Institute. If we don't get $10,000 this year from the graduates I shall seriously consider discontinuing the Institute. This is not for publication but will have to be done . There is no other way. We can give ourselves two years to wind up, admit no more students, give the professors an extra year's salary, and then "Good Night." I have no right to go on even though I stay alive unless I have some assurance that the work can be carried out. At present I have not.

One proposed solution that arose periodically involved reaching some sort of agreement with the UAHC. Throughout the decade there were sporadic attempts to tie the Institute in to the organizational structure of the Reform movement. Julius Morgenstern of Hebrew Union and Charles Bloch of the Free Synagogue had an extended conversation concerning this in November 1923. More serious discussions took place in 1929, when the Union initiated negotiations to provide cooperation between College and Institute. Although here again JIR trustees moved cautiously and hopefully, they found that the champions of Hebrew Union were unwilling to allow any arrangement that did not place the New York school in a decidedly inferior positon. In fact, Hebrew Union began formulating plans for a graduate program, a proposal for which Wise had been denounced in 1922, and which he now saw simply as a maneuver to postpone any rapprochement between the two schools. Although the talks dragged on for several months, nothing came of them. The Cincinnati people really wanted no ties at all with JIR, while Wise and his associates would yield little to the Union.[25] No matter how difficult it might be to sustain the Institute, it still represented their dream of a modern rabbinical seminary, one attuned to the precepts of prophetic Judaism and to the social needs of modern American Jewry.

And Wise, for all the difficulties, derived enormous pride and pleasure from JIR. He could boast of good students and excellent faculty. The quality of the teachers, as a matter of fact, led to an unexpected problem that must have given Wise somewhat questionable satisfaction—other schools were stealing his teachers! Harvard lured away Harry Wolfson, for example, while Columbia took Salo W. Baron, two of the greatest Judaic scholars of the century. As Wise noted, such "dubious compliments" might be a great honor, but they entailed major losses for the school.[26]

On May 26, 1926, the Jewish Institute of Religion graduated its first class as ten men received the degree of Master of Hebrew Literature and Rabbi. No other group in the long history of Judaism had ever received such training. Compared to traditional rabbinical graduates, they no doubt lacked much in Hebrew, Talmud, and Halachah (Jewish law), but they certainly knew more about the world and its problems. In the course of their studies they had been exposed not only to Jewish ideas, but had also spent time with noted Christian scholars and community leaders as well. Wise opened the charge to his graduating students with words from Ezekial: "Son of man stand upon thy feet, and I shall speak with thee, and men, whether they hear or forebear, shall know that I the Lord thy God, have sent thee." Each of the ten then came forward for a private word from Wise and his personal blessing. Interestingly, in these early years the word "ordination" was never used, nor did the graduates receive the traditional *s'micha*, two ommissions designed to point up the professional nature of the Institute's training.

In additional to the rabbinic degrees, the Institute that year also awarded two honorary Doctorates of Hebrew Literature, the recipients representing not only polar opposites in Jewish Life but the catholic view of JIR as well. Claude Montefiore, the English scholar and leader of British Liberal Judaism, completely opposed Zionism, while Chaim Nachman Bialik, the great poet of modern Hebrew, epitomized the Zionist renaissance. Montefiore could not attend owing to illness, but Bialik, then on a visit to America, received his degree in person. He lauded Wise's work, and referred to the honor as symbolic of a covenant between Jewish scholarship and Hebrew literature.[27]

Continuing friction with the UAHC and the blatant discrimination practices against JIR graduates by Reform leaders for many years prevented the school from exercising the influence in American Reform which Wise had hoped it would. The Depression dealt a severe financial blow to JIR, dependent as it was on annual solicitations for its operating expenses. So tied was the school to Wise for its funds that the trustees took out several life insurance policies on him, with the proceeds payable to the Institute.

Yet in the end the Jewish Institute of Religion did set a new pattern for Reform and even Conservative rabbinical training. Gradually Wise's views on the desirability of a college education preparatory to professional studies, the importance of the social sciences, the need for sensitivity to societal issues and exposure to community agencies, the awareness of the importance of Zionism and a Jewish homeland—all became accepted. Before that could happen, however, nearly a whole generation of classical Reform leaders would have to die out, paving the way for those attuned to the needs Wise had recognized decades earlier.

14

"Ivri Anochi"

For Wise, Judaism was neither an anachronism nor a fossil, but a living dynamic religion, with Zionism signaling the modern renascence of Jewish creativity. He did not fear Christianity as a rival religion, nor did he want to isolate Judaism from contact with other creeds. Many rabbis of the time "explained" Judaism to Christians, but Wise went much further; he accepted the historical and credal connection between the two, and told Christians they were not living up to the teachings of the man they professed to worship.

There is a continuing interest in Jesus throughout Wise's career, and he seems to have studied the Nazarene's life quite carefully, "I have given much thought to the problem," he wrote in 1922, and "it is my deepest conviction that Jesus was not God in the form of man but a man who was God-like—not like God come to earth but a man aspiring to reach life's highest nearness unto God." Wise took great pains to separate Jesus from Christianity; the one he respected, the other he charged perverted the high moral teachings of the former. "The world," he once declared, "is far from Christianized as yet," and few people had ever had a chance to see its lofty principles translated into action. Once at the Student-Faculty Forum of Union Theological Seminary, a student asked Wise, "Why don't the Jews accept Jesus Christ?" In the tense silence, Wise replied: "We Jews take Jesus seriously. Do you Christians?" Not one of the students had an answer. Wise criticized Christianity often, pointing out, however, that he did not attack the religion of Jesus. "The religion of Jesus is not Christianity," he averred. Christianity is a substitute for the religion of Christ. I am not an anti-Christian; I am an ante-Christian."[1]

Carl Voss once said that "Stephen Wise was the most Christian man I ever knew," meaning that Wise tried to live out in his own life the teachings of brotherhood enunciated by the Galilean Jew two millennia earlier. Wise spoke frequently at Christian forums and for Christian causes, such as a fund raising dinner for the Cathedral of St. John Divine or the annual banquet of the Presbyterian Labor Temple. He invited Christian ministers to speak at both the Jewish Institute of Religion and the Free Synagogue. In turn, he often occupied the pulpits of Christian churches, and became the first rabbi invited to give the sermon at the American Church in Paris on his trip to Europe in 1927, at a service crowded to the doors.[2]

Perhaps the finest example of Wise's involvement and commitment to Jewish-Christian relations can be found in his close personal ties and friendship with John Haynes Holmes. Each man deserved the title of *ex officio* minister in the other's congregation, so often did they exchange pulpits and work with the various clubs and service groups. When Holmes's church burned down, Wise and the Free Synagogue made a substantial donation to help rebuild it, and Holmes once jokingly suggested that on his tombstone he should be remembered as the master of ceremonies at Wise's annual birthday celebrations. On June 8, 1930, Holmes received what he considered and valued as one of the great honors in his life, an honorary doctorate from the Jewish Institute of Religion. The citation read in part: "Religionist, humanist, battler for divine values and human life . . . hospitable to truth whether uttered by Isaiah or Marx, or Lincoln, Tolstoy or Ghandi, mighty apostle of justice and relentlessly militant prophet of peace . . . defender of Israel because friend of man, servant of justice and helper of the wronged."[3]

Wise had less trouble in explaining Judaism or even non-Pauline Christianity to Christians than he had attempting to inform his fellow Jews of the life and teachings of Jesus. One of his sermons on this subject, delivered to the Free Synagogue in Carnegie Hall on December 20, 1925 and entitled "A Jew's View of Jesus," nearly split the community, and had enormous impact for years to come.

Wise built his sermon that day around the recent English translation of Joseph Klausner's 1922 study, *Jesus of Nazareth: His Life, Times and Teaching.* Klausner, a professor at the Hebrew University in Jerusalem, had impeccable credentials as a Jewish scholar. His work, reflective of late-nineteenth-century "higher Biblical criticism," attempted to look at Jesus and his ministry in the context of his time and place, Jewish Palestine under Roman rule. Much of the teaching credited to Jesus in the synoptic gospels reflected contemporary rabbinic thought; the famous Golden Rule, for example, restated one of Hillel's dicta.

Wise's sermon, delivered the Sunday before Christmas, had four basic points: (1) Jesus was man, not God; (2) Jesus was a Jew, not a Christian (3) Jews have not repudiated Jesus the Jew; and (4) Christians have, for the most part, not adopted and followed Jesus the Jew. In his talk, Wise denied that Jesus was a myth; all the evidence indicated that a man, Jesus of Nazareth, had indeed lived and then died upon a cross. "For years I have been led to believe, like thousands of other Jews, that Jesus never existed,'' Wise said. "I say this is not so. Jesus was.'' But the Jesus of history was not the Jesus Christ of the New Testament. Jesus was a Jew, Wise declared, a link in the great chain of Jewish teachers stretching from Abraham to Moses to Isaiah, Amos and Micah. The Christ figure developed by Paul and the Church Fathers distorted the historical Jesus, whose Jewish teachings were twisted to form a new doctrine. The essential and historical Jesus could still be accepted by Jews, although Christians no longer followed the true Jesus, who had lived and taught as a Jew.[4]

Ironically, Wise said nothing new in his 1925 sermon. For years "The Christlessness of Christianity" had been his favorite lecture topic before Christians, especially ministerial groups, and he took special delight in charging them with failing to obey Jesus and his ethical teachings. When a newspaper once misquoted him in such a way as to imply disrespect on his part, he immediately wrote to set the record straight: "I never made any reference to Jesus save in terms of that profound reverence which I feel for the spiritual character which is the possession of Israel and Christendom alike." Another time, when asked, "What do you think about Jesus?" he responded, "Jesus is my elder brother." As early as 1906 he had publicly discussed the relation of Judaism to other faiths, noting always that Jesus "is our own. He belongs in the eternal order of the prophets whose crown perhaps is radiant, uniquely benignant and beneficent." In a 1916 sermon at the Free Synagogue, he had said:[5]

> What man, who thinks of the example of Jesus, can escape the mystery and the marvel of it, can resist its appeal? The great power of Christianity rests in that ethical and spiritual compulsion which that personality brought about. The Jewish position is as great and wondrous and appealing as is that radiant personality. That personality is not divine in any unique sense. We desire to emulate that high personality, but not to limit our emulation to and of that personality. The Jew recognizes, marvels at the radiance, the benignity of the personality of Jesus, the Nazarene Jew, but we do not class that personality by the side of God. God is One—unique, not humanly inimitable, but humanly attainable.

These earlier comments, while they may have disturbed some people, Jew and Christian alike, had aroused no public controversy. This time, however Wise stood as the best-known rabbi in America, recognized as a leader of his people, and the Orthodox section of the community exploded.

The Yiddish *Der Morgen Journal*, which represented the strict Orthodox viewpoint, responded to Wise's 1925 sermon by means of a black-bordered editorial on its front page, in which Gedalia Bublick charged Wise with near apostasy and a betrayal of Judaism. The *Tageblatt*, another representative of traditionalism, accused Wise of directing "the younger generation to the baptismal font." Young Israel of Brooklyn censured him, labeling his ideas "a grave menance to Judaism," while the Union of Orthodox Rabbis condemned him for an act "which may drive our children to conversion." The ultra-orthodox rabbinical group, the Agudath Harabonim, went so far as to impose *cherem*, excommunicating Wise from the Jewish people. Equally exacerbating to some Jews was the fact that the day after the sermon, the Philadelphia Methodist and Episcopalian Ministers Association hailed Wise as a brother. As he later wrote somewhat ruefully, "I know not which was more hurtful—the acceptance of me as a brother and welcoming me into the Christian fold or the violent diatribe of a fellow rabbi."[6]

Nor were the Orthodox the only ones upset by the Jesus sermon. Wise's old nemesis, Rabbi Samuel Schulman, grabbed at the opportunity to flay this man who had once again disturbed the peace and quiet of the Reform rabbinate. "The sensationalist of the Jewish Pulpit is again on the rampage." He charged, "Rabbi Wise's remarks were entirely uncalled for. It is an indisputable fact that to the consciousness of Christendom Jesus is more than man. He is therefore impossible for any Jew. When Christians wil cease calling Jesus God, Israel will know what to do with him as a man. . . . It does not help religion much to make such superficial, sensational and facetious statements as those in which Rabbi Wise indulged." Louis Marshall, while agreeing with the substance of Wise's sermon, rather unctuously commented: "I am sure Dr. Wise did not intend to express any opinion looking to apostasy. It is regrettable that he has been misunderstood and misinterpreted both by Jews and non-Jews. It merely proves how circumspect a preacher must be when those whom he addresses have varying points of view. They naturally apply to his words conflicting definitions. The unfailing consequence is a war of polemics, which is always deplorable."[7]

For the most part, however, the Reform rabbinate this time rose to Wise's defense, as did many lay leaders. William Fineshriber wrote: "My dear Wise—Be of good courage, neither be thou dismayed, and forgive them for they know not what to say." Other rabbis could preach much the same message without stirring such an alarum, he said, and for this Wise ought to be rather flattered. Above all else, Fineshriber counseled, "Laugh, for that blessed Yiddish press, for tolerance of spirit, gets the cheesecake." For Samuel Untermyer, president of the Keren Haysod, wrote to say that Wise could count on his support, while Nathan Straus, the grand old man of American Jewry, urged him not to lose heart. Rabbi Nathan Kraus of Emanu-El also came to Wise's defense, charging that "a small group of ignorant fanatical Jews passed a bigoted, vicious, nasty resolution condemning a rabbi who has given his life in the service of Israel. [They and] the so-called liberal rabbis who attack Dr. Wise . . . ought to be ashamed of their inexcusable conduct."[8]

The controversy might have been less upsetting for Wise had it remained solely in the realm of historical or theological debate. But the Orthodox groups, in condemning his stand, also labeled him as unfit to head the United Palestine Appeal and called for his resignation as chairman of that fund-raising agency, which had just set as its goal for that year the unprecedented sum of $5 million. Leading the clamor was the Mizrachi, the religiously oriented Zionist organization, but many Zionists who were far from orthodox or even observant also felt strongly. Unless peace could be made, the collections for the *yishuv* would suffer, the UPA, which Emanuel Neumann and Wise had nurtured from its inception a few years earlier, would collapse.

Wise asked for an interview with the Orthodox leaders and received it. The atmosphere at the meeting, in Judd Teller's words, "must have been not unlike that which prevailed at the religious court in Amsterdam when Spinoza was summoned to answer charges of heresy." Wise donned a *yarmulke* (skullcap) for the occasion, and looking every bit the penitent, assured the grim-faced audience that he had never called upon his congregation to "accept Jesus as teacher." In fact, as he explained to Edmund Waterman, "I feel deeply that I must show to Jews, particularly young Jews in America, that Jesus is not alien to us, that his faith and life are a part of the Jewish possessions, and of the very fiber of our Jewish heritage. I do this not that they may go over to Christianity, but that they may remain loyal to Judaism. I would sooner cut off my hand than weaken the loyalty of any Jew to the heritage of his faith and life."[9]

The Free Synagogue's leader left the meeting without a verdict, to learn a few hours later that the more than one hundred rabbis assembled had unanimously called for his resignation from the UPA. "The Orthodox, of course, don't like me," he told a friend, "and they have been trying to get me for twenty years. I never gave them a good enough chance to decapitate me, but when I seemed to have said that Jews must accept Jesus and embrace Christianity, they felt my day had come." Much as he might have wanted to stand and do battle, the cause of Palestine must not be hurt. He sent in his resignation as UPA chairman. In his letter to Louis Lipsky, then head of the Zionist Organization of America, he wrote in part:[10]

I must, however, make it clear that I do not wish my resignation to be construed as assent on my part to the justice of the attacks which have been made upon me, culminating in the incredible edict against me issued by the Agudath Harabonim. I am grieved to think that a body of rabbis should, in deliberative assembly, have done the un-Jewish thing of passing a verdict of condemnation against a man on hearsay evidence, without hearing of witnesses, without inviting his own testimony, even though it were not necessary for him to offer a defense of any word of his before the bar of Jewish opinion in America. I should have thought that thirty years and more of service to Jewish life in all its aspects and to all those causes which lie near to the heart of the Jew should, in the scales of justice, have outweighted misleading headlines of a newspaper report of what I said.

Although I know that the vast majority of Jews of America place entire confidence in my loyalty to Judaism, to Zionism, to every standard of Jewish life, I am not prepared to permit any word or act of mine to be used to the hurt of the Zionist cause. If the Executive Committee accepts my resignation I mean to continue to serve in the ranks of that cause which I have sought to serve throughout my ministry.

What for many Jews, especially Zionists, had up to now been an amusing or at most irritating matter, suddenly assumed more serious proportions. Whether or not they agreed with Wise's interpretation of Jesus as man and Jew, they rcognized that one of their finest leaders and most effective fundraisers might be lost to them because of the narrowmindedness of a bigoted minority. They resented the Orthodox attack on Wise because it violated the American spirit of an open and tolerant pluralism, in a society in which freedom of speech and personal belief did indeed count for something very important. The American system prevented the majority from exercising the tyranny of its beliefs over a minority, a fact which the Jews, everywhere and always a highly visible minority, cherished. For an intolerant minority to silence Wise over his sermon, even one on such a highly controversial subject, affronted their feelings of fairness.

The news of his resignation, therefore, brought in dozens of letters and resolutions from individuals and groups all over the country. Northern California rabbis urged the UPA not to accept his withdrawal, and labeled the Orthodox faction "a small group not representative of the masses of American Jewry." Wise's resignation, warned Rabbi Gerson B. Levi of Chicago, "would be a very serious matter to the Zionists. It might make the gathering of funds absolutely impossible." Temple Knesseth Israel of Philadelphia overwhelmingly passed a resolution pledging its support to Wise. A number of rabbis deliberately preached sermons on the theme of Jesus as Jewish teacher to indicate that Wise's idea—or to be more precise, Klausner's thesis—was widely held in the rabbinate.[11]

Moreover, several Christian ministers also came to his defense. In some instances, Wise might have asked whether with such friends he needed enemies. Those Christians belonging to the more liberal denominations had no trouble acknowledging the role of Jewish thought in the teachings of Jesus, but the Right Rev. Msgr. Joseph H. McMahon of the Church of Our Lady of Lourdes in New York misinterpreted Wise's views in words that buttressed the Orthodox charges:[12]

There can be no everlasting peace on earth until everyone accepts the teachings of Jesus and recognizes God. We who have accepted the teachings of Jesus and have entered Christ's Church and abide by the precepts of His Church please the Lord. We understand the Scripture and comprehend the meaning. The eye of the Jew is still folded.

The Orthodox groups only stiffened their resistance in the face of this show of support. *Der Morgen Journal* declared that Wise's resignation "ought to be accepted without debate and that it is the duty of Dr. Wise himself to insist that it be accepted. . . . There ought to be no place for him at the head of the Jewish movement, in the work of the [Zionist] revival which is based on religious sentiment." The *Jewish Daily News* carried statements from Orthodox rabbis each day demanding Wise's ouster. In a joint meeting of the 400 member Agudath Harabonim and the Mizrachi, reprensenting 10,000 Orthodox laymen, the executive boards threatened that unless the UPA dismissed Wise, they would withdraw from the appeal. Amid hisses and disorder, the majority shouted down a resolution sent by the American Jewish Congregation which called for giving Wise a hearing before condemning him.[13]

In the midst of the controversy, a little-noted incident took place which illustrated Stephen Wise's innate greatness and genuine warmth of spirit in contrast to the petty and narrowminded outlook of his critics. The Mizrachi had reason to honor Gedalia Bublick, the editor of *Der Morgen Journal* who had written several editorials denouncing Wise and his Jesus sermon, and they arranged a luncheon for Bublick at Siegal's Kosher Restaurant in Manhattan. The cream of American Orthodoxy sat at a long table with Bublick at the head, engaged in eating and conversation, when the door suddenly opened and in stalked Stephen Wise. The group was stunned, and a pall of anxiety fell over the crowd. Someone finally offered Wise a seat and something to eat. The tall, slightly stooped figure with the leonine head sat down but growled, "I did not come here to eat." The atmosphere of camaraderie that had pervaded the room was gone, replaced by an almost palpable tension.

The assembly finished the rest of the meal in embrassed silence, and then the chairman rose to begin the serious part of the luncheon. At this Wise stood up and demanded the floor. In the midst of collectively held breath, he asked, "Did you think, gentlemen, that you were going to honor my friend, my comrade in arms, my fellow Zionist, Gedalia Bublick, without my participation? True, Bublick wrote what he did about me, and we have had and will have some differences of opinion. What friends do not? But, gentlemen, please remember: *Bublick* opinion is not yet *Publick* opinon!" Then Wise, with genuine affection, stepped over to Bublick and embraced him, while the rest of the crowd jumped to their feet clapping and shouting, not a few with wet eyes.[14]

It was this largeness of the man—there is no better term—which more than anything swung the support of the community behind him. Even those who, for one reason or another, opposed him on certain issues willingly declared that he had always given body and soul and substance in the cause of his fellow Jews. Samuel Untermyer, for example, wrote: "I have, as you know, criticized the wisdom and manner of your appointment as chairman of the United Palestine Appeal for reasons that need not now be discussed, but now that this issue has been raised, I earnestly protest against the acceptance of your resignation and urge you to remain. You owe this to Palestine and to the cause of Judaism for which you have sacrificed so much." A straw vote by the *Jewish Daily Bulletin* of 205 Zionist leaders showed 190 wanting Wise to remain. Julian W. Mack, Louis Lipsky, Abba Hillel Silver, and dozens of others voiced their strong backing of him, and demanded that the executive board of the UPA reject the resignation. Messages of support even came from overseas. In Jerusalem the Va'ad Leumi, the *yishuv's* National Council, indicated it wanted Wise to stay on. David Yellin, the vice-mayor of Jerusalem, cabled: "I consider the acceptance of Dr. Wise's resignation as most undesirable. Use every possible effort to retain him at the head of the Palestine campaign. We cannot, on account of the calumnies based on perverted statements, be deprived of the unparalleled service of him who gave the best of his life to the Jewish cause."[15]

By now, Wise recognized that the great majority of American Jewry backed him, regardless of whether or not they agreed with his views. Emanuel Neumann went to the Free Synagogue to urge Wise to stay, and later described him as a "lion at bay." He would indeed fight, Wise said, and then laughed as he told Neumann about his grandfather, Reb Yosef, who had carried on a battle with his congregation for decades. Wise issued a statement explicitly denying that he had said "Jews must accept the teachings of Christianity" or that "the teachings of Jesus are an unparalleled code of ethics." "I did say that Jesus was a historic being, not a myth; a man, not a god; a Jew, not a Christian. I must again repeat that I stand exactly where my fathers have always stood in unequivocal denial of the uniqueness or divinity of Jesus. What a mournful commentary upon the infinite hurt which the Jew has suffered at the hands of Christendom, that a Jewish teacher cannot even at this time speak of Jesus, his completely Jewish background and his ethical contribution to his time and all time, without being hailed as a convert to Christianity or misunderstood by some of his fellow-Jews."[16]

Perhaps the greatest boost to Wise's morale came from his old friend Nathan Straus. Recognizing that Wise had offered his resignation because he feared the loss of funds for Palestinian work, Straus not only publicly expressed his personal support but made a concrete gift to show that Wise's fund-raising ability had not been impaired. Straus had already contributed a half-million dollar trust fund whose income would be used for welfare work in the *yishuv*. He now asked Wise to announce two more gifts, $50,000 to the general fund of the United Palestine Appeal and $100,000 for the erection of the Nathan Straus Welfare and Relief Center, which would also house the Palestine administrative offices of Hadassah. "Suppose you did say something with which some Jews did not agree! What of it?" Straus publicly asked, continuing:[17]

> Is all your life of service for Jews and for America to be ignored by those people who take a newspaper headline and are prepared to destroy you and are ready to sacrifice your usefulness in connection with our great work for Palestine? I can hardly believe the newspaper reports that a lot of rabbis, in good standing, should condemn a man like you, with your record and your position, without giving you a chance to explain what you meant. They should have known that no word would ever come out of your mouth that would not have the effect of making Jews still stronger Jews and better Americans, and that, if you said anything at all about Christianity, it would only be in order to remind Christians, as you and I always do, that the first thing for them to do is be just to Jews.

On Sunday morning, January 3, 1926, exactly two weeks after Stephen Wise had preached his sermon on Jesus, the executive committee of the United Palestine Appeal met to consider its chairman's resignation. Earlier, the national committee of the Zionist Organization of America, by a vote of 71 to 1, had instructed its representatives on the UPA to insist that Wise stay. After more than four hours of discussion, the board, by a vote of 59 to 9, declined to accept the resignation. Wise, who had come to the meeting after concluding his regular services at the Free Synagogue, then gave what many considered a confession of faith:[18]

> Words cannot convey how deeply I am moved by the expressions of confidence and trust which have come to me during the past fortnight from my fellow-Jews and fellow-Zionists throughout the land and even of other lands, culminating in the decision of your body not to accept my resignation. This I placed in the hands of the chairman of the Zionist Organization of America not because of any sense of wrong-doing, not because of any fear of censure, but because of my instinctive unwillingness to endanger or hurt, even in the slightest degree, the cause of Zionism. . . .

> Now that the decision has been reached, I may confess to you that it would have been the most grievous hour of my life if you had concluded otherwise, not because of hurt that I would have suffered, but because any action other than that which you have taken would have involved a grave impairment of that freedom of opinion and utterance which is essential to Zionism. Nor do I feel that you have based your decision chiefly upon my service to the Zionist movement beginning in the days of Theodor Herzl. No service, however

great, by any Jew to Zionism could be suffered to stand in the balance as against any disloyalty on his part to the Jewish faith, to Jewish life, to the Jewish People. I have felt confident from the beginning that . . . ultimately the sanity and justice of Jewish opinion would make itself felt and thus save American Israel from perpetrating a deep injustice against a fellow-Jew.

He concluded with words from the Book of Jonah, *Ivri Anochi*—"I am a Jew."

Congratulations flooded in on the vindicated hero. Old friends like Felix Frankfurter and Solomon Goldman rejoiced with him, while from Baltimore came a typical letter from a member of an Orthodox congregation, declaring that the Agudath Harabonim did not represent the feelings of young, traditional but Americanized Jews. Privately Stephen Wise took much satisfaction from the outcome, and blamed the controversy on distorted newspaper headlines. At a public meeting of the United Palestine Appeal, however, he called for an end to the discussion of what he termed "past history."[19]

In a long-term context, Wise's interpretation of Jesus as Jew anticipated what is by now a common historical argument. But even more than that, the 1925 Jesus controversy marked an end to a twenty-year battle for a free pulpit. In 1905, when he had turned down Emanu-El, Wise had stated in his credo the need for a free and unmuzzled pulpit:

The chief office of the minister, I take it, is not to represent the views of the congregation, but to proclaim the truth as he sees it. How can he serve a congregation as a teacher save as he quickens the minds of his hearers by the vitality and independence of his utterances? But how can a man be vital and independent and helpful, if he be tethered and muzzled? A free pulpit, worthily filled, must command respect and influence; a pulpit that is not free, howsoever filled, is sure to be without potency and honor. A free pulpit will sometimes stumble into error; a pulpit that is not free can never powerfully plead for truth and righteousness.

In the debate over the Jesus sermon, nearly all segments of the Jewish community, with the obvious exception of the Orthodox, came to his defense with arguments that directly reflected his earlier statement on a free pulpit. In his sermon on Jesus the Jew, Stephen Wise broke no new theological ground, but he did confirm the triumph of free speech and open inquiry over narrow dogmatism in the American Jewish pulpit.

15

Great Betrayals

The decade of the 1920s appeared to many Americans as a time of inevitable forward progress, as years of prosperity and peace, marred only by some unfortunate incidents such as the Sacco-Vanzetti and Scopes trials. For Jews and Zionists, however, even the social and economic advances they made could not cover completely the unease fostered by increased anti-semitism in the United States and the abandonment by Great Britain of its wartime promises.

Events at home troubled Stephen Wise as much if not more than those abroad, as social and economic developments in the United States tracing back more than five decades unleashed the largest outburst of nativism in the country's history. The demands of industrialization, as well as the hope of freedom and opportunity, had brought millions of immigrants to the United States, but those coming after 1880 had differed in many ways from the earlier settlers. The so called "new immigrants" derived primarily from eastern and southern Europe, and consisted mostly of Catholics and Jews rather than Protestants. Where earlier immigrants had tended to move into the country and farm the land, the newcomers settled in cities, providing the muscle for America's burgeoning factories. The slower rate of immigration, the large numbers who came from the English-speaking isles, and their dispersal throughout the land had made it easier for the "old immigrants" to assimilate into American society. Those who came after 1880 had much more difficulty, and their ghettoization in the large cities not only slowed their absorption into American society but highlighted their "differentness."

By the end of the World War, it had become obvious that America had been transformed. It no longer had large blocs of open territory that could absorb new immigrants, and the economic base had shifted from agriculture to industry. Moreover, the nation's values had shifted, and in years to come the culture and ideals of the big cities would replace those of the farm or small village. Although in fact economic and social opportunity had not shrunk, it appeared that the openness of America, its Jeffersonian values and the general quality of its life were being undermined. Many who feared and did not understand these changes sought a scapegoat, some one or some group to blame for the apparent loss of innocence. To many "real Americans," the answer lay before their eyes in the overcrowded urban ghettos populated by foreigners who had no stake in or commitment to American ideals. The drive to cut off immigration, the attacks on blacks and other minorities, the Palmer raids and the Sacco-Vanzetti trial, the anti-evolution law in Tennessee all reflected the fears of old-line Americans that the newcomers would corrupt and destroy the country.

The nativist outburst pained Wise doubly; he not only opposed attacks on Jews, but lamented that America had betrayed its historic ideals. In no other area was this clearer than in the move to restrict immigration. During the Progressive era a number of attempts had been defeated before the anti-immigration forces had pushed through a literacy test over Wilson's veto. The triumph of the Republicans in 1920 had given the restrictionist a clear path, and they enacted a temporary measure in 1921. Three years later they massed in support of a permanent quota system that would not only greatly reduce the total immigration, but would discriminate against groups from eastern and southern Europe, in effect raising insurmountable barriers against Jews and Catholics.

The American Jewish Committee and American Jewish Congress lead the Jewish opposition to the Johnson bill, with Louis Marshall and Stephen Wise appearing together frequently to denounce America's betrayal of its historic policy toward those fleeing oppression and privation in order to find a freer life and greater economic and social opportunity on this side of the Atlantic. "Were Jesus and his twelve disciples on earth today." Wise told one audience, "they would have to cast lots as to which one of them would have the privilege of coming to the United States under the Johnson bill quota system." Before a congressional committee, Wise vigorously denounced the pseudo-scientific racial theories of Lothrop Stoddard and Madison Grant which provided a rationale for excluding supposedly inferior non-Nordic peoples. When asked whether foreigners had any vested rights in the United States that forced this country to accept them, Wise replied in the negative but declared that he did not believe that a person in Germany of England had or should have a greater right to enter the United States as an immigrant than did someone in Hungary or Italy. He went on to extol the various heritages which immigrants had brought with them to add to America's greatness, and while discussing the spiritual legacy of the Jews, lapsed into Hebrew to recite several verses of Isaiah. It was an impressive performance, one Louis Marshall generously praised.[1]

Throughout the winter and spring, Wise addressed one rally after another, calling upon audiences to oppose the Johnson bill not as Jews or Russians or Italians, but as Americans fighting for the ideals of Washington and Lincoln, Roosevelt and Wilson. The responses of these crowds, composed overwhelmingly of immigrants, as well as the editorial campaign in the liberal press, led Wise to misjudge the restrictionist sentiment of the country. "I think that we have the immigration bill beaten," he told his son. "We have put the fear of votes, if not the fear of the Lord, into the hearts of the Republican leaders." The Coolidge administration, however, had a much more accurate perception of public feeling, and after Congress passed the Johnson bill on May 15, 1924, the president wasted little time in affixing his signature. After nearly three centuries of open immigration, the United States practically closed its doors to those seeking refuge and opportunity, thus mocking the words of Emma Lazarus inscribed on the Statue of Liberty. The terrible results of this decision would include the deaths of hundreds of thousands, perhaps millions of people, who might have escaped the Nazi horror if they had only had a place to go. But there is no doubt that most Americans, disturbed by social changes beyond their control and agitated by nativist hysteria, supported the intent of the Johnson Law to keep Jews and other allegedly inferior groups out the United States. And the bill worked. From 1921 to 1924, an average of 67,570 Jews had entered the United States as immigrants each year; in the four years after the implementation of the quota system, the number dropped to 10,643. Similar figures held for other eastern and southern European groups.[2]

Advocates of immigration restriction denied any antisemitic intent, but their protests rang hollow in light of the rising and obvious anti-Jewish sentiment in the country. Quotas limiting or excluding Jews sprang up in colleges, professional schools, and clubs, while more blatant examples of prejudice could be found wherever one chose to look. "The only profession I know of which does not bar Jews," Wise rather bitterly jested, "is the rabbinical profession." Week after week, month after month throughout the twenties, defenders of Jewish rights such as Marshall and Wise found one incident after another designed to discriminate against Jews or to arouse passions against them. Here one could not afford to pick and choose battles; all cases of antisemitism, large or small, had to be opposed, whether they were passion plays or movies depicting Jews in vicious caricatures.[3] The two leading purveyors of this material and thus major objects of Wise's wrath were Henry Ford and the Ku Klux Klan.

Wise's attacks on Ford and the Klan were, as could be expected, emphatic, public, and grounded in the argument that their conduct and ideals were the antithesis of the true Americanism they allegedly extolled. "God pity and forgive Henry Ford!" Wise declared in one sermon. "God keep America true to the American hope of goodwill and brotherhood among men!" Ford, despite his prominence, was but one man, and after he had to retract many of his statements because of a lawsuit brought by Aaron Sapiro, he struck many Americans as foolish. The Klan, however, numbered in the tens of thousands at the height of its popularity, and it scared Wise much more than did Henry Ford. He began speaking out against the hooded bigots as early as 1922, denouncing them as un-American and anti-American. The fact that the Klan hated blacks and Catholics more than Jews mattered little to Wise, for prejudice against any group ultimately threatened all minorites.⁴ Before the National Democratic Club Wise, who had been invited to speak on the Klan from a "Jewish point view," declared: "There is no such thing as a Jewish point of view in regard to the Klan. The Klan is an attack upon the integrity of American life and may be, therefore, repelled from only one point of view, that of unequivocal faith and devotion to America. Every member of the Klan is a traitor to his country." At the 1924 Democratic convention Wise, who supported Klan target Alfred E. Smith, called upon the Resolutions Committee to adopt a strong anti-Klan plank. He also urged Christian groups to oppose those who made a mockery out of the message of love and compassion which Jesus had bequeathed to his followers.⁵

While the temper of the times precluded the level of tolerance that Wise sought, his attacks on bigotry did manage to upset at least one group, the *yahudim*. The American Jewish Committee and its president, Louis Marshall, still clung to the belief that no good ever came from a public airing of Jewish problems. Rather, "quiet" negotiations would somehow convince the offenders that it would be a better policy not to discriminate against Jews. In late 1922, for example, Marshall wrote to Wise following a Congress-sponsored protest meeting on the Klan, urging that caution be exercised. "Of course every rightly constituted man is opposed to the Ku Klux Klan," he said, "but I doubt the wisdom of Jews going to the front upon this subject." It would be far better, he believed, to let Protestant organizations fight the battle, with Jewish groups providing unpublicized support.⁶ While Wise agreed that Protestants ought to lead the fight, he could not accept a passive rule for Jews, who were, after all, a Klan target. The white-sheeted night-riders affronted not only Jews and blacks and Catholics, but insulted all Americans.

Marshall's comments and actions in a number of areas during the twenties aroused Wise's ire. The Committee had attempted to secure Henry Ford's retraction of antisemitic remarks but had done so in its usual quiet manner. Most people believed that it was not Marshall's efforts that had caused Ford to recant, but that the auto magnate had apologized only because a young lawyer, Aaron Sapiro, had sued Ford for libel. Sapiro claimed that not only had he received no help or encouragement from the Committee leaders, but that the "King of Jews [Marshall] . . . hurt me rather than helped." In a sermon, Wise attacked "the private managers of the affairs of American Israel . . . [who looked on Sapiro] from the heights of their impeccable, withal futile, leadership as if he were some wanton vandal invader of the holy of holies who had not even asked the sanction of them that sit in the seats of the mighty." Marshall also did little to endear himself either to Wise or to the eastern European community by suggesting that some Jews overreacted to every little example of bias, or that some of the hostility they faced might be justified. "We are always talking too much about Jews, Jews, Jews and we are making a Jewish question of almost everything," he charged. The American Jewish Committee could not waste its time on every petty complaint or lunatic diatribe. While there is no doubt that Marshall opposed and fought antisemitism, he also believed that Jews shared some of the responsibility for the prejudice against them because of their own conceit, arrogance, and chip-on-the-shoulder attitude. At one point he confessed less worry about antisemitism than of "the consequences of Jewish indiscretion in dealing with these matters." Among the culprits, he singled out the Yiddish press, Stephen Wise and the American Jewish Congress.[7]

Marshall and Wise often failed to see that in combatting antisemitism, both quiet and public approaches could be effective. Marshall assumed that bias resulted from misinformation, and that an explanation of the true facts and the possible harmful effects would lead a rational person to pursue a more logical and less biased path. In a number of instances, this strategy could and did work. But prejudice is irrational, and like a disease, spreads virulently unless strong measures are taken to stamp it out. Here public protests might be effective, if not in changing the minds of Klan members, then at least in warning others of the danger while rallying forces to oppose the disease. Wise preferred the open protest, but on occasion, he too could exploit his contacts and work quietly.

On the eve of Yom Kippur, September 22, 1928, a little girl wandered away from her home in the small upstate village of Massena, New York.[8] When an exhaustive search yielded no clue to her whereabouts, a State Police corporal, Harry M. McCann, knocked on the door of a Jew named Morris Goldberg. The trooper asked if it were true that Jewish people in the Old World used human blood for holiday services. Goldberg, who knew little about Jewish ritual, replied that he did not know about what happened in Europe, but that he was certain American Jews did not have any such custom. He suggested that the trooper talk to the town's rabbi, and accordingly Rabbi Berel Brennglass was summoned to police headquarters, a little after noon on Yom Kippur day. When he arrived he found a large noisy mob milling outside the building, but to his credit he showed no fear and berated McCann for daring to ask "such a foolish and ridiculous question." A few hours later the little girl was found in the woods about a mile from her home, but by then Massena was ablaze with rumors of ritual murder. Brennglass told his congregation at the late afternoon services that peoples were already saying that Jews had only given up the child because the police had scared the rabbi.[9]

For the Jews of Massena, this sequence of events appeared all too similar to circumstances that had so often preceded a pogrom or riot in Europe. The president of the congregation, Jake Shulkin, hurriedly wrote a letter to Stephen Wise setting forth the details, with a carbon copy to Louis Marshall. Wise immediately began utilizing his contacts within the state government, one of the fringe benefits of his friendship with and support for Governor Alfred E. Smith. Wise wrote to Major John Warner, commander of the State Police, recounting the facts he had received, and demanding a full investigation. "Amends must be made to the Jewish community of Massena," he told Warner, and "nothing less than a most explicit apology will be satisfactory." He urged Warner to act promptly in order to squelch the vicious rumors then circulating about the town. The same day, Wise also wrote to the mayor of Massena, W. Gilbert Hawes, calling for an apology, and called Governor Smith urging him to push Warner's investigation. Smith, himself a target of prejudice, responded promptly. He could hardly believe that the old blood libel had been resurrected, or that a civil official and state policeman had taken part in such an outrageous incident; he promised immediate action with full disciplinary measures imposed on those responsible.[10]

Wise's proddings soon bore fruit. Mayor Hawes, under fire from the governor and from irate townspeople incensed at the bad name being given to their village, called upon the congregation's leaders and asked that they accept his apologies and those of Trooper McCann. Shulkin and Brennglass refused, on the grounds that the whole matter had been referred to a higher authority, and they would all have to await the results. Attempting to head off any further publicity, Hawes wrote to Wise begging him to accept his apologies over an incident that had been blown out of all proportions. By now the consequences of their actions bore in on all concerned. The governor publicly rebuked Hawes, and an official investigation found Trooper McCann guilty of gross lack of discretion and conduct unbecoming an officer; Major Warner wasted no time in imposing the penalty of indefinite suspension from duty.[11]

Less than two weeks elapsed between McCann's knock on Goldberg's door and a press conference in the state capital where Wise stood next to Governor Smith and listened to him condemn prejudice and offer official apologies to the Jews of Massena. Wise, after thanking Smith for his prompt actions, then declared that the lesson of Massena was "for all Americans to banish religious intolerance and bigotry and all their hateful consequences, and to be firm and resolute against everything that savors of injustice between faith and faith, people and people."

Although it was clear from Wise's presence next to Smith that he had played an important role in the affair, he said little publicly, and in fact played down his activities when queried by the press. Very little appeared in the non-Jewish press because, as Wise told his children, he thought it best to keep the entire blood libel as quiet as possible. He wanted results, not publicity, and the prompt action of Smith and Warner assured that.[12]

Wise never took the various antisemitic events of the decade as "proof" that America was becoming as inhospitable to Jews as Europe, nor did he share the attitude of many continental Zionists that Palestine had to be prepared as a refuge as quickly as possible before the whole world turned against the Jews. Palestine would, of course, serve as haven for those fleeing persecution, but more important, it would provide the focus for modern Jewish creativity and spiritual renewal. Because the 1921 schism at Cleveland harmed Judaism, in Wise's view, as well as Zionism, he more than any member of the Brandeis/Mack faction worked to restore harmony in the American Zionist movement.

In the months following the Cleveland debacle, Wise took on several assignments at Brandeis's request. He became chairman of the administrative committee of the Palestine Development League and went on a speaking tour of the Midwest to raise funds for the agency, designed to procure investment capital for Palestinian projects. When Arthur Balfour visited the United States in February 1922, Wise accompanied Brandeis to meet with him and to explain that despite the break, the Brandeis group would still be involved in Zionist work.[13] When Wise traveled to Europe that summer, he met not only with British officials, but decided to sound out Zionist leaders concerning the possibility of reconciliation. The talks left him even more suspicious of "the same old Weizmann . . . I do not trust him and I can never tell what is really in his mind. The only thing I see anew is that he is not a man with whom one can work and upon whom one can build."[14]

Wise's despair over the Zionist leadership gave way in turn to hope and pride in the achievements of Jewish settlers in Palestine, which he visited that July. He arrived just in time to celebrate the award of the mandate, and British officials treated him royally. He and Louise toured over a dozen colonies, and marveled at the changes since their earlier visit. "Things are really wonderful," he enthused. "The old Jewish lack of spirit is gone. Britain and Zionism together have become the transformation of the land. We have England to thank and our young Jewish men who are simply superb." But as he told Brandeis, the only hopeful thing he found in the Jewish world was Palestine, and he feared that that, too, could be lost as long as the Zionist organization lacked real leadership.[15]

Conditions in American Zionism certainly did not fill him with any hope. He labeled fund-raising events for Palestine, even if successful in terms of the number of dollars raised, vulgar and subversive of true Jewish values. An approach that honored big givers and paid no attention to their lack of spiritual commitment would prove "the undoing of things Jewish in America." Wise did not object to fund-raising, of course, but feared that Zionism could be reduced to a charity, a beggar at the tables of the rich, who gave much but cared little about the Jewish renascence Zionism had evoked. He himself paid in over $1,600 to the Palestine Development League in 1923, a considerable contribution for a man of his means.[16] He recognized that something better had to be arranged for the sake of Zionism as well as Zion, and thus in 1924 he proved receptive to the overtures of Emanuel Neumann regarding a new organization, the United Palestine Appeal.

The impetus for the UPA came from a three-year $15,000,000 drive launched by the Joint Distribution Committee to aid Jewish communities in eastern Europe that were still suffering from the devastation of the war and from postwar pogroms. But the JDC also intended to use this money for the controversial Crimea colonization scheme. This plan had been broached in early 1924, and called for the resettlement of large numbers of Russian Jews in the fertile province on the border of the Black Sea. Several Jewish groups within the Soviet Union believed it possible to establish enough cooperative farms peopled by Jews then living in Russian cities to one day transform the Crimea into a Jewish Soviet Socialist Republic. The long-term plan would be financed by the Joint Distribution Committee, with the Russian government facilitating the population moves and land transfers.

Wise opposed the project from the beginning, believing it would divert interest and funds from Palestine. At the 1925 Zionist Congress in Vienna, he attacked the Committee and the Crimea proposal, declaring: "There cannot be any competition between a Russian colonization plan and Palestine. The Zionist Congress cannot remain silent on this question. It must tell American Jewry to consider Palestine first because the funds spent in Palestine will be more useful to the Jewish cause then in any other country."[17] Upon his return to the United States, Wise continued to hammer away at the Crimea plan, and threw a JDC fund-raising meeting in Philadelphia into an uproar when he denounced the scheme. Julius Rosenwald, who had just pledged a million dollars to the Committee, argued that it would be cheaper to settle Jews in the Crimea than in Palestine. Wise shot back: "It may be cheaper as Mr. Rosenwald affirms, but the Jewish people will not stoop to bargain at the counter of Redemption." He then managed to get a compromise resolution passed which did not even mention Russia, but emphasized the continuous support of American Jewry for colonization in Palestine.[18]

The failure of the conference to endorse fully the Crimea plan marked its eventual demise within American Jewry philanthropy, a fact Wise did not recognize at the time. Although Louis Marshall blamed Wise's attacks as the reason the resettlement plan died, the proposal would have foundered anyway. Few Russian city dwellers proved willing to move to the farms, and Stalin's forced collectivization program in 1930 led many who had come to the Crimea to leave. This latter group, most of whom were enamoured of the idea of the small Palestinian *k'vutza*, had no desire to live on large-scale government-managed farms. All told, a little over five thousand Jewish families actually settled on new farms between 1924 and 1931, when the scheme was abandoned. Neither Wise nor Marshall could know this in 1925, but Wise instinctively perceived that support of the plan meant selling out "the soul of Zionism."[19]

The Crimea plan and the obvious bias of the Joint Distribution Committee toward Jewish colonization in Palestine drove home to Zionist leaders the need for a large fund-raising program of their own. Emanuel Neumann, who had been national director of the Keren Hayesod since 1921, now proposed that all Zionist groups consolidate their various drives into one United Palestine Appeal. Recognizing the controversy this might engender, Neumann sought someone with "fire in his belly" to head the effort, and decided to approach Stephen Wise. Despite the fact that he and Wise had been on opposite sides at Cleveland, Neumann knew that the New York rabbi, unlike the other Brandeisians, harbored few personal animosities and had maintained cordial relations with the Lipsky faction. In early February 1925, Neumann met with Wise to present his case, and found him immediately interested in the proposal. The only problem, as far as Neumann was concerned, was Wise's insistence that Neumann serve as executive director. Although Neumann had planned to leave Zionist activity for private business, he finally agreed to chair the executive committee, but only as a volunteer; Bernard Stone would be hired as full-time, paid staff director.[20]

Formal announcement of Wise's return to active Zionist work came on April 2, 1925, at a rally in the Manhattan Opera House celebrating the dedication of the Hebrew University on Mount Scopus. Wise began his speech with "Mr. Chairman and fellow-Zionists" and got no further before the audience rose to applaud. "There have been differences in the ranks of Zionism," he finally continued:[21]

> We have honestly expressed the reasons for these differences as we saw them. Not one of us, so far as I know, ever stepped out of the ranks of Zionism. We stood outside in a sense, while other men took up the burden; while Lipsky assumed command and bore the burden of leadership with great power and with an effectiveness that was unexpected only by those who did not know Lipsky. The business of every Zionist in America is to take his place once again among the number of those who build up the Hebrew University at Jerusalem and will give their complete and unequivocal support to every agency

and instrumentality of our Zionist movement, remembering the critical hour has come. . . . We who for long were among the builders may not stand outside the gates, but must return as I have returned tonight within the gates, and become a soldier in the army of our common cause.

The applause drowned out the last part of his speech, and the three thousand men and women in the audience stood cheering and clapping. Led by Louis Lipsky, the leaders of American Zionism walked over to Wise one by one to embrace him and welcome him back to the cause. The return of the first of the Brandeisians was major cause for rejoicing, and Wise threw himself into a round of fund-raising speeches later in the spring. Before he left for the Zionist Congress that summer, he had been unanimously elected to the executive committee of the ZOA, and as chairman of the United Palestine Appeal had announced a campaign goal of $5,000,000 for 1925/26.[22]

The Vienna Congress did little to bolster Wise's confidence about the condition of the Zionist movement or the ability of its leaders, nor did incidents outside the halls bode well for the Jewish people. An Austrian proto-fascist group, the *Hakenkreuzier*, secured the government's permission to hold a mass rally on Saturday afternoon near the Congress, and that week pasted antisemitic placards and posters all over Vienna. The authorities barely managed to prevent violence, and Wise and other Zionist leaders denounced both the *Hakenkreuzier* and the Austrian government.[23] The debate over the Crimea and the general acquiescence of Zionists to Weizmann's demands evoked anew the resentment over the 1921 debacle. To Brandeis Wise wrote:[24]

Things are not very different from what they were at Cleveland, with the one important difference that the American group is for the most part, like the Congress in its entirety, made up of "functionaries" who are not free to form a judgment. Weizmann does not take the Congress seriously; makes brilliant speeches; but he put it better than he knew: "My business is to keep the Zionist movement from committing suicide at the Congress."

Every encouragement is given to the wretched method of crowding two years' discussion and wrangling into a fortnight of quasiparliamentary debate. The strong men ranged against Weizmann are unwise and unsafe; he is wise and shrewd and as safe as a leader can be; but he lacks character. The most hopeful thing, among others, is the place in the counsels of the movement which has been gained by the Labor party.

My Carthaginian cry throughout has been: "O for the noble leadership which we in America *had!*"

Wise repeated this theme over and over again. He still found the Lipsky administration inadequate, although he could deal with its members on a friendly basis; he did not doubt their sincerity, only their competence. "We were right to fight at Cleveland," he told Max Heller, "but wrong to turn things over to them after our defeat." Nor were the Brandeisians wrong about Weizmann, but they had erred in leaving the field open to him.[25] The Congress experience confirmed Wise in his beliefs that no further good could come from the Brandeis faction staying outside of Zionist affairs. All the ills they had opposed had not gone away, but instead had grown unchecked. With the many problems besetting the Jewish people, they no longer could afford the luxury of remaining aloof while pointing an accusatory finger. Moreover, Wise saw a new proposal being put forward by Weizmann and Louis Marshall as posing a distinct threat to the very essence of Zionism.

The treaty awarding the mandate over Palestine to Great Britain had provided for "an appropriate Jewish Agency for the purpose of advising and cooperating with the Administration of Palestine." This agency would have responsibility for facilitating Jewish immigration and encouraging settlement on the land; until the establishment of such an agency, the World Zionist Organization would be recognized as the body responsible for these tasks. From the beginning, there had been debate within Zionist ranks as to who should be involved in the Agency. The Brandeis group had proposed that prominent non-Zionist experts should be given the administrative responsibilities but that policy should remain in the hands of elected Zionist officials. Weizmann's purpose in creating the Keren Hayesod had been, in part, to appeal to Jews outside Zionist ranks. A number of American Jews who had opposed Zionism before the Balfour Declaration now insisted that they too should be allowed the privilege of helping rebuild the Holy Land. Louis Marshall, while reaffirming that he was still not a Zionist, insisted that "I am greatly concerned in the rehabilitation of Palestine, and I regard it to be the duty of every Jew to aid the cause." Felix Warburg felt a strong need to save Palestine, not only for the Jews but from the Zionists. "If Palestine is going to be anything but a trash basket to satisfy Jews or Jewish politicians," he declared, "it has to become more than an arrogant, conceited, perhaps Hebrew-talking mob devoid of the humility of the Jewish religion."[26] Not all of *yahudim*, however, shared these sentiments, and they saw any Jewish activity in Palestine as tainted by nationalism. "The Jews are not a nation," fumed *Times* publisher Adolph Ochs. "They only share a religion." What would happen to him and the "100 percent Americans" if a Jewish nation came into being?[27]

To Chaim Weizmann, however, the restoration of *Eretz Yisrael* would require the help of all Jews and, in financial terms, would need resources which only the wealthy, non-Zionist Jews had. When he established the Keren Hayesod, Weizmann had predicted that it would bring in

$100,000,000 in five years; at the end of that period less than a tenth of that sum had been realized. In the United States alone, Jews gave over $7,800,000, more than three-fourths of the world total, but only 30 percent of what the Zionist Organization had expected.[28] For Weizmann the message could not have been clearer: A rapproachement was necessary with the *yahudim*, and the vehicle he chose was an enlarged Jewish Agency, a partnership between Zionist and non-Zionist Jews to rebuild their ancient homeland. He began his campaign in the spring of 1923 when he won approval from the WZO Actions Committee to negotiate with the non-Zionist groups all over the world. The key to success, of course, lay in the United States with Louis Marshall and his associates, and Weizmann now brought to bear all his charm and salesmanship to win the support of the American Jewish Committee for his plan.

On February 17, 1924, the leaders of the German-Jewish aristocracy in America convened a conference at the Hotel Astor in New York; among the more than one hundred participants, few if any had ever espoused the cause of Jewish restoration. Marshall, elected chairman of the meeting, delivered a strong statement declaring that the Balfour Declaration and the mandate had made the Zionist/anti-Zionist debate sterile and outdated; all Jews now had the opportunity, in fact the duty, to help settlers in Palestine. "We have no right to be different. . . . Indifference can do us a thousand times more harm than all the Ku Klux Klans and Henry Fords." In his response, Chaim Weizmann went out of his way to play down any political or nationalistic elements in the Zionist movement. The Jewish efforts in Palestine, he predicted, "will create a center of Jewish learning and Jewish culture in a country where our sacred traditions still exist and continue to exist. New visions and new ideas may come forth once more from Palestine, and the word of God from Jerusalem." The meeting turned into a lovefest between Weizmann and the *yahudim*, who agreed to undertake a survey of Palestine needs to determine what the Agency could do.[29] It would ultimately take five years of hard negotiation, meetings, conferences, charges, countercharges, and compromises before Marshall and Weizmann could sign the "pact of glory" at the Zionist Congress in Zurich in August 1929. During most of that time Stephen Wise opposed the entire scheme.

For Wise, the heart of Zionism could be found in the determination to build a Jewish homeland in Palestine, and this in effect meant a Jewish state. Wise never shrank from the political implications of Zionism, nor did he believe that support of Jewish nationalism undermined his own credentials as a patriotic American. He had no qualms about allowing non-Zionists to participate in the work of rebuilding, but he objected strenuously to giving them fifty percent control. "While their help was certainly both desireable and welcome," he later wrote, "admitting them to a position of political leadership and responsibility meant a serious compromise with the basic principles of Zionism. A philanthropic, economic, cultural or spiritual interest in Palestine was laudable and helpful. But it was not Zionism."[30] He had opposed the tendency within Zionist ranks that reduced find-raising to a mere charity drive, and he feared that no matter how much the non-Zionists gave in terms of money, the great enterprise in Palestine would never be anything more to them but a charity.[31]

During the five-year debate over the Agency, Wise gradually drifted away from both the Lipsky and Brandeis groups. He was certainly not alone in his opposition to the Agency. Yitzchak Gruenbaum considered the plan a capitulation to "salon" Jews, while Menachem Ussischkin declared that he much preferred that Palestine be rebuilt by *kranker yidden* (sick Jews) than by *gezunter goyim* (healthy gentiles).[32] But the vision of German-Jewish wealth being used to rebuild the Holy Land won over most of the Lipsky/Weizmann followers, while Brandeis had his own reasons for cautiously endorsing the scheme. Between 1918 and his departure from leadership in 1921, he had initiated a lengthy dialogue with Marshall, Jacob Schiff, and other *yahudim* looking toward cooperation. These meetings had actually laid the groundwork for Weizman, and at the 1920 London Zionist Conference Brandeis had suggested bringing non-Zionists into an enlarged framework. Above all, Brandeis distrusted the philosophy and methods of the European Zionists. A Jewish Agency in which Marshall would be the dominant figure would in all likelihood adopt ideas and programs which the Brandeis faction had endorsed all along.

While Wise never lost his admiration for Brandeis and continued to have good personal relations with "the Chief," a note of exasperation and even condemnation crept into many of his letters during the latter part of the decade.[33] He did not share Brandeis's personal animosity toward Lipsky, and his new role in the UPA made it impossible for him to attack the people with whom he worked on a daily basis. Beyond that, he considered Brandeis's olympian attitude no longer productive; Zionism needed workers and leaders in the arena, not aloof condemnations from on high. Had Brandeis been willing to rejoin the Zionist leadership and take an active role in shaping the Jewish Agency, Wise possibly might have gone along, convinced that Brandeis's Zionism would overcome dangers inherent in the Weizmann-Marshall approach. Failing that, he entered a solitary campaign against the Agency plan.

In a speech for the UPA in early 1926, Wise openly attacked the *yahudim*, declaring that he "would give one thousand Warburgs for one Bialik. Warburg gives out of his surplus, while Bialik gives out of his soul." Nor did he spare Marshall, despite the fact that during the twenties he and the Committee president cooperated a number of times in defending Jewish interests. In a lengthy letter of complaint to Chaim Weizmann, Marshall singled out Wise as one who never lost an opportunity to attack him and the

other non-Zionists.[34] Weizmann tried to get Wise to desist from such condemnations but in vain; the Free Synagogue rabbi continued to oppose what
he believed would be the creation of "an American Jewish peerage" that
would render no real service to Zion. There were times when Wise, as head
of the UPA, had to work with Weizmann, such as during the latter's visit to
the United States in the fall of 1927. At such moments he had to "endure"
the European, but as he told his daughter, "It is really hard to want to serve
a great cause and to be all but debarred from serving it because of the quality
of the men who lead."[35] When Felix Warburg unilaterally canceled a
meeting of the Hebrew University committee, Wise fulminated to Julian
Mack: "It is typical of the way in which the University is being conducted as
though it were the more or less private possession of Mssrs. Warburg and
Magnes [the university president]. But I suppose our poverty compels us to
endure even this shame." The hope of vast sums of money for Palestine
simply did not justify the betrayal of Zionism. Beyond that, Wise doubted
that the non-Zionists would really contribute that much, in either money or
service.[36]

A good example, to Wise at least, came at the Fifteenth Zionist Congress
in Basle in early September 1927. Wise attended as a member of the
American delegation, and was elected chairman of the important Political
Committee. With his support, Abraham Tulin of the United States and
Philip Guedella of Great Britain introduced a resolution in the Committee
protesting the high taxes imposed by the British on the *yishuv* and the cor-
responding lack of services and economic support given to the country by
the mandatory power. Weizmann immediately perceived the political implications of the resolution, and feared it would scare off non-Zionists leery
of the Agency becoming embroiled in political matters. Weizmann declared
that he could not remain head of the WZO should the resolution be
adopted, thus turning the issue into a vote of confidence on his policies. The
bulk of the American delegation, controlled by Louis Lipsky and loyal to
Weizmann, dissociated itself from the resolution. Wise thereupon resigned
as chairman of the Political Committee and took the next boat home to
America.[37]

There is no evidence that Wise had anything else in mind but a protest
against British policy, but Weizmann's reaction confirmed his fears of what
the Agency agreement might do to the Zionist movement. The non-Zionists
would limit the Agency's activities to noncontroversial economic or cultural
projects and would steer away from any confrontation with or protest to the
mandatory government, thus leaving the *yishuv* bereft of any voice to speak in
its behalf. Weizmann had not changed, Wise believed, but had in fact
become more dictatorial than ever, stifling internal debate or criticism, and
opposing any activity that might adversely affect the Agency scheme.

Despite requests from both Lipsky and Weizman that he withdraw his resignation, Wise declared that he could not in good conscience take part in a Zionist gathering that suppressed free speech and thought. Moreover, he did not want to enter a power struggle which he could not win against Weizmann, whose leadership he termed "indispensable at this time." But he took pains to point out that "I have not broken and I do not intend to break with the Zionist Organization. I am a Zionist and have been since the founding of the movement."

Despite the fact that Wise had again walked out, his actions reflect a careful consideration of the available options and the various interpretations and misinterpretations that might attach to them, but the implications of the dispute were clear to all who could see or understand. Even before the conclusion of the Agency agreement, here was evidence that the Zionist Organization, the supporter and champion of Jewish settlement in Palestine, had failed to defend the *yishuv* because Weizmann feared the effect a forthright political statement would have on the non-Zionists. As Wise told Henrietta Szold: "I did not leave either in haste or in anger. I had considered virtually the whole of the night before of what to do, and when Dr. Weizmann. . .threatened to resign, inasmuch as I felt that his resignation would be inadmissible at this time, I had as a matter of self-respect to withdraw."[38]

Wise believed that had he forced the issue, the Congress might have passed the resolution in spite of Weizmann's threat, and that would have smashed the Agency. But the process had gone too far, the non-Zionists stood ready to enter an agreement, and while the Congress might have been willing to accept Chaim Weizmann's resignation, few of the delegates Wise spoke to reacted with anything but horror at the thought of losing the Jewish Agency. He still opposed the Agency and Weizmann, but the Russian-born chemist undeniably had devoted his life and his considerable talents to the movement. Until another leader came along—or one came out of retirement—driving Weizmann out of office would have little benefit and many drawbacks.[39]

When a preliminary pact between the Zionists and the non-Zionists was signed by Marshall and Weizmann, Wise surprised many people by endorsing the new partnership.[40] As chairman of the United Palestine Appeal, it is likely he thought it best to accept the inevitable, at least publicly, and to hope that perhaps the *yahudim* might after all give generously to the needs of the *yishuv*. Or perhaps he perceived that the Agency had inborn deficiencies that would, within a few years, see the non-Zionists do little more than hold a few ceremonial positions, while the effective power within the Agency rested completely in Zionist hands.[41] Or maybe his own disgust at the general trend of Zionist affairs expressed itself in a "why bother to fight" attitude. Shortly after his return from Congress, he seriously considered the possiblity of taking a year off from all responsibilities and living in Palestine, both to do more for the *yishuv* and to escape the incessant clash of personalities in Zionist politics.[42]

Yet Wise, as one of American Zionism's leading personalities, could hardly escape such struggles, and in 1928 he reluctantly found himself drawn into another round in the fight to control the Zionist Organization of America. For all his personal liking of louis Lipsky, Wise found it more and more difficult to work with the man, partly because of Lipsky's ineptitude as a leader and partly because the ZOA president was little more than a puppet, jerked from one position to another whenever Weizmann pulled his strings. On a number of occasions, members of both the ZOA and the Brandeis faction approached Wise, suggesting that he ought to seek the presidency of the organization, that he would be acceptable to both sides and would have wide backing in securing needed reforms within American Zionism.[43] Wise resisted these overtures because he already had too much to do, and because he wanted to avoid a power struggle that would in all likelihood degenerate into a question of personalities and name-calling. "We must not make the fight on Lipsky," he said, "otherwise we will have a repetition of the Cleveland fiasco. . . . The thing to be done is to fight for principles, principles of honesty, efficiency and unafraid management, no matter who must go."[44]

But Brandeis still did not understand the old adage that "you can't beat a somebody with nobody," that so long as the opposition could not propose a man who could inspire the rank and file with confidence in his leadership, the majority would prefer to keep Lipsky, whose devotion to the cause they knew and appreciated. Even Mack tried to tell Brandeis that if the latter remained "silent and invisible except to a selected few, defeat becomes a certainty."[45] But Brandeis would not leave the Court, Mack and Wise refused to lead the fight, and the Brandeisists had no one else of equal stature.

Such a situation doomed the effort to unseat the Lipsky administration in 1928. At Brandeis's request, Wise resigned his seat on the ZOA administrative committee in March, along with Sam Rosensohn and Lawrence Berenson. But where they wanted to make Lipsky the issue, Wise refused, and gave Weizmann and the Agency as the cause of his unhappiness with the ZOA policies.[46] Moreover, Wise told Mack and the other Brandeisians that he would not attack Lipsky, and that he differed from the Chief's views in a number of areas. Above all, Wise suffered growing frustration with Brandeis's refusal to participate openly in Zionist affairs and with the jurist's reliance upon Jacob deHaas, whose grating personality had antagonized many would-be supporters. All of them had put their eggs into a single basket marked "Brandeis," but as long as Brandeis refused to work openly with them they had no chance of success. In essence, Wise told Mack and others, he would fight against the Lipsky administration because it had pursued wrong policies, but he would neither be party to Brandeis's dislike of Lipsky nor an ally of deHaas, whom he considered in many ways worse than Lipsky.

When Abraham Tulin objected that the situation was not as bad as Wise had painted it, that there were leaders, most notably Wise himself, the rabbi replied: "No, we have decided that our only leader is Brandeis. We have made ever other leadership impossible. I will fight for Brandeis and with Brandeis, but I will not serve as a corporal in an army in which Brandeis is the honorary field marshall and deHaas is the commanding general.[47]

Wise refused to go to Washington to meet with the faction in a planning session. He had no desire, as he told Lee Tulin, to attend "a pow wow where the Oracle of Oracles will look beautiful and speak nobly and then we will come back and the chocolate eclairs or cream puffs (which is a rather sweet way to talk about the rest of my colleagues) will flatten down and the field will be left to deHaas." A few days later he strongly attacked the administration of Zionist affairs, singling out Chaim Weizmann as the person responsible for the failure to protect the interest of Palestinian Jewry; he made no mention of Louis Lipsky.[48]

Brandeis now sent a personal invitation for Wise to confer with him. From the notes Wise jotted down immediately afterward, the normal demeanors of the two men were reversed, with the ice-cool jurist aflame with passion and the fiery orator exercising rigid self-control. The meeting highlighted the differences between them, not in regard to the long-term goals which they shared, but to short-run objectives. Brandeis wanted to cleanse the Augean stables of the ZOA and rid the movement of the evil Lipsky; Wise saw the villain as Weizmann, with the real problems to be found in the WZO offices in London and Jerusalem. To Brandeis the Jewish Agency held potential for good, while Wise saw it as further debasement of Zionism from a Jewish renascence to a Jewish charity. In a sharp exchange, Brandeis angrily rejected deHaas's veiled promises that the jurist would once again lead the movement, and Wise countered, "But that is the man whom American Zionists believe speaks for you." "My name cannot be used in any way," Brandeis insisted. "Even if I were not on the Supreme Court, my years make it impossible."[49]

The two-hour meeting confirmed Wise's analysis of the situation, and deepened his despair over the failure to develop an American Zionist leadership tied to Brandeisian principles but not dependent upon the man himself. A number of people believed that such a leadership did exist, and that the obvious candidate for the mantle was Wise himself. Wise received personal appeals from Weizmann to retain his posts, while Mack, Rosensohn, and others in the Brandeis faction importuned Wise to lead the fight on their behalf.[50]

Wise was, in fact, a leader, but one who refused at this time to assume the role. "If I were a free man," he wrote to his son-in-law, "and able to put everything aside and to give all to the battle, it would be a different thing. But I have little stomach for a fight, however just, which for the most part is bound to be in hands either unclean or incompetent."[51] So Wise decided to be, as he so often was, a voice crying in the wilderness, pointing out the sins of omission and comission he saw in the Zionist Organization, especially criticizing Weizmann's failure to stand up for Jewish rights in Palestine.[52]

An issue arose in the summer of 1929, however, which galvanized the Brandeis group into action. On August 23, Arab mobs rioted in Palestine, leaving 125 Jews dead. While Jewish groups around the world called for His Majesty's Government to live up to its obligations, Chaim Weizmann, the president of the World Zionist Organization, proved totally unable to influence his British friends, and the Colonial Office issued a White Paper temporarily stopping all Jewish immigration into Palestine. Louis Marshall, who had been elected chairman of the Jewish Agency at its inception a few weeks before the riots, had died suddenly as a result of an emergency operation, and his successor, Felix Warburg, resigned in protest against the British policy. Louis Lipsky, like Weizmann, appeared impotent; he carried no influence with the American government or with his alleged non-Zionist colleagues in the Agency. In the face of this unprecedented crisis confronting the *yishuv*, the once powerful American Zionist movement literally came apart at the seams. Its membership dwindled, its resources shrank while debts piled up, and its leadership appeared incapable of leading.

The inability of Zionist officials to affect English policy resulted from a number of factors, but certainly among the more important had to be Weizmann's refusal to protest the policies of His Majesty's Goverment. Wise had tried to point this out on a number of occasions, such as the 1927 Congress and in a speech before Avukah, the student Zionist group, in May 1928. At the latter conference, he had declared: "England will not do anything more until it is compelled to. The right kind of Zionist leadership is necessary and a stronger and more aggressive policy toward the mandatory power must be adopted if the Balfour Declaration is to be carried out. Until this change is brought about, England will do very little toward the creation of a Jewish National Home." Referring to a comment by Weizmann in which the WZO president had said that "a struggle with England would last five minutes and that will settle it," Wise asked: "How can a self-respecting Jew utter such words as those voiced by the leader of the World Zionist Organization? It means no change or improvement in Zionism until the Zionist leadership is deposed. As one who helped Brandeis to obtain President Wilson's endorsement of the Balfour Declaration, I will not cease to demand the maximum from England unless you want her promise to become a 'scrap of paper'." After the Arab riots Wise still publicly affirmed his faith in Great Britain, and told the Free Synagogue that he spoke against British policy "not in anger nor in hatred, but in sorrow."[53]

The crisis in Zionism and in Palestine quickened the pace of American Zionist affairs. In November 1929, Brandeis spoke out openly for the first time in eight years to a conference of *yahudim*, members of the Brandeis/Mack faction and some of the *nouveaux riches* eastern Europeans, with the Lipsky group conspicuous by its absence. Soon afterward a delegation of twelve members of the ZOA administrative committee met with the Brandeisians to negotiate terms that would somehow save face for the discredited Lipsky. In June 1930, nine years after the schism, the ZOA convention returned to Cleveland. On the eve of the first session, Wise issued a statement to the Associated Press declaring that "in the things that matter most, morally and politically the [ZOA] is bankrupt."[54] The charges, which no one denied, nonetheless caused a furor because Wise had aired "internal problems" before the gentiles; undoubtedly members of the American Jewish Committee, had they been present, would have understood. Zionism in America had come to a sad state.

Negotiations between the Lipsky and Brandeis factions stuck on the question of what to do with Louis Lipsky. Mack and Wise insisted that it would not be right to throw the man out in the cold after his years of devoted, albeit misguided, service. Moreover, Wise still saw Chaim Weizmann as the real culprit. The Lipsky backers insisted that some room must be found in the new adminstration for them, and at one point declared that only Wise could be the new president of the ZOA.[55] In the end, Lipsky and some of his lieutenants received honorific but powerless positions, while the Brandeis faction took over the reins of power. Wise returned to the administrative and executive committees to work with Robert Szold, to whom Brandeis had delegated the unenviable job of bringing American Zionism out of the financial morass and low morale left by the Lipsky regime. It would be a thankless task, but the healing of the second Cleveland convention allowed American Zionism to begin rebuilding its strength for the great trials ahead.

The initial British reponse to Arab riots had absolutely infuriated Wise. He had diplomatically tempered the public criticism while the Hope-Simpson commission held its hearings, but privately he began "to doubt the possibility of doing anything in Palestine with and through England. It almost seems to me that in the future whatever can be achieved will come to pass not because but in spite of the British government." He took England's policy as a personal affront. "No Jew I know," he wrote, "has more truly the right to feel betrayed, because personally I gave myself to the limit to the British during the war. No one knows of the services, big and little, that I rendered the British government. . . . I have never known such disillusion and betrayal."[56]

The full extent of British perfidy became manifest on October 21, 1930.

That day the Colonial Office released the Hope-Simpson Report and Lord Passfield (Sidney Webb) issued a White Paper clearly attempting to redefine the Balfour Declaration and the mandate so as to arrest further development of the *yishuv*. Instead of a promise to the Jews, Passfield declared, the mandate laid down obligations to promulgate equally the growth of Arab and Jewish communities and to maintain a balance between them. Hope-Simpson, whose past experience had been completely in India and who knew little or nothing about the Middle East, had concluded that no more arable land remained in Palestine, and the Zionist agencies had pursued policies inimicable to Arab rights. Passfield therefore limited all further land purchases by the Jews, and suspended immigration as long as any unemployment remained in Palestine.[57]

It is difficult to tell what upset American Zionists more, the Passfield White Paper or Chaim Weizmann's passive response to it. The WZO president, in words that would come back to haunt him, declared that "never can there be a Jewish state. . . . The fogs have vanished. I see clearly now, and I no longer believe in the Jewish state." American Zionists lambasted Weizmann mercilessly. At every turn, Wise noted, all Weizmann did was yield to the British.[58]

Even before the issuance of the White Paper, Wise had begun assembling lists of statements by previous British governments and statesmen to prove that the Balfour Declaration and the mandate had specifically promised Palestine to the Jews. Midway through the task, he suffered a physical breakdown, the result of a dozen years of incessant work and tension. Despite his professed dislike of deHaas, Wise turned to him for help to complete the indictment. Their joint product, *The Great Betrayal*, appeared five weeks after the White Paper, and received wide play in the Zionist and Jewish press.[59]

The state of Zionist affairs at the end of the decade certainly seemed to have resulted from not one but several "great betrayals." Above all, Britain retreated from the high idealism and promise of the Balfour Declaration. First Churchill had lopped off the large territory east of the Jordan River to establish a Hashemite kingdom, and then Passfield closed off land purchases and immigration into the truncated area west of the river. The once mighty Zionist Organization of America split in Cleveland in 1921, and while the Brandeisians returned to power at the end of the decade, the intervening years of the Lipsky regime had severely damaged the movement. The Jewish Agency reduced Zionism to a charity, and the interests of the *yishuv* rested in the hands of non-Zionists and social workers who knew little and cared less about the meaning of Jewish nationalism. The Agency vitiated the Zionist spirit, Wise believed, and crippled the movement in its greatest crisis. Worst of all, Zionism had been betrayed by its leaders. Brandeis, by walking out in 1921 and boycotting "Lipsky and his ilk," had deprived American Zionism of his talents and those of his close associates, thus making it impossible for a new American Zionist leadership to emerge. Weizmann had betrayed the movement by his passivity, his kowtowing to the moguls for the sake of the Jewish Agency, and his inaction in the face of the White Paper. "If we are so poor that only one man can lead the Zionist movement," Wise wrote, "then we are not a people but a gang of slaves, and we do not deserve a national home of our own."[60]

Yet there was a leader, and throughout the 1920s Stephen Wise had moved, albeit reluctantly, to assume that role. With Brandeis recused on the Supreme Court and Marshall and Schiff dead, Wise's own work in defense of Jewish rights in the United States and overseas had made him the pre-eminent Jewish leader in the country. A number of things detained him from claiming this role until the thirties, including his hope that Brandeis would again take control, as well as the many other causes and institutions that claimed his attention and time. For Wise, like Brandeis, exercised influence within the Jewish community not only for his activities on its behalf, but because of his role in the secular world as well.

16

In the Prime of Life

On March 17, 1924, Stephen Wise celebrated his fiftieth birthday, an occasion that called forth widespread comment and congratulations from both Jews and non-Jews. "You won't recognize your father in the letters which have come from men of distinction all over the country," he told his son. "Mother may be shameless enough to send you copies. I could not possibly."[1] The many messages from friends and longtime colleagues brought him great joy, but he derived special satisfaction from the ungrudging compliments of perennial critics. The *Jewish Tribune*, for example, editorialized that though it had often disagreed with Wise's views and disapproved of his methods, "no one can help admire his wonderful personality, matchless eloquence, boundless energy and unflagging devotion to his people and to all humanity." Millions of Jews and gentiles, it continued, "here and abroad, unite in wishing him many happy returns and in hoping that the years ahead of him might be as rich in service, distinction and beauty as those behind him." The *New York Times*, with which he had maintained a running dispute for years, sent a reporter to mark the event, and the interviewer caught him in a typical moment, hosting a party at the Free Synagogue House for boys and girls from a nearby orphanage. As the children went in to eat, moving slowly and hesitantly, Wise's face clouded over. "They never run like other children," he told the reporter, who noted "one could see why he had fought for years against child labor, and would fight for years more if he had to."[2]

During these years, Wise maintained his daily routine much as he had before. On doctor's advice, he now slept six or even six and a half hours a night instead of his previous five. He retired around midnight and fell asleep immediately. When he went to bed, he once explained, he shut out of his mind all of the day's problems. "I concentrate in the matter of sleep by night as I do in the matter of work during the day. I sleep more in an hour than most people can."[3] And, of course, he took his famous catnaps wherever and whenever he could.

Once awake in the morning, Wise spent an hour reading—novels, history, philosophy, articles, whatever caught his eye. Publishers, authors, and friends constantly sent him material, and thanks to his catholic interests, he devoured everything. Justice Brandeis frequently sent him copies of opinions; with the *Milwaukee Leader* dissent came a note: "Don't think I am trying to demote you to the legal profession, but free speech is your special province." While Wise welcomed and read much of what came his way, he refused to allow other people to choose his reading for him. He turned down an invitation to join the Literary Guild, declaring that book clubs "are for the half-literate. Perhaps I flatter myself unduly in imagining that I have crawled just a little beyond the stage of semi-literacy."[4]

Wise also found time to publish several books. Most were expansions of sermons, such as *Child Versus Parent* (1922) and *How to Face Life* (1924), although he wrote *The Great Betrayal* out of anger at Great Britain. He somehow found time to begin work on his memoirs, writing when he could snatch a few minutes in the morning or longer stretches during the summer at Lake Placid. He started at Placid in 1923, and when he returned to the city that fall thought he had about half of the book written.[5] His friend Lowell Brentano had been pressing him for several years to undertake the task, and finally in May 1924 managed to have Wise sign a contract to deliver a manuscript on *My Thirty Years Battle in the Ministry*. Over the next several years dozens of letters passed between Brentano and Wise, the former pushing him to deliver the book, the latter giving one excuse after another about why he had been unable to finish. "I confess I have never procrastinated in quite the same way as I seem to have procrastinated in the matter of *My Life*," Wise wrote. All or parts of the manuscript were at one time or another written, only to have Wise or Louise or one of the children find fault with it, and so he would start in all over again. In 1927 Brentano declared it would be a thirty-year battle just to get the book from Wise, and later offered to send over secretaries so that Wise could dictate the contents to them. Even though Wise often confessed himself "thoroughly ashamed," Brentano received no book. Finally the publisher gave up. "Suppose we leave the situation this way," he wrote. "Sometime thirty or forty years from now you will come into the Brentano offices and ask to see my grandson. You will then tell him in a quavering voice that here is the book that his grandfather spent his life chasing, and you suppose he will want to publish it. He will. I'll leave a special proviso in my will to that effect."[6] Brentano's estimate was not too far off. It would be twenty-nine years before Wise's autobiography, *Challenging Years*, would be published, and by then both rabbi and book-seller had died.

After his morning's reading, a light breakfast, and perhaps some writing, Wise left for his office at the Free Synagogue House, walking the mile and a half if weather permitted. He arrived promptly at 8:00, in his study, a large room with stone walls on the third floor. In the middle, an enormous refectory table held piles of mail, memoranda, and other materials that had come in for him. Wise always took care of the mail promptly, calling in a series of secretaries. To one he dictated letters relating to the Free Synagogue, to a second he dictated about matters affecting the Institute, while a third came up from the American Jewish Congress office to take his letters for that organization. If he had just returned from a trip, he conscientiously sent out the "bread and butter" letters thanking his hosts, the people who had handled arrangements, and reminding communities, organizations, and individuals of pledges made to support the Institute or the Congress.[7]

At 8:45 he walked up one flight of stairs to a small chapel where students in the Institute conducted *shacharit*, morning prayers. By 9:00 he was back in his office, answering phone calls and seeing visitors. Students from JIR came to see him, some with academic difficulties, others with personal problems. His secretaries tried to get members of the Free Synagogue to see one of the assistant rabbis, but as often as not, "Only Rabbi Wise will know what to do." Some of his visitors were important, men of affairs in the Jewish community or in the outside world; others were ordinary people who needed advice or solace. With every one of them, great or small, Wise sat and listened carefully, giving to each what he or she needed, words of advice or encouragement or comfort. Many people passed through his office each week, and no matter how little time each one received, Wise managed to make all feel as if they were the most important. In between visitors, J. X. Cohen, Sidney Goldstein, or another aide was likely to pop in needing advice or a decision. The last visitor, however, had to leave by 11:00, so that Wise could meet with his Homiletics class at the Institute.

Lunch frequently consisted of little more than a sandwich and a cup of coffee, gulped down during a meeting with colleagues at the Congress or in one of the Zionist groups. Then Wise returned to his study to sign letters, see more people, make more phone calls, and very often, perform a wedding or funeral. But no matter how busy or hectic his schedule, a phone call or a visit from his wife or children halted everything. Whatever the crisis, it had to wait a while as Wise chatted with his family or slipped away for some tea.[8]

Since his schedule always included several speeches a week, Wise frequently left the office late in the afternoon to travel to a nearby city. Some of these talks brought him handsome fees, which he used to supplement the relatively small amount he received as a rabbi of the Free Synagogue; these "professional" engagements were arranged by a lecture bureau, normally

White's. Most of the time, however, such forays were to raise money for the Zionists, the American Jewish Congress, or the Jewish Institute of Religion. Every day brought several invitations for him to speak both to Jewish and to non-Jewish groups, for a personal fee or in the service of a cause.

The varieties of subjects upon which he spoke reflected the catholicity of his interests and reading. He debated with Judge Ben Lindsey on "companionate marriage," spoke to civic forums on "The Best and Worst in American Life," asked religious groups "Do We Need a New Religion?," and discussed "The New College Student" at universities. Of all his activities, Wise enjoyed public speaking most; he was in his natural element when standing on a rostrum. Regrettably, while the written records of his talks give some indication of their contents, they tell little about his delivery or the impact on audiences. Wise "played" an audience, loosening it up with an anecdote or sharing a confidence before pulling his listeners in for the serious part. By then they were hooked, ready to give sympathetic attention to his message.

Despite his reputation, Wise knew that not every speech could be a masterpiece, and his letters are full of deprecatory remarks about particular talks. "We had a lovely service . . . [except for] my address being a pretty poor sort of thing, " he told one friend, and to another he confided that of all his public utterances, his after-dinner remarks were consistently the poorest. After speaking to a group of students at Columbia University, he informed his son, "I was supremely bad. I was stiff, stilted, formal, meaningless and a few other things. I say this not only because it is good for my soul to say it, but because it may be good for you to hear how exposed an old preacher is to failure."[9]

In the large majority of his sermons, speeches, and debates, however, Wise turned in masterful performances. He loved to talk! Once he visited a Quaker meetinghouse, and the clerk invited him to speak if the Spirit moved him. Wise assured the man that It would. Toward the end of the decade Wise's baritone voice reached a new and immeasurably larger audience when he agreed to broadcast a sermon every Sunday evening over the National Broadcasting Company chain—a development, according to the network, generated by public interest in hearing the New York rabbi.[10] His contemporaries, especially fellow orators, considered him the finest Jewish preacher of his day, and one of the half-dozen truly great speakers, Jew or gentile, in the country.

He was at his best and his feistiest, however, on Sunday mornings in Carnegie Hall. Here he stood on home ground, the audience his own congregation, and although his views might now and then drive one or two members to resign, the majority of the Free Synagogue belonged because of Wise. They wanted and expected him to challenge their ideas, to jab their consciences, to stimulate their minds. This and more he did every Sunday, and while he often spoke on secular topics, a large number of sermons dealt with religion in general and Judaism in particular.

Wise was no theologian; he did not develop an elaborate philosophy of Judaism. For him the God of the Jews, the ethical beliefs of the Jewish people and man's everyday experience, were discrete entities, part of an integrated but never complete unity. God would always remain a mystery beyond the comprehension of the human mind, but the meaning of God grew out of human experience. Much to the anger of the Orthodox, he renounced his earlier view of the Bible as divinely inspired. "Much of it is mistaken," he told the Free Synagogue; "much of it is even morally and spiritually erring, in the Old and New Testaments alike." In direct opposition to both Jewish and Christian fundamentalists, he declared that a person "who believes that God has revealed Himself but once in the first chapter of Genesis and that He has since hidden the truth from mankind is an impious blasphemer."

Religion, like any social institution, could not be static, frozen in modes and beliefs decreed centuries earlier, Wise believed. It had to change, adapting to the needs of people. Prayer at one time represented the crude begging of primitive beings for supernatural intervention in daily life, the sending of rain or good crops or children. People ought no longer to see prayer as "asking" but as a "speaking," a human way of communicating with God, a means of growth and understanding. Similarly, early religions had made fear a central element of their structure. "Fear is the beginning of religion," Wise averred, "but freedom from fear is the end and aim of religion." Judaism remained alive, Wise declared, because "the God of the Jews grows with the Jews and reveals Himself more and more as the Jews' insight grows." Early people believed that God created man in His image; Wise intimated that now religion thrived because man created, and recreated, God in the human image in order to meet human needs. This did not debase the idea of God, but placed man and God in a fruitful partnership.

Through that partnership, people did God's work on earth, fulfilling the prophet's command that "Justice, justice shalt thou pursue." To Wise, the prophetic teachings were godly in that they represented God in man. The teachings of an Amos or Isaiah, a Micah or Hosea called for man to exert himself, to reach for the best and noblest within him; these were attributes which Wise saw as the links between man and God. To put God entirely beyond reach, to make religion incomprehensible, to reduce it to a list of do's and dont's, all defeated the essential purpose of religion, the ennoblement of man. "What does the Lord require of thee?," Micah asked. "Only to do justly, and to love mercy, and to walk humbly with thy God." This was a call for a living religion, one attuned to human potential for good.[11]

It is little wonder that the fundamentalists, especially those within

Judaism, feared and condemned him. Wise preached a religion which in effect said: "Away with priestly rituals and anything else which closes man's mind or which prevents him from assuming responsibility for his deeds, for his life, and for his fellow man." Yet even he had to laugh when a friend sent him a report of an Orthodox attack delivered in Yiddish over a radio program originating in Odessa. The man had once seen Wise, in 1916, and described him as a "tall, clean-shaven man who endeavors and succeeds in bringing fatted American capitalism to the black folds of religion, who smokes Havana cigars Saturdays and weekdays, whose efforts are duly limited to an automobile trip on Sunday to the magnificent temple in which two or three thousand moneybags await him. There he delivers his 35-minute weekly sermon, at the end of which he raises diamond-bedecked hands and with difficulty pronounces the only two words he knows in Hebrew, *Bruchim Habaim*, and then motions to a chorus of conservatory-trained pretty young girls to begin the musical program. Do you know what he does the rest of his time? He gambles in Wall Street, then sits in counsel for finding ways to defeat communism." [12]

Wise doubled over with laughter when he read this, and later commented on the description. While admitting he was tall and clean-shaven, he observed that he had failed to notice many "fatted American capitalists" in the Free Synagogue. And not only did he not smoke cigars on the Sabbath, but he never smoked at all. "We have not yet, after twenty-three years, built that magnificient temple. I never preach for 35 minutes, but always speak for 45 to 65 minutes. As for my 'diamond-bedecked hands,' I have never owned a diamond, even in my wife's name, though I do wear a marriage ring. As for the pretty young girls in our choir, they may have been young and pretty in 1916 . . . but I should describe them now only as good singers. As for gambling in Wall Street, perhaps I would if I knew how but I have never learned the art, and anyway I have some scruples about it." [13]

Wise indeed had scruples about stock gambling, and often attacked speculation in his sermons. He once told an investment banker that he and his wife did not want any of their money in profit-making businesses, and had put all their savings into government bonds. They did, however, own a fair amount of silver and antiques which Louise had inherited, as well as her jewelry. In August 1924, while the family vacationed at Lake Placid, they nearly lost all this to a burglar. Fortunately, an alert detective, Patrick Giery, managed to apprehend the thief and recover practically all the stolen property. [14]

Wise did live comfortably and never claimed poverty. He and his family ate and dressed well, lived in a pleasant middle-class house, owned a summer cottage in Lake Placid, had a few servants, and traveled frequently. They were by no means rich, and their generosity prevented any accumulation of capital; throughout their lives they gave above their means to numerous charities. In October 1927, for example, Wise told Julian Mack that he had to raise nearly $3,000 to meet pledges he had made to different organizations, including the Habimah Theater of Palestine, and this was far from the amount for the entire year. Louise Wise on her own sent money to a number of causes that interested her, including Henrietta Szold's work for children in Palestine. They both helped dozens of young writers and artists with cash, letters of introduction, or through purchase of their works.[15] They also helped their children, Jim and Justine, from whom they received much joy and not a little pain and anxiety during these years.

Wise's cup had overflowed when Jim decided to enroll in the first class at the Jewish Institute of Religion. After a year there, however, he went off to study at Cambridge University, developing ideas he had about Judaism into a book entitled *Liberalizing Liberal Judaism*, published in 1924. Upon his return he resumed classes at the Institute, served as a student rabbi for a new Jewish group in White Plains, and also put in time as director of social activities at a settlement house. From all reports, the son had inherited many of the traits that had made his father so effective a pastor—a sense of concern about people, a commitment to social justice, a capacity for moral outrage, and a good speaking style from the pulpit. But he lacked the deep, abiding faith which he felt a rabbi should have.

In his book, the younger Wise argued that religion was made for man, not man for religion. The proper test for religion, therefore, is its ability to help individuals live highly moral and ethical lives. If a religion fails to do this, he argued, its particular future matters little; the important thing is to carry on the mission of ennobling human life. The liberalization of Judaism had so far failed because the necessary reforms had been inadequate. Shunned by Orthodox Jews and ignored by other religions, Reform Judaism was neither fish, flesh, nor fowl. Despite its apparent success in America, according to James Wise, it had lost the vitality of the early reformers, and as the years passed, its doctrinal and ritualistic faults had undermined its program. As things now stood, Reform or Liberal Judaism had little to say to the modern Jews. The younger Wise went on to attack a number of Reform beliefs, and here the father parted company with his son. While he and Jim undoubtedly shared many ideas, Wise had a more optimistic view of the Liberal mode. He did not defend everything in Liberal Judaism; he had, in fact, been a critic of the movement for many years. But Stephen Wise spoke from a position of faith, his son from one of doubt.[16]

As time drew near for the first class to graduate from the Institute, the younger Wise grew increasingly uncomfortable. Despite the aptitude he had shown for the ministry, he knew he could not be a rabbi; he did not believe strongly enough to take on that burden. In April 1926 he told this to his father privately, but the news of the decision somehow leaked out and exploded in a headlined story in the New York *World*. Suddenly, rumors spread that not only had Stephen Wise's son left the ministry and his father's seminary, but he had also abandoned Judaism.

Wise painfully and reluctantly agreed to speak to reporters to set the record straight. He read a telegram from Jim, then in Minnesota speaking for the United Palestine Appeal, denying that he had ceased to be a Jew, and pledging that he would continue "to serve my people Israel." Nervously pacing up and down, Wise admitted that he had hoped his son would follow in his footsteps, but that "intellectual scruples and doubts, which appear to [James] insurmountable, stand in the way. The only decent and honorable thing for him to do is to reach the decision that he has reached, however much I regret it."[17]

James Wise later recalled that his father never once reproached him for the decision, and there is certainly no evidence that Wise ever turned his back, even briefly, on Jim. For the next twenty years he helped his son in many ways, introducing him to people, praising his work, making sure his writings were reviewed, working with him in a number of causes, and from time to time advancing him money. Privately, Wise grieved over his son's decision, but respected him for his intellectual and moral courage. "I cannot feel that my son is wrong," he told Barnett Brickner. "Inasmuch as he cannot offer a prayer he has no place as a rabbi in a synagogue. He really has been prompted by rigidly scrupulous motives." To his close friend Holmes, Wise admitted that Jim was "a source of great concern," and he had been urging the young man to see someone to whom he could talk, perhaps some friends of the family such as Holmes himself or Felix Adler. Letters from longtime friends such as Holmes, Brickner, and Max Heller calmed Wise, but did not ease the pain; eventually, however, even that subsided.[18]

Justine Wise, like her brother, proved a remarkably spirited child. The two to them went to a number of schools before settling down, or at least calming down to some degree. But both children recalled that no matter what problems they had, their parents remained supportive. It was a close family, and the Wises missed the two youngsters terribly when they went off to college. One day Louis Marshall ran into Wise and asked him why he looked so sad. "Jim and Justine are both at school," Wise replied, "and the house seems so empty without them." Marshall, looking rather smug, informed Wise that he had prevented the situation from ever arising. "I told my children that they could go to any college they wanted, providing it was in New York."[19] By giving them freedom, however, Wise tied his family closer together than Marshall, with his strict paternalism, ever could. Jim's collaboration with his father came mainly in the thirties and forties, when they founded and edited *Opinion* and fought in a number of antifascist groups. One of Justine's first ventures into the public sphere, however, soon dragged Wise into the fray.

In 1924, in her senior year at Barnard, Justine and her friend Bertha Paret went to work in a textile mill in Passaic, New Jersey. Several large companies, including Botany and Forstmann & Huffmann, ran factories there and had brutally prevented the unions from securing any toehold in the mills. Under the name of Justine Waterman, she labored as a quiller at $18 a week, and during the winter of 1924/25 applied to the Central Employment Bureau for a better job. The Bureau, run by mill operators, had an extensive spy system to prevent union organizers from getting jobs. One of the inspectors noted that Justine's hands were in too good a condition for a factory girl, and a little investigation soon turned up her real identity. She was invited to leave town before she was arrested, but chose to remain in the sweatshop for a while longer, gathering additional data. She then told her father and John Haynes Holmes of what she had learned: of starvation wages, the espionage system, the brutal and degrading working conditions, and the terrible effects upon family life. When 4,500 workers finally went out on strike in January 1926, Holmes, Wise, and Justine all went immediately to the defense of the strikers.

Wise, however, accurately perceived the weakness of the strike committee. Most of the people at the strike headquarters spent too much time debating ideology and too little on tactics. The leader of the strike, a young lawyer named Albert Weisbord, had been accused of being a communist, and while Wise personally liked him, he considered the young firebrand naive and impractical. As for the parent American Federation of Labor, which Wise termed "an almost medieval institution" most of its leaders hesitated to help the strikers lest they too be accused of radicalism. After a session with the mill owners themselves, however, Wise wrote that "it did more to take me over into radicalism than any experience of a lifetime."[20] Confronted by determined management, a hostile police, and judicial power, lacking support from organized labor and hampered by inept leadership, the strike showed little promise of success.

As tensions and emotions rose on both sides, Wise attempted to put together a committee which, if acceptable to workers and owners, might mediate the dispute. A bitter rabbi found one clergyman after another saying no; they saw no reason for the church to be involved in labor disputes. Finally, John Lovejoy Elliot, head worker at the Hudson Guild; Paul Underwood Kellogg, editor of *Survey*; and the Rev. John Howard Melish, rector of Trinity Church in Brooklyn agreed to serve with Wise. The committee offered its services to the workers, who immediately accepted. The four men now turned to the owners, who just as quickly refused. Charles F. H. Johnson, vice-president of the Botany Worsted Mills and regarded as the spokesman for the owners, declared: "There is no strike in Passaic in the commonly accepted sense of the term. There is a Communist demonstration, led by professional Communists, not for the purpose of helping the mill workers of Passaic but, to use the words of their organ, to give the textile workers schooling in Revolution."[21]

Both father and daughter were incensed. Justine traveled down to Passaic to address the strikers, in words she could only have learned from the rabbi of the Free Synagogue: "You will hear much of the menace of the violence of 'Reds' or Bolsevism, but it is Forstmann & Huffman, the Botany and their kind that constitute the greatest menace to the peace and lawfulness of Passaic and of our country. No outside agitator, however radical, can be as menacing to the life and ideals of America as the interests which invoke our flag solely to protect their profit." Basil Henriques, an English social worker in the United States to lecture at the JIR, told Wise: "Justine made such a speech to the strikers that you can retire." A delighted Wise showed off pictures in the New York newspapers of Justine with her fist clenched in the air "smashing in true Stephenesque fashion."[22]

In turn, Wise rose in the Free Synagogue and attacked the mill owners as "breeders of communism and fomenters of revolt." It would be nothing short of treason for the striking workers to settle without a guarantee of at least the right to organize. The mill owners "were mad to have ordered a ten percent cut in wages at a time when the nation is fairly reeking and raving amid the fumes of prosperity." As could be expected, some of the parishioners disapproved both of Wise's views and of his daughter's activities. But at least one member of the Free Synagogue, Harry Meyers of Passaic, showed how well Wise had taught his people. Meyers told Wise that he disagreed with this stand completely, and felt that the strikers had done irreparable damage to Passaic. Then he handed over a check for $25,000 in full payment of his pledge to the synagogue building fund.[23]

The strike dragged on for almost a year. Eventually Wise's appeals to William Green, president of the American Federation of Labor, bore fruit. The leadership of the strike passed from the hands of Weisbord into more experienced hands, free from the alleged taint of communism. Wise received an enthusiastic welcome when he addressed the annual convention of the Federation, and urged the delegates to support the Passaic strikers with food and financial aid. With this new help, the mill workers took a fresh grip on the strike; in mid-December the Botany Company agreed to the union's terms, and the other mills soon fell into line. The workers won the right to organize and to bargain collectively, while the companies promised to rehire the striking employees without discrimination.[24] It had been a long battle, but one of the few which workers won during Republican prosperity.

Justine's role in the Passaic strike came back to harass her in a minor way in late 1928, when she applied for admission to the Connecticut bar. One of the examiners asked her a routine question—had she ever used another name? She told him about working in a mill under the name of "Justine Waterman," at which an ultraconservative member of the committee protested vociferously, insisting that her application be examined more closely. One of Justine's professors asked her afterward if she or her father knew anyone important who carried influence with Yale. She responded that both Chief Justice Taft and Justice Brandeis had known her for years. Shortly afterward, Taft, speaking for himself and Brandeis, wrote a strong endorsement of Justine to the examining committee. "I am quite sure," declared the Chief Justice of the United States, "that in point of character there is no one who comes before you that is better equipped for the bar than she is, from my knowledge of the atmosphere in which she lives and from her history." At its next session, the committee unanimously approved her.[25]

By this point, Justine Wise had become Mrs. Lee Tulin. Much to her father's delight, she married one of her professors at the Yale Law School in a small ceremony in the spring of 1927, and in the fall of 1928, Wise became a grandfather for the second time. Jim and his wife Joan had produced a son a year earlier, and now Justine and Lee also had a boy. Both babies were named Stephen, which pleased Wise enormously. Although his grandchildren would be a source of much joy to him in the remaining twenty years of his life, this initial happiness soon turned sour. Jim's marriage did not work out, and he and Joan agreed to separate in May 1928. "I am afraid that it is inevitable," Wise wrote, "but oh, what a pain to have that precious boy pass out of our life, as he in large part will and must." Then shortly after Stephen Tulin's birth, Lee became ill with what doctors ultimately diagnosed as leukemia. The Wises helped them first with a loan for a mortgage, then with the medical bills, and in the latter part of Tulin's sickness, they moved out of their house on West 90th Street so that Lee and Justine could be more comfortable.[26]

Wise's own health also gave his family and friends much concern at this time. Always the picture of robust vitality, Wise certainly seemed to be in the prime of life in the 1920s. He carried an enormous load of responsibilities, however, and began to suffer from physical ailments compounded by overwork and exhaustion. The first sign came in the White Mountains of New Hampshire, where the Wises had gone in July 1921 so he could recuperate from a relatively minor operation. For some reason, the healing took much longer than normal, and Wise felt wretched most of the time. In sending some materials back to his secretary, he noted, "I am not at all well. I had a local doctor, but for some days Mrs. Wise had been in telephonic and telegraphic communication with Dr. [Harlow] Brooks . . . In any event, going to New York is out of the question . . . for if I had to go now it would not be an easy matter. I should practically have to go on a stretcher." The following spring, the Travelers Insurance Company turned down Wise's application for additional life insurance. The agent, a member of the Free Synagogue, assured Wise that nothing serious had turned up in the physical examination, but that the company felt him to be in generally run down condition. "It would be well for you to cut down somewhat on your 'speed'," the agent wrote. "You may not feel any ill effects of your strenuous life at present, but this may come back later when you least expect it."[27]

Wise received this advice constantly throughout the decade. "Will you never learn the lesson of conserving your energy?," William Fineshriber admonished him. "Those of us who admire you feel that you ought to put the brakes on."[28] Just as consistently, Wise ignored this advice, and took on ever greater burdens. Yet his mortality weighed heavily on his mind, especially as he approached his fifty-second birthday, the age at which his father had died. His friend, Dr. Leon S. Medalia, to whom Wise confided his fears, tried to reassure him. "It seems to me," Medalia wrote, "that you keep your father's passing away too much on your mind. While it will help you as a matter of precaution, yet you can carry it a little bit too far, and at times when you are not feeling quite right, that fear and worry may cause you much worse conditions than what you are entitled to, and what you will have without the fear."[29]

Wise's symptoms, however, were far from psychosomatic. A complete physical examination by the noted Harlow Brooks in April 1926 showed Wise suffering from heart and liver irregularities, as well as severely inflamed tonsils and bursitis. Most of the problems, Brooks declared, resulted from "physical neglect on the part of Dr. Wise, and from his excessive and emotional nervous stress . . . a characteristic of the man and his great ability." Brooks and Wise's personal physician, Milton Rosenbluth, insisted that Wise slow down, go on a diet, and above all, get some rest. They also advised that his tonsils be removed, and a reluctant Wise, after drawing up instructions for his funeral, consented to the surgery in late June. While recuperating, he received a note from Brooks. "Do not be in a hurry to get out again, and try to take a good vacation before you return to work. Please make your life hereafter a bit more selfish. Be more generous to your wife's husband 'for the good of the service'."[30] Wise now slept a bit more at night, and to some extent adhered to the diet; but he knew not how to slow down.

Part of Wise's morbidness resulted not only from his own health problems, but from the deaths of several people close to him. The decade began with the untimely passing of his elder brother Otto; before it ended his younger brother Joe, the "baby" of the family, succumbed to multiple sclerosis in a Boston hospital. In December 1929, an auto struck and killed his sister Ida. Wise, not knowing what had happened to her, went from one hospital to another until he found her battered body in the morgue. In addition, good friends such as Martin Meyer, Norvin Lindheim, and Israel Zangwill died, with Wise officiating at the funerals of the latter two. In June 1929, his longtime chauffeur Ralph died suddenly of a cerebral hemorrhage hours after cheerfully bidding Wise good evening. Only a little while earlier, an epidemic of scarlet fever had hit the Wise household. Jim had a rather light attack, but Justine had to be hospitalized and then operated upon for inflamed mastoids.

Considering Wise's poor health during so much of the decade, one can only marvel at all he accomplished. Yet one must also wonder at his perverse drive and energy, his refusal to slow down voluntarily, the constant overwork that ceased only when he collapsed. No doubt Wise drove himself relentlessly, as if fearful that he might not have enough time to accomplish all he wanted to do. As a youth, he confessed himself overshadowed by his brilliant older brother Otto, and undeniably saw his father as a larger-than-life figure. Wise set up near impossible goals for himself to prove he was as good as if not better than his childhood heroes.

Some confirmation of this drive came from the father of psychoanalysis, Sigmund Freud. Wise distrusted much of Freud's theory, and especially the abuses inflicted upon Freud's ideas by his alleged disciples. But he also recognized that mental patterns and aberrations existed which undergirded much of human behavior. In 1925 when he attended the Zionist Congress in Vienna, Wise went to visit Freud at Berggasse 19. There the two men discussed Jewish leadership, and Freud asked his American visitor to name "the four greatest living Jews."

"Oh, that is easy," replied Wise. "Einstein, Ehrlich, Freud and Brandeis."

"And you," suggested Freud.

"No, no, no, no, you cannot include me," Wise protested.

"If you had said 'no' once, I would believe you," Freud observed, "but four 'no's' leads me to suspect that you protest too much."

Wise shrugged his shoulders and grinned. "I have gotten a free psychoanalytic reading from the greatest authority on the subject."[31]

Even when he had been younger, this driving need to accomplish, to be great, had taken its toll. As he grew older and punished his system even more, only his innate physical stamina prevented a fatal collapse. Fortunately, his body could not be pushed beyond certain limits, and then, whether he wanted to or not, Wise had to rest. By the end of the twenties, a decade of great exertion and accomplishment, Wise's body demanded rest, a fact his family and friends recognized even if he refused to see the obvious. At the Free Synagogue the trustees insisted that he take longer vacations and delegate more work to his associates. George Kohut and others pleaded with him not to attend the World Zionist Congress in 1930. "For once," Kohut burst out, "the world will have to function without your all-pervasive presence."[32] Wise's physical collapse finally put an end to the argument.

So he rested, his strength gradually returned, and the graph of his activities leaped upward. After all, how could he stay in bed when there was so much to do? The worst depression in the nation's history had wrought economic chaos in which, as usual, the poor and the powerless suffered the most; in New York City, Tammany roared unchallenged, its minions battening on graft and corruption; in Palestine, Great Britain threatened to undo the great promise of a Jewish homeland while ineffectual Zionist leaders stood helplessly by; and in Europe a new nightmare, horrible beyond imagination, took shape and gathered strength.

17

The Political Rabbi

The Depression that devastated the United States at the end of the 1920s gave new vigor to the reform impulse, which had apparently waned after the great crusade of the war. Reform had never died, of course, but had merely been dormant, its advocates fighting rear-guard battles to protect earlier victories. Wise had been part of this struggle, and throughout the years of Republican prosperity had continued to call for economic and civic equality for all Americans. Reform, however, meant politics, and as the level of reform activity rose, so did Wise's involvement in civic, state, and national politics.

During the 1920s, not only had industry prospered, but so had urban machines, especially Wise's old nemesis, Tammany Hall. Throughout the decade, Wise had kept up a barrage against corruption in municipal affairs, even though he realized that few people were paying attention. "The fight for good government in American cities is losing ground," he told the Chicago City Club, "because the masses are weary of the futility of antigraft agitation and unsatisfied even with the technique of improved city administration. They are weary of fighting the Murphys in New York and equally corrupt political machines of both parties in Chicago and elsewhere." Time and again he spoke out against Tammany's candidates and endorsed third-party or independent nominees, but to no avail. As he noted, people seemed not to care so long as the times were good.[1]

Yet even as he opposed the Democrats in New York City, Wise established close and fruitful ties with the Democratic leader of the state, Governor Alfred E. Smith. The two men had first met in 1911, when Smith, then a state assemblyman, participated in the investigation following the Triangle fire. That experience helped turned Smith into a progressive, and his four terms as governor provided the people of New York with a reform-minded and efficient administration. Wise found Smith the most attractive political

238

figure of the twenties, and supported his bid for the Democratic presidential nomination in 1924.

During Smith's last two terms, he and the New York rabbi became friends. Wise sought no personal advancement, and had no hesitation in telling Smith exactly what he thought of the governor's policies or appointments. In 1926, for example, Wise learned upon his return from Europe that the chief justice of the state's highest court had retired, and rumors abounded that Smith would elevate Cuthbert Pound instead of Benjamin Cardozo to the seat. Even before unpacking, Wise dictated a letter to the governor expressing his incredulity that Cardozo might be passed by, or that political considerations would play any role in the choice.

Wise received no reply, but a month later upon returning home from the Free Synagogue on Yom Kippur, the Day of Atonement, he found a message that Smith wanted to see him. After hurriedly breaking fast, Wise went over to the governor's suite at the Biltmore. There Smith asked him point-blank what he had against Judge Pound.

"Absolutely nothing," Wise replied. "He is an ideal man for the post. Unfortunately for him he stands by the side of a man with whom no one on the court can be compared."

To bolster his argument for Cardozo, Wise alluded to the fact that most lawyers considered him one of the finest appellate judges in the country.

"Well, then," Smith asked, "why doesn't the Bar Association get up and say so instead of monkeying around as it does?"

"Most of the big lawyers in New York are Republican, Governor, and you know how embarrassed they would be to come out openly for Cardozo."

It also turned out that Smith had more or less assured the Republican party leader, James Wadsworth, that Pound would be appointed, and here the rabbi quietly but forcefully told the governor that such a promise had been not only rash but wrong. After a lengthy discussion, the two men hit upon a scheme of having eight or ten prominent lawyers, Republicans and Democrats, issue a public appeal to Smith to name Cardozo.[2] The strategy worked, triggering a groundswell of support, and Smith soon afterward named Cardozo Chief Justice of the New York Court of Appeals.*

---

*Five years later Wise again interceded on behalf of Cardozo, who was not only a universally respected jurist but also a close friend of the Wise family. In January 1932, Oliver Wendell Holmes, Jr., retired from the Supreme Court after three decades, and liberals demanded that President Hoover appoint a successor worthy of the seat. At the top of nearly everyone's list stood Cardozo, but Hoover was reportedly leery of naming a second Jew to the High Court; at one point he suggested to Senator Robert F. Wagner that if Brandeis resigned, it would be easier for him to nominate Cardozo. Wise went down to Washington to see Senator Borah, who

Wise campaigned for Smith for governor in 1926 and for president in 1928. "I am in favor of the election of Governor Smith," he told a cheering rally, "because Governor Smith is a servant of all the people, because Governor Smith has been and is as vigilant and as effective in safeguarding the public interest and the public welfare as Senator Wadsworth has been diligent and prominent in safeguarding the interests of the privilege-seekers and the monopoly-hunters."[3] In 1928, Wise also stumped for the state ticket Smith had hand-picked to carry on his policies—Franklin D. Roosevelt and Herbert Lehman. The Republicans nominated Albert Ottinger in the hope of picking up some of the normally Democratic vote among the state's large Jewish population. Wise consistently declared that religion should have no place in judging a candidate's qualifications for office. "Unless we stamp out the anti-American heresy that there will be religious tests," he warned the Free Synagogue, "then we shall really enter upon the most bitter of civil strife." Jews had a golden opportunity, Felix Frankfurter suggested, "to show their patriotism as well as discernment by voting for the Catholic Smith for president, the Protestant Roosevelt for governor, and the Jewish Lehman for lieutenant-governor," a proposal Wise strongly endorsed. Not all Jews shared this sentiment, and one vice-president of the American Jewish Congress resigned because of Wise's political statements. For the most part, however, leading Jewish figures like Wise opposed the idea of a "Jewish vote," especially the assumption that a Jewish candidate automatically commanded Jewish votes.[4]

The victory of Roosevelt and Lehman cheered Wise, although the anticipated defeat of Al Smith left him dispirited. Wise expected, perhaps unreasonably, great things from the new governor, and also assumed that the cordial relationship he had enjoyed with Smith would be continued under Roosevelt. The new governor did move quickly to carry out his campaign promises and show his commitment to social justice, acts which greatly pleased Wise. In January 1929, Roosevelt called upon the state legislature to enact an old-age assistance program. Upstate Republicans, who strongly opposed the measure, tried to bury it in committee, but the governor sent another special message calling for action. More than a half-million people

---

agreed that Cardozo stood head and shoulders above everyone else talked about for the job. At Wise's urging, Borah went to the White House and convinced the president that a religious issue did not exist. The appointment of Cardozo would, in fact, bring nothing but praise to the beleaguered Hoover for rising above petty partisan and regional considerations. A few days later, Hoover sent in the nomination, and, the Senate quickly confirmed. Few people knew of Wise's exertions, but Felix Frankfurter, lobbying by himself for the same end, discovered evidence of Wise's labors and wrote that "your tentacles of effort and enterprise reach out everywhere and cover the country."

in the state were over 65; in New York City alone, 45,000 aged persons depended upon relatives or outside assistance. The legislature reluctantly opened hearings on March 5, and over 200 representatives of business, civic, and welfare groups crowded into the committee room.[5]

First the lobbyists for manufacturers and real estate associations denounced the measure, which they warned would require such high taxes as to drive industry out of the state and depress the value of all property. In response, Stephen Wise rose to defend Roosevelt's proposal. He certainly felt sorry for the "poor and down-trodden real estate owners" and expected that since the situation was so terrible, they would soon introduce legislation to relieve their plight. But in the meantime, men and women who owned little or no property were suffering and needed help. He suggested a compromise measure which he had worked out with Roosevelt a few days earlier: The legislature would name some of the members of the investigating commission, but the data gathering and evaluation would be done by a staff of experts appointed by the governor. "You did a splendid piece of work before that hard-boiled committee," Roosevelt wrote. "I wish you could come up here once a week regularly to give me courage and enthusiasm." Despite their best efforts, however, he and his allies could not get the Republican-dominated legislature to fund any sort of impartial commission.[6]

Throughout Roosevelt's first term, relations between him and the rabbi of the Free Synagogue remained cordial. The governor managed to work several important bills through the legislature, including a modified old-age pension law. About a year after Roosevelt's election, Wise reported a conversation he had with a friend who in 1928 had voted against the Democratic tickets. "Governor Roosevelt is splendid," he enthused to Wise. "He has a fine insight into social problems and a real passion for social welfare and social justice. . . . He is the type of man we need in the White House."[7] Within a few months, however, the governor and the rabbi had split and were exchanging bitter recriminations over the song-writing playboy mayor of New York, James J. Walker.

Jimmy Walker was as much a part of New York as Al Smith or Stephen Wise. A product of the Irish tenement district, he had always been torn between his twin loves—show business and politics; some people said he solved his problem by becoming the best political entertainment of his day. Certainly Walker personified New York in the 1920s, high-living, quick-witted, and fun-loving. His exquisite clothes and expensive tastes seemed to sum up the American dream in the golden glow of Republican prosperity. In 1925 Smith had picked Walker to run for mayor; Tammany needed a new face, and Walker had proven himself popular with the voters. Smith had, in fact, asked Wise on more than one occasion to endorse Walker, but the rabbi had refused on the grounds that he just did not know enough about him.[8]

During Walker's administration, Tammany Hall continued to enjoy a level of power and wealth not seen since the legendary years of Boss Tweed. The Hall had already carved up the city into enclaves, each under a district leader chosen for his loyalty to the party and a willingness to share his loot. Each district leader held a sinecure on the city payroll paying upward of $7,000 a year, but this was only the beginning. For fixing tickets, quashing citations for fire-law violations, securing exceptions from zoning ordinances, or keeping juvenile offenders out of jail, the local party chieftain received thousands in bribes and kickbacks, some of which he distributed to his lieutenants, some of which he forwarded to Tammany, and the rest of which he pocketed. In the classic case, Sheriff Thomas Farley, who had an annual salary of less than $10,000, amassed over $400,000 in a little tin box. But after all, New York was a big city, with a population of seven million and more than $20 billion worth of taxable real estate. There was plenty to go around, and Boss John F. Curry saw to it that all the party faithful got their share. "I am the political leader of the dominant party in New York City," he declared; as for reform, "I will carry out the policies in which I grew up."[9]

The state of New York City politics was no secret. Tammany operated openly, its control of all branches of the municipal government secure. While Curry had not controlled Al Smith, they evidently worked out an accommodation. The governor would leave the city to Tammany, which in turn would back Smith in his state policies and drive for national office. Curry did not like Franklin Roosevelt, but recognized the new governor would have to deal with Tammany and, if the Hyde Park patrician ever wanted to be president, he would have to keep Tammany and its power on his side.

Wise, of course, had loathed Tammany since his youth, and periodically he would loose a blast against political corruption in his beloved city. Starting in early 1929, however, the tempo of his attacks increased, and he began discussions with reform-minded friends about "doing something in respect of the New York situation." In that fall's elections, he endorsed Socialist candidate Norman Thomas, whom he labeled the ablest and most honest man running. Out of the campaign, he hoped, would come a new Independent Municipal party dedicated to the principles of good government. Referring to the other two mayoral candidates, he termed Walker "a delightful farceur" and Fiorello H. LaGuardia "a decent adventurer." As a teacher of religion, he lamented, "I am sick that I live in a city where I cannot speak with pride of the leader of my city."[10] But it was still too early for most people to share Wise's despair; it would take the Depression to make them realize how little they could afford Tammany's corruption.

About a month after the election, which Walker easily won, a series of events began to undermine Tammany's stranglehold on the city. The Tippecanoe Democratic Club of the Bronx honored one of its own, Magistrate Albert H. Vitale, at a dinner in the Roman Gardens restaurant. Vitale, the "honorary president for life" of the club, had worked hard to line up the Italian vote for Walker, and rumors of his close ties to the underworld failed to deter any of his many friends from paying him tribute. In the middle of the celebrations, six masked gunmen, with pistols drawn, entered the private dining room and lined the guests up against a wall. A city detective meekly handed his revolver to the robbers, who then collected thousands of dollars in cash and jewelry from the assembly. Vitale, greatly embrassed by the episode, left the Roman Gardens at 2:00 a.m. and went immediately to the party clubhouse. Within two hours he had rounded up all the money and jewels, as well as the detective's stolen gun, and restored them to their rightful owners.[11] The Vitale incident provided a moment of comedy, but drove home the close ties of Tammany leaders to the city's criminals.

A few days later, Walker and his lieutenants on the city payroll decided that they needed more money, and arranged for several bills to be introduced before the Board of Estimate to that end. At the crowded hearings, Wise led the opposition, declaring the salary grab an "immoral and unfair" measure. Walker protested that the beneficiaries of the bills had not proposed them, and he saw no reason why they should refuse. "Is this an abhorrent thing to do?" he asked.

"Yes," Wise thundered. "The proposed beneficiaries might have said to 'the playboy' who proposed the measure: 'We are very grateful to you, but we must add in Biblical language, "Is thy servant a dog that he should do this thing?" ' "

An audible gasp ran through the chamber, and when Wise sat down opponents of the bills applauded loudly. Walker, his face grim, called the meeting back to order and, after hearing from a few friendly witnesses, announced he would sign the salary increases into law.[12]

The forces of good government realized they would have to organize if ever they hoped to bring Tammany to its knees. No serious investigation of Democratic machinations could be expected from the city's own police force, nor did it appear that the governor's office had any interest in cleansing the municipal stables. The New York Bar Association did manage to have Vitale removed from the bench, but demands for a full-scale examination of the city's courts went unanswered. The legislature's Republican leaders, hopeful of embarrassing Roosevelt in the fall gubernatorial election, pushed through a bill creating a commission to investigate corruption in the city; Roosevelt vetoed it, but the pressure for some action could no longer be ignored.

Wise, John Haynes Holmes, Norman Thomas, Samuel Untermyer, the Bar Association, and other civic leaders kept up a constant barrage of embarrassing questions and scathing denunciations directed not only against

Tammany, but increasingly against Roosevelt for his failure to act. Over the summer, after District Attorney Thomas C. T. Crain had failed to secure grand jury indictments in a blatant fraud case involving city officials, Roosevelt reluctantly took one small step. He called for Crain to turn over all papers bearing on the case to his office for review. Wise, then on vacation at Lake Placid, applauded the decision, but insisted that it must be followed by a wide-scale investigation.[13] Such an examination, however, did not materialize. Roosevelt hoped that by ameliorating minor problems he could evade a full-scale probing of city affairs. Tammany, for its part, felt confident that the governor would not challenge its powers.

On a summer day in 1930, Norman Thomas and Paul Blanchard called upon John Haynes Holmes and asked him to lead a citizens' committee to clean out City Hall; Holmes agreed provided that Stephen Wise served as vice-chairman. In mid-September, the City Affairs Committee ("a nonpartisan committee for civic reconstruction") opened offices at 112 East 19th Street. Its letterhead listed, besides Holmes and Wise, Bishop Francis J. McConnell, Norman Thomas, columnist Heywood Broun, Rabbi Sidney E. Goldsetin of the Free Synagogue, lawyers Morris Ernst and Louis Waldman, Joseph D. McGoldrick, and, as executive secretary, Paul Blanchard. An appeal for funds quickly brought in a little over $1,000, enough to pay rent, furnish the office, and begin operations. Within a year the CAC grew from 50 to 1,500 members with a budget of $9,000, enough to generate reams of information collected by four full-time researchers.[14]

The work of the Committee devolved upon a number of people, but three men comprised the heart of the crusade: Holmes, Wise, and Blanchard. In his memoirs, Holmes recalled that some people warned him that Wise would "hog" the leadership, and rumors abounded that the rabbi really ran the show with Holmes as front man. "The truth of the matter," wrote Holmes, "is that Wise and I worked together in perfect harmony, as equal partners in an enterprise which held the allegiance of us both. We agreed on policies. We divided responsibilities. It fell to my lot to write most of the documents, public letters, etc., while Wise exercised his superb oratory at the public meetings which we arranged from time to time. . . . As time went on in this bitter fight, we became, as it were, 'a band of brothers,' rejoicing in our happy and fruitful work."[15] In the public mind, especially after the Walker fight, Wise and Holmes seemed inextricably linked. A 1933 Broadway comedy, *She Loves Me Not*, had one scene in which a newspaper editor yells at one reporter, "Call Stephen Wise and get a statement," and then to another, "Get John Haynes Holmes on the telephone and have him dictate a paragraph."

The CAC's own research into municipal corruption started slowly; its directors wanted to document Tammany's sordid affairs so thoroughly that neither the state government nor the public would be able to ignore the issue any longer. Then in February 1931, a shocking murder aroused the citizenry and gave further impetus to the Committee's work. A high-priced call girl, Vivian Gordan, had been indicted on a morals charge after she had refused to pay off some policemen. She then offered to produce evidence that she had been framed, and declared that she had information relating to some of the city's leading politicians. A few days later, her body was found in Van Cortland park; she had been strangled. A week afterward, her fifteen-year-old daughter committed suicide, horrified and shamed by publicity. The tabloids had a field day. Miss Gordan's address book listed more than five hundred "sugar daddies" as well as the number of the country's most famous madam, Polly Adler. Police Commissioner Edward P. P. Mulrooney declared there would be "a stain on the shield of every policeman in New York" until they apprehended Miss Gordon's murderer. From Albany, Roosevelt sent word that the police themselves were on trial.[16]

But the culprit remained free, while the police declared they had no clues to his identity. Reformers had no doubt that somehow Tammany had been involved in the crime, and the inactivity of the police provided additional evidence of the arrogance of the political thieves who ran the city. The CAC pounded away at Roosevelt to do something, and demanded that District Attorney Crain, "a dear, nice old man," be removed from office and that an independent prosecutor be appointed to look into municipal corruption. On March 15, clergymen in pulpits throughout the city called for Roosevelt to act. Before the Free Synagogue, Wise called upon the governor to "exercise the power of leadership and compel his party to join the creation of a legislative committee of inquiry which should search out the truth about the mayor and many of his underlings."[17]

Two days later, on Wise's birthday, he and Holmes went to see Roosevelt at the home of the governor's mother on East 65th Street, carrying with them a document prepared by the CAC staff charging the Walker administration with corruption, failing to administer the city in the interests of the people, ignoring inefficiency and corruption, and appointing incompetents to public office. The maid led them upstairs to a second-floor study where Roosevelt received them cooly. Holmes briefly summarized the document and handed it to the governor, who promised to read it as soon as he had an opportunity. The two men then rose to leave, when Roosevelt said, "I have listened to you. Now you sit down and listen to me." He then proceeded to lecture them on their meddling in political affairs, and in particular to denounce Wise for a letter he had sent criticizing one of Roosevelt's judicial appointments. Wise, used to the frank exchanges he had enjoyed with Al Smith, sat in bewildered silence throughout the half-hour diatribe. It would be the last time he saw Roosevelt in person for five years.[18]

The City Affairs Committee released the document the same day, and it immediately drew praise from civic reformers across the country. Newton D. Baker wrote that "everybody I meet in or from New York seems aroused." From Washington Justice Brandeis sent word that "I am glad that you and Holmes are making Jew and Gentile face the shame of the city." An attorney with close connections to the district attorney's office wrote: "I can't very well stand up and cheer you for the splendid job you are doing. But I can whisper to you in the privacy of the confessional that I am thrilled by it and tremendously proud." In light of this response Holmes exulted: "We never did a better job in our lives . . . How glorious it has been to work on this together!"[19]

Later historians have evaluated the release of the CAC indictment as premature and insufficiently documented to justify the charges. William H. Allen, director of the Institute of Public Service, recalled that Henry J. Rossner of the CAC staff had brought him a copy before Wise and Holmes presented it to Roosevelt. He found some of the charges misleading, others undocumented, and some he considered worthless or false; he advised against making it public. Walker himself, after a delay of several weeks, submitted a rambling 15,000-word statement which, despite important omissions and a great superficiality, Roosevelt accepted at face value; the governor then announced that there was insufficient justification for removing the mayor from office. In his reply, Walker characterized the CAC as "an annex of the Socialist party," and Holmes as "a leader in a group of agitators and Soviet sympathizers."[20]

By then, however, it was too late to hold back the public clamor for a full-scale investigation. The legislature named a special committee headed by Senator Samuel H. Hofstadter; the committee in turn hired Judge Samuel Seabury to lead the examination. On April 8, 1931, Seabury began his work for the Hofstadter Committee, work which would continue until December 1932. He and his staff interviewed 2,260 people privately and put another 175 witnesses on the stand in thirty-seven public sessions. The Seabury staff generated over 52,000 pages of testimony and hundreds of thousands of documents detailing the political and financial transactions of the Walker administration and of Tammany Hall.

The CAC watched the Seabury investigation carefully, and no doubt took much pleasure in the astute manner by which the judge forced Roosevelt to act. When the State Court of Appeals ruled that the Hofstadter Committee had no power to grant immunity to witnesses, Seabury followed Judge Cardozo's dictum that the problem could be easily solved by a simple legislative act. Seabury immediately asked Roosevelt to recommend such a measure, and the governor, with his eye on the 1932 presidential race, had no choice but to agree.

Roosevelt had little love for Tammany nor any illusions about Walker.

"Our little Mayor can save much trouble in the future by getting on the job, cleaning his own house and stopping wisecracks," Roosevelt remarked acidly in March 1931. "If he does not do all this he can have only himself to blame if he gets into trouble."[21] But attacking Walker meant attacking Tammany, which might swing its weight behind Al Smith for the 1932 Democratic presidential nomination. Efforts to place the onus for continuing the investigation upon the Republicans failed, as GOP leaders gleefully watched the Democrats taking swings at one another. Outside New York, the nation's Democrats waited to see how Roosevelt would handle the situation. If he caved in to Tammany, they would have nothing to do with him; if he fought the Hall, Boss Curry might deny him the backing of his own state. Each step he took, such as calling a special session of the legislature for the immunity bill or removing Sheriff Farley, he took hesitantly and reluctantly, thus gaining praise from neither the reformers nor the politicians.

The CAC and other reformers refused to ease their pressure on Roosevelt, and whenever he took a high-minded stance, they found a means to turn it to their own purposes. During the hearings on removing Sheriff Farley, for example, Roosevelt had declared that "where a public official is under inquiry . . . [he] owes a positive public duty to the community to give a reasonable or credible explanation of the sources . . . which enable him to maintain a scale of living beyond the amount of his salary." On March 17, 1932, exactly one year after they had issued their original charges, Wise and Holmes called for Roosevelt to remove John Theofel, chief clerk of the Queens County surrogates court, and James A. McQuade, the Kings County sheriff, neither of whom could explain enormous bank accounts. Here was a clear analogy to the Farley case, but an exasperated Roosevelt vented his anger on the two clergymen in a strident four-page letter:[22]

> The time which you two gentlemen now spend bringing charges and asking your governor to perform unconstitutional functions and to ignore the principles of representative government could be more profitably spent. If you would exert yourself patiently and consistently in pointing out to the electors of New York City that an active insistence on their part would result in better qualified and more honest and more efficient servants, you would be rendering a service to your community which at the present time you are not performing.

The following Sunday in Carnegie Hall, Wise rose in the pulpit and noted that in a few weeks the Free Synagogue would celebrate its twenty-fifth anniversary. "My service as a rabbi here for twenty-five years may have been good, bad or indifferent," he commented. "If the judgment of Albany is to be taken, it has been bad." But the Free Synagogue had been founded and kept going because of an ideal, a commitment to preaching the truth however uncomfortable it might be. A surrender to that ideal, Wise said, could only result in a moral and spiritual death, an acquiescent attitude toward corruption and the evils found in everyday life. That course, he declared, would be a far worse fate than mere physical death.[23] Wise, Holmes, and other reformers refused to give up, and constantly called upon Roosevelt to act, to release documents, to make clear just where he stood.

In May, Seabury's investigation reached a climax when he put Mayor Walker on the stand. Up until now the hearings, while exposing the misdeeds of underlings, had failed to produce any evidence of wrongdoing by the mayor personally. Then Seabury's investigators discovered that Walker had been issued letters of credit by a group of businessmen who had created the Equitable Coach Company in a plan to take over all the city's surface transit operations. They had never actually given Walker cash, but had so arranged it that Jimmy had all the money he needed on his high-living jaunts to California, Florida, and the French Riviera. Moreover, despite the fact that the Equitable did not own a single bus, Walker had pushed a franchise through the Board of Estimate, and then kept it alive through one extension after another while the holding company vainly tried to negotiate its deals. For the first time, Seabury had hard evidence linking the mayor of New York to actual corruptions.

On the stand, a tensely smiling Walker listened carefully as Judge Seabury put one question after another to him. How did a $60-a-week bookkeeper in Walker's old law firm manage to deposit nearly one million dollars in a private account, out of which he paid many of the mayor's bills? Why had a publisher split stock profits with Walker, so that while the mayor had not put up a dime of his own money, he received $246,000? All this was really quite simple and honest, Gentlemen Jimmy replied; all his good fortune resulted from having generous and loving friends.[25]

Seabury dramatically recessed the hearings after Walker's appearance, and left the state for a brief vacation, while newspapers and reformers howled for the governor to act. Roosevelt disingenuously declared that he could do nothing until the special investigator reported to him; he had received nothing, and only knew what he read in the newspapers. Seabury immediately responded by sending the governor a transcript of the hearings, an analysis of the evidence, and a list of fifteen charges against Walker. After nearly two years of political evasion, Roosevelt had backed himself into a corner. He had to act, and no matter what course he chose, to pay the political penalties. As Walter Lippman noted, "The problem is entirely the consequence of Governor Roosevelt's indecision during the last year."[26]

On June 21, six days before the Democratic national convention met in Chicago, Roosevelt sent Seabury's charges to Walker and asked for an immediate reply. The mayor politely informed the governor that he was about to leave for the convention, and would reply as soon as he returned. At Chicago, despite Tammany's enmity and "the putrefying Walker albatross around his neck," Roosevelt captured the nomination. But as he well knew, his problems in New York were far from over. He still had to deal with Walker, and in such a way as to minimize any damage to his presidential campaign. Harold Ickes warned Roosevelt that "while many independents and Republicans are favorably inclined toward you at this time, I find that they are not prepared to make up their minds until you have passed upon the case of Mayor Walker."[27]

On July 28 Walker finally sent a long and evasive response to Seabury's charges, and reformers now turned expectantly toward Roosevelt. "How the governor can fail to remove him passes my understanding," Wise wrote. "I hope Jimmy will go, but I can't help regretting that after years of shilly-shally and other cowardice in dealing with the problem, Roosevelt shall now gain advantage by doing an inevitable thing if he screws up the courage to do it." About to leave for Europe, Wise feared that the governor would try to get by with a tongue-lashing of Walker, and then call it a day.[28]

But Roosevelt at last understood that the only course open to him was dealing firmly with the problem. On August 11 the governor opened hearings and personally questioned Walker. In three weeks of tough grilling of the mayor, Roosevelt established a reputation with out-of-state voters as a man free of Tammany's control. He called in Raymond Moley, Felix Frankfurter, and other members of the Brains Trust to advise him; he wanted a solution that would be fair, honest, and, he hoped, politically advantageous. At the same time, party regulars from the city bombarded him with pleas to let Walker off the hook. In the midst of one such session with Tammany representatives on September 1, an aide came in bearing a telegram from Walker announcing his resignation. A relieved Roosevelt quickly accepted.

For Wise, Holmes, and other members of the City Affairs Committee, Walker's resignation marked the climax of a long battle stretching back more than two years. Wise noted that suddenly they had a great many friends, people who until recently had been attacking the CAC now stopped him in the streets to say, "You and Dr. Holmes were right." The real fight, though, had never been against Walker but against Tammany Hall and the corruption it had fostered in New York. In a sermon at the Free Synagogue, Wise declared that "Walkerism" had not departed on the boat to France with the former mayor. "New York City is not going to be changed by a change of mayors, however just and inexorable any new mayor might be. What we must have is not a change of mayors, but a change in New York, a demand for high standards of public life." Wise saw little to suggest that Acting Mayor McKee would initiate such changes; in his seven years on the

Board of Aldermen, McKee was a loyal follower not of civic integrity but of Boss Curry.[29]

The two-year battle with the Tammany tiger had been difficult, and Wise had been the target of much abuse. There had also been threats against him which he had shrugged off but which his wife had taken seriously. Without letting him know, Louise had hired a detective to follow her husband closely and protect him from possible physical attacks. But the fight had been worth it, and as he told Holmes, "I am proud of the City Affairs Committee's part in the job."[30] But defeating Walker was only the first step in ridding New York of the curse of Tammany; now an honest and able administration had to be elected, and before long Wise found himself a supporter and close friend of Fiorello H. LaGuardia.

First elected to Congress in 1916 on a Republican ticket, the feisty half-Italian, half-Jewish LaGuardia had quickly made a name for himself as an independent progressive, tied to no political party, and with an uncanny ability to exploit dramatically almost every situation to his political advantage. He resigned from Congress to enlist in the war, but on his return had run into the immense power of the Tammany machine. During the 1920s he had attacked Curry and Walker continuously, and then the scandals brought him back to center stage. In 1933 he headed the Fusion ticket, a rag-tag assemblage of reformers, Republicans, Socialists, disillusioned Democrats, and just about anyone else who wanted to defeat Tammany.

Wise had not at first been enthusiastic about LaGuardia, and the City Affairs Committee had tried to talk Judge Seabury into running. But Seabury, despite Roosevelt's suspicions, really had no political ambitions; he did not want to be mayor of New York. Perhaps he recognized that his talents lay in prosecutorial investigation rather than in the political wheeling and dealing and administrative detail of which New York's mayor had to be a master.[31] Once Seabury finally convinced the reformers that he would not be a candidate and that LaGuardia was their man, Wise and the others threw their energies into the Fusion campaign. At first it looked as if Joseph V. McKee might win, but the continuous recital of Tammany's sins as well as LaGuardia's panache finally convinced the electorate that a housecleaning in City Hall was long overdue. Wise spoke at numerous rallies, including an overflow crowd at the Madison Square Garden just a few days before the election, a gathering he described as "almost religious in its fervor." The Fusion team miraculously won, and on Juanuary 1, 1934, Wise stood proudly in the alderman chambers as Fiorello LaGuardia was sworn in as mayor of New York. A few minutes after the ceremony, he penned a note to his colleague on the CAC. "I thought much of you today," he wrote Holmes. "A better day has come and we have had a little part in bringing it to pass.[32]

Wise and LaGuardia would maintain a close if at times hectic relationship over the next dozen years. Both men had large egos and could become angry over both real and imaginary slights. Yet they shared a deep respect and real affection for each other, and tended to take the other's advice seriously, even if they did not always follow it. A friend once described Wise as LaGuardia's *Uzona Yevsey*, referring to Jews who advised Czarist officials in the nineteenth century; the Wise–LaGuardia relationship, however, rested as much on friendship as on political alliance. On one occasion when the two men had been arguing, Wise threw up his hands in exasperation. "Fiorello," he yelled, "you may sue me, but you're crazy. You're a crazy Italian. You're a crazy Jew. You're generally crazy!"

His Honor stood up on one foot, put his index finger on his nose, and smiled back. "But I'm a pretty good man, aint't I?"[33]

LaGuardia began to seek Wise's advice on appointments shortly after the election, a practice he continued throughout his tenure. When the mayor named a commission to revamp the city's charter, Wise worried that it had too many respectable "shirt fronts" on it and not enough reformers, and managed to get a few more CAC types added. Later on, LaGuardia practically turned over to Wise responsibility for naming Jewish chaplains to the city's prisons and hospitals.[34] Yet at the same time the mayor often showed a stubborn streak and seemingly went out of his way to ignore the suggestions of friends and reform groups. At one point, Wise complained to attorney Louis Nizer: "I don't know what's the matter with Fiorello. He will consider recommendations from anyone but those who worked with him and have his interests at heart." Nizer suggested that LaGuardia sometimes took his crusade for civic honesty to extreme lengths; he had denounced political bosses for so long, he would not risk being accused of paying off even his dearest friends.[35]

LaGuardia's first years in office were difficult, not only because of the Depression but because he had inherited a city nearly bankrupted by Tammany's depredations. The new administration had to keep expenses down whenever possible, much to the chagrin of some city employees, who felt they were carrying an unfair share of the burden. Wise consistently defended LaGuardia against such charges, and pointedly reminded critics that if they had been half as vocal protesting the waste of the Walker regime the city would not have been brought to such an impasse.[36] Yet at the same time Wise opposed what he considered ill-conceived schemes to increase the city's revenue, such as the proposal for a municipally sponsored lottery. Before the Board of Estimate, Wise declared that "lotteries are a swindle which some people consider adventitious, but they are not worth the thought of any intelligent person. That is a fantastic, childish and basically unethical way of obtaining money."

Bronx Borough President James J. Lyons suggested that Wise was

"behind the times," and pointed to the recent legalization of race-track bet-
ting. "Even with your great temple, you were unable to stop that bill from
becoming law."

"Even if I couldn't cure it, I didn't minister to it," Wise shot back. "I've
been fighting against racing measures for the last twenty years."[37]

When the lottery passed, Wise lectured LaGuardia on its immorality, terming a measure worthy of "the Noble Jimmy" but not of a reform administration. To Holmes he also admitted chagrin but noted that, in
LaGuardia's defense, the mayor had pushed through a number of worthwhile financial proposals, and evidently had had to accept the lottery in
order to get the rest.[38] Despite this incident, Wise did not abandon the Fusion group, and supported LaGuardia and his allies in all the ensuing
municipal elections. In 1937, Wise urged the Free Synagogue to vote for the
man who had cleansed City Hall, and he continued to advise the mayor on
how he and other reformers hoped to see New York redeem itself from the
shame of Tammany.[39]

Wise's visibility on the political scene was not limited to New York. He
added a new forum from which to speak out on issues when he agreed to
help his son launch a new magazine, *Opinion*. After leaving the Institute,
Jim had pursued his literary interests, publishing several books and a
number of articles. He eventually decided to start a weekly magazine addressed to Jewish interests as defined in a broad and liberal manner. Wise
enthusiastically endorsed the idea, agreed to serve on the editorial board,
and set about contacting his many friends and acquaintances to raise money
for the enterprise. In several instances, he agreed to guarantee loans made
to the journal.[40]

The first issue of *Opinion*—"A Journal of Jewish Life and Letters"—appeared on December 7, 1931, with James Waterman Wise as editor and
Johan J. Smertenko as managing editor. The board included, besides
Stephen Wise, Erwin Edman, John Haynes Holmes, Mordechai Kaplan,
Ludwig Lewisohn, Maurice Samuel, and George Kohut. From its very
beginning, *Opinion* was well-written, stimulating, and controversial. Wise
wrote a regular column, "As I See It," which provided him still another
forum to attack antisemites, corrupt politicians, and stuffed shirts. Jim's
broad view of what should interest Jewish readers brought in not only compliments but some complaints that *Opinion* was not really a "Jewish"
magazine. To one such critic Wise heatedly replied: "My son is editing a
paper which is vigorously, frankly and courageously Jewish. Jewishness is
very much more important than the recital of the 'Sh'ma' or even
monotheism. . . . I think it of a very great importance to have a weekly
such as *Opinion* which deals bravely and kindly with every manner of
Jewish problem."[41]

Lively as *Opinion* may have been, the Wises had chosen a difficult moment in which to found a new journal. Like all such ventures, it lost money at the beginning—nearly $18,000 in the first four months and $30,000 for the first year. By September, 1932 Wise felt desperate about the chances of keeping it going. "Unless some miracle happens," he told George Kohut, "*Opinion* is through. The forthcoming issue is a magnificent one, but I am afraid there will be no other." In a last-ditch effort to save the magazine, Wise went back to some of the original subscribers, such as Bernard Baruch, to coax additional money out of them. Finally, the board decided to discontinue weekly publication and change *Opinion* into a monthly. "It has been a terrible struggle," Wise noted, "but we are going to fight on another year, hoping to keep the subsidy down to somewhere between $10,000 and $12,000."[42]

Opinion slowly but surely began to carve out a niche for itself in the Jewish world. It ran comments on current social and political problems, criticism, poetry, reviews, and fiction by some of the better writers of the day. At the same time, though, Jim's personal philosophy was veering leftward. A visit to the Soviet Union led him to believe that America's economic problems needed a radical solution, and that the Russian model might be the answer. Gradually, a more radically political note crept into the page of *Opinion*, causing some unease on the editorial board. Wise and Holmes were at this time sympathetic to socialism but Jim himself recognized the difficulty of the situation. They had founded a journal of Jewish affairs, and had begged and borrowed money to sustain it as a Jewish magazine; to have it follow Jim's steady drift leftward might appear as a betrayal of the original proposal to its backers.

Jim approached his father to discuss the matter in early 1935, and explained that rather than embarrass the members of the board, he would resign. Once again, Wise admired his son's integrity, but lamented the abortion of such a promising beginning; at the very least, he told Holmes, he prayed that Jim would not forsake the field of Jewish work in which he had shown such promise.[43] Once Jim finally decided to leave, the question of a new editor had to be resolved. For a few months *Opinion* was edited by a committee and by whomever happened to have some time to devote to its affairs, but gradually the editorial board began pushing Wise to succeed his son. Now over sixty years old, head of the American Jewish Congress, president of the Jewish Institute of Religion, chairman of the United Palestine Appeal, and president-elect of the Zionist Organization of America, the rabbi of the Free Synagogue protested he already had too much to do. Jim, however, promised to help out with the non-political literary articles, while other people agreed to take more active roles. Wise believed in the value of *Opinion*, not so much as a personal forum, but as a stimulating voice in the Jewish community, and rather than see it fold, he finally agreed to assume the editorship in April 1936.

Many things affected the Jewish people in the 1930s, and Wise dealt with all of them in the pages of *Opinion*. American politics also received wide notice, for the Wises believed that Jews both as Jews and as Americans had obligations to participate in the electoral process, to make their representatives in the city council, the state legislature, or the national government know what their constituents thought and wanted. And as in so many areas, Wise would not call upon others to enter arenas he himself avoided. During the early thirties, Stephen Wise—for better or for worse—was the most politically active rabbi in America.

The Depression demanded political action. The administration of Herbert Hoover, by adhering to a strict policy of nonintervention, had refused to undertake any positive programs to alleviate the economic misery, and thus earned the opprobrium of the American people. By 1930 it had become clear that the animus against the Republicans would practically guarantee victory to the Democrats in the next presidential election. As a result, a number of contenders vied for the nomination, knowing that its capture all but ensured four years in the White House. Al Smith, despite his defeat in 1928, still enjoyed the support of large segments in the party. John Nance Garner, Newton D. Baker, William Gibbs McAdoo, and others all tossed their hats into the ring, but the man with the best chance seemed to be the governor of New York. Franklin Roosevelt's positive and creative response to depression problems in New York, later to be called "the little New Deal,"[44] won praise from many liberals including Wise, who had talked favorably of Roosevelt as presidential timbre after the impressive gubernatorial victory of 1930. But the Walker affair had soured Wise on Roosevelt, and he began casting about for an alternative.

In the spring of 1931 he sounded out former Secretary of War Newton D. Baker, whom Wise considered the most liberal and idealistic of the major Democratic politicians and the true heir of Wilsonian progressivism. He reported a conversation he had had with William E. Borah, in which the Idaho senator had declared that Baker would make the strongest Democratic candidate, able to carry the South, the Middle West, and the entire West with the exception of California. Following a newspaper article headlined "Baker Talk Frets Roosevelt Forces," Wise did his best to keep such talk going, even arranging parlor meetings to plan strategy, but all to no avail. When Roosevelt captured the nomination at Chicago, Wise sadly wrote to Baker: "It should have been you and only you. Personally I cannot give my support to the candidate for the party. I went into the [Democratic] party with Wilson. I go out thanks to Roosevelt; I may come back in 1936 with Baker."[45]

The selection of Roosevelt deeply troubled Wise, who considered the New York governor weak, untrustworthy, and untruthful. In letter after letter that fall he poured out his sense of outrage and betrayal. Roosevelt has "no deep-seated convictions," he told Felix Frankfurter, "no bed-rock in him. He is all clay and no granite. We shall have another four years such as we have had under Harding, Coolidge and Hoover." The Democratic Party, with its noble heritage of Cleveland and Wilson, had fallen to the point where it was indistinguishable from the GOP. As the election neared, Wise resigned himself to the inevitability of Roosevelt becoming the next president, but resolved to cast his ballot in protest for Norman Thomas.[46]

Roosevelt's election, of course, changed the entire political situation of the country and Wise, as a realist, decided to keep open some contact with the new administration. He composed a letter, which both he and John Holmes signed, offering their best wishes to the president-elect and holding out an olive branch of peace. "We trust," they wrote, "that whatever have been the differences between us with regard to civic affairs you may feel free to call upon us for whatever service lies within the power of American citizens to render to their government and president." Roosevelt, eager to build as wide a range of popular support as possible, responded in a similar vein to their "mighty nice letter," and noted that although they had differed over means, they all stood in agreement on the ultimate objectives of good government. As Holmes mused, Wise's gesture had been well worth the effort, and the day might soon come when they would want to work together with Roosevelt. Wise told a friend about the pleasant response, and noted that would not be able to "barb" his sermons as he had intended. "But then I greeted Hoover with a cordial welcome, so I suppose I can be equally hopeful about Roosevelt."[47]

The New Deal, in fact, marked a watershed in American Jewish political life. Roosevelt put together a powerful coalition of old-line party regulars and urban ethnic groups; in this coalition, American Jews played a major role. For the first time a national administration appointed a large number of Jews to important political offices. Samuel Rosenman, Felix Frankfurter, Benjamin Cohen, Henry Morgenthau, Jr., and others exercised great influence in defining and implementing the New Deal, and in return American Jews gave Roosevelt an unbelievable measure of political loyalty. The extent of Roosevelt's appeal in the Jewish community can be seen in Republican Jonah J. Goldstein's pun that the Jews have three *velten* (worlds): *die velt* (this world), *yener velt* (the world to come), and Roosevelt!

Moreover, the traditionally liberal community welcomed the activist measures which the New Deal championed. Roosevelt recognized, as he declared in his inaugural, that the Depression was an emergency as grave as war itself, and his administration stood prepared to respond in heroic fashion. The bank holiday, the abandonment of the gold standard, the NRA, AAA, and other proposals all brought warm applause from many of the old progressives.[48] "The Messiah has not yet come," Wise wrote a few weeks after Roosevelt took office, but the president "is a man and is tackling things admirably." As the Hundred Days progressed, Wise's comments grew more positive and enthusiastic. After hearing the inaugural: "Roosevelt has made a magnificent beginning." On April 18: "Roosevelt is deeply concerned and greatly cares. . . . Is he not doing magnificently?" On May 1: "The President has made a great start. I really believe he is doing big, yes wonderful things."[49]

In the months following, Wise's grudging tolerance of Roosevelt gave way to full-blown enthusiasm. When conservatives objected to the New Deal and charged that the president was a dictator, Wise denounced them before the Free Synagogue. On the first anniversary of the administration, he praised Roosevelt's accomplishments in contrast to the hated Nazi regime in Germany. Felix Frankfurter gently chided his rabbinical friend that perhaps it was time to recognize that Roosevelt and not Baker was the true heir of Woodrow Wilson's vision.[50]

Yet the break had not been completely healed. Some of the president's political advisors, especially Louis McHenry Howe, never forgave Wise for the embarrassment he had caused Roosevelt in the Walker scandal. Despite Roosevelt's post-election suggestion that Wise visit him, a formal invitation never came. Both David K. Niles and Frankfurter told Wise that he would be welcome at the White House, but Wise chose to stand on ceremony. If Roosevelt wanted to see him, then he should invite him directly. So the two men kept a stiff distance until late 1935, when Howe's influence waned as a result of illness. A number of people now suggested that Wise formally be invited, and that his support might be helpful in the 1936 election. On January 12, 1936, while he was visiting with Justice Brandeis, a call came asking if he could come over to the White House. Later that day, Wise entered the executive mansion for the first time since the Wilson administration, and after a few awkward moments, rabbi and president settled into a comfortable conversation.[51]

It was a fateful moment, for from that time until his death, Wise gave to Franklin Roosevelt the unswerving loyalty he had once reserved for Woodrow Wilson. He spoke frequently in favor of New Deal measures and stumped for Roosevelt in the 1936, 1940, and 1944 campaigns. One of the truly strong traits of Wise's character was loyalty, and at times it blinded his judgment. Because Roosevelt had done great things, because he had opened the door for a reconciliation, and because the president frequently expressed himself as sympathetic to Jewish problems, Wise ignored the less appealing facets of the Roosevelt personality, traits which he had seen so clearly during the Walker affair. Roosevelt was devious, he was willing to be all things to all people, he did mislead Wise and others into believing that he gave full support to their programs. The benefits and liabilities of Roosevelt's relations with American Jewry, and especially Stephen Wise, would not be clear for many years.

In 1936 Wise came out openly for Roosevelt, and aligned himself in the fight to continue the New Deal against the conservative assault. Wise's new enthusiasm more than compensated for his earlier disdain; Roosevelt had no more ardent admirer than the New York rabbi. In fact, as Roosevelt rose in his estimation, Al Smith declined. The one-time progressive governor had grown increasingly bitter over Roosevelt having "stolen" the 1932 nomination from him, and during the New Deal's first four years, Smith, now the president of the Empire State Building, moved consistently rightward. He spoke out often against the administration, and then joined the patently anti–New Deal Liberty League. A few days after his visit to the White House, Wise and his wife sat in front of their radio listening to Smith deliver a blistering attack on the New Deal to a Liberty League banquet. When the broadcast ended, Wise reached over to turn off the set, and then said to Louise: "Al Smith is dead." He felt as if he had been to a funeral, he told Felix Frankfurter. "Both of us believed in Al, trusted him and served him. . . . We now can see how lightly rooted was his philosophy of social justice, and that the moment it collides with those interests which have come to overwhelm them it evaporates." Actually, the Happy Warrior had not changed so much as the times. He still clung to his progressive beliefs with their inherently conservative biases, while the enormity of the Depression had led other liberals to positions which many old-line progressives like Smith now saw as radical.[52]

Wise himself had moved leftward since 1928, the year he had stumped the country for Smith. Always a believer in social justice and economic fairness, he found the capitalist system wanting after it "went bust" in 1929. He saw the very rich inconvenienced slightly while the rest of society suffered terribly. The Republican Party, which had claimed prosperity as its own special preserve, had done nothing to alleviate misery other than to mouth platitudes. At the opposite end of the spectrum, Wise also found communism unacceptable. The changes in economic and social life instituted after the overthrow of the Czar pleased him enormously, but as he told his daughter, he could never have complete confidence in any political or economic system that did not respect freedom of conscience. Roosevelt's bold experimentation, which so terrified the Liberty League, appeared to Wise and many liberals as halfway measures, the program of an administration unwilling to give up the old-time religion. After meeting with the president, Wise told Holmes: "I really was sorry for the President. He has not been fought for the things that are wrong, but for the things you and I believe to be right. He has not quite wholly been converted from his faith in the present social system, but the reactionaries may yet achieve that notable victory."[53]

Wise correctly assessed that Roosevelt would be pushed toward more radical reform by the conservatives. The efforts of the "first" New Deal, with its deliberate modeling upon business–government cooperation in the

World War, had led to only partial economic recovery; moreover, business had failed to keep its end of the bargain. Large corporations had been more than willing to join in price-fixing and market distribution, but balked at living up to the labor provisions of the National Recovery Administration, with its standards for fair wages and hours and the right to bargain collectively. Roosevelt once remarked that he had found capitalism like a man drowning; the president had jumped in to rescue him and then, once on shore, the victim had berated his rescuer for not saving his hat as well. In 1935 the New Deal entered its "second" phase, one marked by the spirit of Louis D. Brandeis and his disciples. Here the emphasis shifted from recovery to reform, with specific measures ensuring labor rights as well as limits upon what business and finance could do. As the New Deal moved stongly into this spirit of reform, Wise and other liberals cheered. "I grow less and less fearful that Roosevelt will capitulate," Wise declared. "If he will stand and act in conformity to the promised terms of his acceptance [speech], I shall be entirely happy in my support of him."[54]

That summer in Europe, Wise spoke to both English and French officials, and reported to Roosevelt the wide faith that Europeans had in his leadership and his programs. He added his personal promise to speak for the Democrats if the president and his advisors thought it would be of any help. Upon his return to the United States, Wise received an invitation to spend a day at Hyde Park, and soon afterward the rabbi took to the stump, praising Roosevelt and his accomplishments and contrasting the New Deal to the fascist governments of Italy and Germany. He lashed out with special vigor at Republican innuendos of "alien influence" within the administration, charging there would not be a "Jewish issue" in the campaign had conservatives not resorted to lies in their attacks upon Rooseveltian reform. There ought not to be a "Jewish vote" either, Wise declared, but Jews as Americans ought to support the president for what he had done for the country.[55]

Roosevelt's record-shattering victory on November 3 brought exultation in the Wise household. To the president Wise wrote: "What a glorious vindication! What a mandate for America to go forward! The enemies of liberalism and progress under your great leadership did their worst and nastiest. May God give you and the nation four more wondrously blessed years." A few days before Roosevelt took the oath of office for the second time, Wise dropped him another letter with his prayer for a successful term in which to heal the economic and social wounds of the nation. The rising antisemitism in Europe led Wise to suggest that a word regarding America's continuing commitment to freedom and democracy for all peoples might be in order, and Roosevelt added that sentence verbatim to his inaugural—"Nor will the American democracy ever hold any faithful and law-abiding group within its borders to be superfluous."[56]

Not everyone approved the highly visible political role Wise took in these years. After he had endorsed reform candidate Joseph McGoldrick for Brooklyn district attorney, for example, an irate Jewish citizen of that borough chastised Wise for injecting himself into "local matters" out of his domain. "As a professed leader of Jewry, your extracurricular activities should be confined to only the broadest phases of political endeavor, and not to local issues. You cannot afford to jeopardize the good name of Jewry since other faiths will judge us by your actions." An indignant Wise responded: "You may not say to me that I cannot afford to jeopardize the good name of Jewry. The good name of Jewry is being jeopardized by those who are tolerant of political indecency and civic corruption. The citizens of New York know that I, as a Jew and a rabbi, will speak out whenever I feel it necessary to speak out against unworthy conduct in public office. . . . May I venture to suggest that you do your duty as Jew and American in every sphere of life, and leave it to me to decide for myself how to safeguard the good name of Jewry, for which I have done something in the last forty years."[57]

Wise, it must be recalled, did not initially enter the political arena in the 1930s; he had been a politically active rabbi ever since he stood in his first pulpit in New York in the 1890s. His philosophy of politics as an extension of one's religious obligations had deep roots in the ethical teachings of the Hebrew prophets and the preachings of the American Social Gospel movement. By the thirties, however, Wise had undoubtedly become one of the best-known Jews in America and led a highly active and visible life. Moreover, the reform groups with which Wise had been affiliated for years all seemed to reach fruition in the Depression decade. He had long fought for good government in the cities, and the CAC had helped replace Tammany with LaGuardia's Fusion ticket. He had been a progressive Democrat since Wilson's era, and he personally knew many of the New Deal leaders. He had battled for labor rights, for the protection of children and minorities and in other crusades which now dominated the political scene. Political figures sought him out not only as an ally, but because he did carry political "clout." Although he denied the existence of a Jewish vote, bloc voting did take place. When Wise endorsed Roosevelt or Lehman or LaGuardia, Jews did take notice. Wise was not unaware of his influence, and husbanded it carefully. He gave his advice to politicians who sought it, and publicly lectured those he thought in the wrong; he did not begin this practice in the thirties, but had done so all through his rabbinical career. He endorsed men and women for political office, but whether they were Jew or gentile, his blessing came only if he believed in their abilities and integrity. He asked nothing for himself, but as the decade wore on he began to ask more and more for the Jewish people.

18

A Voice in the Wilderness

The rise of Adolf Hitler and the National Socialist Party in Germany would ultimately affect every nation, every group, every individual on earth, cause a war of global proportions and immense horror and suffering, and lead to the deaths of upwards of thirty million persons. No people suffered more than the Jews, whom the Nazis picked out as a special target for their hatred, yet it would take most Jews several years to realize the danger posed by fascism. Jews in Germany traced their roots back over a thousand years, and saw themselves as proud citizens of the Reich. Hitler, in their view, was an aberration, his tenure a temporary although uncomfortable interlude that had to be tolerated until the nation of Beethoven, Goethe, and Schiller returned to its senses. In America, beset by its own political and economic problems, the Jewish community initially refused to take Hitler seriously, and followed the lead of German Jews such as Leo Baeck who advised against protest. It was an "internal" German matter, one they hoped would soon disappear.

Only a handful of American Jews knew better and tried to rally their people against the fascist danger. Pre-eminent in this miniscule coterie stood Stephen Wise, and for a while his was the only prominent voice raised against the Nazi evil. He was almost sixty years old when Hitler came to power, and it seems as if all Wise had done and stood for previously had been but a prelude to this, the most important fight of his life. Wise's battle against Nazism took many forms and was articulated through a variety of vehicles including the Zionist Organization of America, *Opinion*, the American and World Jewish Congresses, and others. The number of refugees he sponsored and put up in his own home ran into the hundreds, perhaps thousands. From 1933 until the end of the Second World War, Wise's overriding preoccupation was somehow to save his people.

Nearly a decade before Hitler assumed the chancellorship, Wise noted the rising antisemitism in Europe, especially in Germany. In November 1923 he received word of anti-Jewish riots in Berlin in which dozens of Jews were beaten, as many as ten killed, and hundreds of shops looted. He immediately called together the executive committee of the American Jewish Congress and sent a telegram to the German ambassador to the United States expressing shock and dismay at the disorders, and calling upon the German government to protect its Jewish citizens.[1] Two years later at the Zionist Congress in Vienna he personally saw protofascist groups parade in the streets chanting *Juden Heraus*—"Out with the Jews!" In 1927 Michael Franklin, a student at the Jewish Institute of Religion, sent Wise newspaper clippings from Germany about Nazi activites, and reported his own experiences of fascist youth gangs roaming the streets.[2]

Wise never claimed to have foreseen the full measure of depravity to which Hitler would take Germany, but he did recognize a very important point early—namely, that fascism itself represented a danger to democracy. In Italy, for example, Mussolini made no reference to Jews, who until the German occupation were treated like other Italian citizens. Wise's opposition to fascism at this point, as he noted, "has nothing to do with any Jewish question." He adopted a personal boycott of Italy, a land whose culture he and his wife both loved, and swore he would not return there until the Mussolini regime had ended.[3]

The German brand of fascism, of course, had a great deal to do with Jewish questions, and an increasingly apprehensive Wise watched as Hitler's influence grew. In October 1930 he told the American Jewish Congress that a Germany of Hitler, of rowdyism, of antisemitism, had to be opposed, until the Germany of culture and wisdom would triumph. But Germany did not recover its equilibrium, and a year later the incidence of antisemitic brutality had increased.[4] To the German-Jewish scholar Ismar Elbogen, Wise wrote: "We are aghast over things as they are developing in your country. Perhaps it is fairer to say we are nauseated by the things we read. . . . I can hardly bring myself to believe that Germany will lapse into the madness to which Hitler invites it, though when a people is hungry and suffering it is not difficult to incite them to wrong doings and wrong thinking."[5]

In late 1931 Wise received another batch of news clippings, this time from Felix Frankfurter, which alarmed him even more. By then, the Nazis had ceased to be a splinter group; with 107 seats they constituted the second largest faction in the Reichstag, and worries of their seizing power no longer appeared fantastic. Moreover, the Depression had begun to spawn fascist groups in America which, Wise feared, would imitate the street violence and antisemitic outrages of the Hitler party. Wise attempted to convince Felix Warburg and Cyrus Adler of the American Jewish Committee of the seriousness of the situation, but to no avail. He wrote: "These are awful times. It almost seems to me that a century hence this day of ours is to be included in the annals of Jewish misery, unrelieved but for the gleam of Palestine."[6]

Wise stood practically alone in taking Hitler seriously, yet his prescience is even more remarkable since to the world at large in early 1932, Adolf Hitler was a joke, a caricature even more bizarre and unbelievable than that later portrayed by Charlie Chaplin in *The Great Dictator*. Jews had lived in Germany for centuries, had contributed to German culture and economic greatness, had assimilated to the point that the German-Jewish community was beginning to decrease because of intermarriage. Few could comprehend that the German people would succumb to this madman; conversely, optimists blithely pointed out that even if the Nazis took office, they would soon be sobered by responsibility. The ranting Hitler, they said, confronted by the difficult tasks of managing Germany's affairs, would quickly abandon his insane rhetoric and become as conservative as his predecessors.

This latter argument failed to convince Wise, and in the pages of *Opinion* and elsewhere he tried to point out its fallacy. The reality of the situation was that Hitler had made a great many promises which he could not possibly redeem, but it would be all too easy to carry out his pledges against the Jews. Albert Einstein predicted that "Hitler will be powerless to halt the forces of evil he has let loose, even though he has no present intention of carrying out his threats against the Jews."[7] Hitler, as it turned out, controlled events far better than anyone had expected, and did, in fact, intend to make Germany *Judenrein*—free of Jews.

In 1932, the inevitable tragedy slowly unfolded. Hitler failed to win the presidential election in the spring, but that July the Nazis captured more than thirty percent of the popular vote and won over 200 seats in the Reichstag, making it the largest party. The Communist party comprised the next largest group, and as the center parties collapsed, so did democracy in the Weimar Republic. Yet even then, German Jewry remained blind.

That fall, the American Jewish Congress sent a special representative to Germany. Sidney Matz interviewed over thirty of the country's leading Jews, and asked all of them two questions: What should American Jewry do to avert Hitler's coming to power; and if he did assume control of the government, what could be done to prevent harm to the Jews? Matz reported that with one exception, the leaders of German Jewry assured him that Hitler would never come to power. One told Matz: "Say to Rabbi Wise that he need not concern himself with Jewish affairs in Germany. If he insists upon dealing with Jewish affairs in Europe, let him occupy himself with Jewish problems in Poland and Rumania." Only Georg Bernhard, editor of the *Vossische Zeitung*, told Matz that the Congress was right to be fearful: "Hitler will come to power and will destroy German Jewry."[8]

Hitler did both. In the fall of 1932, the depression in Germany worsened and the government, gripped by paralysis, proved unable to respond.

Chancellor Kurt von Schleicher found his plans for a grand coalition stymied and asked President von Hindenburg to suspend the constitution and allow him to rule by decree. The 85-year-old general feared such a course, and finally agreed to a plan put forward by the Junkers. "Make Hitler chancellor," they urged, "and the Nazis and Conservatives will form a parliamentary majority. The man is a drummer and we will be able to control him." Finally von Hindenburg agreed, and on January 30, 1933, Adolf Hitler became chancellor of Germany.

Even before the Nazis took power, a rising antisemitism infected much of the world. In Rumania, frontier guards shot and killed five young Jews without justification. In Poland, authorities barred Jewish students from schools. In London, a Jewish sailor jumped from an American ship on which he had been serving after repeated persecution and Jew-baiting by his crewmates. Even in far-off China, the president of the Jewish community of Harbin was murdered by a gang of White Russian emigrés.[9]

In the United States, the Jewish community stood paralyzed by indecision, nor was it alone. The editorial responses of the country's leading newspapers showed confusion over exactly who Hitler was and what he stood for, and a general apathy toward the fate of German Jewry permeated the articles.[10] Jewish Congress officials met with the leaders of the B'nai B'rith and the American Jewish Committee and Wise repeatedly asked: "What shall we do if Hitler comes to power?" Cyrus Adler, the Committee president, blandly replied, "We will cross that bridge when we come to it, not before."[11]

Within days of this meeting, the Jewish people came to the bridge, and discovered that Adolf Hitler fully intended to carry out the policies he had enunciated for more than a dozen years. On February 4, the Nazis issued a decree prohibiting public meetings and suppressing all publications that "endangered public security." There followed a string of "emergency measures" suspending all the basic freedoms of speech, press, assembly, and privacy culminating in an enabling act on March 23 which granted Hitler full dictatorial powers. In the streets Nazi brigands beat up Jews and any other groups or individuals opposing Der Fuehrer's policies. Jewish professors were forced to cancel their classes, Jewish performers had to leave the Dresden and Berlin operas, while the famed Jewish conductor, Bruno Walter, was barred from leading a concert in Leipzig. Day in and day out, the government kept up a steady stream of antisemitic propaganda; one estimate held that eighteen million copies of anti-Jewish papers were distributed in Germany daily.[12]

During the first week of the Hitler regime, Wise journeyed to Washington to see the German ambassador, a man known for his anti-Nazi attitudes (he would soon be dismissed from office), and found him embarrassed and sorrowful over what was happening in his beloved homeland. Wise then met with Justice Brandeis. The jurist, after hearing Wise's report of the meeting and of the depradations in Germany, astounded Wise by saying, "They must leave. All of them. There is no other way."

"How can 600,000 people be taken out of Germany?" the rabbi asked.

"They must all leave," Brandeis repeated. "I would have the Jews out of Germany. They have been treated with the deepest disrespect. I urge that Germany shall be free of Jews. Let Germany share the fate of Spain. No Jew must live in Germany."[13]

For Brandeis, the departure of German Jews would not be a victory for Hitler, but a terrible punishment to the Reich. German Jews had added enormously to the nation's wealth, and the loss of their capital, their skills, and their imagination would be a blow the jurist felt Germany could ill afford. Even Brandeis could not foresee that Germany would soon be *Judenrein*, but at a terrible price not only to Germany but to the Jews and the world as well.

Wise and other Jewish leaders anxiously awaited the next decree, feeling, as he put it, "utterly impotent in the presence of impending danger and disaster." Wise wanted Julian Mack and Felix Frankfurther, both of whom were on good terms with Franklin Roosevelt, to try to get him to act, but Brandeis advised against this course; the president had just taken office at the beginning of March, and had his hands full with domestic problems. Brandeis did suggest that Wise contact some of his friends in Congress, such as William Borah and Key Pittman, to see if they could help. But, of course, no one did.[14]

Before the Free Synagogue Wise called the German situation "the greatest tragedy in the history of the Jewish people during my lifetime," and called upon Christians as well as Jews to help restore Germany to its sanity. Privately he confessed his despair: "Things are very, very difficult. We are terribly worried about the situation in Germany. Oh, what a tragic fate my poor fellow Jews have! Some of the greatest representatives of the Jewish people in Germany are in hiding. It is just too awful."[15]

Then came word of the planned Nazi boycott of all Jewish shops and services on April 1, 1933, and Stephen Wise at last found a way to respond to Nazi persecutions. Under the sponsorship of the American Jewish Congress, Wise called upon the nation to show its revulsion against the fascists by a boycott of German goods. The idea spread quickly, with boycott committees set up in Great Britain, France, Poland, Belgium, Mexico, and Canada, as well as the United States.[16] A huge rally was scheduled in Madison Square Garden on March 27, and support elicited from prominent politicians and Christian leaders. As momentum picked up, however, Wise found a significant segment of the Jewish community—that group he had always referred to as "Sh-Sh Jews"—aghast at the whole idea.

The American Jewish Committee and the B'nai B'rith, who as late as

January 1933 had practically dismissed the possibility of Hitler ever coming to power, issued a joint statement on March 20 warning against "public agitation in the form of boycotts and mass demonstrations." These would "serve only as ineffectual channels for the release of emotion. They furnish the persecutors with a pretext to justify the wrongs they perpetrate and, on the other hand, distract those who desire to help with more constructive efforts." These "more constructive efforts" involved members of the two organizations traveling to Washington for private, behind-the-scenes meetings with high-ranking government officials. Secretary of State Cordell Hull received one such delegation and expressed sympathy with their goals, but maintained a legalistic posture throughout this early phase of the crisis. Inquiries made to the Wilhemstrasse only brought a response from the German Foreign Office that the fate of German Jews was an internal matter.[17]

The Committee adhered to this approach until March 1938, and the B'nai B'rith did not join in the boycott movement until August 1939. In their defense, it must be noted that a half-million German Jews were essentially hostages of the Nazis, who could quickly and brutally retaliate against hostile actions by Jews outside the Reich. Moreover, in order to facilitate emigration of those Jews who wanted to leave Germany, some contact had to be maintained with the new regime.[18] Given the *yahudim's* bias against any public airing of Jewish problems, it is clear why they immediately broke off negotiations for joint action with the Congress when that body, at the insistence of Wise and President Bernard Deutsch, decided to press ahead for public protest meetings and a boycott of German goods.

Wise and the boycott advocates were not unaware of these considerations ("regarding the German Jewish hostages, we *NEVER* forget them"[19]), but believed that quiet representations to the German government would have little effect. Moreover, Wise wanted non-Jews to join in the protest, to show that the Nazi actions affronted not just the immediate victims but all decent people. "How can we ask our Christian friends to lift their voices in protest against the wrongs suffered by Jews if we keep silent?," he asked a luncheon honoring him on his fifty-ninth birthday. "What is happening in Germany today may happen tomorrow in any other land on earth unless it is challenged and rebuked. It is not the German Jews who are being attacked. It is the Jews. We must speak out. If that is unavailing, at least we shall have spoken."[20]

His efforts to speak out, he soon discovered, were being undermined by the *yahudim*, whom he accused of trying to pretend that nothing serious was happening in Germany. When he invited Herbert Lehman to attend the Madison Square Garden rally, he found the governor curiously evasive, and Lehman finally told Wise that he had received advice that such a meeting would have negative results. Threats that German Jews would suffer because of the protest, as well as purported messages from German Jews asking him not to interfere, also gave Wise reason to pause, but then he received a batch of private letters smuggled out of Germany reporting tortures, the cutting of swastikas on human flesh, night arrests, and sudden disappearances of prominent Jews. One person who had escaped into France cabled Wise: "Do not believe the denials. Nor the Jewish denials." Confirmed by this information, Wise determined to proceed.[21]

The threat of the boycott actually worried the German government more than Wise or anyone else knew at the time. Hitler had promised to end the depression and unemployment, and his base of popular support would diminish unless he could produce some results. A foreign boycott of German goods could have serious effects on the economy, a fact the chancellor's economic advisors well knew. The Wilhemstrasse now contacted the American State Department with a message for Rabbi Wise: If the planned protest meetings and boycott were called off, and agitators stopped spreading lies about atrocities, then there would be a moderation of anti-Jewish measures. The day before the Garden rally, the German consul called Wise and again offered amelioration provided the protest was canceled. In Berlin that same day, Foreign Minister Constantin von Neurath scheduled an unusual press conference to condemn "the deliberate, sudden rebirth of the vilification campaign conducted during the World War against the Germans," and denied stories of anti-Jewish acts of terrorism and looting. A shaken Wise called Brandeis to get advice. Should he proceed or gamble that the Nazis would honor the proferred bargain? "Go ahead," came the succinct reply, "and make the protest as good as you can."

On Monday, March 27, 25,000 people crowded into Madison Square Garden; outside another 30,000 heard the proceedings over loudspeakers, while hundreds of thousands listened in over a national radio hookup.[23] Several Christians, including former governor Alfred E. Smith, Bishops William Manning and Francis McConnell, and Senator Robert F. Wagner attacked the Nazi measures, but the main speech of the evening came from Wise, and it was one of his best.[24]

> Not out of the bitterness of anger but out of the deeps of sorrow and the spirit of compassion do we speak tonight. For Germany we have asked and we continue to ask justice and even magnaminity from her erstwhile foes. We demand in the sight of humanity the right for Germany from the nations and the right from Germany for the Jewish people. No wrong under the heavens could be greater than to make German Jews scapegoats because Germany has grievances against the nations. We who would secure justice from the nations for Germany and justice to the Jews from Germany affirm tonight that Germany cannot hope to secure justice through injustice to its Jewish people.
>
> The protest of tonight is not against the German people, who we honor and revere and cherish. How could we, of the household of Israel, fail to cherish

and honor the German people, one of the great peoples of the earth, a people that has made monumental, indeed eternal, contributions to human well-being in the domains of religion, literature and the arts? How could we fail to cherish and to revere the people of Goethe and Schiller, Immanuel Kant and Hegel, Beethoven and Wagner, Heine and Einstein? . . .

We understand the plea and the plaint of our brother-Jews in Germany. They are German patriots who love their Fatherland and have had reason to love it. Some of their leaders are under the impact of panic and terror, others under some form of compulsion. . . . We have no quarrel with our Jewish brothers in Germany and their leaders, but their policy of uncomplaining assent and of super-cautious silence has borne evil fruit. They who have virtually been silent through the years of anti-Jewish propaganda cannot be followed by us as the wisest of counselors.

And if things are to be worse because of our protest, if there are to be new penalties and new reprisals in Germany, which I cannot bring myself to believe, then humbly and sorrowfully we bow our heads in the presence of the tragic fate that threatens, and once again appeal to the public opinion of mankind and to the conscience of Christendom to save civilization from the shame that may be imminent. . . .

I close as I began. We are not met in the spirit of bitterness, hatred of revenge. We do not desire that the German people be punished because of the un-wisdom of the measures and the injustice of some practices of a temporary government. Whatever nations may ask in the spirit of reparation and reprisal, we who are Jews know that our spirit must be in consonance with the high and classic tradition of Jewish forbearance. But there must be no further reprisals against our fellow-Jews, no penalizing them as German hostages because the conscience of the world utters its mighty protest. God help the German people to be equal to themselves.

As he told Julian Mack a fews days later: "I tried to be as prudent and as cautious as I could. The easiest thing in the world could have been to arouse that audience, that mighty meeting, the most wonderful meeting you have ever seen in your life, to murderous rage."[25] Wise's restraint surely stemmed from his uncertainty of the effects of the protest. "I am going through days and nights of hell," he admitted, "for I am mindful of our awful respon-sibility."[26]

On April 1, the Nazis instituted their boycott of Jewish goods and ser-vices, but much to Wise's joy, the government reversed itself within two days. At this early stage of their regime, the need to protect the economy outweighed Hitler's mania against the Jews. There is little doubt that the American reaction played a role in the Nazi decision, and Wise perceived that force might be the only way to affect Hitler, a realization that most of the world failed to understand until it was far too late.[27] The future of the American boycott remained indefinite as its proponents waited to learn Germany's next step.

The pattern soon emerged. A series of laws passed between April and October 1933 forced Jews out of the civil service, restricted their practice in the professions, established quotas in schools, and slowly strangled the economic life of what had hitherto been a prosperous community. In America the leaders of the American Jewish Committee and B'nai B'rith still tried to deal with these "internal matters" in a quiet way, while Wise agonized over the failure of the world to stop the fascist madness. To Julian Mack he lamented, "I wish I could go on and on fighting, but for the first time in my life I feel that it will be good when the fight is over, seeing that one could do so little."[28]

The early weeks of the Nazi regime proved extremely trying for Wise. In most of his other fights there had been allies, men and women who followed and fought alongside him. There had been identifiable enemies whose tactics and goals, no matter how Wise might disagree with them, at least appeared rational and familiar. The Reform opposition to Zionism, for example, or the *yahudim's* attack on the Congress, grew out of a historical experience which Wise understood even if he did not share. Now he seemed to stand alone, a solitary voice crying out in the wilderness against a madness which otherwise sane and sensitive people chose to ignore or dismiss.[29]

For Wise, this battle against fascism seemed doomed from the beginning, and there is a note of despair in his correspondence that is absent from any of his other campaigns, no matter how bitterly they had been fought or how outrageous the odds. "I am in the midst of a hideous job," he wrote, "with timid and fearful German Jews both in Germany and America at my heels to desist." The failure of the American government to react publicly left him feeling betrayed and sick; Roosevelt might be doing great things for the American economy, but why did he not speak out in favor of decency and humanity abroad?[30] Perhaps most painful to him was the accusation that his activities had played into the hands of the Nazis. An old friend, Rabbi William Rosenau of Baltimore, charged that the protest meeting and proposed boycott had only aggravated the plight of German Jewry, and if such activities continued, "Dr. Wise will kill the Jews of Germany." An overwrought Wise wrote several angry letters to Rosenau, and the two never spoke to each other again.[31] He now devoted practically all his waking moments to the fight. "I can write on nothing else," he told friends. "I am giving so much of my time to it that beginning this week I shall give up both synagogue and Institute work in order to devote every minute of my time to this."[32]

Wise, of course, was not completely alone. A handful of other Jews, mostly from the ranks of the Congress or the ZOA joined him, and he gratefully recognized that Christians such as Senator Borah and his old friend John Haynes Holmes stood up to protest Nazi measures. His family also provided him the moral support he desperately needed, and Jim's increasingly vocal participation in anti-fascist activity filled him with pride. And from Washington Justice Brandeis, whom he now revered more than ever, made it a special point to tell Wise that no matter what the odds, despite the indifference of the world or the attacks by friend or foe, he was in fact pursuing the right and just course. Shortly after the Madison Square Garden meeting, Wise went to Brandeis. The elderly jurist met him at the door saying, "You have done a mighty fine job." Then, in a rare display of feeling, Brandeis took Wise's hands in his own and told him, "You must go on and lead. No one could have done a finer piece of work." There must be no compromising, no negotiations; the protest had to continue, Brandeis urged. A few weeks later, after another attack on him by the *yahudim*, Wise opened his mail to find a one-line message scribbled on Supreme Court letterhead: "Merely to say you are doing 'splendid'."[33]

The forces of passivity proved so strong in these months for a variety of reasons. The Nazi propaganda apparatus took great pains to emphasize the movement's conservative tone, pointing out that it fought primarily against the communists and that its anti-Jewish measures were only incidental to this struggle. This was a strategy that appealed to a number of Americans. In April 1933, Edmund A. Walsh of the Georgetown University School of Foreign Service wrote to Matthew Woll of the National Civil Federation that he opposed the Nazi persecution of Jews and hoped that "the offensive and wholly reprehensible practice of Jewish Communists in Germany shall not be visited on innocent Jews." But, he added, nothing should be done to oppose the German suppression of communism. A few months later, an unsigned memorandum in the Federation files noted that "if the world is to find in Hitler a conservative force fighting against a revolutionary war, it may forgive him his anti-Jewish insanities and offer a prayer for his success."[34]

A number of Jewish-American leaders also feared that the Depression in the United States might trigger an outbreak of nativist antisemitism. Historically, economic distress had caused local populaces to vent their frustrations and anger on Jews. The statements of Committee spokesmen, especially president Cyrus Adler, constantly cautioned that the American public might easily turn against the Jews, and even Christian and liberal leaders who collaborated with the Committee shared this attitude. Jews with entree to the administration were, for the most part, seemingly indifferent to the plight of German Jewry. Henry Morgenthau, Jr., Herbert Lehman, Bernard Baruch, Herbert Feis, and James Warburg did not speak out at all in the early years of the Hitler regime; while Felix Frankfurter discussed the Nazi situation with the president, Roosevelt concentrated all his energies on the domestic economic crisis.[35]

Wise and his colleagues never ceased trying to get American political leaders to oppose publicly anti-Jewish measures in Germany. The Congress organized a letter-writing campaign to senators and representatives, and like the Committee, met whenever possible with State Department officials trying to elicit some positive response from the American government. When Roosevelt named William E. Dodd, an old friend of Woodrow Wilson's, as ambassador to Germany, Wise, together with Julian Mack, Felix Warburg, Judge Irving Lehman, and Max Kohler, arranged an interview with Dodd on July 3. For an hour and a half, they told the ambassador of their reports on Nazi rampages; in turn he responded that the American government could not intervene officially, but he promised to use all his personal efforts to prevent unjust treatment of German Jews and any maltreatment of American Jews in Germany. On the boat to Europe, Dodd discovered that Wise was a fellow-passenger, and on at least a half-dozen occasions during the trip, the two men discussed the German situation.[36]

Wise went to Europe that summer to attend the second World Jewish Conference, a gathering out of which ultimately developed the World Jewish Congress. But it also gave him an opportunity to see firsthand the reaction to Hitler in countries other than the United States. In London, he found the establishment Jews of the Board of Deputies acting exactly as their counterparts on the American Jewish Committee, but joyfully discovered several political figures publicly criticizing Hitler. The New York rabbi urged the British to adopt a more liberal immigration policy for Palestine so that Jews fleeing Germany would have a place to go. This latter proposal caught the attention of the Nazi press, which praised Wise and offered to provide him a list of Jewish families whose emigration to Palestine would be especially welcomed by the Reich.[37]

Wise wanted to go personally to Germany in order to see conditions there firsthand, but Ambassador Dodd warned him that not only would it be unsafe for him but it might in fact complicate the situation. So Wise stopped in countries bordering the Reich, such as Austria and Czechoslovakia, and there saw rallies of Nazi supporters; at night, he could hear roving bands of Hitler youth singing their songs of hate outside his hotel window. In Prague, Wise also came out strongly for the continued boycott of German goods, after a silence of several weeks during which he had waited to see whether the German government would relent in its policy.[38] Undoubtedly his encounters with literally scores of refugees from Germany now convinced him that only the most forceful protests had any hope of affecting Nazi policy. One young German Jew told him that nothing but the American demonstrations had prevented a pogrom, and that a huge massacre was still not impossible. "We go to bed wondering what hour in the night the police will pull us out of bed," the young man declared. "We arise wondering what the day will bring forth."[39]

On the train from Geneva to Paris, a young girl of sixteen or seventeen kept looking at Wise rather furtively. Finally she drew up her courage and asked him in German, "Are you coming, sir, from the World Jewish Conference in Geneva?"

"Yes, why do you ask?"

The girl, obviously scared, now refused to say anything, but after repeated urging by Wise, she poured out her story. "One night three friends and my brother, all twenty-six years of age, were sitting together in our home—please don't mention any names, because my old father and mother still live there—and the police came for them. The next day four coffins were delivered to the families with instructions that the boxes were not to be opened. All were tagged *'Erschossen in Flucht'*—'shot in flight'."

"Did you open the coffins?"

"Yes, and my brother's face had been shot away while he was 'in flight'."

Before the girl got off at a small town in France where she now lived as a governess with a Jewish family, Wise asked her if the American protests had helped or done damage.

Die vielleicht geschadet, aber es muss sein, es muss sein. "Perhaps it does cause damage, but it must be done, it must be done."[40]

Once back in the United States, Wise resumed the seemingly futile task of awakening his fellow-Jews and fellow-citizens to the dangers of fascism. He reached a few, pitifully few, and his sense of frustration increased daily. By November 1933, he began to vent his anger at Roosevelt, whom he described as "immovable, incurable and even inaccessible excepting to those of his Jewish friends whom he can safely trust not to trouble him with any Jewish problems."[41] Generally, Roosevelt preferred that the State Department handle specific administrative matters, especially as they affected refugees, while from time to time he let leading Jewish figures know that he sympathized with the plight of their brethren overseas.[42] The State Department did try to protest some of the more flagrant antisemetic outbursts, but each note from the Americans received the same response from the Wilhemstrasse: Such incidents were entirely internal German affairs. Ambassador Dodd, as he had promised Wise, also tried to use his personal offices and soon found himself virtually isolated in the Berlin diplomatic community.[43]

About the only area in which Wise and other foes of fascism derived any sense of accomplishment was in the boycott. Whatever actual effects the movement had on the German economy, it provided a focus for the growing sense of frustration in the American Jewish community. One could believe that by boycotting German goods a blow—however feeble—was being struck against the the Reich. Even Louise Wise, who had never before participated publicly in any of her husband's crusades, stepped out on a picket line for the first time in her life in late December 1933. Wise had heard that a Jewish toy firm, Shackman's, was still selling German-made items, and confirmed this by a personal visit to the store and a twenty-five-cent purchase. The next day Louise, accompanied by two other members of the American Jewish Congress Women's Division, showed up with sandwich-board signs urging passers-by to boycott Shackman's. When some policemen tried to disperse the pickets, Mrs. Wise informed them that the boycotters were merely exercising their constitutional rights. A group of photographers then asked the women to stop for a moment so they could take pictures, but Louise, with all the aplomb of a veteran picket, told them that she might be arrested if she did not keep walking. "I feel I ought to share in this important work," she explained. "I'm here to do my bit in horror that any American Jewish firm should sell German goods." When Shackman, exasperated, asked a policeman if anything could be done to get rid of the pickets, the patrolman began to lecture him on the evils of Nazi Germany, and told the toy-store owner that Mrs. Wise was a great lady who should be helped and not hindered in her work.[44]

The boycott movement, while worldwide in scope, centered in the United States, where a rather loose coordination existed in the Joint Boycott Council, of which the American Jewish Congress and the Jewish Labor Committee were the chief sponsors. Several labor unions and coalitions, including the American Federation of Labor and the International Trade Unions Congress, endorsed the boycott, and in 1934 the American Jewish Congress sponsored a world trade fair that excluded German products. Although Secretary of State Cordell Hull condemned "a racial or political boycott" that might hurt American exports, few people paid much attention. People joined, abstained, or opposed the boycott in practice not out of lofty considerations of international trade but out of their personal reaction to German policy. Available figures indicate that in free countries in which governments did not oppose the boycott movement, German imports dropped sharply.[45] In the long run, however, Nazi rearmament provided a spur for the domestic economy which more than offset the losses caused by the boycott.[46]

Yet even as he realized that the boycott would not cripple Germany nor his own protests bring the terror to a halt, Wise knew he could not desist from his efforts. The analogy of a prophet crying in the wilderness is apposite, because the prophet, no matter how forlorn, believes that at some point people will hear and understand his message. Thus, week after week, month after month, Wise continued his crusade, slowly picking up allies along the way. The American Jewish Congress had, of course, backed him from the start, and soon the Zionists joined as well. His son Jim developed into a strong voice against fascism, speaking and writing regularly on the Nazi menace.[47] Slowly, very slowly, people who had opposed Wise or had been indifferent came to see that the dangers he described really existed. By the time war broke out in Europe, nearly all American Jewry understood the menace of Hitler. Not all the credit, of course, belongs to Wise, but his was the major voice in awakening his fellow-Jews and fellow-Americans to the danger.

Yet in those six and a half years between Hitler's accession to power and his invasion to Poland, parts of the scenario hardly changed at all. Leading members of the German-Jewish community in the United States continued to attack Wise.[48] Faint hearts quailed at the thought of Jews acting publicly as Jews, while the Committee, increasingly unhappy over the situation, clung to its policy of *shtadlaniut*.[49] Nor could the Jews of Germany help very much. Some persisted in their delusion that their "Germanness" would eventually be accepted, while other remained silent out of fear.[50] A more grievous silence was that of the American government, which stood mute in the face of increasingly barbarous acts.

There was one source of attack, however, that Wise probably welcomed. The Nazis had singled him out as the chief instigator of anti-German propaganda in the United States. During one of his trips to Europe, German newspapers carried his photo with the caption: *Der Haupt juedischer Hetzer in Amerika gegen Deutschland*—"The major Jewish instigator in America against Germany."[51] In 1936, J. X. Cohen, one of Wise's associates, went to Berlin to see Chief Rabbi Leo Baeck. When he introduced himself, Baeck's secretary turned pale, and whispered that the rabbi was out of the city. Moreover, when he returned, he could not see an emissary of Rabbi Wise without a Gestapo official present. Didn't the man know that Hitler had called Stephen Wise his prime American enemy?[52]

Nor did Louise escape the Nazis' ire. In early March 1936, the Women's Division of the Congress tendered a luncheon in honor of Fiorello LaGuardia in appreciation of his outspoken criticism of German policies. The next day, *Der Angriff*, the official organ of the German Labor Front and the former property of Reich Propaganda Minister Joseph Goebbels, described the 1,200 persons attending the affair as "women of the street" who had gathered in order to be entertained by their "pimp and procurer," the mayor of New York. Had the Nazis singled out Louise Wise, she might have remained silent, following her husband's customary practice of publicly ignoring such abuse. In vilifying the entire group, however, the fascists angered Louise as she had rarely been angered before. This was not an insult merely to her and her associates, but an assault on all American women and their right as free and equal citizens to speak their minds. She publicly demanded that the State Department protest the slur, and Ambassador

Dodd delivered the American note to a furious German Foreign Office. On the floor of Congress, Representative Edith Nourse Rogers condemned the German attack. "There are certain insults the United States cannot stand," she declared, "and the men of the United States bitterly resent the attitude of the German Government."[53]

There were other victories, small ones for the most part, but they kept Wise's hopes alives. When he and Franklin Roosevelt patched up their quarrel in January 1936, Wise could finally begin to counteract the information fed into the White House by the "Sh-Sh Jews." At their meeting, the president told Wise: "Max Warburg wrote to me lately that things were so bad in Germany, there was nothing to be done." Roosevelt then threw his hands up and said, "Well, if Max thinks nothing can be done, then nothing can be done." Discussing this meeting afterward, Brandeis expressed to Wise his belief that the administration might have spoken out in 1933 but for the caution advised by Warburg and the other *yahudim*. Now at least Roosevelt would hear from those advising action and not despair, although it is still a matter of dispute whether the American government could, in fact, have done anything.[54]

Wise, however, felt some things could be done. He urged Secretary of the Treasury Henry Morgenthau, Jr. to foreclose any economic negotiations between Germany and the United States that might in any way help the Reich's economy.[55] He tried to urge Roosevelt to speak out publicly, and advised Jewish athletes not to participate in the 1936 Olympic games in Berlin.[56] Within Congress, a few figures such as William E. Borah began to protest more openly about Nazi depradations. All these things kept Wise's hopes alive.[57]

And in one of the most moving events of his life, Wise saw that the masses of European Jewry understood and appreciated his efforts to avert the impending catastrophe. In the summer of 1936, on his way to attend the first World Jewish Congress, Wise made a brief detour to Poland, whose three million Jews made it the third largest Jewish community in the world. As the train from Vienna to Warsaw passed through the Polish countryside, Louis Posner, a New York lawyer accompanying him, noted crowds gathered at every train station and suddenly called out: "Listen! The people are calling 'Stephen Weisz'." At one stop a delegation entered his car and presented him with a citation enthusiastically praising what he was doing. In Warsaw, tens of thousands of Jews led an overwhelmed and tearful Wise through the throng.. As he heard the cheers he thought to himself, "Was ever a people on earth so grateful, so deeply and inordinately grateful for even the least? So often and so cruelly have we been hurt that a normally friendly act is regarded and rewarded as if it were a benediction." That same day he spoke to thousands jammed into a firetrap of an auditorium in *Kongress Deutsch*, an imperfect German sprinkled with Yiddish, Hebrew, and English; few of those who cheered him that day would survive the Holocaust.

In the evening he met with Zionist groups, and learned of the self-defense committees, the same ones to spear the Warsaw ghetto uprising in 1943, and also witnessed the pride—the Jewish pride—of these people. "We are not *Gezwungener Juden* [Jews by compulsion]," they told him. "If we lived in Palestine, we could defend ourselves. We are ready to die for the Jewish land and to endure for Jewish honor. Life is not so dear to us, and if we fall, it will be for Eretz Yisrael that we die." Nor were these people newcomers to Poland, recent immigrants; one man told Wise that in the cemetery of his town were *Mazevot* [tombstones] six hundred years old. Neither were these Jews prosperous, as were their brethren in Germany who still had not comprehended the truth about Hitler. Many of the families he met lived in hovels or crowded into slums, living on an income of three of four dollars a week.

Wie kann Mann mit so wenig auskommen?, he asked. "How can one survive on so little?" Quickly came the answer.

Gott mir helfen—"God will help."

"I went to Poland to observe and learn," Wise wrote on his return home. "What I beheld of Jewish misery and learned of Jewish nobility touched my heart with sorrow not unmingled with pride."[58]

The small gain, the touching gratitude of the common Jews, gave him the strength to go in the face of one calamity after another. All the while his own sense of futility and of impending doom grew. "I lie awake at night," he told Julian Mack. "I have ceased to be able to sleep. I cannot shake off the awful responsibility." After the Anschluss brought Austria into the Nazi domain, he lamented that "for me life is chiefly pain and gloom."[59] That September at Munich, Neville Chamberlain sold out Czechoslovakia for "peace in our time," and for Wise "the moral foundation of the universe has been shaken . . . There is no morality left in the world."[60] Still he fought on, for what alternatives did he have?

American Jews such as Wise labored under the terrible misapprehension, as Henry Feingold has so perceptively noted, that somewhere in the world, at the White House or the Vatican or Downing Street, existed "a spirit of civilization whose moral concern could be mobilized to save the Jews."[61] Certainly Wise's activities through these years bear out such evaluation; he consistently sought some great moral force to rise and fight the Nazi evil. At the same time, one sees a growing despair that even if this goodness existed, it lay asleep and might awaken too late. But to rouse it he tried, and as the thirties passed, this voice calling in the wilderness gradually became the voice of most American Jews as well.

19

Non Possumus!

The Zionist organization the Brandeisians reclaimed in 1930 was a far cry from that which they had lost nearly a decade earlier. Membership declined to about the same level as 1914 when the new leadership had first come to power, and the Zionist Organization of America owed more than $180,000, the result of years of mismanagement by the Lipsky administration.[1] The shock of the Passfield White Paper had led to the demand for the Brandeisians' return; the growing threat of fascism to European Jewry would by the end of the decade restore the movement's vitality and membership. As the nations of the world refused to allow Jews within their borders, Herzl's analysis regained its driving force: Only a homeland of their own would provide Jews with protection from persecution.

Wise had no doubt that with the Brandeis/Mack faction once again in power, he would have a role to play in Zionist affairs. The nature of that role remained undefined, nor was it any clearer just what policies the new administration, headed by Robert Szold, would follow other than attempting to restore the ZOA's financial integrity. As Wise noted, "I am not sure that anything we could do will help an impossible situation very much."[2] One thing that particularly disturbed Wise was the increased power of the *yahudim* through their position on the Jewish Agency, and the apparent willingness of Brandeis to cooperate with Felix Warburg. If American Zionism were ever to regain its old influence, then it would have to stand firmly for unquestioned principles, and stop the useless effort to appease the non-Zionists. Mack and Wise worried that instead of building a national center in Palestine, the movement would accept the vague non-Zionist ideal of a cultural center. When he sent in his contribution to United Palestine Appeal in early 1931, he complained that the Agency would probably divert it to non-Zionist use.[3]

Wise, like most American Zionists, neither developed nor adopted a complex ideological Zionism. He began as and remained a disciple of Herzl, with all the simplicities, strengths, and weaknesses of his mentor. Jews were everywhere persecuted because they lacked a homeland of their own; let them have Palestine as a refuge, as a place in which to build their own lives, and the Jewish problem could be solved. Brandeis had taken Herzl's notion and added to it a Jeffersonian belief in progress, democracy, and human decency, and had also resolved any potential discrepencies between love for the old and for the new Zions. Wise understood what the socialists, orthodox, and cultural factions wanted, and did not necessarily oppose them in principle. His American respect for pluralism allowed him to envision a heterodox society in Palestine in which every group could pursue its own vision without intruding on the rights and dreams of others. All of them, whether in the Holy Land or in the Dispersion, would be ennobled by their adherence to these visions. Zionism, he told one critic, "lifts up the hearts of our young people, and exercises an enriching influence over their lives."[4]

But for the movement to have this beneficial effect, its implementing agencies had to be uncorrupted. This meant a cleansing of the ZOA at home and of the WZO abroad. The return of the Brandeis/Mack group had begun the process in America; now Weizmann and his cronies had to be ousted from the world leadership.[5] At the 1931 World Zionist Congress, Wise led the attack on Weizmann's record, his abandonment of Zionist ideas for the sake of winning over the *yahudim* to the Agency, his failure to stand up for the *yishuv* before His Majesty's Government. "You have sat too long at English feasts," Wise charged the Russian-born chemist. "Only men who believe in their cause can talk to the British, but not a leadership which says in effect, 'You are big and we are small, you are omnipotent and we are nothing'." When Wise characterized the British White Paper as the "Passfield Pogrom," Weizmann stormed from the platform in protest, and Morris Margolies, a member of the Lipsky faction, issued a statement declaring that Wise did not speak for the majority of American Zionists who still revered Weizmann. To his friend George Kohut, Wise wrote: "The Congress has been very exciting. . . . Weizmann and others are furious but I know I did my duty and said what needed to be said, and that my word will be a warning for the future administration."[6]

In the end, the Congress repudiated Weizmann; it had little choice, for to have retained him in office would have meant approval of his minimalist policies. Weizmann blamed the Americans for his defeat, charging that they had come over in the spirit of a vendetta to avenge what had happened at Cleveland in 1921. But a number of the American delegates who voted to censure Weizmann, such as Emanuel Neumann, Ida Silverman, and Ab Goldberg, had been on the Lipsky/Weizmann side in the earlier struggle. Wise, who engineered the vote of censure, rejoiced for the movement, but took no personal pleasure in Weizmann's defeat. "I could have wept for Weizmann," he told his children, "because after all, fifteen years of work,

good, bad and indifferent, were ended by a vote of censure. He deserved it
and I voted for it. At the same time, it was a sad spectacle."[7]

Although the Congress repudiated Weizmann as punishment for his
failure to prevent the Passfield White Paper, it did not really repudiate his
program. To replace him, the Zionists chose Nahum Sokolow, one of the
movement's elder statesmen who differed not one whit in policy or
philosophy from his predecessor. There was, after all, little choice. The
Americans opposed Weizmann's policy, but had no alternative leader to
propose, and none of the other factions had enough appeal to secure the
support of the centrists. The most pronounced alternative to Weizmann's
minimalism could be found in Vladimir Jabotinsky and his Revisionist Party,
but much as most Zionists, including Wise, found "Jabo" personally attractive, they feared the authoritarian and doctrinaire position of Revisionism.[8]

While in Basle, Wise spent a number of hours conferring with the leaders
of Palestine's Labor Party, including Berl Katznelson and David Ben-
Gurion. Wise's original sympathy toward the left had diminished the more
he had learned of the actual workings of the people's paradise in Russia,
and he felt that the labor group in Palestine often acted in much too highhanded and dictatorial a fashion. He told the Palestinians that he had
nothing against their movement in the abstract, but that in practice he considered them as unprincipled as any group within the Zionist movement.
Things were not perfect in the *yishuv*, a fact clear to anyone, yet the Labor
Party often seemed quite willing to barter away ideals for the sake of preserving its own political strength. "I cannot understand," he declared, "how
you with your ideals can stick through thick and thin to a man of the
character and spirit of Weizmann as you have done for ten years or more."[9]
Katznelson and Ben-Gurion patiently explained their policies and program
to the American, and while he was not totally convinced, relations between
him and the Palestinian socialists did improve over the decade, especially as
he came to know and work with Ben-Gurion.

Upon his return to America, Wise sought to determine just what role he
would play in Zionist affairs. The recent transfer of power in the ZOA had
left matters totally confused, with some members of the Brandeis faction
calling for severe financial retrenchment as the first order of business, and
others demanding immediate spiritual regeneration. While the membership
had recalled the old leadership, whether the rank and file also wanted a
change in direction was far from clear. "Lipskyism," as Wise noted, remained popular, and while he and the other Brandeisians knew what they
opposed, they lacked a comprehensive program of reform.[10] Regarding his
own role, Wise agreed to join the administrative committee, but he told
Robert Szold that he just could not take on new responsibilities. When he

was mentioned as a possible president of the ZOA, he immediately set out to quash the idea. At times he wanted to, as he put it, "get out of the ZOA altogether," but realized that if he did that, he would lose any influence he might have in the movement.[11]

The rise of Nazism brought new life and meaning to Zionism. The Zionists had the only likely solution to the problem, a homeland in Palestine. For Wise, the movement would provide additional strength in the fight against Hitler. The old divisions could no longer be tolerated; the great danger from the Third Reich made it imperative that the Zionists put away their internal squabbling. At the 1933 Congress Wise, who only two years earlier had led the fight against Weizmann, now called for unity, but cautioned against the movement reverting to a minimalist approach. Jews could expect little from a world that permitted a Hitler; they must not make the mistake of trying to be too polite, too moderate, of asking for too little. "If we start to compromise," he prophesied, "every year they will push us backwards, and we will lose our position and our rights."[12] His speeches filled the great hall, and triggered some of the bitterest debates of the Congress. In the end, however, the Eighteenth Congress turned not toward Wise's militancy but back to Weizmann. He had, after all, been the architect of the Balfour Declaration, and was well-known and respected in British circles; the times needed a friendly administration in Palestine, and the Zionists hoped Weizmann would be the man to smooth relations with His Majesty's Government.

Wise viewed the Congress as a disaster. In *Opinion* he wrote that it had been "the worst of Congresses," in which the petty interests of party triumphed over the need to unite before common foes. The Revisionists and the Labor Zionists were ready to come to blows, and the murder of the brilliant young labor theoretician, Chaim Arlosoroff—allegedly by a Revisionist—had poisoned not only the atmosphere at the Congress but the *yishuv* as well.[13] Soon afterward Wise, whom the Revisionists had originally seen as a kindred spirit because of his militant demand that Great Britain live up to its promises, began to attack Jabotinsky and his followers for their extremeness and authoritarianism. "Revisionism," Wise told the Free Synagogue, "is counter to every idea of the Jewish people and the Jewish tradition. Revisionism does not mean peace in Palestine. . . . Revisionism is a species of fascism, uttering its commands in the Hebrew language and therefore doubly baleful to us who believe that Hebrew should be the medium of a forward-looking hope, not of a dangerously reactionary movement. Revisionism is a surrender to the stark acceptance of the rightfulness of fascism."[14]

Wise hoped to see in Palestine the development of an egalitarian and democratic society, one with values exactly opposite those allegedly preached by the Revisionists. In 1935, he and Louise traveled to the Holy Land for the first time since 1922, and he marveled at the changes that had taken place in the intervening years.[15]

While in Jerusalem the Wises stayed at Government House as the guests of the British High Commissioner, Sir Arthur Wauchope, probably the ablest and most sympathetic of all the Crown administrators to rule Palestine. After dinner, Sir Arthur chatted with Louise and chivalrously asked if he could grant her any request.

"Yes, Sir Arthur, I do have a favor to ask of you. Dr. Wise and I today again visited the grave of his grandmother. As I stood there on the Mount of Olives I noted a funeral procession, and I saw how hard it was for the cortege to carry the dead over the rough stone road. Would it be possible for Your Excellency to have that road made a little less rough and uncomfortable for the mourners?"

The High Commissioner smiled and said, "Mrs. Wise, your wish shall be granted."

The Wises heard no more about this until they stood on the pier at Haifa a few weeks later, ready to depart Palestine. A courier drove up and presented his compliments to Louise, saying, "His Excellency directs me to inform you before you leave Palestine that the work of improving the road to the Mount of Olives cemetery has begun."[16]

During the time they were in Palestine, Wise took to heart the advice of Arthur Ruppin, the elder statesman of the *yishuv* who had headed the Zionist land office from its inception. Wise had sought his opinion on a number of problems, but Ruppin had told him: "Forget problems and see Palestine. Give yourself the joy of looking upon the land and its people and their achievements, and forget all problems until you return to America." This Wise did, and everywhere he went, he received a warm welcome. Moshe Kol, later to be head of Youth Aliyah and Israeli Minister of Tourism, first met Wise on this trip, and recalled that the *yishuv* looked on him as the greatest American Jew of his generation. Wise spoke everywhere he went and, Kol said, always spontaneously and from the heart; he loved the people he met, and they reciprocated his affection.[17]

Wise was most impressed with the reclamation work done by Jews in the once swampy Valley of Jezreel, now renamed the Emek. But at the same time he despaired that Jews owned only six percent of the land. "We cannot say 'our land' as long as we hold only six percent," he told the settlers at Mikve Israel. "Upon our return to America, our cry will be 'Land! Land! Land!'" To his secretary he declared, "I do not know such a miracle as our young fellow-Jews have wrought. I am more Zionist than ever I was. I have moved from 100 to 200 percent." And seeing the work of the Histadrut, the General Federation of Workers, at close hand, Wise also revised his views of Labor Zionism. He had earlier averred that he did not oppose the ideas but only the practices of the Federation. Now he saw the labor movement not as an abstraction but as a vital force in Palestine, and recognized that he could not judge it from afar. "Labor," he told Kol, "is one of the great forces here for the implementation of Zionism. It must not be broken."[18]

From the joy of *Eretz Yisrael* Wise traveled to the heartbreak of the Zionist Congress at Lucerne. Although thirty German delegates attended, it was obvious that they suffered severe restaints on what they could say. Each had family members literally held hostage against any public criticism of conditions within the Reich. The Congress re-elected Chaim Weizmann to the presidency, a situation Wise regarded as sad but inevitable; after all, who else was there to whom the Zionists could turn for leadership? The shadow of Nazi Germany hung over the assembly like a pall. "One could not even for an hour," Wise wrote, "forget the lot of them to whom every day brought the tidings of some new refinement of torture, some new fiendishness of destructive malice."[19]

The failure of the WZO to take a strong public stand against facism was understandable; Hitler could easily retaliate against the Jews still living in Germany. The *yishuv* wanted to help, but Great Britain controlled immigration into Palestine. And back home in America, Wise found some but not all Zionist leaders aware of the danger, but unable to agree in a policy. Arrangements for the Joint Appeal broke down in the fall of 1935 over disputes between Zionist and non-Zionist forces, and among groups within the Zionist fold. The Mizrachi and Hadassah refused to cooperate, and the general Histadrut drive fought with everyone.[20] Brandeis urged Wise, who had chaired the UPA in the 1920s, to reassume that role, but Wise demurred. He did not want to become enmeshed in endless petty bickering or in handling the thousands of administrative details. Finally, however, Wise agreed, provided he had a co-chairman who would, in effect, serve as chief executive officer; Israel Goldstein, the young rabbi of B'nai Jeshurun in New York, took over those chores. Citing the pressing need of developing Palestine as a refuge for those fleeing HItler, Wise set the UPA's 1936 goal at $3.5 million, a stupendous sum in the midst of depression.[21]

The imperative of Zionism never seemed stronger to Wise than during these years, and he realized that of all Jewish causes, this one demanded more of him than all the others, because, perhaps, it had the most to offer the Jewish people. He was now over sixty years old, and while still possessing far greater energy than most men half his age, his physical health had been showing signs of strain. To the trustees of the Free Synagogue he broached the idea of gradually withdrawing from the daily routine and responsibilities of the congregation. He claimed to be willing to give way to younger men in his pulpit, although it is questionable if he really would have given up the Free Synagogue. His trustees, however, convinced him that he need not choose one at the expense of the other; he had full discretion over how he would divide his time, but they wanted him to remain as leader of the congregation he had founded.

In 1936, Wise assumed what many people considered his rightful place as leader of American Zionism. His resumption of the UPA chairmanship had come at the behest of nearly all the participating groups, which claimed that only he would be acceptable to the competing factions. Similarly, the ZOA, which he had helped found in 1897, turned to him in order to avoid another battle. Morris Rothenberg, who had succeeded Robert Szold, had proven inept yet he wanted to retain the presidency and had built up a cadre of officers loyal to him. Neither the Lipsky nor the Brandeis factions had any faith in Rothenberg, and Wise was the only Brandeisian the Lipskyites would accept. In June, about three weeks before the annual convention, a committee of two dozen prominant ZOA members visited Wise and asked him to become president. Moreover, word came from Brandeis and Lipsky, Weizmann and Ben-Gurion, that they and their followers would welcome Wise's leadership. "Not having enough to do," as he ironically told a friend, he agreed, but only if the convention wanted him; he would not engage in an election battle.[22] For a while it looked as if this unanimous call would not come, and a special negotiating committee worked halfway through the night before Rothenberg finally withdrew. With an irony which Wise later found delicious, it was Louis Lipsky who conducted the proceedings that secured the presidency for his onetime nemesis.

Wise himself did not attend the ZOA convention in Providence, having left a week earlier for London where he, as a member of the WZO Actions Committee, gathered with other Zionist leaders to discuss British policy in Palestine. The repudiation of the Passfield White Paper had not ended efforts to dilute or repudiate the Balfour promise. Throughout the decade, one investigating commission after another tried to analyze the cause of Arab-Jewish tensions in the Holy Land, and the political answers that came out of these studies put the blame on the Jews. If no Jews came to Palestine, then there would be no problems. The same British leaders who appeased Hitler at Munich were equally willing to pacify the Arabs, even to reneging on England's sworn word.

Jewish leaders were far from united over what to do about either the disturbances in Palestine or British policy. The non-Zionists of the Jewish Agency stood resolutely opposed to any militant action by the *yishuv*, even in self-defense; the Mandatory had the responsibility to maintain order and to protect lives, and Felix Warburg believed that the Agency should do no more and no less than insist that the British administration fulfill its obligations. When the Haganah, the defense force created by the settlers, asked for money to purchase arms, Warburg angrily denied the request. Chaim Weizmann and his followers supported the Haganah, but believed that cooperation with Great Britain remained the Jewish people's only option in rebuilding a homeland. With Hitler now entrenched on the Continent, Weizmann argued, how could any Zionist even think of antagonizing His Majesty's Government?

But a new breed of Jew in Palestine, led by David Ben-Gurion, Moshe Sneh, and others, had no intention of waiting supinely for fate to deliver them still another blow. They had founded the Haganah to show that the new Jews of the *yishuv* did not have the getto mentality; they would not meekly accept riots and pogroms, but would fight back. They did not seek trouble, but neither would they run away, and their courage and policy won them the admiration and support of Wise, Brandeis, and other American leaders. "Ben-Gurion is a morally and spiritually energizing personality," Wise wrote, and American Zionists would do well to get some of the "guts" of the young man from Palestine. When Wise learned that Warburg had decided to withhold money from the Haganah, he quietly went to Washington; shortly afterward Brandeis began providing Wise with funds to be put at Ben-Gurion's disposal. This secret fund ultimately ran upward of $45,000.[23]

But while the *yishuv* would now be able to defend itself from Arab marauders, the real enemy was to be found in Whitehall, not east Jerusalem. His Majesty's Government seemed determined to abrogate the intent of the mandate, and to quiet Arab worries by closing off Jewish immigration into Palestine. This was, in Wise's view, "the most critical hour for us since the Balfour Declaration." Once in London, Wise secured an appointment with the Colonial Secretary, William Ormsby-Gore. Wise found the minister personally pleasant and friendly, but totally "under the dominance of the underlings, relentlessly pursuing their [pro-Arab] policy." He told Ormsby-Gore that while American Jews had always felt grateful to Great Britain for its acceptance of the mandate, any attempt to limit immigration would be construed as a danger to be fought at all costs. Given the world situation, the idea of closing Palestine was unthinkable.[24]

The London meetings placed Wise in almost daily contact with Weizmann, Melchett, Ben-Gurion, and other European and Palestinian leaders, while he alone spoke for the American Zionists. None of them had any real plan, although each had his own version of the catastrophe to come. Ben-Gurion in particular worried that the *yishuv* would rather go up in flames, fighting both the British and the Arabs, than suffer slow death through economic strangulation.[25] Some Zionist leaders wanted to mount a dramatic yet passive resistance, modeled on Gandhi's policy in India. In the end, Wise hit upon the strategy which, temporarily at least, averted the closure of Palestine.

Ormsby-Gore had indicated that the British would, of course, be sensitive to world opinion, especially that of the United States. Wise wondered, therefore, if perhaps the Zionists ought to try to influence British policy by appealing to the president of the United States. Felix Frankfurter, spending a sabbatical year at Oxford, came down to London frequently to consult with Wise and believed this might be the worst thing to do. But Wise refused to let go of the idea, especially after an exchange of letters he had had with Roosevelt a few months earlier. Wise had written to the president calling his attention to the disorders in Palestine, and suggesting that a word to the British ambassador might be appropriate, especially because the riots endangered American Jews and non-Jews traveling in the Holy Land. Roosevelt had not sent for the ambassador, but did contact the American consul in Jerusalem and through him had let the British authorities know that the American government expected the mandatory power to maintain order.[26]

After the World Jewish Congress meeting in Geneva, Wise returned home and immediately went to Hyde Park. Roosevelt, alert to the potential political benefits, quickly agreed to Wise's request that he let the British know that the American government hoped no steps would be taken to halt or curtail Jewish immigration into Palestine. The British, for a variety of reasons, decided that it might be to their benefit not to adopt the policy being pushed by the Arabists in the Foreign and Colonial Offices. Talk of a proposed White Paper had already evoked considerable criticism in the House of Commons, and with the situation on the Continent so unpredictable, it would be well to reinforce traditional Anglo-American ties. Word came back to Washington early in September that, for the while, there would be no change in British policy in the Holy Land.

In one grand gamble, Wise had done the seemingly impossible. The normally laconic Brandeis wrote to him that "you have performed a marvelous feat. Nothing more important for us has happened since the mandate," words of unusual exuberance for the Justice.[27] Ultimately the gates of Palestine would close, but in the intervening years more than 50,000 Jews, mostly from Germany and Austria were able to join the *yishuv*—men, women, and children who would undoubtedly have perished had the 1939 White Paper been issued three years earlier. Wise, as president of the ZOA and the American and World Jewish Congresses, and chairman of the United Palestine Appeal, now stood as the pre-eminent Jew in America, and his contacts with those in power had wrought great things.

Yet his success also had its price, one which in later years would have grave results. Wise failed to understand that Roosevelt had acted less out of humanitarian concern or friendship for the Jews than out of a calculated political expediency. At little cost to his administration, he made a gesture which, for reasons of British self-interest, paid off. Wise, whose loyalty was one of his noblest virtues as well as a handicap, failed to see that Roosevelt would have no compunction about ignoring the plight of European Jewry when it became politically useless or undesirable.

In his two years as president of the ZOA and his slightly shorter term at the UPA, Wise worked extremely hard and at times under the most frustrating conditions. Just because he had been acceptable to all groups did not mean they were about to put aside their differences to work harmoniously with him.[28] Moreover, of all the Zionist leaders, he was probably the least sympathetic to non-Zionists in the Jewish Agency, who in turn found him as objectionable and as overly nationalistic as ever.[29] But Wise's accomplishment could not be denied, and it provided a much-needed fillip to American Zionism. Membership increased, and the ZOA became an increasingly vocal and influential presence within the American Jewish community. When the Peel Commission was convened to examine the future of Palestine, the ZOA took the lead in drafting the formal memorandum setting forth American interests in preserving the original terms of the mandate and in resisting Weizmann's appeal for a more moderate approach.[30]

The Peel Commission was generally considered the most able and distinguished of all the investigatory bodies to visit the Holy Land. It conducted full and comprehensive hearings from November 1936 through January 1937, and its report, issued in July 1937, presented a lucid and critical analysis of the dilemma facing the Crown. The British had won Palestine as a prize of war, and could have done almost anything with it. In fact, had His Majesty's Government immediately drawn up boundaries and established a Jewish state, the Arabs, after initial opposition, would probably have been reconciled to it within a decade or two. The Commission praised the Jewish settlers for all they had accomplished in transforming the desert into fertile land, and suggested that the Arabs really had no complaints regarding the purchase of land by the Jews. But because of its vacillation, Britain now faced irreconcilable obligations in its promises to both Jews and Arabs, and the troubles required more than mere palliatives. Radical surgery would be required, dividing Palestine into three zones—one Jewish, one Arab, and a neutral area, including Jerusalem, which would remain under British control.[31]

The Zionists had awaited the report amid growing concern that the Commission would endorse partition, an idea that had been discussed episodically for nearly a decade. The Jews of Europe and Palestine, while not enthusiastic over having the promised land truncated still further, argued that half a loaf, a small *yishuv* but one whose access they controlled, was better than a homeland into which Jews could not come. The Americans, on the other hand, argued that the British had given their word, and should not be allowed to break it even more than had already been done.[32]

When the Commission report appeared, Wise and the American Zionists immediately began their campaign to prevent its implementation. They contacted Secretary of State Hull in a vain effort to have the American government protest partition as a violation of the mandate. "I need hardly tell you," Wise wrote to Chaim Weizmann, "that we are leaving no stone unturned on this side. Naturally we are working with and through our government . . . though I cannot be too reassuring."[33] Publicly, Wise damned partition, condemning it as a scuttling of the Balfour promise, and threatened that the Jewish people would not let England "reduce a sacred obligation to a scrap of paper." In Palestine, he told the press, "We found an almost abandoned waste. We transformed that waste into a high civilization, investing energy, substance and life in the process, and this [Peel Report] is our recompense." Privately, as he wrote Brandeis, "I am sick over the whole business. I never dreamed that we would fare so badly at Britain's hands."[34]

At the Zionist Congress in Geneva that summer, the delegates divided bitterly over how to respond to the Peel plan. Weizmann stood opposed to his longtime colleague, Menachem Ussischkin. Ben-Gurion of the Labor Party wanted any form of autonomous Jewish state, while Berl Katznelson, Labor Zionism's leading philosopher, and Goldie Meyerson, both attacked the idea of a Jewish state without Jerusalem; it would, they said, be a body without a head. The Mizrachi opposed partition on religious grounds; the covenant with God had promised all of *Eretz Yisroel.* The Revisionists argued that the covenant with Great Britain, the mandate, had also promised all and not part of Palestine. Hashomer Hatzair, the idealistic leftist group, had another viewpoint; its members still clung to the vision of a binational state in which Arab and Jew could live together in peace.[35]

From the moment Wise stepped off the train he found himself besieged by opponents and proponents of partition. Weizmann sent a car to bring him over immediately, so the WZO president could try to persuade the American leader to modify his stance. In turn Wise tried in vain to convince "the Premier of the Jewish Republic" that rejection combined with a high moral insistence on England keeping its word would win the respect of the world. "Imposition is one thing," he told Weizmann, "but it does not involve the guilt of assent. Assent is another thing, and we must withhold it."[36] Even though a majority of the 23 American delegates were willing to accept partition, Wise delivered a strong attack on the failure of the Zionist leadership to stand up for its rights. As trustee of the Jewish people, he declared:[37]

> The Congress cannot enter into any contract with Britain that would give less than the whole of Palestine to the Jewish people. . . . If you tell me that the *yishuv* wants partition, then I will tell you that if the British government could have maintained order in [the 1936 riots], you would not now agree to a partition scheme. I never expected to find labor in favor of partition. We do not want an illusory hope to be held out to our suffering brethren. I believe that eight million Jews would be willing to settle in Palestine in the next twenty years, but you may have room for only a tenth. I cannot accept a minimized

and bagatelline Palestine. The Jewish people's answer to Britain must be not 'yea' or 'nay,' but *'non possumus'*—we cannot. The British people would respect us more if we refuse it. We have to justify conduct not to the British government but to our own consciences. . . . My answer to Great Britain is clear on all points. Partition, No! Palliative, No! Jewish state, Yes! Fulfillment of the mandate, Yes!

The final vote, however, had 300 delegates favoring the Peel plan but with reservations, and 158 against; had the resolution not been so vague on details, it is doubtful that it would have received so large a majority. To Wise, the vote provided just one more example of the moral cowardice and failure of the Weizmann regime. In the end, the qualified Zionist acceptance was nullified by an unequivocal Arab rejection. An unhappy Wise returned home and there Brandeis, who also opposed partition, counseled him not to despair. "Nothing is impossible," the jurist said, "because the British have lost their heads. They lack now judgment and decision and persistence."[38]

Despite the failure of the partition proposal, it was clear to all that the *status quo* in Palestine could not be maintained. The refugee situation worsened as conditions in Germany grew increasingly difficult for Jews, and the nations of the world made it quite clear at Evian that they would not open their lands to the refugees. Each batch of Jewish immigrants into Palestine evoked new Arab protests and violence, and His Majesty's Government determined that somehow an answer must be found. Recognizing that the American government might object to any drastic solution, the Foreign Office began plying the State Department with figures designed to show that Palestine could not absorb any more people. The British ambassador to the United States made it a special point to "educate" Franklin Roosevelt on this point. Wise recognized the extent of this campaign when he met with the president in January 1938. After a general discussion of political affairs, Roosevelt leaned forward and in a conspiratorial tone said, "I have got something that I have got to talk to you about. I haven't told a soul as yet, but I am thinking about it. You know there is no room in Palestine for many more people, and don't you think the time has come for your people to consider settling someplace else, in large unoccupied territories where they could build new homes?"

Wise immediately objected to the premise that Palestine had been filled, and then added, "I don't know how large Hyde Park is. I suppose a few hundred acres in extent. I wonder, Chief, whether you would be willing to 'swap' it for the million acres of the King Ranch in Texas?"

"No, I would not, but I might be glad to have both. Hyde Park is alright for me, but I would like the King Ranch for my five children."

"It isn't the same thing," Wise persisted. "They haven't lived in Hyde Park for four thousand years, and my people have lived in Palestine for more than that. Do you realize, Chief, that apart from life and sweat and blood, we have put one hundred million pounds into the development of Palestine in the last forty years? Outside of those Jews who live in free democracies such as our own and England and France, it is the only place on earth Jews care for.''

"Well," said Roosevelt, "I am not offering a substitute for Palestine, but Palestinian possibilities are going to be exhausted. You ought to have another card up your sleeve.''[39]

The conversation greatly disturbed Wise, but he still did not grasp the fact that Roosevelt's sympathy for the Jews did not represent a commitment to nor even an understanding of the Zionist attachment to Palestine. The president, right up to his death, believed that the Middle East imbroglio could be settled in a political manner; all that was necessary was to strike the right bargain. The intense fervor and ideological commitment of both Arab and Jew never impressed him; one could always negotiate a deal. There was little Wise could do other than continue vain efforts to educate the president and to refute some of the misinformation reaching the Oval Office.

In the meantime, Wise prepared to step down from the UPA and ZOA, thus fulfilling a pledge he had made not to serve more than two terms. The bane of Jewish organizations, he had declared, was perpetual officeholders, and he wanted younger men to assume the power and the burdens. At the UPA, he was succeeded by Abba Hillel Silver, the brilliant and acerbic Cleveland rabbi, while in the ZOA, he watched with satisfaction as the convention chose Solomon Goldman of Chicago, a rabbi whom both Wise and Brandeis believed would make a fine Zionist leader. Yet even without office, Wise remained the pre-eminent Zionist of his time, and it was he, not Silver or Goldman, who led the fight against the newest British perfidy.

By fall 1938, many Zionist leaders began to fear a restriction of immigration into Palestine similar to that which had been averted in 1936. In early October, Weizmann alerted the Americans that His Majesty's Government might implement a plan at almost any time unless Wise could secure another intervention by Roosevelt. Wise immediately wrote to the president warning that all the dreams of a Jewish homeland might soon be liquidated. A few days later a more formal communication on behalf of all the major Jewish organizations, including non-Zionist bodies such as the American Jewish Committee and B'nai B'rith, petitioned Secretary of State Hull to "take suitable action to urge upon the British Government a reaffirmation and a fulfillment of its pledge of facilitate the establishment of a Jewish National Homeland." Led by Zionists, scores of demonstrations were held around the country on November 2, the twenty-first anniversary of the Balfour Declaration. Wise, Lipsky, Goldman, and Henry Monsky, the president of B'nai B'rith, visited Hull, while Brandeis made an unusual call at the White House and spent more than an hour with the president, urging him to do all he could to keep the gates of Palestine open. Although Roosevelt issued a statement which suggested that the mandate terms should not be altered, he conceded that the United States was powerless to prevent any British action.[40]

In a final effort to achieve some mediated solution to the Arab–Jewish conflict, the British called a conference at the St. James palace in London for February 7, 1939. Wise, together with Robert Szold and Louis Lipsky, prepared to attend in behalf of American Zionism, but had little hope that the impending disaster could be averted. As he told John Haynes Holmes, "We know we are going to be bamboozled. I know that England is going to fool us to the top of her bent. But what can we do about it? If we poor Jews withdraw from the conference with the Arab kings, the world will say that we are afraid to meet with them. We have got to take our chance, though it is a rotten chance."[41]

As Wise predicted, the conference did nothing other than provide Great Britain with the excuse that it had tried to solve the impasse. The Chamberlain government continued its policy of appeasement, and in May 1939 issued the long-feared White Paper on Palestine, restricting Jewish immigration to 50,000 over the next five years, and then no more unless the Arabs gave their permission. Wise tried desperately in the last few days before its publication to move Roosevelt to action, but the president, aware of the lowering clouds of war, was unable or unwilling to intervene.[42] For Wise, the British policy marked not only the end of an era, but the beginning of a new and tragic period in Jewish history. Nearly a quarter-century of hope and trust in England as the shield of the Jewish people had shattered, while a new and horrendous disaster loomed just ahead. The Zionists in the 1930s had managed to keep open the gates of Palestine, nullify the Passfield White Paper, and delay further restrictions for nearly a decade. They also learned that in the end, Jews could rely only upon themselves. Wise, however, still stood ready to trust Roosevelt, an understandable decision but one that would ultimately have terrible results.

20

In Congress Assembled

The lone hero riding into a troubled town to singlehandedly rescue good from evil is a familiar figure in American legend, but it is not part of the Judaic tradition. David sallying forth against Goliath or Samson fighting the Philistines are, of course, the well-known exceptions, but exceptions they remain. Judaism is primarily a community-oriented religion, and its greatest leaders over four millennia have been those who created and sustained the organizational and philosophical apparatus that fostered the survival of the Jewish people. That Stephen Wise often appeared as a loner is undeniable, as is the fact that he often threw himself into battles with little more on his side than his own sense of moral duty. But while Wise may have been the individualist supreme in American Jewish affairs in this century, he was also one of the community's master builders; he fought, more often than not, at the head of an organization, and this is also true of his battle against fascism.

The chief instrument in this fight, the American Jewish Congress, had suffered lean years following its moment of glory at the Paris Peace Conference, and had proved slow in developing its own style and sense of purpose. Part of this indecision might be attributed to the generally amiable nature of its first president, Nathan Straus. In 1923 Wise finally acceded to the insistent demand that he become president. He neither wanted the responsibility of the Congress nor needed any of the so-called glory leading it, but it had become obvious that the Congress under Straus had little chance of developing into the effective agent of Jewish communal opinion that Wise, Brandeis, and the other founders had envisioned. He hoped, he told Charles Bloch, to find a successor quickly;[1] as it turned out, Wise remained president of the American Jewish Congress, with the exception of a few brief years, from 1923 until his death in 1949. Eventually, he would be able to transform the Congress into a powerful instrument with which to fight transgressions against Jewish rights. But in the 1920s he had all he could do to keep the Congress from falling apart.

Unlike the American Jewish Committee, whose founders had been wealthy men generously willing to subsidize the organization's activities, the Congress had few members of means, and thus depended on a large number of relatively small donations. When Max Steur suggested an appeal to Felix Warburg or Simon Guggenheim, he quickly learned how little the Congress could expect in sympathy or aid from the *yahudim*. Wise did what he could, but his primary obligation in terms of fund-raising lay with the Jewish Institute of Religion, and he resisted the suggestion that he undertake a series of home parlor meetings to solicit funds.[2]

By 1925 Wise and several of the other leaders of the Congress were so discouraged that they debated closing down completely. At a meeting in Wise's home that summer, he seemed willing to let the Congress fold and leave the field of Jewish defense to the Committee. Outside afterward, Bernard G. Richards, the executive director of the Congress, stood talking with George Fox, David Shapiro, and a few other members of the executive committee about the apparent demise of the Congress. Finally Shapiro, one of the owners of the Yiddish newspaper *Der Tag*, said, "Richards, you are not going to close up. Let's see what we can do. I'll send you a couple hundred dollars tomorrow."[3] The money came, in dribs and drabs, never very much, but somehow the Congress stayed alive. During the fifteen-month period ending December 31, 1927, the Congress had a total income of $41,666 with expenditures of $48,621. Its assets amounted to $1,280.45, with liabilities of $20,936.93, mostly in the form of private notes to people who had lent the Congress emergency loans to tide it over from one month to the next. The list of major creditors of the Congress included Stephen Wise.

Wise found this constant shortage of funds ennervating, and his letters indicate his weariness at continuously trying to make ends meet on inadequate income. Time and again it appeared the Congress would collapse; time and again someone who believed in the cause came through with enough, barely enough, to keep it alive. In May 1928 Wise declared, not for the first time, "that unless heroic measures be taken now and something done to enable us to go on, it would be indecent and immoral for is to go on piling up debts which there is no hope of meeting."[4]

For Wise, this second act of the Congress finally played itself out in 1929, after a row with his executive director. Bernard Richards had complained that the Congress relied too heavily on Wise for its direction and had become too identified with him; as a result, it had become a target of hostilities generated by Wise's more controversial battles, such as his tilt with Tammany Hall. When the directors indicated that, despite these alleged drawbacks, they preferred Wise, Richards resigned.[5] Wise nonetheless recognized that Richards' accusations bore much truth; the Congress had become too much a "Wise organization," and he did not want the Congress to become like the American Jewish Committee, which for more than twenty years had been dominated by and identified with Louis Marshall.

At the annual meeting of the Congress in Atlantic City in May 1929, Wise announced he would not accept re-election because "one of the most serious evils in Jewish life grows out of the all but perpetual tenure of Jewish office. Organizations and persons must not become interchangeable terms, regardless of how valuable persons may be." Although most of the delegates would have willingly re-elected him, Wise resisted all pressure, and watched with satisfaction as the assembly chose Bernard S. Deutsch as the new president of the Congress.[6]

Wise's tenure as president of the Congress from 1923 to 1929 stands out in stark contrast to his earlier involvement with the Congress movement during the war years and his later leadership of the organization in the fight against fascism. There is an almost lackadaisical attitude during the 1920s on his part, as if the Congress were an unwanted burden, a sort of stepchild having to wait in line after the Free Synagogue, the Institute, and other projects to see what, if any, interest and energy Wise might give to it. There is no doubt that in Wise's priorities the Congress at that time did not rank very high, and one can surmise why this was so. Despite his immense energy, Wise for once had taken on too much, and the Congress, because it seemed to be accomplishing so little, appeared more and more useless to him in his battles. Beyond that, what the Congress needed in those years is exactly what Wise could not give it, a sense of order and purpose. The Congress required a master of organization, someone who could do what Brandeis had done for American Zionism a decade earlier. Wise founded and led many organizations, but he never had Brandeis's skills in this area; management was just not his forte.

Wise, of course, did not abandon the Congress idea, and when he spoke out for Jewish rights during the 1920s, usually did so as president of the Congress. Thus, when he began the fight against fascism, it was logical for him to turn to the Congress. His absence, however, had led to a near paralysis of the organization. Bernard S. Deutsch, a capable vice-president when Wise had headed the Congress, proved ineffective as president, and there seemed little choice but for Wise, the honorary president of the Congress, to assume a more active role in its affairs.

During 1933 and 1934, a majority of Wise's public protests against the persecution of German Jewry took place under the auspices of the American Jewish Congress. When the Congress objected to domestic activities it considered prejudicial to Jewish interests, Wise nearly always appeared alongside Deutsch, and took the lead in issuing statements or answering questions.[7] As the fascist menace increased, so did Wise's public involvement in Congress affairs. When Morris Rothenberg, president of the ZOA, wrote to inquire about the attitude of the Congress in creating a unified Jewish front against fascism, Wise and not Deutsch responded for the Congress. Shortly after the April 1933 boycott, Wise declined an invitation to speak to a B'nai B'rith convention with the explanation that "I have given up all work in connection with the [Free] Synagogue and the Jewish Institute of Religion in order to devote myself to the work of the American Jewish Congress." By the fall of 1933, although Deutsch remained president, Wise had effectively reclaimed the real leadership of the Congress.[8] Utilizing the Congress much as the Free Synagogue as his podium, Wise struck out more and more against the forces of intolerance spreading across Europe and America.

In 1935, a mortally ill Deutsch resigned from the presidency of the American Jewish Congress, which then elected its real leader as its nominal one as well. As Brandeis wrote from Washington, "I am glad you resumed your natural position." Although Wise claimed that he had agreed to the election only on an interim basis, he held the presidency until his death fourteen years later.[9] Through the Congress he fought the Nazis, battled for more liberal immigration laws, and in the 1940s committed American Jewry to the civil rights struggle. The Congress, in its commitment to democracy and its emphasis on public action, had always reflected Wise's own beliefs and personality. Now, despite his reservations, he and the Congress became totally identified with each other in the public eye, much as Louis Marshall and the American Jewish Committee had been in the 1920s. From that base, he launched the most ambitious organizational venture of his career, the effort to unite Jews all over the globe into a World Jewish Congress.

The idea of a world confederation had long been discussed, and its possible effectiveness demonstrated by the alliance of Jewish delegations at the 1919 Paris conference. The Comité des Delegations Juives, led by Leo Motzkin, managed to keep going in the decade after the peace treaty, and constantly sought means of strengthening Jewish unity and cooperation. In August 1926, Motzkin convened a meeting in London to discuss a larger organization, and the participants decided to hold a major conference the following year. Invitations to this assembly issued from the Comité, led by Motzkin and Nahum Sokolow, and from the American Jewish Congress over the signatures of Wise and Julian W. Mack. Sixty-five Jewish leaders from thirteen countries, representing forty-three organizations, gathered in Zurich on August 17, 1927 in the Conference for the Rights of Jewish Minorities. Notably absent were the American Jewish Committee and its elite counterparts in England, France, and Germany. But Wise and the other American delegates showed so much enthusiasm and support for the idea of mutual cooperation that Sokolow exclaimed, "The bridge across the Atlantic has been built!"

It would take several more meetings and much preparatory work before the bridge could be used, but the depressing reports on the condition of Jewish communities, especially in eastern Europe, left no doubt that some organization had to be created to deal with the problems. Without the American Jewish Committee, the English Joint Committee, the French Alliance, and the German Hilfsverein, no permanent body of strength could emerge, but the Zurich conference did restructure the Comité, now to be called the Council on the Rights of Jewish Minorities, with headquarters in Geneva. Nahum Sokolow became the Council's president, with Motzkin, historian Simon Dubnow, and Wise as vice-presidents.[10]

The Council watched and noted but could do little to stem the rising tide of antisemitism, and in 1931 Wise decided that stronger action would be necessary. That summer he attended the Seventeenth World Zionist Congress in Basle, and asked several Jewish leaders to stay on for a few days to discuss the situation. They agreed with the American rabbi on the need for a new organization, and constituted themselves into a provisional committee with Wise as chairman. The following June, the annual convention of the American Jewish Congress endorsed the proposal to call a World Jewish Conference preparatory to establishing a World Jewish Congress.

Even as this discussion occurred, a familiar scenario began to unfold. The *yahudim* of the American Jewish Committee, now led by Cyrus Adler, attacked the proposed conference in tones identical to those which Marshall and Schiff had employed in 1915 to condemn the organizers of the American Jewish Congess. Jewish affairs should not be aired in public, while an international organization would generate even more hostility and give credence to the belief that Jews comprised a worldwide conspiracy. At the Congress convention, Wise criticized Adler's "intemperate and abusive attack," and declared: "If we are not strong enough and brave and wise enough to meet together in the sight of men to consider what can be done to lighten the burdens laid upon our people, then in truth we do not deserve a better fate." It was not too late, he concluded, to achieve unity. "But the time is short. The need is great. The work presses."[11]

In the following weeks the debate between pro- and anti-congress advocates grew more heated, and Wise emerged, as he had before, as the champion of a comprehensive, unified, and democratic organization. Before two thousand delegates of the fraternal order B'rith Shalom he argued:[12]

> We Jews cannot afford to quarrel. We do however have the right to stand united. We believe that we Jews are and of right ought to be free to come together and consult with one another regarding our Jewish affairs. We

believe no one is wise enough or rich enough or powerful enough to do this without taking advice from the Jewish people. The Jewish people are not Haiti to be governed from afar without the consent of the governed. The Jewish people are believers in democratic government. While it would be easier to let a half-dozen people in Philadelphia and New York tell us how to think and what to do, we of the American Jewish Congress believe we are too old, too wise, too learned and too confident to surrender the right of self-government and self-determination.

The Committee in turn denounced Wise and other pro-conference champions for arrogating unto themselves the right to speak for four and a half million American Jews. The *American Hebrew*, which mirrored the opinion of the *yahudim*, constantly criticized the conference in general and Wise in particular, while behind the scenes the Committee labored, sometimes successfully, to dissuade other Jewish organizations from attending. Moreover, a number of Jews not aligned with the Committee, while not necessarily opposing a world congress, did question the timing and impact an international conference might have. Louis Brandeis, for instance, regretted that he would not have a chance to discuss the matter with Wise before the latter sailed for Europe, "because I am not sure that action is wise at this time."[13] But the jurist did not try to dissuade the rabbi, who left a few days later for Geneva.

There, ninety-four delegates representing Jewish communal organizations in seventeen countries met on August 14 to discuss the increasingly perilous situation of European Jewry. Even before Hitler came to power, spokesmen from Poland, Rumania, Germany, Austria, Czechoslovakia, Lithuania, and Latvia reported on the growing antisemitism. The only way to avert catastrophe, Leo Motzkin warned, was for the Jews of the world to put aside their internal differences and stand united against common foes. In his speech, Wise defined the congress idea as "the right of open and free assembly in the sight of the world for full and complete discussion of Jewish questions and problems and tasks." The Jewish people, he declared, "has nothing to consider and discuss which does not invite and welcome and, indeed, require the light."[14]

Wise attempted at the conference to learn more about conditions inside Germany, and found the Jewish representatives from that country invariably optimistic. But the growing power of fascism could not be ignored, and just before the conference, Nazi sympathizers set off a stink bomb in the assembly hall. The Swiss police decided to provide personal protection for some of the Jewish leaders, including Wise, and that entire week he walked around the city with a burly guard, for whom the teetotaling Wise ordered two beers at every meal. This incident and the information gleaned from recent visitors to Germany led Wise to warn the delegates that Hitler did indeed pose a real threat. "Schiller and Lessing more truly express the soul of Germany than Hitler and Goebbels," he told the conference, but in perilous times the Jews should expect difficulty. But come what might, he did not believe that Jews would be physically exiled from the land of Heine, Wasserman, Rathenau, and Einstein. No other point in his speech received such warm applause.[15]

On the last day of the gathering, Wise again attacked antisemitism in Germany. At a luncheon meeting of the Geneva International Club, he denounced the Nazi program. "It is infamous to provoke race feeling against the Jews in Germany," he insisted. "Adolf Hitler is stirring up hate. It is the duty of Christian nations to protest against this evil." At the closing session of the conference, Wise declared: "If I were a German, I would say, 'Judea does not perish; Judea does not die'." But he warned the Jews of Germany not to shut their eyes and pretend that no danger existed; they and the Jews of other countries had to stand united in common defense.[16]

On his return to the United States, Wise took a less restrained view of what might be expected if the Nazis gained power. In the Free Synagogue on September 25, he reported that "the high and courteous cry of the Hitlerites is *Pereat Judea! Juden Verreckt!* Jews perish! Jews in every city and village and town in Germany find themselves followed by men, women and children who cry *Juden Verreckt*—You Jews perish and croak."[17] But the conference had been a success, the first step on the road toward creating a democratic, international organization to deal with threats such as Nazi hooliganism. A second conference would take place no later than the summer of 1934, during which time Jewish organizations in different countries would be able to discuss the nature of the proposed congress and its relation to the national communities.

Still another task would be to win more support for a World Congress, and in the United States Wise became the idea's leading prosletyzer. In an almost endless stream of correspondence he encouraged congress supporters, tried to persuade those still undecided, and chided those who opposed the congress and who, he thought, should know better. When an old friend, William Fineshriber, wrote to say that he agreed in principle with the ideal but doubted that it would work, Wise responded: "Are you *sure* that it is impossible? I am not. One of the theses of the World Jewish Conference was that we Jews are one people . . . not merely a collection of *Shma Yisroel* reciters." When Lord Melchett and Selig Brodetsky, both of whom had enormous influence among English Jewry, spoke out for the Congress, Wise knew that it would only be a matter of time before the idea became a reality.[18]

The attainment of power by the Nazis and the implementation of anti-Jewish measures led Congress leaders to advance the date of the next conference from the summer of 1934 to September 1933. In the intervening months, the executive named at the First Conference petitioned the League of Nations against the application of Nazi racial laws to Upper Silesia and to the City Free of Danzig. In the latter case, the Jewish leaders were able to stall the pro-Hitler regime long enough for most of Danzig's 10,000 Jews to escape.[19]

On his way to Geneva that summer, Wise stopped in London to participate in negotiations with the Board of Deputies to determine whether that group would join in the Congress movement. Wise found a strong minority with views even more elitist than those of the American Jewish Committee.

"I do not want to meet with the Jews from eastern Europe in a conference," declared Claude Montefiore. "I am willing to give them advice but I do not want to take advice from them."

"I wish, Montefiore," Wise responded, "that I could rid myself of the superstitions of democracy as completely as you have succeeded in doing."

"You must remember, Wise, that I am an old fogey and a reactionary."

"Montefiore," burst out Melchett, "you're the worst person I ever met. You ought to be ashamed of yourself."[20]

The atmosphere at the opening of the Second World Jewish Conference differed enormously from that of the earlier session. While there had been trouble then, the threat of Nazism still seemed distant; now that the menace had become an all-too-real horror, the Jewish leaders in Geneva knew they would have to convince the rest of the world of the danger of fascism. In his opening address, Wise captured this mood perfectly:

> When little more than a year ago we met in Geneva, the sword of Damocles hung over our heads. We of the World Jewish Congress were the only organized group of Jews who recognized and sought to make provision against the day of evil. . . . We knew and know that we were not and are not exhibitionist beggars, but manly and proudly self-referring Jews, resolved to call the world to account for the wrong wreaked upon the heads of the Jewish people. . . .

> One year ago we insisted that such things would come to pass, for we read the dread handwriting on the wall of German life. Our warnings were ignored, every Hitler threat was explained away, we remained for the most part unprepared and in every sense defenseless and divided. Even to this day only a light degree of unity in Jewish life has been achieved. For world Jewry is still divided between those prepared to deal with Hitler's persecutions and terrorism as a passing German phenomenon and those of us who recognize that what Hitler will and would initiate is world war upon the Jewish people.

Although Wise had come to the conference still undecided about the proper measures to take, his conversations with the delegates soon convinced him that the proposed boycott of German goods had to be adopted on a world-wide basis. "Have we not waited," he asked, "until we can no longer expect the Jewish people to stand at our side and to place their faith in us unless we declare before this conference that the time has come to organize, *organize, ORGANIZE* the boycott, *Tuchtig und Grundlich* against Germany?'' To those who argued that an anti-German boycott would harm German Jews, Wise attempted to place the issue in a broader perspective. ''We are not the authors of the misfortunes and the sorrows of the German Jews. We suffer with them. And God knows every Jew would like to take his place at the side of the German Jews in their defense. But the final decision in the matter of a worldwide boycott rests not with German Jews, who are not free, but with world Jewry outside of Germany which is free.''[21]

Here was the heart of the boycott issue for many people, Jews and non-Jews alike, and one reason Wise waited so long before wholeheartedly endorsing the boycott movement. He too wondered how much the Jews outside Germany could presume in taking such drastic steps which very conceivably could rebound and harm their German brethen even more. Although the idea had begun almost as soon as the Nazis had called for the April First boycott of Jewish shops, Wise had hesitated in giving total approval. The American Jewish Congress had been active as an organization in the boycott movement, but Wise himself had stayed to some extent on the sidelines. Some critics have suggested that he was waiting to see which way the winds of public opinion blew, but given Wise's past history, this is not likely. Despite the charges of Cyrus Adler and the *yahudim* that Wise lacked sensitivity in the matter, Wise well understood the dangers of a Nazi backlash. His trip to Europe that summer exposed him to firsthand accounts of the new hell within the Reich, and led him to determine that Jews everywhere—the Jewish people—should not take this new pogrom supinely.

The second Conference closed on September 8 after unanimously adopting three resolutions. The first called for continuation of the boycott, and a second asked the League of Nations to intervene in behalf of German Jews seeking political and humanitarian asylum, especially those desirous of going to Palestine. Wise, who offered the boycott resolution, explained that the measure did not constitute a declaration of war against Germany. ''We do not believe in war, but we take up the weapon of self-defense, which is an honorable, legitimate and peaceable instrument . . . We do not declare war against Germany, but we are prepared to defend ourselves against the will to destroy us of Hitler's Germany. We must defend ourselves because we are a people which lives and wishes to live. My last word that I wish to speak to you is this—our people lives—*am Yisrael chai!*[22]

As a sign of this will to live and in recognition of the danger before them, the delegates in the third resolution called for another session the following year. In the meantime it elected an executive, and named the young Nahum Goldmann to head a permanent office in Geneva to work with the League of Nations High Commissioner for Refugees. Two notes did, however, mar an otherwise harmonious conference. Communist-oriented representatives from Poland demanded that the large American delegation as well as the executive committee include representatives from the miniscule American Jewish communist groups, a proposal Wise finally argued down on the grounds that each country should be free to determine the makeup of its own delegation without external interference. A more touchy issue concerned Zionism. Although most of the delegates favored Jewish nationalism some large and important segments did not, and would have bolted from the Congress had it endorsed a strong Zionist platform. Instead, the Conference expressed its support of Zionist work in Palestine, but noted that the prime responsibility there remained with the World Zionist Organization. Fifteen years later Wise reflected that in adopting a policy of deferring to the WZO, the Congress had made a serious mistake. "It would have been far better," he wrote, "for the World Jewish Congress to have acted freely and independently and thus to have brought help when critically needed from a body committed to Zionism and yet standing somewhat outside of the Zionist organization."[23]

Despite the policy, Zionist leaders definitely saw the Congress as both a threat and a prize: a threat to its prerogatives regarding Palestine, and a prize of prestige in Jewish affairs if it could be captured. Wise believed that the Zionists would prefer to wreck the congress if they could not control it. In late October Louis Lipsky, still Weizmann's chief lieutenant in the United States, sent a circular letter to over two dozen Zionist leaders warning that given the delicate situation, nothing should be done to further a World Congress.[24] A bitter six-hour debate in the ZOA administrative committee in February 1934 pitted the Weizmannites, at this point opposed to the congress, against a majority that had no strong feelings and possibly some real doubts. As a result, Lipsky was able to defeat the request for ZOA endorsement of a world congress, and much to Wise's anger, brought in messages from Felix Warburg of the Jewish Agency and Nahum Sokolow of the WZO opposing the congress. A despondent Wise lamented the state of Zionist politics which allowed men like Lipsky to have such influence. "I am just sick at heart. We are defeated as if we were the enemies of Zionism."[25]

But despite Lipsky and the lack of formal Zionist support, the movement continued to grow. The Third Preparatory Conference met that August in Geneva to approve plans for electing and organizing a permanent World Jewish Congress, and in November the executive effectively interceded to save the Jews of the Saar. A plebiscite scheduled for January 1935 was expected to return the Saarland and its Jews to German control. Nahum Goldmann arranged a Franco-German agreement through the League of Nations under which the Saar Jews could liquidate their assets, emigrate, and transfer their property in an orderly and unpenalized manner.

The growing probability that a world congress would come to pass irritated the officers of the American Jewish Committee and its allies. Once again they charged that Wise and the American Jewish Congress did not represent the Jews of the United States. David A. Brown blasted Wise and the idea of a "Jewish super government." Brown spoke, he declared, "for those Jews in the United States—and their number is legion—who are an integral part of this country and resent, even if by implication, the charge that they owe allegiance to any other government."[26] As the abuse against him increased (one rabbi publicly called Wise and the World Jewish Congress "a greater menace to Jewish life than Nazism"), Wise wrote to the Committee's Sol Stroock, a personal friend since childhood, asking why the *yahudim* ignored the issues, which he believed should be debated and attacked him so falsely.[27] From overseas Neville Laski called Justice Cardozo, asking him to use his influence with Wise and with Brandeis (who actually played an insignificant role in the movement) to stop the congress, which Laski claimed had aroused much fear among English Jews. "They are fighting us in terrific fashion," Wise told a friend, "bitterly as they can. I am being inundated with telegrams of protest against the World Jewish Congress. My comfort is that they did worse than that with Brandeis and the rest of us down at the American Jewish Congress, which has been a tower of strength to the Jewish cause. They were even bitterer and nastier forty years ago when Herzl founded Zionism, and so it goes."[28]

In preparation for the first constituent assembly of the World Jewish Congress scheduled for August 1936, an electoral convention sponsored by the American Jewish Congress met in Washington in June. More than a thousand delegates, elected by ninety-nine communities in thirty-two states, overwhelmingly endorsed the idea of a permanent world body, and chose fifty representatives and fifty alternates to speak for American Jewry at the Geneva gathering. Ironically, the complicated electoral process, designed to provide the widest and most democratic representation, had been worked out by Louis Lipsky, who while objecting to the congress as a Zionist, nonetheless supported it as a member of the American Jewish Congress executive. Moreover, as Lipsky told Weizmann in explaining his change, the very elements opposing the congress were also the most bitter and vociferous critics of Zionism, and he compared the attack of the American Jewish Committee with its assault on the American Jewish Congress two decades earlier. Lipsky, along with Wise and Julian Mack, all original proponents of the American congress movement, were elected delegates-at-large by the Washington conclave.[29]

Amidst much ceremony, the World Jewish Congress came into being on August 8, 1936, the product of nearly a decade of planning, conferences, and negotiations among the leaders of Jewish communities in three dozen countries. At the week-long session, 277 delegates from countries in Africa, Asia, Europe, and North America debated how they might stop the advancing antisemitism. To Wise, who had labored from the start for such a body, went the honor of delivering the opening speech, and he began by invoking the ancient Hebrew prayer, "Blessed art Thou, O Lord our God, who has protected and sustained us, and allowed us to reach this day."

He then explored the means and purposes of the Congress, and emphasized that no one had to defend the legitimacy of the body. As to his—and their—hopes: "What do we expect of a World Jewish Congress? We answer: 'No miracles.' The World Jewish Congress will not solve all, or most, nor even many of the involved problems of the Jewish people." But it would, he said, give them a forum in which to exchange ideas and from which a unified Jewry could fight persecution.[30]

The first Congress did little more than adopt an organizational structure, affirm principles of Jewish unity and resistance to oppression, and elect an executive. The delegates unanimously elected Wise as chairman of the executive committee and Nahum Goldmann as chairman of the administrative body, opening the cooperation between these two men which lasted until the American rabbi's death. Within a year after this initial session, thirty-four affiliates in twenty-seven countries around the world joined the Congress. The agency opened offices in Paris and Geneva, while the New York headquarters of the American Jewish Congress provided staff and an American home for the world body. The Congress immediately began a campaign at the League of Nations to facilitate the exit of Nazi victims from Germany, and developed an effective watchdog system to discover and publicize antisemitic incidents, especially in eastern Europe and the Arab countries. In early 1937, in cooperation with local affiliates, the Congress sponsored mass rallies in protest against new anti-Jewish episodes in Poland.[31]

The similarities between the fight to create the World Jewish Congress and the earlier struggle for the American Jewish Congress are not surprising; the *yahudim* of the American Jewish Committee and their counterparts in Europe still opposed "airing" Jewish problems. A letter Wise wrote to his cousin in 1938 could just as well have been written twenty years earlier. The elite, he declared, "resent the introduction of democracy into Jewish life, and there we part, and part hopelessly and forever. . . . Everything else could be settled, but there is no compromise here."[32]

The World Jewish Congress battle represented this principle even more starkly than did the earlier American fight, for in 1915 and 1916 the struggle for democratic principles was intermingled with a bid by the Zionists for a share of power and influence in Jewish communal affairs. But no international equivalent of the American Jewish Committee existed, and the opposition of the *yahudim* in the United States and elsewhere only reflected the fears of assimilationists that somehow their credentials as loyal citizens would be questioned despite the stark evidence that the most assimilationist Jewish community in the world, the one so at home and loyal to Germany, had been reduced to ruin in less than three years. It was a sobering lesson, but one from which differing conclusions were drawn. For the elitists, it meant maintaining a low profile, keeping "Jewish problems" quiet, having the "best people" handle sensitive matters. For Wise, the answer lay in democracy, participation, and the unity of all Jews. Born out of the response to Nazi tyranny, the World Jewish Congress was designed not only to defend the Jewish people but to reaffirm the noblest Jewish ideals. Through his work in the congresses, Wise directed much of his effort in helping those Jews who managed to escape from the Nazis, but now found themselves without homes or livelihoods.

Wise did not forget that at bottom, all the Reich's policies affected individual Jews—men, women, and children who had names, personalities, homes, and careers, and now found themselves cast out of the world they had known. For those Jews suffering from persecution or attempting to build new and free lives elsewhere, the name of Stephen Wise became a focus of hope, the man who would somehow be able to help them. For thousands, perhaps tens of thousands, Wise's efforts bore fruit, and they—the lucky ones—were able to live. It was a heartbreaking chore for him, because it required immense investment of time and energy and emotion with disappointingly small results. But he never stopped calling for more effort on the part of the free world to save European Jewry, nor working to assist individuals begin new lives.

In the summer of 1933, both Stephen and Louise Wise saw for themselves the first flood of refugees from the Third Reich. In Paris, they went to the train station where scores of Jews arrived each day from Germany, and spoke to them of the conditions they had left behind. "Through their eyes," Wise told Julian Mack, "I have looked in the depths of hell." One day Louise went to the Heine Foyer, where the refugees gathered daily for tea and messages, and that evening she told her husband that upon their return to America, "I shall get the Women's Division of the American Jewish Congress [which she had founded earlier that year] to establish refugee houses." She was as good as her word, and that fall the Women's Division converted three townhouses owned by the Jewish Institute of Religion into temporary shelters to take care of refugees until they found permanent quarters. She personally went around to the stores, badgering the owners for gifts of linens and household goods and beds and sofas, convincing them that she was doing them a favor allowing them to donate to the cause. When a young psychiatrist asked if he could have a table on which to work, his hostess did not telephone or send a secretary, but went out personally to get him a proper desk. Before the war shut off the flow of refugees, 4,000 people passed through the houses.[33]

While Louise Wise and the Women's Division carried a major responsibility for these homes, Wise himself visited them almost daily, talking to the refugees, helping them to find jobs, and often lending them money so they could get started. When the three houses could not accommodate those seeking shelter, the Wises opened their own home to the overflow. Once, coming home late at night from a speech, Wise went into his bedroom to discover a four-year-old girl there. When he asked her what she was doing in his bed, she told him in English heavily tinged with a Bavarian accent, "This is not your bed but my bed."[34]

The real problem, however, was not in taking care of those who managed to reach these shores, but in trying to open the gates of America to the many thousands who wanted to come to the United States. But a country that had been built by those fleeing oppression now turned its back on those trying to escape the latest persecution. Racked by the most severe depression in its history, the United States wanted no more newcomers, especially Jews. Even after the horror of the *Kristallnacht* pogrom shocked many Americans, public opinion polls showed an overwhelming part of the populace opposed to providing haven for the oppressed. In November 1938, a Gallup poll reported that four out of five Americans did not want to let in more immigrants. A few months later, after still another plan for allowing additional refugees into this country had been defeated, the editors of *Fortune* asked: "Would Herr Hitler and his German-American Bunds be safe in the joyful conclusion that Americans don't like the Jews much better than do the Nazis?"[35]

Nothing Wise nor anyone else did in the prewar years changed this situation, and there is probably no sorrier chapter in the history of a nation built by immigrants than this era, when the United States betrayed its legacy. From the White House down, one could find expressions of sympathy, but no new visas, no liberalized quotas, no lives saved. When Wise visited Roosevelt in early 1936, he found the president appalled by the German situation, but totally opposed to a plan then being discussed which would have tied easier egress for Jews out of Germany to a large increase of German imports into the United States. When Jewish groups protested that the State Department was not facilitating the issue of visas, both Roosevelt and Secretary of State Hull promised action, but there was little if any improvement in the situation.[36] After Polish Foreign Minister Joseph Beck threatened to expel three million "surplus" Jews, Wise wrote to a number of government officials seeking aid. The response he received from Senator Borah was typical: "These things are so appalling in this stage of civilization that one is utterly confused to know what to do. . . . I am frank to say at this writing I can only express my deep sympathy for the success of the cause in which you are engaged."[37]

Was there any place for the refugees to go? In the United States, 126,000 places out of the 1937 quota of 154,000 went unfilled, while the British did all they could to prevent Jews from entering Palestine. The Zionists in general, and Wise in particular, have been charged with blocking schemes to find other havens for the Jews, insisting that only the two Zions of America and Palestine would suffice. Wise was more flexible than many Zionists, but most of the areas mentioned in these alternate schemes had little practical appeal. Alaska and British Guiana, one in the Arctic and the other on the equator, were far inferior in land quality to Palestine. When Chamberlain suggested that Jews go to the former German colony of Tanganyika, Wise bitterly rejected the plan. ''I would rather have my fellow-Jews die in Germany than live in lands which bear the imprint of yesterday's occupation by Germany and which may tomorrow be yielded back.'' Even the Wilhemstrasse had not been more indignant over the proposal.[38] Nonetheless, while Wise may or may not have been ideologically intransigent, Franklin Roosevelt was totally naive if he believed that other countries, even those with sparse populations, were willing to take in large numbers of Jews. This became apparent to almost everyone following Roosevelt's refugee initiative in 1938.

In order to mobilize private agencies to carry out rescue work more effectively, the administration invited the leaders of some half-dozen religious and charitable organizations to meet at the White House on April 14.[39] Roosevelt believed that if the government provided access to diplomatic channels in order to facilitate communications, then the private sector would be able to do the rest. At no time did he contemplate active participation by the government, but he hoped to reap maximum political advantage from a minimal gesture. Wise was not on the original list of invitees, with Secretary of the Treasury Henry Morgenthau, Jr., and presidential advisor Bernard M. Baruch nominally representing Jewish interests, although neither of them had ties to organized Jewish life. This oversight was quickly corrected, but it indicated the problems that doomed the President's Advisory Committee on Political Refugees from the start.

Within two weeks Wise, who had originally praised Roosevelt for convening the group, complained to Felix Frankfurter about the Committee's inactivity and the resistence of State Department officials to any other agency attempting to act in the field of foreign affairs. The group could not find a chairman of any stature, and Hamilton Fish Armstrong declined the president's offer, noting that his interest was ''after all [more] international relations than relief or philanthropy as such.'' When the body met for the second time in May, the members chose James G. McDonald as chairman, and began work on a survey of relief and resettlement options. After this step, Roosevelt completely ignored the Committee, which had to v.ork exclusively through the State Department, where it soon became embroiled in a bitter controversy over visa limits.[40]

Roosevelt's second gesture had as little impact as the first, but the conference on refugees that summer at the French resort of Evian-les-Bains drove home the fact that Jews trying to escape Hitler had no place to go. The president hoped that an internationl conference might lead a number of nations to take in the fleeing refugees without any one in particular, the United States or Great Britain, having to take in many. Nahum Goldmann wanted Wise to attend as president of the World Jewish Congress, arguing that he and Chaim Weizmann, as head of the Zionists, could "authoritatively command the best hearing for the general Jewish case," but this was the last thing the State Department wanted.[41] The bureaucrats had selected Congressman Sol Bloom, chairman of the Foreign Affairs Committee, who had a reputation for being "easy to handle." When Wise protested the appointment, he unfortunately referred to Bloom as "the State Department's Jew," a phrase which enabled Breckinridge Long to reply that Bloom "was representative of America." This time Wise had no illusions about what would happen at Evian. In a speech to the ZOA, he predicted that the conference would be a "dismal failure" unless Great Britain offered to open Palestine to mass immigration of Jews from Germany and Austria. Privately, he noted that Roosevelt's call was "a gesture which meant little. . . . One might have expected more from an administration that pretends sympathy."[42]

The conference, as expected, did nothing. England refused even to discuss a Palestinian solution to the refugee plight, while the United States and other democracies claimed their economic difficulties precluded increased quotas. Tiny Santo Domingo alone offered to take in the Jews, but conceded that only a small number could be absorbed in that country. Expressions of sympathy abounded, but little else; as Goldie Meyerson told the press at the end of the meeting, she hoped she would live long enough for the Jewish people not to need any more expressions of sympathy. Ira Hirschman, a New York department-store owner who left the conference in disgust, condemned Evian as a "facade behind which the civilized governments could hide their inability to act."[43] Once again the Zionist analysis had been confirmed: Jews would never be safe until they had a homeland of their own, free from the sympathies or hostilities of other nations.

While the squabble went on, so did the fight to save Jews. Breckinridge Long, the State Department official in charge of visas, ensured that as few spots as possible in the quotas were filled, despite the president's statements about greater flexibility and more liberal guidelines. Jews seeking to enter the United States could only get visas if they were "guaranteed" by a relative or potential employer, so Wise became a one-man resettlement agency, finding jobs and signing affidavits so that "cousins" of the family could enter the land of freedom. "I wrote a rather sharp note to the American consul," he told Karl Grossman, "to say that I am the best judge of how many affidavits I should give to people." Eventually he managed to bring Grossman to America, as he did many other German Jews.[44] When he met

Max Nussbaum in London in 1939, he told the young Berlin rabbi that he should come to the United States. Nussbaum, then on a mission for the Zionists, replied that he had neither money nor connections, and that he could not leave his family behind. Wise promised that he would get a visa, but Nussbaum harbored no great hopes from what he considered a casual comment. He returned to Berlin, but a few weeks later received a cable to the effect that not only had Wise secured a visa, he had also arranged a pulpit. Temple Israel in Hollywood had written Wise asking him to recommend a rabbi, and Wise had told them that by bringing Nussbaum they would not only get a new minister, but could save a Jewish family. Going only upon Wise's word, they immediately agreed to take Nussbaum, who went on to have a distinguished career as rabbi, Zionist, and communal leader.[45]

One can—and should—blame the State Department in general and Breckingridge Long in particular for the lack of sympathy, for the indifference to cruelty and suffering, for what Emanuel Cellar once described as "a heartbeat muffled in protocol." But the State Department did little more than mirror public opinion and political reality. After *Kristallnacht*, Roosevelt declared that he "could scarcely believe that such a thing could occur in twentieth-century civilization." The president ordered a six-month extension of temporary visas, and recalled the American ambassador to Berlin, but did nothing to change the quota system. In response to any inquiry about liberalizing the immigration laws, Samuel Rosenman, one of Roosevelt's advisors as well as a member of the American Jewish Committee, declared "it neither desirable or practicable to recommend any change in the quota provisions." Myron Taylor, speaking for the administration, reassured the public in a radio address that the administration was not contemplating any changes in the immigration law. Public-opinion polls showed that despite the pogrom, Americans were more determined than ever to oppose quota changes. Senator Borach accurately reflected this sentiment when he declared that "this country belongs to the people of this country. I am not willing, myself, while hundreds of thousands in this country are hungry, perhaps millions of children underfed . . . and hordes of young boys and girls coming into active life seeking jobs without ability to get them, to let down the bars. That, to my mind, could not be justified on any theory of patriotism or humanity."[46]

Such a widespread attitude made it questionable at best if any refugee bill could get through Congress, but if nothing else it did require Jewish leaders working for a more humane immigration bill to tread cautiously. Thus when Senator Wagner introduced a measure to allow in some 10,000 refugee children outside the regular quota system, Wise and others pressing for the bill thought it prudent to maintain a low public profile. This led some nativists to charge that the Jews were not that interested in the bill, while historian Saul Friedman later implied that Wise's timidity led to the measure's failure.[47] Yet as long as the American people and its government had no intention of altering immigration policy, the question of tactics is irrelevant. That Wise pushed hard is unquestionable; Breckinridge Long's diary is replete with complaints of the New York rabbi's constant attempts to budge the State Department into issuing more visas. It also indicates that despite Franklin Roosevelt's public statements, the president did not push his subordinates to be more liberal, but expressly approved Long's policy of allowing in as few Jews as possible.[48] For Wise and others, American policy during these years demonstrated a tragic betrayal of all the country represented. Increasingly, American Jews looked toward Zionism as the solution of this latest and most horrendous phase of the Jewish problem.

21

Conflicts

The outbreak of war in Europe in September 1939 posed severe intellectual as well as moral problems for Stephen Wise. The seeming betrayal of Wilsonian ideals following the First World War had led Wise back to pacifism, and despite the menace of Hitler, he found war an even more appalling spectre than he had a quarter-century earlier. Moreover, the entire question of Zionist objectives and actions had to be rethought. What should the movement do now that Great Britain, which had reneged on the Balfour Declaration, and Germany, which threatened the very life of the Jewish people, warred against each other?

Wise, like many other progressives, had found both the postwar settlement in Europe and the new isolationism in the America of the 1920s disturbing. He had followed Woodrow Wilson into war because he had believed that it would lead to a new world order based on justice and democracy. Instead, the foxes of Europe outmaneuvered Wilson at the peace table, turning the treaty into a vengeance-filled document; at home the president's stubbornness allowed his political opponents in the Senate to block American participation in the League of Nations, thus dooming the international organization to impotence. In 1922 Wise warned that the American attitude of "We're through with Europe" would only lead to another war, and he began to wonder if force could every bring about the ideal world society he and other reformers envisioned. In a speech in December 1923 he came, as he put it, "dangerously near the jumping-over point to non-resistance."[1] As the decade wore on, Wise moved even closer to the pacifist position he had held prior to April 1917, condemning military training in colleges and appropriations for a large navy. War, he argued, "solves no problems; instead of war making for peace, it makes for war and war again and yet again war."[2] When the New York City Board of Education considered a proposal for the establishment of a cadet training program, Wise aligned himself fully with opponents to the plan. In the early 1930s, he spoke frequently at pacifist rallies, and

308

called upon religious organizations and individuals to unite in opposition to militarism. Never again, he thundered at one meeting, should religion give its blessing to war. "No state shall so coerce us as to make us violate the will of God that no man slay his brother."³

In early 1932, following the Geneva disarmament conference, Wise and Holmes were allied in a series of debates against advocates of greater expenditures for preparedness. To those who argued that only through an adequate level of defense could aggression be deterred, Wise responded that when all nations were "prepared" war became inevitable. He conceded that preparedness might avert a minor war, but only at the expense of hastening a major conflict. No more false adage existed than "If you desire peace, prepare for war." To the contrary, Wise declared, "If you desire peace, prepare for peace. If you desire war you will have war if you prepare sufficiently for it."⁴ In his sermon on the twenty-fifth anniversary of the Free Synagogue, Wise confessed "in sorrow and in a spirit of penitence" his "great sin" of taking sides in the First World War. Pointing to John Haynes Holmes, who had never wavered from his strict pacifist principles, he avowed: "Without reservation or equivocation, I say now what this man had the courage to say fifteen years ago—that this pulpit, while I stand in it, will never give its support to war, to any war whatever, whether called just or unjust. . . . Though I bore no arms, I gave the fullest measure of my private and public support to the United States and the allied nations in the World War. I will never do so again." He would not, he promised, support even a war to crush Hitler or one to estabish Jewish claims in Palestine. There must be no more war!⁵

There is no reason to question Wise's good faith in this pledge. The early thirties saw the rise of fascism, but also witnessed the growth of a widespread antiwar sentiment. "The war to end all wars" had led only to a perversion of Wilsonian principles at the peace table, and many people now argued that the harsh terms inficted upn Germany had caused, at least in part, the worldwide depression and the rise of Hitler. Books, articles, and congressional hearings all fostered the suspicion that only munitions manufacturers benefited from conflict, at the expense of millions of dead and maimed. In Europe and America, young men took the Oxford pledge never to fight in any war. Idealists once betrayed vowed not to succumb again. No one, including Wise, realized at this time the lengths to which the Nazis would go. People who feared that Hitler would precipitate a war expected that it would be but one more conflict of the type that had plagued Europe for centuries. No one anticipated either the Holocaust or the worldwide bloodbath which Germany would unleash.

Throughout the early and mid-thirties, Wise lent his name and support to a number of pacifist organizations, preached frequently against war and preparedness, and watched with horror as first European countries and then the United States increased appropriations for armaments.⁶ Events in the world were making it more and more difficult, however, for people like Wise to adhere to a pristine pacifism. The Spanish Civil War, for example, raised the issue of the proper response to the use of force. The Free Synagogue's rabbi openly supported the republican cause, and implicitly conceded that in defense, at least, a people had a right to bear arms. Similarly, he denounced Japanese aggression in China, and publicly called upon America "to safeguard China in the name of human justice. The time to avert an American-Japanese war is now by uniting Americans against the crime of Japanese militarism."[7] Yet how, without building up its own armed forces, could the United States undertake to defend China or any other nation victimized by predator states? How could one respond to force other than by presenting a countervailing force? Wise argued that the Nazi boycott could only be answered by an equally forceful anti-German measure. Would not that logic apply to armed actions as well? "I am truly worried," he agonized to Holmes in early 1938. "I do not want my country to go to war, but I don't want the democracies to surrender to the fascist forces." Holmes urged him to hold fast. War, he told his friend, "is the same thing today that it was yesterday, and as it will be tomorrow." If America went to war against the fascists, Holmes warned, it would wind up a fascist state itself. While he recognized the difficulty of Wise's position, he begged, "In God's name don't repudiate your own pledge never to support another war."[8]

But not all churches prayed for peace. A number of Catholic prelates said masses for the success of General Francisco Franco in Spain or defended Hitler's invasion of Austria. These were not, Wise told a peace rally in Madison Square Garden, wars of "old world ideologies" as former president Herbert Hoover had termed them. Rather these conflicts—indeed, wars of any sort in any part of a shrunken world—affected the United States. But if this were true, and if defensive wars against fascism could be legitimized, then how could the United States guard democracy except through preparedness and the willingness to resist aggression? By the spring of 1938, Wise, albeit reluctantly, began slowly to dissociate himself from the more doctrinaire pacifists.[9] When Neville Chamberlain sold out Czech freedom for "peace in our time," a grief-stricken Wise told Holmes that Munich did not mean "England and France are opposed to war; it means that they ignominiously surrendered to Hitler. . . . It is one of the tragic days of all human history. I feel as my forefathers must have felt [at] the destruction of the Temple. Human liberties are fled, democracy is a sham, standards have gone, the moral realm of mankind is laid waste. God help us!"[10] As Europe moved toward war a year later, Wise viewed with horror the prospects of both war and peace. "War is hell," he told a friend "but peace through appeasement and surrender to Hitler would be deeper and fouler than hell."[11]

Yet even after Hitler invaded Poland and Britain and France went to war against Germany, Wise still hoped that the United States might stay out of the conflict. "I loathe everything for which Hitlerism stands," he told Sidney Goldstein, "all that it is and does. But such loathing and my sympathy with England and France will not move me to action in favor of war."[12] He did speak out in support of England, and over national radio argued that the United States should aid Britain as a means not only of self-defense but also of averting American involvement in the war. By this time, his pacifism had been tempered, and he moved further away from the unyielding position of Holmes. This was no mere European quarrel, but a conflict between democracy and dictatorship, and one that had serious implications for the Jewish people.[13] Like many others, Wise hoped that the Allies would defeat the fascists without actual American involvement, but after the German victories in the summer of 1940, it became obvious that Hitler would be triumphant unless the United States entered the war. By May 1941, he wrote English friends that their two counties shared a common cause. Resistance to Hitler, he now averred, could not be called war in the normal sense of the term. "It is a duty laid upon civilization by a menace which . . . is the most imperilling threat that civilization and faith and freedom have ever faced."[14] He continued to defend the right of Holmes and other pacifists, but began to describe himself more and more as an interventionist.[15] To those who reminded him of his 1932 pledge never to support another war, he answered that he now heard another voice, that the horror represented by the fascists and the danger posed to democracy required that the United States, even it it did not enter the conflict, support Britain and France in their struggle. He still loathed war, but recognized that unless the democracies fought back, the aggressors would win by default and impose a loathesome tyranny on the entire world.[16]

Wise had completed his journey by the time the Japanese attacked Pearl Harbor on December 7, 1941. He still despised war, but could no longer argue that any and all wars should be opposed. Moreover, the tyranny of Hitler had few supporters in the United States; a large pro-German faction similar to that of the First World War did not exist in 1941, while the Japanese assault united nearly all Americans in their determination to defeat the Empire of the Rising Sun. Wise did, however, take great care to point out that he was supporting a war to defend democracy, not because Hitler had attacked Jews.[17] But the war did create special problems for Jews and Jewish groups, and they now had to determine a proper response.

The outbreak of war followed the British White Paper closing Palestine by less than four months, and made even more acute the problem of refugees who had managed to flee Nazi-occupied territories. The Zionists now had two battles to fight, one against the British and the other against the fascists. Constant pressure had to be maintained on the Foreign Office and the State Department to get every possible visa, and while the formal leadership worked through diplomatic channels, the *yishuv* organized an underground movement to smuggle Jews from Europe into Palestine.[18] Wise, relying upon the experiences of the earlier war, believed that the ultimate status of Palestine as well as the rights of European Jewry would be decided at the peace conference, and even while engrossed in short-term and daily pressures he tried to establish some sort of planning committee that would prepare for the postwar settlement. In late 1939 he convened a small group consisting of himself, Milton Handler, Jerome Michael, Abe Tulin, and Beryl Levy. Wise suggested that had the Jews been able to make a stronger presentation at the Paris peace conference, they might have secured better political guarantees in Europe as well as in the Palestine mandate. Throughout the winter of 1939/40, while European armies settled into the *Sitzkrieg*, the group commissioned a number of studies which they hoped would serve as bases for future policy. No one in the group, Milton Handler recalled, expected Hitler to win the war, nor did they suspect that he would soon implement his "final solution" to the Jewish problem. The resumption of war in the spring with German armies overrunning western Europe led to the abandonment of the plan, because the group now realized that the war would not be over soon, nor was it so certain that the Allies would win.[19]

Meanwhile, the Zionists had to be organized and just as in 1914, the center of Zionist power began shifting westward across the Atlantic. Chaim Weizmann, as president of the WZO, called for the creation of an Emergency Committee for Zionist Affairs to coordinate the work of the different American groups. Wise reluctantly agreed to head the committee, fearing that the leadership in both London and Jerusalem still considered American Zionists second-class citizens. He declared that he and other Americans refused to be treated as "messenger boys. . .charged with appalling responsibilities and endowed with no power whatever."[20] Wise's fears were soon realized as a number of European and Palestinian Zionists descended upon the United States and, ignoring the local leadership, began soliciting funds for their own pet projects. Vladimir Jabotinsky, much to Wise's anger, campaigned for a Jewish army, thus violating both the president's call for neutrality and American Jewry's reluctance to be labeled as a separate ethnic group. Jabotinsky's first announced his plan at the Manhattan Center on March 19, 1940, before an audience of more than 5,000 people, and the idea appealed to many persons frustrated by the inability of either western Jews or the free democracies to help those trapped in Hitler's grip. Wise, together with other Zionist leaders, went to see the British ambassador, Lord Lothian, to dissociate the American movement from what they termed "Jabotinsky's adventurous scheme," and Lothian soon afterward withdrew his sponsorship of a second Revisionist rally.[21]

Wise recognized the moderate Zionist groups had to unite if they hoped to accomplish anything. Accordingly, he took several steps to bridge the gap that had long existed between Chaim Weizmann and the Brandeis group, unsuccesfully appealing to the retired jurist to meet with Weizmann when the latter came to Washington.[22] During Weizmann's 1940 trip to the United States, the Jewish Institute of Religion conferred an honorary Doctor of Hebrew Letters on him, and Wise cited "a lifetime of most effective work arid eminent service to the Zionist cause." Julian Mack twitted Wise about the fulsomeness of such praise, and Wise responded, somewhat defensively, "Did it occur to you that you cannot confer an honorary degree upon a man and at the same time call him an s.o.b.?" Whatever his past feelings about the British leader, Wise avowed that he would work closely with Weizmann, and over the next several years the two men became real allies as each faced attack by younger and more militant Zionists for being too "conservative."[23]

But even as he and Weizmann were reaching agreement, internal fights within American Zionism threatened to cripple the movement. No one leader, not even Wise, had the stature Brandeis had held in 1914, nor did anyone have a program around which the differing factions would unite. Brandeis, while still involved in Zionist affairs through Robert Szold, was old and ailing, and died before Pearl Harbor. Felix Frankfurter had gone onto the Supreme Court in 1939, Julian Mack lay sick, and Henrietta Szold lived in Palestine. Among both the Brandeis and the Lipsky/Weizmann groups, men and women differed over what policy to pursue and which leaders to follow. Wise had prestige, but no program, and his main concern during these years was to foster Jewish and Zionist unity. Not until 1943 would someone step forward with the charisma and a plan to revitalize American Zionism, and Abba Hillel Silver would bitterly oppose what he considered Wise's temporizing and willingness to accomodate the Roosevelt administration.

In the winter and spring of 1940, the Jewish community in general and the Zionists in particular seemed completely confused over what to do regarding European Jewry, the war, and the mandatory power, as well as who should be doing what. In a replay of the earlier war, the Joint Distribution Committee balked at allocating relief funds to Palestine, thus jeopardizing the continuation of the United Jewish Appeal.[24] Both Silver and Wise wanted the United Palestine Appeal to insist upon apportioning more funds to the *yishuv*, but differed over the best way to push this demand. Within the ZOA, Solomon Goldman, with Brandeis's encouragement, attempted to freeze Weizmann and Louis Lipsky out of any participation in American Zionist affairs, a policy Wise opposed in light of his belief that unity among all Zionist groups was now essential.[25]. Another issue dividing American Zionists involved the proper attitude toward Great Britain. Goldman and

Silver argued that the English ought to be pressed as hard as possible to reverse their Palestinian policy, while Wise, like Weizmann, saw Britain as the last bulwark against Hitler, and therefore deserving all help and cooperation.[26] This conflict within the Jewish community, Wise wrote, "is painful in every way and to me personally it is heartbreaking. I have the greatest affection for Solomon Goldman. I also respect and cherish Mr. Lipsky who, whatever may be said, has been an invaluable servant of the Zionist cause for forty years. I think it 10,000 pities that this dreadful struggle should have broken out at a time when we ought to be united in defense of our sacred cause."[27]

To secure that unity became Wise's overriding concern throughout the war years, and led to his displacement within the ranks of Zionist leaders. In many ways, he relied too heavily on his own past experience, especially the years of accomplishment when Brandeis had led the Provisional Committee and Woodrow Wilson had sat in the White House. Wilson had promised that the Jews would have Palestine after the war, and had counseled trust and patience during the conflict. Wise assumed that Franklin Roosevelt would play a similar role *vis-à-vis* Palestine, if the Zionists would put aside their internal battles and provide the president with a potent ally in the fight to secure a Jewish homeland. Thus he held out his hand to all Zionists, even the Revisionists, in an effort to build this coalition. He accepted Jabotinsky's idea of a Jewish army to be raised in Palestine, not America, and suggested that the Roosevelt administration push the British to accept the proposal.[28] He announced his willingness to cooperate with Abba Hillel Silver, Solomon Goldman, or anyone who could rally the ZOA, and quietly tried to persuade dissident Zionists not to abandon the movement. Yet no matter what he did, the facts remained that the Roosevelt administration did not have the Jewish plight high on its agenda, the European Zionists could not bring themselves to treat the Americans as equals, and the Americans could not agree among themselves on a common platform.[29]

A brief ray of unity appeared in the spring of 1942, when 586 American and 67 foreign leaders, representing every known faction in the Zionist movement, gathered at an extraordinary conference in the Hotel Biltmore on May 10. Wise, as the senior American Zionist leader, gaveled the milling throng to order, and in his opening remarks set the tone of the gathering. "We are met together in order that all American Zionists, irrespective of party affiliation, place the sacred cause of Zionism above party sectarianism." The goal must be nothing less than "the freedom of Jews in all lands and the final establishment under the Victory Peace Conference of a free Jewish Commonwealth in Palestine."

The delegates sat in somber silence as a weary Chaim Weizmann told them of the horrors inflicted upon European Jewry, and predicted that one out of four would not survive the war. Sadly, he admitted that the British had not kept their word in Palestine; had the spirit of the mandate been upheld, tens of thousands of Jews might have been saved. Nonetheless he pleaded with the delegates not to make this a war against Britain, but to fight alongside the brave English in their battle against Hitler's tyranny. The audience, obviously moved by the words of their aging leader, applauded him at length, but the leadership passed to a new and more vigorous group, led by the militant chairman of the Jewish Agency Executive, David Ben-Gurion, and his American counterpart, Abba Hillel Silver of Cleveland. It would be several months before this became apparent, but in historical perspective, the Biltmore conference is the great watershed in modern Zionist affairs. Before the conference, the movement stood divided and unsure of its final goal; after May 1942 it moved slowly but surely with single-minded steadfastness toward the establishment of a Jewish state. In a ringing resolution, the delegates unanimously rejected British policy: "The Conference demands that the gates of Palestine be opened; that the Jewish Agency be vested with control of immigration into Palestine and with the necessary authority for upbuilding the country, including the development of uncultivated lands; and that Palestine be established as a Jewish Commonwealth integrated in the structure of the new democratic world. Then and only then will the age-old wrong to the Jewish people be righted."

In an emotional final session, the delegates unanimously endorsed the Biltmore Declaration, which would now be the official policy of the Zionist movement, and the various factions publicly made peace with one another. As a symbol of this new unity Wise, who had fought with Chaim Weizmann for over twenty years, embraced him on the platform and gave him one of his most treasured possessions, a ring that had belonged to Theodor Herzl. He called on Weizmann to wear that ring when, at the end of the war, he would once again plead the cause of the Jewish people at the peace conference. Clasping hands, the men and women in the audience then rose to sing the Zionist anthem, *Hatikvah*—The Hope.[30]

While the Biltmore Declaration specifically rejected Weizmann's minimalist policy, questions remained on how the resolution would be implemented, and here Wise found himself much closer to Weizmann than to the fire-eaters led by Silver and Ben-Gurion. For Wise, the goal of an independent Jewish state confirmed all that he had believed in since the days of Herzl; the tragedy of fascism and the failure of the democracies to act reinforced the Zionist analysis that in the end, Jews could only rely upon themselves. But if Weizmann was too tied to the British, Wise was equally reliant upon the American government. His faith in the goodwill of Franklin Roosevelt was not only ill-founded, but would prove disastrous. Both Wise and Wiezmann still had important service to perform for their people; each had built up over the years a reservoir of prestige and contacts which would yet prove invaluable in the fight for a

Jewish state. Yet each had already performed his most important service to the cause, and their final years would be shadowed by the rejection of their leadership. Biltmore provided a rallying cry, a goal, around which ultimate unity would be built. But before that could be achieved, Wise and other American Jews would be faced with the most terrible news of their lives: Adolf Hitler's Final Solution to the Jewish problem.

22

Holocaust

Of all the controversies about Stephen Wise, none have matched in bitterness and import the debate concerning his actions during the Holocaust. Critics charged Wise with becoming a *shtadlan*, a court Jew; of failing to act vigorously and effectively when learning the facts of Nazi genocide; and of passively and willingly becoming the tool of the Roosevelt administration's policy of doing nothing to help European Jewry. Although they are made by reputable scholars, these attacks also reflect the *angst* of an American community riddled with guilt over the failure to save six million of its brethren. To evaluate these charges, one must look closely at the Holocaust, how news of it reached outside the kingdoms of death, and how people reacted to this information.

Although antisemitism had been a central tenet of the Nazi party from its inception, no agreement existed within the movement over exactly how the Reich could be made *Judenrein*. In the thirties, Hitler moved to strip the Jews of German citizenship and to exclude them from the economic, cultural, and political life of the nation. These abuses led about half the Jewish community to leave Germany, and had there been open access to either Palestine or the United States, many of the remaining German Jews would have left as well. From all the indications, mass killing of Jews was not a serious option within Nazi discussions before September 1939; while few of Hitler's lieutenants blanched from the occasional riots or executions, they anticipated that Germany would ultimately be rid of its Jews through other means.

The Nazi conquest of Poland and the occupation of most of continental Europe suddenly changed the situation. Instead of a relative handful of Jews, Germany now controlled areas with approximately four and half million Jews, three million in Poland alone. The Third Reich now saw itself as an empire, with the dominant Aryans exploiting slave labor; and in this empire there was no room for Jews. In a speech on September 1, 1939,

Hitler warned the Jews to expect no mercy from Germany; if they continued to wage war against the German people, they would be exterminated. In occupied territories, administrative officers began concentrating the Jewish population in central urban ghettos, a process which later facilitated the Final Solution but which at this time was not seen as part of it. Between September 1939 and January 1942, Jews suffered enormously under German occupation; had there been a haven, thousands upon thousands of European Jews could have been saved.

The decision to exterminate the Jewish people came at a secret meeting in the Berlin suburb of Wannsee on January 30, 1942. Reinhardt Heydrich, chief of the *Sicherheitsdienst* (SD), acting on the direct orders of Adolf Hitler and Herman Göring, proposed the Final Solution to the Jewish problem to fifteen agency heads: Jews of the conquered territories would be transported to the eastern front for slave labor, then killed when they could no longer work; Jews unfit to labor for the glory of the Reich—the sick, the elderly, and the infirm—would be deported to special camps for "elimination." For the next three years, the Nazis carried out this policy, which led to the murder or death of six million Jews.[1] The dream Hitler had articulated in *Mein Kampf*, a Europe free of Jews, had been virtually realized by the time Allies smashed the German war machine.

The first unconfirmed reports of mass killings were made by the German novelist and expatriate, Thomas Mann, in his BBC broadcasts in December 1941, but little specific evidence could be found to confirm these terrible rumors until the following summer. Dr. Gerhard Riegner, representing the World Jewish Congress in Switzerland, learned from a German industrialist not only about the Wannsee conference, but of the mass shootings of Russion Jews by elite Nazi squads and the of use of Zyklon B gas to slaughter hundreds and thousands of Jews in special camps and mobile vans. Riegner gathered corroborative material from refugees fleeing Germany as well as from letters smuggled out of eastern Europe. On August 8, 1942, he met with the American vice-consul in Geneva, Howard Elting, Jr., and gave him a lengthy memorandum for the American government. He also asked Elting to forward the document to Stephen Wise, using the diplomatic pouch to ensure privacy and safe delivery.

Elting, although incredulous about the story, was nonetheless impressed by Riegner, whom he described to his superior as "a serious and balanced individual." Leland Harrison was more skeptical, and when he cabled the essence of Riegner's message to Washington on August 11, he attached a disclaimer, attributing the accusations to "war rumor inspired by fear and what is commonly understood to be the actually miserable condition of the refugees." The director of State's European Division, Elbredge Durbrow, totally discounted the allegations, and recommended that Riegner's "fantastic" story should not be released to Wise and other Jewish leaders.

Moreover, Durbrow asserted, even if the stories were true, the United States could do nothing to help the victims; therefore it would not be in the best interests of the country to publicize the alleged atrocities. On August 17, State wired its Swiss consulate suggesting unconfirmed reports by third parties not be transmitted, and that all dispatches be limited to information involving "definite American interests." This cable was signed by Secretary of State Cordell Hull and Undersecretary Sumner Welles, and initialed by chief officers of the European Division. Following Durbrow's recommendation, the Department did not forward Riegner's report to Stephen Wise.[2]

Wise, however, had already received a copy. At the same time he had approached Elting, Riegner had gone to the British Embassy and asked it to deliver the report to Sidney Silverman, a Labour member of Parliament and chairman of the British section of the World Jewish Congress. The Foreign Office routinely handed the document to Silverman, who immediately sent it on to New York, where Wise received it on August 28. Even as State Department officials debated whether or not to give Wise this information, he was discussing Riegner's findings in a closed session of the American Jewish Congress executive board. A highly agitated Wise then went to Washington at the beginning of September to present the report to Sumner Welles, who, despite his reputation as one of the few State Department leaders friendly to the Jews, had agreed to the decision to withhold Riegner's report from Wise. Welles requested the rabbi not to release the allegations to the public until the goverment had a chance to confirm them. Welles conceded that when "dealing with that madman" anything was possible, but logic would suggest that the Hitler was more interested in utilizing Jewish men and women in munitions factories than in killing off badly needed laborers. The Undersecretary also reminded Wise of the false atrocity stories that had circulated in the First World War, saying that the government did not want to be embarrassed by releasing charges that might prove fraudulent. Wise reluctantly agreed.[3]

It is with this action that the criticism of Wise begins. Elie Wiesel, whose writings have been so potent in informing the world of the inhumanity and terror of the Holocuast, has accused Wise in these words:[4]

What did American Jews do to aid their brothers in Europe? . . . By the time Stephen Wise (whom I consider a very great man and a very great Jew) talked with Under-secretary of State Sumner Welles he already knew of Hitler's "Final Solution." Welles asked Wise not to reveal this information until it was proven conclusively true, and Wise consented. He gave no information to the press. Wise knew that two million Jews had already been exterminated. How could he pledge secrecy when millions of lives were involved? How was he not driven mad by this secret? How could other Jewish leaders pledge silence? How is it they did not cry out in despair? The more important, the more disturbing is this question: What happened after Rabbi Wise was released from his pledge? Not much. Not much at all. Did he and other Jewish leaders proclaim hunger strikes to the end? Did they organize daily marches to the White House? They should have shaken heaven and earth, echoing the agony of their doomed brothers; taken in by Roosevelt's personality, they in a way became accomplices to his inaction.

Historian Saul Friedman has also charged Wise, indeed the entire American Jewish community, with being "docile" and "silent." Friedman quotes a letter from Wise to Roosevelt in which the rabbi admitted knowing of the terrible news for months. "I succeeded," he told the president, "together with the heads of other Jewish organizations in keeping [it] out of the press, and have been in constant communication with the State Department."[5]

That Wise knew of the Final Solution through the Riegner memoranda is indisputable, as is the fact that he withheld this information from the press at the request of Sumner Welles. He did not, however, know that State Department officials, including Welles, had and would continue to ignore and hide reports of mass killings. Did Wise do the right thing in acceding to Welles, or should he, as Wiesel suggests, have cried out the news and attempted to raise a storm of public outrage? Further, assuming Wise had done these things, even if he had been able to stir up the community, would it have made any difference? Would it have in any way affected either the policies of Franklin Roosevelt or Adolf Hitler?

One must recognize that hardly anyone believed such things were happening. Max Gottschalk, a Jewish scholar who had escaped from Belgium just ahead of the Nazi invasion, expressed anger in November 1942 when the rabbi finally released the story. Gottschalk charged that Wise had lent himself to "atrocity propaganda" in believing these "tales." Many people remembered how the British had manipulated American public opinion in the First World War with stories of German massacres and brutalities in Belgium; these accusations inflamed the country but proved to be false. During the 1930s numerous exposés and antiwar tracts pointed to such "atrocity-mongering" as an example of how militarists led nations into war. Beyond this, the idea of deliberately exterminating a whole people seemed incredible, a fantastic nightmare that just could not be true. When the Polish government-in-exile sent Jan Korski to Washington with details of Nazi atrocities, he met with Felix Frankfurter. At the end of Korski's recitation, a white-faced Frankfurter got up and said: "I do not believe you. I do not say you are lying. I just do not believe you. My mind and my heart are made in such a way I cannot believe you."[6]

It took the State Department ten weeks to confirm the news. Welles summoned Wise to Washington on November 24, and informed him that the government now had information to "confirm and justify your deepest fears."[7] The American Jewish Congress could now release the Riegner cable of August as well as additional details he had sent from his Swiss office. Wise, however, had not been idle during these ten weeks, sitting back silently and passively; moreover, despite the State Department's request, news of the mass murders had found their way into the Jewish press in October.

After agreeing to Welles's request, Wise had agonized over whether he had done the right thing, but even more so after receiving additional reports from Europe. "The other day," he told Holmes, "something came to me which has left me without sleep. One hundred thousand Jews within the Warsaw ghetto have been massacred by the Nazis and their corpses have been used to make soaps and fertilizers. . . . I am almost demented over my people's grief."[8] While he waited for the State Department to confirm the stories, Wise utilized his connections with the Roosevelt administration. On September 4, he contacted Felix Frankfurter and sent him a copy of Riegner's cable; about the same time he went to see Henry Morgenthau to tell him the news. He asked both to inform the president. Roosevelt ought to know about this. "Perhaps he will not be able to avert the thing. But one somehow feels that the foremost and finest figure in the political world today should not be without knowledge of this unutterable disaster." A little while later he returned to Washington to talk to Dean Acheson and other officials in the State Department to push them in their investigation.[9] The American Jewish Congress also convened a meeting of the major Jewish organizations, and Wise informed their leaders of the information he had received from Riegner, his promise to Welles, and the status of the government's inquiry; those present immediately confirmed Wise's actions, and constituted the Conference on the Jewish Situation in Europe, with Wise as chairman, to monitor further news and events. By now a number of copies of the Riegner cable were circulating among Jewish leaders, and the Jewish Telegraphic Agency, without waiting for word from Welles, broke the story in the Jewish press in October. On November 2, the World Jewish Congress in London released a collection of authenticated documents from Geneva, and on November 25, following Wise's second meeting with Welles, American newspapers carried Wise's statement that an estimated two million Jews in Nazi-occupied Europe had been killed in extermination camps.[10]

Had this delay of nearly three months affected the course of the Final Solution? If Wise had refused, might anything have prevented the further massacre of hundreds of thousands of Jews? The answer, sadly, is probably not. Hitler had determined to destroy the Jewish people, no matter what the cost, and cared nothing for so-called public opinon. In the summer of 1942 Axis armies seemed invincible, with all Europe and northern Africa under their control. Even when this situation had been totally reversed two and a half years later and the Third Reich teetered on the brink of collapse, Hitler diverted railroad cars from delivering desperately needed supplies to his troops so that death trains could bring more victims to the gas chambers and crematoria. As for the Roosevelt administration, it could not at this time do more than offer sympathy. There were no armies to dispatch, no pressures to bring upon the Nazis other than the promise of retribution at the end of the war, a hollow threat considering the military situation.

Should Wise have gone on a hunger strike, led a protest march on Washington, defied the State Department, or perhaps, like Shmuel Zygelboim, committed suicide to draw attention to the horror of the Holocaust? Wiesel has read the tactics of the antiwar protests of the sixties back to an earlier and far different time. World War Two was not Vietnam, when this nation stood bitterly divided over the rightness and righteousness of American foreign policy. Those who attempted drastic measures soon discovered their futility. Gandhi's hunger strike led the British to throw him in jail as a Japanese sympathizer. When A. Philip Randolph called for a march on Washington in the cause of equal rights, the administration privately threatened to imprison him, and he settled for token concessions. Zygelboim's suicide barely rippled the surface of public awareness. In a nation at war, and a war of unquestioned moral justification, few Americans were willing to tolerate any actions that could have been interpreted as undermining the war effort. In addition, antisemitism as well as widespread racial prejudice existed at the time. One can argue that Wise and other Jews should have done more, although exactly what the "more" should have been remains difficult to define; but the protest tactics suggested by Wiesel would have accomplished little if anything in 1942.

Perhaps the question should be posed in a different manner. Should American Jews have tried harder to rouse public opinon even if the results were uncertain? How do we know they would have failed since, according to some charges, they did not even try? The answer is that they did try. They did stage mass protests; they did lobby government officials; they did call for the relaxation of immigration quotas; they did call for the bombing of rail lines into the death camps; they did suggest temporary havens; they did try to arrange ransoms—and nothing worked. American Jewry was far from silent and passive, but it was powerless. Whether they tried to work within the system, as did Wise, the Zionists and the American Jewish Committee, or from the outside, as did Ben Hecht, Hillel Kook, and the Irgun faction in America, the enormity of the Holocaust overwhelmed them. American Jews tried to do many things, but with little to show for their efforts; we have no reason to assume that doing more would have been any more efficacious.

What did happen after November 24? Once the news was officially released, did it make a difference? The Jewish community reacted with horror, and its religous leaders called for a day of fasting and mourning on December 2. But non-Jews received the news, for the most part, with disbelief or indifference. Perhaps no more callous response could be found than in the pages of the *Christian Century*, which while admitting that terrible things were happening to the Jews, questioned "whether any good purpose is served by the publication of such charges as Dr. Stephen S. Wise gave to the press last week." The journal disputed Wise's claim that Hitler wanted to kill all the Jews of Poland, noting that the Polish government-in-exile claimed that *only half had been marked for extinction and less than 250,000 actually killed.* Wise's "allegation" that Jewish corpses were being processed into soap and fertilizers was "unpleasantly reminiscent of the 'cadaver factory' lie which was one of the propaganda triumphs of the First World War." And this from the country's leading liberal Protestant journal! Wise wrote a heated protest, but it did little good; Charles C. Morrison, the editor of *Christian Century*, may have been more antisemitic than most Americans, but they also seemed to care little for what happened to Jews in Europe.[11]

Soon after the publication of the Riegner material, Wise led a delegation of Jewish leaders to the White House on December 8, and they handed Roosevelt a twenty-page memorandum labeled "Blueprint for Extermination." The document laid out, country by country, the known facts of annihilation. Roosevelt expressed shock that two million Jews had already been killed, but promised that the United States and its allies would take every step to end the crimes "and to save those who may yet be saved."[12]

Some critics have charged that Wise missed a great opportunity by not including demands for relief in the memorandum he gave to Roosevelt. There was no mention, for instance, of Palestine or the White Paper or the lifting of immigration quotas; the delegation requested only that the government create a special commission to gather evidence of Nazi atrocities to present before "the bar of public opinion and to the conscience of the world." The document thus begged the real questions, allegedly to avoid putting Roosevelt on the spot. In fact, disagreement among Jewish organizations on the proper strategy prevented any concrete proposals.

Yet even then, what if there had been some demands? What Wiesel, Friedman, and others ignore is the powerlessness of the American Jewish community. Jews then constituted less than three percent of the population; they lacked the political influence ascribed to them in the 1960s and 1970s; leaders like Wise never claimed to be able to "deliver" the Jewish vote, and recognized that they could not have done so in any event. Roosevelt and his advisors took the line that the best way to save European Jewry from Hitler was to defeat the Nazis as quickly as possible. Wise received constant messages of support and sympathy from the president and other members of the administration,[14] but little else, and there is no reason to believe that demonstrations would have mattered. Wise and his fellow Jewish leaders were not silent, were not passive, were not apathetic, but they did not have the power to change Roosevelt's policy.

Was Wise an accommodationist? In his old age had he become a *shtadlan*, a court Jew, doing all he could to please his friend, the president of the United States? Certainly one can find material that apparently bolsters such an accusation. "I don't know if I am getting to be a *hofjude*," he wrote Felix Frankfurter, "but I find a good part of my work is to explain to my fellow-Jews why our government cannot do all the things asked or expected of them [*sic*]." Wise, according to Saul Friedman, "more than any other figure represented American Jewry, and as such he was patronized by Roosevelt, Hull, and other top-ranking government officials. Because of his longtime friendship with the president and Roosevelt's nodding approval of virtually everything Wise suggested, because he was privy to confidential information that smacked of policymaking, Wise naturally considered himself a person of importance and responsibility. In these crucial years to European Jewry, Wise believed that his larger responsibilities compelled him to silence."[15]

One can by now dismiss the myth of "Jewish silence," the belief that Jewish leaders remained mute throughout the war.[16] Wise, Abba Hillel Silver, Chaim Weizmann, and others spoke frequently and loudly, but to no avail. American Jewish leaders did call for a more liberal immigration policy, did call for the repeal of the White Paper, did call for the establishment of temporary havens and the bombing of rail lines leading into Auschwitz and other camps, but their appeals had no effect on either the Roosevelt or Churchill governments.[17] American and British policy remained based on the belief that the fastest way to stop the extermination of the Jews was to defeat the Third Reich militarily. Within the State Department, officials involved in immigration matters were for the most part antisemitic, while in the Foreign Office the Arabists, opposed to further Jewish colonization in Palestine, held sway. In vain, Wise and other Jewish leaders looked to the White House.

Few American presidents have been so idolized by the Jewish community as Franklin D. Roosevelt. In his administration, Jews rose to unprecedented power and influence, and the community responded by giving him its overwhelming political support.[18] With the exception of Abba Hillel Silver, Jewish leaders in the United States looked to Roosevelt as a friend, as the champion of Jewish aspirations at home and of Zionist hopes in Palestine. Roosevelt did appear to be their ally, and his frequent condemnations of Hitler as well as his intercession with the British in 1936 served to cement this relationship. Of all American Jewish leaders, none championed the president as did Stephen Wise, for he believed that only through Roosevelt's leadership would liberalism and democracy triumph in the United States, and that his friendship would help to fulfill the Jewish agenda.[19]

Whatever Wise's attitude toward Roosevelt may have been following the Walker affair, the Free Synagogue's rabbi had to be counted as among the president's most ardent admirers after their reconciliation in 1936. Wise campaigned for the Democrats that year and in 1940 and 1944 as well, always insisting that Jews should not vote for Roosevelt because they were Jews but because he offered the greatest hope for the country. He did, however, rarely fail to mention that the president had proven a special friend to the Jews, and in turn Roosevelt, when he could, agreed to those requests brought to him by Wise which involved no major policy changes or the expenditure of political capital. Thus in 1941, Roosevelt suggested to Great Britain that Palestinian Jews should be armed for defense against the threatened invasion by Rommel's Desert Korps, and His Majesty's Government dropped its original plans that any Palestinian brigade would have to have an equal number of Jews and Arabs. Throughout the war, Roosevelt periodically reiterated his sympathies for the victims of the Holocaust and his support of the Zionist demand for a Jewish homeland. Unbeknownst to Wise and other Jewish leaders, at the same time he secretly reassured the British and the Arabs that he would not push for any solution to the Mideast muddle until after the war, and then only with their cooperation and approval.[20] As far as Wise knew, "the administration is strongly with us," and he took Roosevelt's frequent statements that "my position is the same as before" at face value. The inconsistencies between the president's statements and administration actions were attributed by Wise to the anti-Zionist and anti-Jewish attitudes of the underlings in the State Department, and to the recognition that wartime exigencies limited the options open to the government.[21] And just often enough, a real achievement could be counted, such as the defeat of a proposed Anglo-American policy statement in 1943 calling for the abrogation of all public discussion of Palestine and its future until after the war.[22] But Wise rarely pushed Roosevelt, and this did give the administration the option to ignore Jewish pressure without fear of political retribution or public controversy.

How little the Roosevelt administration felt inclined to aid the victims of the Holocaust can be seen in its policy of immigration, although here too Wise and other Zionist leaders have been scored for their insistence upon opening the gates of Palestine rather than accepting alternative havens.[23] In October 1939, Sir Herbert Emerson, chairman of the Intergovernmental Refugee Commission, attacked Zionists who would not accept British Guiana as refuge. "The trouble with Jews," he complained, betraying his own antisemitism, is that they always had "some other scheme in the background for which they were prepared to sacrifice schemes already in hand." But while it is true that the Zionists had their eyes on Palestine, it is equally true that they had no control over the immigration policies of the United States, Great Britain, Palestine, or any other country. Given what Henry Feingold has called "the politics of gestures" by the Roosevelt administration—gestures with high publicity value but no substance—it is understandable why Jewish leaders could muster little enthusiasm for Guiana, Alaska, or other impracticable proposals.[24]

Above all, Jewish leaders wanted refugees admitted into the United States and Palestine, two countries where they would be safe and could be cared for by the local communities. The British refused to open Palestine for fear of offending the Arabs, while American policy was lodged in a State Department bureau headed by an antisemite who opposed letting anyone into the country. Breckenridge Long set out, as he openly admitted, to create insurmountable obstacles to any refugee attempting to secure a visa. Long attacked Wise and others who "believe every person, everywhere, has a right to come to the United States. I believe nobody, anywhere has a right to enter the Untied States unless the United States desires."[25] Long undoubtedly reflected the attitude of most Americans at the time. As long as the country opposed a liberalized immigration policy, Roosevelt refused to ask for one or even to do that which was already in his power; direct the State Department to liberalize its adminstrative guidelines.

The battle to save Jewish lives, therefore, became one not of grand strategy involving thousands of people but of desperate ever-changing tactics to rescue a few hundred, a dozen, sometimes one or two lives. A boatload of Jews sailing from France to Mexico was turned back at Tampico when the local authorities declared that the refugee visas had not been properly issued. Had the boat returned to France, the passengers would have gone straight from the dock to concentration camps. Wise entreated Eleanor Roosevelt to help, and at her insistence the president agreed to allow the boat to unload in Norfolk, Virginia, provided Secretary of State Hull agreed. Wise and Nahum Goldmann went to see Hull, who declared that no one, under American law, could enter without a visa. He pointed to the American flag behind his desk and averred: "I have sworn to uphold the Constitution and the laws of the United States. You are asking me to break my oath."

Goldmann then reminded Hull that some anti-Nazi German seamen had recently jumped ship rather than return to the Reich. The Coast Guard had sent a cutter to pick them up, and then had taken the men to Ellis Island where non-visa immigrants were held. "If you like," Goldmann said, "I'll send the refugees a telegram, and they'll all jump overboard at Norfolk. The Coast Guard will have to pick them up, and probably some of the people may catch pneumonia; but in the end they'll all wind up at Ellis Island. So why do we have to go about it in such a devious and complicated way?"

"Dr. Goldmann," Hull snapped, "you are the most cynical man I have ever met."

"I wonder who is more cynical," came the reply, "the Secretary who wants to condemn hundreds of Jewish refugees to certain death, or he who tries everything to save them."[26]

The angry Hull would have preferred to refuse admission, but in the end gave in and allowed the refugees to land. After a brief stay at Ellis Island, these fortunate few received visas and entered the country legally. For the most part, the State Department did as little as it could to save those fleeing Europe; rather, following Long's suggestion, consular officials threw one legalistic roadblock after another into the path of rescue. Wise and others had to fight, literally, not to save masses but to rescue individuals.

While Wise did not receive information on the Final Solution until August 1942, he began receiving detailed reports on refugee movements earlier in the year. Eliahu Elath was stationed in Ankara, Turkey during the first years of the war as a representative of the Jewish Agency's Political Department. Ostensibly, he had little to do other than file reports on matters of interest to the Zionists; secretly, he served as liaison between the *yishuv* and clandestine rescue operations. His instructions included keeping American Zionists informed of refugee movements, but he could not do so openly because the Turks, walking a thin line of neutrality, would not pass any letter to the United States uncensored. Elath approached Ray Brooks of the *New York Times*, who filed his reports nightly by radio, and explained the importance of getting this information to Wise. Brooks and Elath worked out a code, and the *Times* then passed the data on to Wise. In order to preserve the secrecy of the arrangement, Wise had his daughter receive and decode the messages. In some ways, Elath's sources proved better than those of American officials in the area, and Wise provided the State Department with this information. On the basis of Brook's transmissions, for example, Wise got Roosevelt to urge the British to arm Palestinian Jews in the face of an anticipated attack by Rommel.[27]

Other information came more openly, and Wise used all of it in an effort to bring the plight of the refugees before the public. On February 24, 1942, the steamer *Struma,* loaded with Jewish refugees, was towed out of Istanbul after British authorities refused to grant Palestinian visas on the grounds that there were German spies in the group. The ship, totally unseaworthy, sank almost immmediately outside the harbor, and 768 lives were lost. The Zionist Emergency Committee called a mass meeting in New York to protest these deaths, the first of a number of such rallies Wise arranged in a vain effort to develop public opinion that might force the government to adopt a more humane policy. But just as Hull had reflected an administrative attitude utterly callous to the refugee plight, the populace, too, Wise found was silent and indifferent to the problem. Without the leverage of either an aroused public or a caring administration, American Jews could accomplish nothing. Try as they might, they lacked the power. As Wise sadly noted after several fruitless trips to Washington, "The truth is, in the midst of a war, it is very difficult to make anyone see that we are most particularly hurt. These wounds are deeper and sorer than any other wounds inflicted.[28]

Wise knew that the government had the resources to facilitate rescue work. He pointed out that supply ships to Great Britain returned empty, and were certainly capable of carrying refugees. In 1943 the government used these ships to carry 200,000 German and Italian prisoners of war to detention camps in the United States; that same year, less than 25,000 refugees, of whom fewer than 5,000 were Jewish, gained admission to the country. By the end of the war, over 425,000 prisoners of war had been transported to the United States and housed in more than 650 temporary camps, yet the State Department and other military planners complained throughout the war that the country had no means to shelter those fleeing for their lives.[29]

The hypocrisy of the Roosevelt administration came into full view with the Bermuda Refugee Conference in April 1943, and by this time American Jewish leaders knew that all they could expect were some noble words but no action, no rescues, no lives saved. By then the only real question was how many Jews would be able to escape Hitler, although no one could still envision the extent of the destruction. Wise feared there might not be any Jews left alive in Europe after the war, but wrote, "It may be reasonable to expect that . . . at least half if not more will somehow manage to hang on to life." Although he and others would continue to call upon the United States to do something—anything—they recognized that the government would not move. When Justine and Shad Polier had dinner with the Roosevelts in February 1943, the president sent his "affectionate regards" to Wise. A bitter rabbi commented, "If only he would do something for my people."[30]

That nothing would be done was assured by the makeup of the Bermuda Conference, in which Congressman Sol Bloom was the only Jew on the American delegation. Bloom rarely challenged the administration, and Breckinridge Long felt confident that Bloom would go along and follow State Department instructions. Great Britain also assured itself a tranquil time by insisting that Palestine not even be considered as a refuge. Roosevelt's assurances to Wise on the eve of the meeting that the United States would "move, so far as the burden of war permits, to help the victims of Nazi doctrines," were not even given lip service by the State Department organizers. The American Jewish Congress sent Sumner Welles a six-point program for discussion at Bermuda, a program echoed by virtually every other group, Jewish and non-Jewish, concerned with refugee problems. The document recommended that: (1) negotiations be opened with the Axis through neutral parties on release of the Jews; (2) havens for these refugees be established around the world, in particular in Sweden, Switzerland, North Africa, and Jamaica; (3) American immigration laws be liberalized to allow in more refugees; (4) empty troop and cargo ships returning from Europe be utilized to carry the refugees; (5) a new passport be devised for stateless persons; (6) the United States undertake to feed Jewish prisoners in Nazi camps. Wise had this program publicized through full-page newspaper advertisments, and Senator Edwin C. Johnson of Colorado introduced a resolution embodying the six points in the Congress. Moreover, the Zionists organized a letter-writing campaign to the government calling upon the conferees to adopt meaningful proposals at Bermuda. In his diary, Breckinridge Long worried that the campaign might prove successful, and thus become "a definite detriment to or war effort."[31]

He need not have been concerned. The Bermuda Conference did nothing, leading Congressman Emanuel Celler to denounce it as "a diplomatic mockery of compassionate sentiment and a betrayal of human interests and ideals." Rabbi Israel Goldstein, president of the Synagogue Council of America, declared that "the job of the Bermuda Conference apparently was not to rescue victims of the Nazi terror but to rescue our State Department and the British Foreign Office from possible embarrassment." Wise condemned the gathering as a "sad and sordid" affair, and attacked Sol Bloom for his passive acquiescence in the travesty. On July 23, Wise went to the White House to find out why there had been such an "inexplicable absence of active measures to save those who can still be saved." Roosevelt again mouthed platitudes, and Wise, unwilling to attack the president publicly, told the press he had found the chief executive maintaining "a profound and penetrating interest in [Hitler's] victims." Here even Wise's staunchest defenders must agree that far stronger and more honest words were needed.[32]

Wise's visit did, however, have some important results. A few months earlier the Geneva office of the World Jewish Congress had advised Wise that broad rescue activities were possible in France and Rumania, and that 10,000 children could be brought out of Nazi-occupied Europe. Wise raised the issue with the president, declaring that if the necessary currency licenses were issued, American Jewish organizations would raise the money. Roosevelt sent on the request to the Treasury Department, where Secretary Morgenthau quickly approved it, and to the State department, where it ran into immediate opposition. In the end, the State Department approved because, as one bureaucrat noted, not to have done so would have thrown the onus for thwarting the rescue attempt squarely on the Department. But officials did manage to delay issuance of the licenses for several months, during which news arrived through Riegner that 4,000 of the children, aged two through fourteen, had been sent in sealed boxcars to the death camps. Then, when the Americans finally approved the licenses, the Foreign Office objected, claiming that the money would only help the Axis, and that there would be difficulty "disposing of any considerable number of Jews should they be released from enemy territory."[33]

The delay caused by the State Department led Morgenthau to investigate the matter, and gradually he uncovered the full extent of obstruction and double-dealing practiced by Long and his cohorts. The Secretary of the Treasury had his staff prepare a document detailing the "Acquiescence of this government in the murder of the Jews.'' His aides completed their work at the end of 1943, and on January 17, 1944, Morgenthau presented it to the president. Unless Roosevelt acted, Morgenthau threatened to resign and make public the whole sordid affair. Secretary of State Hull, asked to respond, foundered, obviously ignorant of much of the activity of his subordinates even though he shared their attitude, Roosevelt now took responsibility for refugees out of the hands of Long and created the War Refugee Board, headed by Morgenthau's assistant, John H. Pehle, one of the authors of the report. The Board, as Henry Feingold concluded, had only limited success because by this time the Final Solution had gone too far, but it did show that given the leadership of caring officials and the cooperation of the government, some Jews could have been saved.[34] Throughout the rest of the war, Wise worked closely with Pehle, passing on information and plans from Riegner, A. Leon Kubowitzki, and other officials of the World Jewish Congress.[35]

But Morgenthau was a Jew, critics note, and his actions "prove" that Jews were not powerless. Such a claim ignores the fact that at Wise's request, Morgenthau had spoken to the president shortly after the receipt of the Riegner cable, but with no effect. Morgenthau interceded when he discovered a situation fraught with politically embarrassing consequences and Roosevelt acted not out of humanitarian concern but to avoid political problems. The president did not fear that the relatively small Jewish electorate would turn against him, but that the Republicans would seize upon the State Department deceptions to attack the administration in an election year. The Treasury Secretary's Jewishness undoubtedly made him more sensitive to the issue, but Roosevelt would have responded in a similar manner had any of his key advisors alerted him to the potential political danger. Suggestions that American Jews should have threatened Roosevelt with retaliation at the polls in 1944 unless he did something for the Jews of Europe completely ignore the realities of the political situation. The Jewish community had never acted consciously as a political bloc; it was overwhelmingly Democratic, but for a variety of factors, not because of religious beliefs. Moreover, where would Jews have gone in 1944? The Republican Party and Thomas Dewey were hardly attractive alternatives to the man in the White House.

Looking over the charges and countercharges that have beclouded the entire issue of rescue efforts, one can conclude that the original accusations against Wise cannot be justified. Those who have criticized his actions and those of other Jewish leaders have ignored the essential fact that the American Jewish community lacked the political power to move the Roosevelt administration to undertake a serious policy of rescuing those whom Hitler had condemned to ovens. There were undeniably mistakes on the part of the Jewish leaders, but no matter what they might have done, they lacked the leverage to move a government that did not care to act, or to generate a public demand for a wholesale rescue effort. Mass meetings, public protests, alternate schemes, private entreaties—all these were tried, but to no avail. If there is one charge which can be sustained against Wise and the others, it is that they placed their trust in Franklin Roosevelt.

In the time of European Jewry's greatest trial, the president had been morally indignant, but his wariness and not his indignation had set the tone and pattern of administration policy. The State Department must certainly bear a major share of the blame for placing obstacles in the path of rescue, but even Roosevelt admirer and biographer James Burns has conceded that the president "seemed unable to face the main problem—the millions of Jewish men, women, and children trapped in the Nazi heartland and headed for the gas chambers." While Long and his cohorts did all they could to retard rescue work, they never had to fight the commander-in-chief to have their way. Shortly after the war, Frank Manuel attacked the tendency to blame the State Department for American policy; in the end, the decisions belonged to the president.[36]

Numerous theories defend Roosevelt, and they have some merit—he could not lead a nation where it did not want to go, he had to safeguard American military interests, he had hundreds of pressure groups beseeching him to solve their individual crises, and above all, there was the sheer magnitude ot the problem—not hundreds but millions of victims—and the determination of the Nazi regime to liquidate the Jewish people. But where is the moral response of the man who showed such compassion for the ill-housed, the ill-clothed, and the ill-fed? Where, in the entire rescue morass, is the swift decision-making that marked the New Deal's energetic response to the Depression? Franklin Roosevelt personified twentieth-century liberalism; the New Deal was *the* liberal political-economic event of this century. Did Jews expect too much from him? Did they believe that if any democratic society could live up to its most humanitarian aspirations, then the America of Franklin Roosevelt would? But moral and humanitarian responses, claims Henry Feingold, are rare in history and particularly rare in wartime. For Feingold, "the villain of the piece, in the last analysis, may not be the State Department or even certain officials but the nature of the nation-state itself."[37] For all the pious statements, the Western democracies bore out Hitler's prediciton that they would not lift a finger to save the Jews. In the light of this reality, Stephen Wise and his fellow American Jews, despite all their efforts, could accomplish very little.

23

Dissent in Zion

The revelation of Hitler's Final Solution to the Jewish problem drove home, as nothing else could, the need for a Jewish homeland, a place where Jews would not only find refuge from persecution but also be free to build a country that would be theirs as a matter of right. One might have expected that in light of the unity displayed at the Biltmore Conference in May 1942, Zionist organizations would have moved forward to forge a unity in the entire American Jewish community in order to generate political pressure for an autonomous Jewish Palestine after the war. This did happen eventually, and the years between Biltmore and the birth of the State of Israel in May 1948 witnessed the high point of Zionist political power and prestige. But this did not become evident until 1947; during the war, an observer of American Jewish affairs would have noted divisiveness, acrimony, and internal strife apparently crippling the movement. At the center of this struggle stood Stephen Wise, and in the end he found himself deposed as a leader of American Zionism, cast out by a younger and more militant leadership.

The Emergency Committee for Zionist Affairs, nominally responsible for coordinating activities in the United States, found itself crippled even before the Biltmore meeting. David W. Petegorsky, a close friend of Wise and his associate in the American Jewish Congress, resigned from the Emergency Committee in March 1942, complaining that its paralysis resulted from the unwillingness of different organizations to subordinate their individual interests to the common good. A few days later, Emanuel Neumann left, followed by Meyer Weisgal, an old comrade of Wise and now Chaim Weizmann's American lieutenant. Weisgal declared that "what is needed is to burn out of the heart of every Zionist, every group and party and organization the accumulated poison of years of hate and prejudice and distrust for one another."[1] On the eve of Biltmore, Chaim Weizmann moved to fill this void, creating the American office of the president of the

World Zionist Organization to act as liaison among the various factions. This step also proved ineffective, for neither it nor any other organization could establish a dominant position in American Zionist affairs. Instead, over the next three years the movement witnessed a pattern of great shows of solidarity followed by crippling power struggles between the American and overseas leaders and within the Zionist Organization of America.[2]

Following Biltmore, Wise found himself moving closer and closer to Chaim Weizmann. Although appreciative of the strength and dedication of other Zionist figures, as he told Felix Frankfurter, "in this hour Weizmann's course . . . is one of higher statesmanship." But he could never convince Weizmann that in the United States a mature Zionism had developed, one capable of carrying its share of responsibility and leadership. Weizmann never recognized that American Jews could understand the depth of the tragedy in Europe or that they were able and ready to battle for a Jewish state.[3] Moreover, Weizmann's attachment to Great Britain, his unwillingness to push while the English fought for their lives, and his highhanded tactics within the WZO led to his ultimate overthrow as well.

The first attempt took place less than seven weeks after Biltmore, with Wise, once Weizmann's bitterest critic, defending him and trying to restore harmony in the ranks. David Ben-Gurion attacked Weizmann for failing to consult with other leaders of the WZO and Jewish Agency, thus thwarting a desperately needed unity. Ben-Gurion, aware of Wise's previous antipathy toward Weizmann, tried to enlist the American leader to his side, but found no encouragement. Wise urged Ben-Gurion to avoid a confrontation in the light of the anticipated German invasion of Egypt and Palestine, and in an effort to make peace, called a meeting of American leaders together with Weizmann and Ben-Gurion in his study on Saturday afternoon, June 27, 1942.[4]

It was an ugly session, with Ben-Gurion accusing Weizmann of being more loyal to British interests than to the Zionist cause, and Weizmann responding that Ben-Gurion suffered from hallucinations. Wise seemed embarrassed throughout most of the two hours, vainly trying to calm both men down and find an acceptable common ground. At the end, Ben-Gurion realized that he did not yet have the backing to overthrow Weizmann, but he remained determined to oust the moderate leadership. Wise, although admiring the Palestinian, nonetheless backed Weizmann, and in doing so identifed himself as a moderate.[5] One may wonder whether a younger Stephen Wise might not have gone over to Ben-Gurion, whether in the twilight of his life Wise was too tired and worn out. In any event, he chose to back a leader he respected as a dedicated Zionist despite their previous disagreements, and as he too came under attack, the ties between the two men grew stronger.[6]

Wise, however, was no minimalist. He had called for a Jewish state in

Palestine years before Weizmann or even Ben-Gurion had reached that stage. In the fall of 1942, he urged both publicly and privately greater Jewish control of Palestinian matters. "Jewish hopes for Palestine," he wrote, "rest upon large-scale Jewish immigration; and large-scale Jewish immigration in turn depends upon Jewish control; and . . . Jewish control means a commonwealth." Britain had to be pushed, he told a gathering of Christian leaders, to live up to its obligations, and this could only mean an autonomous Jewish homeland.[7] Wise never abandoned this commitment; the criticism against him as against Weizmann was that he was not militant enough, especially *vis-à-vis* the Roosevelt administration, in pushing for Zionist goals. No matter what Wise or other mainline Zionists did, however, they could not please the extremists of American Jewry, the bitter antinationalists at one end of the spectrum and the ultramilitant Revisionists at the other.

Within Reform ranks, the tragedy of European Jewry had led many former opponents to re-evaluate their position. The Central Conference of American Rabbis shifted from opposition to official neutrality, and proponents of the cause no longer found Zionism the stigma it had once been within the CCAR. But there were many Reform rabbis to whom the whole idea of Jewish nationalism in Palestine remained anathema, and they protested at the 1942 CCAR convention when the Zionists, on a roll-call vote, secured the endorsement of a Jewish army in Palestine. Within a short time, denunciations of the resolution began to appear in the Anglo-Jewish press, and a small group of clerics, led by Louis Wolsey of Philadelphia, met to discuss ways of restoring Judaism's "prophetic and universal" ideas. Unless the defenders of the faith acted, Wolsey warned, Reform would be lost to the depradations of "Jewish national chauvinism." Although reluctant to precipitate a schism, the anti-Zionists called a national rabbinical meeting in Atlantic City in early June 1942.[8]

To Wise, the actions of "Cardinal" Wolsey and his friends spelled nothing but trouble. At a time when American Jewry should be striving to speak with one voice, the die-hard reactionaries of Reform were raising all the old spectres of dual loyalty and Jewish chauvinism. Wise hoped the dissidents could be silenced before they did any damage, yet he feared that by attacking them the Zionists would only provide the Wolsey group additional publicity and make it appear stronger than it was.[9]

Ninety rabbis attended the Atlantic City conference; they and six others signed a "Statement of the Non-Zionist Rabbis" which, while noting "how dear Palestine is to the Jewish soul," denounced the "political emphasis now paramount in the Zionist program. We cannot but believe that Jewish nationalism tends to confuse our fellow men about our place and function in society."[10] With this manifesto, Wise recognized that immediate steps had to be taken lest the American government and people believe that the

Atlantic City group spoke for more than a tiny fraction of the Jewish community. He and sixteen other Zionist rabbis, including the presidents of the Synagogue Council of America, the CCAR, and the Rabbinical Assembly, as well as a member of the praesidium of the Union of Orthodox Rabbis, prepared a counterdeclaration entitled "Zionism: An Affirmation of Judaism." They proclaimed that the overwhelming majority of American rabbis regarded Zionism "not only as fully consistent with Judaism but as a logical expression and implementation of it," and castigated the Wolsey group for misrepresenting and distorting "historic Jewish religious teaching." Wise, Abba Hillel Silver, James Heller, and Wise's former student Philip Bernstein secured the signatures of 818 rabbis from all branches of American Judaism, including 215 from the Reform rabbinate. In addition, the student bodies of the five leading seminaries approved the statement, including Reform's Hebrew Union College, where it was endorsed by a vote of 42 to 9, a margin that gave Wise much satisfaction.[11]

But the Wolsey group, augmented by wealthy laymen led by Sears, Roebuck magnate Lessing Rosenwald, went on to form the American Council for Judaism. By the end of the year the original rabbinical protest against the dilution of classical Reform theology had shifted to a lay-dominated attack on Zionism. Even as Wise and others worked to promote solidarity among American Jews, the Council published dozens of pamphlets denouncing any form of Jewish nationalism; this was a step welcomed by Arabists in the State Department and the Foreign Office who could now claim that American Jews did not support the Biltmore Program.

Despite its small membership, the Council generated a great deal of controversy, and did much to undermine the work of the Zionist Emergency Council and the American Jewish Conference. Wise could accept the rabbinical protest as wrong-headed but legitimate within the historic context of classic Reform, but he seethed with rage over the vitriol poured out by the Council, which he attacked frequently.[12] In essence, those who joined the Council were afraid—afraid of too much attention being called to the Jews, afraid of *ma yomru hagoyim?* (what will the gentiles say?), afraid that someone might question their patriotism not because they were *Zionists* but because they were *Jews.* Probably no other group Wise had ever fought symbolized so dramatically all the things he detested within American Jewish life—the self-hatred, the failure to understand the diversity of the American society, the rejection of a living Judaism with ties to the Palestinian renascence. the insularity and provincialism and insensitivity to the problems of modern life. In the end, the Council never spoke for more than a tiny fraction of American Jewry, and its negative impact was more than compensated by the growing unity of the Jewish community around the need for a Jewish homeland.

If the Council harbored those afraid of being identified as Jewish, another extremist group wanted nothing more than to call attention to its members as Jews, and of an especially militant variety. Its members condemned the mainline Zionists as too timid in responding both to the White Paper and to Hitler; inspired by the Revisionists, they denounced all Jews who would not join them in fighting fire with fire. Led by a brilliant young Palestinian, Peter Bergson (Hillel Kook), this American branch of the Irgun generated immense publicity, grabbed headlines, and made it appear as if it and it alone was fighting the Nazis and the British. Through a series of front organizations, the Bergson group garnered the sponsorship of influential Christians and claimed credit as the only Jewish organization effecting rescue operations for European victims of the fascists. The regular Zionists saw the Bergson committees as far more dangerous than the Council, for they appealed to the same raw emotion as did the Zionists, but without being bound by the responsibilities facing Wise, Weizmann, Ben-Gurion, and others.

The centerpiece of the Bergson group was the Jewish Army Committee, which placed full-page ads calling for the raising of a Jewish armed contingent in the United States. Wise opposed this, and had done so from the start. Jews in the United States would fight, but they would do so as Americans in the regular services; the proper place for an all-Jewish unit would be in Palestine, and he worked diligently to explain this difference to those enamored of the Bergson call. Ben Hecht, a playwright and novelist who suddenly discovered his Jewishness through Bergson, bitterly attacked Wise both during and after the war for having killed the Jewish Army plan. According to Hecht, Wise refused to tolerate any other Jewish organization working for Palestine or "stealing honors and publicity from him."[13]

Wise opposed the Bergson committee for the same reason he detested the parent body, for its irresponsibility, and in the case of the Irgun, for its use of violence and terror. Part of the trouble also arose from a lack of coordination between the Bergson group and the Emergency Council. The Zionists, aware of various political pressures and sensitivities, were trying to mount a sophisticated nationwide campaign to break through the apathy confronting them. Bergson and Hecht, under no discipline, could issue the most outrageous statements, well aware that they would face no reprisals. While the regular Zionists discounted so-called Arab might, for example, they at least tried to avoid unnecessarily offending Arab opinion; Bergson damned everyone, scornful of the consequences, indifferent to the fact that potential friends in the government were being alienated. Wherever the Zionists went, they and not the Bergson group reaped the reproaches for the latter's inflammatory advertisements and distorted press releases.[14]

When Bergson and Hecht began attacking specific individuals, however, they drove away sympathizers who recognized the contributions made over the years by Wise and other Zionist leaders. Judd Teller later commented that "however disappointed in Wise, once the roaring lion of Jewish protest, [American Jews] still revered him for a lifetime of Jewish service. Ben Hecht was hardly fit to sit in judgment on him." Perhaps the most ludicrous incident occured when Bergson brought charges against Wise in a rabbinical court, accusing him of obstructing passage of a congressional resolution in favor of a Palestinian homeland. The community recognized the attack for what it was—a cheap publicity stunt—and it backfired badly against Bergson; nearly every Jewish paper in the country defended the Free Synagogue rabbi and condemned Bergson.[15]

The tragedy of Irgun operation in the United States during the war is that it wasted talent, energy and money in a frantic and self-serving search for attention. Bergson and Hecht tapped a vein of eagerness in American Jewry, an eagerness to do something to alleviate the tragedy of the Holocaust. They undoubtedly called attention to the problems, but their pyrotechnics confused both Jewish and non-Jewish supporters of Zionist goals and did much to weaken the unity necessary for the American Jewish community to exert any leverage on the government or on public opinion. In terms of real results—a Jewish army, rescued refugees, altered immigration quotas, changes in British policy—they accomplished little.[16]

For Wise, the experiences with both the American Council for Judaism and the Bergson forces only reinforced his belief that solidarity remained the most important item on the American Jewish calendar, and he recalled his experiences during the First World War with the American Jewish Congress. As early as May 1941, Wise had met with Weizmann, Louis Lipsky, and Henry Monsky, president of the 150,000-member fraternal order of B'nai B'rith. Although the Zionist leaders had no specific plans, they encouraged Monsky to sound out a number of organizations, especially the non-Zionist groups, to see if some basis for cooperation could be found. They recalled that the B'nai B'rith had sided with the Zionists in the 1916 Congress fight and sensed that Monsky, deeply affected by the tragedy in Europe, would ultimately accept the Zionist program. They recognized that the B'nai B'rith president had the necessary prestige among non-Zionists to do the job, and also knew that he resented the elitist attitude of the American Jewish Committee, and especially its new president, Judge Joseph M. Proskauer.[17]

Monsky invited some three dozen Jewish organizations to an exploratory meeting in Pittsburgh on January 23 and 24, 1943, to discuss the role American Jewry would play during the after the war. Only the American Jewish Committee and the Jewish Labor Committee, which harbored a large anti-Zionist bloc, refused to attend. The 78 men and women at the gathering quickly decided on the need for a new umbrella agency that could speak for all segments of American Jewry. Wise could hardly have been more pleased with the results, and wrote that the community finally "has come out of the fog of interminable discussion, that it has finally been placed on the road that will produce a commanding democratic leadership able to cope with the vital postwar problems of the Jewish people."[18] Within a few weeks an executive committee for an "American Jewish Assembly" had been formed, and began the laborious preparations for convening a representative, democratically elected convention.

Once again the American Jewish Committee objected, and once again its leadership recognized that the Committee had no choice but to join the new group or be isolated from the majority of American Jewry. Wise and Monsky spent hours negotiating with Proskauer, attempting to convince him that no one wanted to kill the Committee, that the wartime crisis demanded they bury their differences for the common good. Proskauer finally agreed, provided the name of the new organization be changed to American Jewish Conference ("assembly" evidently smacked of dual loyalty) and Wise, in a gesture he would soon regret, agreed that the Zionists would delay discussion of the Palestine issue until a subsequent meeting of the Conference.[19]

The first session of the American Jewish Conference opened solemnly at the Waldorf-Astoria on August 29, 1943. Monsky greeted the 504 delegates with the same Hebrew phrase which Nathan Staus had opened the American Jewish Congress in Philadelphia a quarter-century earlier: *Hineh mah tov u'mah na'im, shevet achim gam ya'chad.* ("Below how good and pleasant it is for brethren to dwell together in unity.") In his remarks, Monsky emphasized the need for common effort, and Wise in his speech echoed this theme. After reviewing the terrible news from Europe, he noted the "solemn and inevitable obiligation this lays upon us, who have become the largest Jewry in history, not only to bind up the wounds but to take counsel with the surviving, that together we may plan the fate of world Jewry."[20]

In order to achieve this solidarity, Monsky and his colleagues committed what proved to be a major blunder. Instead of electing a single person to lead the Conference, they decided upon a praesidium representing all the major groups. A number of delegates wanted to draft Wise as the single president, but the elderly leader declined, claiming he had had enough honors and burdens in his lifetime, and insisting that Monsky's plan be followed. So Wise, together with Proskauer and others, joined the praesidium.[21] There they watched in horror as their carefully worked out plan to preserve at least the facade of unity fell apart.

When Emanuel Neumann learned of the agreement to defer a Palestine resolution until a later session of the Conference, he hastened to Abba Hillel Silver's room; there the Cleveland rabbi dejectedly confirmed the rumor. Neumann pleaded with his longtime friend to insist upon introducing the Palestine resolution which the militant Zionists had written. Finally Silver agreed, and Neumann hurried off to find a way to get Silver speaking time; through a parliamentary maneuver, Neumann arranged for Silver to gain the rostrum under the sponsorship of Wise's own group, the American Jewish Congress.

It was one of Silver's greatest speeches, and he easily carried the delegates with him. Wise and Monsky had failed to recognize how far American Jews had gone in looking to Palestine as the major and perhaps only solution to the Jewish problem. Unity did exist among American Jews, at least on this issue, and by attempting to placate the American Jewish Committee's fear of statehood, they unwittingly bypassed the one point on which the community stood prepared to rally. When Silver read the Biltmore Platform, the assembly spontaneously rose to sing *Hatikvah*; only Judge Proskauer and the other two delegates of the Committee remained seated.[22] When the Committee withdrew from the American Jewish Conference a few months later, if did so to the near universal condemnation of American Jewry.[23]

The conference also marked the beginning of the bitterest and most humiliating fight of Stephen Wise's life. Shortly after Wise's speech at the Conference, in which he had not said a word about Palestine or a Jewish state, he ran into Silver in a hallway at the hotel. The Cleveland rabbi had just learned of the praesidium's decision to defer debate on Palestine, and was furious. In front of several witnesses, he lashed out at Wise, accusing him of betraying his trust as chairman of the Zionist Emergency Committee. "What happened at Biltmore?" Silver shouted. "We finally have a slogan, a battle cry for a Jewish state, and you, who claim to be a Zionist leader, refuse to talk about it!" According to Emanuel Neumann, it was an embarrassing scene not only for Wise but for the onlookers. Silver treated the older man like a schoolboy, and from that moment worked ceaselessly to depose him as head of American Zionism. In Silver's mind, Wise had given up the fight; the old lion could not or would not battle for a Jewish state.[24]

Silver, like Wise, had a brilliant oratorical style, and beyond that gained a reputation as a scholar for several well-received works on Jewish history and thought. Born in Lithuania, he, like Wise, had been brought to the United States at an early age, and had been a Zionist since his youth. After ordination from Hebrew Union College in 1915, he led a congregation in Wheeling, West Virginia for two years before accepting a call from Cleveland's wealthy and prestigious Tifereth Israel, where he remained until his death in 1963. Wise had recognized Silver as a coming young man during the First World War, and had encouraged him to join the Brandeis group.[25] When he heard that Silver had temporized about his Zionism in order to placate the non-Zionist leaders of the Cleveland congregation, he wrote him an admonitory note, but Silver quickly assured him that he had been and would remain a Zionist and a disciple of Achad Ha'am, the intellectual leader of the cultural faction. Over the years, Silver in fact did lead his

Reform congregation into active support of Jewish nationalism, and joined Wise in the small but growing number of Reform rabbis supporting the Zionist cause. Wise readily acknowledged Silver's talents, at one time calling him "the ablest rabbi in America . . . a remarkable youth, only 27, who if God gives him health and strength, will do great things for Israel."[26] Silver walked out with Wise and the other Brandeisians at the 1921 Cleveland convention, and during the following years the two men worked together on Zionist projects, exchanged pulpits, and on several occasions, Silver and his wife even came as Wise's guests to the Lake Placid home. In the 1930s the New York rabbi arranged for Silver to follow him as head of the United Palestine Appeal, and in many ways looked on the younger man as his heir-apparent in American Zionist affairs.

Yet Silver had a rough edge which frequently irritated not only Wise but others as well. Where Wise could maintain cordial relations with those whom he publicly opposed, Silver tended to group people into two camps—allies and enemies. He had a short temper and no patience for fools. He could command intense loyalty among his followers, but many who agreed with him in Zionist struggles could hardly stand him personally. Meyer Weisgal once noted that "next to Wise [Silver] was the greatest orator to come out of American Jewry. But though when addressing the people *en masse* he had the voice of Jacob, in dealing with individuals he had the hands of Esau. He lacked Wise's broad sympathies and his natural liking for people."[27]

Like Wise, Silver could be a tenacious and effective advocate for the causes he believed in, and he brooked no compromise. Jewish unity was all very good, but not if it meant a surrender of basic principles. The tragedy in Europe confirmed for Silver the essential rightness of political Zionism, and even before Biltmore he began demanding that Palestine become a Jewish state. A Republican and a friend of Ohio Senator Robert A. Taft, Silver distrusted Franklin Roosevelt and believed that Wise and other American Jews were being deceived by the president's apparent friendliness. "Put not your trust in princes!" became his rallying cry, and as the war went on he and Wise found themselves increasingly estranged.

Silver recognized his own limits, his intolerance of shoddy administration, and his short temper, and was therefore initially reluctant to take a leading part in the Emergency Committee. But both Wise and Weizmann believed that the energies and abilities of the younger man could not be wasted, and at Wise's suggestion, Weizmann went to Cleveland in the spring of 1943. There he urged Silver to accept the chairmanship of the Committee, which would soon be reorganized into the American Zionist Emergency Council. Silver, aware of the infighting between the WZO and ZOA, agreed to become co-chairman with Wise provided that the WZO recognized the Council as *the* representative agency of American Zionism.[28] Weizmann agreed, even though he had the authority neither to offer Silver the post nor to commit the WZO to this policy.

Neither Wise nor Weizmann recognized that Silver's militancy would make him a natural ally of David Ben-Gurion, and Weizmann in fact had already begun complaining to Wise about criticism leveled against him by American Zionists dissatisfied with his moderate policies. "If we will achieve the Jewish Commonwealth," Weizmann averred, "it will be not be by a mere repetition of slogans, but by hard work, vast expenditures of money and energy and the application of all our intelligence. . . . I regard the phrase [Jewish State] as our *Shem Hamforosh* and as such, it must not be used in vain." Wise defended the British leader against attack, and in doing so made himself appear less militant and more moderate than in fact he was.²⁹

Increasing criticism of Great Britain's Palestine policy, in fact, had begun to worry the Foreign Office, which proposed to the State Department that a wartime ban be enacted to silence public debate on the Holy Land's future. Preparation for an Anglo-American statement to this effect proceeded secretly, and not until July 27 did a harried Wise and other Jewish leaders learn of the proposal. Their immediate protests to the State Department led the American government to postpone announcement, originally scheduled for the 28th, thus giving the Zionists a chance to rally their forces. Wise, speaking for the Emergency Committee, informed the Secretary of State that American Jews were horrified at the thought that their government might move to limit free speech, even in wartime, without first consulting and demonstrating the need for such a drastic measure. In personal visits to congressional leaders, Wise and his colleagues argued vehemently against stifling discussion of Palestine while millions of Jews in Europe were dying. With the element of surprise now gone, the State Department soon backed down.³⁰

Wise, aware of all these matters, desperately needed assistance, and he had looked eagerly for Silver's help. He soon learned that Silver did not want to help him, but insisted instead on full control of the Emergency Council. A bewildered Wise agreed to step down as co-chairman for the sake of the cause, but his associates on the Council refused to let him, some out of regard for him personally and others out of fear or distrust of Silver. The Cleveland rabbi realized that in order to lead American Zionism on the path he wanted, he would not only have to control the Council, but in addition take over the Zionist Organization of America, which constituted the chief bulwark of the Council, and he announced that he would seek the ZOA presidency. Upon learning of this, Wise penned an angry letter to Silver accusing him of breaking his word that there would be full communication and consultation between them. As for the ZOA, Wise declared that he could not conceive "of any greater hurt coming to the Zionist movement at this time . . . . You know well how we are battling together in order to avert a great peril.'' To Nahum Goldmann, Wise said: "I shall show my fellow-Zionists now that I am not to be shelved; I am not to be displaced; that I will exert my authority as chairman.''[31] The threat of a full-scale fight, one Silver recognized he would probably not win, led him to accept a compromise. He agreed to back Israel Goldstein, then an ally of Wise, for the ZOA presidency, and in turn he would receive the chairmanship of the Emergency Council's executive committee, which would make him the dominant figure on the Council.[32] If Wise thought the issue now settled, he was sadly mistaken.

The real battle began with efforts to secure a congressional resolution calling for recision of the 1939 White Paper. Several congressmen had approached Jewish leaders and indicated their willingness to support such a statement, provided the Zionist leadership wanted it and would fight for it. While nearly everyone on the Council agreed that a resolution, if passed, would be useful, Wise and others argued that that would be of little help unless the proper groundwork could be established and public opinion mobilized behind the Zionists; nothing could be worse than to have the question raised and then fail to pass. While Silver agreed that preparation would be necessary, he nonetheless wanted to push ahead; the policy of the council, he declared, would be an "active and vigorous attack against the White Paper.'' The time for moderation, he implied, had passed.[33] The Council then began a campaign for the resolution, but immediately encountered opposition from both the State and the War Departments. In March 1944 military leaders managed to kill the proposal in committee, claiming it would be detrimental to the war effort. As a result, a number of Zionist leaders asked Silver to tone down his campaign against British policy, especially in a presidential election year. Silver reacted angrily, declaring that quiet diplomacy could not be counted upon to produce concrete results.[34]

In fact, both Wise and Silver wanted the resolution, but differed on how to get it. Wise relied upon Roosevelt's goodwill, and utilized his contacts in the Democratic Party to secure a plank favoring Zionist aims in Palestine in the 1944 platform. The Republicans then adopted a similar plank, and that fall Silver decided to test the sincerity of Roosevelt and the Democratic-controlled Congress by asking the legislators to adopt a resolution in favor of a Jewish homeland. Senators Taft and Wagner introduced the proposal in November, but although the War Department no longer objected on military grounds, complications developed in the Foreign Relations Committee. Both Roosevelt and Secretary of State Stettinius informed the Committee that the time was still not ripe.

Wise, upon learning of this, wired Stettinius that while the Emergency Council naturally wanted the resolution, "if, however, Chief and you should still feel that some postponement [is necessary]. . . I together with many associates do not want to have actions taken contrary to your and President's recommendation." Silver, on the other hand, saw the administration's temporizing as one more example of Roosevelt's duplicity, and of Wise's foolishness in still trusting princes. He publicly denounced the failure of the Democrats to live up to their campaign promise, and Wise privately complained that Silver's outburst had set the cause of Jewish nationalism back for years.[35]

Silver had assumed that the Council reorganization would allow American Zionists to coordinate their efforts under a single leadership, but he soon discovered that the various organizations continued to go their separate ways. Congressman Sol Bloom complained about the large number of Jewish delegations descending upon Washington, each claiming to speak in the name of American Jewry.[36] To Silver the greatest irritant in this area was Nahum Goldmann, who served in Washington as both Weizmann's representative from the WZO and as Wise's lieutenant for the World Jewish Congress. Goldmann had little use for Silver, and by his nature could never take orders. He played a lone hand in Washington, often putting forth his ideas to government officials as if they were the official statements of the Zionist movement. Silver wanted the Goldmann operation closed, because he found it continuously interfering with his direction of Council lobbying in the Capitol. Goldmann acted as if he were the Jewish Agency incarnate, Silver complained, but "nobody has authorized him to speak on those basic Zionist policies, and his actions and opinions are subject to no quick review by the parent body."[37] In late August 1944 Goldmann, who throughout maintained close communications with Wise, saw Secretary of State Edward Stettinius without first consulting Silver, and the Cleveland rabbi exploded. Goldmann had created a situation in which it was impossible for the Emergency Council to function effectively, Silver announced, and then submitted his resignation to the Council. After a round of trans-Atlantic letters and repeated apologies from Goldmann, Silver withdrew his resignation and resumed his post.[38] Throughout this episode, Wise watched with silent amusement.

Large issues were involved, and either Weizmann or Wise could have broken this impasse by ordering Goldmann to stop his completely unpredictable brand of personal diplomacy. But Weizmann, seeing his power base in Europe and Palestine erode, hoped to preserve some control over the American movement despite the rise of the Silver group. His strength had always been in diplomacy, and many considered him the era's greatest emissary of the Jewish people to the non-Jewish world. If he could, through Goldmann, maintain his links with government leaders, then in the end they would deal with him, and not Silver, as *the* head of the Zionist movement. Similarly, the aging Wise had little love for a new leadership that rejected his advice and scorned his influence with the Roosevelt administration. Goldmann served him as well as Weizmann in keeping his contacts with the government current; despite Silver's ascendency on the Council, many government officers continued to regard Wise as the leader of American Jewry.

The "reconciliation" between Silver and Goldman hardly deserved the title. Goldmann "consulted" with Silver for a few weeks, and then kept only his own counsel. Wise, who still believed that the Roosevelt administration would be the best hope for the Zionists in the postwar settlement, actively campaigned for the president in 1944, much to the chagrin of Silver, who felt that the Zionists should lobby both parties, and had gotten the Emergency Council to adopt a resolution of neutrality in the presidential election. At a Council meeting Silver argued that "it was not proper for a Zionist spokesman appearing on Zionist business to give the impression that the whole Zionist movement was tied to the Democratic Party."[39] To add insult to injury, Wise arranged for the president to issue a statement reaffirming his support of Zionist goals, and he did not inform Silver of the much-publicized meeting until afterward. Then, when Silver wanted to test Roosevelt's sincerity after the 1944 election by reviving the congressional resolution against the White Paper, he found Wise working to block him. An anguished Sol Bloom complained that he did not know what to do: One moment Rabbi Silver tells him to go ahead with the hearings, and the next Rabbi Wise tells him to delay. Within the Emergency Council friction became intolerable, with every meeting a battle as advocates of the two men traded charges of "dictatorship" and "cowardice." Silver grew more and more secretive, refusing to discuss matters with any but his most trusted associates, and on several occasions acted as high-handedly as he had accused Goldmann of doing. The situation had gotten completely out of hand, and for the sake of Zion, had to be resolved.[40]

Wise made the first move on December 12, 1944, resigning as chairman of the Council in protest against Silver's alleged dictatorship and insulting manner. At one time, Wise complained, Silver had called him "senile," and he told his wife that "working for a great people is to work side by side with the littlest men." After Wise defended his conduct before the Council, it refused to accept his resignation, a clearcut vote of confidence in him as well as a slap at Silver. Then on December 28, Wise decided to force the issue, and again tendered his resignation. Silver followed suit, and after a lengthy meeting, the Council accepted the withdrawal of both men. Pausing just long enough to express its appreciation to Silver for his "devoted service to the cause," the Council immediately elected Wise as sole chairman and reorganized its structure to give him complete control of the Council and its activities.[41]

Silver retired to Cleveland, sorry that against his better judgment he had ever agreed to join the Council. Left to himself, he probably would not have tried to regain control of the American Zionist apparatus. But the uproar in the Jewish press and the activities of his friends soon convinced him that while he had been outvoted on the Council, he had the support of the lay leadership and of the masses. The editorials in the Jewish papers for the most part did not attack Wise as much as they endorsed Silver's militancy. The *Jewish Morning Journal*, for example, declared: "At this moment we cannot afford to indicate lack of confidence in an outspoken Zionist policy—even when such a policy encounters difficulty," while *Der Tag* insisted that "only an aggressive, dynamic policy can lead to success, and Rabbi Silver is clearly the man to be entrusted with such a policy." Philip Slomovitz, an old friend and ally of Wise, nonetheless editorialized in the Detroit *Jewish News* that Silver "is a consistent and vigorous fighter for justice for Jewry and Palestine, and the Zionist constituency will surely reject any plan to eliminate him from leadership."[42]

Heartened by this response, the pro-Silver faction began its campaign. Two of the Cleveland rabbi's lieutenants, Harry L. Shapiro and Harold P. Manson, resigned from the Emergency Council, and together with Emanuel Neumann and Abraham Tulin created the American Zionist Policy Committee to lobby the rank and file for Silver's return. Their statements not only defended Silver, but included strong and often bitter attacks against Wise, whom they portrayed as the embodiment of timidity and *shtadlaniuth* in American affairs. Wise refused to defend himself, preferring, as he said, for his record and his colleagues on the Council to rebut the charges. At a meeting of the ZOA administrative committee on January 7, 1945, Israel Goldstein, Morris Rothenberg, James Heller, and Louis Levinthal defended Wise, while Neumann and Jacob Fishman presented the Silver case. At one point Wise interrupted Neumann to charge him with carrying on a "sewerage campaign." Neumann slowly turned, offered the opinion that Wise was taking advantage of his years, and then left the platform amidst much applause. But when the vote came calling for Silver's return, it lost by a better than two-to-one margin.[43]

Wise and his backers, aware that the situation had deteriorated beyond saving, began searching for alternatives. While he was ready to resign, neither Wise nor his colleagues wanted Silver in power. As the controversy dragged on through the early months of 1945, the political activities of the Emergency Council ground to a near standstill; only the publication of pro-Palestine propaganda, by now routinized and handled by staff members, gave the organization any semblance of life. Members of the WZO tried to find some solution, only to realize that room for compromise no longer existed. Aside from policy differences, questions of personality beclouded the issue.[44]

The pro-Silver Policy Committee worked feverishly generating support for the Cleveland rabbi through a steady stream of newspaper articles, speeches, and testimonial dinners, with an increasingly personal criticism of Wise. Ostensibly, the Policy committee aimed at winning over the ZOA, the key to power in the American Zionist movement; in fact, it had set itself up as a rival to the Emergency Council. Chaim Weizmann arrived in the United States in April 1945, and found the American Zionists split into bitterly opposed factions, and his efforts at peacemaking yielded only a growing criticism of his own moderate policies. When Hayim Greenberg, an old friend of Wise's and the head of the American Labor Zionists, resigned from the Emergency Council on June 15, Wise recognized that his coalition could no longer survive. Accepting the inevitable, he appointed a committee to negotiate the terms of surrender.

Although the final plan retained Wise as titular co-chairman, Silver had all the power. He controlled appointments to the executive committee, which he chaired, and a majority of the officers as well as key staff members came from among the Silver supporters. At a meeting on July 12, both Silver and Wise listened in silence as the Emergency Council ratified the peace plan.[45] From that moment on, Abba Hillel Silver led American Zionism, and no one could deny that his brilliance and his militancy turned American Jewry into a potent ally in the struggle to secure a Jewish state. While Wise would still have contributions to make to the cause he had championed for nearly five decades, his star had set.

Wise had devoted much of his adult life to the Zionist cause; no one in the Jewish community doubted his love of the Jewish people, his anguish over the Holocaust, or his willingness to fight for a Jewish state. Men and women who worked with Wise recalled his greatness of spirit, his total commitment to Zionism and to Judaism. But as Israel Goldstein, who despite his longtime friendship with Wise eventually backed Silver, explained: "I felt that he was taken in, that out of the goodness of his heart he was taken in by Roosevelt. . . . Wise had in him enough of that beautiful quality of trusting to be at times deluded and deceived."[46]

Wise, like Chaim Weizmann in England, had become too identified with an administration which while proclaiming friendship for Jews did nothing to save them. To the Zionist rank and file, Silver projected a militancy that gave hope for action. It was less a case of rejecting Wise than of electing a different strategy, one which they prayed would somehow redeem both Zion and the Jewish people. In all movements, a time comes when one generation of leaders must give way to the next. With this Wise did not argue, and in fact had anticipated that Silver would one day take his place. He never expected nor did he deserve a transition so bitter and so humiliating.

24

Shehechyanu

The end of the war in Europe brought American Jews a host of problems. As Allied armies liberated the death camps, the stumbling, haggard ghosts of Bergen-Belsen and Auschwitz spoke not only to the conscience of the free world but to the collective social will of American Jewry, which immediately undertook the physical and psychological rebuilding of this pitifully small remnant saved from the ovens. For the Zionists, the time of waiting had ended; Great Britain must now live up to the promise of the Balfour Declaration or give up the mandate and allow the Jewish people freedom to create their own homeland. To do all this, to breathe new life and hope into the Jewish refugees in Europe and achieve the goals of the Biltmore Program, American Jewry entered the political arena as it had never done before, but it was a strangely new arena with many of the old and familiar assumptions suddenly swept away by the death of Franklin D. Roosevelt in April 1945. Now Harry S. Truman sat in the White House, and the policies he would adopt presented unanticipated challenges to the community.

Wise had met with Roosevelt shortly after the president's return from the Yalta Conference. On the trip back, the presidential party had detoured to Cairo so Roosevelt could meet with King Ibn Sa'ud of Arabia, and in his speech to Congress on March 1, 1945, he declared: "I learned more about the whole problem, the Moslem problem, the Jewish problem, by talking with Ibn Sa'ud for five minutes than I could have learned in an exchange of two or three dozen letters." The statement brought a storm of protest from Jewish spokesmen, and two weeks later the president tried to reassure Wise that he still favored the Zionist demands. "I have had a failure," he told the New York rabbi. "The one failure of my mission was Ibn Sa'ud. Everything went well, but not that, and I arranged the whole meeting for the sake of your cause. . . . I have never so completely failed to make an impact upon a man's mind as in his case." After Roosevelt's death Wise continued to defend him as a great and true friend of the Jewish people, downplaying the

Ibn Sa'ud episode with the explanation that the president had been misled by "some supersubtle counselors in the State Department."[1]

Roosevelt's successor, Harry S Truman of Missouri, was relatively unknown to most American Jews, including Wise. As a senator, Truman had, like many other politicians, been willing to sign his name to pro-Zionist statements, but the new chief executive had never been closely involved with the Jewish leadership. Meyer Weisgal reported that what little contact the Zionists had had with Truman had been friendly, but they gave no hint of the new administration's policies. Wise wrote to Truman immediately upon learning of Roosevelt's death, expressing his faith in the new president's "will and capacity greatly to serve our country," and a week later traveled to Washington to meet Truman at the White House.[2] Although Secretary of State Stettinius had sent over a copious file on Jewish affairs, including Roosevelt's various statement on Palestine, Truman evidently did not have the chance to read through it carefully, and he failed to realize how contradictory Roosevelt's comments had been. With unconscious irony Truman promised to carry out Roosevelt's policy, and said he would do everything he could to fulfill the purpose of the Balfour Declaration. A delighted Wise told reporters that he fully expected the new president to support Zionist goals.[3]

But while Truman would eventually carry out this promise to help Jews establish a homeland in Palestine, in his first months in office he allowed himself to be guided by the State Department, whose officials had no desire to aid the Zionists. Roosevelt had told Wise that he hoped to see the Jewish Agency officially invited to the United Nations Peace Conference scheduled in San Francisco for May 1945. Wise informed both Truman and Stettinius of this promise, but the Secretary of State resisted the suggestion, declaring that such issues as Palestine would have to await resolution until the formal organization of the United Nations.[4] Despite Stettinius's assurances that only procedural matters would be on the San Francisco agenda, Wise and other Jewish leaders knew better. The structure the U.N. adopted, the obligations it assumed from the defunct League of Nations, as well as the presence of several Arab nations at the conference, could well determine how the new agency would act in the future on Zionist proposals. Moreover, with the war in Europe nearly over, it would be disingenuous to claim that no substantive measures were to be discussed.

Wise did not want to go to San Francisco. His poor health as well as the strain of the Silver fight left him unenthusiastic about the arduous cross-country trip. He also suspected that the conference would be inundated with far too many Jewish leaders, each clamoring to be heard by the press and the delegates, giving out daily statements contradicting one another, and in general getting in each other's way.[5] He agreed to address a mass rally in New York sponsored by the American Jewish Congress on the eve of the

United Nations gathering, but his fellow Zionists demanded that as head of the Emergency Council he go to California. Only he had the prestige to gain audience with many of the foreign dignitaries, they argued, and despite attacks from the Silver faction, he still spoke as the voice of American Zionism. Reluctantly, he and Louise boarded the train, and when he arrived at the conference, found his worst fears confirmed. Representatives of countless Jewish organizations milled around the hotel lobbies and conference rooms, while many of the foreign diplomats apparently had little idea of how much Jews had suffered during the war nor of Zionist hopes for Palestine. There were several bitter confrontations, especially with Rabbi Herbert Goldstein and with Judge Proskauer, as Wise labored in vain to impose some unity among the Jewish groups. Although Eliahu Elath, representing the Jewish Agency, saw Wise as the dominant Jewish figure at the conference, battling strenuously for the Zionist cause, the overall influence of the Jewish delegates remained minimal, a result of the factionalism that often made it appear more important to belittle one another than to unite in common cause.[6]

The internal conflict at San Francisco reflected the confusion within American Jewry about the future of Palestine and the related question of Jewish survivors. For the Zionists, emigration to Palestine constituted the only acceptable answer, but the non-Zionist groups, especially the American Jewish Committee and the Joint Distribution Committee, wanted to explore other options, including resettlement in Europe or, if that proved unfeasible, emigration to the United States or to Latin America. Wise did not oppose these ideas, provided the displaced person could exercise free choice in where they wanted to go. He vehemently attacked the proposal of forcing Jews to resettle in Germany or Poland, and while acknowledging that new lives could be built in Latin American insisted that the best hope was Palestine. If the Joint Distribution Committee refused to aid the survivors in going to Palestine, then the Zionists should withdraw from the United Jewish Appeal and run a separate campaign.[7]

Despite the charges of timidity made against Wise by the Silver faction, his public statements in the fall of 1945 were often closer to the ideas of David Ben-Gurion and the militants than to those of Weizmann and the moderates. The prospect of armed conflict between the *yishuv* and England still appalled him, but he insisted on the right of Jewish settlers to arm themselves in defense against Arab raids, and to use those weapons in the aid of Jews seeking to enter Palestine.[8] Wise's patience with Great Britain was nearly exhausted by this point, and he welcomed Truman's call to admit 100,000 displaced persons into Palestine immediately. The British response to the president's proposal, to set up still another commission of inquiry, horrified him and he charged the Labour government with trying to "enmesh the United States in the toils of British policy and to make this country a partner of British betrayal.'''⁹ Truman, however, had little choice but to agree to the Anglo-American Committee. He recognized that the British were stalling, but believed that unless he went along with the investigation he would have no leverage to push his plan for getting 100,000 refugees into Palestine.

Nearly all Zionist leaders opposed the Anglo-American Committee, for they had seen too many royal inquiries in the past turn into attacks on Zionism and a subsequent whittling away of the Balfour promise. At first, they seriously considered boycotting the proceedings, but then realized that this would only leave the field open to Arab spokesmen and anti-Zionists. So when the Committee opened hearings in Washington in January 1946, Wise agreed to testify. He consulted with Milton Handler and Abe Tulin over the best approach, and agreed with them that an attack on past British perfidies would not help the Zionist cause. On January 8, 1946, Wise took the chair and set out to emphasize that only a Jewish state would alleviate the agony of those who had survived the Holocaust. For centuries Jews had been homeless, and he detailed how throughout that long period of trial and suffering, the Jewish people had held firm to their love of Zion. "The Christian world, and I include England, of course, in the Christian world, suffered six million of the people of Jesus of Nazareth to die in a most horrible manner," he concluded. "The Christian world owes the Jews some reparation.''¹⁰

One reporter wrote that by the time Wise finished, he could discern tears in the eyes of several Committee members, and he described Wise "with his grey mane and strong worn face [as] an aged lion, rousing himself for a heavy effort." Each member of the Committee rose to shake his hand and thank him for his presentation, and an elderly Orthodox rabbi called out that Wise's words were *kiddush ha-Shem*, a sanctification of the Holy Name. Eliahu Elath told him that "Your seventy years were a preparation for this hour," but his greatest joy came when his grandson, Stephen Wise Tulin, who had skipped school to hear him, came up to give him a hug.¹¹

Two days later the old lion showed he could still roar. Seated in the hearing room, he listened in growing anger as Lessing J. Rosenwald, head of the American Council for Judaism, declared that Jews did not want any special privileges or separate state, and compared Zionism to "the Hitlerian concept that the Jews are a race or nation." At this point Wise could no longer control himself, and he took the floor to reprimand Judge Joseph C. Hutcheson, the American co-chairman, for appearing to agree with Rosenwald, shaking an admonitary finger at him, he shouted that "your courtesy to the preceding witness does not excuse his defamation of the dead." He then read passages written by Louis Brandeis years earlier, especially the phrase that "loyalty to America demands that each American Jew becomes a Zionist . . . Let no one imagine that Zionism is inconsistent with American patriotism.'' Wise characterized Rosenwald's remarks as defaming men such as Brandeis, Cardozo, and Mack, as well as casting doubt on the patriotism of living Zionists such as himself or Justice Felix Frankfurter. Hutcheson retorted that he had known Justice Brandeis and had the greatest respect for his opinions, but did not necessarily agree with all of them, and he reminded Wise that he needed no guidance in the art of respecting differing opinions.[12]

Wise's presentation was probably the best of the Zionist testimony which the Committee heard in the United States, and it helped set the stage for subsequent hearings in London and Palestine, as well as for the visits of individual members to the death camps and internment centers. In the end, much to the Attlee government's anger, the Committee brought in a unanimous report endorsing Truman's 100,000 proposal and calling for the establishment of Jewish and Arab states in Palestine. The British rejection of the report eventually worked to the Zionists' benefit, for it annoyed Truman and led to the dumping of the Palestinian problem in the lap of the United Nations. But even as the Committee pursued its investigation, Wise astounded and outraged many of his fellow Zionists by coming out in favor of American aid to Great Britain.

Like most of the shattered nations of Europe, England looked to America for financial assistance in rebuilding its economy. Before the United States rationalized its aid program through the Marshall Plan, it treated each country's application on an individual basis. When Great Britain applied for a loan of $3.75 billion, some Zionist leaders saw a chance to pressure the English into agreeing, at the least, to admit 100,000 refugees into Palestine. Several other groups, particularly Irish–Americans and isolationists, wanted to kill the loan outright, and for several months stalled the enabling bill in Congress. The Zionists by themselves would not have been able to defeat the measure, but their oppositon joined with that of other factions could possibly succeed. In essence, the Zionists hoped to force His Majesty's Government to open Palestine or lose the loan. In a speech in June 1946, Abba Hillel Silver declared that ''in view of the shocking record of broken pledges . . . American citizens have the right to turn to their representatives . . . and inquire whether the Government of the United States can afford to make a loan to a government whose pledged word seems to be worthless. They should also inquire whether American money, including that of Jewish citizens of the United States . . . should be used to back up a government whose Foreign Secretary has repeatedly given evidence of a virulent anti-Jewish bias.'' The Zionist Emergency Council, because of opposition by the moderate faction, never came out publicly against the loan, but it did agree to work through congressional contacts to delay the bill until the English admitted the refugees.[13]

Wise and other American Jews, however, refused to tie British performance in Palestine to the loan application. Wise drew a sharp distinction between His Majesty's Government, which he detested, and the British people, whom he greatly admired.[14] Golda Meir later expressed similar sentiments when she wrote that "despite the long, stormy, and often terrible conflict between us and the British . . . we Israelis still hold the British people in great and truly affectionate esteem . . . Jews have never forgotten the lonely British stand against the Nazis."[15] Wise had adhered to this view throughout the years when he had been sharply critical of British policy in Palestine, and now believed that innocent people who had shown great bravery ought not to be punished for the deceit of their leaders. In the April 1946 issue of *Opinion* he publicly endorsed the British loan. Even as he damned Britain for failing to live up to its promise, he argued that to deny the loan would be wrong, and "a great wong will not condone another wrong. Wrong is wrong, and if the general denial of the loan to Britain is wrong to the British people and to our own Country, we as loyal American Jews have no right to insist upon that." On July 9 Wise released a message he had sent to Congressman Sol Bloom favoring the loan, which at the White House's request was read into the *Congressional Record.*[16]

Many Zionist leaders, especially Abba Hillel Silver, were furious, for they had viewed the loan as practically the only club they had to force the Attlee government to allow Jews to leave the stinking internment centers and join the *yishuv.* Moreover, British action during this time hardly showed any sensitivity to either the Jews in the DP camps or to public opinion. On June 19, 1946, the "Black Sabbath," British troops in Palestine launched a nationwide search for arms and arrested dozens of Jews, including nearly all the leaders of the *yishuv.* The Attlee government could not even recognize its friends, and when Wise applied for a visa in order to visit Palestine and examine conditions there, the Colonial Office turned him down.

The Emergency Council had decided that in light of the disturbances in Palestine, American Zionists needed firsthand information on the physcial and mental condition of the *yishuv.* Originally Wise, Louis Lipsky, Silver and Nahum Goldmann were to go, journeying on to the Holy Land after a meeting of the Zionist Executive in Paris, but on reconsideration it appeared unwise to have all four men out of the country at the same time. Wise and Lipsky were then delegated, and later Goldmann decided to attend the Paris meeting as well. Wise's secretary routinely called the British Embassy to request a visa for Palestine, and was told that no more visas to that country would be issued. The Americans immediately condemned the British action, and demanded to know what the mandatory power was trying to hide.[17] To add to this ludicrous situation, less than a week after denying Wise the visa, the Crown named Louise Wise as Honorary Member of the Order of the British Empire in recognition of her work as head of the Congress Houses, which had sheltered thousands of British troops during the war. In a dignified letter to Lord Inverchapel, the British ambassador to the United States, Louise rejected the honor, declaring that she could not with self-respect accept an award from a government that had so shamelessly broken its sacred word.[18]

The meeting of the Zionist Executive in Paris opened in a gloomy atmosphere with Palestine under martial law, many of the *yishuv's* leaders in Atlit prison, and the survivors of the Holocaust still languishing in refugee camps over a year after the defeat of Germany. Zionist leaders wondered if perhaps they should have accepted the partition proposal a decade earlier, and over Wise's objections, agreed to approach His Majesty's Government with an offer to accept a smaller Jewish state providing 100,000 refugees were admitted into Palestine immediately. Wise quoted Brandeis's dictum that "what you renounce, you can never regain. What is taken from you, you may regain." But Wise also toured the detention centers, and realized that some place had to be found for these tragic souls. Much as he abhorred the idea of truncating Palestine even more, at least there would be a new home for the displaced persons. Together with Berl Locker and Nahum Goldmann, Wise traveled to London for a fruitless meeting with Foreign Secretary Ernest Bevin. Afterward, the Foreign Office announced that it would convene still one more conference of Jews and Arabs to try to find a solution to the Palestine problem.[19]

The question of attending this conference became the crucial question at the 1946 Zionist Congress which met that winter in Basle. In many ways a meaningless issue, since no one expected the conference to do anything, it served as the focal point of the militant attack on Chaim Weizmann and, to a lesser degree, on Wise. Weizmann, ever willing to place his hope in Britain, called for the Zionists to attend the conference and work for partition. Wise, still unhappy over the division plan, nonetheless backed Weizmann and declared his willingness to abide by the Paris decision of the executive. Silver, who had not attended the meeting, condemned the entire idea of partition, and demanded that the Zionists boycott the London conference, while Ben-Gurion, tired of Weizmann's pro-British leanings, called upon the WZO to endorse a militant policy. Ben-Gurion found strong support for his position among American Zionists. Silver, firmly in control of the Emergency Council, now headed the ZOA as well, and the pages of the *New Palestine* and the minutes of the Council clearly reflected a newly aroused militancy.[20]

Because of the complicated electoral procedures, Wise and some of the more moderate Americans could not be denied seats in the Congress. Beyond that, Wise and Nahum Goldmann still had access to government officials, many of whom refused to talk to Silver because of his attacks on the administration. But Wise's efforts to have the Council enlist the support of the Truman administration to advance the partition proposal ran into the stone wall of Silver's opposition,[21] and there is no doubt that Silver read the situation correctly. There was little the American government could do so long as Bevin remained committed to solving the Palestine muddle by himself. For the Zionists to ask Truman for help would only expose their own weaknesses and internal divisions. Beyond that, Silver enraged Wise by blessing several front committees organized by his lieutenants which attacked the Democrats in that fall's election. So alienated did Wise feel from the leadership that for the first time in years he refused to attend the annual convention of the ZOA.[22]

With a strong sense of foreboding, Wise left for Europe at the beginning of December, aware that representatives of Silver had already met with Ben-Gurion and Moshe Sneh to map out their strategy. It turned out to be "the worst Congress" Wise ever attended, with the militants mercilessly forcing their will on every issue.[23] Supporters of Wise wanted the WZO to at least recognize his decades of service to the cause, and Hadassah proposed that Wise, now 72 years old, be elected chairman of the Actions Committee, a purely honorary position. Rose Halprin went to see Silver and said "Look, your star is rising; Dr. Wise's is waning. Be generous and let us elect him to this office." Silver angrily snapped out a "No!" and turned on his heel.[24]

But if the leadership rejected Wise, the survivors of the concentration camps still held his name dear. During the Congress, a meeting was arranged at which some of the DPs told of their experiences. A small group of delegates, including Wise and Joachim Prinz (whom Wise had brought over from Germany before the war), gathered in an unpretentious back room and heard of the various journeys through hell. One of the refugees, a young red-headed youth, used the word "stephanim," and sensing that many of his listeners did not understand, explained: "You must know that when we spoke of America we spoke of 'Stephania,' and when we spoke of dollars we spoke of 'stephanim.' " In the language of the concentration camps, America had been identified with Stephen Wise. The aging rabbi covered his face with his hands to hide his tears, and whispered to Prinz, "This I do not deserve."[25]

Wise found the last days of the Congress intolerable, as the opposition humiliated Weizmann and prevented his re-election as president of the WZO. On the controversial London conference, the delegates denounced the meeting but left it up to the new Executive whether or not to attend. Wise left Basle before the Congress adjourned, and learned by mail that he had been elected senior vice-president of the Actions Committee, a meaningless post which he promptly declined.[26] A few days later, in a gesture reminiscent of 1921, Wise resigned from all his Zionist offices, refusing, as he told reporters, to "substitute the Zionism of the present imperilling regime of the Zionist Organization of America for the Zionism of Weizmann, Brandeis, Nordau and Herzl." He conceded the right of the Congress to chose by majorty vote the course advocated by Silver and Ben-Gurion, but there were important moral issues at stake, and he could not hold office in an organization he believed had betrayed the cause of Zion. In an echo of Brandeis a quarter-century earlier, he told Eliahu Elath that he would never leave the movement, but would continue to work for Palestine as best he could.[27]

The Silver group immediately attacked him for sowing dissension in the movement, and some commentators saw the gesture as the petty reaction of a loser.[28] But at the age of 72, Wise would not have reacted as he did to the Basle Congress if it were just a political defeat; he had endured worse losses in his life. Rather, he saw the Zionist movement taking on a new tone, one that was not merely militant—that he could have accepted—but, in his eyes, venal as well. Silver may have read the new realities better than Wise, but his authoritarian attitudes and dictatorial demands affronted Wise's lifelong belief that for Zionism to be worthwhile it had to be democratic. The fellowship he had found in fifty years of Zionist activity, the accomplishments, the betrayals—all paled before the prospect of a Zionism every bit as authoritarian in approach as that of the Revisionists whom he detested. How much Wise had the 1921 schism on his mind is difficult to determine, but consciously or not, he patterned his withdrawal on that of Brandeis, and in a manner the great jurist would have understood and approved.

Wise, of course, did not resign from Jewish life, nor did he withdraw from Zionism. In the last years of his life he worked ceaselessly for Palestine and for Jewish rights, but did so primarily through the American and World Jewish Congresses. It was the World Jewish Congress which served as a watchdog for signs of renewed anti-semitism in Europe, and which lobbied the Paris Peace Conference on behalf of Jewish rights. But Zionism remained the great passion of his life, and in 1946 Herzl's dream never seemed closer to fruition.[29] The tragic irony is that in these months Wise stood on the sidelines, ignored by the new leaders of the movement he had helped create.

He did not, of course, remain quiet. Silver could exclude him from power, but could not silence him. Every violation of Jewish rights, every effort to keep Jews out of Palestine, every apparent retreat by the American government, evoked his wrath.[30] Slowly, ever so slowly, a Jewish state in Palestine came into being. Frustrated beyond endurance, Bevin turned the problem over to the United Nations, and in the fall of 1947 the world organization began to debate the Holy Land's future. All the years of joy and sorrow and effort now came to fruition. On November 29, 1947, the General Assembly voted to partition Palestine into Jewish and Arab states, and Wise knew nothing but joy. His former student, Philip Bernstein, who spent the afternoon with Wise, later recalled: ''Gone were the bitterness, the resentment, the enmities. His great heart just overflowed with the spirit of *Shehechyanu* [the traditional prayer of thankfulness]. Although he had not delivered the final and decisive blows, he had helped to prepare the way. And he cared, how much he cared!"[31]

That evening, a jubilant Zionist rally in Madison Square Garden gave Wise a standing ovation, and although he was not scheduled to speak, Wise gladly gave in to demands that he address the crowd. There was still much to do, of course, between the partition vote and the establishment of the State of Israel on May 15, 1948. Still excluded by the leadership, he carried out his promise to work for the cause. When a unknown Goldie Meyerson came to the United States in February 1948 to raise money for the Haganah, Wise traveled with her, introducing her to different audiences and then sitting quietly on the stage as the impassioned young woman raised millions to arm the *yishuv*, each million code-named a "stephen."[32]

When Israel declared its statehood, Wise spoke to still another rally in New York, and proclaimed that at last the infamous 1939 White Paper had been repealed, and Jews could now enter their rightful home. And he recalled that over forty years earlier, as he had walked the streets of Vienna early in the morning, Theodor Herzl had told him that he, Stephen Wise, would live to see the Jewish state. "I am here tonight," he told the crowd, "to thank God that Herzl's prophecy has been fulfilled, that you who are young and I who am no longer young have lived to see, to welcome, and to rejoice in the Jewish state. May God bless it ever more."[33]

25

Final Fruits

Stephen Wise's later years, despite the agony of the Holocaust and the humiliating battle with Silver, were not devoid of accomplishment, nor did they see a diminution of Wise's activities. Instead, he carried almost as many responsibilities as before, both in secular and Jewish affairs, and lived not only to see the State of Israel established, but some of his own projects secured for the future.

One must again recall that through all these years Zionism, despite the vast amount of time it took, constituted but one part of Stephen Wise's life. Wise remained an active and vocal supporter of the economic and social reforms of Franklin Roosevelt and the Democrats on the national scene and of Fiorello LaGuardia in New York. His endorsement of the Roosevelt administration derived not from his perceptions as a Jew but as an American. For all the attacks on him as a political rabbi, Wise never called upon Jews to vote as Jews; time and again he warned that in the polling booths Jews had to decide who would do the best job for the country.[1] American Jews, however, needed to remember how much the Democratic Party had done for the Jewish people, dating back to Wilson's endorsement of the Balfour Declaration.

In New York, Wise continued to back LaGuardia and his Fusion ticket, and saw his friend remain in office for twelve years, during which the power of Tammany, if not destroyed, was at least held in check. But whenever the administration did not live up to the high standards which Wise thought proper he did not hesitate to scold LaGuardia in public. The two men had their share of disagreements, but nonetheless maintained their friendship, uniting to fight Tammany and good-naturedly heckling each other when they had nothing better to do.[2]

Other issues that had interested him across the years also received his attention. Wise reacted angrily to any efforts to abridge individual or group rights in the United States the Council Against Intolerance, which he had helped to found and which his son had led, remained active through the war years, and Wise personally spoke out as often as he could in defense of civil rights. The United States could not fight a war against facism abroad, he told the House Labor Committee in 1944, and tolerate injustice and discrimination at home. The country needed a permanent Fair Employment Practices Commission, he argued, because the work of the temporary FEPC "has made millions of Americans feel that our Government is not only fighting for democracy in Yugoslavia but is preparing to battle for democracy at home." Any efforts to whittle away that freedom, Wise argued, either through discrimination against Jews or blacks or by denying organized labor its legitimate rights, posed a threat to the United States as serious as facism.[3] Seven years before the United States Supreme Court ruler school segregation unconstitutional, Wise told Senator Allen J. Ellender of Louisiana that it was wrong for the South to keep black children in separate schools. The Republican 80th Congress, out to undo twelve years of New Deal reform, came in for its share of criticism as well, especially over the Taft–Hartley law, which Wise viewed as the worst antilabor measure since the turn of the century.[4]

Even the sacrosanct halls of academe did not escape Wise's wrath, and he publicly accused his alma mater, Columbia University, of discrimination. In May 1946 Wise filed an application with the New York City Tax Commission to cancel the university's tax exemption. With help from his son-in-law, Shad Polier, Wise introduced a study conducted by the American Jewish Congress covering the years 1920 to 1940, showing a steady decline in the number of Jewish students admitted into the medical school, despite an increase in the number of qualified Jewish applicants. In 1920, the school accepted forty-six Jews; in 1940 it accepted only eight. The university at first denied that it practiced bias, but then under pressure from the State Commission against Discrimination, Columbia agreed to remove all questions relating to race, religion, or nationality from its application and employment forms.[5]

To speak up for reform and against prejudice, to stand for liberal causes, proved more difficult in the postwar years than had been anticipated. One might have thought that after a war against the forces of intolerance and repression, the mood of the country would swing left rather than right. But the threat of Soviet aggression in Europe, as well as the inevitable reaction to twelve years of persistent reform, left many people in the United States leery of liberals and their causes. Wise heard the growing rhetoric of the Cold War with alarm, and called Winston Chruchill's "Iron Curtain" speech in 1947 "one of the most mischievous and hurtful utterances ever made by a person of authority and responsibility." To give in to such ideas, he warned, could only lead to a needless war with Russia. Before the American Jewish Congress in April 1948, he declared "There must not, there shall not, be war between us," and called on the leaders of the United States and Russia to commit themselves to a policy of peace. Perhaps indiscriminately Wise allowed his name to be used by a number of "peace committees" later charged with being communist front groups.[6]

Wise's espousal of liberal causes, his defense of unpopular views, and his attacks on the Cold War did not sit well with many people bent on witchhunting. The red scare which erupted fully in the McCarthy madness of the early fifties began shortly after the war, and Wise would not accept that responsible men and women should be publicly attacked or dismissed from their jobs because they exercised their right of free speech. He condemned the Columbia Broadcasting System for dropping several commentators, including William L. Shirer, because they had offended some ultrapatriotic fanatics. On his seventy-fifth birthday, Wise rose in the pulpit of the Free Synagogue to condemn the Episcopal Bishop of New York for removing the Rev. John Howard Melish, then 74 years old, from the Holy Trinity Church in Brookly where he had ministered for 45 years. Melish, an old friend of Wise and a companion in many reform battles, had refused to fire his son as assistant rector because of accusations that the young man had communist sympathies.[7]

Inevitably, Wise's defense of the unpopular brought down the wrath of the righteous on his head. In October 1947, Rabbi Bejamin Schultz of Temple Emanu-El in Yonkers and a JIR graduate, called Wise a Communist dupe who "consistently encouraged the Communist and pro-Soviet movement in this country by addressing and joining Communist fronts." Wise's criticism of church groups that participated in witch hunts and opposed peace efforts led a group of Catholic professors to condemn Wise for stirring up relgious hatred even while he showed that he lacked true patriotism.[8] Wise, of course, had long made clear his opposition to communism, but in these troubled years a number of people could not distinguish support of liberalism from support of communism. The charges went on for several years after Wise's death, subsiding only with the fading of the McCarthy era.

If anything, Wise's loyalty to the United States constituted the bedrock upon which he built his ministry and his life. To his son he once wrote: "I thank God for America—my parents' and ours and yours! And I have tried to repay my debt to America in part. Anything you and Justine will in the future do is to be a further installment of my indebtness to America."[9] He gloried in the country, its culture and freedom and opportunity, and he often confused European Zionist leaders who could never understand how a Jew could feel so at home anywhere except Palestine. Once during the war Wise and Nahum Goldmann traveled by train to Washington. Goldmann, dozing while Wise read the newspapers, was suddenly awakened by Wise excitedly calling out.

"What's the matter?" Goldmann asked.

"Look, tomorrow night there is going to be a championship boxing match; listen to what the sportswriters say."

"Who the hell cares?" a sleepy Goldmann responded.

"Oh Nahum," Wise laughed. "You may get two American passports and never become a real American."[10]

His love for sports included that most American of pastimes, baseball, and he enjoyed receiving his annual clergy pass from the New York Yankees, to whose games he often took his grandson, Stephen Tulin. He promised the Yankee front office not to forget the team and, "I must frankly add, the Dodgers, in my prayers."[11]

During the dark days of the World War Two, Wise expressed his credo in the pages of *Opinion.* "I am an American," he wrote:[12]

I am doubly an American, because I am foreign-born. It may be that native-born Americans take America for granted. Foreign-born Americans like myself do not take America for granted. We look upon American citizenship as the most precious and sacred of boons. We understand what it is that we have left behind us—of denial of the freedoms of man, and we know what it is that has come to be our high destiny, to be a sharer in American freedom, to be a bearer of American responsiblity, to be a devotee of the American Democracy, to use American freedom not for one's own advantage but for the service of the American Democracy . . . .

I am an American, I thank God that my parents brought me to this country. I thank God that my children and children's children have been born in this country. They have entered into and become sharers in the most precious heritage which can fall to the lot of man, and I have faith that they will prove equal to and worthy of the high opportunities of life which American citizenship affords. They, like me, will give their deepest, truest loyalty to the America which is today, to the greater, freer, nobler America that is to be on the morrow.

He was once taken to task for allegedly saying that he placed his Jewishness before his Americanism, and he vehemently denied the charge. "What I did say," he declared, "was that I was a Jew thousands of years before I became an American. In other words, our Jewishness goes back three thousand years and more, while my Americanism dates from the year after my birth. I was not weighing the relative values of Jewishness and Americanism. There is the most perfect concord between them. My Jewishness strengthens my Americanism; my Americanism deepens my Jewishness."[13] And it was his Americanism that led him to support throughout his life the liberal ideals of democracy whose roots he found in the writings of the bibilical prophets.

His greatest forum to express these ideals remained, as always, the pulpit of the Free Synagogue, and throughout his years Wise remained the rabbi of the Free Synagogue, delivering sermons, officiating at weddings and funerals, and overseeing the affairs of the congregation. Many of Wise's old friends and congregants died during these years, and he insisted on conducting the funeral services. But the congregation did lighten his load considerably. In May 1943 the trustees granted Wise "leave of absence for the duration" so he could devote most of his time to war problems, preaching, if he chose, once a month and on the High Holy Days.[14] The following month Rabbi Edward Klein, a graduate of the Institute, was appointed associate rabbi of the Synagogue, in charge of pulpit, education, and pastoral duties, with Sidney Goldstein continuing to direct the social service department and J.X. Cohen serving as executive director. One of Wise's favorite students, Klein had been in California heading a Hillel group and had returned to New York for a visit. He stopped by to see Wise, and without any preliminaries, Wise told Klein he wanted the younger man to succeed him.[15] Klein assumed his new duties in September 1943, became rabbi of the Free Synagogue upon Wise's death in 1949, and remained in that post until his retirement in 1980.

Wise still cherished his dream of the Free Synagogue having a home of its own, and work had actually begun on such an edifice in early 1941. Architects had prepared plans for a building with a sanctuary, social hall, educational, and administrative offices, and on November 28, 1941, the Building Committee received bids from contractors. With Pearl Harbor, however, all building plans had to be postponed, because the government limited new construction to essential war-related projects.[16] On April 5, 1942, its thirty-fifth anniversary, the Free Synagogue finally dropped Sunday services at Carnegie Hall, and Friday evening worship in the Synagogue House auditorium, which held about a thousand people, became the focus of congregational prayer. With the end of the war, Wise urged the trustees to resume building, but once again difficulties arose owing to postwar shortages of labor and material. At the dinner celebrating the Free Synagogue's fortieth anniversary, a disappointed Wise, while proud of what had been accomplished, could only hope that he would live to see his congregation housed in an appropriate home.[17]

That dream would be denied, but the following year, in honor of his seventy-fourth birthday, the Free Synagogue consecrated the future building's cornerstone, a large block of Jerusalem limestone from the ruins of the Temple Mount which Wise had received from Sir Wyndham Deedes nearly three decades earlier. Governor Herbert Lehman of New York gave the main address, and Rabbi Leo Baeck, president of the World Union for Progressive Judaism and a survivor of Theresiendstadt, called Wise "the revered man who established the Free Synagogue as a home and an inexhaustible well-spring of Jewish life and spirit and hope."[18] The building was completed after its founder's death, and the congregation named it the Stephen Wise Free Synagogue.

Wise did live to see the future of the Jewish Institute of Religion secured through the long-discussed merger with Hebrew Union College. Negotiations, which had begun before the war, took on an added urgency as both the Institute and the College suffered drops of enrollment and income. But Wise, supported by his school's trustees and alumni, refused to accept any arrangement that diluted the original goals of the New York seminary, while Julian Morgenstern, personally opposed to any union that did not leave the College dominant, threw one roadblock after another into the path of merger. In early 1941, when it appeared that most of the details had been worked out, the Cincinnati president demanded that the Institute stop admitting students immediately, although HUC would be free to enroll another class. At a special meeting of JIR trustees on February 26, Dean Henry Slonimsky spoke for the faculty in arguing that merger should only take place if the integrity of the Institute could be assured and a seminary of liberal Judaism remained in New York. To this the trustees agreed, but also decided to continue the discussion.[19]

The pattern of negotiation and withdrawal, seeming agreement and then an unexpected stumbling block, continued for the next several years. Wise declared that he could agree to almost any arrangement provided the merged institution would abandon neither New York nor the principles for which he fought. He met several times with Morgenstern, who appeared more and more reluctant and who apparently was continuing the negotiations only to please his lay trustees.[20] When Morgenstern signed the 1942 Atlantic City statement of the non-Zionist rabbis, Wise wanted to call the whole thing off; there could be no way he would be "yoked" to a man like that, even for one year. By mid-1943, Wise spoke as if the merger had been shelved indefinitely, and he began a new fund-raising campaign to ensure the survival of the JIR. As his seventieth birthday approached, he told people that the best tribute they could pay to him would be to support the Institute. At a dinner at the Waldorf-Astoria marking Wise's birthday, Rabbi Max Maccoby, an Institute graduate, announced the establishment of a $70,000 fund to be presented to the JIR in honor of Wise.[21]

Unfortunately, the money did not materialize, and in the spring of 1945 a million-dollar campaign was initiated to solve the Institute's financial woes. Albert Einstein agreed to serve as honorary chairman, and a professional fund-raising organization was hired. A year later, the campaign had taken in only $60,453, and the solicitation had cost more than half that sum. A number of factors hindered the campaign, among them the enormous UJA drives to help the DPs, but as one commentator noted, it looked as if Wise was running out of steam as well. At one meeting of the faculty, he threw up his hands and said in despair: "Gentlemen, what can I do? The congregations are not supporting me. Our graduates are not as loyal to the school as they should . . . I've reached the end of my tether." As late as October 1945, it appeared that the JIR would neither merge with HUC nor be able to raise a permanent endowment fund large enough to carry it beyond the life of its founder.[22]

Then on October 16, Wise opened his morning mail to discover that the Cincinnati school desired to award him an honorary Doctorate of Divinity. One can imagine his amusement while reading Morgenstern's pompous letter, explaining that the degree was "in recognition of your unique and fruitful service to Jewish causes as president of a sister institution, a great American Jewish leader who for a generation has commanded the respect and affection of the great mass of American Jewry." Sensing that this might signal a breakthrough in the long-stalled negotiations, Wise accepted, and traveled to Cincinnati in December for a special convocation marking the college's seventhieth anniversary. That day HUC awarded eighteen honorary degrees; novelist Thomas Mann, former Treasury Secretary Henry Morgenthau, Jr., Eleanor Roosevelt, philosopher Harry A. Wolfson, and others joined Wise on the platform. When he recieved his award, he told the men and women in the audience that he had no intention of giving a Zionist speech, but with over 150,000 Jews still languishing in the internment camps, he had little else on his mind but the necessity of opening the gates of Palestine. The captive audience, which included many persons indifferent or opposed to Jewish nationalism, stirred uncomfortably, and the editors of *Liberal Judaism* complained that Wise "missed a rare opportunity to cement firm friendships between JIR and HUC." But the citation for his honorary degree specifically acknowleged his role as a "pioneer American Zionist and world Zionist leader," and even for the sake of merger he would not hide one of the essential tenets upon which he had founded the Institute.[23]

The real breakthrough came with the unanimous endorsement of the merger by the Executive Council of the Union of American Hebrew Congregations in 1946, and the retirement of Julian Morgenstern as president in early 1947. The new head, noted archeologist Nelson Glueck, did not oppose Zionism, and Wise had on several occasions helped raise funds for Glueck's expeditions. Glueck immediately offered his hand in friendship to Wise, and expressed his hope that "our two institutions can unite to labor mightily for our single task." At a meeting in Wise's study on May 21, 1946, Glueck assured the JIR leaders that the school's integrity would be preserved, and that it would remain a New York institution. The Institute trustees soon afterward adopted a resolution approving a merger, and appointed a committee to work out the details. Wise still had some doubts, fearing that necessary compromises might endanger the Institute's principles, but the school's financial problems left no choice but to proceed.[24]

In 1948 the union of the two schools, discussed and negotiated for nearly a quarter-century, came to fruition. The trustees issued a statement that[25]

The Hebrew Union College and the Jewish Institute of Religion resolve to unite for the strengthening and advancement of Judaism in America and throughout the world. The right to serve the Jewish people in its entirety (Klal Yisroel), with freedom for faculty and students alike, is axiomatic.

This united institution shall continue to maintain schools in Cincinnati and New York, with Nelson Glueck as president and Stephen S. Wise and Julian Morgenstern as presidents emeriti. Upon this union we invoke the blessing of God.

In June JIR trustees accepted Wise's resignation and named him president emeritus. Earlier in the year Wise had gone to Cincinnati to participate in Glueck's inauguration as president of the college, and in October installed him as head of the Institute in New York. It would be several more years before the two schools became one institution in fact as well as name, but the future of Wise's seminary was now secure.[26]

At the Institute's commencement in 1948, its last as an independent school, Wise spoke movingly to the newly ordained rabbis, perhaps aware that he would not live to see another graduation:[27]

If men ask of you, "Are you a citizen of the State of Israel?" or "Are you a citizen of the American Republic and a teacher of its people?" answer them, "The memories, the traditions, the hopes, the dreams, the sufferings, the sorrows of four thousand years have not sundered me from the blood and the race of the people of Israel. I am one of them. As a citizen I belong wholly to America. America is my country and I have no other. To it I give the utmost of my loyalty, the deepest of my love, the truest of my service."

I have been thinking of new way of translating that phrase I love, the words of the second chapter of the Prophet Ezekial: "Son of man, stand upon thine own feet and I will speak not with thee, but through thee." Remember, you must strengthen the infirm, you must reassure the timid, you must rebuke the cowardly. Remember you are teachers in Israel; you have not only the right to speak frankly, simply, sincerely to those who hear you in your congregations, but you must speak as men to your fellow-Americans of Christian faith. When they deserve your praise, praise them, but when you must speak harshly and bitterly, be not afraid. Sometimes it is more important to utter the clearest disparise of that which is wrong than to speak in terms of praise, even when that praise is deserved.

This be my last word to you if we never meet again. God speak not to you chiefly or alone, but through you to your congregation, to your people, to American Israel. I part with you in sorrow but with limitless hope and with deep affection for you, my dear boys. And I pray that the God of our fathers may bless you, bless you now and always.

The Jewish Institute of Religion may not have been either the best known or the most important of Wise's achievements, but it had a major and lasting impact upon the Reform rabbinate in America. Its small but distinguished faculty included some of the best scholars in the Jewish community, and of the nearly two hundred graduates, a number became outstanding leaders in American Jewish life. Through them, Wise implanted the ideals of social service and communal responsibility based on prophetic Judaism, the belief that *kol Yisroel arevim zeh lazeh,* every Jew is responsible for his fellow Jews and his fellow men. Moreover, the Institute became a focus for anchoring the legitimacy of Jewish nationalism within the principles of Liberal Judaism. And while Wise was not the scholar he occasionally dreamed of being, the affection and respect shown for him by his students, even to this day, undoubtedly mark him as one of the great teachers in American Jewish life. The effort to build and sustain the Institute had been great, but so was the satisfaction it afforded him.

26

At Last to Rest

As America passed through the war years, longtime congregants and associates still found Stephen Wise a master of the pulpit and often energetic, but they also noticed that he now tired more easily and the slight stoop in his shoulders became more pronounced. Those who looked closely could also see lines of pain and sorrow etched in his face, yet few people outside his family and circle of friends realized how sick he was or how much agony he endured from the ravages of illness and old age. The work continued apace in the Congress, the Free Synagogue, the Institute, and in Zionism; he still wrote every editorial in *Opinion*, and his voice still thundered out whenever he discerned injustice. He remained to the end a center of controversy, determined to go out not as a lamb, but as the lion he had always been.

As much as possible, he made light of his afflictions. When he had to have several of his teeth removed, he joked with Julian Mack that he worried about trying to preach with the replacements. He recalled William Jennings Bryan telling him years earlier: "Wise, never let them take your teeth out and replace them with store teeth. Sometimes when I am in the midst of my greatest perorations, my store teeth begin to rattle and ruin the performance." His doctors urged him to rest, put him in a brace to ease the pain in his back, but although at time illness forced him to bed, he kept up his usual schedule. Once when he could hardly walk, he allowed Louise to pack him off to Lake Placid for a month, and despite protests about all the work he had to do, he enjoyed sitting on the front porch reading, deriving special enjoyment from Carl Sandburg's *Lincoln*.[1] His blood disease grew progressively worse, and the X-ray treatments more painful and debilitating. His spleen was swollen to three times its normal size, and a double hernia could not be operated upon because of the danger of uncontrolled bleeding. "Up to fifty or sixty," he remarked rather ruefully, "it is rather good to have a body. But after that we should be permitted to walk around or move about without the encumberance of physical frame." He feared death less than the thought that he would not be able to complete his work. On the fiftieth anniversary of his graduation from Columbia, he had, as he told Holmes, "a weepy day. . . . So much to do; so little done."[2]

But if he suffered, he saw others suffering even more, and the whole purpose of his ministry had been to bring comfort to those in need. When an old Zionist friend, Joseph Barondess, died penniless, it was Wise who put together a fund to allow his widow to live free from want. He traveled to Holyoke, Massachusetts, in the dead of winter to keep a lecture engagement, and learned that the elderly father of his host had fallen and broken his hip. At the end of the speech, he cut short the question period saying: "I'm sorry I cannot take any more questions. I must visit a sick friend in the hospital before I leave your city." Even when he took a short vacation in Florida during the war, he insisted on visiting a military hospital to talk to the wounded soldiers. While on that trip, he learned that Justine and Shad's six-month-old son, Michael, who had been ill from birth, had died, and he rushed home to comfort them.[3]

He still found time to help friends, although they rarely asked him for anything, trying to avoid taxing his strength; but he insisted anyway, the joy, as he told them, more for his sake than theirs. When Milton Handler's niece wanted to get married, she asked if Wise would perform the ceremony and the elderly rabbi said he would be delighted. But the boy's parents, who were Conservative verging on Orthodox, upon discovering that a Reform rabbi would officiate, objected strenuously. Caught in the middle, the young couple went to Handler, who in turn explained the situation to Wise. With a big grin on his face, Wise said: "They want a Conservative ceremony? I'll give them a Conservative ceremony. They want an Orthodox ceremony? I can make an Orthodox ceremony as well."

Three days before the wedding, Wise's companion of nearly a half a century died. Although Louise had been in poor health for several years, her death from pneumonia on December 10, 1947, devastated Wise, who together with their children were at her beside when the end came. More than a thousand people crowded into the Free Synagogue House for her funeral two days later, and Wise sat in stunned grief among the mourners as his close friend, David Petegorsky, eulogized her. "Her life was a restless and passionate pursuit of justice, beauty and truth," Petegorsky said, adding that "she knew and felt profoundly that the world would never be molded in the image of God and His purpose unless it rested on those foundations. . . . She waged relentless battle not against the men of evil but against the evil in men, for she was certain that active participation in causes which served justice and truth could transform those of ill will or no will into persons of good will."[4]

As Wise sat the period of mounring, Milton Handler came not only to bring comfort but to tell Wise that he should not even think about marrying his niece. "It was an imposition on you to begin with, and now no one expects it." "Oh, no," Wise responded, "I have agreed, and I will do it." Perhaps in his grief he saw this new marriage as a celebration of the life and love he himself had shared. He married the couple but slipped out quietly before the festive dinner began. Handler later recalled that of all the things he knew about Wise, this more than anything demonstrated the man's basic commitment to be a pastor to his people.[5]

With Louise's passing, Wise knew that his own days were numbered, and he resumed writing his long-planned, often-postponed memoirs, working on the manuscript in between the still hectic round of meetings, weddings, and other work. Justine took a leave of absence from the bench to become his research assistant, sorting through the thousands of letters and documents he had accumulated in his lifetime. In crabbed, at times almost illegible scrawl, he set out his memories in *Challenging Years,* downplaying the personal and recalling the great historic events of which he had been part.

In the summer of 1948 he made his last trip to Europe to attend the second session of the World Jewish Congress in Montreaux, Switzerland. His body racked with pain, Wise nonetheless wanted to see once again his comrades in the organization he hoped would one day speak as the voice of a united world Jewry. His speech at the close lasted ten minutes. He spoke without notes and in English, which many of the delegates did not understand, but they intuitively knew what he was saying. He recalled Herzl and the dream of a Jewish state which had now come to pass. The two great experiences of his life, he told them, had been the Zionist movement and then meeting and coming to know the Jewish people. As Joachim Prinz recalled, "he seemed to bless the people with his life."[6]

On his return home he promised his doctors that he would try to take better care of himself. "I find that if I lie down and rest after I have risen and shaved and bathed [in the morning], I can remain comfortable for the rest of the day. I have gained a little weight, but not enough to speak of, and I have regained some appetite, eating almost normally and with some zest." To his great joy and comfort, his family rearranged their plans to spend as much time with him as possible. "I could not have gone through this year," he told Justine's son Stephen, "without your Mother's love and tenderness. It is balm to my wounded soul."[7]

As his seventy-fifth birthday approached in 1949, Wise found himself showered with the admiration and affection not only of his congregation but of Americans, Jews and non-Jews, across the country. The president of the United States sent him as a birthday gift one of the pens he had used to sign the *de jure* recognition of Israel, and lauded him not only for his work as a religious teacher but as a fighter for social justice. Two old foes, Chaim

Weizmann and David Ben-Gurion, now president and prime minister of the Jewish state, joined in behalf of the government and people of Israel to send him greetings, and to thank him for all he had done to make the Zionist dream come true. To James G. McDonald, the American ambassador to Israel, Wise declared that he had but one wish before he died, and that was to visit the Jewish State of Israel.[8] But even if his doctors had allowed the trip, Wise was now too sick, and his time was to be measured not in years or months, but in weeks.

On March 17, 1949, twelve hundred friends and colleagues came to the Hotel Astor to celebrate his life's work. He took particular pleasure in the presence of his beloved friend John Haynes Holmes, who had written a poem for the occasion. The last stanza read:

The years have flown, God's hammer droops and dips,
And you are weary from the ceaseless fight.
But still the living coal burns on your lips.
And high the sword is pointed to the light.

After others had also spoken his praise. Wise slowly went to the rostrum, his hands shaking as he spread out his hand-written talk. It was unusual for him to do this, but he feared the emotions of the evening. Slowly and eloquently he listed what he considered his achievements, first among them Zionism, but he also spoke of all the work still unfinished. The forces opposed to freedom and individual dignity had not been defeated; they still threatened democracy and, he declared, so long as he had breath, he would oppose them. As he finished, he raised his fist and shouted, "I'll fight! I'll fight!" and the audience came roaring to its feet, the applause rolling on and on as Wise stood there with tears in his eyes. As his family helped him on with his coat afterward, he turned to his friend and said, "I should never have tried it, Holmes, I should never have tried it."[9]

The following week, against doctors' orders, he went to Boston to see the newly opened Brandeis University, and accompanied its president, Abram Sachar, on a tour of the campus. At a luncheon with the faculty, Wise sensed a tension over the salaries, and before the astonished professors, he took out his wallet and began passing around pictures of his grandchildren. Before anyone could conclude that the guest of honor had suddenly become senile, he smiled and said, "Gentlemen, see how many grandchildren you can carry in your wallet if you don't care about money." A day later on March 27, he spoke at the historic Ford Hall Forum, where he had first lectured forty-one years earlier. He took as his title "My Challenging Years: A Seventy-Fifth Birthday Address," and declared: "I have lived to see the Jewish State. I am too small for the greatness of the mercy which God has shown us." Then, as many in the overflow audience wept, he did something he had never done before in his many appearances at the Forum: he gave the benediction in Hebrew.[10] The following morning he returned to New York, and on March 30 entered Lennox Hill Hospital.

On April 7, doctors operated on what they described as a "malignant stomach ailment," but his weakened condition and the extent of the cancer allowed little hope for recovery. Over the next ten days he occasionally rallied, and when his grandson, Stephen Wise Tulin, flew in from Oberlin College, Wise shooed everyone else out of the room so he and his namesake could talk about philosophy and other important things in life. On Tuesday morning, April 19, he lapsed into a coma, and at 4:00 that afternoon, with his sister Ella, Jim and his wife Helen, Justine and her husband Shad at his side, he died. In his wallet was a letter he had written to his children several months earlier:[11]

> I am not tearful or maudlin as I write this, but I am so wretched that I would be insensitive and stupid not to write as I do. When something happens to me, Ed [Klein] knows about the things I prefer for the Service.
>
> Ed, of course, is to have charge of the service, whether at the Synagogue House or in Carnegie Hall, where I preached for thirty years and with which I became associated during the stronger years of my life—or, best of all, in the new building.
>
> In view of the large part which the [American Jewish] Congress and Zionism have had in my life, I think that, just as in the case of Mummie, I would like Dave [Petegorsky] to speak the word of farewell if he were equal to it. Dave has grown very dear to me. He knows what it is that I most deeply care for: the State of Israel and freedom and justice for Jews everywhere. If an address is to be made, it shall be made by Dave. He has become very dear to me and he is a loyal and faithful comrade.
>
> I would like a prayer or the reading of a poem by my beloved friend Holmes.
>
> You won't see this while I am alive. When you do see it, I beg you to understand that my release, whenever it comes, is a great mercy. I am far from well and comfortable. As you know, I hate to leave you both and Shad and Helen and my precious grandchildren, but I feel the time is drawing very near for me to go Home. If God will, it will mean the reunion of my spirit with that of Mummie's, and you know that I want my dust to be placed in the niche wherein she lies.
>
> All love forever to you who have taken such wonderful care of me and will do so, I know, to my end, whenever it is to be. You will love and care for each other always.

Into the Hand of God I commend my spirit. May He continue to vouchsafe me His grace and mercy.

Tributes poured in from all over the world, testifying to the greatness of the man and the impact he had exercised on people's lives; newspapers across the country lauded the work he had done. But none of this would have meant as much to him as the more eloquent testimony of the nearly fifteen thousand men and women who filed past his bier in the Free Synagogue. An old, gnarled charwoman, who had waited in line for hours for the doors to open, walked by first, stopped and whispered, "God bless his soul." After her came the poor as well as the rich, black and white, Hispanic and Oriental, Jew and gentile, the unknown and the famous—to all of whom he had dedicated his life. He lay in a simple pine coffin, in accordance with Jewish tradition that in death all men are equal. The only flowers were a spray of daffodils which his son Jim had picked that morning in his garden.

On Friday, April 22, 1949, Wise's body was carried for the last time into Carnegie Hall. Three thousand people jammed the auditorium, and another fifteen thousand stood outside in the drizzling rain, listening to the services over loudspeakers. His coffin stood in the center of the stage covered by a blanket of flowers; two flags, those of the United States and of Israel, flanked the bier, behind which stood an honor guard of the Shomrim Society, Jewish members of the New York City Police Department. Shortly after two o'clock, Rabbi Klein opened the service reading Psalms 90 and 94 in Hebrew, followed by the Rev. John Haynes Holmes, who chose verses from Milton's *Samson Agonistes* and Matthew Arnold's *Rugby Chapel*. His longtime associates in the Free Synagogue, Sidney Goldstein and J. X. Cohen, conducted parts of the service and, as Wise had requested, David Petegorsky delivered the eulogy.

"He was a simple man," Petegorsky declared, "who dared to remain simple in an age which rewarded cunning and cold calculation and deceit. He was a man of profound faith and piety, and he dared to retain his faith in a world which mocked and seemed to disprove any faith. He was a man overflowing with love, and he dared to continue to love during a generation when hate and prejudice and ill-will stalked the earth and crept into the hearts of millions." To all this, Petegorsky noted, Wise added "an overflowing love, and abounding love for his people Israel, his country America, his family, his friends, his associates, for ordinary and humble men and women.

"History will inscribe Stephen Wise among the truly great men of our era. It will record that he was a pioneer, a fearless crusader, in every worthwhile field of social concern; in the cause of justice and freedom for all men and for all peoples; for public morality and social welfare; for the deepening of religion and the extension of knowledge; for international peace and understanding.''

After the ceremony, the funeral cortege moved slowly up Manhattan and through Harlem, past tens of thousands of mourners who stood silently in the rain, many sobbing, paying their last respects to the man and to his life. In the late afternoon his body was placed in the family mausoleum in the Westchester Hills Cemetery of the Free Synagogue. He had finally come to rest.[12]

To measure a man's life is not easy, for surely it is more than just an accounting of achievements and failures. Wise was the last of a generation of titans in American Jewish life, people who by the force of their personalities and will shaped the Jewish community into a self-respecting, self-reliant force. Such individuals are no longer on the scene, for American Jewry, like American society, has matured to the point where no one person can exert the influence a Wise or a Brandeis or a Louis Marshall was able to exercise in the earlier part of this century. In large measure, the success of Wise and others in creating the institutional structure of American Jewish life has shifted the focus away from the charismatic leader toward the organizational manager. The inchoate Jewish society in which Wise lived and worked has now become structured, and in the eyes of many observers overly rigid and terribly uninspired.

What set Wise apart was not his great accomplishments but his less publicized work as a caring and devoted shepherd of his people. He fought Hitler not only because fascism threatened democracy, but because the Nazis tortured and killed individuals, men and women and children. He opposed Tammany Hall and worked for numerous reforms not only because of the larger principles involved, but because of the terrible effect that corrupt politics, stinking tenements, and unsafe factories had on people. For Wise, the Talmudic dictum that ''he who saves a single life saves the entire world'' had a special meaning, and as Nahum Goldmann said, he not only loved the Jewish people, he loved every individual Jew, and beyond that, every person in need. The thousands of common people who filed past his bier or stood bareheaded in the rain as the funeral cortege passed loved him not for his great acts but for the greatness of spirit he showed in his small deeds.

He was not a saint, a role he would have found rather uncomfortable to play. He had his share of failings, his ego and temper at times got the best of him, and on occasion he could be maddeningly self-righteous, assured that he alone knew what was right. But these failings pale to insignificance when measured against, if nothing else, the love and care he lavished so prodigiously on his people. He fought for decency and democracy, for the rights not only of the Jewish people but of all men and women. Throughout Stephen Wise's long life and career, he was indeed a voice that spoke for justice.

Notes

1. Goodly Beginnings

1. "A memoir of Rabbi Joseph Hirsch Weisz by his student, Rabbi Issac Klein, prepared by his grandson, David Klein Fisher," typescript, n.d., courtesy of Justine Wise Polier [JWP]; interviews with JWP, 7 January 1975 and 14 February 1979; Stephen S. Wise [SSW] to John Haynes Holmes, 27 April 1938, Wise MSS [all citations, unless specified for another source, are to this collection]. Reb Joseph's large library was eventually given to Columbia University by his grandson.

2. David de Sola Pool, "Aaron Wise," *Dictionary of American Biography* (New York, 1936, 1964 reprint), 10: 421–22; notes of interview with SSW by the Rev. William K. McKinney, 23 January 1934; "A Magyar Porcelain," *Irta Ruzioska Ilona* (Budapest, 1939); interview with JWP, 7 January 1975.

3. Moshe Davis, *The Emergence of Conservative Judaism* (Philadelphia: Jewish Publication Society, 1963), part III.

4. *American Hebrew*, 3 April 1896; interview with James Waterman Wise [JWW], 14 June 1975; SSW to Mrs. Karl T. Smart, 22 April 1927.

5. SSW to Ruth W. Thompson, 22 January 1935; SSW, "To Aaron Wise," in Sidney Strong, ed., *What I Owe to My Father* (New York: Holt, 1931), pp. 161–66.

6. SSW, *Challenging Years: The Autobiography of Stephen S. Wise* (New York: G. P. Putnam's Sons, 1949), p. xxiii; notes of interview with SSW by the Rev. William K. McKinney, 23 January 1934.

7. SSW, *Challenging Years*, pp. 3–4; Carl Hermann Voss, *Rabbi and Minister: The Friendship of Stephen S. Wise and John Haynes Holmes* (Cleveland: World Publishing Co., 1964), pp. 31–32.

8. Nathanael Beirs to SSW, 20 December 1910; interview with JWP, 14 February 1979.

9. A. Emerson Palmer, *New York Public Schools* (New York: Macmillan, 1905), p. 223; SSW to Florence Luntz, 1 November 1939.

10. SSW, "Abraham Lincoln," *The Literary Review*, 1 (August 1889).

11. Philip Cowen, *Memories of an American Jew* (New York: International Press, 1932), p. 58.

12. Alfred Mark Sugarman, "A Study of the Ethos of Stephen S. Wise in Selected

Speeches on Social Justice," doctoral dissertation (State University of Iowa, 1964), pp. 36, 38.

13. SSW, *Challenging Years*, p. 122. In later years when any student tried to imitate SSW he would invariably repeat his father's rule, and warn the young man: "One of me is quite enough, perhaps too many. Be yourself."

14. Rebekah Kohut, *His Father's House: The Story of George Alexander Kohut* (New Haven: Yale University Press, 1938), p. 166, and *My Portion: An Autobiography* (New York: Thomas Seltzer, 1925), pp. 189–90.

15. Sugar, "A Study of the Ethos . . . ," pp. 39–40.

16. Notes of interview with SSW by the Rev. William K. McKinney, 23 January 1934.

17. Isaac Mayer Wise to SSW, 4 September 1892, Correspondence Files, American Jewish Archieves; Max Margolis to SSW, 17 and 19 September 1982.

18. SSW, *Challenging Years*, pp. 38–39.

19. Morris Raphael Cohen, *A Dreamer's Journey* (Boston: Beacon Press, 1949), pp. 110–11, 117; Gaynell Hawkins, "Thomas Davidson, Teacher," *Southwest Review* 13 (1928): 334.

20. William James, "A Knight-Errant of the Intellectual Life," *McClure's Magazine* 25 (May 1905): 1–9; for additional information on Davidson, see William Knight, ed., *Memoirs of Thomas Davidson, The Wandering Scholar* (London: Ginn & Co., 1907), and Hugh MacDarmid, *Scottish Eccentrics* (London: G. Rutledge, 1936), ch. 7.

21. SSW, Diary of Stay at Glenmore, 1892; SSW to Thomas Davidson, 17 September 1892 and 4 February 1898, Davidson MSS; SSW to Louise Waterman, 14 September 1900, JWP; Davidson to SSW, 7 June 1900, JWP; SSW statement on S. Parkes Cadman, 18 December 1941.

22. Voss, *Rabbi and Minister*, pp. 34–35; SSW, "Dr. Adolf Jellinek," *The Menorah Monthly* 16 (February 1894): 137–44.

23. Trial sermon, March 1893, Wise MSS-AJA; SSW, *Challenging Years*, xiii; *American Hebrew* 52 (April 1893): 825.

24. Israel Goldstein, *A Century of Judaism in New York: B'nai Jeshurun 1825-1925* (New York: B'nai Jeshurun, 1930), pp. 210–16; circular letters to members of B'nai Jeshurun, 5 and 20 December 1893.

25. SSW, *Challenging Years*, p. 56.

26. Louis Lipsky, *Memoirs in Profile* (Philadelphia: Jewish Publication Society, 1975), p. 194.

27. Solomon ibn Gabirol, *The Improvement of the Moral Qualities*, with an introduction by SSW, Columbia University Oriental Studies No. 1 (New York: Columbia University Press, 1902).

28. Quoted in Carl Hermann Voss, "The Lion and the Lamb—An Evaluation of the Life and Work of Stephen S. Wise," *American Jewish Archives* 21 (April 1969): 13; interview with Harry Starr.

29. In 1923, Professor Israel Davidson of the Jewish Theological Seminary wrote an introduction and notes for Israel Zangwill's edition of ibn Gabirol's poetry, and provided an extensive bibliography on works by and about ibn Garbirol, but did not list SSW's book. Wise was furious, and termed Davidson's work "exactly the sort of thing that is characteristic of this high-minded and pious Jew of the Seminary who

makes Orthodoxy a stench in the nostrils of decency." SSW to Richard Gottheil, 26 November 1923; see also SSW to Charles Bloch, same date. For a typical example of rumor-mongering, see Julian Morgenstern to Martin B. Ryback, 26 February 1952, Morgenstern MSS.

30. The study of Gershoni (1844–1897) is in Jacob Kabakoff, *Halutzei ha-Sifrut ha-Ivrit ba-Amerika* (Tel Aviv: Machon L'lmodei HaYehudit, 1966), ch. 2. A prolific writer, Gershoni served at times as a rabbi in Atlanta and Chicago before returning to New York in 1893, where he lived by his pen until his death.

31. Quoted in Jacob Kabakoff to the author, 2 March 1979; the original is in the Felsenthal Papers in the library of the American Jewish Historical Society.

32. SSW to Richard Gottheil, 30 July 1894, Wise MSS-AJA.

33. SSW to Gottheil, 5, 8, 12 and 21 July 1895, ibid.

34. SSW to Gottheil, 1 August 1895, ibid.

35. SSW to Gottheil, 15 and 23 August 1895, ibid.

36. *Hamazkir* 2 (1902): 125 ff.; Noah Braun, ed., Hebrew translation of ibn Gabirol's *Ethics* (Jerusalem: Mossad Harav Kook, 1961), preface. For this information I am indebted to Professor Meyer Passow of Bar-Ilan University, in letter to author of 11 March 1979.

37. SSW to Gottheil, 4 December 1899, Wise MSS–AJA.

38. *The Holy Scriptures* (Philadelphia: Jewish Publication Society 1917), p. v.

39. Telephone interviews with Dr. Solomon Grayzel, 11 May 1979, Dr. Maurice Jacobs, 17 May 1979, and Dr. Jacob R. Marcus, 31 May 1979; all three were long associated with the Jewish Publication Society. In addition, circumstantial evidence that none of the listed translators did the work can be found in the David Philipson Papers, American Jewish Archives, files relating to JPS Bible. I am indebted to Dr. Harry Orlinsky for first providing me with this information in a letter of 10 May 1979. It is also worth noting that while SSW made ocasional references to his work on ibn Gabirol throughout his correspondence, I found no comments by him regarding the JPS Judges.

40. *American Hebrew*, 3 April 1896.

41. SSW, "What I Owe to My Father," p. 164.

42. SSW to Benjamin Blumenthal, 24 November 1896.

2. The Cause and the Lady

1. Rose G. Jacobs, "Beginnings of Hadassah," in Isadore Meyer, ed., *Early History of Zionism in American* (New York: Herzl Foundation, 1958), pp. 231–32.

2. For Zionism in general, see Walter Laqueur, *A History of Zionism* (New York: Holt, Rinehart and Winston, 1972). The literature on Herzl is immense, but the best single volume is Amos Elon, *Herzl* (New York: Holt, Rinehart and Winston, 1975).

3. Laqueur, *History of Zionism,* p. 8; Rufus Learsi [pseud. Israel Goldberg], *Fulfillment: The Epic Story of Zionism* (Cleveland: World Publishing Co., 1951), p. 82.

4. For Reform opposition to Zionism, see Melvin I. Urofsky, *American Zionism from Herzl to the Holocaust* (Garden City: Anchor Press, 1975), pp. 92–99; the

Hirsch speech is in *Publications of the American Jewish Historical Society.* [*PAJHS*]14 (1906): 148–60; see also *CCAR Yearbook* 4 (1892): 25.

5. Urofsky, *American Zionism,* p. 97–99.

6. *American Hebrew,* 17 December 1897; *CCAR Yearbook* 11 (1901): 31; Herschel Levin, "The Other Side of the Coin," *Herzl Year Book* 5 (1963): 33–56; Norman T. Mendell, "Glimpses into the Life of a Famous Rabbi and Zionist: Max Heller," rabbinic thesis (HUC-JIR, 1965); *New York Times,* 11 June 1900.

7. New York *Herald,* 31 August 1897, quoted in Marnin Feinstein, *American Zionism, 1844–1904* (New York: Herzl Press, 1965), pp. 114–15; see also Richard Gottheil, *The Aims of Zionism* (New York: Federation of American Zionists, 1898).

8. Louis Lipsky, *A Gallery of Zionist Profiles* (New York: Farrar, Straus and Cudahy, 1956), pp. 147.

9. Hyman B. Grinstein, "The Memoirs and Scrapbooks of the Late Dr. Joseph Isaac Bluestone of New York City," *PAJHS* 35 (1939): 57; Feindtein, *American Zionism,* ch. vii; SSW to Richard Gottheil, 3 June 1898, Wise MSS-AJA.

10. Julius Haber, *Odyssey of an American Zionist* (New York: Twayne, 1956), p. 166; Feinstein, *American Zionism,* pp. 130–31; SSW, "The Beginnings of American Zionism." *Jewish Frontier* 14 (August 1947): 7.

11. Ibid.

12. SSW to Theodor Herzl, 26 June 1898; SSW, *Challenging Years,* p. 23; New York *Journal,* September 1898.

13. SSW to Herzl, 26 October 1898 and 28 November 1899; Herzl to SSW, 26 December 1898, and to Jacob de Haas, 26 October 1898.

14. SSW to Herzl, 28 November 1899; Richard Gottheil to Actions Committee, 4 January 1899, Gottheil MSS; *Worcester Spy,* 20 November 1899, quoted in Myles Martel, "A rhetorical analysis of the Zionist speaking of Rabbi Stephen S. Wise," doctoral dissertation (Temple Universtiy, 1975).

15. Bernard G. Richards, "Following the Leader," *Congress Weekly* 16 (30 May 1949): 7; *Emanuel* (San Francisco), August 1899, quoted in Martel, "A rhetorical analysis," p. 46; Josef Fraenkel, "Three Jews from Budapest," *Congress Weekly* 16 (21 March 1949): 9, citing Herzl in *Die Welt,* 15 December 1899.

16. *New York Times,* 19 June 1899; Feinstein, *American Zionism,* pp. 151–52.

17. SSW to Herzl, 28 November 1899, and to Isidore Morrison, 22 September 1900.

18. *New York Times,* 11 June 1900.

19. Guido Kisch, "Two American Jewish Pioneers of New Haven: Sigmund and Leopold Waterman," *Historic Judaica* 4 (1942): 7–11.

20. Leopold Waterman to family, September 1844, Waterman Family Papers.

21. James Waterman Wise, *The Legend of Louise: The Life Story of Mrs. Stephen S. Wise* (New York: Jewish Opinon Publishing Corp. 1949), pp. 9–10.

22. Arthur Hertzberg, "Louise Waterman Wise" in Edward T. James, ed., *Notable American Women, 1607–1950* (Cambridge: Harvard University Press, 1971), pp. 634–36.

23. Louise Waterman Wise (LWW) to Felix Adler, 6 March 1933, Adler MSS. For Adler's influence on SSW, see Benny Kraut, *From Reform Judaism to Ethical Culture: The Religious Evolution of Felix Adler* (Cincinnati: Hebrew Union College Press, 1979), pp. 211–12.

24. Wise, *Legend of Louise*, pp. 22-23.
25. Interview with JWP, 7 January 1975.
26. Ben Selling to SSW, 22 July 1899; Simon Blumauer, Solomon Hirsch, and Charles Kohn to SSW, 31 July 1899.
27. SSW to Blumauer, Hirsch, and Kohn, 2 August 1899, and to Solomon Hirsch, same date.
28. SSW, "The Beginnings of American Zionism," *Jewish Frontier* 14 (August 1947): 7.
29. Julius J. Nodel, with Alfred Apsler, *The Ties Between: A Century of Judaism on America's Last Frontier* (Portland: Temple Beth Israel, 1959), p. 84.
30. SSW to Richard Gottheil, 31 August 1899, Wise MSS-AJA.
31. SSW to J. P. Solomon, 29 August 1899; SSW to president and board of B'nai Jeshurun, 3 October 1899.
32. SSW to LWW, January 1900.
33. Thomas Davidson to Felix Adler, 13 January 1900, JWP.
34. SSW to LWW, 18 August 1900.
35. Nodel, *The Ties Between*, p. 87.
36. SSW to LWW, 21 September 1900.
37. Voss, *Rabbi and Minister*, p. 47.

3. Bishop of Oregon

1. SSW to Marcus Arnheim, 26 March 1900, and to Solomon Hirsch, 26 March and 23 April 1900.
2. SSW to president and board of trustees of Beth Israel, 6 October 1899.
3. Hirsch to SSW, 3 November 1899; SSW to Hirsch, 22 December 1899.
4. Nodel, *The Ties Between*, p. 88.
5. SSW to LWW, 8 September 1900; Nodel, *The Ties Between*, p. 88.
6. Nodel, *The Ties Between*, pp. 89-90; SSW to Edgar Jones, 20 May 1932; Voss, *Rabbi and Minister*, p. 47; *Annual Report of President Adolphe Wolfe, Congregation Beth Israel, October 29th, 1903* (Portland: Beth Israel, 1903).
7. Nodel, *The Ties Between*, p. 91.
8. Quoted in Wolfe, *Report of the President*; Richard Gottheil to SSW, 13 February 1901.
9. SSW to Gottheil, 9 July 1900, Wise MSS-AJA; Gottheil to SSW, 7 January 1902.
10. SSW to Gottheil, 16 February, 3 and 9 May 1901, 22 March 1902, Wise MSS-AJA; Voss, *Rabbi and Minister*, p. 49.
11. SSW to Gottheil, 16 February 1901, Wise MSS-AJA; Isidore Morison to SSW, 28 February 1901.
12. Laqueur, *History of Zionism*, p. 122 ff.; SSW to Actions Committee, 8 July 1905, Vienna Office Records; SSW to Gottheil, 12 October 1905, Wise MSS-AJA.
13. SSW to Gottheil, 21 April 1904, Gottheil MSS.
14. Theodor Herzl to SSW, 25 April 1904; SSW to Herzl, 4 May 1904.
15. SSW, *Challenging Years*, p. 37.
16. SSW to Gottheil, 11 July 1904, Gottheil MSS.

17. Voss, *Rabbi and Minister*, pp. 38-39; SSW to Gottheil, 16 February 1901, Wise MSS-AJA; SSW to LWW, 1902, in Justine Wise Polier and James Waterman Wise, *The Personal Letters of Stephen Wise* (Boston: Beacon Press, 1956), p. 92.

18. Polier and Wise, *Personal Letters*, pp. 95-96.

19. SSW, *Challenging Years*, p. 9; SSW to Richard Neuberger, n.d. [1939].

20. Polier and Wise, *Personal Letters*, pp. 93-94; clipping. *Oregon Daily Journal*, n.d. [1902].

21. Abigail Scott Duniway to SSW, 29 January 1901; SSW to Theodore Roosevelt, 22 May 1903, T. Roosevelt MSS.

22. Harold U. Faulkner, *The Quest for Social Justice, 1898-1914* (New York: Macmillan, 1931), pp. 184-88.

23. *SSW, Challenging Years*, pp. 56—57; Polier and Wise, *Personal Letter*, p. 84.

24. Nodel, *The Ties Between, p. 95; Personal Letters*, p. 95; SSW, "Minister and Congregation," *Beth Israel Pulpit,* October 1906.

25. Alexander Blackbirn to SSW, 17 April 1901.

26. SSW to Jennie and Leo Waterman, n.d. [1901]; *Beth Israel Pulpit,* March and October 1905.

27. *Beth Israel Pulpit*, September 1905. For his views on the Philippines, see also SSW to Jacob Schurman, president of Cornell University and a leading anti-imperialist, 5 February 1904, Schurman MSS.

28. SSW to Julilus Hochfelder. 5 April 1933; SSW, *Challenging Years*, pp. 109-10.

29. SSW to LWW, 18 November 1903.

30. Leon M. Nelson to SSW, 22 November 1903, and SSW's reply, 1 December 1903; SSW to Maximillian Heller, 5 February 1904, Heller MSS.

31. Wise, *Legend of Louise,* p. 27.

32. SSW to LWW, 17 July 1902.

33. SSW to LWW, 14 April and 24 September 1902.

34. Wise, *Legend of Louise*, pp. 29-30.

4. Emanu-El

1. Sol Stoock to SSW, 5 April 1902.

2. Polier and Wise, *Personal Letters,* p. 76.

3. Ibid., pp. 88-89. In another letter regarding Emanu-El's desire for a "good speaker," he wrote: "there be nothing behind the voice, then let the nothingness or the nakedness stand revealed."

4. James Seligman to SSW, 9 November 1903; SSW to LWW, 11 November 1903.

5. Polier and Wise, *Personal Letters,* pp. 113, 115.

6. Fanny Garrison Villard to SSW, 27 November 1905, JWP.

7. J. X. Cohen to James Marshall, 28 March 1944.

8. Details of this meeting have been reconstructed from SSW, *Challenging Years*, pp. 84-85; *New York Times,* 8 and 10 January 1906; Voss, *Rabbi and Minister*, pp. 54-55.

9. Louis Marshall to SSW, 1 December 1905; J. X. Cohen, "A Prophet in Israel," *Congress Weekly* 11 (17 March 1944): 21; Wise, *Legend of Louise,* pp. 35-36.

10. SSW to Louis Marshall, 3 December 1905.

11. *New York Times,* 7 and 8 January 1906.

12. Ibid., 8 January 1906.

13. SSW to Rabbi Max Raisin, 27 January 1906; Richard Gottheil to SSW, 5 and 8 December 1905; SSW to Gottheil, 11 January 1906; Wise MSS-AJA; SSW to E. R. A. Seligman, 24 February 1906, in Seligman MSS.

14. David Solis Cohen to SSW, 6 June 1906.

15. SSW to Gov. George Chamberlain, 19 September 1906; Nodel, *The Ties Between,* p. 97.

16. SSW, "Minister and Congregation: A Farewell Sermon, *"Beth Israel Pulpit,* October 1906.

5. The Free Synagogue

1. See, among many works on New York Jewry at this time, Moses Rischin, *The Promised City* (Cambridge: Harvard University Press, 1962); Irving Howe, *World of Our Fathers* (New York: 1976); Stephen Birmingham, *Our Crowd* (New York: Harper and Row, 1967); Ande Manners, *Poor Cousins* (New York: Coward, Mc-Cann & Goghegan, 1972); Naomi W. Cohen, *Not Free to Desist: A History of the American Jewish Committee, 1906-1966* (Philadelphia: Jewish Publication Society, 1972); and Arthur A. Goren, *New York Jews and the Quest for Community: The Kehillah Experiment 1908-1922* (New York: Columbia University Press, 1970).

2. Richard Gottheil to SSW, 7 November 1906.

3. *New York Times,* 31 December 1906.

4. Voss, *Rabbi and Minister,* p. 17; SSW, *Challenging Years,* pp. 96-100.

5. Sheldon H. Blank, "Bible," in Samuel E. Karff, *Hebrew Union College-Jewish Institute of Religion at One Hundred Years* (Cincinnati: Hebrew Union College Press, 1976), p. 293.

6. Free Synagogue, *Constitution and By-Laws . . .* (New York, 1917).

7. Voss, *Rabbi and Minister,* pp. 79—80.

8. SSW to LWW, 12 September 1907; SSW to Richard Gottheil, 14 September 1907, Wise MSS-AJA.

9. See, for example, SSW to Hyman G. Enelow, 24 June 1907, Enelow MSS.

10. Jacob S. Minkin, "When the East Side Discovered Him," *Congress Weekly* 16 (30 May 1949): 11-13; SSW to Henry Fleischman, 23 January 1912; Howe, *World of Our Fathers,* p. 197. In 1914, when Wise heard that a new settlement house would be built, he suggested that it include an auditorium large enough to house the Downtown branch, but nothing came of the idea; SSW to Alice and Irene Lewisohn, 22 April 1914, Wald MSS. He did engage Abraham Cronbach in 1915 as assistant rabbi for the Downtown branch, but a severe cutback in expenses forced the Free Synagogue to drop the venture during the First World War; SSW to Abraham Cronbach, 4 November 1915, 1 February and 9 July 1917, Cronbach MSS.

11. Voss, *Rabbi and Minister*, p. 81.

12. SSW to M. I. Silver, 17 February 1913.

13. Voss, *Rabbi and Minister*, pp. 109-11; Gerson Rubenovich, "Stephen Wise's New Role," *Maccabaean* 19 (December 1910): 199; SSW to Jacob H. Schiff, n.d. [November 1910].

14. SSW, *Challenging Years*, p. 97.

15. Not all people, of course, found the service dull; many found it moving and even spiritual. One visitor from England wrote:

> The services are held in a hall packed with about 700 men and women, far more men than women and mostly young men and women, who hang on the words of the preacher with an earnestness I have never witnessed in a synagogue before, and, who join in the prayers of that service, every word of which they comprehend, with a fervour unusal in congregations in Great Britain, or London, whether the prayers are said in the East or in the West. And if you tell me that such a service is a "menace to Judaism," then I say, with as much energy as I can convey in writing, that I believe such services will tend to the salvation of Judaism rather than its "menace."

16. Much of the following information on the Free Synagogue's social service program is drawn from Sidney E. Goldstein, *The Synagogue and Social Welfare: A Unique Experiment, 1907-1953* (New York: Bloch Publishing Company, 1955).

17. Sidney E. Goldstein, "The Social Function of The Hospital," *Charities and Commons* 18 (4 and 18 May 1906): 160-66, 205-11.

18. SSW to Mrs. Max Danziger, 14 October 1912. SSW asked Mrs. Danziger and several other well-to-do congregants to subscribe to a special fund to pay Goldstein's salary.

19. Celia Hendel, "Report on Downtown Branch Social Services for the Year Ending September 1912." [October 1913].

20. SSW to Mrs. Lewis Wolff, 30 October 1912.

21. SSW to Morris Waldman, 13 December 1909, and to Henry L. Stimson, 22 September 1913.

22. Morris Waldman to SSW, 10 May 1912.

23. Wise, *Legend of Louise*, pp. 47-51.

24. SSW to S.N. Bernard, 7 August 1930.

25. See, for example, SSW to Henry Morgenthan, Sr., 29 August 1914 and 2 March 1915, Morgenthau MSS.

6. The Rabbi of the Free Synagogue

1. Israel Goldstein, *Transition Years* (Jerusalem: Maas, 1962), p. 67.

2. William Inglis, "Celebrities at Home, Rabbi Stephen S. Wise, Ph.D.," *Harpers Weekly* 52 (5 December 1908): 13.

3. Voss, *Rabbi and Minister*, pp. 83-84.

4. Interviews with JWP, 7 January 1975, and with JWW, 14 June 1975. Jim remembers being spanked only once, when he was about seven or eight, and stole some marbles from a store. Another time, when he did something that provoked his father and it looked as if his father would hit him, his little sister flew to his defense, threatening to "kill" anyone—including Wise—who touched her brother.

5. Interview with Meyer Weisgal, 29 May 1975.

6. N. H. Batchelder to SSW, 7 May 1917.

7. Interview with JWP, 14 February 1979.

8. SSW to Henry Morgenthau, 6 April 1915; Carl Grossman to SSW, 18 June 19[?].

9. Willam McAndrew to SSW, 28 October 1910; SSW to William Feakins, 7 December 1911.

10. Analyticus [James Waterman Wise], *Jews Are Like That!* (New York: Brentano's, 1928), p. 93. Louis Lipsky, who heard Wise speak many times, wrote in a similar vein in *Memoirs in Profile*, pp. 198-99.

He preached many a sermon well; he delivered many a eulogy with great pathos; he was good-humored and captivating at dinners at which he presided with grace and dignity; he was a tempestuous political orator comparable to the best in American political life. But he was superb when he freed himself of form and manuscript and gave unbridled sway to his emotions. He often missed the bull's eye of accuracy; his logic was faulty, but the range of his vocabulary, the power of his invective, the wrath he was able to pour into his polemics gave these improvisations the quality of incomparable oratory.

11. SSW to Cyril Clemens, 20 November 1942; Allen Nevins Memoir, Columbia Oral History Collection [COHC], p. 87; Samuel Skolnick to SSW, 19 February 1934, and SSW's reply, 21 February 1934.

12. Bernard Gershon Richards Memoir, COHC, p. 112; Voss, *Rabbi and Minister*, p. 82; SSW to Edgar Jones, 20 May 1932.

13. Westwood (Los Angeles) Temple *Bulletin*, High Holydays 1964, p. 3.

14. Sugarman, "A Study of the Ethos . . . ," p. 1; Ben B. Lindsey to Morris Wertheim, 27 December 1911, JWP; John Haynes Holmes, *I Speak for Myself: The Autobiography of John Haynes Holmes* (New York: Harper & Bros., 1959), pp. 94-95.

15. Quoted in Morris N. Kreuter, *Today's American Jew* (New York: McGraw-Hill, 1967), p. 173.

16. "That cause I have served by the means, however poor and meager at times, of preaching. To me preaching has never meant talking or sermonizing or discussing. I have claimed the high office of preaching as the only means of uttering my soul on great causes in the spirit and freedom of truth." SSW, *"Gaudium Certaminus*—Why I Have Found Life Worth Living," *Christian Century* 45 (11 October 1928): 1224.

17. Rabbi Hyman J. Schactel, "Some Preachers I Have Known," lecture to HUC Homiletics class, 20 January 1964, quoted in Floyd L. Herman, "Some Aspects of the Life of Stephen S. Wise to 1925," rabbinic thesis (HUC-JIR, 1964), p. 106.

18. Henry Bloch to SSW, n.d.; SSW to Lorraine B. McClelland, 29 June 1934. See also, among many other, SSW to Jerome Adler, 16 March 1943 (Stephen had married the Adlers 45 years earlier); to Lazarus Joseph, 20 November 1942; and to Maurice J. Karpf, 20 October 1937. When SSW heard of the death of congregants he had known at B'nai Jeshurun or in Portland, he wrote to their families as well.

19. SSW to Edward Lubbin, 3 April 1928.

20. See, for example, SSW to Mrs. Carl Morse, 2 November 1943. On 4 July 1917, SSW wrote to Rabbi Samuel Rosinger: "I have made it a rule since the founding of the synagogue not to accept any personal gifts in any connection and in any circumstance whatever."

21. SSW to Irvin Getnick, 25 January 1940; SSW, *How to Face Life* (New York: B. W. Huebsch, 1917), p. 14.

22. Interview with Israel Goldstein, 12 September 1973.

23. *New York Times*, 6 November 1949; Philip S. Bernstein, "Stephen S. Wise—Some Personal Recollections," *CCAR Journal* 11 (April 1963): 11.

24. Nahum Goldmann, *Sixty Years of Jewish Life: The Autobiography of Nahum Goldmann,* tr. by Helen Sebba (New York: Holt, Rinehart and Winston, 1969), pp. 123-24.

25. SSW to C. L. Powell, 5 February 1914.

26. Abraham J. Cronbach, "Autobiography," *American Jewish Archives* 11 (April 1959): 49; Voss, "The Lion and Lamb" *American Jewish Archives* 21:13.

27. *"Gaudium Certaminus,"* 1223; see a similar statement made toward the end of his life, "Why I Remained a Jew," *Progressive Jew* (October 1948): 10.

28. SSW, *How to Face Life*, pp. 22-23; SSW to P. C. MacFarland, 14 February 1912; see also SSW to Alex Laven, 9 October 1942.

29. Harry Orlinsky, "The Legacy of Stephen Wise," *Founder's Day Addresses* (Cincinnati: HUC-JIR, 1978), pp. 19-21.

30. *New York Times*, 7 March 1912.

31. Ibid., 22 May 1911.

32. Cohen, *Not Free to Desist,* ch. 4; *New York Times,* 26 November 1911.

33. See SSW to Henry Morgenthau, Sr., 6 March and 22 December 1914, 18 May 1915, Morgenthau MSS; SSW, "The Case of Leo Frank," *Free Synagogue Pulpit* 3 (May 1915): 80.

34. *CCAR Yearbook* 7 (1901): 76, 81, 82.

35. Ibid., 20 (1909): 432-94.

36. Ibid., p. 16 ff.

37. SSW to J. L. Luect, 25 November 1911; Jewish *Abluck,* 18 February 1910; Sidney E. Goldstein to SSW, 17 July 1912.

38. SSW to LWW, 27 June and 1 July 1914; Sidney E. Goldstein to SSW, 10 July 1914; SSW to Martin A. Meyer, 3 August 1914; see also SSW to Meyer, 20 October 1914 and to J. Leonard Levy, 5 November 1914.

39. *CCAR Yearbook* 24 (1914): 83-84; Rabbi Cornfeld to SSW, 22 December 1914; SSW to Max Heller, 25 December 1914, Heller MSS.

40. SSW to Heller, 28 December 1914, Heller MSS.

41. Meyer, "History of HUC-JIR," p. 78; SSW to Max Heller, 17 and 18 March and April 1915, Heller MSS.

42. SSW to Max Heller, 3 August and 15 November 1915, Heller MSS.

7. The Rabbi as Progressive

1. *Historical Statistics of The United States* (Washington: Government Printing Office, 1960).
2. Jacob A. Riis, in *How the Other Half Lives* (New York: Scribner's 1890), gives a graphic contemporary account of slum life for the new immigrants.
3. SSW, *Challenging Years*, p. 64; James Panken (of the ILGWU) to SSW, 26 October 1914, inviting him to be an arbitrator, and SSW's reply, 4 November 1914.
4. Richard O'Connor, *The First Hurrah: A Biography of Alfred E. Smith* (New York: Putnam, 1970), pp. 64–66; Voss, *Rabbi and Minister*, p. 114; Leon Stein, *The Triangle Fire* (Philadelphia: Lippincott, 1962), pp. 141–45, 207.
5. Stein, *Triangle Fire*, p. 208; *New York Times*, 5 December 1911; Irwin Yellowitz, *Labor and the Progressive Movement in New York State, 1897–1916* (Ithaca: Cornell University Press, 1965), p. 155.
6. *New York Times*, 1 and 15 January 1912; cf. Louis D. Brandeis, "How Far Have We Come on the Road to Industrial Democracy?," *LaFollette's Weekly Magazine*, 5 (24 May 1913): 5, 14; see also SSW to Benjamin Schnierer, 11 February 1913.
7. Clarence Darrow, *The Story of My Life* (New York: Scribner's, 1932), chs. 21, 22; the Brandeis statement is in Boston *Globe*, 3 December 1911.
8. SSW, *Challenging Years*, p. 57; Voss, *Rabbi and Ministers*, pp. 117–18; see also SSW speech to Methodist Ministers Association, *New York Times*, 30 April 1912; see also "Larger Bearings of the McNamara Case," *Survey* 27 (30 December 1911): 1419–29.
9. *American Industries* 12 (January 1912): 7.
10. SSW, *Challenging Years*, p. 58.
11. *New York Times* editorial, 22 February 1916.
12. A copy of the petition can be found in *Letters of Louis D. Brandeis* (Albany: SUNY Press, 1971–1978), 2: 531–35; for the Commission and its history, see Graham Adams, Jr., *The Age of Industrial Violence, 1910–1915* (New York: Columbia University Press, 1966).
13. *New York Times*, 7 July 1914.
14. SSW, *Challenging Years*, pp. 60–61.
15. Langston Hughes, *Fight for Freedom: The Story of NAACP* (New York: Norton 1962), pp. 20–22; Mary White Ovington, *The Walls Came Tumbling Down* (New York: Harcourt, Brace, 1947), pp. 112–13; *New York Times*, 31 March and 13 December 1915; SSW, "Abolition Fifty Years After," *Crisis* 5 (February 1913): 188.
16. SSW, "Women and Democracy," *Free Synagogue Pulpit* 3 (1915).
17. Interview with JWW, 14 June 1975; *New York Times*, 1 November 1915; Free Synagogue sermons: "Unrest Among Women," 1 March 1914; "The Drama of Today," 21 December 1913; "Are the Morals and the Manners of Our Time Decadent?," 4 January 1914.
18. *New York Times*, 11 December 1911.
19. SSW, *Challenging Years*, p. 12.
20. Thomas M. Henderson, *Tammany Hall and the New Immigrants: The Progressive Years* (New York: Arno Press, 1976), ch. 2; Goren, *New York Jews*, p. 151; William J. Gaynor to Murray W. Stand, 16 October 1912, in *New York Times*, 19 October 1912.

21. Lately Thomas, *The Mayor Who Mastered New York: The Life and Opinions of William J. Gaynor* (New York: Morrow, 1969), pp. 411–35.

22. SSW to editor, New York *Post*, 18 July 1912, and to Charles S. Whitman, 21 November 1912; Whitman to SSW, 2 June 1914.

23. *New York Times*, 30 January 1911.

24. Ibid., 2 November 1913.

25. SSW, *Challenging Years*, pp. 14–15; SSW to Henry Morgenthau, 22 December 1913, Morgenthaus MSS; SSW to Richard W. Montague, 5 February 1914.

26. *New York Times*, 30 January 1911, 3 November 1913, and 16 April 1915; SSW to Oswald Villard, 9 November 1911; SSW to John A Dix, 22 March 1912; SSW to Martin Glynn, 25 November 1913 and 4 May 1914.

27. SSW to Theodore Rousseau, 22 April 1914.

8. Wilson and the New Freedom

1. The literature on Wilson is enormous, but the best single volume on his early life is Arthur S. Link, *Wilson: The Road to the White House* (Princeton: Princeton University Press, 1947); Link has also written a fine overview, *Woodrow Wilson and the Progressive Era, 1910–1917* (New York: Harper & Row, 1954).

2. SSW, *Challenging Years*, p. 161.

3. SSW Diary, entries for 10 and 11 February 1911.

4. SSW to Walter L. Hauser, 18 October 1911; Wilson's speech of 6 December 1911 at the Free Syngagoue can be found in *Congressional Record*, 62nd Cong., 2nd Sess., 48: 497–99.

5. Cohen, *Not Free to Desist*, ch. 4.

6. *New York Times*, 1 April 1911; SSW to S. J. Douglas, 27 September 1911 and to William Howard Taft, 21 November 1911.

7. *New York Times*, 15 January 1912.

8. Voss, *Rabbi and Minister*, p. 122.

9. SSW Diary, 17 and 23 May 1912.

10. Merlo J. Pusey, *Charles Evans Hughes*, (2 vols., New York: Columbia University Press, 1963), 1: 300; Frederick C. Tanner Memoir, COHC, 63; *New York Times*, 21 June 1912.

11. Link, *Wilson: Road to the White House*, ch. 13.

12. SSW Diary, 2 July 1912; SSW, *Challenging Years*, pp. 164–65.

13. SSW Diary, 7 July and 19 August 1912; SSW to J. H. Holmes, and Henry Morgenthau, both 8 July 1912.

14. *New York Times*, 20 July 1912; William Hotchkiss to SSW, 25 July 1912, and SSW's reply, 28 July 1912.

15. Melvin Urofsky, "Wilson, Brandeis and the Trust Issue," *Mid-America* 49 (January 1967): 3–14.

16. SSW to George F. Peabody, 16 September 1912; SSW to Woodrow Wilson, 28 September 1912, Morgenthau MSS.

17. SSW Diary, 5 November 1912.

18. Woodrow Wilson to SSW, 20 November 1912; SSW Diary, 25 November 1912; SSW, *Challenging Years,* pp. 167–68.

19. SSW to William Borah, 18 December 1912; SSW, *Challenging Years,* p. 168; SSW Diary, 20 January 1913.

20. Woodrow Wilson to United States Diplomatic and Consular Offices, 31 March 1913; Arthur S. Link, *Wilson: The New Freedom* (Princeton: Princeton University Press, 1956), ch. 5; SSW to Henry Morgenthau, n. d. [late June or early July 1913], Morgenthau MSS.

21. Louis D. Brandeis to Alfred Brandeis, 2 March 1913, Brandeis MSS; Brandeis to Woodrow Wilson, 19 May 1913, Wilson MSS; Yonathan Shapiro, *Leadership of the American Zionist Organization 1897–1930* (Urbana: University of Illinois Press, 1971), 65–66.

22. Henry Morgenthau, *All in a Lifetime* (Garden City: Doubleday, 1922), p. 162; SSW to Morgenthau, 7 July 1913.

23. SSW Diary, 19 November 1913; *New York Times;* 20 November 1913; SSW to Henry Morgenthau, 21 November 1913, Morgenthau MSS; Morgenthau to SSW, 6 December 1913.

24. SSW to Wilson, 21 January 1914, Wilson MSS; SSW to Morgenthau, 21 January 1914, Morgenthau MSS.

25. SSW to Wilson, 29 January 1915; Link, *Wilson and the Progressive Era,* pp. 60–61.

9. Zionism Redivivus

1. Harry Friedenwald to David Wolffson, 4 November 1908, and Federation to Actions Committee, 24 June 1909, Cologne Office Records; for the status of American Zionism in these years, see Urofsky, *American Zionism,* pp. 111–18.

2. SSW, *Challenging Years,* pp. 40, 43.

3. SSW to Julius Rosenwald, 24 November 1913.

4. Jacob Schiff to SSW, 27 January 1914, Schiff MSS; for SSW's comments on the language controversy, see his letter to Hilfsverein der Deutsche Juden, 19 August 1914, deHaas MSS.

5. SSW to Morgenthau, 16 February 1914, Morgenthau MSS.

6. Jacob Schiff to SSW, 1 May 1914; SSW to Schiff, 12 and 19 June 1914, and Schiff to SSW, 18 and 25 June 1914, Schiff MSS; see also SSW to Abram Elkus, 11 August 1914, and to Lee K. Frankel, 14 and 31 August 1914, as well as Schiff to Frankel, 31 August 1914.

7. SSW to Rosenau, 18 May 1914, and to Rosenau, Bloomfield, and Bogen, all on 19 May 1914; Louis D. Brandeis to SSW, 3 June 1914; memorandum of announcement, 10 June 1914.

8. Urofsky, *American Zionism,* especially ch. 4; see also Shapiro, *Leadership of the American Zionist Organization,* ch. 3.

9. *Boston Post,* 28 September 1914.

10. *The Maccabaean* 24 (July 1914): 17–38; Richard Gottheil to Horace Meyer Kallen, 6 March 1914, Kallen MSS.

11. Urofsky, *American Zionism*, pp. 118-21.

12. Louis D. Brandeis to SSW, 16 September 1914, and SSW response, 16 September and 18 November 1914, Brandeis MSS.

13. SSW to Henry Morgenthau, 27 October 1914, Morgenthau MSS; SSW to Horace Kallen, 27 October 1914, Wise MSS-AJA; SSW to Martin A. Mayer, 4 November 1914.

14. SSW to Richard Gottheil, 12 November 1914, and to Horace Kallen, 3 December 1914, Wise MSS-AJA.

15. *Jewish Advocate* (Boston), 5 February 1915; Polier and Wise, *Personal Letters,* p. 148.

16. *Evening Tribune* (Providence), 28 June 1915; *Jewish Monitor*, 1 July 1915.

17. Henry Morgenthau to SSW, 3 August, 1 and 6 December 1915, Morgenthau MSS; Cyrus Adler, *Jacob Schiff: His Life and Letters*, (2 vols., Garden City: Doubleday, 1928), 2:296-99.

18. Cincinnati *Times-Star*, 10 and 13 October 1914; SSW to Brandeis, 15 January 1915, and Brandeis to Horace Kallen, 10 February 1915, Brandeis MSS; SSW to Brandeis, 3 March 1915; New York *Sun*, 27 April 1915; Martin Mayer to SSW, 4 May 1915.

19. SSW to Kallen, 27 October 1915; Wise MSS-AJA; *New York Times*, 24 January 1916; SSW to Kallen, 4 February 1916, Kallen MSS.

20. *New York Times,* 1 May 1916; SSW, "Zionism, Religion and Americanism," *The Maccabaean* 28 (June 1916); 125-26.

21. *CCAR Yearbook* 27 (1917): 201-202, 139-40.

22. SSW, "Reform Rabbis and Zionism," *The Maccabaean* 29 (August 1917): 316.

23. An extensive analysis of the congress fight can be found in Urofsky, *American Zionism*, ch. 5; for the origins of the congress idea, see Bernard G. Richards, "Where the Congress Idea Originated," *Congress Bi-Weekly* 10 (9 April 1943): 11; Marie Syrkin, *Nachman Syrkin: Socialist-Zionist* (New York: Herzl Press, 1961), p. 167; Moses Rischin, "The Early Attitude of the American Jewish Committee to Zionism (1906-1922)," *PAJHS* 49 (1959): 192.

24. Horace Meyer Kallen, *Zionism and World Politics* (Garden City: Doubleday, 1921), pp. 143-44; see also Kallen to Louis D. Brandeis, 5 January 1916, Brandeis MSS.

25. Brandeis to Marshall, 31 August 1914, and reply of the same date, Marshall MSS.

26. Morton Rosenstock, *Louis Marshall: Defender of Jewish Rights* (Detroit: Wayne State University Press, 1965), p. 53; Julian W. Mack to Adolph Kraus, 12 November 1914, Magnes MSS; Alvin S. Roth, "Backgrounds and Origins of the American Jewish Congress," rabbinic thesis (Hebrew Union College, 1953), pp. 134-35; Goren; *New York Jews,* pp. 221-22.

27. Nathan Schachner, *The Price of Liberty* (New York: American Jewish Committee, 1948), p. 65; Adler, *Jacob Schiff,* 2:297-98; Goren, *New York Jews,* p. 220; see also Louis Marshall to Solomon Schechter, 19 February 1915, in Charles Reznikoff, ed. *Louis Marshall: Champion of Liberty, Selected Papers and Addresses* (2 vols., Philadelphia: Jewish Publication Society, 1957), 2:506.

28. Horace Kallen to SSW, 7 January 1915, Wise MSS-AJA; SSW to Otto Wise, 15 March 1915; *American Israelite,* 1 April 1915.

29. Richard Gottheil to Brandeis, 6 May 1915, Brandeis MSS; Judah Magnes to Brandeis, 30 June 1915, Magnes MSS; Judah Magnes to Chaim Weizmann, 2 September 1915, Weizmann MSS; interview with Bernard G. Richards, 7 September 1967, New York City.

30. SSW to Henry Morgenthau, 23 August 1915, Morgenthau MSS.

31. *New York Times,* 21 June 1915; Boston *Evening Transcript,* 28 June 1915.

32. Felix Frankfurter, "Memorandum of meeting . . . ," 12 July 1915; Cyrus Adler to Brandeis, 21 and 28 July and 3 August 1915, and Brandeis to Adler, 28 July and 10 August 1915, all in Brandeis MSS; Cyrus Adler, *I Have Considered the Days* (Philadelphia: Jewish Publication Society, 1941), p. 306.

33. Louis Marshall to Harry Friedenwald, 2 August 1915, Brandeis MSS.

34. Brandeis to SSW, 26 August 1915, Brandeis MSS; *American Hebrew,* 10 September 1915.

35. SSW, "Jewish Conference or Congress: Which and Why?" *Free Synagogue Pulpit* 3 (October 1915).

36. Boston *Post,* 4 October 1915; SSW to Henry Morgenthau, 6 November 1915, Morgenthau MSS.

37. Horace Kallen to Brandeis, 20 October 1915, Julian Mack to Brandeis, 15 November 1915, Charles A. Cowen to Brandeis, 8 November 1915, Brandeis to Bernard G. Richards, 16 November 1915, Brandeis MSS.

38. Kallen to SSW, 21 January 1916.

39. Jacob Schiff to Brandeis, 29 March 1916, Schiff MSS; *American Hebrew,* 3 March 1916; Brandeis to Louis Lipsky, 13 March 1916, Brandeis MSS.

40. Kallen to SSW, 16 March 1916, Wise MSS-AJA; SSW to Kallen, 4 February 1916, and Kallen's reply on 15 February 1916, Kallen MSS; see also SSW to Max Heller, 13 February 1916, Heller MSS.

41. Otto Wise to SSW, 20 March 1916.

42. American Jewish Congress, *Proceedings of Preliminary Conference . . .* (New York: Jewish Congress Organizing Committee, 1916), pp. 5–8, 37–38; SSW to Bernard G. Richards, 3 April 1916.

43. SSW to Simon Wolf, 8 April 1916; Roth, "Congress," pp. 140–41; *American Israelite,* 8 June 1916.

44. Urofsky, *American Zionism,* pp. 175–77; *New York Times,* 18 July 1916.

46. SSW to Bernard Richards, 27 July 1916, and Richards to SSW, 21 August 1916; SSW to Richard Gottheil, 27 July 1916, and to Kallen, 23 October 1916, and Kallen's response, 31 October 1916, all in Wise MSS-AJA.

10. War . . .

1. SSW to Nissim Behar, 4 June 1912, and to William H. Shorten, 29 July 1912; SSW to George Kennan, 9 August 1912, Kennan MSS; *New York Times,* 10 February 1913.

2. Link, *Wilson and the Progressive Era,* ch. 5; SSW to Henry Morgenthau, 27

April 1914, Morgenthau MSS; *New York Times*, 27 April 1914.

3. SSW to Henry Morgenthau, 13 and 31 August 1914; Robert L. Duffus, *Lillian Wald: Neighbor and Crusader* (New York: Macmillan, 1938), p. 151.

4. Link, *Wilson The Struggle for Neutrality, 1914-15* (Princeton: Princeton Unversity Press, 1960), pp. 138-40; SSW to Wilson, 8 December 1914, and Wilson's reply, 10 December 1914, Wilson MSS.

5. "Must we have a larger army and navy?" and "Peace preparedness vs. war preparedness," *Free Synagogue Pulpit* 3 (1915).

6. *New York Times*, 16 January 1915; SSW to Henry Morgenthau, 18 and 28 May 1915, Morgenthau MSS.

7. *New York Times*, 22 May 1911 and 9 September 1915.

8. SSW to Henry Morgenthau, 22 October 1915, Morgenthau MSS.

9. SSW to Woodrow Wilson, 12 November 1915, Wilson MSS.

10. Wilson to SSW, 18 November 1915, Wilson MSS.

11. *New York Times*, 10 February 1916; Lillian Wald to SSW, 4 March 1916, Wald MSS.

12. SSW to George Foster Peabody, 9 May 1916, and to Jesse F. Orton, 22 May 1916; *New York Times*, 15 May 1916.

13. *New York Times*, 17 April 1916; SSW to Henry Morgenthau, 18 January 1916, Morgenthau MSS.

14. SSW to Hamilton Holt, 25 August 1916; *New York Times*, 17 October 1916.

15. SSW to Frank Thilly, 20 October 1916, Thilly MSS; SSW to Horace Kallen, 15 November 1916, Kallen MSS.

16. *New York Times*, 4 January 1917; SSW to Horace Kallen, 8 February 1917, Kallen MSS.

17. *New York Times*, 12 February and 24 March 1917.

18. Oswald Garrison Villard, *Fighting Years: Memoirs of a Liberal Editor* (New York: Harcourt, Brace, 1939), pp. 323-24; Voss, *Rabbi and Minister,* pp. 142-43.

19. Link, *Wilson and the Progressive Era*, pp. 281-282.

20. New York Times, 9 April 1917; Voss, *Rabbi and Minister*, pp. 146-48.

21. SSW to Lillian Wald, 19 July 1917, and her reply, 30 July 1917, Wald MSS.

22. SSW to Richard Ward Montague, 4 June 1917, see various speeches reported in *New York Times,* 3 and 24 September 1917 and 15 March 1918.

23. SSW to E. M. House, 10 April 1917, House MSS; *New York Times,*, 5 November and 31 December 1917; SSW to LWW, 28 June 1918.

24. SSW, undated memorandum [c. 1945]; *New York Times,* 27 and 28 July and 18 August 1918; Voss, *Rabbi and Minister,* p. 153. A few years later Wise was invited to give a speech to the Pennslyvania Society of New York, and was introduced by Charles M. Schwab, president of Bethlehem Steel, which had operated the Shippen Point yard. In his remarks Schwab spoke most generously of SSW, and said that during the war, on one of the hottest days in the summer of 1918, he had gone to the Hog Island shipyard, and there found SSW working as a riveter in the broiling sun. To much applause, SSW replied: "I bow to everything my boss Charlies Schwab may say except for some slight inaccuracies. I was not a riveter but an unskilled worker at $3 a day, and he never saw me at Hog Island. What kind of a rabbi would I be to take a job, even for the government, at a place called Hog Island?"

25. SSW to David Yellin, 27 October 1914; SSW Henry Morgenthau, 26 October 1914, Morgenthau MSS.

26. *Menorah Journal* 1 (January 1915): 18; *Maccabaean* 25 (November/December 1915): 155; SSW to Richard Gottheil, 2 February 1917.

27. SSW to Jacob deHaas, 9 April 1917, deHaas MSS; SSW to Horace Kallen, 12 Apriil 1917, Kallen MSS.

28. Henry Morgenthau to Robert Lansing, 15 June 1917, State Department Records; SSW, Memorandum of meeting with President Wilson, 29 June 1917; *New York Times*, 30 June 1917.

29. Jacob Schiff to Bernard G. Richards, 5 July 1917, and to Cyrus Adler, 16 July 1917, Schiff MSS.

30. SSW to Harry Cutler, 26 September 1917; SSW to Horace Kallen, 24 September 1917, and Kallen's reply, 27 September 1917, Kallen MSS; SSW to Louis Brandeis, 5 October 1917, and SSW to Horace Kallen, 31 October 1917.

31. Brandeis to SSW, 14 February 1917, and SSW's reply, 16 February 1917.

32. SSW to Harry Friedenwald, 28 May 1917, cited in Alexandra Lee Levin, *Vision* (Philadelphia: Jewish Publication Society, 1964), pp. 233–34; SSW to Richard Gottheil, 30 June 1917, Wise MSS-AJA.

33. See Leonard Stein, *The Balfour Declaration* (New York: Simon and Schuster, 1961); Isaiah Friedman, *The Question of Palestine, 1914–1918* (New York: Schocken, 1973) and *Germany, Turkey and Zionism: 1897–1918* (Oxford: Oxford University Press, 1977). For the American role, see Urofsky, "American Zionists and the Balfour Declaration," *Midstream* 24 (December 1978): 28–34.

34. SSW to E. M. House, 29 January 1917, to Brandeis, 9 April 1917, and to Clarence I. deSola, 19 June 1917, SSW, *Challenging Years*, p. 189.

35. *Challenging Years*, p. 189; Urofsky, *American Zionism*, pp. 202–13.

36. Charles I. Goldblatt, "The Impact of the Balfour Declaration in America," *AJHQ* 57 (June 1968): 476–80.

37. *New York Times,* 24 December 1917; SSW to Sir Cecil Spring-Rice, 20 December 1917; SSW, *Challenging Years,* p. 191.

38. Robert Lansing to Woodrow Wilson, 13 December 1917, State Department Records; Cecil Spring-Rice to Foreign Office, 21 and 27 December 1917, Foreign Office Records.

39. SSW to Woodrow Wilson, 27 August 1918, and Wilson's reply, 31 August 1918, Wilson MSS.

40. Felix Frankfurter to SSW, 4 September 1918; SSW to Bernard G. Richards, 16 October 1918.

41. Chaim Weizmann *et al.* to Brandeis, 10 January 1918, Foreign Office Records; SSW to Brandeis, 11 January 1918, deHass MSS.

42. SSW to Brandeis, 25 February 1918; Brandeis to SSW, 27 February 1918, deHaas MSS.

43. On 26 February 1918, Lansing informed Wilson of the Provisional Committee's request for passports for a medical unit to go to Palestine, and suggested that it be turned down. Brandeis and Wilson then prepared a response to Lansing's objections, arguing the humanitarian rather than political nature of the unit, which Col. House showed to the president, and on 3 March Wilson approved the Zionist re-

quest. Lansing to Wilson, 26 February 1918, with hand-written notation dated 3 March, "President authorized the unit," State Department Records; SSW to E. M. House, 2 March, and House to Wilson, 3 March 1918, Wilson MSS.

44. For details, see Urofsky, *American Zionism*, pp. 253–57.

45. Jacob deHaas to Brandeis, 26 October 1918.

11. . . . *and Peace*

1. SSW to Horace Kallen, 18 October 1918, and Kallen to SSW, 20 October 1918, Kallen MSS.

2. Letters of introduction from Brandeis to Nahum Sokolow, Chaim Weizmann, Herbert Hoover, Arthur Balfour, and others, 26 November 1918; SSW to Max Heller, 29 November 1918.

3. Chaim Weizmann and Aaron Aaronson to Brandeis, 5 December 1918, London Office Records.

4. Bernard Richards memoir, COHC, pp. 88—89.

5. Reznikoff, *Marshall*, 2:526; *New York Times,* 19 December 1918.

6. SSW to Jacob deHaas, 20 December 1918; notes of interview, SSW with Balfour, 19 December 1918, de Haas MSS.

7. SSW to JWP, 23 December 1918, see also SSW to Henry Morgenthau, 30 December 1918, Morgenthau MSS.

8. LWW to JWW, 21 December 1918.

9. Ibid.

10. Cable, SSW to Brandeis, 20 December 1918, State Department Records; SSW, "Memorandum of meeting with Chaim Weizmann, 30 December 1918," Weizmann MSS; SSW, "Report to National Executive Committee of ZOA," 1 February 1919, Sokolow MSS.

11. SSW, Reports to National Executive Committee, 1 and 9 February 1919, Sokolow MSS.

12. Memorandum of conference, SSW, Mary Fels, Chaim Weizmann, and Joseph Cowen, 6 January 1919, Sokolow MSS.

13. SSW to Brandeis, 15 January 1919; SSW, *Challenging Years,* p. 196; SSW to Woodrow Wilson, 15 January 1919, Wilson MSS; Voss, *Rabbi and Minister,* pp. 166–67; Frank E. Manuel, *The Realities of American-Palestine Relations* (Washington: Public Affair Press, 1949), pp. 234–35.

14. SSW to Max Heller, 4 February 1919; SSW, "What will come out of the Peace Conference?" *The Maccabaean* 32 (February 1919):29.

15. *New York Times*, 3 March 1919; SSW to Nathan Straus, 6 March 1919.

16. London *Jewish Chronicle,* 25 May 1914; SSW, *Challenging Years*, p. 105; Morgenthau, *All in a Lifetime,* pp. 293–94; Voss, *Rabbi and Minister,* pp. 135–36; Henry Morgenthau to executive committee of the Free Synagogue, 5 March 1919, Morgenthau MSS.

17. *New York Times,* 9 March 1919.

18. SSW to E. M. House, 3 February 1919, House MSS; SSW to Brandeis, 27 May 1919.

19. SSW to Bernard G. Richards, 24 July 1919, and Richard's response, 31 July 1919.

20. Louis Marshall to Jacob Schiff, 24 April 1920, and Schiff to Bernard Richards, 24 April 1920, Schiff MSS; Julius Simon to Zionist Bureau, London, 7 May 1920, London Office Records.

21. *New York Times,* 31 May 1920.

22. SSW, *Challenging Years,* p. 208; Louis Marshall to Jacob Schiff and Schiff to Bernard Richards, 1 June 1920, Schiff MSS.

23. SSW to Brandeis, 2 June 1920.

24. SSW to Julian Mack, 19 November 1918, deHaas MSS; SSW to Brandeis, 22 April 1919.

25. Louis Marshall to Cyrus Adler, 11 August 1919, in Reznikoff, *Marshall,* 2:725-26; Polier and Wise, *Personal Letters,* p. 181; SSW to Julian Mack, 29 November 1919.

26. SSW to Brandeis, 19 January 1920, Brandeis MSS; minutes, National Executive Committee of ZOA, 12 February 1920, London Office Records; SSW to Brandeis, 31 March 1920.

27. SSW to Nathan Straus, 26 February 1920, and to Brandeis, 9 April 1920; Urofsky, *American Zionism,* ch. 7, passim.

28. SSW to Brandeis, 14 April and 2 June 1920, Brandeis MSS; *New York Times,* 11 July 1920.

29. SSW to Nathan Straus, 3 August 1930; SSW to Julian Mack, 11 and 24 August 1920; Mack to SSW, 13 August 1920, deHaas MSS.

30. Minutes of National Executive Committee, ZOA, 29 August 1920, deHaas MSS.

31. Emanuel Neumann, *In the Arena* (New York: Herzl Press, 1976), p. 47; Morris Margolies to SSW, 24 September 1919.

32. Minutes of National Executive Committee, ZOA, 29 and 30 September 1920, deHaas MSS; SSW to Richard Gottheil, 2 October 1920, Wise MSS-AJA.

33. Buffalo *Courier,* 28 November 1920.

34. Brandeis to SSW, 29 November 1920.

35. Brandeis to SSW et al., 19 March 1921; SSW to Brandeis, 4 April 1921, Brandeis MSS; summary of conferences, 4-9 April 1921, Weizmann MSS; Polier and Wise, *Personal Letters,* pp. 190-91.

36. SSW to Felix Frankfurter, 18 April 1921.

37. Memorandum of luncheon with Chaim Weizmann, 26 April 1921; SSW to Frankfurter and to Brandeis, both 26 April 1921.

38. *Report of Proceedings of the 24th Annual Convention of the Zionist Organization of America* (New York: ZOA, 1921), pp. 16-17; Bernard Rosenblatt Memoir, Oral History Collection of The Institute for Contemporary Jewry, The Hebrew University, Jerusalem, pp. 43-44.

39. *Report of Proceedings,* pp. 119-21; Bernard Richards Memoir, COHC, p. 206.

40. SSW to Mary Fels, 14 June 1921.

41. Chaim Weizmann to Sir Herbert Samuel, 8 August 1920, Weizmann MSS.

12. "Slightly Dispirited"

1. SSW to Richard Gottheil, 7 October 1920, Wise MSS-AJA.

2. O. E. Miller to SSW, 14 November 1946, inquiring if the story were true; Florence Eitelberg (SSW's secretary) to Miller, 20 November 1946, confirming the details; SSW to Woodrow Wilson, 1 July 1919, Wilson MSS.

3. SSW to Editor, *New York Times*, 8 July 1919, in *Times* of 13 July 1919; SSW to William Howard Taft, 24 February 1920, Taft MSS.

4. See M. I. Urofsky, *Big Steel and the Wilson Administration* (Columbus: Ohio State University Press, 1969), ch. 7.

5. SSW to Samuel Gompers, 18 June 1919, and to William Z. Foster, 10 July 1919; David Brody, *Labor in Crisis: The Steel Strike of 1919* (Philadelphia: Lippincott, 1965), p. 94.

6. *Free Synagogue Pulpit* 5 (1919); Voss, *Rabbi and Minister,* pp. 177-78; *New York Times*, 6 October 1919.

7. SSW to Arthur Kaufmann, 7 October 1919.

8. See, for example, Daniel Kline to SSW, 7 October 1919.

10. *New York Times,* 14 and 16 October 1919; Louis Brandeis to SSW, 13 October 1919; George Foster Peabody to SSW, 18 October 1919.

11. SSW to Maurice Abner, 5 April 1920; Charles H. Joseph to SSW, 6 August 1920.

12. *New York Times,* 23 November 1919; Isidor Lubin Memoir, COHC, p. 33.

13. SSW to Brandeis, 4 April 1921; *New York Times,* 1 and 14 September 1920; James Cox to SSW, 2 September 1920; Pat Harrison (Democratic Speakers Bureau) to SSW, 27 October 1920.

14. *New York Times,* 17 October 1920, see also Brandeis to SSW, 27 October 1920, deHaas MSS.

15. SSW to JWP, 3 November 1920.

16. *New York Times*, 4 June 1928; SSW to Moses Einhorn, 26 December 1923.

17. SSW to Moses Einhorn, 21 March 1921 and 2 January 1922.

18. Ibid., 16 May and 21 November 1927, 27 January 1928; SSW to Rev. Joel B. Hayden, 13 January 1928, and to Lee and Justine Tulin, 9 January 1928.

19. *New York Times,* 13 March 1922 and 10 January 1927.

20. Ibid., 13 December 1926 and 16 March 1925.

21. Sermon on *King of Kings,* 4 December 1927; SSW to Louis I. Newman, 6 and 15 December 1927 and 25 January 1928, and to Rudolph I. Coffee, 8 December 1927.

22. *New York Times,* 14 February 1927; see also SSW, endorsement of the Catholic Theater Movement, *New York Times,* 12 August 1930; John Haynes Holmes to SSW, 16 December 1926.

23. SSW to Harry Weinberger, 6 April 1923 and 11 May 1924; Weinberger to SSW, 6 April 1923, 26 January 1925 and 25 March 1926; SSW, "Some Impressions of 'The God of Vengeance,' " all in Weinberger, MSS.

24. *New York Times,* 23 April 1923.

25. Ibid.

26. SSW to Jacob Billikopf, 25 April 1923, Billikopf MSS; SSW to Woodrow Wilson, 15 December 1921, Wilson MSS.

27. Henry A. Wallace Memoir, COHC, p. 2305, reporting conversation with SSW.

28. SSW to JWW, 5 November 1923, and to Max Levy, 17 June 1924.

29. SSW to Mary Fels, 30 June 1924; to Owen Lovejoy, 8 July 1924; to John Haynes Holmes, 7 July 1924; to Abram Elkus, 16 July 1924; to Newton D. Baker, 22 July 1924; and to Julian W. Mack, 26 July 1924.

30. SSW to John Haynes Holmes, 25 September 1924; *Jewish Daily Bulletin* 1 (4 November 1924); 2; "a devoted member" to SSW, 3 November 1924; Houston Thompson to SSW, 4 November 1924; SSW to Newton D. Baker, 6 November 1924.

31. A. Simonson to SSW, 15 October 1928; see also John R. Stratton to SSW, 19 October 1928.

32. *New York Times,* 4 November 1928.

33. SSW to Julian Mack, 5 November 1928 and to Felix Frankfurter, 7 November 1928; SSW to Gretchen Cunningham, 23 April 1929.

13. The Jewish Institute of Religion

1. Solomon Goldman, *A Rabbi Takes Stock* (New York: Harper and Brothers, 1931), p. 7.

2. SSW to Arthur Abdelson, 2 October 1923, and Abraham Feldman, 13 March 1924; see also SSW to Abraham Cronbach, 30 April 1919, Cronbach MSS.

3. SSW to Israel Goldstein, 11 February 1920. Goldstein stayed on at New York's B'nai Jeshurun Congregation for a distinguished ministry of more than four decades.

4. Polier and Wise, *Personal Letters,* p. 131; SSW to Richard Gottheil, 5 August 1910, Wise MSS-AJA.

5. SSW to Mordecai Kaplan, 6 April 1920; minutes of meeting, 2 November 1920, JIR Records; SSW, *Challenging Years,* p. 131.

6. Goldstein, *The Synagogue and Social Welfare,* pp. 72–73.

7. SSW, *Challenging Years,* p. 134.

8. Abram I. Elkus to executive board of UAHC, 19 May 1921; SSW to JWP and JWW, 24 May 1921; "Dr. Stephen S. Wise Makes a Proposal to the Union. The Committee's Reply" (pamphlet, 1922).

9. David P. Hayes to Lee K. Frankel, 6 April 1922; SSW to Max Heller, 3 April 1921 and 6 May 1922, Heller MSS; see also SSW to Louis J. Kopald and Richard Gottheil, 11 April 1922, and to James Heller, 12 April 1922.

10. A. H. Silver to Charles Shohl, 21 April 1922; Max Heller to SSW, 28 April and 11 May 1922, JIR Records.

11. SSW to Max Heller, 8 August 1922, Heller MSS; memorandum of 9 June and 4 July 1922.

12. SSW to Martin A. Meyer, 14 September 1922.

13. Michael Meyer, "A Centennial History," in Samuel E. Karff, ed., *Hebrew Union College-Jewish Institute of Religion at One Hundred Years* (Cincinnati: HUC Press, 1976), pp. 146–48.

14. SSW to Mordecai Kaplan, 31 May 1922; SSW to Ismar Elbogen, 13 September 1923, Elbogen MSS; Kaplan to Carl Herman Voss, 23 January 1955; interview with Dr. Voss, 9 September 1975.

15. Meyer, "A Centennial History," pp.156-57.
16. *Ibid.*, p.152, quoting Philip Bernstein.
17. Voss, *Rabbi and Minister*, pp.212-13.
18. Story told by Rabbi Jerome R. Malino (JIR 1935) in "Hebrew Union College Jewish Institute of Religion: A Documentary History," *American Jewish Archives* 26 (November 1974): 185.
19. Wise did in fact have the gift of being able to snatch catnaps at any moment—in his office, in a taxi, or at meetings—a valuable asset, considering his hectic schedule. Yet he appeared able to follow a conversation even while apparently dozing. At one time Morris Raphael Cohen was talking to JIR students and noticed Wise with his eyes closed and head nodding. "What year were we in the Adirondacks together at Davidson's camp?" he suddenly asked. Wise opened his eyes, said "1892," and then immediately closed them again.
20. Philip S. Bernstein, "Stephen S. Wise: Some Personal Recollections," *CCAR Journal* 11 (April 1963): 8.
21. *Ibid.*, pp.6-7.
22. Albert Vorspan, "A Disciple of the Wise: Jacob X. Cohen," *Congress Bi-Weekly* 38 (21 May 1971): 14-15.
23. SSW to Martin Mayer, 7 April 1923; to Fannie Saxe Long, 27 September 1923; to Harry L. Glucksman, 11 April 1924.
24. SSW to Julian W. Mack, 8 May 1924, to William W. Green, 5 February 1924, and to Solomon Goldman, 18 March 1925, complaining that Abba Hillel Silver had refused to allow him to talk on the JIR to the Men's Club at Tifereth Israel in Cleveland; SSW to Morton Berman, 20 January 1928.
25. Memorandum, 5 November 1923; Walter Hilborn to SSW, telegram of 13 February 1929 and letter of 19 February 1929; Louis Newman to SSW, 22 February 1929; SSW to Julian Mack, 12 March 1919 and to James Heller, 5 June 1929; Ludwig Vogelstein to SSW, 7 June 1929, all in JIR Records. See also SSW to Hilborn, 11 June 1930.
26. SSW to Ismar Elbogen, 18 January 1926, and to Walter S. Hilborn, 10 January 1930
27. *New York Times*, 23 May 1926; Morton Berman, "Rabbi, Teacher and Leader," *Congress Weekly* 16 (30 May 1949): 14; Meyer, *A Centennial History*, pp.159-60.

14. Ivri Anochi

1. SSW to Mrs. Frank Lukens, 28 April 1922; *New York Times*, 22 October 1922 and 25 December 1924; Voss, *Rabbi and Minister*, p.100.
2. *New York Times*, 22 January and 4 February 1925 and 11 July 1927; SSW to Julius Fohs, 11 May 1923, and to Charles Bloch, 13 July 1927.
3. For Holmes's private emotions, see his letter to Wise, 21 March 1930.
4. SSW, *Challenging Years*, p.283; *New York Times* 21 December 1925. According to Myles Martel ("A rhetorical analysis," p.127), no copy of the original speech has ever been found, although there are references to a stenographic transcript in some of SSW's letters.

5. Voss, *Rabbi and Minister*, pp.224–25; SSW to Hutchins Hapgood, 17 July 1912, to James N. Whiton, 14 March 1913, and to C. L. Powell, 5 February 1914.

6. Judd L. Teller, *Strangers and Natives: The Evolution of the American Jew from 1921 to the Present* (New York: Dell, 1968), p.76; *New York Times*, 22, 29, and 30 December 1925; SSW, *Challenging Years*, p. 281.

7. *New York Times*, 22 December 1925; Reznikoff, *Marshall*, 2: 828–29.

8. William Fineshriber to SSW, 24 December 1925; Samuel Untermyer to SSW, 26 December 1925; Nathan Straus to SSW, 25 December 1925; *New York Times*, 28 December 1925.

9. Teller, *Strangers and Natives*, p.78; SSW to Edmund Waterman, 31 December 1925.

10. SSW to Louis Lipsky, 23 December 1925, in *New York Times*, 25 December 1925.

11. *New York Times*, 26, 27, and 28 December 1925.

12. Ibid.; see also comments of other Christians in this article.

13. *Jewish Morning Journal*, 30 December 1925; *New York American*, 30 December 1925; *New York Times*, 31 December 1925.

14. Harry Orlinsky, "The Legacy of Stephen Wise." *Founders' Day Addresses* (New York, 1978), 22–23.

15. Samuel Untermyer to SSW, 26 December 1925; *New York American*, 30 December 1925; *New York Times*; 3 January 1926.

16. Neumann, *In the Arena*, p.89; *New York Times*, 31 December 1925.

17. Nathan Straus to SSW, 25 December 1925.

18. Extra edition of *Jewish Daily Bulletin*, 3 January 1926.

19. Felix Frankfurter to SSW, 4 January 1926; Solomon Goldman to SSW, 5 January 1926; E. Milton Altfeld to SSW, 12 January 1926; *New York Times*, 9 January 1926; SSW to Richard Montague, 3 January 1926, and to Edward Nathan Calisch, 17 March 1926.

15. Great Betrayals

1. *New York Times*, 7 January 1924; Bernard G. Richards, "Following the Leader," *Congress Weekly* 16 (30 May 1949): 10; SSW to JWW, 4 January 1924.

2. *Jewish Week*, 14 February 1924; SSW to JWW, 14 February 1924; *American Jewish Year Book* 27 (1925/1926): 428–36; J. X. Cohen to SSW, 4 December 1929.

3. *New York Times*, 3 May 1929; Rosenstock, *Louis Marshall*, pp. 261–62.

4. Voss, *Rabbi and Minister*, p. 240; SSW to Rev. B. Gallagher, 2 December 1922. Although Wise did not play an active role in the NAACP, he remained friendly to the cause of civil rights and willingly lent his name to many groups seeking equitable treatment for blacks. On more than one occasion he noted his regret that he could not do more in this area because of the demands of his other commitments.

5. *New York Times*, 3 February and 26 June 1924, and 9 March 1925; SSW to Nathan Strauss, Jr., 28 May 1923, and to Rev. Frank Norris, 1 April 1924.

6. Louis Marshall to SSW, 29 November 1922.

7. Rosenstock, *Louis Marshall*, pp. 40, 196.

8. A detailed narrative of these events is Saul S. Friedman, *The Incident at Massena* (New York: Stein and Day, 1978).

9. Jake Shulkin to SSW, 25 September 1928.

10. SSW to Major John Warner and to W. Gilbert Hawes, both 20 September 1928; memorandum of telephone conversation between SSW and Alfred E. Smith, 29 September 1928; Smith to SSW, 3 October 1928.

11. Jake Shulkin to SSW, 1 October 1928; W. Gilbert Hawes to SSW, 2 October 1928; John A. Warner to Alfred E. Smith, W. Gilbert Hawes to SSW, Harry Mc-Cann to SSW, and John A. Warner to Louis Marshall, all 4 October 1928.

12. SSW to JWW and JWP, 3 October 1928; *New York Times*, 5 and 8 October 1928. Ironically, the resultant publicity in the case came mainly from Louis Marshall, who normally prided himself on keeping Jewish problems out of the press. It is possible that Marshall resented that the Massena Jews had written to Wise and sent him only a carbon of the letter. Marshall did dispatch journalist Boris Smolar to Massena to investigate, but by the time Smolar arrived, Wise's intercession had determined the future course of events. Marshall then wrote a long and rather legalistic letter to Smith, demanding that he force Hawes to resign as mayor of Massena, and released the document to the press. An angry governor told Wise that unless Marshall took care, Hawes would wind up "a victim and a hero and the KKK will send him to Congress or make him governor." After the disciplinary action and public apologies, Wise helped Shulkin and Rabbi Brennglass draft a letter to Marshall "thanking" him for all his help, but asking him to desist from any more public statements, lest he make the life of Massena's Jews intolerable.

13. Brandeis to SSW, 22 August 1921; SSW to Brandeis, 26 September and 9 November 1921; SSW to Felix Frankfurter, 1 February 1922.

14. SSW to Julian W. Mack, 26 and 28 June 1922.

15. SSW to Gertrude Wolfe, 28 July 1922, Wolfe MSS; SSW to Max Heller, 8 August 1922, Heller MSS; *New York Times*, 17 December 1922; SSW to Brandeis, 14 September 1922.

16. SSW to Julian Mack, 22 January and 31 December 1923.

17. SSW to Bernard G. Richards, 11 March 1924; *New York Times*, 21 August 1925.

18. *New York Times*, 14 September 1925; SSW to Chaim Weizmann, 14 September 1925; JWW to author, 10 July 1975.

19. Reznikoff, *Marshall*, 2:753; SSW to Leo Motzkin, 28 August 1925, and to S. Bernstein, 15 September 1925; SSW to Harry Friedenwald, 12 December 1925, Friedenwald MSS.

20. Neumann, *In the Arena*, p.85; interview with Emanuel Neumann; SSW to Richard Gottheil, 4 February 1925, Wise MSS-AJA.

21. *New York Times*, 3 April 1925.

22. "Dr. Wise's return," *New Palestine* 9 (24 April 1925): 501; Emanuel Neumann to SSW, 24 April 1925; SSW to Louis Lipsky, 26 May and 1 June 1925; SSW to LWW, 1 June 1925; Lipsky to SSW, 6 August 1925.

23. *New York Times*, 20 and 21 August 1925.

24. SSW to Louis D. Brandeis, 27 August 1925, Brandeis MSS.

25. SSW to Bernard G. Richards and to Abram Elkus, both 28 August 1925; SSW to Max Heller, 9 September 1925, Heller MSS; SSW to Felix Frankfurter, 11 September 1925.

26. Louis Marshall to Henry Cohen, 6 February 1925; Reznikoff, *Marshall*, 2: 745; Felix Warburg to Louis Marshall, 12 July 1923, Warburg MSS.

27. Diary entry for 14 November 1922, in Alex Bein, ed., *Arthur Ruppin Memoirs, Diaries, Letters* (New York: Herzl Press. 1972), p.201.

28. Urofsky, *American Zionism*, p.313.

29. Verbatim transcript of the conference in *Zionist Review* 7 (April 1924): supplement.

30. SSW, *Challenging Years*, pp.306–307.

31. See SSW to Julian Mack, 11 February 1926; to Max Heller, 23 February 1926, Heller MSS.

32. Urofsky, *American Zionism*, pp.317–18.

33. See, for example, SSW to Lee and Justine Tulin, 30 March 1926.

34. Louis Marshall to Fred Kirsch, 23 April 1926, and to Chaim Weizmann, 28 May 1926, Weizmann MSS.

35. SSW to Bernard G. Richards, 5 August 1926; to Louis D. Brandeis, 11 January 1927; and to JWP, 18 January 1927; *New York Times*, 9 November 1926.

36. SSW to Julian Mack, 2 June 1927; to Louis D. Brandeis, 8 June 1927.

37. SSW to Louis Lipsky, 6 and 7 September 1927; Lipsky to Political Committee, 6 September 1927; "Dr. Wise Returns from Basle," *New Palestine* 13 (16 September 1927): 209; editorial, *New Palestine* 13 (23 September 1927): 228; *New York Times*, 1 October 1927.

38. SSW to Henrietta Szold, 13 October 1927.

39. SSW to Lee and Justine Tulin, 13 October 1927, reporting meeting with Julian Mack, Abraham Tulin, Norvig Lindheim, Sam Rosensohn, and Louis Lipsky.

40. SSW, "Why I Favor the Jewish Agency," *New Palestine* 15 (28 December 1928): 537.

41. For the history of the Agency, see Zelig Chinitz, "The Jewish Agency and the Jewish Community in the United States," master's essay, Columbia University (1959), and Melvin I. Urofsky, "Fifty Years of the Jewish Agency,"*Midstream* 25 (November 1979): 42–46.

42. SSW to JWP, 29 September 1927.

43. SSW to Louis D. Brandeis, 8 June 1927; Norvig Lindheim to SSW, 20 July 1927; Sam Rosensohn to SSW, 11 October 1927.

44. SSW to Lee Tulin, 27 October 1927.

45. Julian Mack to Louis Brandeis, 26 March 1928, deHaas MSS.

46. *New York Times*, 20 and 21 March 1928; SSW to Louis Lipsky, 22 March 1928; Shapiro, *Leadership of American Zionist, Oraganization*, pp.225–26.

47. An extensive report of this meeting is in SSW to Lee and Justine Tulin, 23 March 1928; *New York Times*, 2 April 1928.

48. SSW to Lee Tulin, 22 March 1928; *New York Times*, 2 April 1928.

49. SSW, memorandum of meeting with Justice Brandeis, 3 April 1928.

50. SSW to Lee and Justine Tulin, 30 March 1928; memorandum of meeting with Mack et al., 11 April 1928; SSW to Nahum Goldmann, 8 May and 12 June 1928.

51. SSW to Lee Tulin, 22 March 1928; SSW to Lee and Justine Tulin, 3 April 1928.

52. SSW to Barnett Brickner, 1 May 1928, and to Samuel Rosigner, 3 May 1928;

Julian Mack to Abba Hillel Silver, 7 May 1928, Silver MSS.

53. *New Palestine* 14 (4 May 1928): 498; *New York Times*, 28 October 1929; see also SSW to George Kohut, 18 November 1929.

54. *New York Times*, 29 June 1930.

55. SSW to Vladimir Jabotinsky and to John Haynes Holmes, both 2 July 1930, and to Nahum Goldmann, 7 July 1930.

56. SSW to Rober Kesselman, 8 May 1930 and to Harry Snell, 26 May 1930; SSW to Meyer Weisgal, 3 June 1930, Weizmann MSS.

57. His Majesty's Government, *Parliamentary Papers*, Cmd. 3692 (1930).

58. Chaim Weizmann to Felix Warburg, November 1930, Weizmann MSS; SSW to N. E. Bezer, 26 September 1930.

59. SSW and Jacob deHaas, *The Great Betrayal* (New York: Brentano's, 1930); SSW to John Haynes Holmes, 28 November 1930; Brandeis is SSW, 18 December 1930.

60. SSW to Robert D. Kessleman, 23 December 1930, and to Israel Rosoff, 17 December 1930.

16. In the Prime of Life

1. SSW to JWW, 21 February 1924.

2. *Jewish Tribune*, 23 March 1924; *New York Times*, 16 March 1924.

3. Memorandum to Dr. Israel Braun, 4 March 1927.

4. Louis Brandeis to SSW, 9 March 1921; SSW to Sue Michaelis (Literary Guild), 29 March 1927.

5. SSW to Mary Fels, 19 August 1923.

6. SSW to Lowell Brentano, 22 April 1925. Brentano to SSW, 3 May 1927, 10 August 1928, and 20 January 1930.

7. Interview with Gertrude Adelstein, 20 October 1977.

8. M. Boraisha, "Dr. Wise's Art of Living," *Congress Weekly* 11 (17 March 1944): 15–18; Voss, *Rabbi and Minister*, pp. 240–41.

9. SSW to Charles E. Bloch, 6 June 1922; SSW to A. H. Thorndike, 13 December 1922, Thorndike MSS; SSW to JWW, 25 January 1924.

10. Voss, *Rabbi and Minister*, p. 188; *New York Times*, 27 September 1929.

11. Wise's sermons can be found in the *Free Synagogue Pulpit* and in the many reports of his sermons published over a forty-year period in the *New York Times*.

12. Robert D. Kesselman to SSW, 14 March 1930. Kesselman had heard the broadcast in Palestine the night before.

13. SSW to Kesselman, 11 April 1930.

14. SSW to A. M. Lamport, 19 January 1924; *New York Times*, 30 August and 6 September 1924. To show his appreciation of what Giery had done, Wise contacted Nathan Straus, Jr., and set in motion events that led to Giery's promotion in November. As Wise well understood, advancement in the police department under a Tammany administration depended more on politics than on ability.

15. SSW to Julian W. Mack, 20 October 1927; Jacob Billikopf to SSW, 16 December 1926.

16. James Waterman Wise, *Liberalizing Liberal Judaism* (New York: Macmillan, 1924).

17. *New York Times*, 27 April 1926.

18. Interview with JWW, June 1975; SSW to Barnett Brickner, 5 May 1926, and to John Haynes Holmes, 8 May 1926; Brickner to SSW, 5 May 1926; Holmes to SSW, 6 May 1926; JWW to Max Heller, 1 May 1926, Heller MSS.

19. Interview with JWP, 14 February 1979.

20. SSW to JWP, 28 January and 3 March 1926.

21. SSW to JWP, 5 March 1926; Albert Weisbord memorandum, 4 March 1926; *New York Times*, 6 and 8 March 1926; New York *Herald Tribune*, 8 March 1926.

22. Voss, *Rabbi and Minister*, p. 233; SSW to Bertha Paret, 10 March 1926.

23. *New York Times*, 22 March 1926; Harry Meyers to SSW, 15 March 1926; SSW to Meyers, 19 March 1926, and to JWP, 20 March 1926.

24. SSW to William Green, 21 and 27 September 1926; *New York Times*, 12 October 1926; news release, United Textile Workers Union, 14 December 1926.

25. William Howard Taft to F. H. Wiggin, 3 December 1928; Taft MSS; interview with JWP, 18 November 1979.

26. SSW to Florence Luntz, 17 May 1928, and to JWP, 30 July 1929; JWP to author, 6 January 1978.

27. SSW to Gertrude Wolfe, 26 July 1921, Wolfe MSS: Lionel Haas to SSW, 3 April 1922.

28. William Fineshriber to SSW, 4 February and 1 December 1925.

29. Dr. Leon S. Medalia to SSW, 24 November 1925.

30. Dr. Harlow Brooks to Dr. Milton Rosenbluth, 1 May 1926; SSW memorandum on funeral arrangements, 16 June 1926; Brooks to SSW, 26 June 1926.

31. SSW told the story to Nathan Ziprin, who reported it in an editorial for the Seven Arts Features Syndicate, 9 March 1944.

32. Charles Bloch to George Kohut, 23 October 1930; Kohut to SSW, 15 October 1930.

17. The Political Rabbi

1. *New York Times*, 25 January and 8 October 1921, 6 November 1922, 26 October 1923, and 26 May 1925; SSW to Felix Frankfurter, 9 November 1921; Goldstein, *Synagogue and Social Welfare*, pp. 245–46.

2. SSW, *Challenging Years*, pp. 147–49; SSW to JWP, 20 September 1926.

3. *New York Times*, 31 October 1926.

4. Ibid., 12 March 1928; Felix Frankfurter to Julian Mack, 17 October 1928; SSW to Henry Margowitz, 19 October 1928; SSW to Franklin Roosevelt, 13 November 1928.

5. Frank Friedel, *Franklin D. Roosevelt: The Triumph* (Boston: Little, Brown and Co., 1956), pp. 41–42.

6. Roosevelt to SSW, 19 March 1929, F. Roosevelt MSS.

7. Roosevelt to SSW, 7 January 1929, SSW to Roosevelt, 10 April 1930 and 18 December 1929, SSW to Roosevelt; SSW to Abram Elkus, 15 April 1929.

8. Gene Fowler, *Beau James: The Life and Times of Jimmy Walker* (New York: Viking Press, 1949), passim; SSW to Abram Elkus, 9 and 14 September 1925.

9. Herbert Mitgang, *The Man Who Rode the Tiger: The Life and Times of Judge Samuel Seabury* (Philadelphia: Lippincott, 1963), pp. 160–65.

10. Nathaniel Zatlowitz to SSW, 3 January 1929; SSW to C. C. Burlingame, 1 April 1928, and to Leonard M. Wallstein, 23 December 1929; *New York Times*, 28 October and 4 November 1929.

11. Mitgang, *Man Who Rode the Tiger*, pp. 166–67.

12. SSW, Memorandum of Remarks, 30 December 1929; *New York Times*, 31 December 1929.

13. SSW to Holmes, 16 June 1930; *New York Times*, 17 August 1930.

14. Paul Blanchard to SSW, 17 September 1930; CAC, *Fight for Civic Reconstruction*, First Annual Report, October 1931.

15. Holmes, *I Speak for Myself*, pp. 215–17.

16. Mitgang, *Man Who Rode the Tiger*, pp. 204–205.

17. *New York Times*, 10 and 16 March 1931; see also SSW to William H. Allen, 10 March 1931.

18. Voss, *Rabbi and Minister*, pp. 275–76; Bernard Bellush, *Franklin D. Roosevelt as Governor of New York* (New York: Columbia University Press, 1955), p. 271; see also SSW to Felix Frankfurter, 18 March 1931.

19. Newton D. Baker to SSW, 30 March 1931; Louis D. Brandeis to SSW, 22 March 1931; Neumann Levy to SSW, 18 March 1931; Holmes to SSW, 18 March 1931.

20. Mitgang, *Man Who Rode the Tiger*, p. 246; William H. Allen Memoir, COHC, p. 470; Bellush, *Roosevelt as Governor*, p. 271.

21. Friedel, *Roosevelt: The Triumph*, p. 256.

22. Ibid., p. 258; Roosevelt to Holmes and SSW, 30 March 1932.

23. *New York Times*, 4 April 1932.

24. Mitgang, *Man Who Rode the Tiger*, p. 248.

25. Friedel, *Roosevelt: The Triumph*, p. 295.

26. Statement by Holmes and SSW, 5 June 1932; Mitgang, *Man Who Rode the Tiger*, p. 265.

27. Friedel, *Roosevelt: The Triumph*, pp. 296, 324.

28. SSW to Jerome Michael, 29 July 1932.

29. SSW to Holmes, 7 September 1932; *New York Times*, 19 September 1932.

30. Wise, *Legend of Louise*, p. 43; SSW to Holmes, 7 September 1932.

31. Mitgang, *Man Who Rode the Tiger*, p. 313 ff.

32. SSW to Carl Grossman, 10 October and 6 November 1933; SSW statement to the press, 20 October 1933; SSW to Holmes, 1 January 1934.

33. Richards Memoir, COHC, p. 255.

34. SSW to Felix Frankfurter, 7 December 1933; to Holmes, 18 January 1934; to Bernard S. Deutsch, 18 January 1934; to Joshua Goldberg, 22 December 1936; to Fiorello H. LaGuardia, 34 December 1936.

35. Louis Nizer, *Reflections Without Mirrors: An Autobiography of the Mind* (Garden City: Doubleday, 1978), p. 710.

36. SSW to Harry L. Cohen, 16 February 1934, and to Sigmund Goldschmidt, 18 April 1934.

37. *New York Times*, 12 July 1934.

38. SSW to LaGuardia, 20 September 1934, and to Holmes, 19 September 1934.

39. SSW to C. C. Burlingame, 7 November 1934; *New York Times*, 22 October and 1 November 1937; see, for example, suggestions on expanding the Civil Service list, SSW to LaGuardia, 3 December 1936, LaGuardia MSS.

40. SSW to Sol Stroock, 9 November 1931, and to Helena Rubenstein, 8 December 1931.

41. SSW to Benjamin A. Laven, 25 March 1932.

42. SSW to George Kohut, 29 September 1932; to Bernard Baruch, 30 September 1932; to Florence Luntz, 11 October 1932; to Walter S. Hilborn, 30 November 1932.

43. SSW to Holmes, 27 February 1935; see also SSW to Gertrude Wolfe, 2 March 1935, Wolfe MSS.

44. Bellush, *Roosevelt as Governor*, passim.

45. SSW to Newton D. Baker, 6 May 1931 and 2 August 1932; *New York Times*, 12 September 1931; SSW to John Stewart Bryant, 12 May 1931.

46. SSW to Felix Frankfurter, 8 September 1932; to Mrs. G. Cunningham, 5 August 1932; to Edward I. Israel, 9 September 1932; to Florence Luntz, 11 October 1932.

47. SSW and Holmes to Franklin Roosevelt, 17 November 1932; Roosevelt to SSW and Holmes, 16 December 1932; Holmes to SSW, 21 December 1932; SSW to Philip Bernstein, 3 January 1933. In his sermon to the Free Synagogue shortly before Roosevelt's inaguration, Wise spoke in guarded but friendly tones: "We have a right to expect of Mr. Roosevelt certain qualities of leadership and decision, but we must not regard him as a miracle man. He is a simple, honest, unafraid American who, by his election, is entitled to our confidence, cooperation and forbearance." *New York Times*, 6 March 1933.

48. William E. Leuchtenburg, "The New Deal and the Analogue of War," in John Braemen et al., eds., *Change and Continuity in Twentieth-Century America*, (Columbus: Ohio State University Press, 1964), pp. 81–143; Otis L. Graham, Jr., *An Encore for Reform; The Old Progressives and the New Deal* (New York: Oxford University Press, 1967), pp. 110–11.

49. SSW to Ida Silverman, 12 April 1933; to Carl Grossman, 20 March 1933; to Richard Ward Montague, 18 April 1933; to Mrs. G. Cunningham, 1 May 1933.

50. *New York Times*, 8 January and 5 March 1934; "If ever a man deserves to be loved for the enemies he has made, it is Roosevelt," SSW to Robert S. Marx, 3 March 1934; see also Felix Frankfurter to SSW, 28 November 1934.

51. SSW to David K. Niles, 26 September 1935; Bernard G. Richards Memoir, COHC, p. 263. Felix Frankfurter told Wise how much the president had enjoyed renewing their friendship and healing the breach; Frankfurter to SSW, 30 January 1936.

52. SSW to Frankfurter, 28 January 1936; SSW to Heywood Broun, 28 January 1936, and *New York Times*, 15 and 27 January 1936; Frederick Rudolph, "The American Liberty League, 1934–1940," *American Historical Review* 56 (1950): 19–33.

53. JWP to author, 17 October 1978; SSW to John Haynes Holmes, 3 February 1936.

54. SSW to Julian W. Mack, 29 June 1936.

55. SSW to Roosevelt, 28 August 1936, and Roosevelt to SSW, 7 September 1936, F. Roosevelt MSS; Marvin McIntyre to SSW, 24 September 1936; *New York Times*, 25 October and 2 November 1936; *Opinion* 7 (November 1936):19.

56. SSW to Roosevelt, 4 November 1936, F. Roosevelt MSS. Colonel Beck, the Polish foreign minister, had recently declared that the three million Jews in that country were "superfluous" and must migrate. SSW to Roosevelt, 15 January 1937, and Roosevelt's response, 23 January 1937, ibid.

57. H. B. Sussman to SSW, 7 November 1935, and SSW's response, 12 November 1935.

18. A Voice in the Wilderness

1. E. W. Lewin-Epstein to SSW, 18 November 1923; SSW, N. Straus, and Aaron J. Levy to German ambassador, telegram, November 1923.

2. Michael Franklin to SSW, 18 October 1927.

3. SSW to Jacob Gilbert, 7 January 1927, and to E. C. Lindemann, 27 November 1928.

4. *New York Times*, 20 Octgober 1930 and 21 September 1931.

5. SSW to Ismar Elbogen, 11 December 1931.

6. SSW to Julian W. Mack, 30 December 1931, and to Ludwig Lewisohn, 31 December 1931. See also SWW speech to United Rumanian Jews: "In all my life I have never seen a more serious hour for the Jew than now," *New York Times*, 11 January 1932.

7. *Opinion* 1 (8 February 1932):110-11.

8. SSW, *Challenging Years*, pp. 234-35. Bernhard, than a member of the Reichstag, was stripped of his citizenship soon after the Nazis took power. He fled to Paris, where he edited an emigré newspaper, and when war broke out he came to the United States. He died in New York in 1944.

9. Jacob Rader Marcus, "Zionism and the American Jew," *The American Scholar* 2 (May 1933):286.

10. Margaret K. Norden, "American Editorial Response to the Rise of Adolf Hitler: A Preliminary Consideration," *American Jewish Historical Quarterly*, 59 (March 1970):290-301.

11. SSW, *Challenging Years*, p. 236.

12. Martel, "Stephen Wise," pp. 416-18.

13. SSW to Carl Grossman, 10 February 1933; SSW, *Challenging Years*, pp. 237-38.

14. SSW to Julian W. Mack, 1 and 6 March 1933.

15. *New York Times*, 20 March 1933; SSW to Adrienie Battey, 9 March 1933.

16. *Unity in Dispersion*, pp. 103-104.

17. *New York Times*, 21 March 1933; Henry L. Feingold, *The Politics of Rescue: The Roosevelt Administration and the Holocaust, 1938-1945* (New Brunswick: Rutgers University Press, 1970), p. 12.

18. Frederick A. Lazin, "The Response of the American Jewish Committee to the Crisis of German Jewry, 1933-1939," *American Jewish History* 68 (March 1979): 283-304.

19. SSW to Madeline and Benjamin Schloss, 18 May 1933.

20. *New York Times*, March 1933.

21. SSW to Ludwig Lewishon and to Louis D. Brandeis, both 23 March 1933; memorandum of telephone conversation with Governor Lehman, 20 March 1933; SSW, *Challenging Years*, pp. 240–41.

22. *Challenging Years*, pp. 244–45; *New York Times*, 27 March 1933.

23. NBC had originally agreed to carry only an hour's worth of the meeting, and Wise had insisted that the network broadcast the talks of the Christian speakers. But NBC officials listening to the proceedings decided, without Wise knowing about it, to continue the broadcast in order to carry his speech as well.

24. *New York Times*, 28 March 1933; *Opinion* 3 (April 1933):16–17.

25. SSW to Julian W. Mack, 29 March 1933.

26. Wise received a cable from three former presidents of the German Zionist Federation urging him to call off the anti-German boycott. Another message declared: "German Jews accuse you and associates to be tools of outside political influences. Your senseless overrating of own international importance and lack of judgment damages largely those you pretend to want to help." As he later discovered, all these messages had been sent under compulsion of Nazi officials, and the overly insolent tone had been deliberately adopted in the hope Wise would recognize that the writers did not mean what they said. SSW, *Challenging Years*, pp. 248–49.

27. SSW to John Haynes Holmes, 3 April 1933, and to Madeline and Benjamin Schloss, 4 April 1933.

28. SSW to Marion and David Greenberg, 7 April 1933; to Julian W. Mack, 8 April 1933; to George Kohut, 26 April 1933.

29. In May 1933, the American Jewish Committee called a meeting to explain and discuss its policies, and hardly anyone attended. Sol Stroock bitterly commented: "It is somewhat disappointing to me to receive a letter from one gentleman that he could not come tonight because he had to go out to dinner. It is equally disappointing, and possibly more so, to receive a letter from another gentleman saying that he is not interested in this because 'I have too many other things that take my time and action'." Quoted in Lazin, "Response of American Jewish Committee," pp. 303–304.

30. SSW to Felix Frankfurter and Julian W. Mack, both on 15 April 1933, and to Richard W. Montague, 18 April 1933.

31. SSW to William Rosenau, 10 and 19 April 1933, and Rosenau to SSW, 15 April 1933, in Rosenau MSS; see also charges in *American Hebrew*, 21 April 1933, and in *B'nai B'rith Magazine*, May 1933.

32. SSW to Helen and Max Lowenthal, 18 April 1933.

33. Polier and Wise, *Personal Letters*, p. 220; SSW to Albert Einstein, 9 May 1933; Brandeis to SSW, 28 April 1933. Julian Mack also provided encouragement, even while he worried about danger facing his daughter Ruth, then studying psychiatry in Vienna. "If at times I disagree with you on this, that or the other point," Mack wrote on 18 May 1933, "I need hardly tell you how deeply gratified and satisfied I am that you have been given the strength to take a lead and to carry on so wonderfully."

34. Zosa Szajkowski, "A Note on the American-Jewish Struggle," *American*

Jewish Historical Quarterly 59 (March 1970):272.

35. Lazin, "Response of American Jewish Committee," pp. 291-92; SSW to Ludwig Lewisohn, 7 June 1933.

36. SSW to Julian W. Mack, 4 May and 14 July 1933; William E. Dodd, Jr., and Martha Dodd, eds., *Ambassador Dodd's Diary, 1933-1938* (New York: Harcourt, Brace and Co., 1941), p. 9.

37. SSW to Ludwig Lewisohn, 15 July 1933; *New York Times*, 1920 and 21 July 1933.

38. SSW, *Challenging Years*, pp. 252-53; *New York Times*, 15 August 1933. For Wise's caution regarding the boycott, see SSW to John Haynes Holmes, 3 April 1933, and to Ruth Mack Brunswick, 6 April 1933.

39. SSW to John Haynes Holmes, 18 August 1933, and to Louis D. Brandeis, 19 September 1933.

40. Minutes of American Jewish Congress Administrative Committee, 23 September 1933.

41. SSW to Benjamin Schloss, 8 November 1933.

42. Cyrus Adler of the American Jewish Committee rebuked Rabbi Samuel Schulman, who suggested a petition to have the president publicly protest Nazi measures. The White House would not deal in any public way with the German situation, "although I am assured that the President has spoken most directly to Dr. Schact and to Dr. Luther. I understand his point of view to be that anything which would mar the interest of this country . . . would be bad for the world and of course for the Jews of the world. It might fall even more heavily on the Jews in Germany." Adler closed, "I am sure that you will agree with me that Jews in the country cannot, as good American citizens, expect any more than this." Quoted in Lazin, "Response of American Jewish Committee," p. 288.

43. Feingold, *Politics of Rescue*, pp. 18-19.

44. Jewish Telegraphic Agency dispatch, 27 December 1933; Wise, *Legend of Louise*, p. 68.

45. SSW to Jacob Billikopf re:cooperation with the AF of L, 24 October 1934, Billikopf MSS; *Unity in Dispersion*, pp. 101-10.

46. In 1934 SSW noted that while the boycott seemed to be having some effect, Germany appeared to be preparing for war. SSW to Carl Grossman, 22 June 1934.

47. James Waterman Wise and Pierre Van Paassen, eds., *Nazism: An Assault on Civilization* (New York: Smith & Haas, 1934).

48. SSW to Walter S. Hilborn, 10 April 1934, Hilborn MSS; Dodd and Dodd, *Ambassador Dodd's Diary*, pp. 138, 145; SSW to Morris Lazaron, 23 November 1934.

49. Lazin, "Response of the American Jewish Committee," p. 289; SSW to Harry Friedenwald, 14 May 1934, Friedenwald MSS; SSW to Albert Einstein, 31 November 1934.

50. SSW to John Haynes Holmes, 27 May and 3 September 1935; Louis Nizer to SSW, 4 October 1934; *Opinion* 5 (March 1935): 22.

51. SSW to David Pearlman, 28 November 1934.

52. J. X. Cohen, "A Prophet in Israel," *Congress Weekly* 11 (17 March 1944): 24.

53. Wise, *Legend of Louise*, p. 69; LWW to Cordell Hull, 8 March 1937; *Opinion* 7 (April 1937):7–10.

54. SSW to Louis Brandeis, 12 January 1936; to Albert Einstein, 13 January 1936; to John Haynes Holmes, 12 February 1936.

55. SSW to Henry Morgenthau, Jr., 24 December 1936, and Morgenthau's reply, 8 January 1937, Morgenthau, Jr. MSS.

56. SSW to Felix Frankfurter, 2 March 1936; SSW to Alexander S. Gottlieb, 11 March 1936; SSW to Walter S. Hilborn, 20 April 1936, Bisno MSS.

57. William Borah to SSW, 9 June 1937, Borah MSS.

58. *Challenging Years*, pp. 268–72; *Opinion* 6 (August 1936):7.

59. SSW to Julian Mack, 10 October 1937; to Grover Seelig, 3 June 1938; to Justine and Shad Polier, 21 March 1938.

60. SSW to JWP, 19 September 1938; *New York Times*, 10 October 1938; see also SSW to James G. McDonald, 2 September 1938, McDonald MSS.

61. Henry L. Feingold, "Who Shall Bear Guilt for the Holocaust: The Human Dilemma," *American Jewish History* 68 (March 1979):279.

19. Non Possumus!

1. Urofsky, *American Zionism*, pp. 363–7.

2. SSW to Marvin Lowenthal, 11 March 1930, Lowenthal MSS; SSW to Richard Gottheil, 14 March 1930, Wise MSS-AJA.

3. Shapiro, *Leadership of American Zionist Organization*, p. 243; SSW to Jacob de Haas, 19 January 1931, deHaas MSS.

4. SSW to Ismar Elbogen, 15 June 1931.

5. See SSW statement of 28 June 1931, ZOA Records.

6. Laqueur, *Zionism*, p. 496; *New York Times*, 4 and 6 July 1931; SSW to George Kohut, 7 July 1931.

7. Emanuel Neuman, "Whither Bound?" *New Palestine* 19 (September 1930): 53; SSW to Israel Rosoff, 17 December 1930, Weizmann MSS; SSW to JWW and JWP, 13 July 1931.

8. For Revisionism, see Joseph B. Schechtman and Yehuda Benari, *History of the Revisionist Movement* (Tel Aviv: Hadar, 1970), as well as Schechtman's two-volume *The Jabotinsky Story* (New York: Thomas Yoseloff, 1956, 1961).

9. SSW to JWW and JWP, 16 July 1931; memorandum of conversation, SSW, Katznelson, and Ben-Gurion, 18 July 1931.

10. SSW to Louis Brandeis, 18 September 1931, "Plain Speaking About Zionism," *New Palestine* 21 (2 October 1931):20.

11. SSW to Robert Szold, 8 December 1931, ZOA Records; SSW to Emanuel Neumann, 16 May 1932, and to J. X. Cohen, 5 July 1932.

12. Interview with Moshe Kol, 4 June 1975; *New York Times*, 30 August 1933.

13. *Opinion* 3 (October 1933):19; SSW to Ludwig Lewisohn, 31 August 1933, and to Adolph Lewison, 3 October 1933. Fear that the proposed World Jewish Congress would somehow reduce Zionist influence led some Zionist officials to strike out against the supposed usurper of their role. See SSW to Nahum Goldmann, 9 February 1934.

14. SSW to Robert L. Baker, 17 January 1934; *Rassviet*, 15 April 1934 (containing text of Jabotinsky's birthday message to SSW of 17 March 1934); Jabotinsky to LWW, 18 October 1934; SSW to Jabotinsky, 29 October 1934; Felix Frankfurter to SSW, 12 December 1934. For Wise's most sustained attack on Revisionism, see SSW speech to Free Synagogue, 10 March 1935, carried in the *New Palestine* 25 (15 March 1935):2-3, and reported in nearly all the major Palestinian newspapers.

15. SSW to Maurice Levin, 25 July 1935; see also *Opinion* 6 (November 1935): 13-14; SSW to Jacob Billikopf, 4 October 1935.

16. SSW, *Challenging Years*, pp. 43-44.

17. Ibid., pp. 53-54; interview with Moshe Kol, 4 June 1975.

18. Memorandum of SSW visit, 4 August 1935, Political Department Records; *Personal Letters*, 228; SSW to Gertrude Wolfe, 19 August 1935, Wolfe MSS; SSW to Isaac Hamlin, 14 March 1935; interview with Moshe Kol, 4 June 1975.

19. SSW to Fiorella H. LaGuardia, 27 August 1935; Goldmann, *Sixty Years of Jewish Life*, pp. 182-83; interview with Nahum Goldmann, 21 April 1975; *Opinion* 5 (October 1935): 11; *New York Times*, 23 and 28 August 1935; SSW to JWP, 11 October 1935.

20. SSW to Moshe Shertok, 11 November 1935, Political Department Records; SSW to Irma Lindheim, 21 November 1935.

21. SSW to Robert Szold, 12 January 1936; *New York Times*, 3 and 16 February 1936.

22. SSW to Louis Brandeis, 16 June 1936; to JWP, 25 June 1936; to Samuel Wohl, 2 July 1936; to Margaret Soloman, 30 June 1936; *New York Times*, 5 July 1936.

23. The complicated transactions can be traced in SSW to Louis Brandeis, 5 May 1935, and to Julian W. Mack, 7 May 1936; David Ben-Gurion to SSW, 20 August 1936; Eliezar Kaplan to SSW, 17 December 1936; SSW to Ben-Gurion, 24 May 1937 (Mack MSS); SSW to Kaplan, 15 October 1936, enclosing $25,000, and 9 November 1936, enclosing an additional $10,000.

24. SSW to Julian Mack, and to JWW and JWP, both 5 July 1936; memorandum of visit to Ormsby-Gore, 8 July 1936, and SSW to the Colonial Secretary, 10 July 1936, Political Department Records.

25. SSW to JWW and JWP, 5 July 1936.

26. SSW to Franklin Roosevelt, 18 May 1936; Roosevelt to Cordell Hull, 22 May 1936; Hull to American consul in Jerusalem, 23 May 1936; Roosevelt to SSW, 8 June 1936, all in F. Roosevelt MSS.

27. Louis Brandeis to SSW, 4 September 1936; see also SSW to Ben-Gurion, 10 September 1934, and to Shertok, 24 September 1936, Political Department Records; SSW to Harry Friedenwald, 12 October 1936, Friedenwald MSS.

28. For his exasperation with the UPA, see SSW to Gertrude Wolfe, 5 February 1937, Wolfe MSS; SSW to Irma Lindheim, 18 November 1936, to Julian Mack, 9 February 1937, and to Henry Montor, 16 April 1937.

29. SSW to Martin Rosenblueth, 20 November 1936, and to L. Bokstansky, 8 December 1936.

30. *Memorandum submitted to the Royal Palestine Commission . . .* (New York: ZOA, 1936); SSW to Chaim Weizmann, 26 October 1936, Szold MSS.

31. Parliamentary Papers, Cmd. 5479 (1937).

32. See cable, SSW to Chaim Weizmann, 13 May 1937, London Office Records, reporting opposition of American Zionist leaders to partition.

33. SSW to Cordell Hull, 4 and 8 June 1937; Hull to SSW, 16 June 1937, Mack MSS; SSW to Charles C. Burlingame, 13 July 1937; SSW to Chaim Weizmann, 18 June 1937, London Office Records.

34. *Opinion* 7 (July 1937): 7; *New York Times*, 9 July 1937; Neumann, *In the Arena*, p. 136; SSW to Brandeis, 5 July 1937, Szold MSS.

35. Laquer, *Zionism*, p. 519.

36. SSW to JWW, JWP and Shad Polier, 1 August 1937; Polier and Wise, *Personal Letters*, p. 243; SSW to Chaim Weizmann, 4 August 1937, London Office Records.

37. *New Judea* 13 (August–September 1937): 222–23; *New York Times*, 9 August 1937.

38. SSW to Brandeis, 17 August and 1 September 1937, Szold MSS; SSW to Linley Gordon, 31 August 1937, CRIA Records; Brandeis to SSW, 30 December 1937.

39. Memorandum of meeting with President Roosevelt, 22 January 1938.

40. SSW to Roosevelt, 6 October 1938, and Marvin McIntyre to SSW, 12 October 1938, F. Roosevelt MSS; Robert Silverberg, *If I Forget Thee, O Jerusalem!* (New York: Morrow, 1970), pp. 165–66; Brandeis to Felix Frankfurter, 16 October 1938.

41. Polier and Wise, *Personal Letters*, pp. 253–54; see also SSW to Harry Friedenwald, 26 January 1939, Friendenwald MSS.

42. SSW to Roosevelt, 10 and 17 May 1939, F. Roosevelt MSS.

20. In Congress Assembled

1. SSW to Charles Bloch, 17 October 1923.

2. SSW to Max Steur, 26 May 1924, and to Bernard G. Richards, 13 March 1925.

3. Bernard Richards Memoir, COHC, p. 132.

4. SSW to Marvin Lowenthal, 18 June 1926; to Bernard G. Richards, 22 May 1928; and to George I. Fox, 7 June 1928.

5. Richards Memoir, COHC, pp. 112, 218; Richards to JWP, 7 September 1966; Richards to SSW, 4 April 1928.

6. *New York Times*, 20 May 1929.

7. SSW to JWW, 23 September 1932; *New York Times*, 7 May 1934.

8. SSW to Morris Rothenberg, 17 March 1933, ZOA Records; SSW to Joseph Salus, 26 April 1933, and to J. X. Cohen, 16 October 1933.

9. Louis Brandeis to SSW, 19 March 1935; SSW to Brandeis, 21 March 1935, but note SSW to Sidney Goldstein, 13 April 1935: "Someone must take command, and it might as well be I."

10. *Unity in Dispersion*, pp. 29–31.

11. *New York Times*, June 1932; see also SSW to Nahum Goldmann, 13 June 1932.

12. *Jewish Daily Bulletin*, 21 June 1932.

13. *New Jewish Unity* 1 (8 July 1932): 1; SSW to John Haynes Holmes, 11 July

1932; SSW to Salo W. Baron, 27 July 1932, reporting that the Berlin Centralverein had originally voted to attend, but under pressure from the Committee had changed its mind. The votes in the Hilfsverein and the Anglo-Jewish Committee had been close, and no doubt the American *yahudim* had intervened there as well; Louis Brandeis to SSW, 4 August 1932.

14. *Unity in Dispersion*, p. 32; SSW, *Challenging Years*, pp. 313–14; *New York Times*, 15 August 1932.

15. *New York Times*, 15 August 1932.

16. Ibid., 18 August 1932.

17. Quoted in Martel, "Stephen Wise," p. 416.

18. SSW to William F. Rosenblum, 21 September 1932; William Fineshriber to SSW, 16 March 1933, and SSW's response, 17 March 1933; Lord Melchett to SSW, 27 September 1932; Selig Brodetsky to SSW, 23 January 1933.

19. Isaac I. Schwarzbart, *25 Years in the Service of the Jewish People: A Chronicle* (New York: Jewish Congress, 1957), p. 7.

20. SSW to JWP, 19 July 1933.

21. *Protocol of The Second World Jewish Conference* (Geneva: World Jewish Conference, 1933), p. 24; *New York Times*, 6 September 1933.

22. *New York Times*, 9 September 1933; *Second Conference*, pp. 93, 102.

23. SSW, *Challenging Years*, pp. 318–19, 322–23.

24. SSW to J. X. Cohen, 21 October 1933; Louis Lipsky to Solomon Goldman, 27 October 1933, and same letter to others, ZOA Records; see responses of Goldman and Barnett Brickner, both on 1 November 1933, agreeing with Lipsky.

25. SSW to Nahum Goldmann, 16 February 1934.

26. *New York Times*, 21 September 1934; *American Hebrew*, 31 August 1934.

27. Solomon Goldman to SSW, 25 March 1935, reporting the incident; SSW to Sol Strook, 30 October 1934. See also Abba Hillel Silver to SSW, 4 June 1936.

28. Benjamin Cardozo to SSW, 26 October 1935, Wise MSS-AJA; SSW to Florence Luntz, 5 June 1936.

29. *New York Times*, 15 June 1936; Lipsky, *Memoirs in Profile*, p. 396; Lipsky to Chaim Weizmann, 16 June 1936, Weizmann MSS.

30. L. Zelmanovits, *Origin and Development of the World Jewish Congress: An Historical Survey* (London: British Section, 1943), pp. 18–19.

31. *Unity in Dispersion*, pp. 77–79, 95–96; see Schwartzbart, *25 Years*, pp. 8–10.

32. SSW to Rosemary Krensky, 28 May 1938.

33. SSW to Julian W. Mack, 24 July 1933; Wise, *Legend of Louise*, pp. 71–76; SSW, *Challenging Years*, p. 254.

34. SSW to Eric Mosse, 5 March 1935; SSW to Rosemary and Milton Krensky, 8 January 1939.

35. Saul S. Friedman, *No Haven for the Oppressed* (Detroit: Wayne State University Press, 1973), pp. 31–32.

36. SSW to Office Committee of American Jewish Congress, 12 January 1936; Herbert Samuel to Felix Warburg, 27 May 1936; Warburg to Herbert H. Lehman, 5 June 1936; Lehman to Franklin Roosevelt, 15 June 1936; Roosevelt to State department, 17 June 1936; Roosevelt to Lehman, 2 July 1936, noting that the "State Department had already taken several steps to . . . facilitate processing," F. Roosevelt MSS.

37. SSW to William Borah, 12 January 1937, and Borah's reponse, 14 January 1937, Borah MSS.

38. Feingold, *Politics of Resuce*, pp. 124–25; for Guiana, see SSW to Robert Szold, 13 January 1939, Szold MSS.

39. Franklin Roosevelt to SSW, 11 April 1938, Roosevelt MSS.

40. SSW to Roosevelt, 28 March 1938, Roosevelt MSS; SSW to Felix Frankfurter, 25 April 1938, and to Robert Szold, 9 May 1938; Feingold, *Politics of Rescue*, pp. 21–26.

41. Feingold, *Politics of Resuce*, p. 195; cable, Nahum Goldmann to SSW, 29 May 1938; SSW to James G. McDonald, 29 May 1938.

42. *New York Times*, 4 July 1938; SSW to Harry Friedenwald, 18 August 1938, Friedenwald MSS.

43. Golda Meir, *My Life* (New York: Putnam, 1975), p. 159; Feingold, *Politics of Rescue*, p. 33.

44. SSW to J. X. Cohen, 27 April 1938; SSW to Karl Grossman, 31 August 1938, Grossman MSS.

45. Max Nussbaum to Carl Herman Voss, 15 April 1969; Nussbaum "Stephen S. Wise, Master Builder and Friend," *Congress Bi-Weekly* 41 (24 May 1974): 10. SSW personally and through contacts with the Union of American Hebrew Congregations urged a national policy of having larger congregations bring in German rabbis either to fill vacant positions or to serve as adjunct rabbis ministering mainly to refugees in the community. See SSW to Max C. Carrick, 12 January 1939.

46. Feingold, *Politics of Rescue*, p. 42; William Borah to James P. Roe, 25 November 1938, Borah MSS.

47. SSW to Emil Lengyel, 8 May 1939; Friedman, *No Haven for the Oppressed*, p. 98.

48. Fred L. Israel, *The War Diary of Breckinridge Long: Selections from the Years 1939–1944* (Lincoln: University of Nebraska Press, 1966), pp. 128, 134–35, 161; Feingold, *Politics of Rescue*, pp. 145–47.

21. Conflicts

1. *New York Times*, 9 December 1922; SSW to JWW, 13 December 1923.

2. SSW statement, 6 May 1927; SSW to Henry Atkinson (Church Peace Movement), 23 February 1928; to Geoffrey Franklin, 1 March 1928; to editor, Winston-Salem (N.C.) *Journal*, 9 June 1927; *New York Times*, 29 February 1928.

3. *New York Times*, 14 and 27 February 1930, 27 October and 12 November 1931; *Opinion* 1 (28 December 1931):7.

4. *New York Times*, 9 and 28 February 1932; SSW to Frederick Adams, 1 March 1932; to James Eikman, 1 March 1932; *New History* 1 (March 1932):9–11.

5. *New York Times*, 18 April 1932.

6. SSW to Frank Holmstead, 25 October 1934, and to Frank W. Nye, 10 January 1935; *New York Times*, 4 May 1936.

7. SSW to Amador Marin, 23 September 1936; to Israel Harburg, 7 April 1937; and to William Loveb, 21 September 1937.

8. SSW to John Haynes Holmes, 3 February 1938; Holmes to SSW, 4 and 7 February 1938.

9. *New York Times*, 5 April 1938; SSW to Evelyn West Hugham (War Resisters League), 29 June 1938.

10. SSW to Holmes, 20 September 1938; see also SSW to Josiah Wedgewood, 21 September 1938 and to Rosemary Krensky, 30 September 1938.

11. SSW to Florence Luntz, 31 August 1939, and to Julian Mack, 31 August and 5 September 1939.

12. SSW to Sidney Goldstein, 16 October 1939; to Alan Gilbert, 1 February 1940. Yet in a letter to Major Selig on 2 October 1939, Wise wrote: "I believe that nothing can permanently keep us out of the war."

13. SSW to Lord and Lady Melchett, 27 January 1941; *New York Times*, 24 November 1940.

14. *New York Times*, 27 June 1940; SSW to Milton L. Bernstein, 17 March 1941; to Lady Mary Marsten, 8 May 1941; to Reverend Harold Bosley, 27 June 1941.

15. SSW to Warren Marks, 24 October 1941; to Paul Killian, Jr. (Boston America First Committee), 14 November 1941. On 4 September 1941, SSW met with Franklin Roosevelt, and the president asked him: "Can't you do anything about John Haynes Holmes? What is the matter with him?" Wise replied: "Holmes believes that wars are evil. He obeys his conscience and his God in opposing war in any and all circumstance." Roosevelt then said: "That is all right, so do I. But . . . " SSW to Holmes, 5 September 1941.

16. SSW to Rev. T. H. Ressler, 21 November 1941.

17. SSW to Nathan Lithzin, 15 January 1942; to Joseph M. Lonegan, 6 February 1942; to George M. Stockdale, 29 May 1944; *New York Times*, 15 October 1941.

18. See Ehud Avriel, *Open the Gates!* (New York: Atheneum, 1975).

19. Interview with Milton Handler, 15 March 1979.

20. David Werner Senator to Rose Jacobs, 8 November 1939, Non-Zionist Section Files; SSW to Julian W. Mack, 23 October 1939; Urofsky, *American Zionism*, pp. 419–24.

21. SSW to Selig Brodetsky, 31 January 1940; Joseph B. Schechtman, *The United States and the Jewish States Movement* (New York: Herzl Press, 1966), pp. 47–48.

22. SSW to Louis D. Brandeis, 16 January 1940. Brandeis refused, and until his death in October 1941, would not deal with Weizmann, Lipsky, and their "gang." See Brandeis to Robert Szold, 10 April and 5 July 1940, 13 July 1941, all in Szold MSS.

23. *New York Times*, 27 February 1940; SSW to Julian Mack, 29 February 1940; to J. H. Hertz, 29 February 1940; to Isidore Breslow, 8 April 1940.

24. SSW to Solomon Goldman, 30 November 1939; Friedman, *No Haven for the Oppressed*, pp. 46–47.

25. SSW to Isidore Breslow, 8 April 1940; to Morton Berman, 13 April 1940; SSW to Eliezer Kaplan, 17 September 1940, Kaplan MSS.

26. SSW to Felix Frankfurter, 16 September 1940; for Silver's attitude see Silver to Emanuel Neumann, 2 December 1940.

27. SSW to Philip Slomovitz, 9 June 1940; see also SSW to Florence and Darwin Luntz, 11 July 1940.

28. SSW to Joseph Beder, 26 June 1941, and Beder's reply, 9 July 1941, London Office Records; *New York Times*, 7 May 1941 and 22 March 1942; SSW to Henry Morgenthau, Jr., 29 May 1941, Morgenthau Diaries.

29. SSW to Robert Szold, 18 August 1941, Szold MSS; SSW to Philip Slomovitz, 16 September 1941, and to Louis Brandeis, 31 March 1941; Chaim Weizmann to Louis Levinthal, 15 October 1941, Levinthal MSS.

30. American Emergency Committee for Zionist Affairs, "Minutes of the Extraordinary Conference . . . at the Biltmore Hotel," typescript of stenographic record, Zionist Archives and Library, New York; see also *New York Times*, 10–12 May 1942.

22. Holocaust

1. Raul Hilberg, *The Destruction of the European Jews* (Chicago: Quadrangle, 1967), pp. 262–66; William L. Shirer, *The Rise and Fall of the Third Reich* (New York: Simon & Schuster, 1960), pp. 963–67.

2. Interview with Gerhard Riegner, 23 February 1978; Morse, *While Six Million Died*, pp. 7–9; Saul S. Friedman, *No Haven for the Oppressed: United States Policy Toward Jewish Refugees, 1938–1945* (Detroit: Wayne State University Press, 1973), pp. 130–31.

3. SSW to Nahum Goldmann, 4 September 1942.

4. Elie Wiesel, "Telling the Tale," *Dimension* 2 (Spring 1968): 9–12.

5. Friedman, *No Haven for the Oppressed*, pp. 139–40; SSW to Roosevelt, 2 December 1942.

6. Neumann, *In the Arena*, p. 186; comments by Korski, 23 March 1980, American University Holocaust Synposium; interviews with Louis Levinthal, 22 December 1972, and with Israel Goldstein, 12 September 1973.

7. For the nature of this information, see Friedman, *No Haven for the Oppressed*, pp. 131–37, and Feingold, *Politics of Rescue*, pp. 169–70.

8. SSW to John Haynes Holmes, 9 September 1942.

9. SSW to Felix Frankfurter, 4 and 16 September 1942; speech of Henry Morgenthan, Jr., 20 April 1947.

10. *Unity in Dispersion, p. 162;* Morse, *While Six Million Died*, pp. 16–17; *New York Times*, 25 November 1942.

11. *Christian Century*, 9 December 1942 and 13 January 1943; see also SSW to *Time* magazine, 18 January 1943.

12. SSW to Roosevelt, 2 December 1942; Morse, *While Six Million Died*, p. 28; Eliyho Matzozky, "An Episode: Roosevelt and the Mass Killing," *Midstream* 26 (Aug–Sept 1980):17–19.

13. Silverberg, *If I Forget Thee, O Jerusalem!* pp. 226–27. Disagreements on strategy plagued the Jewish community throughout the war. In 1944 Rabbi Jacob Rosenheim, director of the Vaad Ha-Hatzala, the rescue committee of Orthodox Jewry, explained why he prefered to act alone. The rescue scene "was a dog-eat-dog world [in which] the interest of religious Jews [is] always menaced by the preponderance of the wealthy and privileged Jewish organizations, especially the Agency and the Joint." As Henry Feingold commented, "Clearly for Rosenheim the Nazis were not the only enemy." "Who Shall Bear the Guilt for the Holocaust?," pp. 274–75.

14. See, for example, Eleanor Roosevelt to SSW, 28 December 1942, E. Roosevelt MSS.

15. SSW to Felix Frankfurter, 16 September 1942; Friedman, *No Haven for the Oppressed*, p. 151.

16. Bernard Wasserstein, "The Myth of Jewish Silence," *Midstream* 26 (Aug-Sept 1980):10–16.

17. For bombing of the rail line, see "A Question of Priorities," *Jerusalem Post*, international edition, 25 April–5 May 1980; interview with Moshe Kol, 4 June 1975; Feingold, *Politics of Rescue*; Bernard Wasserstein, *Britain and the Jews of Europe, 1939–1945* (London: Oxford University Press, 1979).

18. Samuel Lubell, *The Future of American Politics*, (Garden City: Doubleday, 1956 rev. ed.), pp. 220–21.

19. Interviews with Eliahu Elath, 5 June 1975, and with Arthur Lourie, 9 June 1975; see also SSW, "In Memorium," *Opinion* 15 (May 1945):6.

20. Roosevelt to SSW, 30 August 1943; Hull, *Memoirs*, 2:1536; SSW to Chaim Weizmann 23 July 1943, Weizmann MSS; SSW to Samuel Rosenman, 29 September 1943, Rosenman MSS; diary entry for 10 March 1944, Henry Wallace Memoir, COHC; SSW to David K. Niles, 13 March 1944.

21. SSW to Eliezer Kaplan, 17 March 1944, political department files; Roosevelt to SSW, 9 October 1944, F. Roosevelt MSS; SSW to Chaim Weizmann, 23 July 1943, Weizmann MSS; SSW to John Haynes Holmes, 25 March 1943.

22. Monty N. Penkower, "The 1943 Joint Anglo-American Statement on Palestine," *Herzl Year Book* 8 (1978):212–41.

23. The Zionists did not so much dismiss other options as insist upon the Jewish right to Palestine. In April 1944, for example, Wise commented that he had no objection to the Virgin Islands as a temporary refuge, but it would be better to bring the people to the United States, and better still to Palestine. SSW to Maurice Perlsweig, 12 April 1944.

24. Feingold, "Who Shall Bear the Guilt?", pp. 267–8.

25. Breckinridge Long to A. A. Berle and J. C. Dunn, 26 June 1940, in Feingold, "Who Shall Bear the Guilt?", pp.265–66; entry for 4 September 1941, Israel, *War Diary of Breckenridge Long*, pp. 216–17.

26. Goldmann, *Sixty Years of Jewish Life*.

27. Eliahu Elath, *Zionism at the U.N.—A Diary of the First Days*, tr. by Michael Ben-Yitzchak (Philadelphia: Jewish Publication Society, 1976), pp. 42–43; interview with Elath, 5 June 1975.

28. *New York Times*, 13 March and 17 May 1942; SSW to Margaret Solomon, 6 August 1942, and to Florence Luntz, 1 November 1942.

29. SSW to Felix Frankfurter, March 1941; Friedman, *No Haven for the Oppressed*, p. 196.

30. SSW to Bernard Baruch, 4 January 1943, Baruch MSS; *New York Times*, 1 March 1943; SSW to JWW, 16 February 1943, and to Julian W. Mack, 22 March 1943.

31. Roosevelt to SSW, 23 March 1943, F. Roosevelt MSS; Friedman, *No Haven for the Oppressed*, p. 165; entry for 20 April 1943, Israel, *War Diary of Breckenridge Long*, p. 307.

32. Feingold, *Politics of Rescue*, pp. 208–209; *Opinion* 13 (June 1943): 5; *New*

York Times, 23 July 1943.

33. *Unity in Dispersion*, pp. 178–79; Morse, *While Six Million Died*, pp. 79–80. At about this same time, the Committee for a Jewish Army, co-chaired by playwright Ben Hecht, received word that the Rumanian government would allow 70,000 Jews to leave at a cost of $50 each. After confirming the story through the underground, Hecht took out a large advertisement in the *New York Times* of 16 February 1943 which proclaimed "FOR SALE 70,000 Jews. Guaranteed Human Beings at $50 apiece." A week later Wise issued a statement denying Hecht's claim, and called it a hoax. Wise should have known better, since the original source was the WJC representative in Switzerland, Gerhardt Riegner. While the story is not entirely clear, it would appear that Wise responded partly because the regular Zionists and the Revisionists (who sponsored the Hecht group) were fighting bitterly at this point, and partly because he recognized that nothing could be done without government approval of a license to export money. It is debatable whether the Hecht group had any real chance of success, but its actions were more in the mode of what critics of American Jewry believe should have been done. See Friedman, *No Haven for the Oppressed*, pp. 148–49.

34. Feingold, *Politics of Rescue*, pp. 240–41; SSW to Henry Morgenthau, Jr., 27 January 1944, Morgenthau Diaries.

35. See, for example, A. Leon Kubowitzki to John Pehle, 26 June 1944; SSW to Pehle, 14 August 1944 and 19 January 1945, WRB Records.

36. James MacGregor Burns, *Roosevelt: The Soldier of Freedom* (New York: Harcourt, Brace, 1970), p. 396; Manuel, *The Realities of American-Palestine Relations*, pp. 314–15.

37. Feingold, *Politics of Rescue*, p. xiii; see also Selig Adler, "Franklin D. Roosevelt and Zionism—The Wartime Record," *Judaism* 21 (Summer 1972):265–76, which shows the diverse pressures on the president.

23. Dissent in Zion

1. Petegorsky Memorandum, 30 March 1942, Manson MSS; Emergency Committee Minutes, 14 April 1942, AZEC Records; Meyer Weisgal to SSW, 23 April 1942, London Office Records.

2. Chaim Weizmann to SSW, 29 April 1942, ibid. For full details of these struggles, see Urofsky, *We Are One!*, chs. 1, 3.

3. SSW to Felix Frankfurter, 21 May 1942; Weizmann to Berl Locker, 3 June 1942, Weizmann MSS.

4. David Ben-Gurion to Weizmann, 11 June 1942, ibid.; Ben-Gurion to SSW, 19 June 1942; SSW to Ben-Gurion, 22 June 1942, Weizmann MSS. For an extended analysis of the philosophical differences between Ben-Gurion and Weizmann, see Yehuda Bauer, *From Diplomacy to Resistance: A History of Jewish Palestine* (Philadelphia: Jewish Publication Society, 1970), pp. 236–42.

5. Memorandum of meeting, 27 June 1942, Weigal MSS; SSW to Weizmann, 29 June 1942, and Weizmann to SSW, 30 June 1942, Weizmann MSS; SSW to Lavey Bakstansky, 29 September 1942. Present at the meeting were SSW, Ben-Gurion,

Weizmann, Nahum Goldmann, Hayim Greenberg, Louis Levinthal, Louis Lipsky, Robert Szold, and Meyer Weisgal.

6. At Wise's urging, however, Weizmann set up what ultimately became the American Section of the WZO, consisting of those members of the Zionist Executive in the United States. If Wise expected this to reassure Ben-Gurion that consultation would now take place, he was mistaken. The American Section, however, eventually did carve out for itself an influential place in Zionist affairs.

7. SSW to Israel Goldstein, 28 September 1942, Goldstein MSS; *New York Times*, 15 December 1942. See also Wise statement to House Foreign Affairs Committee, *New York Times*, 3 December 1943.

8. Howard Robert Greenstein, "The Changing Attitudes toward Zionism in Reform Judaism, 1937–1948," doctoral dissertation (Ohio State University, 1973), pp. 68–69; Halperin, *Political World of American Zionism*, pp. 82–83. For the Council, see Herman (Chaim) Leiberman, *Strangers to Glory: An Appraisal of the American Council for Judaism* (New York: Rainbow Press, 1955); Isaac Deutscher, "The Non-Jewish Jew," in *The Non-Jewish Jew and Other Essays* (London: East-West Press, 1968); and Urofsky, *We Are One!*, pp. 66–72.

9. SSW to James G. Heller, 28 April 1942.

10. Barry Silverberg, "Beyond the Communal Consensus: The American Council for Judaism," seminar paper (Brandeis University, 1974), p. 11. I am indebted to Mr. Silverberg for allowing me use of this paper as well as generously sharing the materials he collected on the Council.

11. Greenstein, "Changing Attitudes," pp. 77–78; Halperin, *Political World of American Zionism*, pp. 287–88; Louis Wolsey, "The Meaning of Reform Judaism," in *Sermons and Addresses* (Philadelphia: Cong. Rodeph Sholom, 1950), pp. 6–7.

12. SSW to Isadore Breslau, 3 February 1943; to Henry Luce, 8 July 1943, American Section Records; to Jacob Kaplan, 27 June 1945; *Opinion* (March 1944):3.

13. SSW to Eliezar Kaplan, 14 May 1943; Weizmann to SSW, 29 May 1943, Weizmann MSS; Harry S Truman to SSW, 1 June 1943, American Section Records; Ben Hecht, *A Child of the Century* (New York: Simon & Schuster, 1954), p. 547.

14. SSW to Eliezar Kaplan, 17 March 1944, Kaplan MSS; memorandum of conversations, Meyer Weisgal with Henry Morgenthau, Jr., 4 August 1943, and with Samuel Rosenman, 6 and 12 October 1943, American Section Records.

15. Teller, *Strangers and Natives*, p. 207; I. L. Kenen to Charles B. Kramer, 21 February 1944, Waldman MSS.

16. Urofsky, *We Are One!*, pp. 72–81.

17. Daisy Monsky and Henry Bisgyer, *Henry Monsky: The Man and His Work* (New York: Crown, 1947), p. 86; Isaac Neustadt Noy, "Toward Unity: Zionist and Non-Zionist Cooperation," *Herzl Year Book* 8 (1978): 149–65; Nahum Goldmann to Eliezer Kaplan, 21 December 1942, Political Department Records; Arthur Lourie to Leo Lauterbach, 2 September 1943, London Office Records.

18. SSW, "A Vindication of Faith," *Congress Weekly* 10 (29 January 1943):3–4.

19. SSW to Weizmann, 16 February 1943, Weizmann MSS; Morris Waldman, *Nor by Power* (New York, 1953), pp. 253–54.

20. American Jewish Conference, *Organization and Proceedings of the First Session* (New York: Am. Jewish Conf., 1944), pp. 67, 70–71.

21. Monsky and Bisgyer, *Henry Monsky*, p. 93.

22. Interview with Emanuel Neumann, 1 July 1975; Neumann, *In the Arena*, p. 191; American Jewish Conference, *Proceedings*, pp. 100–101.

23. Urofsky, *We Are One!*, pp. 29–30. Wise worked arduously to convince Proskauer to stay in the Conference, but in vain. Waldman, *Nor by Power*, p. 258; SSW to Henry Monsky, 15 November 1943. Here, as in so many other battles, one finds a discrepancy between public and private statements. Wise and Proskauer castigated each other mercilessly in public statements, accusing each of undermining Jewish unity. Privately, however, they maintained a cordial, even fond, relationship, one that dated back nearly two decades, when Wise had endorsed Proskauer's candidacy for the bench. See Proskauer to SSW, 25 October 1943, and SSW to Proskauer, 12 November 1943. Wise also enjoyed good personal relations with the executive director of the American Jewish Committee, Morris Waldman. See Waldman to SSW, 30 April 1942, and Wise's reply, 4 May 1942. Waldman MSS.

24. Neumann interview, 1 July 1975; Neumann, *In the Arena*, p. 192.

25. SSW to Max Heller, 15 April 1920, and to Louis Brandeis, 6 January 1920.

26. SSW to Abba Hillel Silver, & May 1917; Silver to SSW, 11 May 1917, enclosing Silver to Moses Gries, 26 April 1917; SSW to Nathan Straus, 22 April 1920.

27. SSW to Charles Bloch, 19 October 1925; Meyer Weisgal, . . . *So Far*, p. 168, interviews with Israel Goldstein, 12 September 1973; Rose Halprin, 23 March 1973; Eliah Elath, 5 June 1975; and Meyer Weisgal, 29 May 1975.

28. SSW to Weizmann, 10 February 1943, Weizmann MSS; Neumann, *In the Arena*, pp. 187–88.

29. Nahum Goldmann to Moshe Shertok, 16 June 1943, Political Department Files; Weizmann to SSW, 25 June 1943, Goldstein MSS; SSW to Leon Gellman, 12 June 1943, American Section Records.

30. SSW to Nahum Goldmann, 27 July 1943; to Cordell Hull, 3 August 1943; to Jacob Billikopf, 13 August 1943; SSW to Samuel Rosenman, 24 August 1943, Rosenman MSS; Schechtman, *U. S. and Jewish State Movement*, pp. 78–79. The best source for the abortive proposal is Monty N. Penkower, "The 1943 Joint Anglo-American Statement on Palestine," *Herzl Year Book* 8 (1978):212–41.

31. Israel Goldstein to Silver, 2 August 1943, and SSW to Silver, 3 August 1943, Goldstein MSS; SSW to Nahum Goldmann, 4 August 1943.

32. SSW to Goldmann, 5 August 1943, American Section Records; Meyer Weisgal to Weizmann, 11 August 1943, Weizmann MSS; minutes of meeting, 26 August 1943, AZEC Records; Arthur Lourie to Leo Lauterbach, 10 September 1943, Organization Department Files; Goldmann to Moshe Shertok, 16 September 1943, Political Department Files; Neumann, *In the Arena*, pp. 188–89.

33. Minutes of meeting, 5 October 1943, AZEC Records.

34. Silver to Weizmann, 3 March 1944, Weizmann MSS; *New York Times*, 10 March 1944.

35. SSW to Stettinius, 3 December 1944, and to Joseph M. Levine, 12 December 1944.

36. Memorandum of confidential interview with Bloom by Nahum Goldmann, 11 October 1943, American Section Records; see also Bloom to Israel Goldstein, 13 December 1944, Goldstein MSS.

37. Meyer Weisgal to Weizmann, 6 April 1944, Weizmann MSS; Silver to Emanuel Neumann, 17 July 1944, and to David Wertheim, 25 August 1944, Manson MSS;

minutes of meeting, 14 August 1944, AZEC Records.

38. Minutes of meetings, 28 and 31 August 1944, AZEC Records; Moshe Shertok to David Ben-Gurion, 2 September 1944, and Ben-Gurion to Silver, 17 September 1944, Political Department Records; Meyer Weisgal to Weizmann, 7 and 23 September 1944, Weizmann MSS.

39. Minutes of meeting, 12 October 1944, AZEC Records.

40. Maurice Boukstein to Meyer Weisgal, 5 December 1944, Political Department Records; Sol Bloom to Israel Goldstein, 13 December 1944, Goldstein MSS. For a detailed although biased account and chronology of the events beginning at the end of October 1944 until their denouement, see the draft of a proposed pamphlet, possibly written by Herman Shulman, in Goldstein MSS, hereafter cited as Wise-Silver memo.

41. Polier and Wise, *Personal Letters*, p. 266; SSW to John Haynes Holmes, 27 December 1944; minutes of meeting, 28 December 1944, AZEC Records; *New Palestine* 35 (19 January 1945):81.

42. *Jewish Morning Journal*, 22 December 1944; *Der Tag*, 23 December 1944; Detroit *Jewish News*, 26 January 1945; see also *Jewish Spectator*, January 1945, *American Jewish World* (Minneapolis), 5 January 1945, and *Jewish Daily Forward*, 11 January 1945.

43. Abba Hillel Silver, *Vision and Victory*, (New York: ZOA, 1949), pp. 72-73; *Jewish Morning Journal*, 8 January 1945; Wise-Silver Memo; *New Palestine* 36 (19 January 1945):82-83; SSW to Israel Goldstein, 5 February 1945, and to Herman Shulman, 9 February 1945.

44. Cable, Wise, and others to Weizmann, 9 January 1945, and Goldmann to Shertok, 31 January 1945, Political Department Records; Weisgal to Weizmann, 10 January 1945 Weizmann MSS.

45. Weisgal to Weizmann, 9 March 1945, Weizmann MSS; Israel Goldstein to Herman Shulman, 12 March 1945, Goldstein MSS; minutes of meeting, Hadassah National Board, 21 March 1945, Hadassah Records; minutes of meetings, 19 June and 12 July 1945, AZEC Records.

46. Interviews with Golda Meir, 10 June 1975, Eliahu Elath, 5 June 1975, Rose Halprin, 23 March 1973, and Israel Goldstein, 12 September 1973.

24. Shehechyanu

1. *New York Times*, 2 March 1945; Urofsky, *We Are One!*, p. 62; SSW to Chaim Weizmann, 21 March 1945, Weizmann MSS; Schechtman, *U.S. and Jewish State Movement*, p. 122.

2. Meyer Weisgal to Weizmann, 20 April 1945, Weizmann MSS; SSW to Harry S Truman, 13 April 1945, Truman MSS.

3. Harry S Truman, *Memoirs*, 2 vols. (Garden City: Doubleday, 1955), 1:68-69; *New York Times*, 21 April 1945.

4. SSW to Max Nussbaum, 26 March 1945; to Edward Stettinius, 21 April 1945; Stettinius to SSW, 23 April 1945.

5. SSW to James G. Heller, 26 March 1945.

6. Elath, *Zionism at the U.N.*, pp. 45, 81-82, 113; Joseph Proskauer to SSW, 14

May 1945; Leon Gellman to SSW, 6 June 1945, AZEC Records; interview with Eliahu Elath, 5 June 1975.

7. *New York Times*, 27 January 1945; SSW to Herman Weisman, 28 January 1945, and to Monroe Goldwater, 19 June 1945; *Opinion* 15 (August 1945):5; see also SSW to John Haynes Holmes, 4 April 1946.

8. *New York Times*, 27 October 1945; SSW to Abram Elkus, 9 November 1945; SSW to Truman, 7 October 1946, Truman MSS; *Opinion* 15 (December 1945):3.

9. SSW and A. H. Silver to Truman, 30 October 1945, Truman MSS; Truman, *Memoirs*, 2:142–44; *New York Times*, 11 and 24 December 1945.

10. Interview with Milton Handler, 15 March 1979; *New York Times*, 9 January 1946.

11. Voss, *Rabbi and Minister*, pp. 324–25.

12. *New York Times*, 11 January 1946.

13. Silver, *Vision and Victory*, pp. 92–93; minutes of meetings, 21 June and 1 July 1946, AZEC Records.

14. See, for example, SSW to Lord Halifax, 18 May 1943; to Felix Frankfurter, 19 May 1943 ("I have been an Anglophile almost to the point of Anglomania. I am and will remain an Anglophile."); SSW to Truman, 31 August 1945, and to David Niles, 9 July 1946, Truman MSS.

15. Meir, *My Life*, p. 135.

16. *Opinion* 16 (April 1946):6–7; SSW, *Challenging Years*, p. 304; SSW to Lady Eva Reading, 10 July 1946; *New York Times*, 10 July 1946; ZOA minutes, 15 July 1946.

17. *New York Times*, 1 and 9 July 1946.

18. Wise, *Legend of Louise*, pp. 93–95; New York *Herald-Tribune*, 17 July 1946.

19. SSW to Justine and Shad Polier, 17 August 1946; *New York Times*, 18 August 1946; SSW to Truman, 29 July and 21 August 1946, Truman MSS; SSW to John Haynes Holmes, 9 October 1946.

20. See, for example, *New Palestine* 35 (13 July 1945):235, and 36 (14 December 1945):51; minutes of Council meetings of 22 June, 14 and 26 November 1945, AZEC Records.

21. Will Clayton to Truman, 12 September 1946, Truman MSS; SSW to Silver, 12 September 1946, and Silver's answer, 14 September 1946.

22. New York *Herald-Tribune*, 30 September 1946; SSW to Nahum Goldmann, 11 September 1946, Weizmann MSS; minutes of 14 October 1946 meeting, AZEC Records; SSW to Louis Levinthal, 8 October 1946; SSW to Jacob Billikopf, 4 November 1946, Billikopf MSS.

23. Interview with Jacques Torczyner, 4 November 1976; SSW to David Petegorsky, 22 December 1946; *Opinion* 17 (January 1947):4.

24. Interview with Rose Halprin, 23 March 1973; Nahum Goldmann to SSW, 31 December 1946, Weizmann MSS.

25. Joachim Prinz, "Stephen S. Wise—His Fifteenth Yahrzeit."

26. Nahum Goldman to SSW, 31 December 1946, Weizmann MSS.

27. *New York Times*, 4 January 1947; SSW to Eliahu Elath, 17 February 1947.

28. *New York Times*, 6 January 1947; T. Weiss-Rosmarin, "The Case of Dr. Wise," *Jewish Spectator* 12 (February 1947):5.

29. *New York Times*, 6 July 1946; *Unity in Dispersion*, pp. 252–53; SSW to Eliahu Elath, 3 July 1947.

30. *Opinion* 17 (March 1947):5; SSW to Truman, 30 April and 1 August 1947, Truman MSS; *New York Times*, 23 and 31 July, 19 September 1947.

31. SSW to Felix Frankfurter, 31 October 1947; Bernstein, "Personal Recollections," p. 10.

32. SSW to LWW, 29 November 1947; interview with Golda Meir, 10 June 1975.

33. *Congress Weekly* 15 (21 May 1948):4.

25. Final Fruits

1. SSW to James G. O'Hare, 1 November 1940; *New York Times*, 13 May 1944; Allen Nevins, *Herbert H. Lehman and His Era* (New York: Scribner's, 1963), p. 306.

2. *New York Times*, 27 October 1941 and 14 February 1944; transcript of radio talk endorsing LaGuardia for re-election, 29 October 1941.

3. SSW to N. Morroff, 14 November 1944; to Laverne Wilson, 14 February 1945; *New York Times*, 14 June 1944 and 21 November 1946; Walter Reuther to SSW, 2 January 1946.

4. *New York Times*, 5 and 13 June 1947; SSW to Philip Murray, 17 April 1947; to Jacob M. Zinamen, 5 June 1947.

5. *New York Times*, 15 March and 18 May 1946, 25 February 1947.

6. Ibid., 15 November 1946 and 3 April 1948; memorandum of speech on Churchill's address, n.d. [1947]; SSW to Mack Kaufman, 13 November 1947; to John Haynes Holmes, 22 March 1948; to R. Brainin, 30 December 1947. Responding to birthday greetings from William Zuckerman in 1948, SSW wrote: "I am afraid you are quite right in your description of me as a lonely liberal. I am afraid that all liberals are lonely these days" (1 April 1947).

7. SSW to David Taylor (CBS program director), 22 October 1947; William L. Shirer to SSW, 24 November 1947; see also SSW to Maurice Bloom, 6 January 1949; notes of sermon on Melish case, 18 March 1949.

8. New York *World-Telegram*, 16 November 1947; SSW to Louis I. Newman, 23 October 1947; Washington *Times-Herald*, 20 March 1949; New York *Post*, 22 March 1949.

9. Polier and Wise, *Personal Letters*, pp.201-02.

10. Interview with Nahum Goldmann, 21 April 1975.

11. SSW to Edward G. Barrow, 2 May 1944.

12. "I Am An American," *Opinion* 12 (July 1942): 5.

13. SSW to Leo Fassberg, 14 April 1942.

14. SSW to Jacob Billikopf, 11 October 1941; Meyer Weisgal to SSW, 3 November 1943; Free Synagogue *Bulletin*, 28 May 1943.

15. *New York Times*, 26 June 1943; interview with Edward Klein.

16. Cohen, "Prophet in Israel" p.21; SSW to William C. Alexander, 30 March 1943.

17. Report of Building Fund Committee, 1 June 1945; SSW to David K. Niles, 7 May 1946 and 14 January 1947; George Brussel to Civil Production Agency, 28 February 1948; excerpts from SSW speech, Vanderbilt Hotel, 20 April 1947.

18. *New York Times*, 15 March 1948.

19. See, for example, Morton Berman to SSW, 5 February 1941; minutes of meeting, 26 February 1941; SSW to Berman, 28 March 1941, JIR Records.
20. Julian Morgenstern to SSW, 11 April 1941; memorandum of meeting, 9 November 1941; SSW to James G. Heller, 14 October 1941, JIR Records.
21. SSW to Heller, 28 December 1942 and 11 January 1943; Heller to SSW, 31 December 1942, JIR Records; SSW to John Haynes Holmes, 14 June 1943, and to Usher Kirshblum, 16 February 1944; *New York Times*, 13 March 1944.
22. Meyer, "A Centennial History," pp.163–64; SSW to Heller, 9 October 1945.
23. Morgenstern to SSW, 16 October 1945; Voss, *Rabbi and Minister*, p.323. The citation in full read:

Distinguished leader and spokesman for the entire household of Israel, eloquent preacher, contending constantly and courageously for a liberal interpretation for Judaism and for every worthy, just and humanitarian cause, powerful voice of the battle against economic exploitation of the underprivileged, valiant fighter for fellow Jews and other minority groups at the Versaille Peace Conference, pioneer American Zionist and World Zionist leader, zealous defender of the freedom of the pulpit, champion of the principle of democracy in communal and national Jewish organizations, capable and devoted founded and president of our sister institution, the Jewish Institute of Religion.

24. Nelson Glueck to SSW, 16 May 1947; SSW to Joseph M. Levine and others, 19 May 1947; minutes of meeting, 19 June 1947, all JIR Records; SSW to J. Brachman, 23 October 1947.
25. Meyer, "A Centennial History," p.168.
26. Ibid., pp.168–69, 185–87.
27. SSW, *Challenging Years*, pp.140–41.

26. At Last to Rest

1. SSW to Julian W. Mack, 4 March 1941; to Rosemary Krensky, 6 March and 12 April 1941; to Joseph M. Levine, 18 July 1941.
2. Voss, *Rabbi and Minister*, pp.328–29; SSW to Julian Mack, 24 December 1941; to John Haynes Holmes, 3 June 1942.
3. SSW to Frank Abelson, 5 February 1942; *Congress Weekly* 40 (February 1973): 2; Voss, *Rabbi and Minister*, p.319; SSW to Ed Kapman, 15 March 1945.
4. *New York Times*, 11 and 13 December 1947.
5. Interview with Professor Milton Handler, 15 March 1979.
6. Prinz, "His Fifteenth Yahrzeit," p.5.
7. SSW to Dr. Irving Graes, 16 August 1948; to Stephen Wise Tulin, 27 October 1948.
8. Harry S Truman to SSW, 8 February 1949, Truman MSS: Chaim Weizmann and David Ben-Gurion to SSW, cable, 16 March 1949; SSW to James G. McDonald, 23 February 1949.
9. Voss, *Rabbi and Minister*, pp. 347–48; *New York Times*, 18 March 1949.

10. Voss, *Rabbi and Minister*, p.348.
11. Voss, ed., *Servant of the People*, pp.295-96.
12. *New York Times*, 20-23 April 1949; Voss, *Rabbi and Minister*, pp.350-51.

Bibliographical Note

Secondary works are fully cited in the preceding footnotes. The main source for this biography is the voluminous Stephen Samuel Wise Papers in the Library of the American Jewish Historical Society in Waltham, Massachusetts; all citations not otherwise attributed are to be found there. In addition, the following manuscript collections were consulted:

Adler MSS Felix Adler Papers, Special Collection, Columbia University Library, New York

American Section Records Records of the American Section, World Zionist Organization/Jewish Agency for Palestine, Record Group Z5, Central Zionist Archives, Jerusalem, Israel

AZEC Records Records of the American Zionist Emergency Council and of its predecessor, the Emergency Committee for Zionist Affairs, Zionist Archives and Library, New York

Baruch MSS Bernard Baruch Papers, Firestone Library, Princeton University Princeton, New Jersey

Berman MSS Morton Meyer Berman Papers, privately held, Jerusalem, Israel

Billikopf MSS Jacob Billikopf Papers, American Jewish Archives, Cincinnati, Ohio

Bisno MSS Julius Bisno Collection, American Jewish Historical Society, Waltham, Massachusetts

Borah MSS William E. Borah Papers, Manuscript Division, Library of Congress, Washington, D.C.

Brandeis MSS Louis Dembitz Brandeis Papers, Law School Library, University of Louisville, Louisville, Kentucky

CRIA Records Records of the Council on Religion and International Affairs, Special Collections, Columbia University Library, New York

Cronbach MSS Abraham Cronbach Papers, American Jewish Archives, Cincinnati, Ohio

Davidson MSS   Thomas Davidson Papers, Sterling Library, Yale University, New Haven, Connecticut

deHaas MSS   Jacob deHaas Papers, Zionist Archives and Library, New York

Ehrenreich Genealogy   Ehrenreich Family Geneology, American Jewish Historical Society, Waltham, Massachusetts

Elbogen MSS   Ismar Elbogen Papers, Leo Baeck Institute, New York

Enelow MSS   Hyman Gerson Enelow Papers, American Jewish Archives, Cincinnati, Ohio

Foreign Office Records   Records of H.M.G. Foreign Office, Public Records Office, London, England

Frankfurter MSS   Felix Frankfurter Papers, Record Group A264, Central Zionist Archives, Jerusalem, Israel

Friedenwald MSS   Harry Friedenwald Papers, Record Group A182, Central Zionist Archives, Jerusalem, Israel

George Junior Republic   Papers of the George Junior Republic, Department of Manuscripts and University Archives, Cornell University, Ithaca, New York

Goldstein MSS   Israel Goldstein Papers, Goldstein Archives, Jersalem, Israel

Gottheil MSS   Richard James Horatio Gottheil Papers, Record Group A138, Central Zionist Archives, Jerusalem, Israel

Hadassah Board Minutes   Minutes of the National Board of Hadassah, the Women's Zionist Organization of America, Hadassah Archives, New York

Heller MSS   Maxmillian Heller Papers, American Jewish Archives, Cincinnati, Ohio

Hilborn MSS   Walter S. Hilborn Papers, American Jewish Archives, Cincinnati, Ohio

Hilles MSS   Charles D. Hilles Papers, Sterling Library, Yale University, New Haven, Connecticut

House MSS   Edward Mandel House papers, Sterling Library, Yale University, New Haven Connecticut

Hurwitz MSS Henry Hurwitz Papers, American Jewish Archives, Cincinnati, Ohio

JIR Records   Records of the Jewish Institute of Religion, American Jewish Archives, Cincinnati, Ohio

JWP   Materials supplied through the courtesy of Hon. Justine Wise Polier, New York; much of this has since been interfiled with the main body of Wise Papers

Kallen MSS   Horace Meyer Kallen Papers, American Jewish Archives, Cincinnati, Ohio

Kaplan MSS   Eliezer Kaplan Papers, Office of Jewish Agency Members, Record Group S53, Central Zionist Archives, Jerusalem, Israel

Kennan MSS George Kennan Papers, Manuscript Division, Library of Congress, Washington, D.C.

LaGuardia MSS Fiorello H. LaGuardia Papers, New York City Municipal Archives, New York

Lehman MSS Herbert Henry Lehman Papers, School of International Affairs Library, Columbia University, New York

Levinthal MSS Louis Levinthal Papers, privately held, Philadelphia, Pennsylvania

London Office Records Records of the World Zionist Organization/Jewish Agency for Palestine, Central Office in London, Record Group Z4, Central Zionist Archives, Jerusalem, Israel

Lowenthal MSS Marvin Lowenthal Papers, American Jewish Historical Society, Waltham, Massachusetts

McDonald MSS James G. McDonald Papers, School of International Affairs Library, Columbia University, New York

Mack MSS Julian William Mack Papers, Zionist Archives and Library, New York

Manson MSS Harold P. Manson Papers, Archives of Temple Tifereth Israel, Cleveland, Ohio

Marshall MSS Louis Marshall Papers, American Jewish Archives, Cincinnati, Ohio

Meyer MSS Annie Nathan Meyer Papers, American Jewish Archives, Cincinnati, Ohio

Morgenstern MSS Julian Morgenstern Papers, American Jewish Archives, Cincinnati, Ohio

Morgenthau MSS Henry Morgenthau Papers, Manuscript Division, Library of Congress, Washington, D.C.

Morgenthau Jr. MSS Henry Morgenthau, Jr., Papers, Franklin D. Roosevelt Library, Hyde Park, New York

Organization Department Records Records of the Organization Department of the Executive of the World Zionist Organization/Jewish Agency for Palestine, Record Group S5, Central Zionist Archives, Jerusalem, Israel

Perkins MSS Frances Perkins Papers, Special Collections, Columbia University Library, New York

Philipson MSS David Philipson Papers, American Jewish Archives, Cincinnati, Ohio

Political Department Records Records of the Political Department of the Executive of the World Zionist Organization/Jewish Agency for Palestine, Record Group S25, Central Zionist Archives, Jerusalem, Israel

Rosenau MSS William Rosenau Papers, American Jewish Archives, Cincinnati, Ohio

E. Roosevelt MSS Eleanor Roosevelt Papers, Franklin D. Roosevelt Library,

Hyde Park, New York

F. Roosevelt MSS   Franklin Delano Roosevelt Papers, Franklin D. Roosevelt Library, Hyde Park, New York

T. Roosevelt MSS   Theodore Roosevelt Papers, Manuscript Division, Library of Congress, Washington, D.C.

Rosenman MSS   Samuel I. Rosenman Papers, Franklin D. Roosevelt Library, Hyde Park, New York

Schiff MSS   Jacob Henry Schiff Papers, American Jewish Archives, Cincinnati, Ohio

Schurman MSS   Jacob Gould Schurman Papers, Department of Manuscripts and University Archives, Cornell University Library, Ithaca, New York

Seligman MSS   Edwin R. A. Seligman Papers, Special Collections, Columbia University Library, New York

Silver MSS   Abba Hillel Silver Papers, Archives of Temple Tifereth Israel, Cleveland, Ohio

Sokolow MSS   Nahum Sokolow Papers, Record Group A18, Central Zionist Archives, Jerusalem, Israel

State Department Records   Records of the United States Department of State, Record Group 59, The National Archives, Washington, D.C.

Stimson MSS   Henry Louis Stimson Papers, Sterling Library, Yale University, New Haven, Connecticut

Szold MSS   Robert Szold Papers, Zionist Archives and Library, New York

Taft MSS   William Howard Taft Papers, Manuscript Division, Library of Congress, Washington, D.C.

Thilly MSS   Frank Thilly Papers, Department of Manuscripts and University Archives, Cornell University, Ithaca, New York

Thorndike MSS   Ashley H. Thorndike Papers, Special Collections, Columbia University Library, New York

Truman MSS   Harry S Truman Papers, Harry S Truman Library, Independence, Missouri

Vienna Office Records   Records of the Central Zionist Office in Vienna, Record Group Z1, Central Zionist Archives, Jerusalem, Israel

Wald MSS   Lillian D. Wald Papers, Special Collections, Columbia University Library, New York

Waldman MSS   Morris David Waldman Papers, American Jewish Archives, Cincinnati, Ohio

Warburg MSS   Felix Warburg Papers, American Jewish Archives, Cincinnati, Ohio

Waterman MSS   Waterman Family Papers, American Jewish Archives, Cincinnati, Ohio

Weinberger MSS   Harry Weinberger Papers, Sterling Library, Yale University, New Haven, Connecticut

Weisgal MSS   Meyer Weisgal Papers, privately held, Rehovoth, Israel

Weizmann MSS   Chaim Weizmann Papers, Library of Yad Chaim Weizmann, Rehovoth, Israel

Wilson MSS   Woodrow Wilson Papers, Manuscript Division, Library of Congress, Washington, D.C.

Wise MSS-AJA   Stephen Samuel Wise Collection, American Jewish Archives, Cincinnati, Ohio

Wolfe MSS Gertrude Wolfe Papers, American Jewish Historical Society, Waltham, Massachusetts

WRB Records   Records of the United States War Refugee Board, Franklin D. Roosevelt Library, Hyde Park, New York

ZOA Records   Records of the Zionist Organization of America, Zionist Archives and Library, New York

Wise's sermons while he was in Portland were published in the *Beth Israel Pulpit* (1902–1906); his talks to the Free Synagogue were frequently reported in the *New York Times*, and a number published in the *Free Synagogue Pulpit* (published irregularly from 1907 to 1949). Two of his books, *Child Versus Parent* (1922) and *How to Face Life* (1924), were essentially reprints or expansions of sermons or lectures. Wise was also a prolific writer, with letters or articles appearing in a number of journals. The most important outlets for his views were *The New Palestine*, *Opinion*, and the *Congress Weekly*. His autobiography, *Challenging Years* (1949), which was published posthumously, was written while he was quite ill, and lacks analysis or introspection. Wise tended to eschew the personal side of his life and concentrated more or less on an anecdotal recall of great people and events. Two volumes of his letters are available in print, *The Personal Letters of Stephen Wise*, edited by Justine Wise Polier and James Waterman Wise (1956), and *Stephen S. Wise: Servant of the People, Selected Letters*, edited by Carl Hermann Voss (1969). In addition Carl Voss, *Rabbi and Minister: The Friendship of Stephen S. Wise and John Haynes Holmes* (1964) is an invaluable source of material not to be found elsewhere.

Much insight into Wise and his times came not from any written materials, but from men and women who knew him and who worked with him. Transcripts of the following interviews have been deposited in both the Oral History Collection of the Hebrew University in Jerusalem and in the Wise Papers at the American Jewish Historical Society: Gertrude Adelstein, Morton Berman, Eliahu Elath (Epstein), Nahum Goldmann, Israel Goldstein, Rose Halprin, Milton Handler, Edward I. Kiev, Edward Klein, Moshe Kol, Louis Levinthal, Arthur Lourie, Golda Meir, Emanuel

Neumann, Meyer Passow, Justine Wise Polier, Shad Polier, Gerhardt Reigner, Ezra Shapiro, Aryah Tartakower, Jacques Torczyner, Carl Hermann Voss, Meyer Weisgal, and James Waterman Wise.

Index

Abbott, Lyman, 40
Abrahams, Israel: offered presidency of JIR, 186; 89, 185, 187
Achad Ha'am, 20, 63, 339
Acheson, Dean, 321
Addams, Jane: nd Industrial Commission, 97; and peace movement, 135
Adler, Cyrus: negotiates with Brandeis, 127; opposition to world congress, 294; 261, 263, 269, 298
Adler, Felix: association with LWW, 27; 31, 47, 65, 231.
Adler, Hermann: opposition to Zionism, 18
Adler, Polly, 245
Agudath Harabonim: attacks SSW, 196; 199, 202
Allen, William H., 246
Allenby, General: captures Jerusalem, 146
American Council for Judaism, 334-35
American Hebrew, 23
American Jewish Assembly. *See* American Jewish Conference
American Jewish Committee: relations with Provisional Committee, 119; opposition to Zionism, 122; opposes American Jewish Congress, 124-25; loses congress fight, 131; salvages loss at Hotel Astor meeting, 132; and antisemitism in twenties, 206; and Jewish Agency, 214; and anti-Nazi measures, 269-70; opposes world congress, 294, 301; opposes American Jewish Assembly, 337-38; walks out of American Jewish Conference, 339; and postwar plans, 349; 159
American Jewish Conference, 87, 337-40

American Jewish Congress, 87; early history, 124 ff; March 1916 meeting, 130; SSW address to, 130-31; postponed, 143; endorsed by Woodrow Wilson, 144; meets after war, 153; delegation to White House, 157; second session, 159-60; decision to reconvene, 160; difficulties in twenties, 290-92; and news of Holocaust, 321; program for Bermuda conference, 328-29; and postwar discrimination, 358; Women's Division, honors LaGuardia, 273; attacked by Nazi press, 273
American Jewish Relief Committee, 121
American Jews: reaction to rise of Hitler, 260
American Union Against Militarism, 135, 139
American Zionism: and friction with European Zionists, 149-50, 153
American Zionist Policy Committee, 345
"Analyticus." *See* Wise, James Waterman
Anglo-American Commission on Palestine, hearings, 350; report, 351
Anglo-American Statement on Palestine, blocked by Zionists, 341
Anti-Defamation League, 177
Antisemitism in Europe in twenties, 261
Arab riots of 1929: and British reaction, 220; Zionist reaction, 220
Arlosoroff, Chaim, 279
Armistice (1918), 152
Armstrong, Hamilton Fish, 304
Astor Hotel meeting, 132
Atkinson, Henry, 187
Auschwitz, 347